Lecture Notes in Computer Science 9731

Commenced Publication in 1973
Founding and Former Series Editors:
Gerhard Goos, Juris Hartmanis, and Jan van Leeuwen

More information about this series at http://www.springer.com/series/7409

Masaaki Kurosu (Ed.)

Human-Computer Interaction

Theory, Design, Development and Practice

18th International Conference, HCI International 2016
Toronto, ON, Canada, July 17–22, 2016
Proceedings, Part I

Editor
Masaaki Kurosu
The Open University of Japan
Chiba-shi, Chiba
Japan

ISSN 0302-9743 ISSN 1611-3349 (electronic)
Lecture Notes in Computer Science
ISBN 978-3-319-39509-8 ISBN 978-3-319-39510-4 (eBook)
DOI 10.1007/978-3-319-39510-4

Library of Congress Control Number: 2016939992

LNCS Sublibrary: SL3 – Information Systems and Applications, incl. Internet/Web, and HCI

Printed on acid-free paper

This Springer imprint is published by Springer Nature
The registered company is Springer International Publishing AG Switzerland

Foreword

The 18th International Conference on Human-Computer Interaction, HCI International 2016, was held in Toronto, Canada, during July 17–22, 2016. The event incorporated the 15 conferences/thematic areas listed on the following page.

A total of 4,354 individuals from academia, research institutes, industry, and governmental agencies from 74 countries submitted contributions, and 1,287 papers and 186 posters have been included in the proceedings. These papers address the latest research and development efforts and highlight the human aspects of the design and use of computing systems. The papers thoroughly cover the entire field of human-computer interaction, addressing major advances in knowledge and effective use of computers in a variety of application areas. The volumes constituting the full 27-volume set of the conference proceedings are listed on pages IX and X.

I would like to thank the program board chairs and the members of the program boards of all thematic areas and affiliated conferences for their contribution to the highest scientific quality and the overall success of the HCI International 2016 conference.

This conference would not have been possible without the continuous and unwavering support and advice of the founder, Conference General Chair Emeritus and Conference Scientific Advisor Prof. Gavriel Salvendy. For his outstanding efforts, I would like to express my appreciation to the communications chair and editor of *HCI International News*, Dr. Abbas Moallem.

April 2016 Constantine Stephanidis

HCI International 2016 Thematic Areas and Affiliated Conferences

Thematic areas:

- Human-Computer Interaction (HCI 2016)
- Human Interface and the Management of Information (HIMI 2016)

Affiliated conferences:

- 13th International Conference on Engineering Psychology and Cognitive Ergonomics (EPCE 2016)
- 10th International Conference on Universal Access in Human-Computer Interaction (UAHCI 2016)
- 8th International Conference on Virtual, Augmented and Mixed Reality (VAMR 2016)
- 8th International Conference on Cross-Cultural Design (CCD 2016)
- 8th International Conference on Social Computing and Social Media (SCSM 2016)
- 10th International Conference on Augmented Cognition (AC 2016)
- 7th International Conference on Digital Human Modeling and Applications in Health, Safety, Ergonomics and Risk Management (DHM 2016)
- 5th International Conference on Design, User Experience and Usability (DUXU 2016)
- 4th International Conference on Distributed, Ambient and Pervasive Interactions (DAPI 2016)
- 4th International Conference on Human Aspects of Information Security, Privacy and Trust (HAS 2016)
- Third International Conference on HCI in Business, Government, and Organizations (HCIBGO 2016)
- Third International Conference on Learning and Collaboration Technologies (LCT 2016)
- Second International Conference on Human Aspects of IT for the Aged Population (ITAP 2016)

Conference Proceedings Volumes Full List

1. LNCS 9731, Human-Computer Interaction: Theory, Design, Development and Practice (Part I), edited by Masaaki Kurosu
2. LNCS 9732, Human-Computer Interaction: Interaction Platforms and Techniques (Part II), edited by Masaaki Kurosu
3. LNCS 9733, Human-Computer Interaction: Novel User Experiences (Part III), edited by Masaaki Kurosu
4. LNCS 9734, Human Interface and the Management of Information: Information, Design and Interaction (Part I), edited by Sakae Yamamoto
5. LNCS 9735, Human Interface and the Management of Information: Applications and Services (Part II), edited by Sakae Yamamoto
6. LNAI 9736, Engineering Psychology and Cognitive Ergonomics, edited by Don Harris
7. LNCS 9737, Universal Access in Human-Computer Interaction: Methods, Techniques, and Best Practices (Part I), edited by Margherita Antona and Constantine Stephanidis
8. LNCS 9738, Universal Access in Human-Computer Interaction: Interaction Techniques and Environments (Part II), edited by Margherita Antona and Constantine Stephanidis
9. LNCS 9739, Universal Access in Human-Computer Interaction: Users and Context Diversity (Part III), edited by Margherita Antona and Constantine Stephanidis
10. LNCS 9740, Virtual, Augmented and Mixed Reality, edited by Stephanie Lackey and Randall Shumaker
11. LNCS 9741, Cross-Cultural Design, edited by Pei-Luen Patrick Rau
12. LNCS 9742, Social Computing and Social Media, edited by Gabriele Meiselwitz
13. LNAI 9743, Foundations of Augmented Cognition: Neuroergonomics and Operational Neuroscience (Part I), edited by Dylan D. Schmorrow and Cali M. Fidopiastis
14. LNAI 9744, Foundations of Augmented Cognition: Neuroergonomics and Operational Neuroscience (Part II), edited by Dylan D. Schmorrow and Cali M. Fidopiastis
15. LNCS 9745, Digital Human Modeling and Applications in Health, Safety, Ergonomics and Risk Management, edited by Vincent G. Duffy
16. LNCS 9746, Design, User Experience, and Usability: Design Thinking and Methods (Part I), edited by Aaron Marcus
17. LNCS 9747, Design, User Experience, and Usability: Novel User Experiences (Part II), edited by Aaron Marcus
18. LNCS 9748, Design, User Experience, and Usability: Technological Contexts (Part III), edited by Aaron Marcus
19. LNCS 9749, Distributed, Ambient and Pervasive Interactions, edited by Norbert Streitz and Panos Markopoulos
20. LNCS 9750, Human Aspects of Information Security, Privacy and Trust, edited by Theo Tryfonas

21. LNCS 9751, HCI in Business, Government, and Organizations: eCommerce and Innovation (Part I), edited by Fiona Fui-Hoon Nah and Chuan-Hoo Tan
22. LNCS 9752, HCI in Business, Government, and Organizations: Information Systems (Part II), edited by Fiona Fui-Hoon Nah and Chuan-Hoo Tan
23. LNCS 9753, Learning and Collaboration Technologies, edited by Panayiotis Zaphiris and Andri Ioannou
24. LNCS 9754, Human Aspects of IT for the Aged Population: Design for Aging (Part I), edited by Jia Zhou and Gavriel Salvendy
25. LNCS 9755, Human Aspects of IT for the Aged Population: Healthy and Active Aging (Part II), edited by Jia Zhou and Gavriel Salvendy
26. CCIS 617, HCI International 2016 Posters Proceedings (Part I), edited by Constantine Stephanidis
27. CCIS 618, HCI International 2016 Posters Proceedings (Part II), edited by Constantine Stephanidis

Human-Computer Interaction

Program Board Chair: **Masaaki Kurosu, Japan**

The full list with the program board chairs and the members of the program boards of all thematic areas and affiliated conferences is available online at:

http://www.hci.international/2016/

HCI International 2017

The 19th International Conference on Human-Computer Interaction, HCI International 2017, will be held jointly with the affiliated conferences in Vancouver, Canada, at the Vancouver Convention Centre, July 9–14, 2017. It will cover a broad spectrum of themes related to human-computer interaction, including theoretical issues, methods, tools, processes, and case studies in HCI design, as well as novel interaction techniques, interfaces, and applications. The proceedings will be published by Springer. More information will be available on the conference website: http://2017.hci.international/.

General Chair
Prof. Constantine Stephanidis
University of Crete and ICS-FORTH
Heraklion, Crete, Greece
E-mail: general_chair@hcii2017.org

http://2017.hci.international/

Contents – Part I

HCI: Theory, Practice and Education

Interaction Design Methods and Tools

Usability and User Experience Evaluation Methods and Techniques

Models and Patterns in HCI

Contents – Part II

Gesture, Motion-Based and Eye-gaze Based Interaction

Multimodal, Multisensory and Natural Interaction

Multi-platform, Migratory and Distributed Interfaces

Contents – Part III

Wayfinding, Mobility, and Transport

HCI: Theory, Practice and Education

Virtual Reality Applications in Rehabilitation

Shi Cao(✉)

Department of Systems Design Engineering, University of Waterloo, Waterloo, Canada
shi.cao@uwaterloo.ca

Abstract. One of the most valuable applications of virtual reality (VR) is in the domain of rehabilitation. After brain injuries or diseases, many patients suffer from impaired physical and/or cognitive capabilities, such as difficulties in moving arms or remembering names. Over the past two decades, VR has been tested and examined as a technology to assist patients' recovery and rehabilitation, both physical and cognitive. The increasing prevalence of low-cost VR devices brings new opportunities, allowing VR to be used in practice. Using VR devices such as head-mounted displays (HMDs), special virtual scenes can be designed to assist patients in the process of re-training their brain and reorganizing their functions and abilities. However, such VR interfaces and applications must be comprehensively tested and examined for their effectiveness and potential side effects. This paper presents a review of related literature and discusses the new opportunities and challenges. Most of existing studies examined VR as an assessment method rather than a training/exercise method. Nevertheless, promising cases and positive preliminary results have been shown. Considering the increasing need for self-administered, home-based, and personalized rehabilitation, VR rehabilitation is potentially an important approach. This area requires more studies and research effort.

Keywords: Virtual reality · Virtual rehabilitation · Cognitive impairment · Biomedical engineering

1 Introduction

Virtual reality (VR) technologies use multimedia devices and computer simulation to allow users to interact with a simulated environment, creating life-like experience. Display devices present sensory information, such as vision, auditory, and touch sense, to the user; control devices collect user actions such as motion, gesture, and voices. The term VR is a very broad term, and researchers have used it to refer to a wide range of systems. A system using motion sensing gloves and a desktop display can be called VR, which emphasizes life-like hand control and feedback. In some studies, especially early studies, a system using standard computer input (keyboard and mouse) and output (desktop displays) devices can also be called VR, which emphasizes the virtual environment generated by the software. In this sense, many first-person computer games can be called VR. Recently, VR is used more to specifically referring to systems using head-mounted displays (HMDs), which can create 3D depth perception and change the view as the head moves.

M. Kurosu (Ed.): HCI 2016, Part I, LNCS 9731, pp. 3–10, 2016.
DOI: 10.1007/978-3-319-39510-4_1

Since VR enables users to gain experience without exposing them to risks in the real environment, VR has been widely used for gaming and training purposes. A relatively new and less explored area of VR applications is rehabilitation, helping patients who have lost some of their physical and/or cognitive abilities to regain the abilities. The goals of the current paper are to summarize recent research efforts, discuss the benefits and potential side effects of VR, and discuss practical issues for researchers who are interested in conducting their studies in this area.

In general, rehabilitation in healthcare refers to the treatment and process to restore good health and regain impaired functions and abilities. The impaired functions can be categorized into physical and cognitive groups. Physical functions include movement and control of physical body parts such as limbs, hands, fingers, and head. In contrast, cognitive functions are related to information processing such as vision, hearing, task execution, memory, and decision. While some loss of physical functions happens in the motor system, the most challenging cases are due to injuries or diseases in the central neuron system (i.e., brain). Different brain areas are in charge of different functions. The type of function loss depends on the damaged area. In Parkinson's disease, the degeneration of brain cells mainly affects the motor system, so the symptoms are mainly related to walking and hand movement. In Alzheimer's disease however, the degeneration of brain cells starts in brain areas that control cognitive functions, so memory and language are mostly affected. For stroke and traumatic brain injuries, the impaired functions can be both physical and cognitive, depending on the specific areas of damage.

Current neuroscience theories commonly believe that adult brains have very limited capability to replace damaged and dead cells, but new connections can be formed between existing cells to support reorganization of impaired brain functions [1, 2]. Rehabilitation therapy and treatment often use repetitive physical and cognitive exercises as a way to stimulate neuron reorganization and achieve restoring and regaining some functions and abilities. Complete recovery is not common, but many patients can gain improved quality of life and do better in their activities of daily life (ADL). In general, there are the following five important components in a rehabilitation program [3].

1. Diagnostic assessment and evaluation.
2. Introducing assistant devices.
3. Educating the patients about the diseases.
4. Repeated practice of exercise and training activities.
5. Developing compensation and adaptation strategies.

Most of the existing studies using VR in rehabilitation mainly focused on applications in Step 1 Assessment. A relatively small number of studies have also examined the effectiveness of VR designed for Step 4 Exercise.

2 Previous VR Applications in Rehabilitation

2.1 VR Applications for Rehabilitation Assessment

Many studies have examined VR as a tool to assess the level and type of cognitive impairment; for reviews, see [4, 5]. The following studies are reviewed as an illustration of typical research in this area. An early study in 1998 used HMD (486 PC platform) to present a household kitchen environment [6]. A meal preparation task was used to evaluate memory and executive functions of patients with traumatic brain injury (TBI). Thirty participants were tested twice within 7 to 10 days, and the results showed good test-retest reliability; however, there was no comparison between VR and traditional assessment methods.

A study in 1999 [7] reported an HMD-VR system (Pentium 166 MHz) developed to assess patients' driving abilities. Driving test performance such as lane keeping and stop sign stopping were compared between 17 brain-injured adults and uninjured participants matched in age, gender, and education. The results showed some trend of worse performance by brain-injured patients, but no statistical significance was reported.

A study in 2008 [8] showed that HMD-VR (Onyx2 Reality; 640 × 480) can be used to differentiate two types of Parkinson's disease. Participants were asked to walk while wearing the system that showed a virtual corridor with optic flow. Patients with predominant left-hemisphere dysfunction deviated right of centre, whereas patients with predominant right-hemisphere dysfunction did not.

In a recent study in 2012 [9], the authors implemented a simple driving simulation with PC and a projector, which allows a user to navigate a virtual city or town passively as a passenger or actively as a driver. After the exploration, participants' episodic memory about the virtual place was tested in recall and recognition questions. The results showed that the method was sensitive enough to tell the difference between three groups, healthy older adults, early clinical manifestations of Alzheimer's disease, and amnesic mild cognitive impairment.

2.2 VR Applications for Rehabilitation Exercise

In contrast to the high number of rehabilitation assessment studies, there are very few studies that have investigated VR applications in rehabilitation training and exercise. In a case report in 2001 [10], a 65-year old woman with impaired memory functions received a 24-week rehabilitation exercise with both music-story therapy and HMD-VR experiences (Pentium III) that visualized the scenes told in the stories. The results showed improved clinical conditions, and the authors suggested that the interactive and immersive features of VR could benefit music-enhanced therapy and better involve the patient during the training.

A later controlled study by the same research group in 2010 [11] compared HMD-VR memory training (Pentium III) and traditional face-to-face music training, where the participants were encouraged to sing and play music instruments, in six months. The VR scenes included home, park, and streets familiar to the participants. The tasks were exploration and navigation using a joystick. The results showed that the VR training was more effective than the music therapy training. The fifteen elderly patients (with memory deficits) in the VR group showed significantly improved memory test scores; in contrast, the sixteen elderly patients in the control group of the face-to-face music therapy showed progressive declined memory.

In addition to HMD-VR studies, there are also studies demonstrating the effectiveness of non-wearable VR systems using computer monitors or projectors as displays.

An early study in 1999 [12] reported the case of an amnesia patient (female, age 53) who received route finding training and testing in eight weeks using a desktop VR system (Pentium 133 MHz; 15″ monitor). She was able to learn the three routes practiced in VR but not the one route practiced in the real world. A potential explanation is that training in VR allows the isolation of the core route knowledge and avoids the distraction of other objects and events in the real world.

A study in 2003 [13] examined a simple VR shopping exercise created by digital photos, programmed navigation steps, and interactive functions on a touch screen. Nine patients with Alzheimer's disease received four-week training. Their performance (speed and error rates) and Mini-Mental State Examination (MMSE) scores improved after the training and sustained after following-up three weeks later.

A recent study in 2011 [14] examined a desktop VR exercise where patients see their image mirrored in a virtual space and wave hands to hit virtual targets. Fifteen stroke patients were assigned to the VR group, where they received the VR exercise and computer-based cognitive rehabilitation training (tasks such as matching cards, memorizing numbers, and finding pictures by names); thirteen patients were assigned to the control group, where they received only the cognitive rehabilitation training. The results after four-week training showed that the VR group had significantly larger improvement than the control group in visual attention and short-term visuospatial memory related tests.

An interesting study in 2013 [15] examined desktop VR vocational training on schizophrenic patients with cognitive impairments. The VR environment (Pentium IV; 38″ monitor) simulates a clothes shop where the patient was trained for a shop clerk job, performing tasks such as sorting clothes and handling customers' requests. The results showed that VR vocational training was more effective than therapist-administered vocational training and conventional training without the shop scenario, in terms of better problem solving and executive control abilities measured by Wisconsin Card Sorting Test and better self-efficacy scores. The findings suggest that an immersive environment and real-world purposes are both important in rehabilitation.

It would be interesting to compare VR implemented on HMDs and desktop displays. Since 2D displays are less expensive and more available, if VR training using desktop displays can be equally effective for certain types of exercises, there will be no need to use HMDs. Previous studies showed that both HMD and non-wearable VR systems have value for rehabilitation. Unfortunately, no study found in the current review directly compared HMD-VR with non-wearable VR.

3 Potential Advantages and Side Effects of VR Rehabilitation

Although there is not sufficient evidence to confirm the effectiveness of VR exercise or its advantages over traditional training methods, it is expected to have several benefits in comparison to conventional computer-based rehabilitation training [16, 17].

1. Increase the degrees of immersion and interaction (especially HMD-VR), making the exercise interesting and motivating persistent practice.
2. Allow tests and exercise of activities (such as driving) that would be too dangerous for patients to do in the real world.

3. Allow tests and exercise (such as visual perception and field of view tasks) that are otherwise too difficult, time-consuming, or impossible to do in the real world.

As a computerized method, VR rehabilitation also has similar benefits as computer-based rehabilitation training over traditional therapist administered training, for example, improved standardization of protocols, better control of stimulus presentation, and easier collection of response measures.

However, the potential side effects of VR must be thoroughly studied before wider rehabilitation applications of the technology. The first major area of concern is simulator sickness. It is a kind of motion sickness experienced by people in motion or vehicle simulation. In most virtual simulators, the visual and auditory stimuli can be presented closer to real-life experience, but real acceleration and orientation are difficult to create. The discrepancies between the stronger motion perceived by vision and hearing and the weaker motion perceived by the vestibular system and proprioception can lead to simulator sickness. Typical syndromes include discomfort, fatigue, nausea, and disorientation.

From the literature, it seems that there is a large individual difference in simulator sickness. There are case studies that reported no or little simulator sickness, e.g., [6]. There are also cases where participants were excluded due to strong simulator sickness. In 2000, Kesztyues et al. [18] compared the difference of side effects between a HMD (800×600; Pentium-II 266 MHz; two Vodoo2 graphic cards) and a projector. Simulator sickness was measured by a subjective questionnaire—Simulator Sickness Questionnaire (SSQ) [19]. The tasks were to navigate (walking) and find targets in relatively simple virtual environments (a maze and a park). Valid results were collected from 21 healthy participants (most in age 20–29). One of them (5 %) could not complete the tasks using HMD due to strong nausea. For both HMD and projector conditions, simulator sickness was reported, but the levels were considered tolerable.

Since the level of simulator sickness also depends on the device (HMD vs. non-wearable displays) and the type of tasks (e.g., walking vs. driving), these factors need be considered for the cost-benefit trade-off of VR rehabilitation.

The second major group of side effects is eye strains related issues, such as eye dryness, redness, discomfort, and reduced visual acuity. Some subjective measuring methods of simulator sickness (e.g., SSQ) include eye fatigue and discomfort as part of the scales. The effects of using standard non-wearable displays have been relatively well-established as the computer vision syndrome [20]. Regarding HMD, previous studies have examined its effects on visual perception (e.g., flicker fusion frequency, distance estimation), subjective comfort (e.g., fatigue, comfort), and visual acuity [21]. In comparison to projectors, HMDs were reported to result in significantly higher levels of subjectively reported eye strains and fatigue [18]. However, there is a lack of evidence for comparison about eye dryness and redness between HMDs and standard displays. These important ocular health concerns require future research.

The third area of concern is related to particular groups of patients who are afraid of new devices or are very sensitive to their environment. For example, introducing VR devices may agitate schizophrenia patients with persecutory delusion and paranoia. The cost-benefit trade-off of using VR rehabilitation needs to be evaluated for each patient based on their specific cases. There is no existing standard or guideline available in the literature.

4 Practical Issues for Researchers in This Field

HMD vs. Standard Display. Wearable HMDs are expected to create better immersion and life-like experience than standard non-wearable displays (e.g., desktop monitor, projector) because HMDs support 3D depth perception through binocular discrepancy and a dynamic field of view through head tracking. However, many participants reported oppressiveness using HMD [18]. It is very difficult to wear HMD while wearing frame glasses. Cost-benefit analysis should be conducted to select a suitable display for each kind of VR rehabilitation applications.

Control Groups. Many existing studies (especially case studies) lack the comparison between VR and traditional rehabilitation methods. A control group that consists of randomly assigned patients with matching background is needed.

Access to Patients. It is important to have access to a large patient pool. This may be achieved by collaborating with hospitals and assisted home care providers. When planning a study, researchers should be prepared that many patients may be ineligible or refuse to participate for various reasons, and elderly patients may die or become unable to continue their participation later in the study. For example, in one study focusing on elderly patients (age 65 years or older) with cognitive impairments, 159 individuals lived in a rest-care home were assessed for eligibility, 123 (77 %) were excluded, 5 died or left the rest-care home during the study, and finally data from only 31 individuals (19 %) were good for analysis [11].

Ethics and Safety. Although VR rehabilitation does not involve medication and drugs, research ethics and safety of patients still require careful planning and administration. The ethics review process may take a long time, especially if the VR device is categorized as a medical device by the reviewing authority. Safety of the participants needs to be considered not only during but also after the experiment. In one case [22], the authors specifically emphasized the importance of arranging transportation for elderly persons after they have participated in a VR study. Because even if one case of a car accident happened after exposing to VR, it would be extremely detrimental to the research project, no matter whether there was a causal link or not between VR and the accident.

Development Cost. The cost of VR devices have dropped significantly during the last decade. An HMD device can be purchased with only a few hundred dollars right now. However, the programming and development of the virtual scenes and interactions still require a lot of effort. Time and programmer salaries should be properly estimated when writing research proposals, especially if customized virtual scenes for each individual is needed.

5 Conclusions

Over the past two decades, VR applications have been proposed and examined for rehabilitation purposes. Existing studies are mostly preliminary ones with low participant numbers, and most studies examined VR as an assessment method rather than a training/ exercise method. The reviewed case studies and control studies showed positive and promising results of using VR for rehabilitation exercise. Considering the increasing availability of low-cost VR devices and the increasing need for self-administered, home-based, and personalized rehabilitation approaches, VR applications are expected to play an important role in reducing healthcare cost and improving rehabilitation outcomes. The existing literature lacks controlled studies to support cost-benefit analysis required for practical applications. More studies are needed to examine the effectiveness and side effects of VR systems, especially HMD-VR, for health and work rehabilitation.

References

1. Lee, W.-C.A., Huang, H., Feng, G., Sanes, J.R., Brown, E.N., So, P.T., Nedivi, E.: Dynamic remodeling of dendritic arbors in GABAergic interneurons of adult visual cortex. PLoS Biol. **4**, e29 (2005)
2. Buonomano, D.V., Merzenich, M.M.: Cortical plasticity: from synapses to maps. Annu. Rev. Neurosci. **21**, 149–186 (1998)
3. Raymond, M.J., Bennett, T.L., Malia, K.B., Bewick, K.C.: Rehabilitation of visual processing deficits following brain injury. NeuroRehabilitation **6**, 229–239 (1996)
4. Rizzo, A., Kim, G.: A SWOT analysis of the field of virtual reality rehabilitation and therapy. Presence **14**, 119–146 (2005)
5. Rose, F.D., Brooks, B.M., Rizzo, A.A.: Virtual reality in brain damage rehabilitation: review. Cyberpsychol. Behav. **8**, 241–262 (2005)
6. Christiansen, C., Abreu, B., Ottenbacher, K., Huffman, K., Masel, B., Culpepper, R.: Task performance in virtual environments used for cognitive rehabilitation after traumatic brain injury. Arch. Phys. Med. Rehabil. **79**, 888–892 (1998)
7. Liu, L., Miyazaki, M., Watson, B.: Norms and validity of the DriVR: a virtual reality driving assessment for persons with head injuries. Cyber Psychol. Behav. **2**, 53–67 (1999)
8. Davidsdottir, S., Wagenaar, R., Young, D., Cronin-Golomb, A.: Impact of optic flow perception and egocentric coordinates on veering in Parkinson's disease. Brain **131**, 2882–2893 (2008)
9. Plancher, G., Tirard, A., Gyselinck, V., Nicolas, S., Piolino, P.: Using virtual reality to characterize episodic memory profiles in amnestic mild cognitive impairment and Alzheimer's disease: influence of active and passive encoding. Neuropsychologia **50**, 592–602 (2012)
10. Optale, G., Capodieci, S., Pinelli, P., Zara, D., Gamberini, L., Riva, G.: Music-enhanced immersive virtual reality in the rehabilitation of memoryrelated cognitive processes and functional abilities: a case report. Presence Teleoperators Virtual Environ. **10**, 450–462 (2001)
11. Optale, G., Urgesi, C., Busato, V., Marin, S., Piron, L., Priftis, K., Gamberini, L., Capodieci, S., Bordin, A.: Controlling memory impairment in elderly adults using virtual reality memory training: a randomized controlled pilot study. Neurorehabil. Neural Repair. **24**, 348–357 (2010)
12. Brooks, B.M.: Route learning in a case of amnesia: a preliminary investigation into the efficacy of training in a virtual environment. Neuropsychol. Rehabil. **9**, 63–76 (1999)
13. Hofmann, M., Rösler, A., Schwarz, W., Müller-Spahn, F., Kräuchi, K., Hock, C., Seifritz, E.: Interactive computer-training as a therapeutic tool in Alzheimer's disease. Compr. Psychiatry **44**, 213–219 (2003)

14. Kim, B.R., Chun, M.H., Kim, L.S., Park, J.Y.: Effect of virtual reality on cognition in stroke patients. Ann. Rehabil. Med. **35**, 450–459 (2011)
15. Tsang, M.M.Y., Man, D.W.K.: A virtual reality-based vocational training system (VRVTS) for people with schizophrenia in vocational rehabilitation. Schizophr. Res. **144**, 51–62 (2013)
16. Schultheis, M.T., Rizzo, A.A.: The application of virtual reality technology in rehabilitation. Rehabil. Psychol. **46**, 296 (2001)
17. Cherniack, E.P.: Not just fun and games: applications of virtual reality in the identification and rehabilitation of cognitive disorders of the elderly. Disabil. Rehabil. Assist. Technol. **6**, 283–289 (2011)
18. Kesztyues, T.I., Mehlitz, M., Schilken, E., Weniger, G., Wolf, S., Piccolo, U., Irle, E., Rienhoff, O.: Preclinical evaluation of a virtual reality neuropsychological test system: occurrence of side effects. Cyberpsychol. Behav. **3**, 343–349 (2000)
19. Kennedy, R.S., Lane, N.E., Berbaum, K.S., Lilienthal, M.G.: Simulator sickness questionnaire: an enhanced method for quantifying simulator sickness. Int. J. Aviat. Psychol. **3**, 203–220 (1993)
20. Rosenfield, M.: Computer vision syndrome: a review of ocular causes and potential treatments. Ophthalmic Physiol. Opt. **31**, 502–515 (2011)
21. Nichols, S., Patel, H.: Health and safety implications of virtual reality: a review of empirical evidence. Appl. Ergon. **33**, 251–271 (2002)
22. McGee, J.S., van der Zaag, C., Buckwalter, J.G., Thiebaux, M., Van Rooyen, A., Neumann, U., Sisemore, D., Rizzo, A.A.: Issues for the assessment of visuospatial skills in older adults using virtual environment technology. Cyberpsychol. Behav. **3**, 469–482 (2000)

Human-Machine Networks: Towards a Typology and Profiling Framework

Aslak Wegner Eide[1(✉)], J. Brian Pickering[2], Taha Yasseri[3], George Bravos[4,5], Asbjørn Følstad[1], Vegard Engen[2], Milena Tsvetkova[3], Eric T. Meyer[3], Paul Walland[2], and Marika Lüders[1]

[1] SINTEF, Oslo, Norway
{aslak.eide,asbjorn.folstad,marika.lüders}@sintef.no
[2] IT Innovation Centre, University of Southampton, Southampton, UK
{jbp,ve,pww}@it-innovation.soton.ac.uk
[3] Oxford Internet Institute, University of Oxford, Oxford, UK
{taha.yasseri,milena.tsvetkova,eric.meyer}@oii.ox.ac.uk
[4] Athens Technology Center, Athens, Greece
g.bravos@atc.gr
[5] Hellenic American University, Athens, Greece

Abstract. In this paper we outline an initial typology and framework for the purpose of profiling *human-machine networks*, that is, collective structures where humans and machines interact to produce synergistic effects. Profiling a human-machine network along the dimensions of the typology is intended to facilitate access to relevant design knowledge and experience. In this way the profiling of an envisioned or existing human-machine network will both facilitate relevant design discussions and, more importantly, serve to identify the network type. We present experiences and results from two case trials: a crisis management system and a peer-to-peer reselling network. Based on the lessons learnt from the case trials we suggest potential benefits and challenges, and point out needed future work.

Keywords: Human-machine networks · Typology · Network profiling · Human-centred design · Case trials · Human-computer interaction

1 Introduction

The world we live in is suffused with interconnected information and communication technology (ICT) components that have become a ubiquitous part of virtually every aspect of our daily lives. At work and in our private lives, when we socialize, create, collaborate or play, we often do so in networks of both humans and machines (e.g. in online social networks, online retail platforms, collaboration platforms, crowdsourcing engines, decision support systems, and massive multiplayer games). Designing and developing for such human-machine networks (HMNs) poses immense challenges.

As technologies and services are integrated into interacting networks of humans and machines rather than being taken up by individual users, classical approaches to human-centred design (HCD) may no longer provide a sufficient degree of design support.

M. Kurosu (Ed.): HCI 2016, Part I, LNCS 9731, pp. 11–22, 2016.
DOI: 10.1007/978-3-319-39510-4_2

This is for example borne out by the challenges involved in establishing sustainable social networks [1], collaborative systems for knowledge workers [2], and citizen-government collaboration systems [3].

To improve the general understanding of HMNs and strengthen our capability to design for such networks, we are developing an HMN typology and associated profiling framework that can be used by designers and developers during the HCD development cycle. A typology is an approach to classification, where the basic concept is detailed according to its salient dimensions [4]. The profiling framework is intended to support access to design knowledge and experience on the basis of the typology.

This paper describes the initial versions of the typology and profiling framework, and illustrates their usefulness through case examples on real-life HMNs. We first present the background on which the typology is based. We then set out the objectives for the typology and profiling framework, before describing their current, initial versions. Finally we present two case trials in which the typology and profiling framework have been applied, before discussing lessons learnt, limitations, and future work.

The typology and associated profiling framework are developed as part of the HUMANE project (http://humane2020.eu). A comprehensive presentation of the typology and framework can be found in the HUMANE technical report *Typology and method v1* [5].

2 Background

In human-centred design, as described in the relevant international standard [6], much emphasis is put on the context analysis and requirements phases of development. However, whereas context analysis and requirements in HCD is skewed towards understanding and specifying the required interactions between individual users and machine interfaces, design for human-machine networks needs strengthened support for identifying and modelling the entire network during these phases. Hence, we need design support that allows human-centred designers and future thinkers to benefit from existing knowledge and experience on the level of HMNs.

A number of theoretical concepts have been developed to understand aspects of what we term HMNs. One example is the theory of socio-technical systems, which provides insight into the dual shaping of technology and the social (work) context in which it is implemented, recognizing organizations as complex systems of humans and technology [7]. Another example, actor-network theory, argues that we explicitly need to take into account that any social system is an association of heterogeneous elements such as humans, norms, texts, devices, machines, and technology, thus granting equal weight to humans and non-human (machine) entities in the analysis of the social [8]. A third and newer perspective, the study of social machines, focuses on online systems that combine social participation with machine-based computation, connecting with Berners-Lee's original vision of the Web more as a social creation than a technical one [9]. Though insightful, these theories tend towards a narrow scope, too restrictive to provide a unified framework for understanding HMNs. Instead, selecting high-level constructs of interactive synergies resulting from the behaviours of all actors, we may begin to develop a unified approach.

To establish the background required for developing the HMN typology, we need to define the term and its scope. Based on a systematic literature review across fields of research that attempt to conceptualize networks comprising both humans and machines [10], we defined HMNs as networks in which the behaviours of different actors result in synergistic effects. That is, in human-machine networks, the interaction of human and machine actors allows for objectives to be set and met that would not be feasible without such networked interaction.

The review suggested four analytical layers for studying HMNs: actors, interactions, networks, and behaviours. Actors are the nodes in the HMNs. We distinguish between human actors, who may be represented by individuals, organizational roles, or entire organizations, and machine actors, which may be represented by single devices, as well as by complex back-end systems, as long as they behave in the HMN as a single node. The human and machine actors interact in the HMN. Thus, at the interaction layer, we focus on the (mediated) human-human interactions, human-machine interactions, and machine-machine interactions. The network layer concerns the integration of actors and interaction into larger compounds and aims towards defining types of such sets of actors and interactions. The behavioural layer concerns the emergent qualities of HMNs. Among these are the changing characteristics or roles of actors depending on network context, emergence of new patterns of interaction in the HMN, new applications of the network, and the overall evolution of the network.

As explained further below, the proposed typology was built upon the four layers of actors, interactions, networks, and behaviours.

3 Objectives

The main aim of this paper is to present an initial typology and framework towards efficient and accurate profiling of human-machine networks. Profiling a human-machine network is intended to identify the network type, thereby facilitating access to relevant design knowledge and experience where successful HMNs are analysed for the purpose of reusing generic design solutions contributing to their success [11]. Moreover, the profiling's process aims to facilitate relevant design discussion, where the stakeholders may address a richer set of aspects pertaining to the network of humans and machines as part of the context analysis and requirements phases than what is typically done today.

To that end, the typology on which the profiling framework is based should include the key dimensions to support HMN design decisions; that is, the dimensions that ICT-developers typically need to consider in analysis, design, and evaluation. Furthermore, the dimensions should clearly discriminate between different human-machine networks of individual ICT projects. The key objectives of the HMN typology and profiling framework are to:

(1) Help design teams reflect upon system characteristics at the level of networks of humans and machines,

(2) Support creation of a profile of the HMN that works as a documentation of its envisioned network characteristics,
(3) Enable designers to identify relevant successful HMNs,
(4) Support elicitation of relevant design implications.

4 HMN Typology and Framework

4.1 Developing the Typology

This first version of the HMN typology was developed following the steps outlined in Fig. 1. Through the initial literature review [10], key constructs were identified and analytical layers established. The literature review also provided insight into relevant dimensions for classification. Then, an initial set of dimensions were suggested and applied to six cases during a workshop. The workshop experiences suggested the initial dimensions be refined into an interim set of dimensions, which was then applied by way of an initial profiling for each of those same cases. Following from the experiences of this initial profiling, a refined set of dimensions were established. This refined set constitutes the first version of the HMN typology.

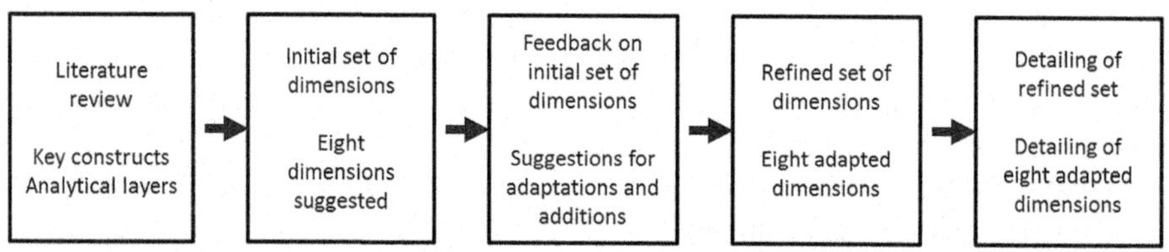

Fig. 1. Overview of the process leading to the initial HMN typology and framework

4.2 The Typology

We structured the typology based on the four analytical layers (actors, interactions, network, and behaviours) detailed in Sect. 2. We assigned two dimensions to each layer representing key defining characteristics of HMNs. The typology dimensions are given in Fig. 2.

The "actors" layer comprises two dimensions – Human agency and Machine agency. Agency is the capacity of the actors in terms of what they can do and achieve in the network. The two dimensions facilitate distinctions between HMNs characterized by varying degrees of automation, artificial intelligence and robot actors, as well as HMN characterized by active collaboration between human and machine agents. We do not imply that machines can exhibit agency on the same level as humans. However, it is practical for the purposes of this typology to refer to machine agency, especially as machines may influence and affect the agency in human actors [12].

At the "interactions" layer, we consider the strength of human to human ties and human to machine interactions as the two dimensions. Tie strength between humans is important for familiarity and trust on the one hand, and social heterogeneity and access to complementary skills and knowledge on the other. While tie strength is much explored, human-machine interaction strength is less studied. However, as machine agency increases, e.g., with the increasing use of social robots, the interaction strength between humans and machines may become increasingly important to HMNs, as is for example seen in some health-care areas [13].

Layer	Dimension	Description	Scale
Actors	1. Human agency	The capacity of the human actors in terms of what they can do and achieve in the network.	low, intermediate, high
	2. Machine agency	The capacity of the machine actors in terms of what they can do in the network, as well as to what extent they enable agency in human actors.	low, intermediate, high
Interaction	3. Tie strength	The tie strength between human nodes in the network.	no ties, latent ties, weak ties, strong ties
	4. H2M interaction strength	The nature and strength of the interaction between humans and machines (H2M) in the network.	independent-optional, independent-necessary, reliant-optional, reliant-necessary
Network	5. Network size	The number of human nodes in the network.	small, medium, large, massive
	6. Geographical space	The geographical extension of the network.	local, regional, global
Behaviours	7. Workflow interdependence	The level of interdependence between actors of in the network.	low, intermediate, high
	8. Network organization	Network organization with implications for predictability and emergence.	bottom-up, intermediate, top-down

Fig. 2. Overview of the typology dimensions

Several dimensions may be considered as critical at the "network" level of HMNs. In the initial version of the typology, we have chosen to include the dimensions of network size and geographical space, due to their importance for the sustainability of HMNs. Growth in terms of size and spread are today seen as key objectives for many HMNs, seen particularly for social networks such as Facebook and Twitter that rely on network effects both for functional and commercial reasons. Furthermore, network size and geographical space have important implications for other dimensions of the network, such as the need for increased machine agency and decreasing of social tie strength with increasing network size.

Finally, at the "behaviours" layer, HMNs are characterized by their workflow interdependence and network organization. Both dimensions concern networks' capacity for emergent change. The former concerns the degree to which the actions of the actors in the network are dependent on and need to be synchronized with the actions of others. The latter concerns the degree of bottom-up vs. top-down organization of the network, where in top-down networks organization is imposed and controlled whereas in a bottom-up network it is self-organising and organic. For example, emergent change may be more prevalent in networks characterized as bottom-up, where initiatives may spread from the grassroots. While efficient spread and refinement of emerging practices may require a certain level of interdependence between the network actors.

4.3 The Profiling Framework

The typology and dimensions alone provide limited support for HCD. To facilitate use by others, we have developed a profiling framework as summarized in Fig. 3.

Steps	1. Define network characteristics Describe and scope the characteristics of the network according to the eight dimensions in the typology	2. Create joint network profile Create a joint profile of the network based on the network characteristics defined in step 1.	3. Identify similar networks Identify similar networks based on the network profile generated in step 2.	4. Extract design principles Extract design principles (design implications, design patterns) from similar networks
Output	Document describing network characteristics	Network profile	List of similar networks	Collection of design principles

Fig. 3. Overview of profiling framework procedure

The profiling framework comprises four steps, during which various levels of interaction and discussion are possible, and lead to a set of comparative descriptors for a given HMN along with some indication of common HCD design features and issues. Step 1, as shown above, involves an initial estimate of the overall characteristics of the network as defined in regard to the four analytical layers and associated dimensions. Human agency, for example, may be seen as high, but machine agency as low or intermediate; this would relate to a network where most activity is initiated by human actors, with technology components simply responding to their requests. Once some indication of values associated with dimensions has been achieved, collectively these would lead to an overall profile of the HMN (Step 2).

Our own experience to date has been largely confined to these first two steps. However, we have begun to characterize multiple networks as part of Step 3 (see also the Sect. 5 below), and in so doing, a set of profiles will be created which may be used to compare similar networks. Such cross-network comparisons will potentially identify common features and designs for similar networks (Step 4 in our methodology), revealing parallels in the HCD of HMNs not previously evident.

5 Case Trials

The initial typology and framework has been applied to case studies pertaining to ICT innovation and development projects. In the following, we present two of these along with experiences and results. The case trials concern human-centred design processes in which the typology and framework is applied, including a crisis management system and a peer-to-peer reselling network. The cases exemplify how the typology and framework provide increased insight during the HCD phases concerning context analysis, user requirement engineering, and design.

5.1 Case 1: Crisis Management System

The eVACUATE project (http://www.evacuate.eu) provides a decision-support system to help operational staff as well as (potentially) emergency services to track and safely guide evacuees in a crisis situation ranging from severe events such as a fire or terrorist threat to less severe operational responses such as responding to overcrowding. Following the initial steps outlined above (Fig. 3), we generated two profiles in connection with this case, one representing normal operations when effectively the HMN is simply monitoring activity, and a second for a possible emergency situation. The resulting profiles are shown in Fig. 4.

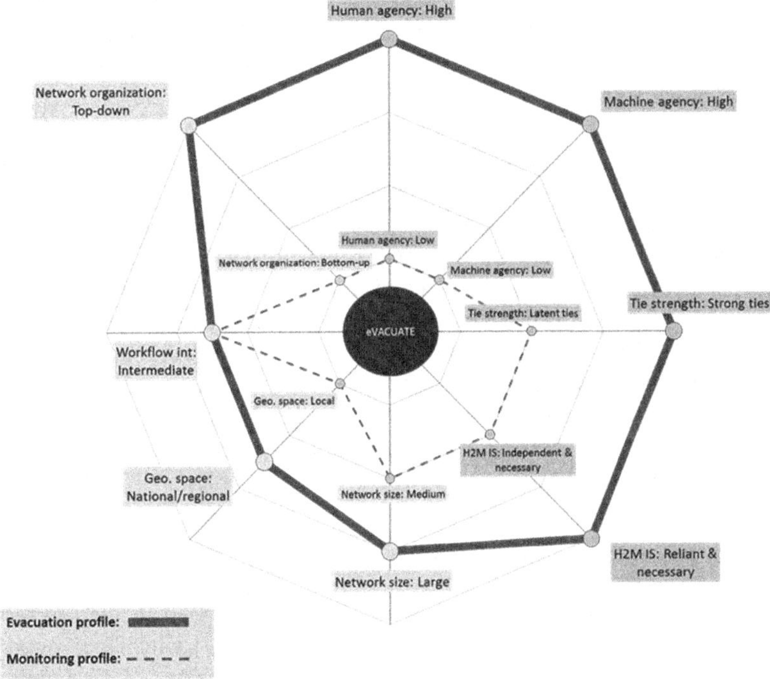

Fig. 4. Joint profile for the eVACUATE HMN

For normal operations ("monitoring": the dashed line in the figure), the network is relatively constrained (shown by network size and geographical space), with low human and machine agency: the network as a whole is simply ticking over (low in both cases), checking that the situation is normal and no intervention is required; human interaction with machines is moderate and confined essentially to operational staff (H2 M interaction strength: independent and necessary), who need to review machine input (sensor data) and reporting from the decision support system itself. In consequence, tie strength, for instance, remains latent: operational staff has little interaction with members of the public being monitored, who in turn have little interconnection beyond family or friendship groups, and incidental proximity to others.

Contrast this, though, with an emergency situation ("evacuation": the solid line in Fig. 4). Focus simply on the machine and human parts of the network: both change dramatically in terms of size, but especially in the level of agency apparent for each. The decision support system may physically increase, for instance, by recruiting additional devices in the crisis situation itself, such as personal communication devices, intelligent signage and so forth, but also by connection from an emergency services network if warranted. Evacuees in extremis will become more interdependent for their own well-being and even survival; operational staff themselves may become evacuees depending on location and situation. In consequence, tie strength becomes 'strong', and human agency 'high'.

An initial validation of the accuracy of the profile was effected through discussion with software engineers with experience of the eVACUATE system and knowledge of the related scenarios. Having introduced them to the rationale behind the profiling framework, they were presented with the profiles in Fig. 4 and asked for their comments. Although in broad agreement with the dimensions and our interpretation in connection with the eVACUATE system, they believed that other dimensions, such as an indication of machine-to-machine dependence or at least interaction, might be necessary to describe such networks accurately. Notwithstanding such omission and a concern about the scalability of the visualisation itself, the software engineers were positive in two important aspects. First, the profile we provide highlights behavioural aspects of the overall system which may not be apparent from more traditional formal methods: a network, as pointed out by one of the engineers, is much more than its constituent parts. Second, they emphasised that this sort of approach would help communication between the engineers and other 'actors' in the network, namely operational staff and even potential evacuees, in providing a common understanding of the network and what it is there to do. These aspects of the profiling framework are now being investigated further in relation to other HMNs as we build up experience and a repertoire of network types and profiles.

5.2 Case 2: Peer-to-Peer Reselling Network

The HMN typology and profiling framework was next applied to the Conserve & Consume project (http://conserveandconsume.wordpress.com/), which focuses on peer-to-peer reselling markets. Here, we have utilized the dimensions of the typology to analyse and discuss a recently launched iOS/Android app for such markets. The app is designed to enable direct selling of goods: sellers snap a photo of the item for sale, add a maximum of 58 character description, and publish the ad. Potential buyers see a thumbnail of the image, the distance to the seller, the price, and the time since the ad was published, and can then choose to open the item to read the description. The analysis has included data from developer and stakeholder collaboration, user interviews, as well as content analyses of classified advertisements posted by users. The resulting profile is shown in Fig. 5. In this paper we will focus on the dimensions network size, geographical space and machine agency.

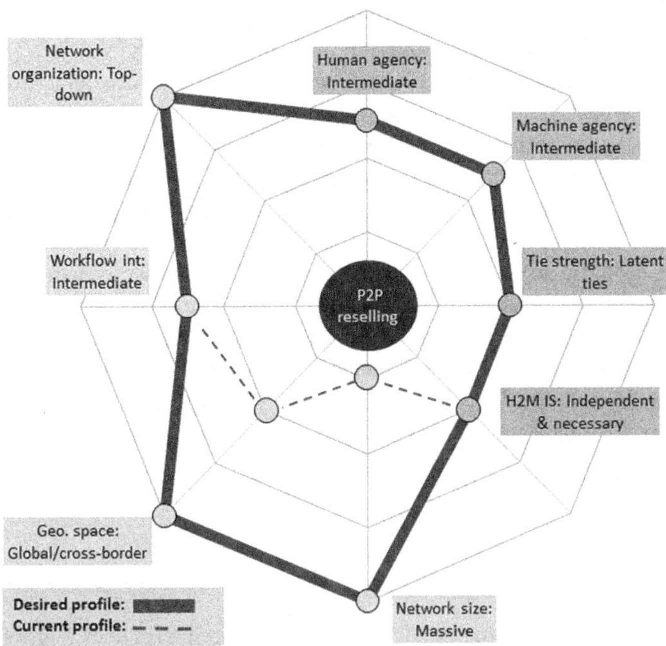

Fig. 5. Joint profile for the peer-to-peer reselling HMN (The joint profile for Case 2 differs from that presented in the HUMANE technical report *Typology and method v1* [5], due to updates following data collection and collaboration with the users and stakeholders.)

As is seen in the profiling, network size and geographical space are scored at different values (desired and current profile), reflecting the developer and stakeholder aim of increasing network size and eventually to become an app with global reach.

Machine agency is considered to be intermediate, with an important role for human nodes in the network. In its current version, the app performs a small set of functions, notifies users, and influences user-experience. The latter is apparent in how the app is designed to take off as much of the work-load in creating ads as possible, and in the features helping users discover items, and follow peers. End-user interviews demonstrate how users appreciate these functions, making the app functional, efficient and enjoyable both for users as sellers and buyers.

From working with the typology and profiling, several aspects of the network design became apparent as a consequence of how network size, geographical space and machine agency interrelate.

First, the desired increase in network size may require increased, or improved, machine agency to facilitate emergent change. As the group of typical users of the network evolves, the categories of items sold through the network also need to evolve. To support this, the developers prioritize functions for automatic classification of content in ads based on image- and text-recognition, and supports automatic updating of filtering categories to keep up with the evolving characteristics of the stuff sold through the marketplace. Hence, the link between machine agency, network size, and network capacity for emergent chance (related to the behaviour layer) has become apparent to the Conserve and Consume project through the profiling activity.

Second, whereas the app has a national reach, with some occasional users present also across the world, networks of human nodes seem to gather locally. Transactions between buyers and sellers are made locally, and end-users request improved functions that limit the availability of items for sale to their region. Such user-patterns and preferences call for design supporting the local, even for HMNs that on an aggregate level are global.

Third, the profiling activity provides terminology for discussing characteristics, and enables stakeholders to consider both the current state of an HMN and the desired state. For example, whereas the local will likely remain important, content-analysis of ads indicates heterogeneous user-patterns. Geographical proximity appears important for transactions to be completed, yet analyses of users' ads show that close-by items do not get more views than far-away items.

6 Discussion

6.1 Lessons Learnt

The application of the proposed typology in the cases described in Sect. 5 provides useful insights into the potential benefits but also the challenges associated with the dimensions. Significant benefits of the typology include the usefulness of the dimensions to support cross-disciplinary discussion of non-functional aspects of design (Case 1) and the novel understanding of HMN characteristics (Case 2). Furthermore, the profiling procedure was found to support the intended first two steps of defining network characteristics and establishing a network profile effectively.

At the same time, a number of challenges were identified. For instance, developers or stakeholders may desire additional dimensions to accurately describe the HMN. Furthermore, whereas the dimensions were found to support dialogue and aspects of analysis, the reliability in classifying HMNs on the individual dimensions were questioned. Future work is needed both to refine and consolidate the dimensions, and also to improve reliability in analysis for the dimensions.

Another critical challenge derived by the implementation of the dimensions concerned the identification of specific network types based on network profiles, that is, step 3 in the profiling process. This step requires the grouping of similar profiles; the mapping of these profiles would make this easier to carry out. However, the grouping rules and network types' identification remain a challenge. Future work is needed to deploy the typology for matching or clustering HMNs on the basis of their type.

Finally, some early indications have been provided concerning how the profiling framework may support the extraction of design guidelines. For example, in Case 2 considerations regarding machine agency serve to clarify the benefit of increasing automatic support for content classification and categorization; that is, increasing machine agency rather than working towards increased human agency to support growth in HMNs that are comparable to such reselling markets. At the same time, the cases only show early indications as to how such profiling may elicit design knowledge and experience, and future work is needed for the profiling framework to deliver more robust design support for future HMNs.

6.2 Limitations

The typology described here is not an exhaustive representation of all possible HMNs. The typology has emerged from and been tested against only a limited number of cases so far, and many more possible configurations will need to be considered as this typology matures. Also, the cases thus far are retrospective analyses of existing HMNs; to be of most value, the typology should also be tested at the design and initiation phases of HMNs to understand the extent to which the typology can help designers achieve their goals for the HMN.

Nevertheless, there are some early signs that there are benefits to this approach based on feedback from people close to the cases where it has been applied. What needs to be done now is work on resolving issues and concerns around both dimensions and methodology to capitalise on such potential. In our initial approach, the risk of overlooking some critical dimensions is inevitable. We attempted to scale each dimension as generally as possible, but the coarseness and the discrete nature of scales in each dimension will limit the applicability of the framework to certain cases.

Even though we believe that our typology can be very useful in understanding HMNs at the theoretical level, we provide no verification of its usefulness as a means to access design support in this paper. This is recognised as a significant gap which needs to be addressed as part of future work.

6.3 Conclusion and Future Work

We have presented an initial typology and framework for profiling HMNs in order to support HCD practitioners in the design of more successful systems, focusing on aiding the context analysis and requirements phases. Initial results from case studies in the HUMANE project have demonstrated value, such as helping system designers understand the relationship between aspects of the technical system and its users in order to achieve their vision of their desired system, and improving cross-disciplinary communication when performing requirements elicitation.

In the short term, we will continue to evaluate the typology and profiling framework against more current ICT projects based on superficially different HMNs. The purpose of this is twofold: first, we can thereby extend the investigation of dimensions; and secondly, we will begin to establish a set of profiles for future comparison. On this basis, the typology can then be assessed and validated against a larger set of case studies to ensure it is widely applicable. Network profiling on an even larger scale will pave the way for an analysis into network types and correlations between the dimensions in order to develop an extended technology for identifying a) similar networks and b) relevant design guidance and shared experience. This will address the two final steps of identifying similar networks and extracting design principles in the profiling framework proposed in this paper in order to maximize the potential value of this work to the system designers.

Acknowledgements. This work has been conducted as part of the HUMANE project (http://humane2020.eu), which has received funding from the European Union's Horizon 2020 research and innovation programme under grant agreement No. 645043.

References

1. Shneiderman, S.B., Plaisant, C., Cohen, M., Jacobs, S.: Designing the User Interface: Strategies for Effective Human-Computer Interaction. Pearson New International Edition. Pearson, Essex (2013)
2. Lüders, M.: Networking and notworking in social intranets: user archetypes and participatory divides. First Monday **18**(8) (2013). doi:10.5210/fm.v18i8.4693
3. Tayebi, A.: Communihood: a less formal or more local form of community in the age of the internet. J. Urban Technol. **20**(2), 77–91 (2013)
4. Collier, D., LaPorte, J., Seawright, J.: Putting typologies to work: concept formation, measurement, and analytic rigor. Polit. Res. Q. **65**(1), 217–232 (2012)
5. Følstad, A., Eide, A.W., Pickering, J.B., Bravos, G., Tsvetkova, M., Gavilanes, R., Yasseri, T., Engen, V.: HUMANE Typology and Method v1. Technical report, HUMANE project (2015). http://humane2020.eu/publications/
6. ISO: Ergonomics of Human–System Interaction — Part 210: Human-Centred Design for Interactive Systems. International Organization for Standardization, Geneva (2010)
7. Leonardi, P.M.: Materiality, sociomateriality, and socio-technical systems: what do these terms mean? How are they related? Do we need them? In: Leonardi, P.M., Nardi, B.A., Kallinikos, J. (eds.) Materiality and Organizing: Social Interaction in a Technological World, pp. 25–48. Oxford University Press, Oxford (2012)
8. Latour, B.: Reassembling the Social-an Introduction to Actor-Network-Theory. Oxford University Press, Oxford (2005)
9. Smart, P.R., Simperl, E., Shadbolt, N.: A taxonomic framework for social machines. In: Miorandi, D., Maltese, V., Rovatsos, M., Nijholt, A., Stewart, J. (eds.) Social Collective Intelligence: Combining the Powers of Humans and Machines to Build a Smarter Society. Springer, Heidelberg (2013)
10. Tsvetkova, M., Yasseri, T., Meyer, E.T., Pickering, J.B., Engen, V., Walland, P., Lüders, M., Følstad, A., Bravos, G.: Understanding Human-Machine Networks: A Cross-Disciplinary Survey (2015). http://arxiv.org/abs/1511.05324
11. Seffah, A.: Patterns of HCI Design and HCD Design of Patterns: Bridging HCI Design and Model-Driven Software Engineering. Springer, Heidelberg (2015)
12. Engen, V., Pickering J.B., Walland, P.: Machine agency in human-machine networks; impacts and trust implications. In: Kurosu, M. (ed.) HCII 2016, Part III. LNCS, vol. 9733, pp. 96–106. Springer, Heidelberg (2016)
13. Broekens, J., Heerink, M., Rosendal, H.: Assistive social robots in elderly care: a review. Gerontechnology **8**(2), 94–103 (2009)

Build or Buy: A Case Study for ERP System Selection in SMEs

Olga Gomez(✉), Patrick Wriedt, and Fan Zhao

College of Business, Florida Gulf Coast University, Fort Myers, USA
ogomez3492@eagle.fgcu.edu

Abstract. The purpose of this paper is to provide enterprises with valuable input when selecting ERP. This study resulted from a case study on an Air Conditioning Company in Florida, USA. Case study research technique evaluated the data collected from interviews, documents, and observations. The results show the importance of embedding every single factor in order to make a decision. The data analysis confirmed the ultimate decision that was reached by the company.

Keywords: ERP selection · SMEs · In-house ERP

1 Introduction

In today's globally competitive environment, a business will find it very problematic to operate without a structured and uniform information system. Currently, all the business companies are now armed with the ERP system in order to follow the environment change and business development (Zouine and Fenies 2014). Also enterprises need to be responsive and flexible, and will require the same from their information systems. Motiwalla and Thompson (2012) point out that these "integrated information systems are needed today to focus on customers, to process efficiency, and to help build teams that bring employees together that cross functional areas. ERP systems are the specific kind of enterprise systems to integrate data across and be comprehensive in supporting all the major functions of the organization". The goal of ERP system is to make data stream be both dynamic and instant, consequently increasing the usefulness and value of the data. Companies chose to implement ERP because they can reduce costs, increase workflow efficiency, respond rapidly to an always changing marketplace, and excerpt business intelligence from the data.

The theory behind implementing ERP system is to make every aspect of business organized and uniform and also to provide an integrated access to all areas of business. While some enterprises choose ERP solutions from vendors, others benefit from constructing an ERP system in-house. When business executives decide to obtain ERP integrated system, they are faced with evaluating possibilities to have an in-house applications or get it from the shelf of a vendor.

In this research paper we would like to find out key factors influencing the decision making process for the ERP solution selection in small and medium enterprises (SMEs). We want to study more toward the reasons whey a medium size company to

M. Kurosu (Ed.): HCI 2016, Part I, LNCS 9731, pp. 23–33, 2016.
DOI: 10.1007/978-3-319-39510-4_3

buy an ERP system or if they should develop their own system in-house. Each option has to provide a suite of software modules that cover all functional areas of a business (Finney and Corbett 2007). For this purpose, we do not only want to highlight all the advantages and disadvantages that already have been discovered by previous studies, but also analyze different opinions from different employees of a company and the reasoning behind their thoughts about buying a vendor-package or developing a new system in-house. Do they prefer to buy a standardized vendor-package even if it means to customize it in addition to their needs and to learn how the new system works? Or do they prefer to develop their own system in-house? This case study will give an overview of key issues that explain such decisions.

2 Literature Review

Nowadays ERP systems are more popular than ever and more specialized in all business areas. On the competition edge many companies try to elevate qualities of their products and services and get the focus of their customers' attentions (Moohebat et al. 2011). Among the most important attributes of ERP systems are their abilities to automate and integrate an organization's business processes, share common data and practices across the entire enterprise, and produce and access information in a real-time environment (Kamhawi 2007). They have developed enormously over time, so they got very complex and expensive. Based on the situation that almost every vendor-package has to be customized to the specific needs of a company - because the standardized vendor-packages does not suit to all needs - it even get more expensive to buy and implement an ERP system, as well as increase the time required (Harrell et al. 2001). Before beginning an ERP implementation, much planning and thought must go into the process (Gargeya and Brady 2005). In order to achieve this, enterprises should consult experts during the implementation process in order to deliver the above-mentioned benefits, and avoid system failure (Shatat 2015).

For this reason there are many companies that are thinking about if they should buy a vendor-package, lease, outsource, or develop their own system in-house (Harrell et al. 2001). Especially, for SMEs it is more complicated to afford the huge expense of buying an ERP system of a vendor.

The decision about if a company should implement an ERP system of a vendor or try to build one in-house could be one of the most important decisions an enterprise has to do because it determines which way a company will go in the future. As we know an ill-conceived decision could break your company up.

Both solutions have their advantages and disadvantages. Starting with an off-the-shelf ERP software, the two main points of buying are that it does not meet all the needs of a company's operations but on the other hand it seems to be faster and the prices are reasonable at the beginning (Harrell et al. 2001). Table 1 summarizes the advantages and disadvantages of both solutions.

Furthermore, buying a software indicates higher upfront costs and less control because companies are more dependent on external (vendor, consultant) support (Panorama Consulting Solutions 2013).

Table 1. Comparison of ERP solutions

System solution	Advantages	Disadvantages
Off-the-shelf ERP	- Based on a good software sophistication there are less complications/"bugs" - If the company's operations can be adjusted to the software then it is a good choice - Provided with long-term training and support from experts - Cost effective - It is continuously improving the software	- The use of customization is often necessary (is often inflexible and has the same functionalities as everyone else who buy the program) - It requires an increase of costs - The time of implementation increases if a customization of the software is necessary - It does not meet all the needs of a company's operations - It creates conflicts if other software are included - To execute an upgrade could be difficulty if your software is already customized
Built-on-house ERP	- Most customized to a company's business and tailored to individual operations - Full ownership of the system - Possibility of a bigger competitive advantage compared to a bought well-known software - Social benefits	- Requires programming skills in the company (hired or subcontracted) - Requires a lot of time to develop the system - Company is responsible for maintenance - Expensive (not only the development and implementation but also maintenance and IT-skilled personnel) - "Bugs" could appear - Hard to upgrade the system

The other alternative of building the software in-house could be the better solution if you want the most customized system which fits perfectly to your business. Also if you want to have most flexibility you should think about develop your own system.

To be sure which alternative should be chosen the managers/companies have to decide well-thought-out how to overcome all of these disadvantages and consider all advantages and disadvantages for both alternatives. For this purpose Harrell et al. (2001) created a few questions to find out if you should consider buying or building a software. Based on your individual situation you have to try to honestly answer those questions, so you are able to find out which alternative suits best to your company.

Olsen (2011) stated that if a small sized company wants to survive it has to be flexible, able to react quickly to market needs, and dynamic and therefore being in control of its own IT system (Olsen and Saetre (n.d.)). Buying an ERP software could be too expensive (customizing, updates, consultants, etc.) and the implementation could be challenging to the company. The company would be too dependent on the vendor. If a small sized company wants to gain an advantage it has to be flexible and the IT system has to go along with the business of the company.

Olsen and Saetre (n.d.) said that one major effect of building the ERP system in-house is the specification part in which the company has to define functionality, terminology, and important processes. Although it needs a lot of time and be a very complex part of the whole system development, it will create many positive side effects so it should not be interpreted as an IT-cost. Another positive effect is that an in-house built ERP implicates social benefits. Employees could feel more comfortable with the system and they possibly can identify themselves with the own developed system of the company. Preferences of the users could be met much easier compared to those companies who buy an ERP package. If you buy a package then you have to adjust your business processes to the bought ERP system, on the other hand if you develop your own system in-house your system will be created based on the company's business processes. All requirements of the company and its users should be met with the use of an in-house ERP system.

In addition, Umble et al. (2002) mentioned that with the use of developing an in-house ERP system a company is able to find more and creative solutions concerning integration problems. All in all you will have more freedom in your solution creation.

Nevertheless, an in-house development is still viewed as expensive and it takes too much time. "The software costs must be included with all the other costs in the business case for the new processes" (Newing 2000). In addition, Ifinedo (2011) mentioned for having success in ERP systems it is very important to have in-house IT professionals and external expertise, otherwise it would even get more difficult to develop an in-house system without external help. Piturro (1999) stated that it is important to make sure having enough people who are able to complete the implementation. Avoiding personnel shortages is a criteria that has to be considered.

Furthermore, if an organization considers to buy an ERP system it often underestimates the costs by 40 % to 75 % (Piturro 1999). An off-the-shelf system rarely fits perfectly to the needs and requirements of the business of an organization, so they need to customize the program and get external help which will immensely increase the costs in an instant.

King (2005) said that most firms buy packaged software from vendors instead of develop their own system in-house because it is still too difficult to develop and additionally too expensive. Furthermore, another point which has to be considered in an in-house development is how stable and strong an IT department of a company is.

Companies entrust the knowledge and the development of an in-house system to its current employees (IT) but this could be a very risky business and situation if the employees would leave the company ("ERP buy versus build", 2002). In that case they would take the unique knowledge with them and in the end the company would have a problem with its system. Without the responsible persons who are in charge of the ERP system the company is not able to take care and handle this situation.

Rao (2000) tried to find out whether an organization should think about buying or building its ERP system in-house. He used a decision tree model that includes four different options:

1. Developing an own ERP package: This option needs many functional specialists who possess the right knowledge and skills to develop the ERP system in-house.
2. Enhancing the capabilities in the existing system: All the non-integrated computerized business functions has to be measured for integration. Also for this option you need specialized skills otherwise it will not be possible.
3. Buying a ready-made package: To use the vendor-package effective it often requires a specific customization to the needs and requirements of a company.
4. Engaging a software company: In this case it is the use of outside resources. There are some companies who already have developed a software for a client, which can also be used for others with or without any changes.

Daneshgar et al. (2011; 2013) analyzed in their study what kind of factors affect the decision of software acquisition method by large organizations and SMEs. The study was based on a survey of Thai SMEs as a general representative of today's SME. They found out that the following factors are more relevant for large companies than for SMEs:

1. Strategy and competitive advantage
2. Intellectual property
3. Risk (of negative outcome)

Factors that are relevant and important to SMEs and large organizations are:

1. Cost
2. Commoditization
3. flexibility/change
4. Time
5. Scale and complexity
6. Support structure
7. Requirements fit
8. In-house experts
9. Operational factors

And finally, factors that are especially relevant to SMEs (Daneshgar et al. 2013):

1. Availability of free download
2. Ubiquitous systems
3. It should be customizable to specific government or tax regulations

Socrates (2015) mentioned in a general study about decision-making criteria concerning make-or-buy issues that the two most significant criteria in such a situation are cost and quality. On the one hand organizations want to achieve cost savings and on the other hand gain operational advantages.

Overall it can be said that strategical factors are not as relevant as operational factors to SMEs and that in general there are some important factors that affect more the decision process depending on the size of the organization. Furthermore, Daneshgar et al. (2013) speculated in their study that compared to larger organizations SMEs do not chase long-term visions too much and competition seems not to be as intense for SMEs as it is for the larger organizations which are more integrated in a global competition and not in a local market (but this statement was only based on their study which analyzed SMEs in the Asian region, so it cannot be used as a general statement).

Proper project planning is widely recognized as a critical success factor for a successful vendor packaged ERP implementation for medium-sized enterprises (Doom et al. 2010). This includes:

The project scope - the identification of the business processes affected by the ERP implementation, the choice of ERP modules and the identification of the changes to the standard ERP packages. It is essential that these choices are made correctly;

- The project plan with phasing and the critical path;
- The milestones and deadlines;
- The resources plan;
- Contingency measures.

Thus it is not surprising to see that having clear goals and objectives, user training and education as well as user involvement in evaluation and implementation were commonly considered by companies as key success factors (Beheshti et al. 2014).

However sometimes, ERP implementation creates a major challenge. It has become common to see a gap between results and the initial objectives (Olivier et al. 2009). The study by Wang et al. (2005) showed that costs average 178 % over budget and implementation periods 2.5 times longer than anticipate. It is a crucial factor in detecting the overall triumph of the ERP implementation, since if the allocated budget is exceeded there is a pressure to reduce the cost on downward phases like training, which are core for implementation project (Saini et al. 2013). "Project managers must grasp technical issues such as system development and process reengineering. But they must also master the human and organizational domains such as change management and end-user involvement." (Olivier et al. 2009). If top management is not actively backing an ERP implementation, there is little hope for it (Akkermans and Helden 2002).

3 Case Study

In order to research questions thoroughly and extensively, case study research method was chosen. This research method allows to dig into true reasons why enterprises go one way or another. Woo (2007) points out that case studies are suitable to explore new areas and issues where little theory is available. The research was conducted on the premise of a middle-size company, which specializes in air conditioning repairs and installations. The research included numerous interviews with executive team using open-ended questions, and multiple observations.

Data for the research study was collected from an air conditioning company in Bonita Springs, Florida, USA. This type of service business was chosen to display how small and middle-sized companies nowadays truly depend on Internet services and software applications. SMEs have such characters as small-scale production, flexible operation, high rate of assets and liabilities, less competitive, etc. (Zhang and Li 2007). The study was conducted by interviewing IT Director of the company, Steven Smith, HR Director, Jennifer Colombo, CFO, Cathy Baker, and CEO, Louis Bruno. Also, the data was collected from multiple observations by one of the researchers, Olga Gomez. She spend about two months diagnosing the need of bringing in the new ERP system to the company.

Bruno Air Conditioning company was founded in 2012 by a young entrepreneur Louis Bruno and grew substantially by 2015. Right now the company has 3 locations: Bonita Springs, Tampa, and Orlando, and by December of 2015, company's sales will exceed 27 million dollars with staff of over 130 individuals. IT director of the company was hired at the enterprise five months ago and recognized the need to have an ERP system for the growing business.

Bruno Air Conditioning Company has multiple departments that structure air conditioning business. From customer service department to accounting department, the enterprise uses at least three different systems to operate.

For instance, dispatch department, and customer service experience department use program AcoWin to efficiently record data and extract information when needed. Accounting department operates on Quickbooks program which is synced with AcoWin. Accountants pull numerous reports from AcoWin database to record profits, losses, sales, and expenses. For human resource management, ADP cloud software was chosen to register all the records of employees and account for their salaries. Sales and lead generation department uses Excel program to track information. Also, each subdivision of Bruno Air Conditioning uses Outlook program to communicate between each other. Platforms that company currently uses include Microsoft 7, which is installed on every work computer in the main office, and IOS platform for technicians who use tablets while they are out on the road or at the job site.

The main Customer Relationship Management (CRM) application, AcoWin was chosen by executive team in order to facilitate growing customer orders. The application was chosen because at that time it did provide the enterprise with aspects that were needed. The application uses FoxPro database, which is outdated for current management and cannot do upgrades. Each license per seat costs 1500 dollars, which makes AcoWin extremely expensive. In addition the license for AcoTruck system used by technicians is also costly.

When company brought AcoWin to become major CRM, a lot of expectations were not met. For example, it was not capable of doing much for the company with extreme growth. With the amount of data, that was pushed into it, and the amount of data that needed to be extracted, often AcoWin would spit out reports with errors, corrupted data, or simply freeze during the work process not allowing the users to finish the job timely. Diagram 1 shows where the process was slowing down and how complicated the structure of software is (red lines are examples of the "bottleneck" processes).

The decision to acquire ERP system was made by executive team in August 2015. CEO and CIO of the company tried to look for an ERP application that will suit their business the most, increase productivity by 30 %, and reduce costs.

The company was considering two opportunities: ERP system from vendor Oracle or build in-house ERP, that will be created with the help of outsourcing company ECOS. In addition, Bruno Air Conditioning was considering cloud-based ERP, however, fast enough refused that prospect, because of Internet Service Provider, Comcast. It was found that Comcast could not support the company on the high level because of the connectivity problems and the geographical area. Also, the company's business is highly dependent on Internet use, thus, a loss of Internet connection can cause the company to fail.

Executive team debated between purchase of Oracle ERP and build-in house ERP for three months. The Chief Financial Officer of the company tried to convince the rest of executive team to go with Oracle. She recognized many advantages for the company if they were to buy from the popular vendor. For instance, all members of the executive team were familiar with the package. They used to work on Oracle platform while they were working at big corporations like Boeing, Hertz, and Gartner. Also, CFO stressed the importance of upgrading opportunities for the growing company. In addition, she pointed out that Oracle is a respected vendor, and will have a lower risk of failure. The disadvantages of buying Oracle were also taken into account. For instance, the company would get little to zero customization, high upgrade costs, and the asking price of three hundred thousand dollars was above company's budget.

The other option of building ERP in house was discussed much more thoroughly than buying from a vendor option. IT director, Steven Smith, was working on in-house ERP project for a long time. He considered working with outsourcing company ECOS from India to acquire the software. Four developers flew from India to meet with executive team for a discussion. The asking price for a project was sixty thousand dollars and project could go to alpha-test in about 6-8 months. The advantages of acquiring ECOS custom-built software seemed very substantial. The company uses DotNet platform and SQL database, which is very convenient for the enterprise. Also, the demos that were demonstrated in front of executive team impressed everybody. Other companies that were considered as candidates for partnership did not even have half of functionalities needed by Bruno Air Conditioning. In addition, the enterprise will own the software, which means that the company does not need to pay anybody for licensing.

In October of 2015, Bruno Air Conditioning reached the decision of building ERP in house. By next year, company projects to operate on a new ERP system, which allows for reduction of costs, user-friendly interface, and full capacity of customization. Projected ERP functionality is counted to be at 90 %.

4 Discussions and Conclusions

Analysis of data was completed through extensive interviews, collections of data, and numerous observations. No surprisingly, most of the key issues we found through our literature review were discussed and emphasized by the company, such as cost, implementation time, requirements fit, and so on. However, there are several interesting findings that we want to share in our case study.

First, even most of the key issues were mentioned during the interview, the company has a full list of all the key factors with different priorities. From the company's perspective, the most important factor they considered was functionality. This seems different with other SMEs who more focus on the cost as the first priority factor. As the IT director mentioned "the main reason we go with in-house system is because we can cover over 90 % of our required functions and features. Other companies that we were looking at only had half of functionalities." Cost was the number 2 in their list. The number 3 factor they considered is customization. They prefer "more ability to change on demand." Next one in their list is the ownership of the ERP package. They enjoy to own the package with "no copyright agreements, no infringements, and no fees." The next factor they talked is time. "We only need 6–8 months to go alfa." This includes both development time and implementation time.

Second, as we mentioned previously, the IT director worked on in-house ERP project for a long time. We believe the technical background of the key decision maker may impact the decision significantly! In this case study, even CFO with Oracle background tried to convince everyone to go with Oracle, because of the technical background of IT director, who is the key decision maker, eventually, the final decision turned to be an in-house system.

Third, the most popular ERP solution for SMEs is cloud ERP. The company did considered this option, but they have a strong reason to not go with cloud: "We cannot completely rely on cloud, because Comcast shuts down quite often." Therefore, the Internet hardware will be another factor to be considered when a company makes the decisions.

Nowadays, numerous SMEs face a decision to acquire ERP system. As we found out many companies implement ERP system from a popular vendor, however, others try to go their own way by building customized application. This research shows that there are advantages and disadvantages of choosing one approach or another. In our research we found the following trend that buying ERP for the middle size company is more efficient. This research was done only on one company which limits its scope. However, there was enough literature research findings supporting our assumption. Nevertheless, more research has to be done to reach a more accepted solution on this topic.

This paper provides valuable insights towards understanding executives' decision when selecting ERP. Overall we can say that every company has to evaluate its current situation in connection with a rating of all advantages and disadvantages of buying or building an ERP system concerning the specific needs and requirements of the company's business. It is also important that if you want to build your ERP in-house you need to have at least internal expertise and personnel who are able to support your decision. If a company wants to gain most control out of its core IT functions then it has to develop its ERP system in-house because only with this option you are able to create the system you need most and that fits perfectly to your business. Based on our selected company - Bruno Air Conditioning - we can say that it would make sense for medium-sized companies to build an ERP system in-house. However, it has to be taken into account that each different type of business is not the same, thus each individual case has to be valuated with additional courtesy.

References

Adam, M.N.K.B.: The critical success factors of enterprise resource planning (ERP) implementation: Malaysian and American experiences. Multimedia University (Malaysia), ProQuest Dissertations Publishing (2010). http://search.proquest.com.ezproxy.fgcu.edu/abicomplete/docview/860327924/1351944351414801PQ/2?accountid=10919 (accessed)

Akkermans, H., van Helden, K.: Vicious and virtuous cycles in ERP implementation: a case study of interrelations between critical success factors. Eur. J. Inf. Syst. **11**(1), 35–46 (2002)

Clydebuild Business Solutions: Developing in-house vs. off the shelf (2012). http://www.clydebuiltsolutions.com/wp-content/uploads/2012/05/Inhouse-VS-Off-the-Shelf-May.pdf (accessed)

Daneshgar, F., et al.: An investigation of 'Build vs. Buy' decision for software acquisition in small to medium enterprises. Inf. Softw. Technol. **55**(10), 1741–1750 (2011)

Daneshgar, F., et al.: An investigation of 'Build vs. Buy' decision for software acquisition by small to medium enterprises. Inf. Softw. Technol. **55**(10) (2013) (revised)

Doom, C., Milis, K., Poelmans, S., Bloemen, E.: Critical success factors for ERP implementations in Belgian SMEs. J. Enterp. Inf. Manage. **23**(3) (2010). http://search.proquest.com.ezproxy.fgcu.edu/abicomplete/docview/220041605/1351944351414801PQ/5?accountid=10919 (accessed)

ERP buy versus build: ComputerWire (2002). http://phamtrung.wikispaces.com/file/view/ERP+BUY+VERSUS+BUILD.pdf (accessed)

Finney, S., Corbett, M.: ERP implementation: a compilation and analysis of critical success factors. Bus. Process Manage. J. **13**(3) (2007). http://search.proquest.com.ezproxy.fgcu.edu/abicomplete/docview/220322969/1351944351414801PQ/19?accountid=10919 (accessed)

Gargeya, V., Brady, C.: Success and failure factors of adopting SAP in ERP system implementation. Bus. Process Manage. J. **11**(5) (2005). http://search.proquest.com.ezproxy.fgcu.edu/abicomplete/docview/220320780/1351944351414801PQ/10?accountid=10919 (accessed)

Harrell, H.W., et al.: Expanding ERP application software: buy, lease, outsource, or write your own? J. Corp. Account. Financ., 37–43 (2001). http://search.proquest.com/abicomplete/docview/201614513/7305FEE2CE434CB5PQ/2?accountid=10919 (accessed)

Ifinedo, P.: Examining the influences of external expertise and in-house computer/IT knowledge on ERP system success. J. Syst. Softw. (2011). http://www.sciencedirect.com/science/article/pii/S0164121211001208 (accessed)

Iivari, J.: Implementation of in-house developed vs application packaged based information systems (1990). http://www.researchgate.net/publication/233817667_Implementation_of_in-house_developed_vs_application_package_based_information_systems (accessed)

Kamhawi, E.M.: Critical factors for implementation success of ERP systems: an empirical investigation from Bahrain. Int. J. Enterp. Inf. Syst. **3**(2) (2007). http://search.proquest.com.ezproxy.fgcu.edu/abicomplete/docview/222696806/1351944351414801PQ/6?accountid=10919 (accessed)

King, W.R.: Ensuring ERP implementation success. Inf. Syst. Manage., 83–84 (2005). http://search.proquest.com/abicomplete/docview/214132903/fulltext/C000F2C713E54573PQ/1?accountid=10919 (accessed)

Beheshti, H.M., Blaylock, B.K., Henderson, D.A., Lollar, J.G.: Selection and critical success factors in successful ERP implementation. Competitiveness Rev. **24**(4) (2014). http://search.proquest.com.ezproxy.fgcu.edu/abicomplete/docview/1658481852/1351944351414801PQ/23?accountid=10919 (accessed)

Moohebat, M.R., Jazi, M.D., Asemi, A.: Evaluation of the ERP implementation at Esfahan steel company based on five critical success factors: a case study. Int. J. Bus. Manage. **6**(5) (2011). http://search.proquest.com.ezproxy.fgcu.edu/abicomplete/docview/867071719/1351944351414801PQ/14?accountid=10919 (accessed)

Motiwalla, L.F., Thompson, J.: Enterprise Systems for Management. Pearson Education Inc., New Jersey (2012)

Newing, R.: Why the cash benefits are notoriously difficult to quantify: MEASURING RETURN ON INVESTMENT by Rod Newing: Industry in general has a dismal record in tracking return on investment - 80 % of companies cannot even compute the total cost of ownership for their ERP solutions: [Surveys edition]. Financial Times [London (UK)] 19 July 2000 (2000). http://search.proquest.com.ezproxy.fgcu.edu/abicomplete/docview/248889899/EDB2B8972CE4EF2PQ/10?accountid=10919 (accessed)

Olsen, K.A.: In-house programming: an option for small and medium sized niche companies (2011). http://www.nik.no/2011/5-1-olsen11InHouseProgramming (accessed)

Olsen, K.A., Saetre, P. (n.d.): ERP for SMEs - is proprietary software an alternative? http://home.himolde.no/~olsen/artikler/P81CompletePaper.pdf (accessed)

Panorama Consulting Solutions: ERP Systems: Build vs. buy (2013). http://panorama-consulting.com/erp-systems-build-vs-buy/ (accessed)

Piturro, M.: How midsize companies are buying ERP. J. Accountancy (1999). http://www.journalofaccountancy.com/issues/1999/sep/piturr.html (accessed)

Rao, S.S.: Enterprise resource planning: business needs and technologies. Ind. Manage. Data Syst., 81–88 (2000). http://search.proquest.com/abicomplete/docview/234920592/780D0E602EB0477DPQ/2?accountid=10919 (accessed)

Saini, S., Nigam, S., Misra, S.C.: Identifying success factors for implementation of ERP at Indian SMEs and large organizations and multinational organizations. J. Model. Manage. **8**(1) (2013). http://search.proquest.com.ezproxy.fgcu.edu/abicomplete/docview/1315354996/1351944351414801PQ/20?accountid=10919 (accessed)

Shatat, A.S.: Critical success factors in enterprise resource planning (ERP) system implementation: an exploratory study in oman. Electron. J. Inf. Syst. Eval. **18**(1) (2015). http://search.proquest.com.ezproxy.fgcu.edu/abicomplete/docview/1697718578/1351944351414801PQ/12?accountid=10919 (accessed)

Sokrates, J.M.: Decision-making criteria in tactical make-or-buy issues: an empirical analysis. EuroMed J. Bus. **10**(1), 2–20 (2015)

Umble, E.J., Haft, R.R., Umble, M.M.: Enterprise resource planning: implementation procedures and critical success factors. Eur. J. Oper. Res., 241–257 (2002). http://down.cenet.org.cn/upfile/94/200526163844188.pdf (accessed)

Wang, E., Chou, H.-W., Jiang, J.: The impacts of charismatic leadership style on team cohesiveness and overall performance during ERP implementation. Int. J. Proj. Manage. **23**(3), 173–180 (2005)

Woo, H.S.: Critical success factors for implementing ERP: the case of a Chinese electronics manufacturer. J. Manuf. Technol. Manage. **18**(4). (2007). http://search.proquest.com.ezproxy.fgcu.edu/abicomplete/docview/208175880/1351944351414801PQ/8?accountid=10919 (accessed)

Zhang, Q., Li, Z.: Study on ERP-based cost control in SME. Manage. Eng. **1** (2007). http://search.proquest.com.ezproxy.fgcu.edu/abicomplete/docview/1355856125/EDB2B8972CE4EF2PQ/1?accountid=10919 (accessed)

Zouine, A., Fenies, P.: The critical success factors of the ERP system project: a meta-analysis methodology. J. Appl. Bus. Res. **30**(5) (2014). http://search.proquest.com.ezproxy.fgcu.edu/abicomplete/docview/1655564764/1351944351414801PQ/3?accountid=10919 (accessed)

Innovation and Collaboration Patterns in Human-Computer Interaction Research

Junius Gunaratne(✉) and Bharat Rao

New York University, New York, NY, USA
{junius, bharat.rao}@nyu.edu

Abstract. Research in human-computer interaction is dominated by institutions characterized by a deep involvement in the evolution of the field, and their ability to successfully network and collaborate with others. Network analysis and information flow visualization are useful techniques to help understand their influence and centrality. We use data visualizations of publication data to examine how collaborative research institutions are with each other in HCI research.

Keywords: Innovation · Collaboration · Research productivity · Data visualization

1 Introduction

Studies of industry research labs show that institutions that collaborate with other institutions tend to produce more research and are generally more innovative [1]. Examining such collaboration and innovation patterns in institutional settings, we compared universities and industry research labs specializing in human-computer interaction (HCI). Research in HCI has greatly influenced everything from graphical user interface prototypes to the notions of ubiquitous computing, and the HCI field at large continues to dramatically influence trends in modern computing. We find that institutions doing research in HCI that actively collaborate with other institutions (both universities and industry research labs) have greater numbers of published research papers (productivity), and possibly higher impact (innovativeness).

1.1 Patterns of Collaboration and Innovation Within HCI

HCI's origins can be traced back to the 1970s when prototype computer systems such as Xerox PARC's Alto system started to emphasize human factors in computing. HCI research activity has seen steady growth over the past few decades and this is reflected in the increasing popularity of ACM's Computer-Human Interaction conference and published papers in the field of HCI [2]. Major contributors to HCI research include Carnegie Mellon University, Georgia Institute for Technology, IBM Research, Microsoft Research and Stanford University. Many theories and concepts from these institutions have defined HCI and continue to influence computing today ranging from research in user interface software development to ethnographic techniques adopted for computing [2].

M. Kurosu (Ed.): HCI 2016, Part I, LNCS 9731, pp. 34–45, 2016.
DOI: 10.1007/978-3-319-39510-4_4

Top institutions are recognized for their research prominence by word of mouth reputation, citations, and so on; however, we attempt to show that these institutions are partially successful because of inter-institutional collaboration. Collaboration not only enhances innovation, but also can help an institution become more central and influential to a field. A number of studies show how centrality is created and why it is useful. Suarez and Utterback [3] discussed how alliances are formed between institutions when a dominant standard is established. At research universities, often the dominant players in a research area are hard to surpass and these key players often remain at the forefront of an established research area for decades. These key research universities often get the best faculty and students. In industry, Cusumano and Nobeoka [4] found that research and development (R&D) used to shape business strategy has a significant impact on overall financial performance of companies. For firms involved in commercial R&D, this means that R&D needs to be an integral part of product planning and strategy [1, 5].

2 Methodology

Network analysis and information flow visualization are useful techniques to help understand influence and centrality with respect to research activity. Polites and Watson [6] studied the influence of journals within the information systems discipline using social network analysis and information flow. Polites and Watson found Communications of the ACM to be one of the most influential and respected publications in the field and demonstrated that prestige does matter in the sense that core journals have substantial effects in influencing the research of many related journals in closely related fields. Therefore, centrality in network graph visualizations is a good indicator of influence.

To discover collaborative relationships within the domain of HCI, we used data from the Association of Computing Machinery's online digital library (ACM DL) to obtain author and institution collaboration data by searching for the keyword "HCI" and grouping results by institution. From each institution, ACM DL lists the top 100 contributing authors for publications affiliated with that institution based on a keyword. Authors are listed in descending numerical ranking, with the authors associated with the most papers at the top of the list. Authors can be either a primary author or a co-author of a paper to show up in an author ranking associated with an institution. Using primary author and co-author institution affiliation data we linked institutions by collaborating authors. Authors may be affiliated with multiple institutions since one author may show up in different institution rankings. We used D3 for Data-Driven Documents, a data visualization JavaScript library to create our network visualizations. This tool is commonly used for data visualization of social networks, amongst other purposes [7]. D3's primary use is for data visualization so deriving relationships between data is limited to spatial analysis and approximating the proximity of nodes in the graph. Because of how D3 animates graphics there is some variability in how graphs are rendered. Despite these limitations Weng and Menczer [8], Wu et al. [9] and others have used the tool for social network data visualization.

3 Analysis and Key Findings

This analysis examined the top 20 institutions contributing to HCI research analyzing the profiles of approximately 2000 authors and co-authors contributing to the field of HCI research. We compared the social network data visualizations to a ranked table of institutions publishing HCI research (Table 1) to provide further analysis of top HCI research institutions.

Table 1. Institutions and the number of corresponding HCI papers. 2014 ACM Digital Library

Institution	Papers	Institution	Papers
Carnegie Mellon University	799	University of Oulu	161
Georgia Institute of Technology	568	University of York	160
Microsoft Research	387	MIT Media Laboratory	160
Stanford University	337	Newcastle University, UK	159
University of Washington Seattle	336	National University of Singapore	157
University of California, Irvine	290	Simon Fraser University	155
Nokia	271	Aalborg University	149
University College London	268	University of Salzburg	148
Eindhoven University of Technology	267	Korea Adv Institute of Sci & Tech	147
Indiana University	254	Delft University of Technology	146
University of California, Berkeley	247	IBM	145
Lancaster University	240	University of Melbourne	144
University of Maryland	235	University of Twente	142
University of Glasgow	230	University of Manchester	141
Pennsylvania State University	228	Ludwig Maximilian Uni of Munich	137
Virginia Tech	226	University of Colorado at Boulder	136
University of Toronto	224	University of Calgary	133
University Michigan Ann Arbor	217	Microsoft	133
IBM T.J. Watson Research Center	216	Brunel University	133
University of Nottingham	212	University of Tampere	131
Massachusetts Institute of Technology	204	Tampere University of Technology	130
The University of British Columbia	202	University of Illinois	127
Microsoft Research Cambridge	189	University of Saskatchewan	127
University of Aarhus	186	RWTH Aachen University	124
Aalto University	181	German Research Center for AI	124
Cornell University	180	Palo Alto Research Center	121
Open University	164	Vienna University of Technology	121
University of Cambridge	163	Intel Corporation	120
University of Tokyo	163	University of Dundee	119
City University London	163		

We used author publication count data and author institution affiliation data to create social network visualizations. In a social network visualization, each node represents an author with the size of the node representing the number of papers an author published as a primary author or co-author. Authors, nodes in the network, are clustered together by institution. Institutions are connected to each other using co-author relationships.

We created social network visualizations on the top 10 and 20 institutions publishing HCI papers. Collaboration trends and connections between institutions became visible through these visualizations.

3.1 Analysis of Institutional Collaboration

The author collaboration visualization by the top 10 HCI institutions (Fig. 1) captures collaboration and influence, showing the most collaborative institutions at the center of the graph. Each node in the social network graph visualization represents an author, where a node's size is based on the number of papers an author has published. These nodes are grouped together by institution so each author is affiliated with a parent institution. Authors are affiliated with their institution and their co-author's institution, creating connections between collaborative institutions. The top 10 institutions publishing HCI research show distinct patterns of collaboration and influence. The most prolific authors are the largest nodes in the graphs—an indicator of influence.

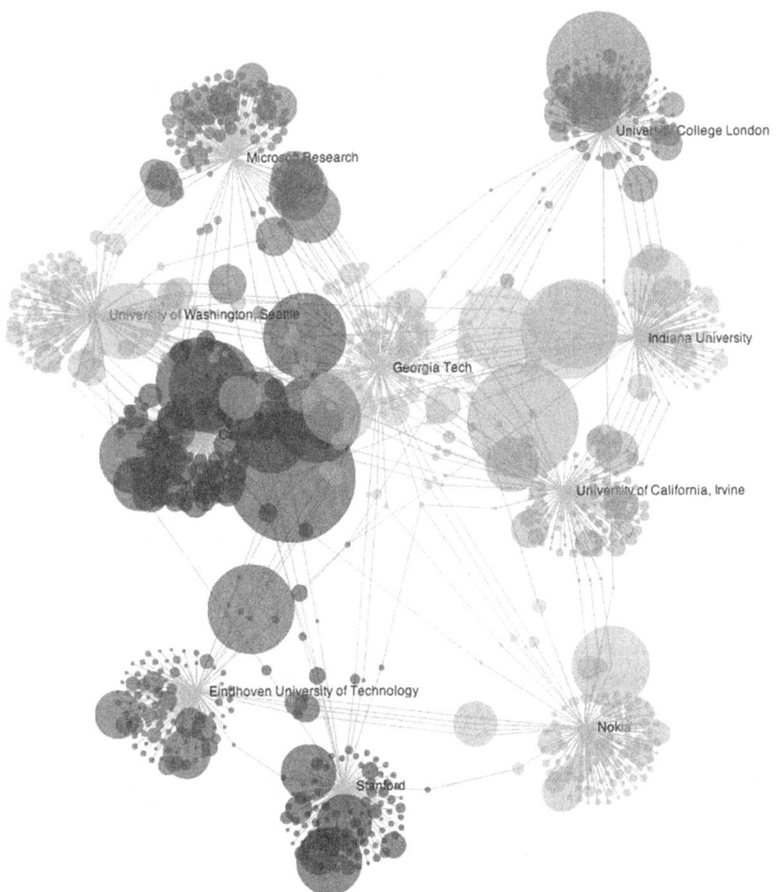

Fig. 1. Author collaboration amongst the top 10 institutions involved with HCI research

There are high degrees of collaboration between Carnegie Mellon, Georgia Tech and Microsoft Research. Georgia Tech is the most central institution in this visualization, demonstrating that it is one of the most collaborative. Nokia collaborates a great deal with Eindhoven University of Technology in the Netherlands, perhaps indicating that geographic distance helps these two institutions collaborate a great deal. University of California, Irvine, is also fairly central in the graph, indicating it also does quite a bit of collaboration with other institutions. Finally, Stanford University has many prolific authors in the field of HCI, but there appears to be little collaboration at Stanford occurring with other institutions within the top 10 HCI publication contributors.

Fig. 2. Author collaboration amongst the top 20 institutions involved with HCI research

Expanding social network analysis to the top 20 institutions involved in HCI research (Fig. 2), some of the patterns of collaboration and influence from the top 10 institutions become clearer. The pattern of geographic collaboration within clusters of innovation becomes more evident. There are clear geographic patterns to collaboration. Institutions based in Europe, for example, collaborate with other European institutions more than they do with American based institutions. Even within the U.S., Pacific Northwest based institutions, such as Microsoft Research and the University of Washington, Seattle seem to collaborate more with each other than with other institutions elsewhere in the country. The University of Nottingham collaborates a great deal with University College London presumably because they are both in the U.K., and so on. Porter [10] found symbiotic, collaborative relationships evolve within many industries based on geography and economies that evolve within a region, and this pattern appears to hold true of institutions conducting HCI research.

Some of the most influential institutions tend to be able to collaborate across geographic clusters. Carnegie Mellon and Georgia Tech are at the center of the social network graph, demonstrating their centrality and influence. Stanford and UC Berkeley, both in the San Francisco Bay area, also collaborate a great deal with each other, but appear to be some of the least collaborative institutions within the top 20 HCI researcher publishers. Because research tends to be very specialized even within the field of HCI, part of this could indicate that those who are in the center of the social network graph do the most interdisciplinary work or have the most diverse set of research interests. Stanford and UC Berkeley, for example, do a great deal of research in HCI with computer science centric topics, whereas UC Irvine focuses more on the social science aspect of HCI [2]. Given Georgia Tech and Carnegie Mellon are more central in the graph indicates that they are perhaps doing both computer science and social science research within HCI.

Another interpretation of centrality could have to do with the immediacy of impact of research. Institutions on the periphery of the social network graph with prolific researchers could indeed be conducting highly impactful research, but researchers at those institutions may be doing research that is many years away from having an impact [3]. Leonoard-Barton [11] has shown that while institutional specialization can increase impact, it can also lead to rigidities that can impede innovation.

3.2 Corporate Research in HCI

While it is common for research labs in private industry to collaborate with universities, firm-to-firm collaboration solely within industry is another matter. Intellectual property and proprietary research tends to be more difficult to disseminate externally due to more legal restrictions and perhaps the fear of losing a competitive edge [1, 5]. Not surprisingly, Microsoft Research in Cambridge, England collaborates a great deal more with Microsoft Research in Seattle, Washington than with any arm of IBM. Similarly, IBM researchers collaborate a great deal with their respective corporate labs.

The author collaboration visualization by the top three research labs (Fig. 3) examines collaboration amongst research labs in private industry and shows that this type of collaboration is more common than one would expect. In fact, avoiding these types of firm-to-firm research lab collaborations appears to put more independent labs outside of the purview of influence in the HCI domain, limiting the influence and depth of research understanding of the firm. Perhaps not surprisingly, research labs that are affiliated under the same corporate parent collaborate with each other a great deal.

Microsoft, IBM and Nokia rank near the top of corporate contributors that publish research in HCI. Google is below average in terms of its contributions to publishing within the HCI community. It ranks 65 in HCI publications with 111 publications. Nokia is one of the top HCI publication contributors, even surpassing Microsoft Research Cambridge. Figure 4 shows the top 10 corporate research labs conducting HCI research.

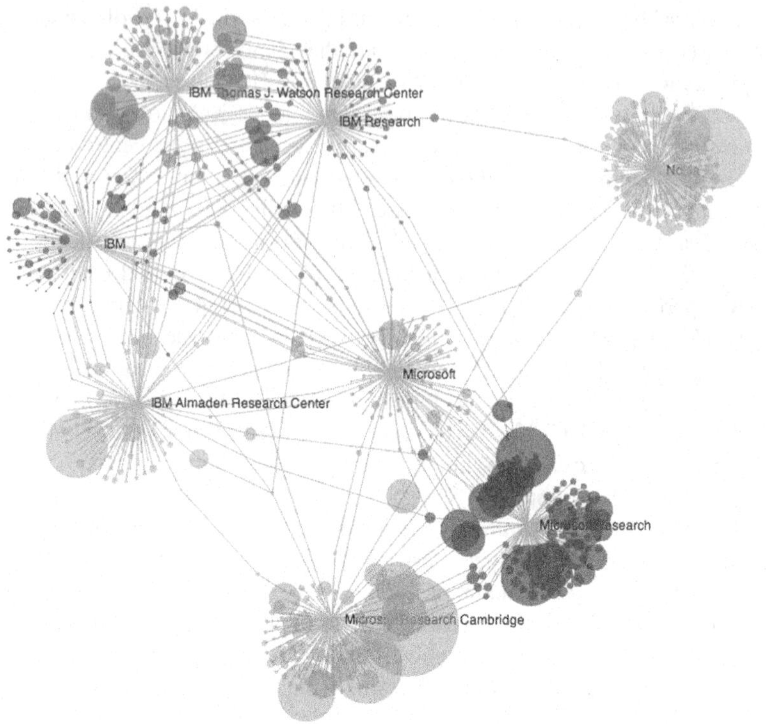

Fig. 3. The top three corporate research labs contributing to HCI research

Corporations are taking advantage of clusters by positioning their research labs in areas where there is a great deal of technological innovation [10]. Silicon Valley, Seattle, New York and Cambridge, England are all thriving technology clusters. IBM, Microsoft and Nokia have all opened research labs in these clusters. While there are benefits from locating a research lab within an existing cluster, this does not necessarily mean that all the benefits of the cluster will benefit the research lab [10, 12]. Silicon Valley arguably has more companies, human capital, financial capital and social networks that are aimed at growing technology than anywhere else in the world. Corporate research labs based in technology-oriented clusters don't necessarily seem to benefit from being in stronger clusters. IBM T.J. Watson Research Center in Yorktown Heights, New York had 216 publications versus IBM Almaden Research Center in San Jose, California with 109. Silicon Valley is typically viewed as the world's center of innovation and clusters with strong ecosystems are supposed to foster innovation, yet IBM's Silicon Valley research center is producing half the amount of HCI oriented research as its New York counterpart. Microsoft Research Cambridge, England produced 189 publications versus U.S. based Microsoft Research in Redmond, Washington that produced 387 publications. In the case of corporate research labs what seems to matter is not necessarily being in the best technology cluster, but rather proximity to corporate headquarters. IBM headquarters are in Armonk, New York. Microsoft is based in Redmond, Washington.

Fig. 4. The top 10 corporate research labs contributing to HCI research

3.3 Company-University Collaborations and Research Productivity

One characteristic that becomes clear from a cursory analysis of collaboration between universities and research labs is that more collaboration is an indication of better corporate research lab performance in terms of HCI publications. More often than not firms are unwilling to share information when it is known how to apply the information in some advantageous way in the market [3, 13]. Typically, it is information with unknown value or seemingly insignificant value that is shared in collaborative endeavors. In other words, firms are only willing to share their lemons, so to speak [1]. Perhaps it is this mentality of conservatism and restriction of information intended to save a firm that ironically leads the firm to lose its competitive position by not being able to collaborate as effectively with partners due to a lack of useful information to share in a collaborative endeavor.

Cohen and Levinthal [14] argue that research and development can help increase a firm's absorptive capacity—their ability to interpret and apply research. Clearly, IBM and Microsoft's research in HCI have increased their absorptive capacity as much HCI related research coming out of the labs have been applied towards improving a product's user experience or towards implementation of innovative user interfaces. Research within the broader HCI community has also influenced work at Microsoft and IBM. For example, research in social network analysis coming from the University of Michigan and Carnegie Mellon University has been applied to research at IBM and

Microsoft. Both firms are prodigious producers of HCI related publications and rank at the top of the list of HCI research contributors. Nokia is also a top producer of HCI publications, but arguably, it's innovation in its research and development labs have not positively affected the company's bottom line in the mobile phone industry.

Nokia's organization structure may not have the same direct connections to product that IBM and Microsoft have. IBM's consulting model has some emphasis on making high value products that commercialize research done within R&D labs. For example, the company spent millions of dollars on R&D for its Watson technology that is able to answer domain specific questions. Watson is best known for competing with humans in Jeopardy and winning. However, the technology has since been commercialized and applied towards medical and financial domains to help answer complex questions [15]. Microsoft has done years of HCI research related to touch interfaces and computer vision. This work has been commercialized in its gaming division and implemented in its Xbox gaming consoles [16]. While long-term research with no commercial application is done at both IBM and Microsoft, there is a culture and directives in place that encourage researchers to find ways to create products that can be commercialized. Product groups are also encouraged to work with researchers to find commercial applications of research products. This sort of organizational structure does not seem to be in place at Nokia. Despite being a major contributor to HCI publications, the firm has not been able to apply this research to commercial products.

Pisano [1] showed that collaborative arrangements between companies can help improve research and development performance. These developments in R&D can help firms develop commercial products faster and efficiently. Firms tend to make these collaborative research arrangements in areas where their expertise is complimentary, for competitive reasons [11, 17]. While outside technology has a higher rate of failure than internal technology, the overall domain-specific knowledge a firm generates through collaborations can help extend expertise to many areas, which can benefit the firm overall. This model of research collaboration seems to work well with companies collaborating with universities.

An indicator of these collaborations between a university and company are co-authored papers and journal articles. Microsoft and Carnegie Mellon University co-authored 478 HCI related publications. IBM and Carnegie Mellon authored 292 HCI publications. Nokia only authored 88 HCI publications with Carnegie Mellon. Collaborations between those same companies and Georgia Tech numbered 255, 153 and 73 respectively. While Nokia is a strong producer of HCI publications in general, it is evident that its university collaborations are far less than Microsoft and IBM. Microsoft has the best track record of working with universities on HCI publications. These numbers may be an indication of the core capabilities and rigidities within each respective company.

Comparing collaboration with Georgia Tech on HCI papers to the total number of HCI papers, 36 % of Microsoft papers have university collaborators, 33 % at IBM and 27 % at Nokia. Similar numbers appear for collaboration with Carnegie Mellon University. As an overall percentage of its HCI publications Nokia does fewer university collaborations than Microsoft or IBM. Work in certain parts of an organization may not be valued as much as in other parts of an organization due to incentive systems and the like [11]. Nokia may not have an incentive system in place that values sharing of information and collaborating with outside universities. Firms that do not collaborate are literally on the edges of network visualizations, while those that do collaborate are in the center of the visualization, benefiting from knowledge coming from a variety of institutions that collaborate within the HCI research ecosystem.

4 Assessing the Strength of HCI Programs

Measuring the quality of HCI programs is in many ways a highly subjective process. Because the research foci of university labs may differ greatly from one to another, sometimes comparing HCI programs from one institution versus another is like comparing apples and oranges. However, a general indication of the research strength of a program can be demonstrated through the number of publications it produces. These data can be captured using data from the ACM DL. ACM DL provides publication data from the top 100 institutions that publish HCI research simply by searching for the term HCI and using institution as a criterion to narrow search results. Sorting by this list provides a rough ranking of research strength.

The top five contributors in the research area of HCI (from ACM Digital Library 2014) in order of rank are Carnegie Mellon University, Georgia Institute of Technology, Microsoft Research, Stanford University and University of Washington, Seattle. From 1977 through 2014, the top 100 contributors to HCI published 15,631 papers and journal articles pertaining to HCI. The top five contributors published 2,427 or 15.5 % of the total amount of publications. The next five contributors published 1,350 papers, or about 8.6 % of total contributions or 55.6 % of the amount of the top five contributors. Institutions on average have 156 publications and have a median of 131 publications.

Some institutions publish under different names though they are affiliated with a larger organization. For example, Microsoft publishes under Microsoft Research, Microsoft Research Cambridge and Microsoft. IBM also publishes under its various research labs including T.J. Watson Research Center and Almaden Research Center. MIT publications fall under the Massachusetts Institute of Technology and the MIT Media Laboratory. Combining total publications of affiliated institutions increases their ranks significantly. MIT, for example, rises from a rank of 21 to 5, replacing University of Washington, Seattle, when its publications are combined with MIT Media Lab (ranked 33). Microsoft and IBM move to 2 and 4 respectively when their affiliated institutions are combined, raising their rankings from 3 and 41 respectively.

By using the simple metric of publication ranking it becomes clear that some institutions are substantially more prolific than others. Few other institutions match the sheer quantity of publications coming from Carnegie Mellon and Microsoft. Georgia Tech and IBM come close, but would have to increase their output close to 30 % to compete with the top two contenders. Georgia Tech has 4,875 academic faculty and staff versus 1,442 at Carnegie Mellon. Similarly, IBM has four times the number of employees as Microsoft, 434,246 versus 100,932 respectively. Yet Microsoft has more than a third more publications than IBM. HCI research is prioritized at leading institutions, but certainly having nearly quadruple the faculty resources or employees should help Georgia Tech or IBM at least have similar output to Carnegie Mellon or Microsoft, though this is not the case.

5 Conclusion

We used quantitative data of academic paper citations and collaborations from the Association of Computing Machinery's online digital library (ACM DL) to construct social network graph data visualizations. We used published conference and journal papers as a proxy to indicate the influence and magnitude of research conducted at the institution. Through these visualizations it became evident which institutions within the HCI community are most central, influential and collaborative; and similarly, which institutions tend to not be as influential and collaborative. These visualizations corroborate some opinions from expert researchers within the HCI community on which institutions are most influential and the type of work that is most important [2]. The social network graph visualizations show greater connections between institutions that collaborate more and these institutions appear closer to the center of the social network graph.

Visualized social network publication data based on quantity of publications and incidence of joint activities clearly shows that the most collaborative institutions, and those that are the most highly regarded in rankings, are at the center of social network visualizations. Visualization data show collaborative institutions at the center and non-collaborative institutions in the periphery. Collaboration occurs within clusters to some degree and geographic clusters evident in collaboration. Merely having highly prolific authors that publish a great deal and do not collaborate leads to less impact and influence, if influence is indicated as being closest to the center of a social network graph visualization. From these visualizations and data it is evident that there is a relationship between collaboration and how prolific an institution is in publishing papers related to HCI. In future research we hope to apply similar network analysis to other measures of influence such as paper citations. There are opportunities to apply this type of analysis to other fields within computer science to understand influential institutions in other areas of specialization.

References

1. Pisano, G.P.: R&D Performance, Collaborative Arrangements and the Market for Know-How: A Test of the "Lemons" Hypothesis in Biotechnology. SSRN, New York (1997)
2. Erickson, T., McDonald, D.W.: HCI Remixed: Reflections on Works That Have Influenced the HCI Community. The MIT Press, Cambridge (2008)
3. Utterback, J.M., Suarez, F.F.: Innovation, competition, and industry structure. Res. Policy **22** (1), 1–21 (1993)
4. Cusumano, M.A., Nobeoka, K.: Strategy, structure and performance in product development: observations from the auto industry. Res. Policy **21**(3), 265–293 (1992)
5. Pisano, G.P.: The R&D boundaries of the firm: an empirical analysis. Adm. Sci. Q. **35**, 153–176 (1990)
6. Polites, G.L., Watson, R.T.: The centrality and prestige of CACM. Commun. ACM **51**(1), 95–100 (2008)

7. Russell, M.A.: Mining the Social Web: Data Mining Facebook, Twitter, LinkedIn, Google+, GitHub, and More. O'Reilly Media, Inc., Sebastopol (2013)
8. Weng, L., Menczer, F.: Emergent Semantics from Game-Induced Folksonomies. ACM, New York (2012)
9. Wu, M.Q.Y., Faris, R., Ma, K.-L.: Visual Exploration of Academic Career Paths. ACM, New York (2013)
10. Porter, M.E.: Cluster and the new economics of competition (1998)
11. Leonard-Barton, D.: Core capabilities and core rigidities: a paradox in managing new product development. Strateg. Manag. J. **13**, 111–125 (1993). Long Range Plan. **26**(1), 154 (1993)
12. Christensen, C.M., Suárez, F.F., Utterback, J.M.: Strategies for Survival in Fast-Changing Industries. Institute for Operations Research and the Management Sciences, Catonsville (1998)
13. Suárez, F.F.: Dominant designs and the survival of firms (1991)
14. Cohen, W.M., Levinthal, D.A.: Absorptive capacity: a new perspective on learning and innovation. Adm. Sci. Q. **35**(1), 128–152 (1990)
15. Hamm, S., Kelly, J.: Smart Machines: IBM's Watson and the Era of Cognitive Computing. Columbia University Press, New York (2013)
16. Research, M. Collaboration, Expertise Produce Enhanced Sensing in Xbox One (2013)
17. Macher, J.T., Richman, B.D.: Organisational responses to discontinuous innovation: a case study approach. Int. J. Innov. Manage. **8**(01), 87–114 (2004)

"Kansei Engineering" as an Indigenous Research Field Originated in Japan

Ayako Hashizume[1(✉)] and Masaaki Kurosu[2]

[1] Faculty of System Design, Tokyo Metropolitan University, Hachioji, Japan
hashiaya@tmu.ac.jp
[2] Faculty of Informatics, The Open University of Japan, Chiba, Japan
masaakikurosu@spa.nifty.com

Abstract. This paper reports on the overview of the research field of Kansei Engineering that originated in Japan. The paper traces back the history of the word "Kansei" and reviews its current use as an indigenous academic term specific to Japan and some Asian countries. The field of Kansei Engineering will be explained and its implication for the international use is examined, and the word "Kansei" could be used internationally more than before and it will help develop the better user interface of products and services. Kansei Engineering set a goal of improving the quality of life with comfort and enjoyment for people.

Keywords: Kansei · Kansei Engineering · Emotion · Feeling · Sensibility

1 Introduction

Kansei Engineering was born by Mitsuo Nagamachi in the 1970 s in Japan. Kansei Engineering and Affective Engineering is "the science of translating the images and emotions representing human desires into physical design components, and specifically designing them [1]." Kansei Engineering is used as a method for translating feelings and impressions into product parameters. It can "measure" the feelings and shows the relationship for certain product properties.

At least in Japan, "Kansei" is used as a word meaning what is outside of the realm of rationalism. Hence MEXT (Ministry of Education, Culture, Sports, Science and Technology) and METI (Ministry of Economy, Trade and Industry) supported to promote the "Kansei" aspects in industrial activity [2–4]. The Japanese government recommended for industries to create high-valued products and services that appeal to user's interests. Kansei value is an "added value", which makes a large impact on the first impression of the customer. It is the key to understanding the buying motive. Hence, the word "Kansei" could be used internationally more than before and it will help develop a better user interface.

In this paper, the historical background and the significance of the word "Kansei" that originated in Japan will be explained and its implication for the international use will be examined.

M. Kurosu (Ed.): HCI 2016, Part I, LNCS 9731, pp. 46–52, 2016.
DOI: 10.1007/978-3-319-39510-4_5

2 The Historical Background of the Word "Kansei"

The term "Kansei" that we use today originates from the "Aesthesis" (an ancient Greek word meaning sensitivity/senses) used by Aristotle and is thought to have similar meaning to ethos [2]. The German philosopher Alexander Gottlieb Baumgarten (1714–1762) specified the study of sensible cognition as "Aesthetics" for the first time in the history of philosophy, and this influenced Immanuel Kant. Baumgarten defined the term "sensible cognition" using the Latin word "Aesthetica" as in "Aesthetica est scientia cognitionis senstivae" [Aesthetics is the study of sensible cognition]. He defined "beauty" as a "perfection of sensible cognition with a coordinated expression" and defined "aesthetics" as "the study of natural beauty and artistic beauty." Lucien Paul Victor Febvre (1878–1956) understood Kansei as the French word "Sensibilite", which can be traced back to the early fourteenth century. He also mentioned that Kansei meant human sensitivity to ethical impressions such as "truth" and "goodness". In the seventeenth century, and in the eighteenth century, it referred to emotions such as "sympathy", "sadness", etc. On the other hand, in Japan, aesthetica was translated as "Bigaku" [science of beauty].

Given this international trend including Japan, Kansei research was activated and attempts were made to understand Kansei from various perspectives [5]. A major argument was that it could be interpreted in many ways based on the meaning of its Chinese characters, such as sensitivity, sense, sensibility, feeling, aesthetics, emotion, intuition, etc. Another argument was that from a philosophical standpoint, the term was created through the translation of the German word "Sinnlichkeit" in the 18th century. Kansei (感性) consists of two Chinese characters – "Kan" [感 (meaning feel and sympathize)] and "Sei" [性 (meaning character and property)], which represent yin and yang respectively, and if combined, constitute the universe. The two different natures of yin and yang influence and interact with each other to exert power [6].

Another interpretation was that "Sinn" in the word Sinnlichkeit includes such meanings as senses, sensuality, feeling, awareness, spirit, perception, self-awareness, sensitivity, intuition, giftedness, talent, interest, character, taste, prudence, discretion, idea, intelligence, reason, judgment, mind, will, true intention, soul, etc. These suggest that the word "Kansei" has not only innate aspects such as giftedness and talent but also acquired aspects such as interest, prudence, etc. It is supposed to be polished while exerting its power through interaction with others in various environments (Fig. 1).

3 Toward the Internationalization of Kansei

Hisorically, "Kansei" is a mixed concept of "Aesthetics" and "Sinnlichkeit" and have been disregarded because of its ambiguity. As described above, the word "Kansei" carries a great deal of meaning, it is multivalent and there are various ways Kansei could be translated, such as sensitivity, sense, sensibility, feeling, aesthetics, emotion, intuition, etc. In addition, the issue we have to deal with is the lack of a consistent definition for Kansei, because each discipline has different viewpoints on it. In Japan

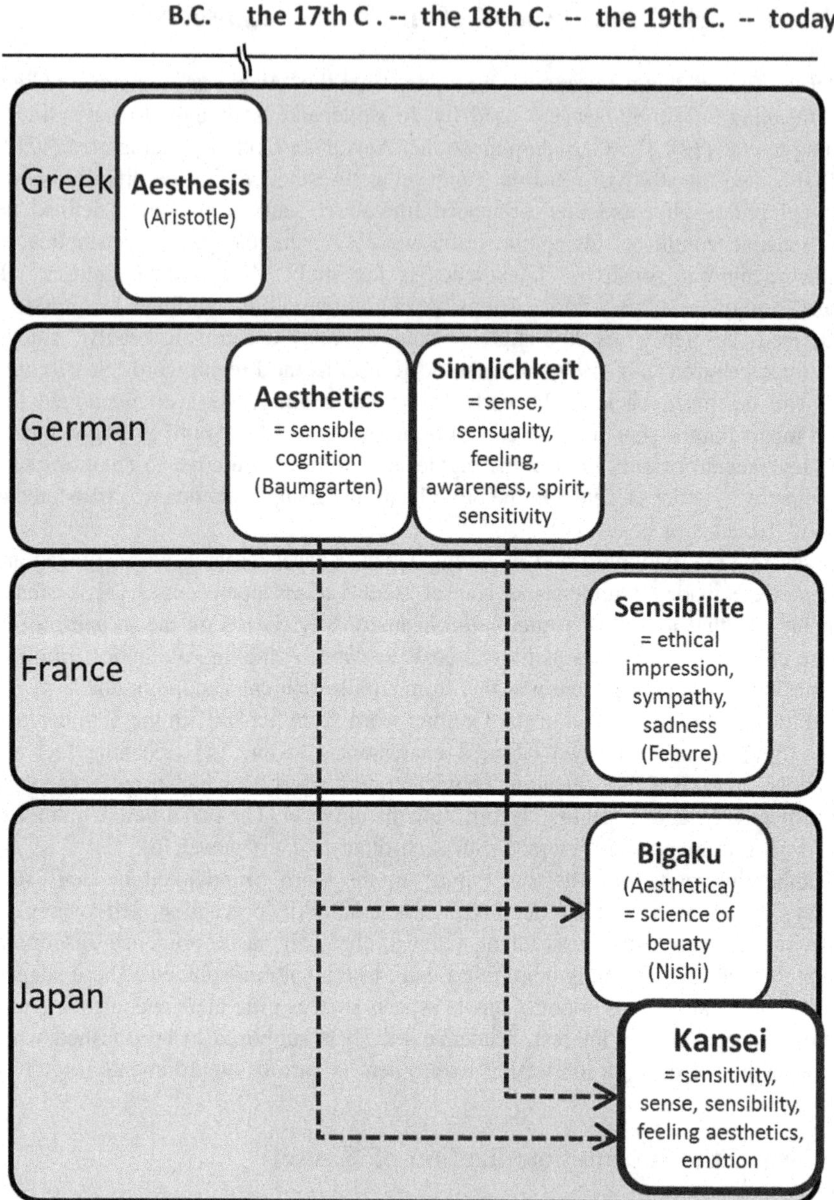

Fig. 1. The root of the word "Kansei"

there are academic societies, such as "Japan Society of Kansei Engineering (JSKE)" and "Japanese Society for Kansei and Well-being (SKW)". Although they focus on Kansei, they do not have the unique and explicit definition of Kansei.

There is no word in English that is an exact translation of Kansei, but occasionally some English words such as "sensibility" and "emotion", are used. They are inaccurate in that they don't convey a subtle sense, though it is very difficult to translate languages without losing some of the meaning and subtle nuances. There are certain typical Japanese expressions that have some difficulties when translating them into English. Lately, some Japanese words that have been adopted in the English language such as "Tsunami," "Karaoke" and "Manga." The word "Kansei" could be another example too.

In fact, most East Asian countries (i.e. China, South Korea, Taiwan, and Japan) adopting the Chinese writing system, use the Kanji word "感性," and they have almost exactly the same meaning. However, as is illustrated in Table 1 the pronunciation is different in each country, with the exception of Taiwan where the pronunciation of "Kansei" is used. Therefore, there is no standard English translation, but in Taiwan and Japan, they normally use "Kansei" as an English word. Although there is no academic society on Kansei research in China, they are using the word emotion or Kansei as English words in research concerning Kansei.

4 The Field of Kansei Engineering

To integrate many different technologies of collaboration from the late 20th century, much attention has been given to Kansei, and spawned a new field called Kansei Engineering. The basic principle in the fields of Ergonomics/Human Engineering and Kansei Engineering/Affective Engineering is the central position of humans as consumers of products and services. This includes the concept of the Human-Centered Design (HCD), wherein goods and services are designed for the primary purpose of meeting human needs. Ergonomics and Human Engineering focus particularly on physical aspects or physiological characteristics of humans and seek to design goods and services that humans can use with the most natural motions and states possible. Kansei Engineering, however, focuses particularly on subjective psychological aspects, such as feelings and images. The goal is to design products that can have a positive effect on humans. Thus, Kansei Engineering includes components that meet the expectations humans would have for certain goods or services and particularly emphasizes the enjoyable experience of their use.

Kansei Engineering covers broad academic fields from humanities and social sciences fields such as philosophy, education, psychology, the arts, politics, economics, management, sociology, etc. to natural science fields such as medicine, physiology, chemistry, materials science, mechanics, information technology, computer system and so on. Kansei Engineering facilitates the progress of industry, economics and culture. It also creates new values from attention on the functions of Kansei. Although "Kansei" is a popular word in Japan, there is no adequate English translation for the word. Sometimes, 'sensibility', 'feeling', and 'emotion' were used to translate "Kansei".

Kansei Engineering has developed as a study of manufacturing for respecting the diversity of human's Kansei, while conventional technologies are purely rational. Hence, Kansei Engineering has relevance to various research fields. Figure 2 is drawn

Table 1. Using the word "Kansei" in East Asian countries

Country	Language of the Country (Pronunciation)	English Translation	Instance (Academic Society)
China	感性 (gǎn-xìng)	emotion, Kansei	-
South Korea	感性 / 감성 (Kam-som)	emotion, sensibility	韓国感性科学会 / 한국감성과학회 (Korea Society for Emotion and Sensibility)
Taiwan	感性 (gǎn-xìng)	Kansei	台灣感性學會 (Taiwan Institute of Kansei)
Japan	感性 (kan-sei)	Kansei	日本感性工学会 (Japan Society of Kansei Engineering)

based on the results of a survey for Kansei researchers on their view of the term Kansei. These findings lead us to believe that Kansei is multifaceted.

There is a little difference in the interpretations of Kansei by Researchers in their fields, even in Japan. For example, researchers in Design think that kansei has secondary aspects that can be acquired through expertise, experience, and learning, such as

1. Subjective and Unexplained Functions:
Kansei has postnatal aspects that can be acquired through expertise, experience, and learning such as cognitive expressions, etc. as well as an innate nature. Many design field researchers have this view.

2. Cognitive Representation of Knowledge and Experience in Addition to Inherent Predisposition:
Kansei is a representation of external stimuli, is subjective, and is represented by actions that can hardly be explained logically. Researchers in information science often have this view.

3. Intuition interaction with intellectual activities:
Kansei is to judge the changes made by integration and interaction of intuitive creativity and intellectual activities. Researchers in linguistics, design, and information science often have this view.

4. Sense of Intuitive Reaction and Perspective to Features:
Kansei is a function of the mind to reproduce and create information based on images generated. Researchers in Kansei information processing have this view.

5. Mind Works of Creating Images:
Kansei is the ability to quickly react and assess major features of values such as beauty, pleasure, etc. Researchers in art, general molding, and robot engineering have this view.

Fig. 2. Interpretations of Kansei by researchers in various fields

cognitive expressions, etc. Those in the Information Science field feel it is a representation of external stimuli, is subjective, and is expressed by actions that can't be defined logically. People in the Linguistics, Design, and Information Science fields tend to agree that Kansei judges the shifts made by integration and interaction of intuitive creativity and intellectual activities. Kansei Information Processing Researchers think it is a function of the mind to reproduce and create information based on images generated. Those in the Art, General Modeling, and Robot Engineering disciplines feel it is the ability to quickly react and assess major features of values.

5 Conclusion

Historically, "Kansei" was brought back from Europe and is the combination of "Aisthesis" and "Sinnlichkeit." At least in Japan, "Kansei" is used as a word meaning what is outside of the realm of rationalism and is an ambiguous from the viewpoint of rationalism. However, the Japanese Ministry of Education and the Ministry of Economy supports the promotion of the "Kansei" aspects in industrial activities in Japan. Kansei Engineering set a goal of improving the quality of life with comfort and enjoyment for people.

In the field of Kansei Engineering, each researcher tries to combine each technology that develops in the various fields with Kansei. It aims to improve the quality of life, and promote a safe and affluent society. Both Kansei Engineering and Ergonomics have a basic philosophy of HCD. While Ergonomics only puts emphasis on the conformance to a human's physiological and somatic aspects, Kansei Engineering also focuses on the mental side. Not only does it try to give physiological Kansei (a good feeling for users), but it also tries to give psychological Kansei so that users can enjoy using the product.

References

1. Nagamachi, M.: Kansei Engineering. Kaibundo Publishing, Tokyo (1989)
2. The Japanese Ministry of Economy, Trade and Industry (MEIT): Kansei Value Creation Initiative (2008)
3. The Japanese Ministry of Economy, Trade and Industry (MEIT): Announcement of the "Kansei Value Creation Mueseum" (2009)
4. The Japanese Ministry of Ministry of Education, Culture, Sports, Science and Technology (MEXT): The Center of KANSEI Innovation Nurturing Mental Wealth (2013)
5. Shiizuka, H.: Kansei system framework and outlook for Kansei engineering. Kansei Eng. **6**(4), 3–16 (2006)
6. Harada, A.: Definition of Kansei, Research papers by Tsukuba University project on Kansei evaluation structure model and the model building, pp. 41–47 (1998)

Classification of Functional-Meanings of Non-isolated Discourse Particles in Human-Human-Interaction

Alicia Flores Lotz(✉), Ingo Siegert, and Andreas Wendemuth

Institute of Information and Communication Engineering, Cognitive Systems Group, Otto von Guericke University, 39016 Magdeburg, Germany
alicia.lotz@ovgu.de

Abstract. To enable a natural interaction with future technical systems, not only the meaning of the pure spoken text, but also meta-information such as attention or turn-taking has to be perceived and processed. This further information is effectively transmitted by semantic and prosodic cues, without interrupting the speaker. For the German language we rely on previous empirically discovered seven types of form-function-concurrences on the isolated discourse particle (DP) "hm".

In this paper we present an improved automatic classification-method towards non-isolated DPs in human-human interaction (HHI). We show that classifiers trained on (HCI)-data can be used to robustly evaluate the contours of DPs in both HCI and HHI by performing a classifier adaptation to HHI data. We also discuss the problem of the pitch-contour extraction due to the unvoiced "hm"-utterances, leading to gaps and/or jumps in the signal and hence to confusions in form-type classifications. This can be alleviated by our investigation of contours with high extraction completion grade. We also show that for the acoustical evaluation of the functional-meaning, the idealized form-function prototypes by Schmidt are not suitable in case of naturalistic HHI. However, the precision of acoustical-meaning prediction with our classifier remains high.

Keywords: Human-human interaction · Human-computer interaction · discourse particles · Automatic form-function classification

1 Introduction

In HHI the behavior of the speaker is mainly characterized by semantic and prosodic cues such as short feedback signals. These signals further the progress and coordination of interaction. These cues transmit so called meta-information about certain dialogue functions such as attention, understanding, confirmation or other attitudinal reactions [1]. DPs such as "ja", "so", "wie" or "hm" belong to these feedback signals and serve as independent small utterance units, occurring at communicative decisive points of the conversation, without interrupting the

M. Kurosu (Ed.): HCI 2016, Part I, LNCS 9731, pp. 53–64, 2016.
DOI: 10.1007/978-3-319-39510-4_6

speaker [16]. As these signals only have a very small semantic content, special attention needs to be paid to their prosody. By changing the intonation, a DP can have several different meanings. Therefore, "hm" is one of the most diverse DP. For the German language seven form-function-relations for the isolated speech signal of the DP "hm" have been revealed by Schmidt [12]. They describe the relation between the functional-meaning of the DPs and specific pitch-contours, see Table 1.

Table 1. Form-function relation of DP "hm" according to [12], the terms are translated into appropriate English ones.

Name	Form-Prototype	Description
DP–1		attention
DP–2		thinking
DP–3		finalization signal
DP–4		confirmation
DP–5		decline
DP–6		positive assessment
DP–7		request to respond

Furthermore, DPs are verifiably used in both HHI and HCI [5,12,15] and specific form-function-relations could be confirmed [8,9]. Also influences of specific subject characteristics, as age and biological gender, as well as certain personality traits on the use of DPs were uncovered [6,14].

To obtain a more human-like interaction in communicating with a technical system, the system needs to be capable of understanding these feedback signals and react appropriately. This enables a more natural interaction and the system thus becomes the users' attendant and ultimately his *companion* [2].

To achieve this aim, we developed a classifier to distinguish between the different functional-meanings of the DP "hm" [8]. The classifier is trained on speech material from HCI. In this paper we describe the adaptation of this classifier to a HHI corpus and show that it is possible to assign non-isolated DPs from HHI. Furthermore, we show the possibility to assign one of the seven prototypes obtained by Schmidt by only applying small changes to the existing algorithm. Compared to the results of HCI we assume an increase of partner-oriented feedback signals in case of HHI [5].

The remainder of the paper is structured as follows: Sect. 2 shortly describes the utilized dataset providing HHI as well as HCI. Then, Sect. 3 describes the DP-classifier developed on the HCI data in detail. Afterwards, Sect. 4 describes the conducted manual labeling process as well as the adaptation of the classifier based on the new obtained HHI data. Section 5 presents and discusses the results of the improved DP classification algorithm and analyses the manual labeling. Finally, Sect. 6 concludes the paper and provides an outlook for further research directions.

2 Datasets

The *LAST MINUTE Corpus (LMC)* contains 130 high-quality multi-modal recordings of German speaking subjects during Wizard-of-Oz experiments [10,11]. The setup of the HCI revolves around an imaginary journey to the unknown place Waiuku. With the help of an adaptable technical system, the subjects have to prepare the journey, by packing the suitcase, and select clothing and other equipment by using voice commands. Each experiment takes about 30 min. For a sub-set of the corpus a total number of 259 DPs are extracted from 25 h of speech material received from 56 subjects. They serve as training data for the basis classification algorithm presented in [8].

The *ALICO Corpus* is recorded to investigate feedback behavior changes in HHI concerning distraction of the listener [4]. The corpus consists of 2×25 dialogues in German language, in which one person is telling the other participant two stories. In the first talk the listener gets the instruction to pay attention, make remarks and ask questions. In the second one an additional distraction task is given to the listener. He gets the instruction to press a button on a hidden counter every time the story teller utters a word starting with the letter 's'. A sub-set of 40 dialogues is annotated, resulting in 1505 feedback signals from 3 h of speech material. Out of these signals 537 are marked as "hm" and used for the investigation presented in this paper.

3 The Discourse Particle Classifier

The DP-classifier uses a rule-based approach. Before the classification a pre-processing step is conducted, see Fig. 1. The following function analysis is based on regression calculation on the pitch-contour. Depending on certain threshold values the classifier decides to which form-prototype the given pitch-contour belongs. The thresholds were set by preliminary investigations. During these investigations, additionally to the seven form-function-prototypes of Schmidt, two more frequently occurring formtypes were identified, see Table 2. No information about the functional use of these formtypes is given, as the work [8] only deals with the course of the pitch-contour and not the identification of its meaning.

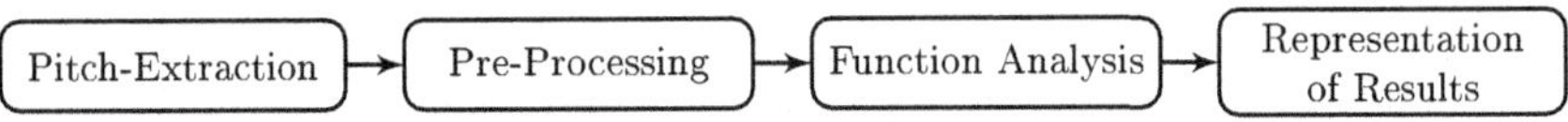

Fig. 1. Structural flowchart of the classification-algorithm

Table 2. Additional form types as stated in [8].

Name	Form-Prototype
DP-8	⌣
DP-9	⌢

Depending on the coefficient of determination (R^2) either a first, second or third order regression is performed. If the coefficient exceeds the threshold value:

$$TH_{determination} = 0.9 \tag{1}$$

It is assumed that the regression function describes the original pitch-contour sufficiently. Only regarding the slope of the first order regression line, the tendency of the contour is determined (horizontal, rising or falling). This allows the classifier to neglect some prototypes for further assignment. For example, if the first order regression line has a rising tendency, all prototypes with a horizontal (DP-2) or falling tendency (DP-1, DP-3, DP-5 or DP-8) can be neglected. This leaves only the prototypes DP-4, DP-6, DP-7 or DP-9 for the later assignment.

Considering the order of regression, the prototype-courses can be distinguished into 3 types: linear (DP-2, DP-3, DP-7), quadratic (DP-4, DP-5, DP-8, DP-9) and cubic ones (DP-1, DP-6). If a pitch-contour is sufficiently described by a linear regression function, it can be unambiguously assigned to a linear prototype by looking at its course tendency. In case of contours described by higher order regression, the course is divided into sections limited by their turning points. Based on the timeratio and slope of these sections the prototypes are assigned. The thresholds for these parameters are:

$$TH_{timeratio} = 1/3 \tag{2}$$

$$TH_{slope} = 40\ \text{Hz/s} \tag{3}$$

If two consecutive sections exceed $TH_{timeratio}$, both sections will be taken into account for further assignment. Otherwise, only the dominant part (longer section) will be considered. For TH_{slope}, the courses (linear regression) and sections (higher order regression) are assumed to be horizontal if the absolute slope is below the threshold and rising or falling for slopes exceeding the threshold, respectively.

As the investigation is implemented on a HCI corpus, most DP samples express talk-organizing or expressive functions. These are mainly DPs of type DP-2. Therefore, an exception in the algorithm is made for regression lines with horizontal tendencies. Disregarding $TH_{determination}$, if the standard deviation of the original pitch-contour is less than 7 Hz the type DP-2 is assigned. Variations of this size can be neglected, as the human ear is not able to perceive them [17]. More information on the classification algorithm especially the pre-processing of the original pitch-contours is given in [8].

To evaluate the implemented classifier a manual annotation of the pitch-contours is performed. A consistency of the results is obtained in approx. 79 % of the given DPs contained in the LMC HCI corpus.

4 Adaptation of the Classifier

As the existing classifier is only trained on the LMC HCI corpus, the amount of training material for partner-oriented prototypes is recognizably low, see row HCI in Table 4. As most of the prototypes detected in HCI are of type DP-2, DP-3 and DP-7, having a linear course of the pitch-contour, a verification of contours described by higher dimensional functions is not given. Another problem is the low number of DPs used to evaluate the classifier, as not all pitch-contours occurring in HHI are considered in the original implementation, leading to impossible assignment of prototypes. Therefore, an adaptation of the classifier is needed.

4.1 Manual Labeling

To verify the results of the algorithm [8] and adapt the classifier to non-isolated DPs from HHI we first utilized a manual labeling. The labeling was conducted in two stages: First, a visual assignment of the intonation curve, based on extracted pitch-values, to one of the seven idealized pitch-contours was performed. DP-8 and DP-9 were left unconsidered on purpose, as no functional-meaning of these types is known. We assumed that these formtypes are variants of the verified form-function-prototypes by Schmidt. Second, an acoustic annotation of the functional-meaning without knowledge of the pitch-contour was conducted (see Table 1). For the acoustic annotation, a modified version of *ikannotate* (cf. [3]) was used. To clarify the results stated in Sect. 5.2: For the acoustic annotation the labelers were not instructed to annotate the perceived intonation-curve but the functional-meaning according to the audible context the DPs occurred in.

4.2 Adjustment of the Threshold Parameter

As already stated in our earlier investigation on DPs in HCI [7], one major problem of a classifier using the intonational-curve of the signals is the subject of pitch-extraction. In our case the considered DP "hm" is a unvoiced utterance. This makes it hard to get a robust pitch-estimation, as there is no stimulation of the vocal cords at the glottis. The pitch-extractor will not be able to continuously estimate a pitch-contour. This leads to gaps and/or jumps in the signal. To ensure the reliability of the classifier, we assumed that at least 50 % of the contour needs to be available to the function analysis algorithm. For all contours with a lower percentage of existence a correct assignment of the prototypes' functional-meaning by the classifier is not implied. Figure 2 depicts a frequently occurring mismatch of prototypes: While the extracted pitch-contour will lead to a DP-3 (finalization signal) assignment, the complete contour will get assigned to DP-4 (confirmation). The made assumption has no influence on the actual assignment of the prototypes, but there is no point in correctly assigning a formtype, if it is not possible to assign the functional-meaning correctly.

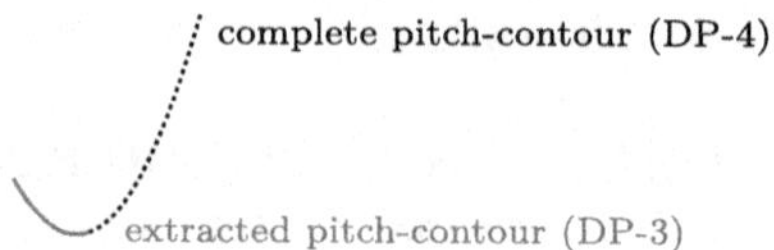

Fig. 2. Frequently occuring mismatch in prototype.

To optimize the performance of the classifier, first, the function analysis algorithm was extended. Therefore, a new threshold was introduced $TH_{sloperatio}$. In cases of the description of the pitch-contours using higher order regression functions, not only the timeratio but also the sloperatio of two consecutive sections needs to be considered for the assignment of the prototypes. This will lead to a better differentiation of linear and higher polynomial (quadratic and cubic) prototypes (cf. Sect. 3), which were rarely considered in the earlier investigation on DPs in HCI [8]. Furthermore, the thresholds were adjusted:

$$TH_{timeratio} = TH_{sloperatio} = 1/6 \tag{4}$$

This is necessary to make the classifier more sensible for higher polynomial prototypes.

5 Results

In this section the results of the original and optimized classifier are compared. The performance of the classifier is determined depending on the visual and acoustic annotation of the labelers. If not indicated differently, all results refer to the 537 extracted DPs obtained from the ALICO HHI Corpus.

5.1 Classification-Algorithm

In the pre-processing of the classifier, all pitch-contours that are too short (114) or failing the requirement made in Sect. 4.2, saying that at least 50 % of the pitch-contour needs to be available to the classifier, (177) were not considered for the classification. In total 537 DPs were given as input to the function analysis loop, leaving 423 for further investigation to the original and 246 to the optimized classifier. The results can be found in Table 3.

In both cases (original and optimized classifier) a high number of DP-2 was recognized. In case of the original classifier there was an assignment of linear courses of type DP-3 and DP-7. This is explainable by the development of the rule-based classifier on a corpus for HCI, including mostly linear prototypes.

Table 3. Frequency distribution of the results of the classification-algorithm. (a) original classifier (423 DPs) b) adjusted classifier (246 DPs); additionally used labels: NSP "no specification possible"

Label		DP-1	DP-2	DP-3	DP-4	DP-5	DP-6	DP-7	DP-8	DP-9	NSP
Item [%]	(a)	0	30.5	15.4	18.0	0.7	2.1	24.6	5.7	1.7	1.4
	(b)	0	31.7	11.8	30.5	0.8	4.9	6.5	11.4	2.4	0

The optimization of the classifier led to a decrease of these linear types and an increase of quadratic and cubic prototypes of type DP-4, DP-6 and DP-8, as assumed and supported by the results of the following Sect. 5.3. In comparison to HCI (cf. Table 4), we obtained a remarkable number of detected DP-4 which corresponds to the assumption made in the introduction, that the number of partner-oriented feedback signals will increase in HHI. This is expectable, as the style of the dialogue is more interview-like leading the listener to use feedback signals such as the DPs to express confirmation.

Table 4. Frequency distribution of the results of the original classifier comparing HCI (LMC corpus) with HHI (ALICO corpus)

Label		DP-1	DP-2	DP-3	DP-4	DP-5	DP-6	DP-7	DP-8	DP-9
Item [%]	HCI	0.5	49.3	30.6	3.7	2.7	1.8	7.8	2.7	0.9
	HHI	0	30.5	15.4	18.0	0.7	2.1	24.6	5.7	1.7

5.2 Manual Labeling

The manual labeling was assessed using majority voting. For both assignments (visual and acoustic) 10 labelers were consulted. Then a majority voting of the results of the 5 labelers with the highest inter-rater reliability (Krippendorff's $\alpha_{visual} = 0.64$ and $\alpha_{acoustic} = 0.16$) was carried out. The low reliability for the acoustic labeling is due to the many degrees of freedom the labelers had, as no further restrictions was given except for the functional-meanings. These meanings, defined by Schmidt, describe sometimes quite similar functional-meanings, which are hard to distinguish acoustically. The low values of $\alpha_{acoustic}$ are rather typical across several databases, as it was shown in [13] for various emotional assessments.

The results of the majority voting are stated in Table 5. Considering the inter-rater reliability and the results of the majority voting we can already see, that it is hard for all labelers to agree on one functional-meaning. The low inter-rater reliability of the annotation of the functional-meaning can also be justified by the calculation algorithm of Krippendorff's α. As the majority of the data is rated as DP-4, all single mismatches are rated as unlikely and therefore are less reliable.

Table 5. ALICO data: Frequency distribution of the majority voting. (a) visual assignment of the idealized pitch-contours (b) acoustic annotation of the functional-meaning; additionally used labels: NSP "no specification possible" and NM "no majority"

Label		DP-1	DP-2	DP-3	DP-4	DP-5	DP-6	DP-7	NSP	NM
Item [%]	(a)	0.6	35.6	7.8	16.8	0.7	1.9	15.3	13.6	7.8
	(b)	0	0.2	0	89.0	0.4	2.6	0	0.7	7.1

5.3 Pitch-Contour Assessment

For the manual labeling process DP-8 and DP-9 were left unconsidered, as no statement about the functional-meaning of these prototypes is given. The pitch-contours assigned to DP-8 or 9 by the classifier will, accordingly, never match with the manually annotated labels and therefore, not be taken into account to calculate the performance of the classifier concerning the visual annotation results. Without any adaptation of the function analysis algorithm or threshold parameters, the original classifier correctly identified 70.5 % of all DPs in non-isolated HHI. By optimizing the classifier this value was raised up to 74.5 %.

Table 6. Confusion matrix of the prototype assignment of the original classifier compared to the manual labeling; additionally used labels: NSP "no specification possible"

		Manual Labeling									
		DP-1	DP-2	DP-3	DP-4	DP-5	DP-6	DP-7	DP-8	DP-9	NSP
Classifier	DP-1	0	0	0	0	0	0	0	0	0	0
	DP-2	1	113	0	7	0	1	0	0	0	7
	DP-3	2	28	29	0	0	1	0	0	0	5
	DP-4	0	6	0	61	0	2	0	0	0	7
	DP-5	0	0	0	0	2	0	0	0	0	1
	DP-6	0	1	0	2	0	4	0	0	0	2
	DP-7	0	16	0	14	0	1	61	0	0	12
	DP-8	0	6	10	2	0	0	0	0	0	6
	DP-9	0	1	0	0	2	0	3	0	0	1
	NSP	0	2	0	2	0	1	0	0	0	1

Table 6 shows the confusion matrix of the manual labeling of the formtypes and the results of the original classification algorithm. Most of the mismatches are noticed between DP-2 and DP-3, DP-7. In these cases only a disagreement in the slope of the course was found. It can be concluded, that the labelers were more likely to identify the perceived signals as sloping than horizontal.

Moreover, we recognized a high confusion between the formtypes DP-7 and DP-4, illustrated in Fig. 3. This also explains the unexpected high number of DP-7 in the visual annotation of the pitch-contours. In these cases the labelers

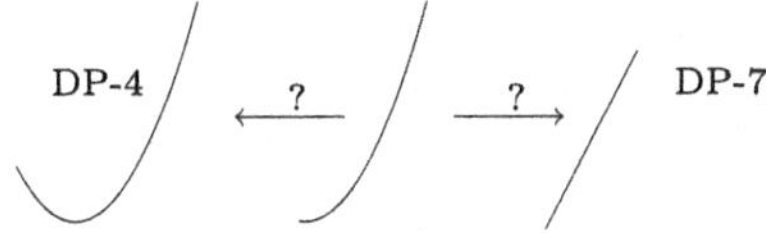

Fig. 3. Illustration of the confusion of real signals between the prototypes of DP-4 and DP-7.

were not sure on which prototype to decide on. Both cases of mismatch were minimized by the adjustment of the classification algorithm described in Sect. 4.2. For the optimized classifier no clear majority in the mismatches of prototype assignment was recognized.

5.4 Functional-Meaning Assessment

We now considered the results of the acoustic functional-meaning assessment. Regarding the results stated in Table 5 (b) a clear majority of DP-4 (confirmation) was recognized. In comparison the results of the pitch-contour assignment showed a distribution over all considered prototypes. The high deviation of both assignments will clearly lead to a low performance of the classifier concerning the functional-meaning of the DPs. Only considering the annotation results of the labelers, will lead to a consistency in 28.45 % of all cases. The classifier obtained a slightly higher performance of 33.49 %. This makes it impossible for the user to get a reliable statement on the functional-meaning of the pitch-contours. A reason for this low agreement is the number of overlaps contained in the DP audio-samples. To still be able to rate the performance of the classifier for the ALICO Corpus a new approach is introduced. As the annotation of the functional-meaning has a strong majority of DP-4 we reduced the classification problem from a seven class problem to a two class problem containing the classes "DP-4" and "other DP". The confusion table of this new classification problem is depicted in Table 7, resulting in a (foreseeable) recall of 31.05 % and a (remarkable) precision of 90.67 %.

This means, almost all prototypes assigned to type DP-4 are true confirmation signals. Furthermore, looking at the idealized pitch-contours of DP-6, DP-4, DP-8 and DP-9 we noticed, that all of these prototypes can be represented within DP-6. This phenomenon is depicted in Fig. 4. As the functional-meaning of DP-6 and DP-4 state similar descriptions (confirmation and positive assessment →

Table 7. Confusion table of the reduced 2-class classification problem. Recall = 31.05 %, precision = 90.67 %

	classified DP-4	classified other DP
Acoustically labeled DP-4	68	7
Acoustically labeled other DP	151	20

positive feedback) we generalized these functional-meanings into one class, also containing DP-8 and DP-9. The acoustic evaluation of these formtypes also confirms this assumption. This led to an even higher recall of 51.10 % and precision of 95.08 %.

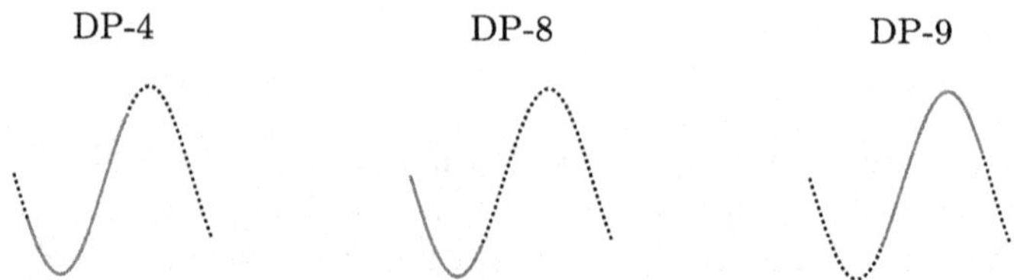

Fig. 4. Comparison of pitch-contours with similar functional-meanings

In case of the LMC HCI dataset we got a higher match (cf. Table. 8) of the acoustic labeling. Only the ratios of the assignments were available and not the direct assignments of the data-samples. Nevertheless, a high agreement in the frequency occurring of DP-2 and DP-4 is recognized. We assume that a direct assignment of the data-samples will also lead to a better match of pitch-contour and functional-meaning compared to the results of the seven class problem presented earlier in this section. This is explainable by the style of interaction: In almost no cases the computer interrupts the speaker. This leads to a low number of overlaps in the DP-samples and an almost "isolated" occurrence of the pitch-contours.

Table 8. LMC data: Frequency distribution of the a) classifier b) acoustic annotation of the functional-meaning; additionally used labels: NSP "no specification possible"

Label		DP-1	DP-2	DP-3	DP-4	DP-5	DP-6	DP-7	NSP
Item [%]	a)	0	66.4	10.9	12.5	3.9	0.8	5.5	0
	b)	2.9	77.0	2.2	14.2	0	1.1	0	2.6

6 Conclusion and Discussion

As a conclusion, we state that a high congruence of the visual manual labeling and the DP-classifier for pitch-contours could be shown (74.53 %). Thus, a cross-usage of HCI-trained classifiers applied on HHI data is viable, and our classifier can be used, to robustly evaluate the contours of DPs in both HCI and HHI. For the acoustical evaluation of the functional-meaning, the idealized form-function prototypes by Schmidt are not suitable in case of naturalistic HHI. For the given

ALICO dataset it was possible to reduce the seven class classification problem to a two class problem obtaining a foreseeable recall of 31.05 % and a remarkable precision of 90.67 %.

Furthermore, we can state that the given audio material of the ALICO corpus is not the most suitable dataset for this investigation. As the annotated feedback signals were not assigned to the different speakers, an overlap of the speakers is possible. This can lead to failures in the pitch-estimation, resulting in a high number of correct assignments of pitch-contours to the prototypes but no correlation of their functional-meaning. A mapping of the DPs to the speakers could lead to an increase of matches in the functional-meaning, as for both, speaker and listener separate headset microphone recordings are available. Additionally, most of the DPs contained in the corpora were of type DP-4. To get a significant statement about the classification of the functional-meaning the dataset should include a balanced distribution of all form-function-prototypes identified by Schmidt in an appropriate audio quality. As the investigation so far only deals with the classification of "isolated" DPs, in terms of no surrounding content of the considered DPs, the desired dataset can be merged from different corpora of the same conversational style (HCI/HHI) and level of naturalness (naturalistic/acted).

Acknowledgment. The work presented was done within the Transregional Collaborative Research Centre SFB/TRR 62 "Companion-Technology for Cognitive Technical Systems" (www.sfb-trr-62.de) funded by the German Research Foundation (DFG).

References

1. Allwood, J., Nivre, J., Ahlsén, E.: On the semantics and pragmatics of linguistic feedback. J. Semant. **9**(1), 1–26 (1992)
2. Biundo, S., Wendemuth, A.: Companion-technology for cognitive technical systems. Künstliche Intelligenz **30**(1), 71–75 (2016)
3. Böck, R., Siegert, I., Haase, M., Lange, J., Wendemuth, A.: ikannotate – a tool for labelling, transcription, and annotation of emotionally coloured speech. In: D'Mello, S., Graesser, A., Schuller, B., Martin, J.-C. (eds.) ACII 2011, Part I. LNCS, vol. 6974, pp. 25–34. Springer, Heidelberg (2011)
4. Buschmeier, H., Malisz, Z., Skubisz, J., Wlodarczak, M., Wachsmuth, I., Kopp, S., Wagner, P.: Alico: a multimodal corpus for the study of active listening. In: Proceeding of the 9th LREC 2014, Reykjavik, Iceland (2014)
5. Fischer, K., Wrede, B., Brindöpke, C., Johanntokrax, M.: Quantitative und funktionale Analysen von Diskurspartikeln im computer Talk. Int. J. Lang. Data Process. **20**(1–2), 85–100 (1996)
6. Giles, H., Coupland, N.: Language: Contexts and Consequences. Cengage Learning, Boston (1991)
7. Lotz, A.F.: Differentiation von Form-Funktions-Verläufen des Diskurs Partikels "hm" über unterschiedliche mathemathische Herangehensweisen. Master's thesis, Otto von Guericke University Magdeburg (2014)

8. Lotz, A.F., Siegert, I., Wendemuth, A.: Automatic differentiation of form-function-relations of the discourse particle "hm" in a naturalistic human-computer interaction. In: Günther, W. (ed.) Elektronische Sprachsignalverarbeitung 2015, Studientexte zur Sprachkommunikation, vol. 78, pp. 172–179. TUDpress (2015)
9. Paschen, H.: Die Funktion der Diskurspartikel HM. Master's thesis, University Mainz (1995)
10. Rösner, D., Haase, M., Bauer, T., Günther, S., Krüger, J., Frommer, J.: Desiderata for the design of companion systems - insights from a large scale wizard of oz experiment. Künstliche Intelligenz **30**(1), 53–61 (2016)
11. Rösner, D., Frommer, J., Friesen, R., Haase, M., Lange, J., Otto, M.: Last minute: a multimodal corpus of speech-based user-companion interactions. In: Proceeding of the 8th LREC 2012, pp. 2559–2566, Istanbul, Turkey (2012)
12. Schmidt, J.E.: Bausteine der intonation. In: Neue Wege der Intonationsforschung, Germanistische Linguistik, vol. 157–158, pp. 9–32, Georg Olms Verlag (2001)
13. Siegert, I., Böck, R., Wendemuth, A.: Inter-rater reliability for emotion annotation in human-computer interaction: comparison and methodological improvements. J. Multimodal User Interfaces **8**(1), 17–28 (2014)
14. Siegert, I., Haase, M., Prylipko, D., Wendemuth, A.: Discourse particles and user characteristics in naturalistic human-computer interaction. In: Kurosu, M. (ed.) HCI 2014, Part II. LNCS, vol. 8511, pp. 492–501. Springer, Heidelberg (2014)
15. Siegert, I., Prylipko, D., Hartmann, K., Bück, R., Wendemuth, A.: Investigating the form-function-relation of the discourse particle "hm" in a naturalistic human-computer interaction. In: Bassis, S., Esposito, A., Morabito, F.C. (eds.) Recent Advances of Neural Networks Models and Applications. SIST, vol. 26, pp. 387–394. Springer, Heidelberg (2014)
16. Sievers, E.: Grundzüge der Phonetik, 5th edn. Breitkopf Härtel, Leipzig (1901)
17. Wendemuth, A.: Grundlagen der stochastischen Sprachverarbeitung. Oldenbourg, Munich (2004)

Automatic Generation of C Source Code for Novice Programming Education

Shimpei Matsumoto[1](✉), Koki Okimoto[2], Tomoko Kashima[3], and Shuichi Yamagishi[1]

[1] Faculty of Applied Information Science, Hiroshima Institute of Technology, 2-1-1 Miyake, Saeki-ku, Hiroshima 731-5193, Japan
s.matsumoto.gk@cc.it-hiroshima.ac.jp

[2] Graduate School of Science and Technology, Hiroshima Institute of Technology, 2-1-1 Miyake, Saeki-ku, Hiroshima 731-5193, Japan

[3] Faculty of Engineering, Kinki University, 1 Takaya Umenobe, Higashi-hiroshima City, Hiroshima 739-2116, Japan

Abstract. To efficiently support novice programming learners feeling programming difficult, clarifying the cause of preventing programming understanding, and developing a new teaching method appropriate for their understanding degree would be necessary. The objective of this paper is to develop a learning support system with reading source codes. This paper also aims to evaluate the effectiveness of the developed system from the subjective viewpoint of learners. The developed system can automatically generate a source code of C programming language in which there is no particular meaning because the source codes as learning materials are generated randomly. The developed system was utilized in a programming lecture for novice programming learners. This paper obtained student responses from a questionnaire, after the students had completed one semester of the instruction in programming, and analyzed the data. From the analysis result, it turned out that different evaluation patterns existed depending on the learner's basic programming skill.

1 Introduction

With the rapid development of information technology, today's society has been requiring a lot of software development engineers. Among software development, programming has been considered as an essential skill. However, usual programming instructional methods cannot afford to neglect an issue: polarization. The polarization consists of two group; the one is a group of learners who are readily acceptable to learn to program, and the other is a group of learners who does not receive any concept of programming. This problem would be uniformly continued to be repeated even though the programming education has promoted and various learning materials of programming have been actively developed. About this problem, Konecki mentioned that programming education comes with many reoccurring problems and difficulties that its novice learners experience, and offered suggestions on these reasons [1]. Our previous study [2,3] also noted

M. Kurosu (Ed.): HCI 2016, Part I, LNCS 9731, pp. 65–76, 2016.
DOI: 10.1007/978-3-319-39510-4_7

a similar tendency. An effective instructional method to support a learner not good at programming has not constructed enough as long as the authors survey. This reason would be in the point that programming requires various skill such as logical thinking, language, imagination, ingenuity, and mathematical ability. On the other hand, we are not still sure what and how much skill is necessary for programming. Additionally, there is no method to indicate learner's detail of the degree of each skill, so a learner is also not sure what kind of skill should be trained to overcome the difficulty of programming. Therefore, a system and a method, which can effectively collect data of learning leading to the definition of understanding degree in each skill field while supporting daily programming education, would be effective for a learner not good at programming.

The aim of this paper is to develop a source code reading based learning support system to enrich a programming lecture, which is available for self-study and mini-examination. The developed system of this paper can automatically generate a source code of C programming language used as a learning material. Since the source code is generated randomly, there is no particular meaning in the source code. The type of question with the source code is to answer the proper value of a variable after the execution of source code. With the developed system, a learner would learn the basis of the processing flow, memory retention, calculation ability, and basic knowledge such as the assignment operator and the increment/decrement which are the difficult concept for learners not good at programming. The developed system aims to equip minimum knowledge, but necessary for programming without describing a source code, and to rebuild his/her confidence to make a program. The authors expect that the writing skill of source code would be eventually improved because the psychological resistance will be reduced from his/her confidence for programming. Additionally, experiencing much source code reading not depending on a particular context will contribute to writing a readable code [4,5]. The developed system would be also useful as a method to grasp what and how much a skill is insufficient for improving programming ability because it can collect each learner's response according to the characteristic of a question from daily education.

This paper also aims to evaluate the effectiveness of the developed system from the subjective viewpoint of learners. The developed system was utilized in a programming lecture for novice programming learners majoring Informatics and tried to support the instruction of source code reading. This paper obtained student responses from a questionnaire, after the students had completed one semester of the instruction in programming, and analyzed the data. From the analysis result, it turned out that different evaluation patterns existed depending on the learner's programming skill.

2 Developed System

2.1 Source Code Reading

The developed system in this paper is for training the skill of reading source code of C language. Writing a program is particularly difficult for learners being not

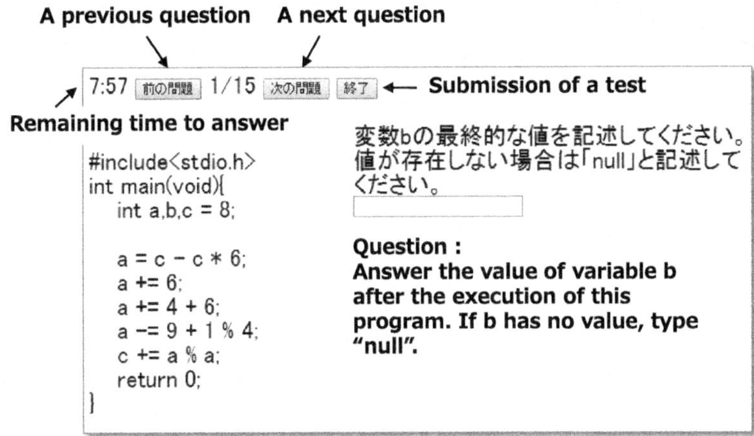

Fig. 1. A screenshot of the developed system

good at programming, so this system tries to reduce the psychological resistance to programming.

The system can automatically generate source codes as a learning material and give a question that requires students to answer the proper value of a variable after the execution of a source code. The source code is randomly generated, i.e., it consists of the series of meaningless procedure, so it does not have a meaning to process. This paper considers that a source code without a certain meaning would be effective to equip the basic knowledge of programming language specification. The total lines of the generated source are several dozen. Such source code is not common because a source code with several dozen lines is too short to process a certain meaning work, but this paper considers that reading source code described in a short sentence is important to get used to a large-scale practical program as a first step. In addition to these, recently since many software development sites have actively adopted programmer-centered software development approach with utilizing open source software, the need for reading technique of source code not depending on comment is now becoming greater and greater. Additionally, most of the time to program is said to be reading [4]. These backgrounds mentioned above are the main reasons that the authors focused on the source code reading blended programming education.

2.2 Specification of Implementation

The developed system is a web application. All functions of the developed system are available through the Internet as long as a client device equips a web browser available the standard of HTML5. The developed system runs on an operating system with Linux kernel 3.16, and uses the following software: Apache 2.4.7, a web server program, to provide web service, PHP 5.5.9, a server-side scripting language, to implement the function, jQuery 1.7.2, a cross-platform JavaScript library, to perform dynamic UI, and MySQL 5.6.16, a database server program, to manage all system data.

Figure 1 shows an example of a screenshot of the developed system, and the source code shown in Fig. 1 is a question for a learner. The question type requires a learner to answer the value of a variable after the execution of a presented source code, and the variable is randomly chosen. Some question styles are available in the developed system, such as a free descriptive question, and a multiple choice question. The details are as follows.

Free Descriptive Question. This type of question is addressed in this paper. All learners should put an integer number into a specified textbox by using a keyboard. The developed system picks up a variable randomly from a presented source code, and the variable is used as a question. There is another type of free descriptive question which requires answering all variable values in a presented source code, but this capability is not mentioned in this paper.

Multiple Choice Question. This type of question requires a learner to select an option whose all variable values after execution are proper. All variable values in an option are different each time except the correct option because they are randomly generated.

Alignment Question. This type of question is multiple choice, and the question requires a learner to select an option with the proper order of statements. The distracter's order of statements is randomly generated. As all variable values after execution are shown, each learner can think the order of statement by using the values. The difficulty level of this question is not influenced much by the combination of the distracters, and this point is different from the above two types of question.

Statement Supplement Question. A source code lacking a statement, and all variable values of this source code after execution are given to a question. This type of question is multiple choice, and the question requires a learner to select an option with a proper statement for the lacked place. The lacked place is randomly given, and the distracters are also randomly generated.

As shown above, this paper addresses only the trial result of free descriptive question. All source codes used as questions consist of only sequential processing, do not include branch and repetition to give learners a firm foundation in programming. Besides, all source codes consist of only integer variables. In the developed system, a question and its difficulty level differ for each learner even though the source code is same. Therefore, a sufficient number of questions statistically guaranteed should provide when executing a test.

2.3 Automatic Generation of a Question

The developed system has the capability to generate a source code automatically as a question. As the statements of a source code are randomly ordered, there is no meaning in the source. The administrator of this system can give following the conditions to obtain a source code by the configuration form:

Table 1. Conditions to generate a source code

Term	S1	S2	S3	S4	S5	S7	S11	S12	S13
1	3	4	3	0.3	+,-,		*		
2	3	4	2	0.3	+,-		*		
3	3	4	3	0.3	+,-,*,/,%	+,-	*		
4	3	4	3	0.4	+,-,*,/,%	+,-	*		
5	3	4	2	0.4	+,-,*,/,%	+,-,*,/,%	*	*	
6	3	4	2	0.6	+,-,*,/,%	+,-,*,/,%	*	*	

- S1: The number of variables: 1–9 variables are available, where variable names are alphabetical sequence, i.e., a, b, c, ...,i or array a[0], a[1], ..., a[9].
- S2: The number of statements: 1–10 statements are available, where a closing curly bracket does not include the number.
- S3: The maximum number of variables calculated: 1–10 variables are available.
- S4: Appearance ratio of variables in a calculation: 0–100% is available.
- S5: Use/disuse of operators: use/disuse of addition, subtraction, multiplication, division, and remainder operators are selectable. A source code consists of only simple assignment statement when all operators are disused.
- S6: Use/disuse of the selection (if) and the repetition (for, while) statement.
- S7: Use/disuse of compound assignment operators: use/disuse of addition, subtraction, multiplication, division, and remainder operators are selectable.
- S8: Constraints for conditional expression: 4 settings are available for conditional expression of "if" or "while": only numerical values (both right and left sides), variables and numerical values (Appearance ratio of variables is stochastically determined), variables and numerical values with a constraint (a variable is certainly in the left side), only variables (both right and left sides).
- S9: Complex condition: use/disuse of complex condition, and the number of conditions (1–9).
- S10: Nest: use/disuse of nest, the number of nests (1–9), and the appearance ratio of nest (0–100%).
- S11: Use/disuse of increment/decrement.
- S12: Use/disuse of initialization.
- S13: Appearance ratio of a redundant statement (0–100%): e.g. "a = 1; a = 2;".

3 Experiment and Result

This paper tried to support a programming lecture by using the developed system. The lecture is for freshman students majoring in Informatics, most of them are a beginner of programming, and used C language. This programming lecture continued one semester, and it consisted of 15 lectures. The developed system was utilized with examination style in 6 lectures among the 15 lectures. The

```
#include<stdio.h>
int main(void){
    int a,b,c = 1;

    c = c - 7;
    a = c - 2 + 5;
    b = 7 + 5;
    c = 9 - a - 9;
    return 0;
}
```

(a) A question in the 1st test

```
#include<stdio.h>
int main(void){
    int a,b;

    b = 5 - 10;
    a = 2 + b;
    b = b - a - b;
    return 0;
}
```

(b) A question in the 2nd test

```
#include<stdio.h>
int main(void){
    int a,b,c = 6;

    a = 3;
    c = 9 % c;
    b = c / a;
    c = a / 6;
    return 0;
}
```

(c) A question in the 3rd test

```
#include<stdio.h>
int main(void){
    int a = 2,b,c;

    a -= a;
    b = a;
    b += 9;
    c = a / 9 + b;
    return 0;
}
```

(d) A question in the 4th test

```
#include<stdio.h>
int main(void){
    int a,b,c = 2;

    b = 8;
    a = ++c;
    c += 7 * 8;
    b += 2;
    return 0;
}
```

(e) A question in the 5th test

```
#include<stdio.h>
int main(void){
    int a = 6,b,c;

    c = a++ * a;
    a -= c-- - ++c;
    b = a;
    a -= 5;
    return 0;
}
```

(f) A question in the 6th test

Fig. 2. Examples of a question in each term

author provided 15 questions for each test, and each testing time is 10 min. The amount of knowledge in each test was related to the contents of the lecture according to the progress of this lecture. Concretely, in the early stage of this lecture, a test includes only simple calculation with addition and subtraction, on the other hand, in the closing stage, svarious operators and techniques are given to generate a source code in the late stage. The detail of the settings to generate a source code is shown as Table 1, and examples of a question in each test are shown in Fig. 2. In this paper, as the source codes only including simple assignment operators were given for students, the settings for generation code S6, S8, S9, S10 are not mentioned. After each test, questions included in a test are available to practice as much as a learner wants.

This paper obtained 108 student responses from the questionnaire, after the students had completed one semester of the instruction in programming, and analyzed the data. The objective of the analysis to check the effectiveness of reading source code, so each question does not ask students for the effectiveness of the developed system itself. Namely, as the developed system is only to facilitate the automation of scoring a test, what this paper wants to do is to clarify the degree of contribution of reading source code for programming learning, and the content of source codes generated by a method in this paper. This paper gave 15 questions asking how much reading source code contributed to the programming learning and obtained student responses with 6 grade Likert scale. Questions given to a student are as follows.

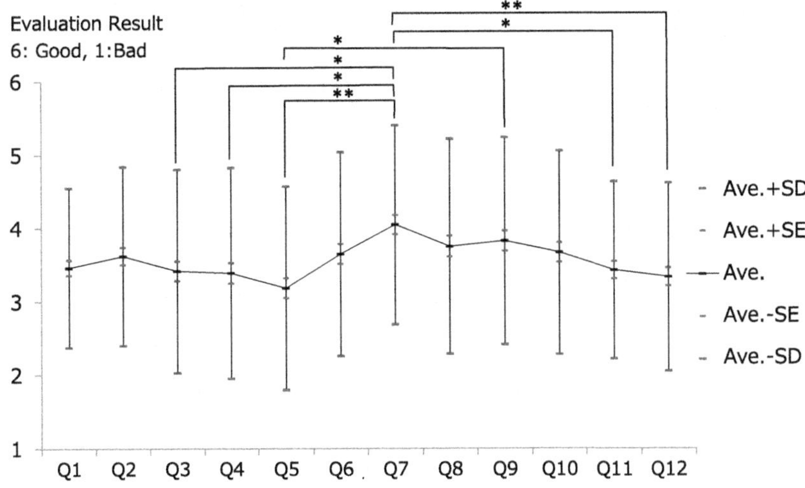

Fig. 3. Evaluation result of all students

- Q1: The degree of contribution for understanding the fundamental concept of programming.
- Q2: The degree of contribution for understanding the mechanism of assignment operator and the sequence of operation in the assignment operator.
- Q3: The degree of contribution for understanding/giving attention to the advanced knowledge such as compound assignment operator and increment/decrement.
- Q4: The degree of contribution to getting used to programming.
- Q5: The degree of contribution to reading another man's program and for fixing a bug.
- Q6: The degree of contribution to getting used to a calculation with a remainder operator.
- Q7: Will you be able to read the remainder operator "%" properly if you continue to train reading source code?
- Q8: Will you be able to read the increment/decrement "++, - -" properly if you continue to train reading source code?
- Q9: Will you be able to read the compound assignment operators "+=, -=" properly if you continue to train reading source code?
- Q10: Will you be able to read the compound assignment operators "*=, /=, %=" properly if you continue to train reading source code?
- Q11: Will you be able to deal with the difference in the sequence of operation depending on compilers?
- Q12: The degree of contribution of reading randomly and automatically generated source code for acquiring knowledge of programming.

Questions Q1–6 are to reveal the contribution of reading source code for programming learning, Q7–10 are to reveal the expectation of reading source

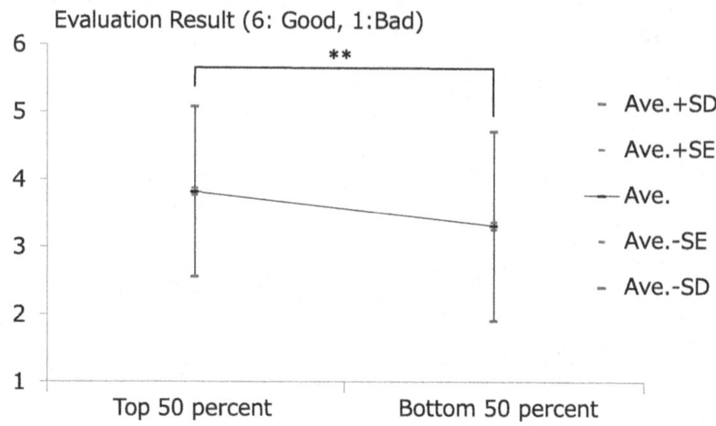

Fig. 4. Gap between top and bottom 50 %

code for improving programming skill, and Q11 and Q12 are to reveal the quality of source code.

From the normality testing with skewness and kurtosis for each item, questions except Q1 indicated normality ($p < 0.05$). Therefore, this paper assumed each learner's response as interval scale and applied parametric testing method. Additionally, from the Bartlett's and Levene's tests, the null hypothesis of equal variances was rejected ($p < 0.01$), and the result suggested that the result of each item's response includes its own feature. The summary of evaluation results is shown in Fig. 3, where * indicates a significant difference $p < 0.05$, and ** indicates $p < 0.01$ respectively. From the high evaluation results of Q7 and Q9, the reading source code blended programming learning would be strongly expected for improving the reading of remainder operator and compound assignment operators +=, -=. On the other hand, the results of Q3, Q4, Q5, Q11, and Q12 were relatively low, and especially the evaluation result of Q5 was worst. From these findings, most students would feel that reading the automatically generated source codes contributed to acquiring the fundamental programming knowledge, but the effectivenesses for getting used to programming, reading another man's program and fixing a bug were less. As these reasons, the source codes in this experiment were strikingly different from a practical source code and were not the contents for fixing a bug. Based on the assumption, the evaluation for fixing a bug will improve if a source code with a bug is used as a question. Similarly, the evaluation of Q4 will improve if a practical source code is used as a question. The results of Q3, Q11, and Q12 are considered to be strongly related, i.e., the factor in Q12 affected the result to Q3 and Q11. Reading randomly generated source codes forced to touch a confusing thing about programming. Concretely, the factor in Q12 would give a strong impact to the evaluation of Q11 because the execution result of a complex statement including both a compound assignment operator and a increment/decrement differs according to compiler. For example, the execution result of the source code (f) shown in Fig. 2 depends on the kind

Table 2. Comparison of each item's average value between top and bottom and its significant difference

Students	Q1	Q2	Q3	Q4	Q5	Q6	Q7	Q8	Q9	Q10	Q11	Q12
Top	3.593	3.833	3.556	3.556	3.389	3.852	4.537	3.944	4.370	4.056	3.778	3.333
Bottom	3.333	3.407	3.278	3.222	2.981	3.444	3.556	3.556	3.278	3.278	3.074	3.333
Sig. Dif		*					**		**	**	**	

of compiler, and also its version. This point would be an extremely troublesome mechanism for students not good at programming. Similarly, the consideration that Q12 would give a high impact to Q3 was based on the assumption that source codes including extremely complex statements as shown in Fig. 2 would cultivate a sense of fear for programming.

All students in this experiment have taken a course in the algorithm at last semester. In this course, students learned a fundamental concept of algorithms, such as sequence, selection, and repetition, which are also the essential knowledge to the program. It is reasonable to assume that the score of the algorithm course would be strongly related to the programming skill because the correlation of score between algorithm and programming was high in the previous data. Based on this reason, students were divided into 2 groups based on the score of the algorithm, the top 50 % of 54 students, and the bottom 50 % of 54 students. Two-way ANOVA analyzed the difference of the averages of all items for each group. As shown in Fig. 4, there was a significant difference $p < 0.01$ between 2 groups. Since the evaluation result of the bottom 50 % students, whose basic skill of programming are not probably enough, was lower than the top 50 % one, the result would suggest that reading the source codes generated by the method in this paper failed to contribute fully to reduce a resistance for programming. However only in this result, we cannot say for sure that a student whose programming skill is insufficient is certainly a student feeling not good at programming. Therefore, shortly we will obtain a subjective evaluation of the developed system from the interview of a student not good at programming. This paper examines the reason of the tendency in Fig. 4 as follows. A student with enough programming skill can realize one's sufficient/insufficient points in programming from the scoring result of reading source codes because he/she had enough skill to make a self-assessment. The developed system gave an opportunity to reflect, so he/she would give the learning of reading source codes a good evaluation. On the other hand, a student whose fundamental programming skill is not enough cannot do them. Therefore, positive correlation between the basic programming skill and the evaluation result of reading source code is considered to be quite natural. Based on this consideration, to make the developed system more acceptable to every student, we ought to give feedback with an easy-to-understand comment just after the scoring to support one's reflection about reading.

Table 2 shows each item's averages of the top and the bottom 50 % students with significant differences. The result of the top and the bottom was same in

Q12, and it is the noted point because the whole trend is that the top's evaluation was over the bottom's evaluation, but Q12 was its exception. The results must be either the high expectation from the bottom or the low expectation from the top about reading the source codes generated by the method in this paper. Considering a balance between Q12 and the other questions, the former assumption is natural. Due to this reason, the significant differences would be generated by the high evaluation of the top 50 % students. So, we might be possible to devise a way to improve the satisfaction of the bottom because there is enough possibility to improve the evaluation of the questions with a significant difference. Namely, this paper considers that we can reduce the gap to the level with no significant difference, and a method to reduce the gap is to give feedback mentioned above.

4 Related Works

Previous studies on programming are roughly classified into three objectives [6,7]: analysis of student's learning history data and discovery of student's characteristic, proposal of a programming teaching method, and development of ICT-based learning support system. So far, researches on programming education have often focused on writing source code, but some of them have addressed reading source code [8]. Reading source code has also been considered to be an important ability for obtaining a deeper understanding of programming, but good reading strategies have not been known so much.

Earlier programming education studies on reading source code provide a lot of valuable knowledge about a characteristic of programming learners, teaching method, and programming learning support system. Firstly, this paper shows the remarkable efforts of software development. A framework on reading source code was proposed [9] where the process of reading code consists of two steps: reading comprehension and meaning deduction. Reading comprehension was defined as the inverse of coding, and meaning deduction was also defined as the inverse of algorithm design. Arai et al. developed a learning support system for programming beginners that facilitates the process of learning by reading source code, and confirmed that the system was effective [10]. Arai's work trained the skill to convert source code into an equivallent abstract processing flow, and the skill was positioned as the reading comprehension. There is also an interesting learning support system for code reading [11,12]. They assumed that learners will understand programs and algorithms by recalling an image consisting of three fields: the program code, objects processed by the program, and a sequence of concrete operations for the objects. Their proposed system visualized the three fields and their relationships to support understanding the relationships and correspondence among their components. Additionally, they discussed how code reading using their proposed system allows learners to cultivate a superior understanding of programming. Tang developed a distributed, social code review tool designed for the specific constraints and goals of a programming course named "Caesar" [13]. Caesar is capable of scaling to a large and diverse reviewer population, provides automated tools for increasing reviewer efficiency, and implements a social web interface for reviewing that encourages discussion and participation.

Busjahn et al. took a further look into the role of reading source code in programming learning from the result of interviews with programming instructors using the miracle question, on the role of code reading and comprehension [14]. They claimed that a possible means to foster programming learning is to teach reading directly, including reading strategies, and besides, reading should probably be made more explicit as learning goal in itself.

Lopez analyzed student responses to an examination, after the students had completed one semester of instruction in programming [15]. He showed that the performance of students on code tracing tasks correlated with their performance on code writing tasks, and a correlation was also found between performance on "explain in plain English" tasks and code writing.

5 Conclusion

This paper developed a learning support system for reading a source code and showed the detail of the developed system. This paper implemented a function of automatic C source code generation for a learning material. This paper also aimed to evaluate the effectiveness of the developed system from the subjective viewpoint of learners and tried to support a programming course by using the developed system. Mini-tests were given several times in the programming lecture by using the function of automatic generation of C source codes. This paper obtained 108 student responses from the questionnaire, after the students had completed one semester of the instruction, and analyzed the data. From the analysis result, firstly it turned out that most students would feel that reading the automatically generated source codes contributed to acquiring the fundamental programming knowledge, but the effectivenesses for getting used to programming, reading another man's program, and fixing a bug were less. From the evaluation result, we can understand that reading randomly generated source codes forced to touch a confusing thing about programming, and it would cultivate a sense of fear for programming. Secondly, students were divided into 2 groups based on the basic programming skill, and Two-way ANOVA analyzed these differences. The analysis result showed that reading the source codes generated by the method in this paper failed to contribute fully to reduce a resistance for programming. Based on this result, it was found that we ought to give feedback with an easy-to-understand comment just after the scoring to support one's reflection about reading to improve the student's satisfaction not good at programming. But, we confirmed that it might be possible to devise a way to improve the satisfaction of the bottom group of students because there would be enough possibility to improve the evaluation from the data of responses.

Acknowledgments. This work was partly supported by Japan Society for the Promotion of Science, KAKENHI Grant-in-Aid for Young Scientists (B), No. 13304922, Grant-in-Aid for Scientific Research(C), No. 26350296.

References

1. Konecki, M., Petrlic, M.: Main problems of programming novices and the right course of action. In: Proceeding of the 25th Central European Conference on Information and Intelligent Systems, pp. 116–123 (2014)
2. Kashima, T., Matsumoto, S., Yamagishi, S.: Knowledge acquisition with eye-tracking to teach programming appropriate for learner's programming skill. In: Proceeding of The Third Asian Conference on Information Systems, pp. 287–292 (2014)
3. Okimoto, K., Matsumoto, S., Yamagishi, S., Kashima, T.: A source code reading based learning support system for novice programming education. In: Proceedings of the 21nd International Symposium on Artificial Life and Robotics, PS3, pp. 765–768 (2016)
4. Boswell, D., Foucher, T.: The Art of Readable Code. (Theory in Practice), O'Reilly Media (2011)
5. Spinellis, D.: Reading, writing and code. ACM Queue **1**(7), 84–89 (2003)
6. Robins, A., Rountree, J., Rountree, N.: Learning and teaching programming: a review and discussion. Comput. Sci. Educ. **13**(2), 137–172 (2003)
7. Pears, A., Seidman, S., Malmi, L., Mannila, L., Adams, E., Bennedsen, J., et al.: A survey of literature on the teaching of introductory programming. ACM SIGCSE Bulletin **39**(4), 204–223 (2007)
8. Lopez, M., Sutton, K., Clear, T.: Surely we must learn to read before we learn to write! In: Proceedings of the Eleventh Australasian Conference on Computing Education, vol. 95, pp. 165–170 (2009)
9. Kanamori, H., Tomoto, T., Akakura, T.: Development of a computer programming learning support system based on reading computer program. In: Yamamoto, S. (ed.) HCI 2013, Part III. LNCS, vol. 8018, pp. 63–69. Springer, Heidelberg (2013)
10. Arai, T., Kanamori, H., Tomoto, T., Kometani, Y., Akakura, T.: Development of a learning support system for source code reading comprehension. In: Yamamoto, S. (ed.) HCI 2014, Part II. LNCS, vol. 8522, pp. 12–19. Springer, Heidelberg (2014)
11. Kogure, S., Okamoto, M., Yamashita, K., Noguchi, Y., Konishi, T., Itoh, Y.: Evaluation of an algorithm and programming learning support features to program and algorithm learning support environment. In: Proceedings of the 21st International Conference of Computers in Education, pp. 418–424 (2013)
12. Yamashita, K., Nagao, T., Kogure, S., Noguchi, Y., Konishi, T., Itoh, Y.: Code-reading support environment visualizing three fields and educational practice to understand nested loops. Res. Pract. Technol. Enhanced Learn. (RPTEL) **11**(1), 1–22 (2016). doi:10.1186/s41039-016-0027-3
13. Tang, M.: Caesar: a social code review tool for programming education, Doctoral dissertation, Massachusetts Institute of Technology (2011)
14. Busjahn, T., Schulte, C.: The use of code reading in teaching programming. In: Proceedings of the 13th Koli Calling International Conference on Computing Education Research, pp. 3–11 (2013)
15. Lopez, M.: Relationships between reading, tracing and writing skills in introductory programming. In: Proceedings of the Fourth international Workshop on Computing Education Research, pp. 101–112 (2008)

Is There a Biological Basis for Success in Human Companion Interaction?

Results from a Transsituational Study

Dietmar Rösner[1(✉)], Dilana Hazer-Rau[2], Christin Kohrs[3], Thomas Bauer[1], Stephan Günther[1], Holger Hoffmann[2], Lin Zhang[2], and André Brechmann[3]

[1] Institut für Wissens- und Sprachverarbeitung (IWS), Otto-von-Guericke Universität, Postfach 4120, 39016 Magdeburg, Germany
{roesner,tbauer,stguenth}@ovgu.de

[2] Medical Psychology, Ulm University, Frauensteige 6, 89075 Ulm, Germany
{dilana.hazer,holger.hoffmann,lin.zhang}@uni-ulm.de

[3] Special Lab Non-Invasive Brain Imaging, Leibniz Institute for Neurobiology, Brenneckestr. 6, 39118 Magdeburg, Germany
{christin.kohrs,andre.brechmann}@lin-magdeburg.de

Abstract. We report about a transsituational study where a representative subsample of twenty of the subjects from the LAST MINUTE experiment underwent two additional independent experiments: an fMRI study and a psychophysiological experiment with emotion induction in the VAD space (Valence, Arousal, Dominance). A major result is that dialog success in the naturalistic human machine dialogs in LAST MINUTE correlates with individual differences in brain activation as reaction to delayed system responses in the fMRI study and with the classification rate for arousal in the emotion induction experiment.

1 Introduction

Empirical research in HCI is conducted by different disciplines with a multitude of approaches. Such empirical investigations range from in-depth analysis of full fledged human dialogs and naturalistic dialogs between humans and Wizard of Oz simulated systems (e.g. [11,22,23]) to psychophysiological and neurophysiological studies utilizing controlled stimuli, e.g. for the induction of emotional responses (e.g. [6,21]) or the neural responses elicited by computer feedback in dialog-like situations (e.g. [8]).

Despite the relative merits of such experiments, their outcome can not easily be combined and generalized when the experiments are performed completely independent and with different cohorts. This changes remarkably in a transsituational setting with a common cohort of subjects undergoing a series of different experiments.

In the following we report about such a transsituational study. A representative subsample of $N_{exps} = 20$ subjects from the LAST MINUTE experiment (LME) [5,15,16] has undergone two additional independent experiments:

M. Kurosu (Ed.): HCI 2016, Part I, LNCS 9731, pp. 77–88, 2016.
DOI: 10.1007/978-3-319-39510-4_8

an fMRI study [9] and a psychophysiological experiment [18,24]. We will present and discuss what the transsituational analysis of data from all three experiments revealed about correlations between dialog success in LME and results from fMRI and analysis of biopsychological data.

2 The Experiments

2.1 The LAST MINUTE Experiment

The LAST MINUTE corpus (LMC) is derived from a large scale Wizard of Oz (WoZ) experiment – the LAST MINUTE experiment (LME) – that required users to solve a mundane task with the need for planning, replanning and strategy change (cf. [5,15]). The LMC comprises multimodal recordings (audio, transcripts, video, biopsychological data, ...) from a cohort of $N_{total} = 133$ subjects. The cohort was balanced in gender (68 women and 65 men) and age group (72 subjects aged between 18 and 28 vs. 61 aged above 60 years).

The LMC has been intensively investigated with respect to differences in dialog success (e.g. [14,15]). For example, significant differences between the age groups could be found, whereas global differences in gender were insignificant [17].

Dialog Acts and Interaction Success. In the transcripts of the LMC all user and system utterances are semi-automatically enriched with dialog act labels in the format of the dialog act representation (DAR) [15]. The DAR employs triples that first encode the speaker (i.e. S for subject, W for wizard), then the dialog act (e.g. R for REQUESTs, A for ACCEPTs or Rj for REJECTs, cf. [3]) and finally an optional subtype (e.g. a REQUEST for an action may be subtyped with the shorthand code for the action: P for packing, U for unpacking, C for changing category, ..., [15]).

These local DAR annotations are exploited for defining measures for global dialog success by integrating over local interaction success or failure in problem solving [15]:

- **DSM1**: ratio between accepted subject requests and total number of subject requests;
- **DSM2**: ratio between accepted subject requests and total number of turns (i.e. not only subject requests).

By definition the following holds for all transcripts: $0 \leq \text{DSM2} \leq \text{DSM1} \leq 1$. In the following evaluations we work with these measures.

Subphases. As a key aspect, an inherent need for re-planning and strategy change was built into the WoZ scenario of LAST MINUTE (cf. [5]). Therefore problem solving was divided into three major subphases which where demarcated by the weight limit barrier (**WLB**, after the eighth of twelve consecutive selection categories) and the weather info barrier (**WIB**, after the tenth selection category).

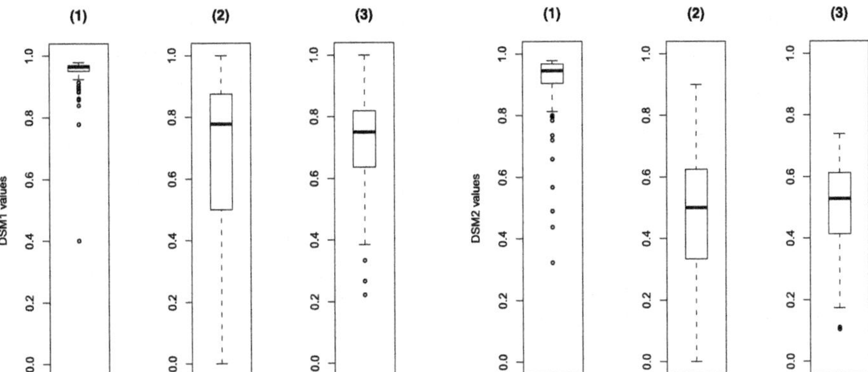

Fig. 1. DSM1 values in the three subphases of problem solving ($N_{total} = 133$): (1) before weight limit barrier (WLB), (2) from WLB to weather info barrier (WIB), (3) from WIB to end of experiment. Please note outliers in (1) and (3).

Fig. 2. DSM2 values in the three subphases of problem solving ($N_{total} = 133$). Please note outliers in (1) and (3).

The WLB enforces re-planning. Up to the WLB there is no need for unpacking, but thereafter it becomes crucial, for no progress can be achieved without at least one successful unpacking attempt.

At the WIB the subject receives a deliberately delayed weather information about the target location. This enforces a strategy change. Now items for cold and rainy weather are needed in exchange for e.g. bathing suits and other summer items.

Reasons to Fail. At first glance packing a suitcase by selecting items from menus seems to be a fairly easy task. How can the resp. dialogs become problematic? The weight limit barrier (WLB) poses a major challenge for many subjects. They have to successfully unpack items in order to make room for additional items. What can prevent subjects from successful unpacking? There are a variety of potential failures:

- Subjects may try to unpack items that are not in the suitcase.
- A variant of this failure is when subjects employ synonyms or hypernyms for items and when the wizards are not accepting these terms. Such rejections often proof to be very puzzling for subjects.
- In its verbal explanation of the weight limit the system has offered the option to enumerate the suitcase contents (verbally). Such a listing may be very helpful. However, subjects have to be aware of this option. Quite a number of subjects seem to be unaware of this option, at least they do not make use of it.

Examples of Transcripts. In the following we shortly present excerpts from transcripts illustrating these points.

The transcript example in Table 1 with DAR labels is taken from a dialog segment where a subject (20110117bsk) hits the weight limit again and successfully overcomes it by unpacking several items (SRU WAU pairs).

The excerpt in Table 2 illustrates that unpacking may fail: the unpacking requests (SRUs) of subject 20110126afw are rejected several times (WRjUs). Therefore the packing request (SRP) after the category change (WIC) is doomed to fail as well (WRjP).

Table 1. Transcript example with DAR tags (subject 20110117bsk; cf. text). Following the GAT-2 minimal standard [19] short pauses are noted as (.) and (-).

Tag	German text	English gloss
	...	...
SRP	((schnalzt)) (-) zwei bücher	((flicks)) (-) two books
WRjP	der artikel buch kann nicht hinzugefügt werden (.) anderenfalls würde die maximale gewichtsgrenze des koffers überschritten werden	the item book cannot be added (.) otherwise the weight limit of your suitcase will be exceeded
SRU	schnorchel entfernen	remove snorkel
WAU	ein schnorchel wurde entfernt	a snorkel has been removed
SRU	taucherbrille entfernen	remove diving googles
WAU	eine taucherbrille wurde entfernt	diving googles have been removed
SRU	kleid entfernen	remove dress
WAU	ein kleid wurde entfernt	a dress has been removed
SRU	((schnalzt)) badelatschen entfernen	((flicks)) remove beach slippers
WAU	ein paar badelatschen wurden entfernt	a pair of beach slippers have been removed
SRP	buch hinzufügen	add book
WAP	ein buch wurde hinzugefügt	a book has been added
SRC	nächste kategorie	next category
WIC	sie können jetzt aus der rubrik technische geräte auswählen ...	you may now choose from the category technical devices ...

Dialog Success in Subphases. The DSM values differ remarkably within the subphases of problem solving (cf. Figs. 1, 2).[1] As shown in Fig. 1, the DSM1 values lie above 0.95 for more than 75 % of the subjects before the WLB. In subsequent phases the medians drop to 0.78 and 0.75, while the means go down to 0.69 and 0.71 respectively.

These differences can be explained as follows: In the first subphase the vast majority of subjects has hardly any problems. The weight limit barrier (WLB)

[1] The distributions are visualized — here and in other figures — as trellis box plots: the rectangles represent the interquartile range (i.e. the range of 25 % of the values above and below the median resp.), the black bar gives the median, the whiskers extend the rectangle to the range of values, but maximally to 1.5 of the interquartile range, outlier values beyond the maximal whisker range are given as unfilled dots (cf. [1]).

Table 2. Transcript example with DAR tags (subject 20110126afw; cf. text). Following the GAT-2 minimal standard [19] short pauses are noted as (.) and (-), longer pauses with their duration in brackets, e.g. (3.0).

Tag	German text	English gloss
	...	...
SRP	ein reiseführer	a guidebook
WRjP	der artikel reiseführer kann nicht hinzugefügt werden (.) anderenfalls würde die maximale gewichtsgrenze des koffers überschritten werden	the item guidebook cannot be added (.) otherwise the weight limit of your suitcase will be exceeded
SRU	hosen herausnehmen	remove trousers
WRjU	der gewünschte artikel ist nicht im koffer enthalten	requested item is not contained in the suitcase
SRU	fünf socken herausnehmen	remove five socks
WRjU	der gewünschte artikel ist nicht im koffer enthalten	the requested item is not contained in the suitcase
SRU	einen hut herausnehmen	remove a hat
WRjU	der gewünschte artikel ist nicht im koffer enthalten	the requested item is not contained in the suitcase
SRU	sonnenhut (3.0) herausnehmen	sunhat (3.0) out
WRjU	der gewünschte artikel ist nicht im koffer enthalten	the requested item is not contained in the suitcase
	(---)	(---)
WIT	die auswahl von artikeln aus der rubrik reiselektüre muss jetzt beendet werden (.) um die aufgabe in der zur verfügung stehenden zeit beenden zu können	selecting items from category travel reading needs to be finished now in order to complete the task in time
	(--)	(--)
WIC	sie können jetzt aus der rubrik technische geräte auswählen	you may now choose from the category technical devices
SRP	fotoapparat	camera
WRjP	der artikel fotoapparat kann nicht hinzugefügt werden (.) anderenfalls würde die maximale gewichtsgrenze des koffers überschritten werden	the item camera cannot be added (.) otherwise the weight limit of your suitcase will be exceeded
	...	...

changes this drastically because without success in unpacking, no further packing is possible. Thus if unpacking is not attempted or is not successful a downward spiral with a series of subsequent rejections – and thus low DSM values – may result. As already discussed above, the task of unpacking demands to remember already packed items (or - as an alternative - to remember that a listing of the suitcase contents can be asked for), to decide which packed items to sacrifice and to request the respective unpacking action.

2.2 The fMRI Experiment

The subcohort of twenty subjects was recruited to participate in a functional magnetic resonance imaging (fMRI) experiment carried out in a 3 Tesla scanner (Siemens Trio, Erlangen, Germany). Three participants had to be excluded due to contraindications for MRI, excessive head motion, or abortion of the experiment before completion. Methodological details of the scanning parameters for anatomical and functional imaging, presentation of acoustic and visual stimuli, and task procedure are published in [8]. In short, the participants had to perform an auditory categorization task on frequency modulated sounds. In 300 trials they had to indicate by left or right button press if a sound was rising or falling in pitch. In 85 % of all trials they received immediate feedback, i.e. visual presentation of a green checkmark for correct responses and a red cross for false responses. In 15 % this feedback was delayed by 200, 400, or 600 ms. The fMRI data were analyzed with a region of interest (ROI) analysis of variance (ANOVA) as implemented in BrainVoyagerQX using the four different feedback times as predictors. As regions of interests, we used five brain areas identified to be significantly activated by feedback that was delayed by 500 ms as compared to immediate feedback [9], i.e. posterior medial prefrontal cortex, bilateral anterior insula, left inferior parietal lobe, and right inferior frontal cortex. Within each of these areas, we identified the beta values resulting from the ANOVA regarding feedback delays of 400 ms and 600 ms and subtracted the beta values for immediate feedback in order to determine the increase of neural activity elicited by delayed feedback as compared to immediate feedback. We did not analyze activity elicited by 200 ms delays because such short delays do not have a significant impact on brain activity and are usually not perceived as delayed [8]. We then calculated a two sided Pearson correlation between the participants' dialog success rate from the LAST MINUTE experiment and the activation data of the participants in each of the five brain areas.

2.3 The Psychophysiological Experiment

In the psychophysiological experiment, the same representative subcohort of twenty from the LME recruited at the university of Magdeburg participated in a controlled emotion induction setting. Numerous studies on emotion recognition based on facial expression, speech, body language, contexts and physiological signals have been performed in the past few decades [2]. Among them, physiological signals have considerable advantages, for example, as honest signals [13], they cannot be easily triggered by any conscious or intentional control. Various classifications, feature selection and evaluation algorithms are currently used for the emotion recognition from physiological data [21,24].

In this experiment, emotions were induced by using standardized stimuli from the International Affective Picture System (IAPS) to represent the VAD (Valence, Arousal, Dominance) space. The advantage of using standardized stimuli relies in the reliability of the induction of a specific VAD value. Prolonged presentations consisting of 10 pictures à 2 s (total of 20 s) are used to intensify the elicitation. A total of 10 picture-presentations à 20 s each were presented to induce a total of 10 VAD-states. 20 s neutral fixation crosses were introduced as baseline between 2 different presentations. The induced VAD-space for the 10 picture-presentations included positive/negative/neutral (+/-/0) Valence, positive/negative (+/-) Arousal, and positive/negative (+/-) Dominance values. For the classification of the emotional states, picture-presentation with similar ratings in terms of Valence (+/-/0) and/or Arousal (+/-) and/or Dominance were combined in one category. In total we evaluated the emotion recognition rates of 5 different category-classes: V(+/-/0), A(+/-), D(+/-), VA(0-/++/-+/+-/–), VAD(10 different picture presentations) [24].

We processed the emotion recognition rates by fusing four physiological signals including skin conductivity, respiration and 2x electromyography signals (corrugator & zygomaticus). The evaluation was conducted using the Augsburg Biosignal Toolbox (AuBT, [20]). The AuBT provides Matlab-based tools to analyze physiological signals for the emotion recognition. The emotion recognition rates were computed for each subject individually. Therefore, for the evaluation of the individual classification rates for each subject, 10 samples from the subject itself were used as test-set and 190 samples from the 19 subjects left were used as training-set. In total 20 different classifications were conducted.

3 Results

3.1 The Subcohort in the LAST MINUTE Experiment

The LAST MINUTE experiments with the total cohort were performed over a time period of nearly a year. The transsituational experiment with the subcohort of twenty subjects was performed in a compact subinterval of two months. The participants in the subcohort were randomly chosen during this interval with the only restriction that finally the subcohort was roughly balanced with respect to gender (9 women vs. 11 men) and age groups (10 young subjects aged between 18 and 28 years vs. 10 elderly subjects aged above 60 years).

When one tests dialog success values (as measured with DSM1 and DSM2) for representativity, the distribution in the subcohort of twenty does not differ significantly from that of the total cohort (Wilcoxon tests; DSM1: W = 1105, p = 0.2243; DSM2: W = 1051, p = 0.1317; see also Figs. 3, 4). Having a representative subsample with respect to dialog success motivates the following investigations about correlations between dialog success in LME and relevant outcomes in the two other experiments.

The discourse success measures DSM1 and DSM2 are strongly correlated. This holds for the whole cohort of $N_{total} = 133$ (Pearson's product-moment correlation 0.85, $t = 18.1972, df = 131, p < 2.2e - 16$) as well as for the sample of twenty (Pearson's product-moment correlation 0.88, $t = 8.022, df = 18, p = 2.357e - 07$). But there is considerable variance with respect to individual differences between the two values. When we take the quotient $DSM2/DSM1$ as a percentage we get distributions as summarized in Table 3 for the whole cohort and for the subcohort of 20.

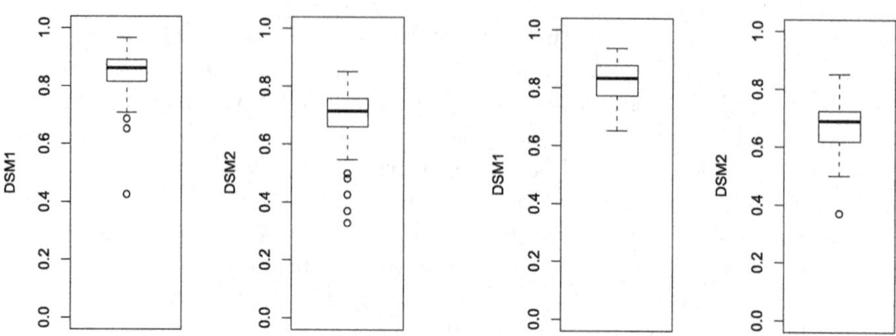

Fig. 3. Distribution of DSM1 and DSM2 values for complete cohort ($N_{total} = 133$)

Fig. 4. Distribution of DSM1 and DSM2 values for subcohort of $N_{exps} = 20$

Table 3. DSM2 values as percentage of DSM1 values per transcript

cohort	Min.	1st Qu	Median	Mean	3rd Qu.	Max.
133	55.29	80.60	83.10	82.34	85.92	92.65
20	56.79	79.50	82.68	80.29	85.45	90.91
Elder	55.29	78.95	82.14	80.79	84.62	89.58
Young	62.12	81.23	84.53	83.66	86.12	92.65

For the whole cohort the age groups differ significantly and with a medium effect size with respect to this quotient, with elderly subjects having greater differences between DSM2 and DSM1 than the younger (Wilcoxon rank sum test W = 1531, p = 0.002695, $d_{Cohen} = 0.503$).

3.2 Results from the fMRI Experiment

Consistent to the previous study, we found that delays of 400 and 600 ms result in significant activation of the selected brain regions. However, we found considerable interindividual variance of the activation increase elicited by delayed feedback in each of the selected brain regions. Pearson correlations showed a significant positive relation between dialog success in the LME and activation increase only in the anterior insula (left insula: DSM1: $p = 0.005$, $r = 0.65$, DSM2: $p = 0.005$, $r = 0.65$; right insula: DSM1: $p = 0.014$, $r = 0.65$, DSM2: $p = 0.018$, $r = 0.57$). The lower significance for the right insula may be due to the fact that the ROIs selected from a previous study with different participants and thus different anatomy matched the location of activation resulting from the group level analysis of the actual participants less well (see overlap of transparent ROI with significant voxels coded in yellow to red in the right panel of Fig. 5). After the fMRI experiment, the subjects filled in a questionnaire whether or not they have noticed delays in feedback and if so how many different delays. Five subjects

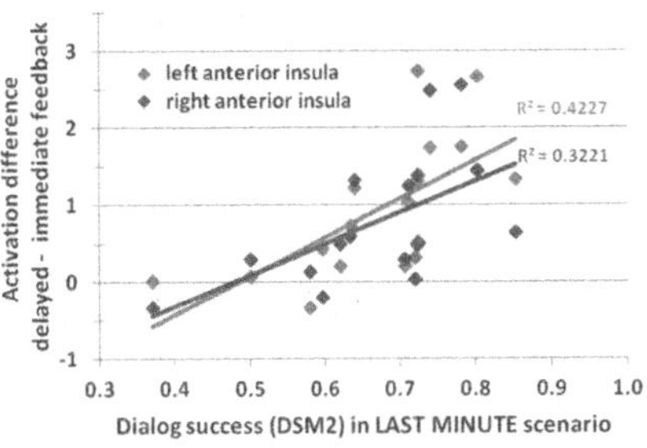

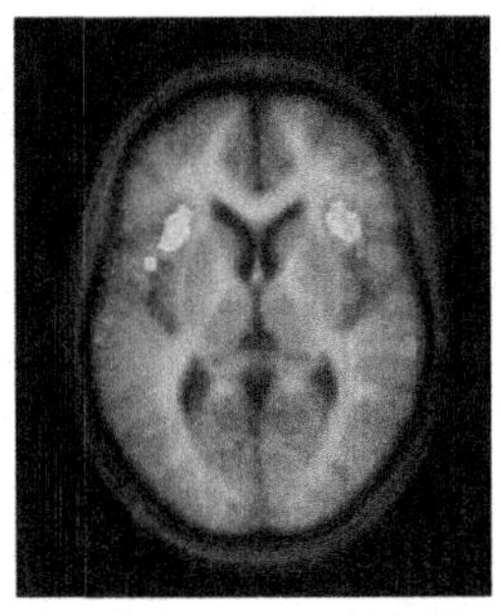

Fig. 5. Correlation between the dialog success (DSM2) in the LAST MINUTE experiment and the increase in fMRI activation in the anterior insula elicited by delayed vs. immediate feedback (left panel). The right panel shows the location of the region of interest (transparent grey cluster) extracted from a previous study [9] and the significant fMRI activation from the group level analysis of the current study (Color figure online).

reported not to have noticed any delay at all, and these subjects are among the lower performers (rank 10 to 14) in the LAST MINUTE experiment.

3.3 Results from the Psychophysiological Experiment

For the analysis of the correlation, the two-category-classes Arousal (+/-) and Dominance (+/-) as well as the three-category-class Valence (+/-/0) are considered in this study. For each subject, the individual recognition rates are correlated with the individual dialog success ratios. The classification data are normally distributed and the Pearson correlation coefficients are used to assess the correlation between the emotion recognition rates and the dialog success DSM1 and DSM2 ratios. Two strongly positive correlations between the emotion recognition rates of the classifiers and the dialog success from the LME were found: (1) A strong positive correlation between the emotion recognition rate of the

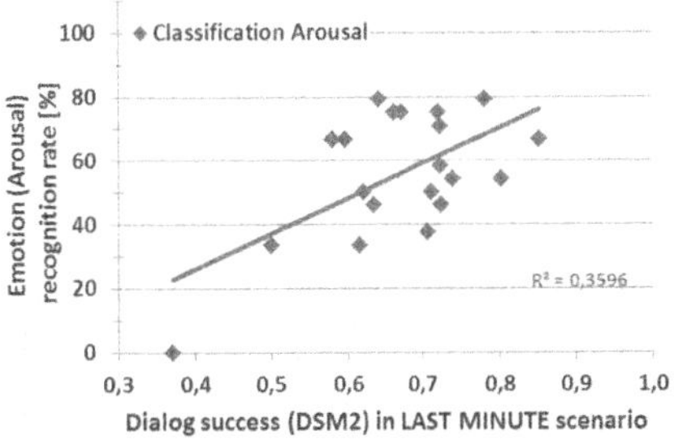

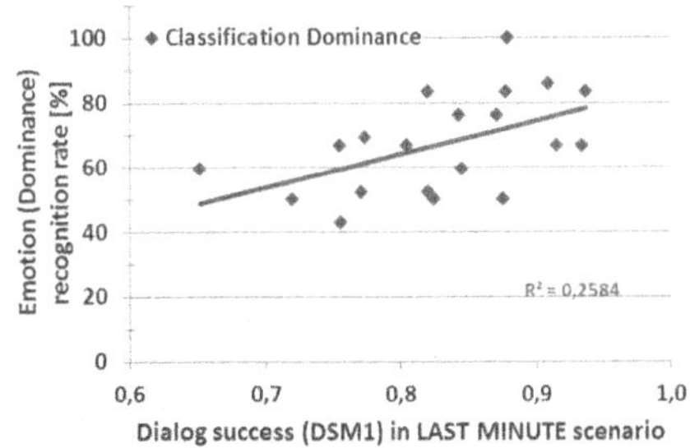

Fig. 6. Correlation between the dialog success DSM2 and the psychophysiological Arousal recognition rate (left-panel) and between the dialog success DSM1 and the psychophysiological Dominance recognition rate (right-panel).

two-category-class Arousal (+/-) and the dialog success rate DSM2 ($r = 0.600$, $p = 0.005$), and (2) A strong positive correlation between the emotion recognition rate of the two-category-class Dominance (+/-) and the dialog success rate DSM1 ($r = 0.503$, $p = 0.024$). The correlations results are illustrated in Fig. 6.

The biophysiological recognition rate results were obtained using the Sequential Forward Selection (SFS) feature selection and the Linear Discriminant Analysis (LDA) model for the two-category-class Arousal classification and using the Sequential Forward Selection (SFS) feature selection and the k-Nearest Neighbor (kNN) model for the two-category-class Dominance classification. No correlation was found between the dialog success and the emotion recognition of the three-category-class Valence (+/-/0) classification.

4 Discussion and Future Work

As a summary we have the following: dialog success in the naturalistic human machine dialogs in LAST MINUTE correlates with individual differences in brain activation as reaction to delayed system responses in the fMRI study and with the classification rate for arousal in the emotion induction experiment.

What do different – and especially low – values of the dialog success measures mean? Not surprisingly, there are quite different dialog courses in the LMC but generally speaking, subjects with low DSMs are locally unsuccessful repeatedly in interaction and they generally take longer (or completely fail) to overcome challenging situations in the dialogs where – by design [5] – re-planning or even strategy change is needed. In contrast high values of the DSMs go with avoiding to repeat errors once encountered and with high flexibility in adapting to unforeseen situations in the dialog course.

The original objective of the psychophysiological experiment was to find feature combinations for classifying emotional states by psychophysiological responding [24]. On an individual level, high classification rates for emotional states mean a consistency between the psychophysiological response and a certain emotion stimulation, e.g. a high arousing IAPS picture series would than lead to high amplitudes of the skin conductance level (SCL). Given that such an interpretation is correct, the obtained psychophysiological correlation implicates that persons with high DSM in a HCI setting show a high correspondence between their dialog activity and their psychophysiological responding and vice-versa. This would render the classification of the arousal state based on psychophysiology more easy in high expressive persons [24]. Since the correlation between classification rates and brain activation was not significant, further analyses e.g. of personality traits are needed to better understand the biological basis of individual success in HCI.

The successful participants in the LAST MINUTE experiment show strong fMRI activation of the anterior insula after delayed SRT. The original aim of the fMRI experiment was to study the effects of breaching a general rule of communication, namely the subjective sense of completion of an action [12]. We have shown that unexpected delays in feedback elicits an emotional response that can be classified as "suspense" according to the accompanying psychophysiological effects of a decelerating heart rate together with an increased skin conductance response [10]. Thus, communication has subjectively been perceived as unsuccessful. The anterior insula has recently been suggested to play a more general role in awareness (beyond interoception), and as neural correlate of consciousness [4]. Since an increase in activity has been suggested as sign of a conscious perception of an error [7], participants with a strong activation in the fMRI experiment may have perceived the delay as irritating. Participants with low activity, however, are less irritated and indeed four subjects with low DSM2 values and low activation of the anterior insula could not remember to have encountered delayed SRT after the MRI scan. Taken together, participants with a higher degree of conscious awareness of maladaptive dialog acts of technical systems seem to be more successful in challenging situations of the LAST MINUTE experiment

Acknowledgements. The presented study is performed in the framework of the Transregional Collaborative Research Centre SFB/TRR 62 "A Companion-Technology for Cognitive Technical Systems" funded by the German Research Foundation (DFG). It is also supported by a doctoral scholarship funded by the China Scholarship Council (CSC) for Lin Zhang and a Margarete von Wrangell (MvW) habilitation scholarship for Dilana Hazer-Rau. The responsibility for the content of this paper remains with the authors.

References

1. Baayen, R.: Analyzing Linguistic Data - A Practical Introduction to Statistics using R. Cambridge University Press, Cambridge (2008)
2. Calvo, R.A., D'Mello, S.: Affect detection: an interdisciplinary review of models, methods, and their applications. IEEE Trans. Affective Comput. **1**(1), 18–37 (2010)
3. Core, M., Allen, J.: Coding dialogs with the DAMSL annotation scheme. In: AAAI fall symposium on communicative action in humans and machines, pp. 28–35 (1997)
4. Craig, A.: How do you feel – now? the anterior insula and human awareness. Nat. Rev. Neurosci. **10**, 59–70 (2009)
5. Frommer, J., Rösner, D., Haase, M., Lange, J., Friesen, R., Otto, M.: Früherkennung und Verhinderung negativer Dialogverläufe - Operatormanual für das Wizard of Oz-Experiment. Pabst Science Publishers (2012)
6. Hazer, D., Ma, X., Rukavina, S., Gruss, S., Walter, S., Traue, H.C.: Transsituational individual-specific biopsychological classification of emotions. In: Stephanidis, C. (ed.) Proceedings of the HCI International 2015, pp. 110–117 (2015)
7. Hester, R., Foxe, J., Molholm, S., Shpaner, M., Garavan, H.: Neural mechanisms involved in error processing: a comparison of errors made with and without awareness. NeuroImage **27**(3), 602–608 (2005)
8. Kohrs, C., Angenstein, N., Brechmann, A.: Delays in human-computer interaction and their effects on brain activity. PLoS ONE **11**(1) (2016). doi:10.1371/journal.pone.0146250
9. Kohrs, C., Angenstein, N., Scheich, H., Brechmann, A.: Human striatum is differentially activated by delayed, omitted, and immediate registering feedback. Frontiers Human Neurosci. **6**, 00243 (2012)

10. Kohrs, C., Hrabal, D., Angenstein, N., Brechmann, A.: Delayed system response times affect immediate physiology and the dynamics of subsequent button press behavior. Psychophysiology **51**(11), 1178–1184 (2014)
11. Legát, M., Grůber, M., Ircing, P.: Wizard of Oz data collection for the Czech senior companion dialogue system. In: Fourth International Workshop on Human-Computer Conversation, pp. 1–4. University of Sheffield (2008)
12. Miller, R.B.: Response time in man-computer conversational transactions. In: AFIPS Conference Prodeedings, pp. 267–277. Thompson Book Company, Washington (1968)
13. Pentland, A., Pentland, S.: Honest Signals: How They Shape Our World. MIT Press, London (2008)
14. Prylipko, D., Rösner, D., Siegert, I., Günther, S., Friesen, R., Haase, M., Vlasenko, B., Wendemuth, A.: Analysis of significant dialog events in realistic human-computer interaction. J. Multimodal User Interfaces **8**(1), 75–86 (2014)
15. Rösner, D., Friesen, R., Günther, S., Andrich, R.: Modeling and evaluating dialog success in the LAST MINUTE Corpus. In: Proceedings of LREC 2014. ELRA, Reykjavik, May 2014
16. Rösner, D., Haase, M., Bauer, T., Günther, S., Krüger, J., Frommer, J.: Desiderata for the Design of Companion Systems - Insights from a Large Scale Wizard of Oz Experiment. Künstliche Intelligenz (2015), 28 October 2015. doi:10.1007/s13218-015-0410-z
17. Rösner, D., Andrich, R., Bauer, T., Friesen, R., Günther, S.: Annotation and analysis of the LAST MINUTE corpus. In: Proceedings of the International Conference of the German Society for Computational Linguistics and Language Technology. pp. 112–121. Gesellschaft für Sprachtechnologie and Computerlinguistik e.V. (2015)
18. Rukavina, S., Gruss, S., Walter, S., Hoffmann, H., Traue, H.C.: Open_emorec_ii-a multimodal corpus of human-computer interaction. World Acad. Sci. Eng. Technol. Int. J. Comput. Electr. Autom. Control Inf. Eng. **9**(5), 1135–1141 (2015)
19. Selting, M., Auer, P., Barth-Weingarten, D., Bergmann, J.R., Bergmann, P., Birkner, K., Couper-Kuhlen, E., Deppermann, A., Gilles, P., Günthner, S., et al.: Gesprächsanalytisches Transkriptionssystem 2 (GAT 2). Gesprächsforschung-Online-Zeitschrift zur verbalen Interaktion 10 (2009)
20. Wagner, J., Kim, J., André, E.: From physiological signals to emotions: Implementing and comparing selected methods for feature extraction and classification. In: IEEE International Conference on Multimedia and Expo (ICME) (2005)
21. Walter, S., Kim, J., Hrabal, D., Crawcour, S.C., Kessler, H., Traue, H.C.: Transsituational individual-specific biopsychological classification of emotions. Systems, Man, and Cybernetics: Systems, IEEE Transactions **43**(4), 988–995 (2013)
22. Webb, N., Benyon, D., Bradley, J., Hansen, P., Mival, O.: Wizard of Oz Experiments for a Companion Dialogue System: Eliciting Companionable Conversation. In: Proceedings of LREC 2010. ELRA (2010)
23. Wolters, M., Georgila, K., Moore, J., MacPherson, S.: Being old doesn't mean acting old: how older users interact with spoken dialog systems. ACM Trans. Access. Comput. **2**(1), 2:1–2:39 (2009)
24. Zhang, L., Rukavina, S., Gruss, S., Traue, H.C., Hazer, D.: Classification analysis for the emotion recognition from psychobiological data. In: International Symposium on Companion-Technology (ISCT) (2015)

Teaching Virtual Reality with Affordable Technologies

Nancy Rodriguez(✉)

LIRMM, University of Montpellier, CNRS, Montpellier, France
nancy.rodriguez@lirmm.fr

Abstract. In 2004, G.C. Burdea published his article *Teaching Virtual Reality: Why and How?* He pointed out that the reduced offer of Virtual Reality courses could be explained by the requirement of specialized and expensive equipment. Even if a VR course could only focus on theoretical principles, hands-on learning allows to increase and clarify knowledge and to directly experience –and then better understand- several concepts as immersion, natural interfaces or motion sickness. At the present time, digital entertainment industry renewal has fostered the development of low cost devices for virtual reality. These affordable technologies as a BYOD approach are used in the « open VR Lab » of the Computer Science department at University of Montpellier. In this paper, the VR Lab as well as our course *Vision and Augmented/Virtual Reality* are described in detail.

Keywords: Virtual reality · Augmented reality · Computer vision · Interaction devices · Display devices · VR laboratory · Higher education · Practical course

1 Introduction

In his article of 2004 Teaching Virtual Reality: Why and How? Grigore C. Burdea [1] discussed several aspects concerning teaching virtual reality. His web worldwide survey [2] found that only 148 universities have virtual reality courses, 273 in the last update (2008). As stated by [3] "today the number of VR courses worldwide has risen, but most of the courses are theoretical and are deriving from computer graphic courses and cannot provide all of the required practical and soft skills". Burdea pointed out that the reduced offer of Virtual Reality courses could be explained by the requirement of specialized and expensive equipment. Even if a VR course could only focus on theoretical principles, hands-on learning allows to increase and clarify knowledge and to directly experience –and then better understand- several concepts as immersion, natural interfaces or motion sickness. As stated by Burdea, hands-on experience is essential for true understanding of the field.

Affordable display and interaction devices for games and virtual reality are now available, going from Google Cardboard [4] to OculusRift [5] or OSVR Hacker Development Kit [6], and motion control devices as the LeapMotion [7] or the Microsoft Kinect [8]. These low-cost technologies have allowed us to set up an « open VR Lab » following a BYOD (Bring Your Own Device) approach. This lab supports the Vision and Augmented/Virtual Reality course offered in IMAGINA (Image, games and intelligent agents), a Master program of the Computer Science Department of the University of Montpellier. In our course, we apply several teaching methods like traditional lectures, devices' demonstrations, hands-on

M. Kurosu (Ed.): HCI 2016, Part I, LNCS 9731, pp. 89–97, 2016.
DOI: 10.1007/978-3-319-39510-4_9

training in form of labs and a final assignment, defined by students themselves, the development of a virtual reality application.

In this paper, our VR Laboratory and the Vision and Virtual/Augmented reality course are described in detail. Final course students' projects are presented, with a focus on immersive displays and gesture recognition. To conclude, I will discuss the issues encountered during the several activities realized in our course.

2 The Vision and Virtual/Augmented Reality Course

The master IMAGINA (Images, Games and Intelligent Agents) is a two-year graduate program (accessible after a Bachelor degree) of the University of Montpellier. The objective of this program is to train engineers and researchers in the imaging industry, video games and simulators, able to master the theories, models and technologies related these industries. The curriculum is developed over four semesters with choices of major elective courses in the third semester. The last semester includes an internship in a company or research laboratory for a period of five months minimum.

The Virtual and Augmented Reality course was created en 2012, to introduce students to the concepts, hardware and software involved in the development of virtual and augmented reality applications. At the end of the course, students should have a thorough understanding of the theoretical and computational tools for the creation of VR/AR systems and the difficulties inherent to this type of technology. Students learn about the historical development of virtual and augmented reality, their theoretical foundations and applications, a reminder of computer graphics concepts (modelling, viewing, rendering, geometric objects and transformations, scene graph, texture mapping) and 3D user interaction. In 2015, our course (HMIN320 - Vision, Virtual and Augmented Reality) was extended to Computer Vision. Students learn about main computer vision concepts and techniques including tracking, stereovision, image processing and registration.

Several labs are proposed, concerning the application of computer vision techniques using Matlab and OpenCV, and also the development of an interactive virtual environment using Unity [9]. The final course project is done in teams of 2-3 students. In addition, students have to summarize a state of the art research article (from Siggraph or Disney Research available articles) and to present (and evaluate) their final course project. This set of learning activities aims to enhance their communication skills, teamwork abilities and critical thinking.

3 The Virtual Reality Laboratory

A virtual environment is a computer-generated world that relies on user's tracking (head, hands, arms or the entire body) and multisensory rendering to create immersive experiences. Training is an application area perfectly suited to virtual reality [10]; environments and situations can be experimented under user's control, at his own pace, without risks, in a very flexible way. Because VR allows to develop skills and to have confidence to work in real conditions with real equipment, it has also showed its potential in several fields as health care and industry.

When learning Virtual Reality, it is important to confront the manipulation of VR technology, to better understand the specific difficulties of this kind of applications in terms of immersion, usability, health and safety. In the first version of our course, some students added control to their VR applications with their own video game controllers. I did a funding request for some low-cost VR devices in order to allow all of interested students to experience this technology. The Computer Science department of University of Montpellier financed the purchase of several interaction and display devices for our course: The Oculus Rift DK1, a space Navigator, a Novint Falcon force-feedback joystick, a 5DT Dataglove, 2 Kinect and 4 video game controllers. More recently, the CS Department acquired a LeapMotion controller. Some other material resources as an Oculus Rift DK2 and a second LeapMotion can be borrowed from one of our industrial partners NaturalPad. This funding and our partnerships had enabled us to implement an open laboratory, with a BYOD (Bring Your Own Device) approach.

The VR lab is an « ephemeral installation ». The project's room of the CS Department is large enough to accommodate a group of 25-30 people. The tables have power sockets and shelves to install the devices that are provided to students upon request. Video projection equipment is also available. Our lab serves as an alternative to highly immersive and expensive infrastructures as CAVEs and reduces licensing and maintenance costs.

After several demonstrations and initiation labs, five practical sessions of 3 h per week, are dedicated to the conception and development of the final course project. Students, organized in teams of 2-3 students, define themselves the nature of their project and the technologies to be integrated. The proposal is discussed and validate by lecturers. The final project presentation takes place the last session of the course. Each team presents its project and receives feedback from lecturers and the other teams. In addition, there is a prize "coup de coeur", awarded to the project which has totalized the more votes during the projects presentation (Fig. 1).

Fig. 1. Students presenting their work at the VR Lab

Videos showing several moments of the final project presentation day and several project trailers are available at our channel http://bit.ly/20XewVR.

4 VR Projects

This year, projects were developed along two main axes: immersive displays and motion capture devices. 3 teams of 8 have chosen to produce a visual immersive experience and 4 teams have integrated gesture recognition devices. The next sections discuss these productions.

4.1 Immersive Displays

Recent years have seen emerge a number of low cost display devices for virtual reality. Head Mounted Displays (HMD) as the Oculus Rift are now affordable for the end user. There are also cheaper alternatives like Google Cardboard or the Archos VR Glasses [11] that made use of smartphones to create lightweight "pocket" VR experiences.

One of the teams of our course have focused on Oculus Rift integration for the project "No Man's Ground". In No Man's Ground, the player, through a choice of 16 height maps, can generate a realistic terrain to be explored thereafter. The terrain appears gradually to create a futuristic feel. To integrate the Oculus Rift DK1, we tested different versions of the runtime, SDK and Unity plugins. Despite of our efforts, it was impossible to use the Oculus Rift DK1 for development in our laptops. One of our industrial partners, NaturalPad, provided us with an Oculus Rift DK2 to successfully finish the project. Given these difficulties, the two others team implementing immersive visual experiences turned to another solution: the Archos VR glasses (Fig. 2).

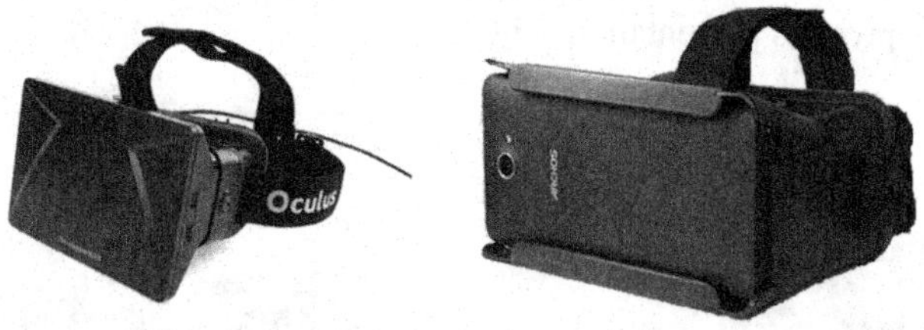

Fig. 2. Display devices: left Oculus Rift DK1, right Archos Vr Glasses

The Archos VR glasses like the Google cardboard, made use of the gyroscope and accelerometer from a smartphone to track the user's point of view. The smartphone is just inserted into the glasses to have a stereoscopic 3D image.

When using VR glasses, the big concern is interaction. The two teams chosen two different solutions: the project "Virtual race" calculates the rendering for each eye and controls the racing car using a Bluetooth keyboard. The project "Experience" uses the Google Cardboard SDK for Unity, which provides stereoscopic view generation and head tracking. Experience is an exploration game where player's movement follows her gaze direction.

As stated by the students, this kind of interaction keeps the game very simple but less dynamic. The integration of another input device is then an interesting perspective (Fig. 3).

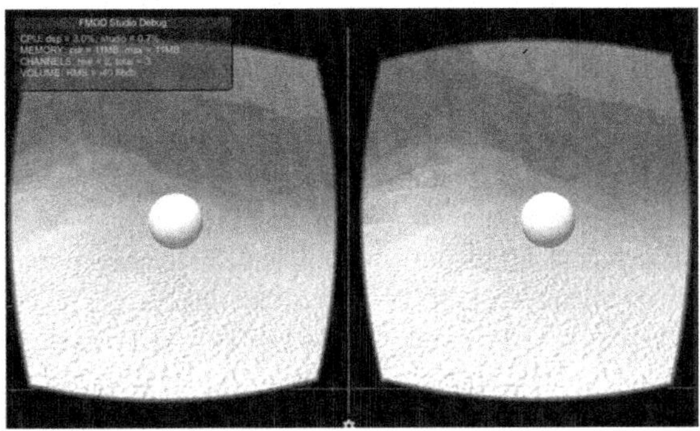

Fig. 3. Screenshot of the project "Experience", designed for the Archos VR glasses or Google Cardboard.

4.2 Gesture Recognition

As display devices, low cost interaction devices have appeared in recent years. Designed primarily for video games, they address "natural" interfaces: intuitive, based on gesture recognition, having a very low learning curve. We can cite the Kinect and the Leap Motion, two wireless touchless devices that allow recognizing the position and movements of the user (Kinect) or of her hands and fingers (LeapMotion).

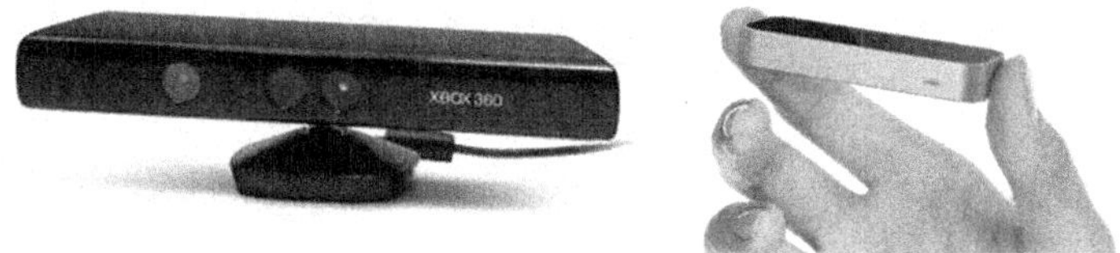

Fig. 4. Gesture recognition devices: left Microsoft Kinect, right Leap Motion

3 teams have chosen the LeapMotion as input device. The Leap is designed to lay on the desktop. To interact, the user makes gestures over the controller with the hands, fingers, or finger-like objects such as a pen or pencil (Fig. 4).

The Leap Motion SDK for Unity provides a hand 3D model mapping user's hands movements. It also detects predefined gestures like swipe or tap. The project "Leap Flowers", based on PS3 game "Flowers", aims to drive an object through a virtual environment using simple actions. Students decided to provides only few commands: turn left/right, go up/down, accelerate/decelerate.

When using LeapMotion or Kinect controller no support can be employed for the user arms or hands, inducing discomfort and fatigue. As shown in figure above, gestures have been chosen to decrease user's fatigue. For example, instead of using a hand movement to accelerate/decelerate, the user open or close his hand. By linking acceleration with hand opened or closed, the user hand is no longer passive and shoulder is less subject to strong efforts. Furthermore, this gesture was more effective and intuitive when tested, a muscle contraction being a natural response to an "emergency" situation (e.g. stopping to avoid a collision).

The "Créa-Main" project used Kinect and a 5DT DataGlove [12] to create objects by assembling simple cubes ("Voxel Art"). Kinect allows detecting the position of the two hands of the user while the Dataglove measures fingers flexures. Right hand controls systems commands (e.g. camera rotation) while left hand, the one wearing the glove, maps to a 3D hand performing interaction with the 3D scene and the virtual cubes.

There are several technical difficulties when implementing gesture recognition as detection of involuntary movements, lack of haptic feedback and user's fatigue. In addition to these technical challenges, it is very important to consider user acceptance. The gestures applications language has to be learned and adopted so it needs to be simple and intuitive.

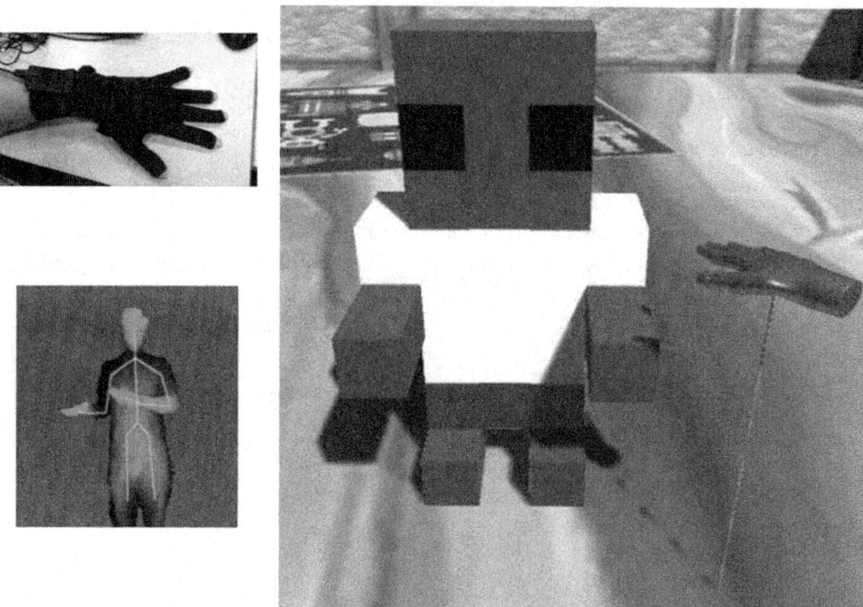

Fig. 5. In the "Créa-Main" project, the virtual hand (right) is controlled by a combination of Kinect and Dat Glove controllers.

5 Discussion

The quality of the projects presented this year show that the goals of our course are fulfilled (acquire knowledge of virtual reality hardware, software and applications). The divers projects also shows the three most important aspects of VR, according to Burdea and Coiffet [13]: immersion, interaction and imagination.

Students have enjoyed their work as spontaneously qualitative feedback points out:

- "Given the scope of its applications and as part of the training of integration of new development tools, learn to use the Oculus Rift is a great way to understand emerging technologies".
- "This project was a good introduction to the issues related to the use of Unity, the Leap Motion and the needs of analysis while working with gestures. Thinking process about player's perspective to make a game pleasant, intuitive and easy to handle has been both rewarding and exciting".
- "This project allowed us above all to be open-minded about new technology as the Leap Motion, cause we hadn't had a chance to tested it before this course. We were able to learn how to integrate it in our application to control a virtual object using hand movements. The project also allowed a reflection about how to integrate this kind of technology into a project. In fact, many times we have made changes on both the game design and the level design during the integration of the device".
- "We are pleased with the final outcome of our game and we were seduced by virtual reality. We created a nice experience that people who had the opportunity to try have appreciated".

As showed before, the final project is a good experience for students. They work in an application defined by students themselves, which leads to higher motivation and better results. Indeed, they use the final project to improve their portfolio and "impress" their personal and professional circles. This is very useful during internship search, next and final phase of the Master curriculum.

6 Conclusion

The IMAGINA Master program of the Computer Science Department of the University of Montpellier aims to prepare graduates for professional activities concerning games, interaction, simulation, and computer vision in a wide variety of industries.

The course HMIN320 – Vision, Virtual and Augmented Reality students learn about essential concepts of these fields, and are also confronted to their technical, ergonomic and social challenges. The Computer Science Department financed the purchase of several VR devices: Oculus Rift, Kinect, LeapMotion and 5DT DataGlove. These low-cost devices, rapidly deployable are combined to a BYOD approach to create a short-lived VR Lab when needed. This classroom space is used in a multimodal and versatile manner; it is also used for our final project presentations day.

At present, several displays and interaction devices are affordable for the end user. We believe it is important to introduce students to these technologies to facilitate understanding of the key issues of their integration into a project. The course has a traditional lecture-based approach combined with practical sessions, in order to ensure a minimal knowledge concerning basic concepts and the tools to be used.

15 h at the end of the course are dedicated to the conception and development of the final course project. Students, organized in groups of 2-3 people, choose the topic of the project and the technologies to be used. We have noticed that this organization strongly

motivate the students, they work on the project in their spare time, and is often used to show their skills during internship research. In addition to their teamwork abilities, the students' communication skills are enhanced by reading of scientific research papers and the presentation of the final course project.

In the article *Teaching Virtual Reality: Why and How?* G.C. Burdea pointed out that the reduced offer of Virtual Reality courses could be explained by the requirement of specialized and expensive equipment. As discussed in this paper, a set of low-cost devices coupled to a versatile academic space, allow us to develop a VR lab targeted to make VR technology accessible to a greater number of undergraduate and graduate students of Computer Science Department (Fig. 5).

Acknowledgements. I would like to thank all the HMIN320 2015 students for their work and feedback. Special thanks to Christophe Dauphin, Bastien Herbaut and Robin Herbaut for have kindly agreed to appear in the VR Lab photo.

References

1. Burdea, G.C.: Teaching Virtual Reality: Why and How? Teleoperators Virtual Environ. **13**(4), 463–483 (2004)
2. World-wide Survey of Universities Teaching Virtual Reality, http://vrtechnology.org/resources/public/survey.html
3. Häfner P., Häfner V., Ovtcharova J.: Teaching Methodology for Virtual Reality Practical Course in Engineering Education. In: 2013 International Conference on Virtual and Augmented Reality in Education. Procedia Computer Science 25, 251 – 260 (2013)
4. Google cardboard. https://developers.google.com/cardboard/
5. Oculus Rift. https://www.oculus.com/
6. OSVR Hacker Development Kit. http://www.osvr.org
7. Leap Motion. https://www.leapmotion.com/
8. Meet Kinect for Windows. https://dev.windows.com/en-us/kinect
9. Unity. http://www.unity.com
10. Watson, D.: Education Inf. Technologies **5**(4), 231–232 (2000)
11. ARCHOS Virtual Reality glasses. http://www.archos.com/gb-en/products/objects/cself/avr/index.html
12. Fifth Dimension Technologies Data Gloves. http://www.5dt.com/?page_id=34
13. Burdea, G., Coiffet, P.: Virtual Reality Technology. Teleoperators Virtual Environ. **12**(6), 663–664 (2003)
14. Araullo, J., Potter, L.E.: Experiences Using Emerging Technology. In: OzCHI 2014 Annual Conference of the Australian Computer-Human Interaction Special Interest Group (CHISIG), Sydney, Australia (2014)
15. Caputo, F.M.: Evaluation of basic object manipulation modes for low-cost immersive virtual reality. In: Biannual Conference of the Italian Chapter of SIGCHI, CHITALY 2015, pp. 74–77. ACM (2015)
16. Desai, P.R., Desai, P.N., Ajmera, K.D., Mehta, K.: A review paper on oculus rift - a virtual reality headset. Int. J. Eng. Trends Technol. (IJETT) **13**(4), 175–179 (2014)

17. Whitman, L., Malzahn, D., Madhavan, V., Weheba, G., Krishnan, K.: Virtual reality case study throughout the curriculum to address competency gaps. Int. J. Eng. Educ. **20**(5), 690–702 (2004)
18. Cliburn D.C., Miller J.R., Doherty, M.E.: The design and evaluation of online lesson units for teaching virtual reality to undergraduates. In: 40th ASEE/IEEE Frontiers in Education Conference FECS, pp. F3F-1-F3F-6 (2010)

What's Wrong with ERP in China?

Hang Shi(✉) and Eugene Hoyt

GP Technologies, Florida Gulf Coast University, Fort Myers, USA
Usa@imagicsmart.com, ehoyt@fgcu.edu

Abstract. ERP was introduced to Chinese organizations for about 30 years. However, the successful ERP implementation rate are always kept low, sometime even lower than 10 %. By adopting Hofstede (2001) national culture dimensions, this study provides substantive explanations and conclusions about the effects of national culture dimensions on organizations' ERP implementation successful rate.

Keywords: ERP · China

1 Introduction

As a central efficient solution strategy, enterprise resource planning (ERP) becomes to a key management package in most of the organizations in the world since last two decades. Benefits from ERP systems are obvious. Through data standardization and process integration, ERP systems have the potential to facilitate communications and co-ordination, enable the centralization of administrative activities, reduce IS maintenance costs and increase the ability to deploy new IS functionality (Gattiker and Goodhue, 2000). When they are well implemented, ERP systems are able to bring operational, managerial, strategic, IT infrastructure and operational benefits to their customers (Shang and Seddon, 2000). ERP systems have spread rapidly among organizations all over the world.

After three decades, China grows up rapidly and has now become the second largest economy. During the development, China adopted tons of new technologies, advanced business and management theories and applications. ERP is one of the blooming market in China for the past twenty years. The evolution of ERP in China can be summarized into three stages:

1. 1988 to 1995: SAP is the first ERP vendor entered China in 1988. After that, more and more international ERP vendors, such as Oracle, PeopleSoft etc., followed in around early 1990s. This was the first time Chinese organizations first heard business process reengineering (BPR) and ERP. According to many reasons including several strong culture reasons, many Chinese organizations tried to implement ERP. Unfortunately, very few succeeded. At this stage, over 90 % of the ERP market were taken up by foreign ERP vendors (Zhang et al. 2002).
2. 1996 to 2002: Because of high failure rate of ERP from foreign vendors and high demand of ERP in the market, many of Chinese domestic vendors began to design

M. Kurosu (Ed.): HCI 2016, Part I, LNCS 9731, pp. 98–104, 2016.
DOI: 10.1007/978-3-319-39510-4_10

and develop small scale of ERP packages. At this stage, domestic vendors took over the ERP market from the foreign giant vendors. Because of complicated and rapid changing accounting and financial policies in China, large foreign ERP vendors were hard to localize their packages in China. However, domestic ERP vendors, most of which were accounting software development vendors before, easily put a lot of unique Chinese characteristics in their agile ERP packages. Therefore, most of the Chinese organizations at this stage went to the domestic vendors for ERP solutions. Unfortunately, the failure rate of ERP implementations got even higher, over 90 % (Liu 2014).

3. 2003 to date: Some Chinese organizations realized issues from domestic vendors, such as unreliable system, non-integrated functions, fatal database systems, etc., then switched to foreign vendors. The rest of the organizations still relied on domestic vendors, mainly because of the cost. In this stage, according to IDC report (2015), there are too many software packages announced to have ERP functions in the Chinese market. However, most of them were not fully functioned ERP systems. Most of the current "ERP" packages are more close to a sub function in one of the ERP modules. Therefore, on one side, most of the Chinese organizations need ERP packages with Chinese characteristics; on the other hand, they are looking for inexpensive packages. For other organizations, they are willing to adopt ERP systems from giant foreign vendors. However, even large companies, like SAP, entered China almost thirty years, there are still not many skilled Chinese consultants available for their packages. In results, the reputation of the ERP systems from these ERP vendors in China are expensive and difficulty to implement. Some of the Chinese researcher even declared that the successful rate of ERP applications in China was close to zero (Liu 2014).

Comparing the ERP adoption and usage in China and western countries, we found an interesting issue that even for the same package of ERP, the results could be totally opposite. Xue et al. (2005) argue that cultural issues could make ERP adoptions and implementations much more difficult. Therefore, in the study, we focus on culture influence on ERP adoptions, especially what are the key factors of Chinese culture influencing the successful ERP adoption of Chinese organizations.

2 Literature Review

Today, a vast amount of the ERP studies focus on management perspectives of ERP on either implementations or post-implementations. However, cultural impact was not addressed in previous research studies as a determinant factor of successful ERP adoption. Only a few of studies concern the culture issues in ERP implementations. After study different dimensions of culture differences, Alhirz and Sajeev (2014) only find a significant influence between uncertainty avoidance and perceived user involvement and user resistance with ERP in a Saudi Arabia case study. By recognizing the cultural differences, a Thai corporation adopted "Cultural Intelligence" strategy in the ERP implementation to ensure the successful ERP implementation (Meissonier et al. 2014).

The culture differences between China and Western countries toward IT/IS implementations have been recognized by many researchers (Martinson and Revenaugh 1998; Martinson and Westwood 1997; Ping and Grimshaw 1992). Martinson and Revenaugh (1998) argue that fundamental values in Chinese culture does conflict with IT-enabled strategic change which generated from Western managerial culture on a "harmonious equilibrium with the system and the respect of hierarchical authority." Sheu et al. (2003) study on four US-Taiwanese manufacturing organizations and find five categories of culture related differences influencing successful ERP implementation: language, culture, politics, regulations and management style. Soh et al. (2000) identified three cultural issues including incompatibilities of data format between organizational requirements and the ERP systems, incompatibilities in processing procedures required, and incompatibilities in information reports and presentations of ERP.

After analyzing the failure cases of Chinese ERP implementations, Liu (2014) points out two cultural characteristics among Chinese organizations while facing to the ERP adoptions: over self-criticizing of management capability, which makes Chinese organizations believe that everything made-in-China cannot be compatible with foreign products, over estimation of the quality from Western countries, which causes Chinese organization being easily persuaded by foreign vendors. Davison (2002) summarizes the cultural differences on ERP implementations between North America and Hong Kong into three issues: different beliefs in providing access to information, misunderstanding/miscommunications due to complications of Chinese language, and significant difficult reengineering processes. Avison and Malaurent (2007), through a case study of failure ERP implementation in a Chinese branch of an international organization, find that four categories of issues: organizational, cultural, political and economic. Additionally, they argue that linguistic factors are crucial.

3 Theoretical Background

Hofstede (2001) introduced a five dimension classification of cultures based on a survey of employees in IBM subsidiaries located in fifty countries.

Power distance index (PDI) identifies how societies under different cultures regulate the behavior of their members. In large power distance countries, the less powerful members expect and accept the inequality of power distribution. Lower power members are required to be obedient and respectful to higher power members. For example, employees are rarely encouraged to challenge their superiors. In countries with lower distance power, children are allowed to contradict their parents or challenge their teachers. In ERP implementations, Chinese organizations always emphasize that ERP is a so called "Leader support project", which is similar to Top management support in Western culture. However, in most of the Chinese organizations, there is only one leader in the organization who is the King of the organization. If the ERP project gain the support from this leader, most likely all the resources will be lean to this implementation and the successful rate gets much higher for the project. Hence, we suggest the following hypothesis:

H1: The higher the country's PDI score, higher leadership support more likely will cause higher successful ERP implementation.

According to Hofstede (2001), uncertainty creates anxiety and people feel threatened by uncertain or unknown situations, for example, knowledge of a life after death. Uncertainty Avoidance Index (UAI) describes how people adapt or cope with these uncertain or unknown situations. In high UAI cultures, people tend to adopt technology, law, rules, and religion to decrease the ambiguity of situations by making events clearly interpretable and predictable. Organizations in high UAI cultures will not take unnecessary risks and only plan and complete those projects with enough value that they can explicitly approve in the market.

Since there are so many uncertainties in an ERP implementation, to avoid these uncertain issues, organizations in high UAI cultures are inclined to stay with trusted vendors and controllable scale of implementations. Hence, we suggest the following hypothesis:

H2: The higher the country's UAI score, the more likely companies in that country are will choose vendors with better reputation implementing with reliable ERP packages. Therefore, the successful rate of ERP implementation will be high.

Individualism and collectivism index (IDV) represents the relationship between the individual and collectivity or the group in a certain society. Individualism and collectivism impact the decision making of a person in the society. Individualism culture is more toward personal decision making with less influence from the surrounding collectivity or group.

For example, converting oneself from believing one religion to another is a highly individual activity in the countries with high individualism score while, in high collectivism countries, it is more reasonable that people tend to change their views together with their surrounding groups. In countries with low individualism culture, organizations are more likely to adopt the BPR and implementation suggestions from the vendors instead of having their unique methods. Hence, we suggest the following hypothesis:

H3: The higher the country's IDV score, the more likely companies in that country are to consider better BPR and implementation solutions, therefore, the implementations will gain the higher successful rate.

The fourth dimension in Hofstede's model is Masculinity (MAS) and Femininity. Basically, Hofstede (2001) argues that gender differences come from the natural differences between men and women. Culture could be more Masculinity or more Femininity according to how the societies define and follow norms in different ways. From his survey, Hofstede found two basic facts.

First, historically, masculine cultures tend to be more militaristic; second, masculine cultures tend to be more competitive while feminine cultures try more to encourage cooperation. Masculine cultures focus more on ambition, making quick decisions with less cooperation. Therefore, organizations with higher MAS scores tend to implement the ERP project alone without too much cooperation. Hence, we hypothesize the following:

H4: The higher the country's MAS score, the more likely companies in that country are to implement the ERP alone without too much involvement of consultants. Therefore, the successful rate of the implementation will decrease.

In his second edition of Culture's Consequences, Hofstede (2001) defines a new dimension of national cultures:

Long- Versus Short-Term Orientation. This Long-Term Orientation Index (LTO) score is based on a Chinese Value Survey (CVS) conducted in 1985 from students in 23 different countries. Cultures with high LTO scores tend to persist for a longer time with higher perseverance. The key words in LTO connotations summary are persistence, perseverance, personal adaptability to different circumstances, and believe of the happening of the most important events in life in future.

On the contrary, people in Low LTO cultures expect quick results, prefer personal steadiness and stability, and believe that the most important events in life occurred in past or occur in present instead of future.

Therefore, we expect that organizations in high LTO cultures are more likely to focus on future results with long strategy and operations planning, and more receptive to changes which may offer better results in the future, while as companies in low LTO cultures tend to emphasize short term benefits and are resistant to change. Obviously, ERP implementation will be a relatively long project, but the benefits will come eventually. Therefore, organizations in high LTO cultures will be patient to work on the project and expect the successful results.

H5: The higher the country's LTO score, the more likely companies in that country are getting higher successful rate for long term ERP implementation.

4 Data Collection and Analysis

A survey was sent to 127 organizations in three US cities (one large city, one mid-size city and one small town) and 432 SMEs in three Chinese cities with similar city size pattern. A total of 186 surveys were completed and 164 (71 from US and 93 from China) were used in the analysis. Table 1 shows the industry distribution of the companies.

Table 1. Industry distribution

Industry	Number	Percentage
Industrial Manufacturing	31	19 %
Public Sector	18	11 %
High Technology	49	30 %
Education	12	7 %
Healthcare	26	16 %
Utilities	7	4 %
Others	21	13 %

The items used in this survey were adapted from Hofstede's IBM and China survey questionnaires. The reliability of the items was evaluated using Cronbach's alpha [17].

The coefficient alphas for the PDI, UAI, IDV, MAS, and LTO were 0.82, 0.80, 0.79, 0.75, and 0.81, respectively. Pearson's correlation coefficients were also determined to assess the convergence validity. Since all the attribute coefficients were somewhere from high to moderate ranges, they were all retained for future analysis. Additionally, there were no concerns about multi-collinearity because none of the coefficients was extremely high.

The data were analyzed using multiple linear regression analysis. The purpose of a regression analysis is to relate a dependent variable to a set of independent variables. Regression analysis, therefore, was the most appropriate analytical technique in this study to determine the relationship between customer commitment and innovation characteristics, between customer attitude and innovation characteristics, and between customer commitment and customer attitude. Table 2 shows the hypothesis testing results along with the conclusions whether the hypothesis is supported by the statistical analysis at $\alpha < .05$.

Table 2. Summary of Regression Analysis Results

Hypothesis	Independent Variable	t-value	Significance	Support
H1	PDI	−4.987	<0.001	Yes
H2	UAI	−2.858	0.021	Yes
H3	IDV	4.066	<0.001	Yes
H4	MAS	2.413	0.028	Yes
H5	LTO	−1.055	0.302	No

5 Discussion and Conclusion

As demonstrated by the data analysis above, this empirical study supports hypothesis 1, 2, 3, and 4, while hypothesis 5 was not supported. Consequently, we can answer the research question in our study. First, national cultural variables, such as PDI, UAI, IDV, and MAS are related to successful ERP implementations; secondly, national culture should be added to the framework in ERP implementation studies.

The findings indicate that level of LTO is not related to successful ERP implementation. The possible reason to explain this result may be because the index was measured in 1985. With the remarkable and rapid economic growth, Chinese culture of LTO may change from the long term expectations to short term visions. Therefore, the results show an opposite direction e between the two countries.

Our study provides substantive conclusions about the effects of national culture dimensions on ERP implementations in organizations. We formulated a number of hypotheses regarding the influences of various national culture dimensions, such as PDI, UAI, DVI, MAS, and LTO. According to our data analysis, we found evidence to support most of our hypotheses. We can conclude that national culture does influence the successful rate of ERP implementations in organizations. Hofstede dimensions appeared to be a good theoretical background for ERP implementation study.

References

Alhirz, H., Sajeev, A.: Do cultural dimensions differentiate ERP acceptance? a study in the context of Saudi Arabia. Inf. Technol. People **28**(1), 163–194 (2014)

Gattiker, T., Goodhue, D.: Understanding the plant level costs and benefits of ERP: will the ugly duckling always turn into a swan. In: Proceedings of the 33rd Hawaii International Conference on System Science, Hawaii (2000)

IDC report. China Business Analytics Services 2015–2019 Forecast and Analysis (2015). http://www.idc.com/getdoc.jsp?containerId=CN25099. (Accessed on Jan. 2016)

Liu, Y.: Analysis of the dilemma between low successful rate and high demand of ERP. Productivity Res. **10**, 2013 (2014)

Martinsons, M., Revenaugh, D.: IT-enabled strategic change in the Chinese business culture. In: Proceedings of AMCIS, MD, USA (1998)

Martinsons, M., Westwood, R.: Management information systems in the Chinese business culture: an exploratory theory. Inf. Manage. **32**, 215–228 (1997)

Meissonier, R., Houze, E., Lapointe, L.: "Cultural Intelligence" during ERP implementation: insights from a Thai Corporation. Int. Bus. Res. **7**(12), 14–28 (2014)

Ping, Z., Grimshaw, D.: A comparative study of the application of IT in China and the West: culture and the stages of growth model. Int. J. Inf. Manage. **12**, 287–293 (1992)

Shang, S., Seddon, P.B.: . A comprehensive framework for classifying the benefits of ERP systems. In: Proceedings of the Americas Conference on Information Systems, Long Beach (2000)

Soh, C., Kien, S., Tay-Yap, J.: Cultural fits and misfits: is ERP a universal solution? Commun. ACM **43**(3), 47–51 (2000)

Xue, Y., Liang, H., Boulton, W., Snyder, C.: ERP implementation failures in China: case studies with implications for ERP vendors. Int. J. Prod. Econ. **97**, 279–295 (2005)

Zhang, L., Lee, M., Zhang, Z., Chan, J.: A framework of enterprise resource planning system implementation success in China. In: Proceedings of the Pacific Asia Conference on Information Systems, Tokyo (2002)

Discourse Particles in Human-Human and Human-Computer Interaction – Analysis and Evaluation

Ingo Siegert[1(✉)], Julia Krüger[2], Matthias Haase[2], Alicia Flores Lotz[1], Stephan Günther[3], Jörg Frommer[2], Dietmar Rösner[3,4], and Andreas Wendemuth[1,4]

[1] Institute of Information and Communication Engineering, Otto von Guericke University, 39016 Magdeburg, Germany
Ingo.siegert@ovgu.de

[2] Department of Psychosomatic Medicine and Psychotherapy, Otto von Guericke University, 39016 Magdeburg, Germany

[3] Institute of Knowledge and Language Engineering, Otto von Guericke University, 39016 Magdeburg, Germany

[4] Center for Behavioral Brain Sciences, Otto von Guericke University, 39016 Magdeburg, Germany

Abstract. Discourse particles are verifiably used in both human-human interaction (HHI) and human-computer interaction (HCI). In both types of interaction form-function-relations could be confirmed. Also correlations with specific subject characteristics, personality traits and the use of these particles could be uncovered. But these investigations are performed on separated datasets containing either HHI or HCI. Moreover, the subjects analyzed in both interaction types are not the same and thus, direct connections could not be made.

In our contribution, we report about analyses of discourse particles in both HHI and HCI with the same subjects. This enables us to draw conclusions of the communication partner's influence in relation to subject characteristics and personality traits. This will prospectively help to better understand the use of discourse particles. By using this knowledge, future technical systems can react to known subjects more individually.

Keywords: Human-human interaction · Human-computer interaction · Discourse particles · Personality · Subject characteristics

1 Introduction

In speech based HHI semantic and prosodic cues effectively communicate certain dialog functions such as attention, understanding or other attitudinal reactions of a speaker [1]. Furthermore, it is assumed that these short feedback signals are uttered in situations of a higher cognitive load [4] where a more articulated answer cannot be given. Among these cues the discourse particles (DPs), as

M. Kurosu (Ed.): HCI 2016, Part I, LNCS 9731, pp. 105–117, 2016.
DOI: 10.1007/978-3-319-39510-4_11

"hm", "uh", and "uhm"[1], recently gained increased attention [2,12] also in HCI [25]. We distinguish two types of DPs: "hms" are used to provide the listener's feedback and "uh" as well as "uhm" are mostly used as filled pauses. Thus, we will shortly denote "hm" as feedback (signal) and "uhm" as well as "uh as fillers. In HHI the interaction partner is able to understand the DPs and is using them himself whereas in HCI the technical system as dialog partner is mostly neither able to understand these cues nor using them. Positive exceptions are presented for instance in [28]. But, DPs are verifiably used in both HHI and HCI [22,27] and specific form-function-relations could be confirmed [15,17]. Also influences of specific subject characteristics and certain personality traits on the use of prosodic cues, such as DPs, were uncovered [9,24].

Enabling technical Systems to understand and use these particles will help to detect crucial points within the interaction. A previous study we rely on, analyzed three different interactions [6]. The considered corpora comprise HHI, indirect HHI, where the subject knew that a wizard simulated the system, and HCI, but with different subjects. A functional analysis shows that even if DPs are used in structurally similar contexts as in HHI they do not always serve the same purposes. For instance, feedback signals are often not directed to the hearer and therefore are unlikely to display perception and understanding [6]. The authors of [7] concluded that the use of partner-oriented signals (e.g. feedback signals) decreases while the number of signals indicating a talk-organizing, task-oriented, or expressive function (e.g. fillers) increased.

For this paper, we were in the advantageous situation to perform our investigations on a dataset providing both types of interaction, HHI and HCI. Thus, we could investigate which similarities in the use of DPs can be observed between these two different types of interaction. Furthermore, different styles of dialogs are present in HCI. As we also have additional knowledge about the subject's age, biological gender, and personality traits, we incorporated this information as additional factors. In this paper, the focus is on identifying similarities and influencing factors on the use of DPs in HHI and HCI.

The remainder of the paper is structured as follows, Sect. 2 shortly describes the methods utilized in the present investigation. Then, Sect. 3 describes the utilized dataset providing HHI as well as HCI. Section 4 presents and discusses the results of our investigation on the DPs use in HHI and HCI. Finally, Sect. 5 concludes the paper and provides an outlook for further research directions.

2 Methods

As DPs are verbalized, we took into account the number of uttered tokens of the subjects. These tokens are words and vocalizations. This measure is denoted as the number of verbalized tokens (#Token). It varies from subject to subject and influences the DPs's use. Therefore, we used the normalized DPs frequency

[1] As the investigations are performed on a German corpus, we decided to rely on a perceptional translation: "ähm" is translated as "uhm" and "äh" as "uh" to be consistent with German sounds.

(||DP||). The subject's number of uttered DPs is divided by the subject's total number of uttered tokens during the (considered part of the) HCI and HHI interaction multiplied by 100:

$$\|\mathrm{DP}\| = \frac{\#\mathrm{DPs}}{\#\mathrm{Token}} \cdot 100 \tag{1}$$

Afterwards, we averaged over all considered subjects and calculated mean and standard deviation. To analyze the impact of the different factors — user characteristics as sociobiographic variables and personality traits, or communication partner — we used a median split to gain two groups of subjects. Afterwards, we used a non-parametric version of the ANOVA, the Mann-Whitney U-test [16].

3 Dataset

For our study we utilize the LAST MINUTE Corpus (LMC) [20]. It contains 130 high-quality multi-modal recordings of German speaking subjects during Wizard of Oz (WOZ) experiments. This part is referred as HCI-part. It is already the object of examination regarding affective state recognition [8,26] and linguistic turns [21]. Furthermore, 73 of these subjects underwent a semi-structured interview, which followed the HCI-part experiment. This part is referred as HHI-part.

The corpus was recorded with several opposing speaker groups, young (y) vs. elderly (e) speakers and male (m) vs. female (f) speakers. The younreg group was represented by subjects being 18 to 28 years old. The elder group consists of subjects being older than 60 years. The combination of both age and gender led to four sub-groups: (ym, em, yw, and ew). Additionally, several questionnaires had to be answered by the subjects after participating in experiment, regarding personality traits (NEO-FFI [5], IIP [10]) and further psychological user characteristics including technical affinity (TA-EG [3]), attributional style (ASF-E [18]) and stress coping behavior (SVF [11]).

3.1 LMC's HCI-parts – Personalization and Problem Solving

The setup of the HCI part revolves around an imaginary journey to the unknown place Waiuku. With the help of an adaptable technical system, the subjects have to prepare the journey, by packing the suitcase, and select clothing and other equipment by using voice commands. Each experiment takes about 30 min. All experiments are transcribed according to the GAT-2 minimal standard [23], enabling the automatic extraction of speaker utterances. For a subset of 90 subjects all DPs are annotated. Furthermore, each HCI-part is distinguished into two modules, with two different dialog styles [19].

The **personalization module**, being the first part of the experiment, has the purpose of making the subject familiar with the system and ensuring a more natural behavior. In this module the subject is asked a set of questions focused on personal details and on recent events which made him happy or angry.

During the **problem solving module** the subject is expected to pack the suitcase from several depicted categories, for instance "Tops"or" Jackets & Coats". The dialog follows a specific structure of specific subject-action and system-confirmation dialogs. This conversation is task focused. This part of the experiment has a much more command-like regularized dialog style.

3.2 LMC's HHI-part – the Interview

After the WOz experiment, nearly half of the subjects took part in a semi-structured interview. Therein, they were asked to described their individual experience of the experimental interaction and the simulated system [13,14]. The interview focused in particular on the subjects' emotions occurring during the interaction, the subjects'subjective ascriptions to the system and the subjects' overall evaluation of the system.

The interview questions were formulated in a way that the subjects were enabled to speak freely, in order to get narrations, which allow examining individual subject's experiences using methods from qualitative social research. Hence, the subjects' part of speech exceeded that of the interviewer. In order to ensure a naturalistic, comfortable, open and friendly dialog atmosphere, the interviewer gave feedback in terms of nodding and DPs, as well as further queries throughout the whole interview (no strict feedback policy). To extract all DPs in the interviews, a manual transcription and annotation has been performed. As this is quite time-consuming not all interviews were translated completely and thus not all interviews could be used further. For a subset of 64 subjects the interviews are transcribed and all DPs are transcribed.

3.3 Utilized Subset

A subset of 44 subjects, having transcribed interviews, transcribed experiment recordings and DPs-annotations for both interactions, were used for this study. This subset of LMC has a total duration of approx. 30 hours of HCI data and approx. 35 hours of interview data. The age and biological gender distribution is nearly balanced, see Table 1.

Table 1. Distribution of speaker groups in the utilized subset of the LMC.

	Male (m)	Female (f)	Total
Young (y)	11	9	20
Elderly (e)	11	13	24
Total	22	22	44

4 Results

At first, we analyzed the different use of DPs in HHI and HCI. Afterwards, we tried to explain these differences by examining different influencing factors.

4.1 Similarities Between HHI and HCI in the Use of DPs

To analyze differences between HHI and HCI the frequency of DPs-occurrence is of major interest. This aspect is depicted in Fig. 1. As noticeable differences in the various speaker groups were observable, the normalized DPs frequency (cf. Eq. 1) is depicted for all groups of speakers.

The interviewer's mean DPs frequency is 0.088, with a standard deviation of 0.043. This is much higher than the observed subjects' DPs frequency and can be explained with the fact that the interviewer's aim is to keep the subject talking and show interest and understanding in order to achieve a comfortable, open communication atmosphere. Thus, mostly short feedbacks, as DPs, were used.

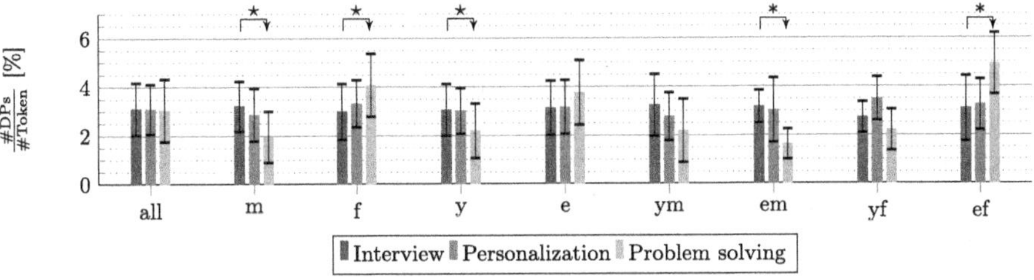

Fig. 1. Mean and standard deviation for the DPs regarding different speaker groups for the HHI and both HCI parts. The stars denote the significance level: * ($p < 0.05$), ⋆ denotes close proximity to significance level.

Regarding Fig. 1, it can be seen that a differentiation into speaker groups has to be used for HCI data, because the specific speaker group differences can be averaged out. Within each speaker group, the DPs frequency of the interview is quite similar to the personalization module. Although male subjects have a slightly higher DPs frequency within the interviews and female subjects' DPs frequency is slightly higher within the personalization module, none of these differences are significant. But in comparison with the problem solving there are remarkable differences. Male and younreg subjects used more DPs during the interview and the personalization, while female and elderly speakers used more DPs within the problem solving. For male, female and young subjects the difference between interview and problem solving module is close to significance (p < 0.07). Significant differences (p < 0.05) between interview and problem solving can be observed for elderly male subjects and elderly female subjects.

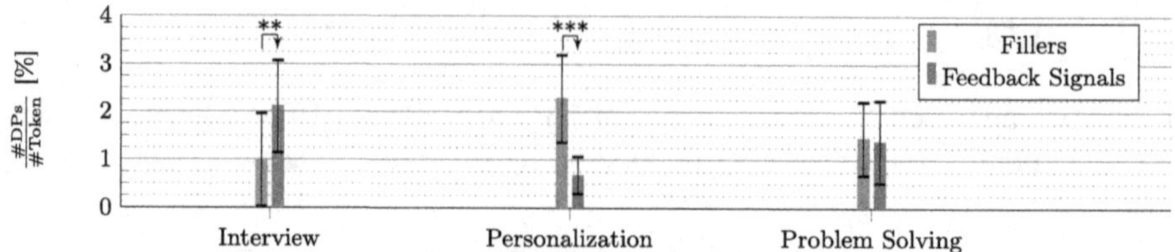

Fig. 2. Mean and standard deviation of fillers and feedback signals for the HHI part and both HCI parts. The stars denote the significance level: ** ($p < 0.005$) and *** ($p < 0.001$).

Further significant differences are prevented by the high standard deviation of our samples.

Besides the average DPs frequency, also the ratio between fillers and feedback signals is of interest, as this analysis reveals further information on the behavior of the subjects in interactions with and without a human conversation partner. In Fig. 2 it can be observed that in the personalization module the use of the fillers is significantly outstanding (p < 0.001) against the use of feedback signals. In problem solving the use of feedback signals and fillers is nearly similar. Analyzing the HHI part, we observed a very different use of DPs. Nearly twice of all DPs occurrences are feedback signals, which is highly significant (p < 0.005).

The frequent use of feedback signals in the interviews is expectable, as feedback signals are used to minimally communicate certain speaker and dialog states and the existing interviewer is able to understand them. The lower use of feedback signals in the personalization module, although of similar dialog style as the interview, indicates an influence of the absent human conversation partner. But the higher use of feedback signals within the problem solving module in comparison to the personalization module indicates that the use of feedback signals is also dependent from additional factors, as for instance in this case a challenging dialog (cf. Sect. 4.3). The distribution of the different DPs-types on the speaker groups is relatively balanced in the interview as well as in the two HCI-modules personalization and problem solving. Thus, group-specific ratios of feedback signals and fillers are not depicted.

4.2 Investigating Different Influencing Factors

As it can be seen in Fig. 1, the standard deviation for all speaker groups is quite high. Thus, additional factors seem to influence the use of the DPs. We investigated the subjects' individual attitude in using DPs and his/her psychological user characteristics.

Influence of the Subjects' Individual Dialog Attitude. To analyze the individual dialog attitude, we distinguished two groups, low scorers and high scorers. Both groups are obtained by a median split regarding the normalized

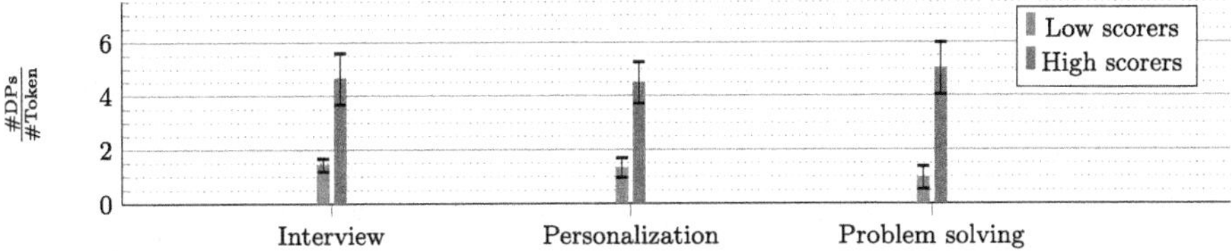

Fig. 3. Mean and standard deviation of low and high scorers for the HHI part and both HCI parts.

DPs occurrences on the particular parts. Low scorers have an individual normalized DPs frequency below the median and high scorers have an individual normalized DPs frequency at or above the median. For all interaction styles (interview, personalization, problem solving), the number of subjects are nearly balanced.

The mean and standard deviation for all groups regarding personalization and problem solving module as well as the HHI part are depicted in Fig. 3. As the distribution of low and high scorers for the different speaker groups according to age and gender is equal in the interview as well as in the two HCI-modules, they are not depicted. The correspondence of subjects along the low and high scorers between the personalization and the problem solving module is 79.55 % and between both HCI modules and the interview the correspondence is 80.65 %. The difference of the DPs use between low and high scorers quite huge. This substantiates the grouping in low and high scorers, as these groups produce verifiably different normalized DPs distributions The subjects' individual dialog attitude remains the same for all interaction styles. High scorers have very similar DPs frequencies. Low scorers are using fewer DPs during problem solving than in the interview and personalization. But this is not significant.

Influence of Personality Traits. To investigate the influence of different personality traits, we differentiated between subjects with traits below the median (low trait) and those at or above the median (high trait). We selected certain personality traits, where in previous studies a relationship with the use of DPs could be verified [24]:

- SVF positive strategies (`SVF pos`)
- SVF negative strategies (`SVF neg`)
- IIP vindictive competing (`IIP vin`)
- NEO-FFI Agreeableness (`NEO agr`)

The results are depicted in Fig. 4. Again, distinguishing according to age and gender of the subjects does not show significant differences and thus the results are not depicted. Analyzing the influence of personality traits for the use of DPs in the interview data, only subjects having a `SVF pos` trait below the median are using significantly more DPs than subjects above the median ($p < 0.05$). This observation shows that, subjects having lower skills in stress management with

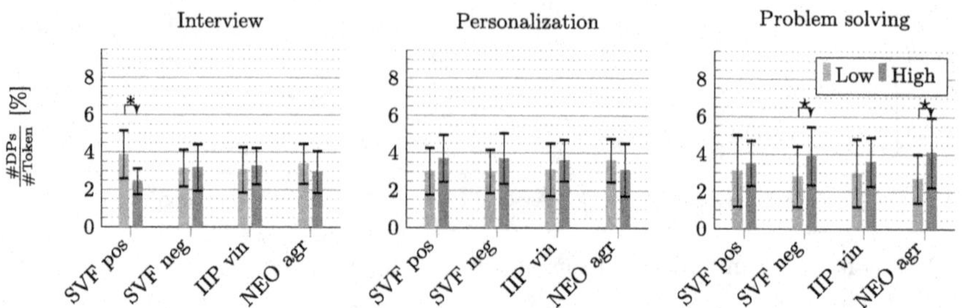

Fig. 4. Mean and standard deviation for the DPs divided into the two dialog styles regarding different groups of personality traits. The stars denote the significance level: * ($p < 0.05$), ⋆ denotes close proximity to significance level.

regard to positive distraction use substantially more DPs. For all other traits, no significant difference and thus no influence is detectable. The normalized DPs frequency is nearly equal for `SVF neg`, `IIP vin` and `Neo age`.

Considering the two HCI parts, no significant differences are noticeable for personalization. For the problem solving module, the differences for `SVF neg` and `NEO agr` have just close proximity to significance level ($p < 0.07$). This is due to the fact, that on the one hand we compare very few users within a very heterogeneous sample. On the other hand, the influence of psychological characteristics heavily depend on the situation in which the subject is located. The distinction between a open dialog and command-like dialog may not be sufficient to describe the situation. Especially in the command-like problem solving module very different situations are induced by the experimental design, which also produce partly contradictory user reactions. This will be analyzed in the next section.

4.3 Subject Behavior After Dialog Barriers

As discussed in Sect. 4.1, the distinction between a open dialog (personalization) and command-like dialog (problem solving) may not be sufficient to describe the subject's situation. Thus, we investigated the problem solving module in detail. Within this module pre-defined barriers occur for all users at specific time points [8]. These barriers are intended to interrupt the dialog-flow of the interaction and provoke significant dialog events: Although **Baseline (BSL)** does not represent a barrier, it serves as an "interaction baseline" from which the other barriers are distinguished. At the **Weight Limit Barrier (WLB)** the system refuses to pack further items, since the airline's weight limit of the suitcase is reached. Thus, the subject has to unpack things.

First, we investigated the ratio between fillers and feedback signals. As it is shown in Fig. 2, subjects use feedback signals and fillers nearly equally in the problem solving module. The same behavior can be seen in Fig. 5. The only difference is that the use of fillers and feedback signals is remarkably lower during BSL than after the WLB (Fig. 6).

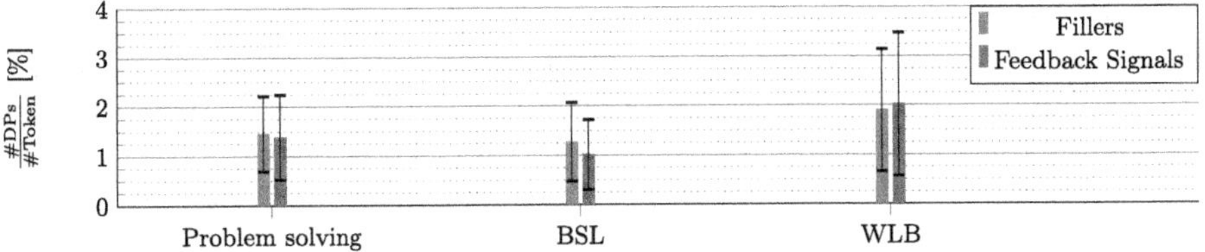

Fig. 5. Mean and standard deviation of fillers and feedback signals for the BSL and WLB dialog parts.

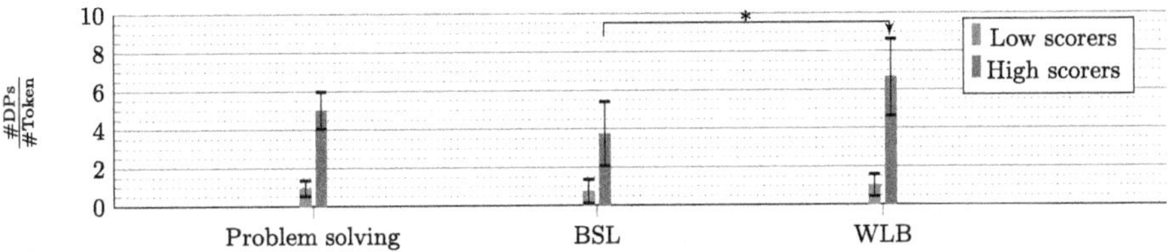

Fig. 6. Mean and standard deviation of low and high scorers for the HHI part and both HCI parts. The stars denote the significance level: * ($p < 0.05$).

Afterwards, we analyzed which influence the dialog situation has on the individual dialog attitude. Again, we distinguished two groups, low scorers and high scorers. Both groups are obtained by a median split regarding the normalized DPs occurrences on both dialog parts. The correspondence of subjects along the low and high scorers for BSL and WLB is 85.31 % and 81.34 % against the two HCI modules. Verifiably different normalized DPs distributions are produced by low and high scorers. It can be seen that low scorers do not differ much between the BSL and WLB dialog parts. But high scorers use significantly more DPs during the WLB dialog part than within the BSL part ($p < 0.05$).

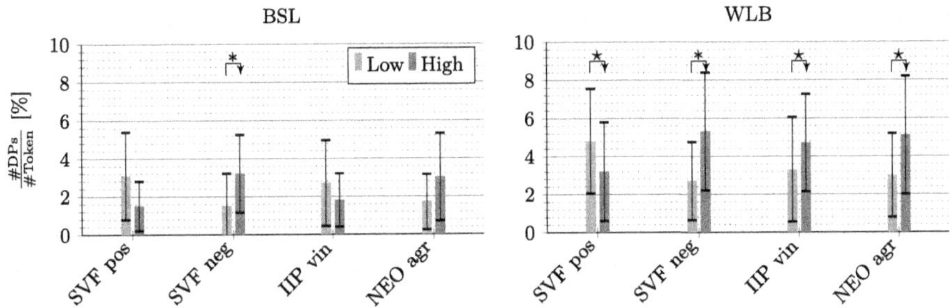

Fig. 7. Mean and standard deviation for the DPs of the two barriers regarding different groups of user characteristics. The stars denote the significance level: * ($p < 0.05$), ⋆ denotes close proximity to significance level.

Finally, we analyzed the influence of personality traits on the use of DPs after the BSL and WLB events. From Fig. 7, the following conclusions can be drawn. Subjects having better skills in stress management with regard to positive distraction use substantially less DPs. The finding on SVF negative strategies (`SVF neg`) confirms this statement. Subjects not having a good stress management or even having negative stress management mechanisms use more DPs. Subjects who use DPs more frequently are also more likely to have problems in trusting others or are suspicious and rather quarrelsome against others (`IP vin`). The interpretation of the NEO-FFI traits also confirms the IIP-findings. Subjects using fewer DPs show less confidence in dealing with other people which is determined by the factor agreeableness (`NEO Agree`).

5 Outlook

Within this paper, we could show similarities and differences in the use of certain DPs within HHI and HCI by analyzing the same group of subjects. Therefore, we used the LMC containing both types of interactions. Furthermore, we distinguished two types of interaction within HCI (personalization and problem solving) and considered interrupted dialog flows after pre-defined barriers.

First of all, we observed similarities in the occurrence of DPs in the case similar dialog styles were used, but the type of DPs varied. In general, the number of DPs between the interview (HHI) and the personalization module (HCI), two similar dialog styles, is roughly equal. But the ratio of the two types, fillers and feedback signals, is significantly different. This could be traced back to the absence of a proper conversation partner within the HCI. This result is in line with the findings of [7], that talk-organizing DPs are increasing in HCI in comparison to HHI.

Another similarity is the constant influence of low and high scorers. Subjects using only few DPs within HHI are also using few DPs during the HCI, with a similar frequency. Thus, the absence of a conversation partner does not lead per se to an increase or decrease of DPs.

Afterwards, we analyzed to what extent personality traits influence the use of DPs. In the interview only an influence of SVF positive strategies was shown. To analyze the influence of personality traits in HCI, we had to take into account the dialog barriers. In this case, a significant difference in the use of DPs for SVF positive strategies, SVF negative strategies, IIP vindictive competing, and NEO-FFI Agreeableness was shown. The use of DPs is mainly stimulated by "negative" psychological characteristics. Bad stress regulation capabilities will cause the use of DPs in situations of higher cognitive load. This supports the assumption that DPs are an important pattern to detect situations of higher cognitive load [4].

By analyzing the subjects' use of DPs after the dialog barriers, we showed that both fillers and feedback signals are used more often in situations of higher cognitive load, although the conversation partner is not able to understand these cues. One possible explanation is that the subjects ascribe this ability to the system because they unconsciously assume humanlike characteristics and mental states to the system [13]. Another insight could be drawn from the comparison of the behavior of low and high scorers after the investigated barriers. High scorers used significantly more DPs during the distorted dialog than during a non-distorted dialog. This again shows the influence of the personality traits, as the frequent use of DPs is an indicator for bad stress regulation capabilities which will lead to an increased use of DPs within the distorted dialog.

Our results are in line with the findings of [7] showing that the use of feedback signals and fillers is different between HHI and HCI. But we could also show that certain dialog situations influence the use of DPs. In future, a deeper analysis of the functional meaning of the uttered DPs, although not directed to the artificial conversation partner, will be performed. Together with the knowledge that subjects in situations of higher cognitive load tend to use more DPs, this enables future technical systems to examine lonreg-lasting natural interactions and dialogs and to identify critical situations.

Acknowledgments. The work presented was done within the Transregional Collaborative Research Centre SFB/TRR 62 "Companion-Technology for Cognitive Technical Systems" (www.sfb-trr-62.de) funded by the German Research Foundation (DFG).

References

1. Allwood, J., Nivre, J., Ahlsén, E.: On the semantics and pragmatics of linguistic feedback. J. Semant. **9**, 1–26 (1992)
2. Benus, S., Gravana, A., Hirschberg, J.: The prosody of backchannels in American English. In: Proceedings of the 16th ICPhS, pp. 1065–1068. Saarbrücken (2007)
3. Bruder, C., Clemens, C., Glaser, C., Karrer-Gauß, K.: TA-EG - Fragebogen zur Erfassung von Technikaffinität. Technical report, TU Berlin (2009)
4. Corley, M., Stewart, O.W.: Hesitation disfluencies in spontaneous speech: the meaning of um. Lang. Linguist. Compass **2**, 589–602 (2008)
5. Costa, P.T., McCrae, R.R.: Domains and facets: hierarchical personality assessment using the revised NEO personality inventory. J. Pers. Assess. **64**, 21–50 (1995)
6. Fischer, K.: From Cognitive Semantics to Lexical Pragmatics. Mouton & Co, Berlin (2000)
7. Fischer, K., Wrede, B., Brindöpke, C., Johanntokrax, M.: Quantitative und funktionale Analysen von Diskurspartikeln im Computer Talk. Int. J. Lang. Data Process. **20**, 85–100 (1996)
8. Frommer, J., Michaelis, B., Rösner, D., Wendemuth, A., Friesen, R., Haase, M., Kunze, M., Andrich, R., Lange, J., Panning, A., Siegert, I.: Towards emotion and affect detection in the multimodal last minute corpus. In: Proceedings of the 8th LREC, pp. 3064–3069. Istanbul (2012)
9. Giles, H., Coupland, N.: Language: Contexts and Consequences. Cengage Learning, Boston (1991)
10. Horowitz, L.M., Strauß, B., Kordy, H.: Inventar zur Erfassung interpersonaler Probleme (IIPD), 2nd edn. Beltz, Weinheim (2000)
11. Jahnke, W., Erdmann, G., Kallus, K.: Stressverarbeitungsfragebogen mit SVF 120 und SVF 78, 3rd edn. Hogrefe, Göttingen (2002)

12. Kehrein, R., Rabanus, S.: Ein Modell zur funktionalen Beschreibungvon Diskurspartike. ln: Neue Wege der Intonationsforschung,Germanistische Linguistik, vol. 157–158, pp. 33–50. Georg OlmsVerlag, Hildesheim (2001)
13. Krüger, J., Wahl, M., Frommer, J.: Making the system a relational partner: users' ascriptions in individualization-focused interactions with companion-systems. In: Proceedings of the 8th CENTRIC 2015, pp. 48–54. Barcelona (2015)
14. Lange, J., Frommer, J.: Subjektives Erleben und intentionale Einstellung in Interviews zur Nutzer-Companion-Interaktion. In: Proceedings der 41.GI-Jahrestagung. Lecture Notes in Computer Science, vol. 192, pp. 240–254. Bonner Köllen Verlag, Berlin (2011)
15. Lotz, A.F., Siegert, I., Wendemuth, A.: Automatic differentiation of form-function-relations of the discourse particle "HM" in a naturalistic human-computer interaction. In: Proceedings of the 26th ESSV, pp. 172–179. Eichstätt, Germany (2015)
16. NIST, SEMATECH: e-handbook of statistical methods (2014). http://www.itl.nist.gov/div898/handbook/
17. Paschen, H.: Die Funktion der Diskurspartikel HM. Master's thesis, University Mainz (1995)
18. Poppe, P., Stiensmeier-Pelster, J., Pelster, A.: Attributionsstilfragebogen für Erwachsene (ASF-E). Hogrefe, Göttingen (2005)
19. Rösner, D., Haase, M., Bauer, T., Günther, S., Krüger, J., Frommer, J.: Desiderata for the design of companion systems - insights from a large scale wizard of Oz experiment. Künstliche Intelligenz **30**(1), 53–61 (2016)
20. Rösner, D., Frommer, J., Friesen, R., Haase, M., Lange, J., Otto, M.: LAST MINUTE: a multimodal corpus of speech-based user-companion interactions. In: Proceedings of the 8th LREC, pp. 96–103. Istanbul (2012)
21. Rösner, D., Kunze, M., Otto, M., Frommer, J.: Linguistic analyses of the LAST MINUTE corpus. In: Jancsary, J. (ed.) Proceedings of KONVENS 2012, pp. 145–154. ÖGAI , Main track: oral presentations, September 2012
22. Schmidt, J.E.: Bausteine der Intonation. In: Neue Wege der Intonationsforschung, Germanistische Linguistik, vol. 157–158, pp. 9–32. Georg Olms Verlag, Hildesheim (2001)
23. Selting, M., Auer, P., Barth-Weingarten, D., Bergmann, J.R., Bergmann, P., Birkner, K., Couper-Kuhlen, E., Deppermann, A., Gilles, P., Günthner, S., Hartung, M., Kern, F., Mertzlufft, C., Meyer, C., Morek, M., Oberzaucher, F., Peters, J., Quasthoff, U., Schütte, W., Stukenbrock, A., Uhmann, S.: Gesprächsanalytisches Transkriptionssystem 2 (GAT 2). Gesprächsforschung **10**, 353–402 (2009)
24. Siegert, I., Haase, M., Prylipko, D., Wendemuth, A.: Discourse particles and user characteristics in naturalistic human-computer interaction. In: Kurosu, M. (ed.) HCI 2014, Part II. LNCS, vol. 8511, pp. 492–501. Springer, Heidelberg (2014)
25. Siegert, I., Hartmann, K., Philippou-Hübner, D., Wendemuth, A.: Human behaviour in HCI: complex emotion detection through sparse speech features. In: Salah, A.A., Hung, H., Aran, O., Gunes, H. (eds.) HBU 2013. LNCS, vol. 8212, pp. 246–257. Springer, Heidelberg (2013)
26. Siegert, I., Philippou-Hübner, D., Hartmann, K., Böck, R., Wendemuth, A.: Investigation of speaker group-dependent modelling for recognition of affective states from speech. Cogn. Comput. **6**(4), 892–913 (2014)

27. Siegert, I., Prylipko, D., Hartmann, K., Bück, R., Wendemuth, A.: Investigating the form-function-relation of the discourse particle "HM" in a naturalistic human-computer interaction. In: Bassis, S., Esposito, A., Morabito, F.C. (eds.) Recent Advances of Neural Networks Models and Applications. SIST, vol. 26, pp. 387–394. Springer, Heidelberg (2014)
28. Skantze, G., Johansson, M., Beskow, J.: Exploring turn-taking cues in multi-party human-robot discussions about objects. In: Proceedings of the 2015 ACM International Conference on Multimodal Interaction, pp. 67–74 (2015)

Green IS in Education Industry: A Case Study

Fan Zhao, Samuel Farmer(✉), Jodi Alejandro, and Adrian Perez-Estrada

College of Business, Florida Gulf Coast University, Fort Myers, USA
smfarmer6243@eagle.fgcu.edu

Abstract. Green IS relates to environmentally sustainable Information Technology practices in order to reduce business cost and lower environmental impact. Currently, much of the discussion of Green IS is focused on businesses, but the same practices can be applied to education or to anywhere IT or IS related. It is viewed as needed in both business and education because it considers the long term impacts of technology. This study conducts several interviews with employees work in an American university to explore motivations behind Green IS adoption. The results are in line with work of Jenkin et al. (2011a, b) showing that Organizations are still in the infancy stage of awareness and Green IS adoption. In addition, we found Green IS education is one critical factor current universities need to focus on in their process of Green IS adoption. We also suggest that standardization and a rating system of Green IS are necessary to encourage universities in adopting Green IS.

Keywords: Green IS · ERP · Education · Adoption

1 Introduction

Technology and information systems specifically, were not known to be environmentally friendly. In recent years, that has changed and information systems that is environmentally conscious is known as 'Green Information System' (Green IS). Due to the concerns of global warming, most of society and many businesses are becoming eco-friendlier and adopting sustainable products and solutions. Technology is constantly evolving and due to our consumeristic society, the impulse of buying the latest gadget to replace two-year-old electronic devices, has had a huge negative impact on the environment (Jenkin et al. 2010). More electronic devices are consuming electricity, companies and even universities need more and more hardware devices and software to store huge amounts of data, analyze, and summarize the data to improve business processes, thereby increasing the need for more data centers and both IT and IS.

Green Information System or Green IS is the effort of reducing the first hand environmental impacts of Information Technology (IT) by making computing more energy efficient. According to Murugsan (2008), Green IS is defined as "the study and practice of designing, manufacturing, using and disposing of computer, servers and associated subsystems … efficiently and effectively with minimal or no impact on the environment" This can be applied to any level or scale and therefore, is applicable to anything from smartphones to large data centers (Fig. 1).

M. Kurosu (Ed.): HCI 2016, Part I, LNCS 9731, pp. 118–127, 2016.
DOI: 10.1007/978-3-319-39510-4_12

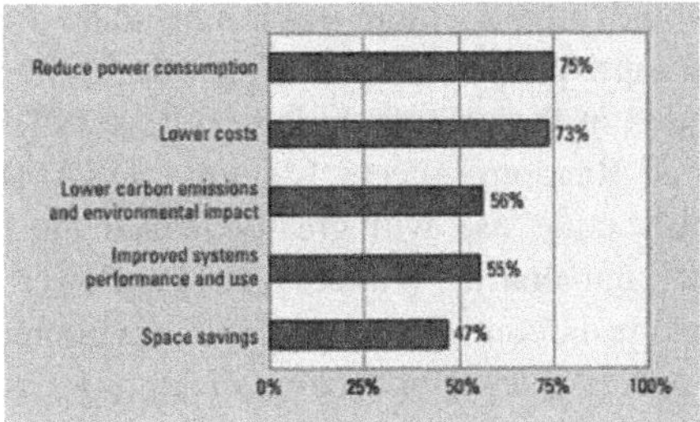

Fig. 1. Green IS by Murugesan (2008)

Green IS is able to reduce IT costs in the long run, which makes it a stronger incentive for its adoption according to a survey conducted by Dedrick (2010) (Communications of the Association for Information Systems). The author points out, however, that businesses are more apt to adopt Green IS if it makes financial sense. He also states that IS managers are beginning to become more interested in the positive impacts of Green IS practices due to the many positive benefits that can be gained from its adoption.

Green IS has many parts such as virtualization of servers and storage, storage consolidation and environmentally friendly IT actions (ex. double-sided printing). Electronic waste management, also known as e-waste management is also necessary in order lower the environmental impact of Information Technology and Information Systems (Jenkin et al. 2011a, b). There has been an increase in remote group collaboration such as teleconferencing and using software such as SharePoint and Office 365.

Prior to the increase of green sustainability among businesses, the design of its information systems and company culture were not environmentally friendly. Inefficient components of their information systems contributed to high electricity costs (especially in data centers), single-side printing resulting in paper waste, not recycling ink toners, and not recycling old electronics (computers, printers, etc.). Data centers, especially, used excessive energy to cool the servers. Instead of businesses having their own data centers, they could switch over to virtual servers, thereby reducing energy costs and decreasing their carbon footprint. One of the main reasons for companies to adopt Green IS practices was to reduce costs (Molla et al. 2009). Adopting Green IS is not just limited to businesses, but to universities as well. Universities such as Florida Gulf Coast University, have implemented environmental sustainability practices on campus.

One example of poor IS design that could be improved with Green IS practices is the traditional data center cooling approach. The traditional approach includes air cooled computer rooms; this has many problems such as wasted energy due to the way that air convection works. There is wasted electricity from constantly running fans, and there is still heat created that dissipates but is not being used in any way (Li and Kandlikar 2015).

Yet another reason for the necessity of Green IS is to respond to pollution caused by population growth. Due to the use of fossil fuels and of fossil fuels being unsustainable (Santoyo-Castelazo and Azapagic 2014), renewable power alternatives such as solar or wind power would provide more environmentally friendly IS. Fossil fuel resources are limited and cause pollution which affects the entire planet. The amount of fossil fuel resources needed in the manufacturing processes of IT infrastructure components such as Dynamic Random Access Memory (DRAM) are so high that IS practices with less infrastructure use will greatly reduce the overall environmental impact of a company or university (Williams 2011). Power consumption from a university's IT infrastructure is contributing to these environmental problems. Thus, changing the source of power is a major factor in adopting Green IS (Blaabjerg and Ionel 2015).

As The Climate Group (2008) announced that Green IS/IT could potentially reduce global emissions by 15 %. In most of the previous studies, Green IS/IT are always mentioned together. However, they are different. Green IT addresses the direct impact from technology perspectives, such as energy consumption and waste associated with the applications of hardware and software, toward upon the environment. Green IS focuses on how to adopt a Green system to support other business initiatives to reduce the negative environmental impacts, therefore it has more indirect impact on the environment. Most organizations are willing to change part of their IT and turn it to Green (Jenin et al. 2011), but update IS to green is more difficult and complicated. In this paper, we focus the study on Green IS.

According to Brooks et al. (2010), there were several stages organizations completed in the past toward Green IS, from recognizing the Green IS, to realizing the importance of Green IS, and eventually willing to accept and adopt Green IS. However, even organizations realize the importance of Green IS and are ready for the Green IS, many of the organizations do not necessarily begin Green IS adoption. Even though studies to date explores some issue of Green IS adoptions, such as using TAM to study the intention of Green IS adoption, few study looks at the motivations in pushing organizations to eventually adopt Green IS. Moreover, we find no study focuses on the Green IS adoption in educational industry. Therefore, we decided to study the motivational drivers of adopting Green IS in universities.

2 Literature Reviews

Green IS adopts Information Systems as one solution to environmental issues and problems (Dedrick 2010). Ryoo and Koo (2013) propose a Green IS framework to reveal the current concerns of environmental sustainability (ES). There are five stages in the model: there should be some ES motivating forces first, such as new laws, or social norms to push the concerns to the organizations; then, environmental strategies and technologies start to initiate the ES projects; organizational internal factors, such as attitudes or intentions from different level of management or groups in the organization, should also be considered after the ES initiation; ES alignment emphasizes the coordination between Green IS and other systems in the organization; the last stage evaluate the impact on environment.

To be more empirical, Grauler et al. (2013) develop a belief-action-outcome research model to demonstrate consumers' attitude and actions toward Green IS adoption. The results indicate that a sophisticated sustainability report that satisfies

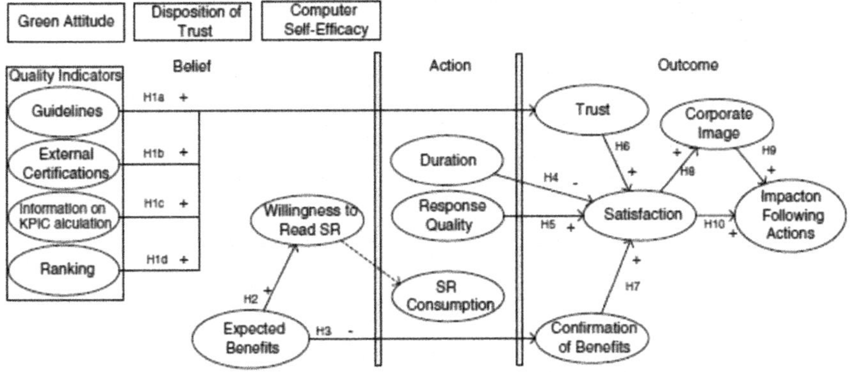

Fig. 2. Research model from Grauler et al. (2013)

consumers' Green expectations could significantly impact/change the organization's reputation and consumers' purchase actions (Fig. 2).

Jenkin et al. (2010) provides exemplary evidence for Green IS/IT. The authors state one of the issues of adopting green information systems and technology, are that most businesses do not put sustainability as a priority. It only becomes a priority if there it is financially driven, meaning if the business will end up saving more money in the long run by adopting sustainability practices. Electronic devices used in organizations such as laptops, desktop computers, printers, and cellphones (company issued) have short lifespans. When businesses replace legacy systems and hardware, it also contributes negatively to the environment. The electronic waste or e-waste is not biodegradable and over time when the metals deteriorate, it may seep into the ground. The authors also point out that IS and IT can also be used to alleviate the negative impacts on the environment and electronic/IT companies such as Apple and IBM, are addressing the issue. IBM's consulting division, Green Sigma, was created to provide green sustainability consulting services to companies (Jenkins et al. 2010).

Even some organizations adopted green IS, their performances may vary. Molla (2013) develops a conceptual framework to identify the sustainability performance indicators of Green IS. He proposed four dements in the framework: Eco-Value governance with measurability of both tangible and intangible Green IS benefits, Eco-Process with embedded environmental criteria design in IS products and services, Eco-Brand with customers' perspectives of the balanced scorecard, and Eco-Learning with ability to educate employees' sustainability behaviors (Fig. 3).

To further study the Green IS and get a full picture of the sustainability performance, researchers have different focus groups from different angle to explain organizational intentions toward Green IS adoptions. Gholami et al. (2013) propose a Green IS adoption model based on belief-action-outcome framework. Through a survey of 405 organizations, the findings indicate that two macro factors in their model shows different results. Coercive pressure is supported to positively relate to attitude whereas mimetic pressure does not (Fig. 4).

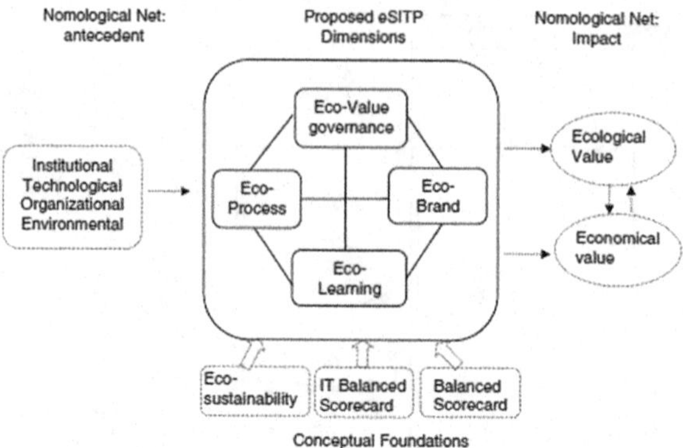

Fig. 3. Sustainability performance framework by Molla (2013)

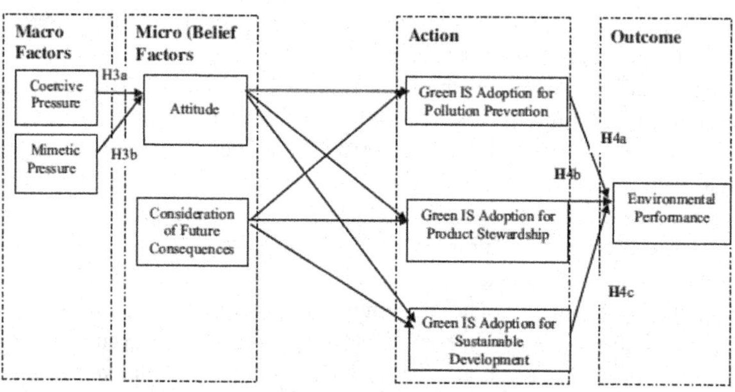

Fig. 4. Green IS adoption model by Gholami et al. (2013)

From employees' perspectives, Jenkin et al. (2011a, b) identify four types of gaps in Green IS adoption based on their proposed research model and the interview results (See Fig. 5).

1. Knowledge gaps: employees are not award of Green IS adoption in organizations;
2. Practice gaps: organizations doesn't follow their intentions in adopting Green IS;
3. Opportunity gaps: after being award of organizations' environmental issues, employees identify additional areas that organizations could improve;
4. Knowing-doing gaps: even employees recognize an environmental issue and know the benefits of Green IS, they do not change their behaviors toward Green IS.

Jenkin et al. (2011a, b) also emphasize that they believe organizations are still in the infancy stage of awareness and adoption of Green IS. Therefore, our research is trying to understand a little bit more toward the motivations behind the Green IS adoption in education industry.

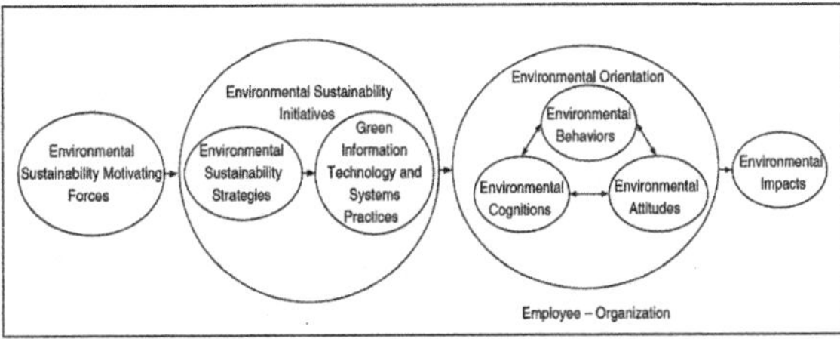

Fig. 5. Green IS research framework from Jenkin et al. (2011a, b)

3 Case Study

This research adopts case study method to study the research question. We conducted several interviews with several IT related employees in one American university. Florida Gulf Coast University's use of Banner by Ellucian, it is hosted at the University of South Florida. The specific name of where it is hosted is the CFRDC or the Central Florida Regional Data Center, which is an entity of its own. CFRDC and USF also currently host this ERP system for a number of other schools in the state of Florida such as University of West Florida, University of North Florida and the State College of Florida. Before implementing Banner, there was a short time the PeopleSoft was used as the university's ERP system. Currently, staff at FGCU in Business Technology Services work very closely with staff at USF in order to report issues with Banner and deploy updates. There are no specialists in Banner at FGCU although there are specialists for Banner, Oracle Database Administrators and IT staff at USF that work directly on Banner, manage updates and troubleshoot problems. The build of all Banner modules at FGCU are based off of a duplicate of the ones in use at USF.

ERP systems for a universities and other higher education institutions are an increasing trend. "Several IS education programs have adopted the hands-on use of ERP systems for instructional purposes with successful results" (Scholtz et al. 2013). This is used for academic purposes compared to business purposes that a traditional organization ERP is used for. Some of the functions that these systems are able to handle include accounting, student class registration, financial aid services, health services and payroll. As with business, there are different sized higher education ERP systems to fit the size of a university.

The primary interview was conducted with the IT director of Applications Group who deal with the use of Banner and other systems in use by FGCU. The second interview was conducted with a Systems Team Specialist at FGCU's Business Technology Services (BTS), he has full access to Banner. The third interview was done with an Analyst and Computer Programmer in the Information Systems part of FGCU's BTS. A fourth interview was conducted with a Banner end user, a Patron Account Manager at the FGCU Library in order to get a different perspective.

4 Discussion and Conclusion

We summarize some of the question answers from our interviews in Table 1. According to the knowledge of Green IS, the interview results show that IT director understands the Green IS best, system specialist are close to the IT director, Business analyst gets less understanding toward Green IS, and Banner end user only knows the term Green IS. Therefore, to show an interesting results, we draw a diagram to compare the knowledge of Green IS Vs. Confidence of Green of current system among the four employees. The graphic (see Fig. 6) shows that the more knowledge of Green IS, the less confidence one employee will have toward current system in the university. This seems to be in line with the work of Jenkin et al. (2011a, b) that current organizations need to educate employees about Green IS. This should be the initial step toward the process of Green IS adoption.

Table 1. Summary of several interview questions and answers

Participant	Do you find Green IS to be important?	Do you think FGCU follows Green IS practices?	Do you think hosting Banner (an ERP system) in a centralized location is a green IS practice?	Additional information
IT Director	Yes	We follow all legally and budget allowed practices	Our current practice is the best we can support	We try our hardest, but there can be budget restraints for getting what could possibly be the best technology
System Specialist	Personally, Yes	We follow all legally and budget allowed practices	There is definitely economics of scale by the way we manage one server compared to multiple servers for running databases	
Business Analyst	Absolutely	Yes, though they could be better if it weren't for legal and budget issues	It's green to have it hosted there	

(*Continued*)

Table 1. *(Continued)*

Participant	Do you find Green IS to be important?	Do you think FGCU follows Green IS practices?	Do you think hosting Banner (an ERP system) in a centralized location is a green IS practice?	Additional information
Banner User	Absolutely	Yes	Yes	I have not given any in depth thought about the possible environmental impact of the technology that I use at the university

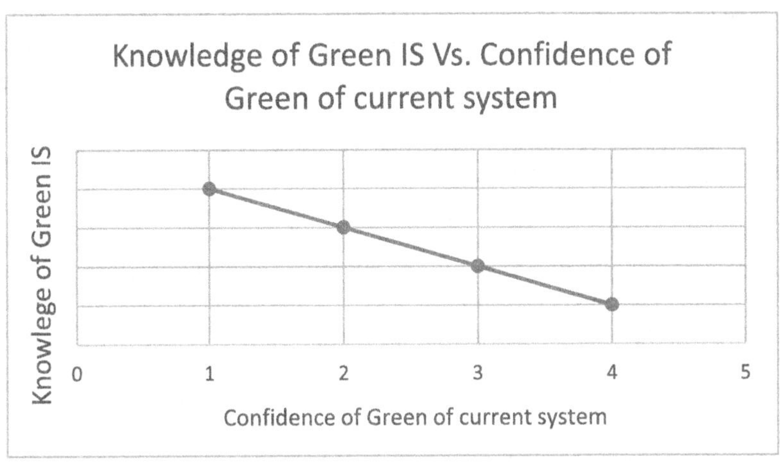

Fig. 6. Knowledge of Green IS Vs. Confidence of Green of current system

Additionally, in the current priority of IS/IT, Green IS is not ranked on the top. That is the reason the IT director emphasized "There may also be more environmentally friendly ways of disposing of some equipment, but because of the requirements such as that all equipment must be completely wiped before disposal. Due to the cost of these legal requirements, it can be difficult to become more sustainable." We believe the four types of gaps summarized by Jenkin et al. (2011a, b) are the main reason.

Another interesting finding is that FGCU ranks top five among colleges and universities in the U.S for its sustainable initiatives according to a student blog website (2014). However, the university and employees focus on the sustainable issues more toward on direct impact factors of environment, such as green grass area, adopting more renewable energy source, recycling policies, and so on. From this view of point, universities need to consider more upon Green IS while they spent most on direct environmental issues.

Throughout all the literatures, we rarely find any standard of Green IS. We argue that this is one reason why it is difficult to educate employees about Green IS. Therefore, the last suggestion we propose is that standardization and a rating system of Green IS are necessary to encourage universities in adopting Green IS.

Future trends of Green IS appear to be moving to a cloud based model for implementation. Cloud computing rents out computing resources which includes infrastructure making it more efficient. In the United Kingdom, environmental factors are one of the reasons for organizational decision makers to adopt cloud computing (Gutirrez et al. 2015). Further supporting that this is a new trend is that much of the literature about this topic was made recently in only the last five years. "Green IT is again one of the most important issues for future development" (Nowak 2011). As discussed earlier, a reduction of IT infrastructure is an example of a Green IS practice, cloud based ERP systems use less infrastructure so they help meet this requirement.

In data centers and other IT rooms where there are large amounts of power usage and heat, different cooling methods are being explored to reduce cost. These include liquid cooled plates which are able to effectively dissipate heat. The way that data cooling systems are being engineered are keeping energy conservation as a concern. The wasted heat from these systems can be repurposed in order to provide building and water heating in order to help other conservation efforts not directly related to the IS practices of a company or university (Li and Kandlikar 2015).

Some limitations that we found were a lack of discussion on Green ERP for universities or other higher education institutions. ERP systems in business have been studied more thoroughly than ERP systems for education. The topic of green IS and IT has become more discussed in recent years, but there has been little that looks at the difference of environmental impact of ERP systems in a university. Authors would not usually mention specific costs of an ERP implementation at a university. They would provide some information such as how much was budgeted to a region's education system, but only a little information about how much was specifically spent on an ERP implementation.

Another limitation that we encountered was the lack of research in the comparison of having higher education ERP systems hosted in a centralized location instead of hosting ERP systems individual at each institution. Due to the lack of research, we have no way of knowing how often the centralized implementation model is used and the potential environmental and cost savings that could be derived from its use.

References

Aldayel, A., Aldayel, M., Al-Mudimigh, A.: The critical success factors of ERP implementation in higher education in Saudi Arabia: a case study. J. Inf. Technol. Econ. Dev. **2**(2), 1–16 (2011). Accessed 28 Oct 2015, from Bussiness Source Premier

America's Greenest Universities (2011). Accessed 28 Nov 2015

Blaabjerg, F., Ionel, D.M.: Renewable energy devices and systems – state-of-the-art technology, research and development, challenges and future trends. Electr. Power Compon. Syst. **43**(12), 1319–1328 (2015). doi:10.1080/15325008.2015.1062819

Bridgestock, L.: Green Universities, 28 October 2012. Accessed 28 Nov 2015

Center for Sustainable Systems, University of Michigan (2014). "Green IT Factsheet." Pub. No. CSS09-07

Brook, S., Wang, W., Sarker, S.: Unpacking IT: a review of the existing literature. AMCIS **2010**, 398 (2010)

Centers, institutes and programs (Centers, institutes and programs). Accessed 10 Dec 2015

Dedrick, J.: Green IS: concepts and issues for information systems research. Commun. Assoc. Inf. Syst. **27**(11), 173–184 (2010)

Hammer, K.: Our Plan, 4 September 2014. Harvard Sustainability Plan. Accessed 10 Dec 2015

Grauler, M., Freundlieb, M., Ortwerth, K., Teuteberg, F.: Understanding the beliefs, actions and outcomes of sustainability reporting: an experimental approach. Inf. Syst. Front. **15**, 779–797 (2013)

Green IT - Information Technology|Emporia State University (Green IT - Information Technology) Emporia State University). Accessed 10 Dec 2015

Gutirrez, A., Boukrami, E., Lumsden, R.: Technological, organizational and environmental factors influencing managers' decision to adopt cloud computing in the UK. J. Enterp. Inf. Manag. **28**(6), 788–807 (2015). ISSN:17410398

Jenkin, T., McShane, L., Webster, J.: Green information technologies and systems: employees' perceptions of organizational practices. Bus. Soc. **50**(2), 266–314 (2011a)

Jenkin, T.A., Webster, J., McShane, L.: An agenda for 'Green' information technology and systems research. Inf. Organ. **21**(1), 17–40 (2011b)

Li, Z., Kandlikar, S.G.: Current status and future trends in data-center cooling technologies. Heat Transf. Eng. **36**(6), 523–538 (2015). doi:10.1080/01457632.2014.939032

Molla, A., et al.: An international comparison of green IT diffusion. Int. J. e-Bus. Manag. **2**(3), 3–23 (2009)

Molla, A.: Identify IT sustainability performance drivers: instrument development and validation. Inf. Syst. Front. **15**, 705–723 (2013)

Murugesan, S.: Harnessing Green IT: principles and practices. IT Prof. **10**(1), 24–33 (2008)

Ryoo, S., Koo, C.: Green practices-IS alignment and environmental performance: the mediating effects of coordination. Inf. Syst. Front. **15**, 799–814 (2013)

Santoyo-Castelazo, E., Azapagic, A.: Sustainability assessment of energy systems: integrating environmental, economic and social aspects. J. Clean. Prod. **80**, 119–138 (2014). doi:10.1016/j.jclepro.2014.05.061

Scholtz, B., Calitz, A., Cilliers, C.: Usability evaluation of a medium-sized ERP system in higher education. Electron. J. Inf. Syst. Eval. **16**(2), 148–161 (2013)

Schuetze, C.: How Green Is your school? 26 March 2013. Accessed 2 Dec 2015

Strategic Initiatives (Green IT: Sustainability: Northwestern University). Accessed 20 Nov 2015

Stuenkel, M.: Green IT Best Practices at the University of Michigan 29 October 2009. Accessed 7 Dec 2015

Williams, E.: Environmental effects of information and communications technologies. Nature **479**(7373), 354–358 (2011). doi:10.1038/nature10682

Interaction Design Methods and Tools

UserX Story: Incorporating UX Aspects into User Stories Elaboration

Joelma Choma(✉), Luciana A.M. Zaina, and Daniela Beraldo

Federal University of São Carlos, Sorocaba Campus, São Paul, Brazil
jh.choma@hotmail.com, lzaina@ufscar.br,
danielaberaldo12@gmail.com

Abstract. In the last decade, many strategies have been employed successfully to incorporate User Experience (UX) practices into agile development in order to increase user satisfaction with the product. In this paper, we present a grammar for stories of interaction called UserX Story, in order to remedy the difficulties encountered by teams to insert UX aspects and usability requirements in the first steps of software conception. An action research approach was applied to carry out the research within the industry, allowing us to work closely with the agile teams. The research cycle was split in three steps. In the first step, we carried out a technical literature survey, aiming to investigate the use of user stories in the agile methodologies, and additionally, an ethnographic study also was carried out in order to understand how the traditional user stories were being developed by product owners. In the second step, we proposed together with both teams - UX and agile - a grammar to UserX Story incorporating two concepts of UX: personas and Nielsen's heuristics. In the third step, six product owners were invited to implement the UserX Stories in real projects. After that, we interviewed the participants aiming to collect their experiences with the implementation of UserX Stories. Thus, we have found out that most of the agile teams approved the use of the stories incorporating UX aspects.

Keywords: Agile · Scrum · User experience · Usability · User story

1 Introduction

Agile software development methodologies, such as Scrum, are being adopted by many software companies, due to their lightweight and adaptive nature, seeking mainly deal with the lack of predictability that is common within the traditional development process. According to agile principles the highest priority is to satisfy the customer through early and continuous delivery of valuable software [13].

Nonetheless, due to lack of awareness about usability issues during agile development, the focus is not specifically on creating a design with good usability [11]. Customers often focus in core functionalities. Especially when customers are involved in providing constant feedback during software development, they are able to verify, for instance, the ease of use of a system under development [25]. However, the usability can be better assessed from the end-user experience perspective [23].

M. Kurosu (Ed.): HCI 2016, Part I, LNCS 9731, pp. 131–140, 2016.
DOI: 10.1007/978-3-319-39510-4_13

Agile approaches emphasize different design styles, once the quality of design is essential to maintaining agility. Design is considered a continuous activity that should be performed throughout the software development process rather than to be an entirely up-front activity [13]. The interest of integrating the User Experience Design (UXD) into agile methodology practices has been increased in the last decade in order to provide high quality user experience, and usability as an important item to add more value to the software [18].

Many strategies have been employed, including some UX professionals who have found ways to incorporate successfully UXD into their agile projects [2, 30]. However, few proposals concern to incorporation of design methods and more suitable artifacts to support the communication between designers and agile teams working closely. Artifacts in an agile environment are important mechanisms to maximize the transparency of information, and support decisions during the software development [27], while the UXD artifacts are produced to outline useful solutions from understanding users' needs, tasks, and context of use [3].

Considering that the shared use of artifacts by both teams (designers and programmers) is an important instrument to support the integration of the UXD methods into agile practices, this paper presents a proposal to the incorporation of UX aspects including usability recommendations in the elaboration of user stories, from interaction scenarios. User story is one of the most popular artifacts for specifying and communicating agile requirements. In most cases, however, the user stories do not address usability aspects, and take no account of real users' needs and behaviors [15]. Recently, in the course of a research project in a software industry, we detected that the Scrum teams were having difficulties to insert UX aspects in their stories to define user interaction requirements. In this paper, we describe the solution found to help practitioners to write user interaction stories called UserX Stories.

The remainder of this paper is organized as follows: Sect. 2 introduces the background about agile requirements engineering, including usability aspects; Sect. 3 some considerations about methodology, and research issues; Sect. 4 presents the research context, the steps to build and evaluate the artifact adapted from user stories, discussing the outcomes found in practice; and finally Sect. 5 presents the conclusions and points out directions for further works.

2 Background

Agile development is more flexible concerning elicitation and management of requirements than traditional software development, for the purpose of a quick reaction to changes in order to match customer needs [13]. The main practices used in the agile methodologies to transfer ideas from the customer to the development team are the face-to-face communication and frequent feedback [26]. These practices allow the adaptation of requirements that are discussed in detail with the customers during the development process. The agile requirement specification is not centralized in one phase before development; instead, this activity is evenly spread throughout development [4]. Rather than written specification for creating extensive requirements documents, agile methodologies usually adopt more simple techniques. In Scrum software projects [27], the most popular agile methodology, the user stories are artifacts adopted to define requirements in a high-level [8].

User stories are defined focusing on customer value, unlike other forms of requirements specification, which focus on system operations [25]. User stories are written throughout the agile project in a common language, intelligible to the users, in an effort to keep the attention and awareness on the needs of the users to emphasize their goals [8]. Everyone on the agile team participates in the writing of the stories with the goal of creating the list of features (product backlog) that describe the functionalities to be added over the course of the project [7]. Once that user stories contain just enough information to drive the development, more details about the requirements can be exploited by the development team through a conversation directly with the customer and/or other stakeholders [16]. Acceptance criteria are commonly added to user stories to guide the acceptance tests, in order to verify whether the stories were developed exactly how the customer expects [7].

According to Ramesh et al. [25] and Inayat et al. [16], a major concern about the iterative requirements engineering in agile development is the inadequate attention given to non-functional requirements - often ill-defined and ignored - during early development cycles. Overall, software engineers deal with usability as a non-functional requirement, believing that it can be considered later in the software development [28].

Usability requirements are qualitative attributes that specify user effectiveness, efficiency, or satisfaction levels that the system should achieve [23]. Some studies have highlighted the relationship between usability and functional requirements, aiming identify functional usability recommendations [19, 20]. According to these studies, usability features, especially those with functional implications, should be dealt as early as possible and included along with all the other requirements features, in order to provide a quality user experience and to avoid any rework and further unnecessary costs due to required adjustments.

3 Methodology and Research Issues

The last years, we have developed a project in partnership with a software industry to integrate UX in their software development process. This company has more than thirty years of experience in the development of ERP (Enterprise Resource Planning) systems for several market segments. Besides mechanisms and techniques to improve the usability of the ERP systems, other objective of this project has been to propose more suitable artifacts to support the integration of UX concepts within Scrum projects, agile method recently adopted by the company. Aiming to improve the communication of usability issues between UX designers and Scrum teams, we proposed previously a protocol for communication of design solutions and usability recommendations, whose findings can be seen in [5]. In this paper we present a new proposal of artifact incorporating UX aspects in user stories.

In order to carry out the research within the software industry, allowing us to work closely with the agile teams, we have applied a research approach called SoftCoDeR

(Software Cooperative Design Research) [6]. This research approach is based on a qualitative method of Action Research called Cooperative Method Development (CMD) proposed by Dittrich et al. [10], matched with the Design Science Research framework proposed by Hevner et al. [14]. On one hand, CMD approach provides a structured process of research, in which three phases are defined: (1) Understanding Practice (qualitative empirical investigations), (2) Deliberate Improvements (aiming to solve the problems identified in the first phase) and (3) Implement and Observe Improvements (checking the effectiveness of the improvements). On the other hand, DSR provides the guidelines to design artifacts of value based on both real need of industry (relevance) and scientific knowledge (rigor of research).

In the following section, we describe the research context and the three phases of the SoftCoDeR approach that was applied to answer the specific research question concerning to the building and evaluating of the artifact adapted from user stories, integrating UX aspects elicited from interaction scenario.

4 UX Aspects on User Stories Elaboration

The aforementioned protocol for communication of design solutions and usability recommendations had been proposed specifically to supply a need of the designers of a formal procedure to report results of user testing to Scrum teams. The proposed protocol was based on two UX concepts: personas and Nielsen's heuristics. Both UX concepts were primarily used to establish a common vocabulary among the developers, testers and UX designers.

Personas have been widely employed in the fields of usability and user experience as an artifact to describe groups of typical users by the creation of hypothetical archetypes. The personas can help create an empathy with users, facilitating the understanding on characteristics, behaviors and their deeper needs [24]. In addition to this, personas also can help in the development of interaction scenarios, and/or to describe tasks to the usability testing planning [9].

Nielsen's heuristics are one of the most used usability guidelines for user interface design, developed by Nielsen and Molich in the early 90's [22]. Also, these guidelines are commonly used to support the critical analysis in usability inspections (heuristic evaluation), and to check the problems identified in usability testing [12].

We have observed in practice that such concepts - personas and Nielsen's heuristics - can to improve the level of awareness and concerns on usability aspects of UX designers and developers (programmers and testers) [5]. The incorporation of both concepts to report the usability problems identified in user tests increased the level of reliability of the agile teams regarding the recommendations proposed by designers. However, we observed that the product owners (POs) were having difficulties in understanding such usability concepts, and also they did not know how to incorporate UX issues in the product requirements.

Considering that the POs were most familiarized with user stories to deal with agile requirements, we have suggested an adaptation of this artifact incorporating the vision of the user experience by employing the same UX concepts used on protocol for communication of usability recommendations. Thereby, a research cycle was started in order to answer the following question:

RQ: How could personas and Nielsen's heuristics concepts be incorporated into the User Stories?

4.1 Understanding Practice

In the first phase, we have carried out (i) an ethnographic study in order to understand how the user stories were being developed by POs; and (ii) a technical literature survey, aiming to investigate the use of user stories in agile practices.

Regarding user stories development (i), we found out that these were being written in a more traditional way, as the template popularized by Mike Cohn [7], shown in Fig. 1. Such user stories were stored in a software used for issue tracking and project management, instead of written on index cards or sticky notes.

As a <type of user>, **I want** <some goal> **so that** <some reason>

Fig. 1. User Story template

As for the results of literature review (ii), we found some recommendations about how to deal with usability issues and user stories together. Moreno and Yagüe [20], for instance, have identified three ways to incorporate functional usability requirements with user stories: (1) adding new stories to represent the requirements that are directly derived from usability (called usability stories); (2) adding or modifying tasks in US (detailing as needed); and (3) adding or modifying acceptance criteria. According to these authors, there are usability recommendations that: have positive impact on the final quality of use of software systems; can be considered as functional usability requirements that complement the traditional requirements; and can be documented as user stories - the usability stories - because both are similar. On the other hand, Barksdale et al. [1] have used conceptual maps to design a complete picture to the user, detailing the connections between user stories and scenarios. Scenarios are a type of design artifact commonly used to describe how a particular user uses the system for a specific task, considering the context and environment where it will be held [17]. The conceptual mapping was proposed to mitigate existing conflict between designers and agile teams to communicate usability and interaction requirements during the agile project. Still on scenarios, Sohaib and Khan [29] also recommended the use of them along with user stories during the exploration phase, and in addition, heuristic evaluation during acceptance testing.

4.2 Deliberate Improvements

Bearing in mind the research question, and from the outcomes of the literature review and the ethnographic study, we proposed to the teams a grammar - incorporating personas and Nielsen's heuristics - to describe interaction stories, that we called UserX

Story. The UserX Stories should be written from scenarios associated with user's actions and respective feedback necessary to achieve goals supported by the system.

Figure 2 shows the first version proposed to the UserX Story, whose traditional grammar of the user story was modified, by replacing (1) <type of user> by <personas>, to provide a clear target for developers to focus on; and (2) <some reason> by <Nielsen's heuristic(s)>, to highlight, from usability point of view, the positive impact on user interaction to achieve their goals.

UserX Story (template)

As a < Persona >**, I want/need** < goal> **so that** < Nielsen's heuristic> **will be met**

Fig. 2. Initial proposal to UserX Story template (1st version)

The initial proposal was discussed between the researchers, POs, Scrum Master and UX designer. From the discussions between researches and practitioners, the artifact had been improved, resulting in a second version to the UserX Story. In the second version (Fig. 3), the user stories would be expanded from the outcomes of the data collected in the user research phase. User research focuses on understanding user behaviors, needs, and motivations through observation techniques, task analysis, and other feedback methodologies, e.g. the usability testing and the recommendations pinpointed in the aforementioned communication protocol.

UserX Story (template)

As a < Persona >**, I want/need** < goal>**, for this** <interaction>,
through/ when [<task> / <context>].
I evaluate that my goal was achieved when <feedback>

Acceptance criteria:

Checks <action> **through** <set of conditions> **to satisfy** <Nielsen's heuristic(s)> **of action, and** < Nielsen's heuristic(s)> **of feedback.**

Fig. 3. UserX Story template (2nd version)

The UserX Stories are told from the perspective of the persona, who needs a particular condition for interaction. Such a condition can meet multiple personas. The stories describe an interactive process wherein the persona has a goal to achieve, for this s/he acts on the interface (interaction), to perform tasks (steps /features to effect the action) in a particular context (usage pattern). The persona will assess whether the objective was achieved interpreting system feedback. Aiming to verify whether stories were developed such that it exactly met the user interaction needs, the acceptance criteria should describe the action, the set of conditions, and the Nielsen's heuristics (action/feedback) that will be satisfied once the goal is successfully achieved.

The workshop entitled "Interaction Stories" was organized in order to make a warm up for the creation of stories adding the vision of UX through the use of personas and Nielsen's heuristics. Table 1 shows some information about the six POs who attended the workshop. All the participants had more than ten years of experience in the IT field. However, five out of the six participants had little experience with agile methodology (less than a year).

Table 1. Overview of the workshop participants

Product Owner	Experience in the IT field	Experience in the Company	Experience with Agile Methodology
P1	14 years	13 years	6 months
P2	11 years	2 weeks	2 weeks
P3	15 years	8 years	6 months
P4	15 years	9 years	9 months
P5	27 years	27 years	3 months
P6	17 years	3 years	3 years

The workshop was divided into (i) explanation of the concept of user story, personas and Nielsen's heuristics (ii) presentation of the UserX Story; and (iii) an exercise of writing stories from the proposed template, including the acceptance criteria. Some data collected with end-users during a workshop about "User Research" techniques previously performed with another group of participants, were provided as supplementary material to support the proposed exercise. Some personas were also included in this material. At the end of the workshop activities we discussed with the POs the next step for implementing the interaction stories in real projects, in order to evaluate the proposed artifact.

4.3 Implement and Observe Improvements

In this phase, the POs had one month to implement the UserX Story into one of their projects. After this period, researchers carried out individuals' interviews with the POs to collect their experiences with the implementation of UserX Stories. Figure 4 shows an implemented UserX Story for the redesign of part related for the issuance of reports for a Tax Bookkeeping sub-module.

Most POs had shared the UserX Story with their respective Scrum teams, which reacted positively, approving the use of the interaction stories, as well as the proposed template. However, two POs had not implemented the UserX Stories in their projects, since they were working on small changes that were related exclusively to business rules (legal requirements), and such changes would have had no impact on user interaction.

As we have discussed with company's practitioners, further tests will be needed to evaluate the procedures in which user stories are written from items reported in the protocol for the communication of usability recommendations. However, it was suggested that, firstly, the items reported in the protocol should be discussed between

UserX Story - Tax Bookkeeping sub-module

As a <Leo Walker> **I need to** <issue financial reporting and balance sheets, filtered by agents>, **for this** < the system allows me to choose the agent that I want to filter >, **through/ when** [<for issuing the report> / < regardless of the organization to which I am placed in the system, it being subsidiary or consolidator>]. **I evaluate that my goal was achieved when** <the report only listed the launches carried for the selected agent >

Acceptance criteria:

Checks < the system will validate if that agent code can be used for the selected organization > **through** < filtering by agent code **> to satisfy** <H5> **of action, and** < H9> **of feedback.**

Checks < the system should display the agent name next to the chosen code > **through** < choosing an agent, either by agent code or searching > **to satisfy** <H1> **of action, and** <H6> **of feedback.**

Fig. 4. UserX Story and acceptance criteria implemented by a PO

UX designer and Scrum team. And then, whether the Scrum team agrees with the recommended item, the item would be written in UserX Story template with the participation of the UX designer. Otherwise, the recommendation is discarded if, for example, there are technical limitations preventing it to be implemented.

One issue identified during interviews was related to the level of detail that acceptance criteria should be written. One of the POs commented that your criteria seemed quite detailed; thinking that reaching a greater level of detail should be the role of testers. Generally, acceptance criteria should be detailed enough to define when the user story is satisfied. Nonetheless, it is worth noting that there is some confusion about acceptance criteria and test cases. According Nazzaro & Suscheck [21], acceptance criteria should answer the question, "How will I know when I am done with the story?" and test cases answer the questions, "How do I test and what are the test steps?" Therefore, test cases can require more detail than acceptance criteria. Remembering that, the main focus of the acceptance criteria in UserX Story is satisfying usability guidelines.

5 Conclusion and Further Work

The outcomes of this work are part of a set of actions performed together with professionals from a company developing ERP systems, whose main objective is the incorporation of interaction design into the software development agile process.

This paper presents a solution to incorporate UX aspects into user stories, aiming to guide and facilitate the work of the agile teams in terms of usability requirements. The UserX Stories are told from the perspective of the persona representing a group of users; and the heuristics are intended to reinforce the acceptance criteria to highlight the positive impact of user interaction if the conditions were satisfied.

Although the proposal of interaction stories has already been approved by the majority of company's agile teams, more research is required in this area through the involvement of further organizations and agile teams. We found out that further tests will be needed to evaluate the cycle in which UserX Stories are written from results reported in usability tests. In the further works, we intend to draw up a set of guidelines to target the use of the UserX Stories. Another issue deserving further research refers to the granularity of the acceptance criteria.

References

1. Barksdale, J., Ragan, E., McCrickard, D.: Easing Team Usability: A Concept Mapping Approach. Agile Conference. IEEE, Chicago (2009)
2. Brown, D.D.: Five Agile UX Myths. J. Usability Studies **8**(3), 55–60 (2013)
3. Brown, J.M., Lindgaard, G., Biddle, R.: Collaborative events and shared artefacts: Agile interaction designers and developers working toward common aims. In: Agile Conference AGILE 2011, pp. 87–96. IEEE Computer Society, Salt Lake City (2011)
4. Cao, L., Ramesh, B.: Agile requirements engineering practices: an empirical study. IEEE Softw. **25**(1), 60–67 (2008)
5. Choma, J., Zaina, L.A., Beraldo, D.: Communication of design decisions and usability issues: a protocol based on Personas and Nielsen's heuristics. In: Kurosu, M. (ed.) Human-Computer Interaction. LNCS, vol. 9169, pp. 163–174. Springer, Heidelberg (2015)
6. Choma, J., Zaina, L. A., Silva, T.S.: Towards an approach matching CMD and DSR to improve the Academia-Industry software development partnership. In: Brazilian Symposium on Software Engineering (SBES). IEEE (2015)
7. Cohn, M.: User Stories Applied: For Agile Software Development, 13th edn. Pearson Education, Boston (2009)
8. Cohn, M.: Succeeding with Agile: Software Development using Scrum, 2nd edn. Pearson Education, Boston (2010)
9. Cooper, A., Reimann, R., Cronin, D.: About Face 3: The Essentials of Interaction Design. Wiley Publishing, New York (2007)
10. Dittrich, Y., Rönkkö, K., Eriksson, J., Hansson, C., Lindeberg, O.: Cooperative method development. Empirical Softw. Eng. **13**(3), 231–260 (2008)
11. Ferreira, J.: Agile development and UX design: towards understanding work cultures to support integration. In: Bajec, M., Eder, J. (eds.) CAiSE Workshops 2012. LNBIP, vol. 112, pp. 608–615. Springer, Heidelberg (2012)
12. Følstad, A., Law, E.L., Hornbæk, K.: Outliers in usability testing: how to treat usability problems found for only one test participant? In: Proceedings of the 7th Nordic Conference on Human-Computer Interaction: Making Sense Through, pp. 257–260 (2012)
13. Fowler, M., Highsmith, J.: The Agile manifesto. Softw. Dev. **9**(8), 28–35 (2001)
14. Hevner, A.R., March, S.T., Park, J., Ram, S.: Design science in information systems research. MIS Quart. **28**(1), 75–105 (2004)
15. Hudson, W.: User stories don't help users. Interactions **20**, 50–53 (2013)
16. Inayat, I., Salim, S.S., Marczak, S., Daneva, M., Shamshirband, S.: A systematic literature review on agile requirements engineering practices and challenges. Comput. Hum. Behav. **51**, 915–929 (2015)
17. Jia, Y., Larusdottir, M.K., Cajander, Å.: The usage of usability techniques in scrum projects. In: Winckler, M., Forbrig, P., Bernhaupt, R. (eds.) HCSE 2012. LNCS, vol. 7623, pp. 331–341. Springer, Heidelberg (2012)

18. Jurca, G., Hellmann, T.D., Maurer, F.: Integrating Agile and user-centered design: a systematic mapping and review of evaluation and validation studies of Agile-UX. In: Agile Conference (AGILE), pp. 24–32. IEEE, Orlando (2014)
19. Juristo, N., Moreno, A.M., Sanchez-Segura, M.I.: Guidelines for eliciting usability functionalities. IEEE Trans. Softw. Eng. **33**(11), 744–758 (2007)
20. Moreno, A.M., Yagüe, A.: Agile user stories enriched with usability. In: Wohlin, C. (ed.) XP 2012. LNBIP, vol. 111, pp. 168–176. Springer, Heidelberg (2012)
21. Nazzaro, W., Suscheck, C.: New to user stories? (2010). https://www.scrumalliance.org/community/articles/2010/april/new-to-user-stories
22. Nielsen, J.: 10 Usability Heuristics for User Interface Design (1995). http://www.nngroup.com/articles/ten-usability-heuristics/
23. Nielsen, J.: Agile development projects and usability (2008). https://www.nngroup.com/articles/agile-development-and-usability/
24. Norman, D.: Ad-hoc personas & empathetic focus. Jnd. org. (2004). http://www.jnd.org/dn.mss/personas_empath.html
25. Ramesh, B., Cao, L., Baskerville, R.: Agile requirements engineering practices and challenges: an empirical study. Inf. Syst. J. **20**(5), 449–480 (2010)
26. Rodríguez, P., Yagüe, A., Alarcón, P.P., Garbajosa, J.: Some findings concerning requirements in Agile methodologies. In: Bomarius, F., Oivo, M., Jaring, P., Abrahamsson, P. (eds.) Product-Focused Software Process Improvement, pp. 171–184. Springer, Heidelberg (2009)
27. Schwaber, K., Sutherland, J.: The scrum guide. Scrum Alliance (2011)
28. Seffah, A., Gulliksen, J., Desmarais, M.C.: Human-Centered Software Engineering - Integrating Usability in the Software Development Lifecycle, vol. 8. Springer, Netherlands (2005)
29. Sohaib, O., Khan, K.: Incorporating discount usability in extreme programming. Int. J. Softw. Eng. Appl. **5**, 51–62 (2011)
30. Sy, D.: Adapting usability investigations for Agile user-centered design. J. Usability Stud. **2**, 112–132 (2007)

POP: An Instrument to Decide on the Adoption of Participatory Design

Helder Cognaco de Oliveira, Marcelo da Silva Hounsell(✉), and Isabela Gasparini

Graduate Program in Applied Computing, Department of Computer Science, Santa Catarina State University, Joinville, SC, Brazil
heldercdo@gmail.com, {marcelo.hounsell, isabela.gasparini}@udesc.br

Abstract. Participatory Design (PD) is an approach that promotes the involvement of end-users in interactive software design. PD can be beneficial to software quality but can also raise concerns on pragmatical levels. There is no technique to help designers decide on adopting PD besides their experience on the matter. This paper proposes an objective questionnaire that gives clear indications for this decision, with confidence grading and coherence analysis. The instrument, called POP, can be used by non experts on PD, designers, developers and software analysts. The instrument has been validated by PD experts and by interactive software developers. POP was conceived for the development of educational video games but can be applied to a wider variety of systems. Results show that POP is able to clearly indicate when a project can benefit from PD, and to also give clues on the difficulties it would be facing. POP allows PD to be considered into projects that otherwise, would never evaluate how beneficial the PD approach could be to system development and to end-users.

Keywords: Participatory design · Decision-making · Questionnaire

1 Introduction

In Human-Computer Interaction (HCI), interactive software development approaches that engage end-users, directly or indirectly (i.e. in which the needs, wants, and limitations of end-users of a product, service or process are given attention at each stage of the design process), are classified as User-Centered Design (UCD). One of such approaches is Participatory Design (PD), in which end-users are involved directly, becoming active members of the development team [1]. According to Abras et al. [2], UCD can help designers by providing an understanding of factors (psychological, organizational and others) that affect the usage of a software. This can help the software development with high efficiency and efficacy, while managing end-users expectations about the final product. However, PD also has its downsides, such as the need for more resources (like time and money) during development, and the possibility that the resulting product will be too specific, or hard to adapt to a different group of users.

M. Kurosu (Ed.): HCI 2016, Part I, LNCS 9731, pp. 141–152, 2016.
DOI: 10.1007/978-3-319-39510-4_14

During the development of interactive software, the development team might have to make a decision on whether to adopt PD practices or not. This paper proposes an instrument to help developers, software analysts and designers on making such decisions, and is structured as follows. The second section presents the fundamentals of PD, while the third section focuses on related works. The content of the instrument is presented in the fourth section, with the instrument validation being described in the fifth section. The discussion regarding obtained results is shown and the conclusions are presented, respectively, in the sixth and seventh sections.

2 Participatory Design

Participatory Design (PD) is an approach that transforms end-users in active members of the development team, helping the construction of different aspects of a software. PD started in Scandinavia (Denmark, Sweden and Norway) in late 60 s, when workers started to pressure their unions for more democracy on deciding which information systems would be used in their work environments [1]. What they were effectively asking for was to choose the systems that they judged more adequate, whether because of its usability or its features.

PD became popular around the globe. In America, it started being used as a mean to develop software that effectively identified and satisfied end-users requirements [3]. In practical terms, PD consists on integrating an end-user in the development team, participating in different steps of a software life cycle, such as requirement analysis, construction/prototyping and evaluation/testing [4].

For the application of PD, there are different techniques that can be used, such as: BrainDraw [4], a round-robin graphical brainstorming technique; CARD [1], which describes processes and activity flows through the usage of cards and; PICTIVE [1], which creates low-tech prototypes of user interfaces.

3 Related Works

There is no instrument that helps designers to decide on choosing to use PD or not. However, following related works defined certain aspects of the PD approach that can be evaluated to a certain degree with the instrument proposed in this paper.

Bratteteig and Wagner [5] proposed a classification of the types of decision made during PD, as a way to analyze how the division of power occurs between developers and users. The decisions are summarized as follows:

- Values and concepts: how the participation occurs and how much will it affect the final design;
- Vision implementation: how the design will be applied; what are the identified solutions to the problems the software is trying to solve;
- Negotiations with the outside world: decisions not directly related to the software like, for instance, the choosing of the users who will participate in the design;

- Non-decisions: decisions made without deliberation or communication; inexplicit decisions. The authors describe the action of "accepting a 'gift'" as a good example of such decision.

These decisions are made considering certain variables, like participants' profiles and applicable techniques. It is necessary to choose a technique that is adequate to the user [6].

Inspired by the work of Greenbaum and Halskoy [7], a classification was proposed by Bergvall-Kåreborn e Ståhlbrost [8], regarding the motivations of software development with PD. According to this classification, there are three distinct perspectives:

- Ethical (democracy): human beings have the right to influence their destinies. Therefore, they also have the right to influence technological decisions that affect their professional and private lives, like choosing an adequate software;
- Curiosity (theoretical): projects motivated by the curiosity regarding the nature of participation, best practices in participation, good and bad outcomes (for the participants and for the software);
- Economic (pragmatic): projects with this motivation focus on achieving best results as possible, regarding software quality and acceptance.

Despite the rationalization made by these works on the motives and values of shared decisions, they do not present an objective way to evaluate whether PD should be opted, or not. The proposal of an objective instrument that is easy to use, can help the analysis of the outcomes that PD can bring to a software development project.

The instrument, named POP, presented in the next section, was based on empirical knowledge from researchers, and do not conflict in anyway with presented classifications.

4 Objective Participatory Questions (POP)

The Objective Participatory Questions (in Portuguese namely *Perguntas Objetivas Participativas*, hereby called POP), is a questionnaire, created to acknowledge and evaluate specific aspects of the participatory process, prior to opting for this kind of approach.

The creation of POP was based on empirical knowledge, obtained by a team that developed persuasive educational video games about drug addiction. Despite being created in a very specific context, POP content is generic enough so that any interactive software development team can benefit from it. The questions in POP were originated from the advantages and disadvantages observed before, during and after the participatory development of educational video games.

The questionnaire is composed of 11 questions, available in Appendix A. Each question deals with a specific topic in the context of PD, as experienced by the researchers. These topics are:

- Technical Benefits: some benefits and harms can easily be identified by designers and domain experts. Therefore, it is important to take their opinion on the necessity of using PD, or not;

- Personal Benefits: a participation that brings personal benefits can be of great value to those involved;
- Logistics: a participation with complex logistics like, for instance, a group of users with limited time to participate, should not be advised;
- Profile: to depend on a very specific kind of user can make it difficult for a participatory process to happen. Generic users are easier to be obtained, so it is more likely that enough participants will be found to help the design process;
- Volatility: a group of volatile users can harm long-term participatory processes, with little homogeneity on the participation and decision making;
- Group Size: large groups of end-users can be hard to coordinate and organize for participatory sessions, which could delay development. Besides, finding a participatory technique that handles a large group of participants can prove difficult. According to Muller [4], PD techniques support up to 14 participants in average, to a maximum of 40 participants;
- Empathy: empathy among developers, domain experts and end-users can facilitate complex multidisciplinary projects, for it helps different teams to work together appropriately. Antipathy, on the other hand, can make software development difficult in important steps of its life cycle, such as requirements analysis;
- Conceptual Contribution: the participation of end-users during requirements analysis is a first step to develop a software with PD that is adequate to end-users expectations;
- Technical Contribution: participation in technical steps of development can help to assure the correct implementation of previously established requirements, with end-users helping to translate them into data, models, code, etc.;
- Conceptual Framework: as conceptual steps in the software life cycle result in the creation of requirements, which are the fundamental to the software development, it is important to use techniques for participation that help to obtain end-users' requirements with clarity, in order to avoid as much rework as possible;
- Technical Framework: inappropriate participatory techniques in technical steps of development may result in a low quality user interface, which is hard to comprehend and to work with.

For each question, there are four possible answers: positive, neutral, negative, and abstentious. The positivity/negativity characterization of each answer is represented by points that are assigned to them. Moreover, each question has a description text to help designers understand its context.

During the development of educational video games using PD, the authors noticed that, regarding decision-making, certain aspects of participation were more important than others. To reflect that, some questions that have bigger influence in the recommendation of PD, have answers with absolute values that are higher than the answers in less influential questions. The definition of which questions have higher valued answers was based on researchers' empirical experiences.

4.1 Decision-Making

The results from the questionnaire can be analyzed through three indicators, which are based on the following variables:

- *s*: is the sum of points assigned to all the questions answered by the designer;
- *r*: is the amount of questions that were effectively answered, meaning questions which answers were different than "d" (abstentious);
- *m*: sum of the absolute value of all questions answered by the designer. It represents the best possible score the designer could have obtained with the set of questions he answered.

With all these three variables, it is possible to calculate the indicators:

- Final Indication (*fi*): it is obtained by analyzing the value of *s*. If the value of *s* is positive, then end-user participation is recommended. If it is negative, than participation is not recommended. If it is zero, then it is not possible to conclude on whether participation is recommended or not.
- Confidence (*cf*): represents how confident the *fi* indicator is, based on the amount of questions effectively answered. The higher the confidence, the more grounded the recommendation is. This indicator is calculated by Eq. 1.

$$cf = (r/11) * 100 \tag{1}$$

- Coherence (*cr*): represents how coherent the *fi* indicator is, based on the trend observed on answered questions. In other words, it shows how many questions were answered positively, if participation is recommended, or answered negatively, if participation is not recommended. This indicator can only be calculated (Eq. 2) if *s* is different than zero.

$$cr = [(|s| + m)/2m] * 100 \tag{2}$$

Analyzing all these three indicators, designers can obtain a recommendation on whether using the participation of end-users or not, how confident that recommendation is, and how coherent among each other the answers were.

For instance, the application of this instrument can result in a final indication that participation is recommended (because s is positive), with a low 13 % of confidence (because many questions were left unanswered), but with a high 84 % of coherence (because most answered were positive).

5 Validation

This instrument was validated in two different ways:

- Experts' Validations, to validate if POP is relevant as a decision making tool for PD supported development, experts were consulted, with unstructured interviews;

- Practitioners' Validation, to validate if the usage of POP reflects decisions taken by designers in real development scenarios, designers used the instrument in both current and past projects (retroactively).

5.1 Experts' Validation

During this initial validation, the questionnaire was evaluated by three PhD professors, with experience in PD whether teaching about it in class or applying it in research projects and software development. To help with this validation, they were provided with a list of justifications for each question, explaining the reasons each of them were created, how relevant they were to PD, etc. These justifications are not present in Appendix A.

After they analyzed the instrument, each one participated individually in an unstructured interview. Based on feedback obtained through these interviews, some adjustments were made to the instrument: removal of some questions; changes in the points assigned to the answers; improvements in the description of certain questions.

Questions removed were focused on applying POP into a specific development methodology. With the removal of these questions, POP was made generic enough so that it can be applied into many other development methodologies.

The point system was changed from a scale of −10 to 10 points, to a scale of −3 to 3 points. This way, it is easier to calculate the questionnaire results, for the variables will have smaller values. Moreover, it was decided that certain questions would have higher valued answers than others, in order to emphasize the importance of certain aspects to the practice of PD. Questions that are more relevant have answers ranging from −3 to 3, while less relevant questions have answers ranging from −1 to 1.

Finally, the description of some questions were improved, in order to clear them up and make them easier to understand. Some professors judged that certain descriptions were not really helping the understanding of the question's context, and some contained words not commonly used by practitioners. Where possible, descriptions were changed to include advantages and disadvantages in each context, and more examples of application.

5.2 Practitioners' Validation

During the second validation, designers, HCI specialists and developers answered the questionnaire in order to see if its results were similar to the decisions they had made. Some designers answered the questionnaire retroactively, that is, as if they were at the start of a project that is already finished. This way, it could be observed if the results were consistent with the choice of the designers.

Professors who participated in the first validation, helped the researchers to select designers for the second validation. In total, eight cases were analyzed (results are shown at Table 1) with designers enrolled to each project using POP, whether it was retroactively, or not. Selected cases were:

Table 1. Results obtained during the second validation of POP

	Case 1	Case 2	Case 3	Case 4	Case 5	Case 6	Case 7	Case 8
PD?	Yes	Yes	Yes	Yes	Yes	No	No	No
fi	4	18	14	16	12	−5	−10	−4
cf	75 %	100 %	66,7 %	83,3 %	100 %	75 %	100 %	83,3 %
cr	62,5 %	90,9 %	100 %	94,4 %	83,3 %	66,7 %	66,7 %	66,7 %
Retroactive?	Yes	Yes	Yes	Yes	No	No	Yes	No

- Case 1: Development of three persuasive educational video games, about the "12 Steps" program to fight drug addiction. Participation helped the creation of end-users' requirements, and graphical elements of the games;
- Case 2: Development of a software for healthcare industry, which managed multidisciplinary medical treatments in a health institute for the elderly. Professionals participated to identify multidisciplinary tasks and to define software interfaces;
- Case 3: Development of a retail software, with end-users participating during requirements analysis and prototyping;
- Case 4: Development of an electronic document management software for law practice. Participants helped on requirements analysis and made suggestions during ergonomic evaluation;
- Case 5: Development of an educational video game to help drug addicts during treatment, to ease their way back into society. Participants helped to create end-users' requirements and the storyline of the game;
- Case 6: Development of an educational video game to help patients who suffered stroke, to reacquire standing balance during rehabilitation;
- Case 7: Development of an educational video game to alphabetize children with Down's syndrome;
- Case 8: Development of an education video game to improve math literacy in children with Down's syndrome.

Each column of Table 1 presents data related to a certain case. The "PD?" row shows whether each case decided to use PD or not. The following three rows shows the results of each indicator generated by POP, respectively, Final Indication, Confidence and Coherence. The last row shows whether POP was applied retroactively or not.

All recommended suggestions (*fi*) obtained by using POP were consistent with the decisions taken by the designers. Low coherence values (below 70 %) were obtained in cases 1, 6, 7 and 8. In particular, case 1 had the lowest value, for the aspects of logistics and volatility had negative answers. The results indicate that, although recommended, the participation could prove to be difficult to execute, since at least some questions were answered negatively. It is up for the person making the decision to analyze whether it is worthy or not to use PD considering the logistical problems he or she is going to face, and if the volatility of end-users participating is harmful or not to the software development.

6 Discussion

POP does not rely on a specific development methodology and therefore, designers can use it to identify if a participatory approach is recommended, regardless of the development methodology.

Experts' validation resulted in changes that made the instrument more adequate to professionals of the field, by using the right vocabulary. Moreover, the structure of questions, explanations and answers were also improved, making the instrument easier to be used.

Practitioners' validation indicates the instrument is consistent with decisions made by designers in real scenarios, meaning POP is a valid instrument for decision making, with relevant contexts being reflected throughout its questions, and its different valued answers.

While answering the questionnaire, the designer responsible for case 2 criticized a question regarding how the resulting software would be used. If the software was to be used spontaneously, then participation would be recommended to motivate users. If the usage was obligatory, like in a class activity or corporate training, then participation would not be recommended. After deliberation, this question was removed from the instrument, because it was judged that both scenarios could benefit from end-user participation. Even if a software is going to be used regardless of users' motivation, it can benefit from better analysis and be more adequate to users.

During both validations, no participant questioned or indicated the existence of a similar instrument for decision making in PD. This suggests that POP is a novel instrument.

Because of the way POP is composed, there is no need for a deep knowledge in UCD, or even PD. Therefore, a designer can analyze if PD is recommended or not and, if necessary, can focus on studying participatory practices.

It seems unusual for designers to consider PD in their projects, unless they have a certain affinity with this approach. With POP, more designers can consider PD, for there is no need for previous knowledge to use it.

POP was created to be a tool in a video game development methodology, but it is structured in a generic way, so that it can be applied to any interactive software development methodology.

The instrument can help designers whose motivation are classified as pragmatic [8], because it helps them evaluate certain viability issues (logistics, volatility, empathy, benefits and contributions) that are important to projects within this classification.

This viability information can also benefit decision making in projects with curiosity (theoretical) motivation [8], because if POP results do not recommend participation (with high confidence and coherence values), then the end-user participation will be difficult to execute, with the risk of incorrect data being generated. These projects can also benefit from POP when the question regarding personal benefits is answered positively. This was observed in cases 1 and 5, during the second validation. In both cases, the direct participation of drug addicts to develop educational video games resulted in the transformation of the participatory process into a therapeutic process, with the appropriate help of field professionals.

However, POP does not help projects with exclusively ethical motivations, because arguments that are fundamental to these projects (such as democracy at workplace) addresses psychological and social concepts that are beyond the scope of this research.

Questions related to participation in conceptual and technical steps of development can help in decisions regarding division of power [5]. These decisions are influenced by the way participation is executed. Besides, by classifying the level of contribution in participation, it is possible to analyze the amount of freedom that will be given to participants.

The final form of POP, presented in Appendix A, is slightly different than the one used during the validation processes. Some questions were removed, in order to address only relevant contexts of PD, and the overall writing was improved, to make POP easier to understand and to use.

Although in certain cases POP may not recommend end-user participation, there are still other UCD approaches that could be considered by designer, developers and software analysts, such as Contextual Design and Collaborative Design.

7 Conclusions

Although there are studies that classified different kinds of participatory practices, motivations, division of power, and other contexts related to Participatory Design (PD), no objective decision-making tools for designers were found.

The instrument proposed by this paper, POP (*Perguntas Objetivas Participativas*, or Objective Participatory Questions in English), is a questionnaire that evaluates the context of a software development project, and generates quantifiable information, in order to help a designer on making a decision about using PD during development. POP can be used by designers, regardless of their previous knowledge on UCD, or even PD itself.

The instrument has been validated in two different ways, by experts and by practitioners, and none of them questioned its novelty. Validation fine-tuned the instrument that is presented in its final form in Appendix A.

Results obtained by the use of POP, indicate whether PD is recommended or not, but the final decision is taken by the designers, which can be opposite to POP's recommendation. In such cases, the results of POP indicate if the project is losing a good opportunity to involve end-users or, oppositely, how difficult and disadvantageous it would be to execute their participation.

It is believed that this is a novel tool for decision-making in PD, and that it can benefit developers and designer, by providing them with information to support their final decision. This could help spread the practice of PD by showing to designers who previously would not consider this approach, how it can be beneficial to their projects.

A. Appendix

Before answering the questions below, reflect about: (a) What is the target audience (end-users and their characteristics)? (b) Where can individuals from the target audience be found, to eventually participate?

POP 1: (Technical Benefits) What is the technical impact of end-users participating in the software development?			
Explanation/Example: Participation can bring technical benefits to development such as requirements that are more adequate to end-users, but can also bring harm such as delays and difficulties in conciliating end-users' desires with domain experts' desires.			
(a) Beneficial (+2)	(b) None (0)	(c) Harmful (−2)	(d) Unknown (0)

POP 2: (Personal Benefits) What is the personal impact for end-users to participate in the software development?			
Explanation/Example: Participation can bring inexplicit personal benefits to end-users, such as improvements in interpersonal relationships, occupational therapy, acquisition of technical knowledge, and others, but can also make users uncomfortable when discussing certain aspects of the software.			
(a) Beneficial (+2)	(b) None (0)	(c) Harmful (−2)	(d) Unknown (0)

POP 3: (Logistics) How difficult are the logistics of allowing end-users to participate in the software development?			
Explanation/Example: Participatory tasks may require end-users transportation, resource allocation, scheduling and etc.			
(a) Easy (+3)	(b) Neutral (0)	(c) Hard (−3)	(d) Unknown (0)

POP 4: (Profile) How difficult is it to find and involve end-users that fit into a desirable profile for participation in the software development?			
Explanation/Example: Generic profiles can be filled by most end-users, while specific profiles can only be filled by a small group of end-users.			
(a) Easy (+2)	(b) Neutral (0)	(c) Hard (−2)	(d) Unknown (0)

POP 5: (Volatility) Considering the duration of the development project, how volatile is the group of end-users that would participate in the software development?			
Explanation/Example: Some groups of end-users are volatile, for they constantly change in formation or organization, while non-volatile groups can remain unchanged during the whole software development.			
(a) Not volatile (+3)	(b) Variable (0)	(c) Volatile (−3)	(d) Unknown (0)

POP 6: (Group Size) What is the size of the group of end-users that would participate in the software development?			
Explanation/Example: Participatory Design techniques can, in average, support groups of 2 to 14 participants. At most, these techniques can support up to 40 participants.			
(a) Up to 14 people (+2)	(b) Between 15 and 40 people (0)	(c) More than 40 people (−2)	(d) Unknown (0)

POP 7: (Empathy) What is the level of empathy between technical staff and end-users?			
Explanation/Example: Technical staff can be composed of programmers, designers, analysts, etc. Empathy must be seen as personal and professional proximity between both groups. With a high level of empathy, both groups share a vision about definitions and objectives of the software, know the specific vocabulary of each domain, have similar previous experience working together, etc. With a low level of empathy, the groups don't know each other from previous works, have difficulties communicating adequately, etc.			
(a) High (+2)	(b) Neutral (0)	(c) Low (−2)	(d) Unknown (0)

POP 8: (Conceptual Contribution) What is the potential for contribution from end-users while participating in conceptual steps of the software development?			
Explanation/Example: Conceptual steps, like requirement elicitation and analysis, are prior to codification and construction of graphical elements of the software. End-users can contribute during analysis by presenting their perspectives about the software. However, in some cases the requirements cannot be interfered by end-users.			
(a) High (+1)	(b) Neutral (0)	(c) Low (−1)	(d) Unknown (0)

POP 9: (Technical Contribution) What is the potential for contribution from end-users while participating in technical steps of the software development?			
Explanation/Examples: Technical steps involve the creation of interfaces, definition of software architecture, codification, evaluation, assessment, etc. Participation in such steps may allow end-users to contribute with graphical elements to the interface, codification with high-level programming tools, evaluations through interviews, interaction tests, focus groups and controlled experiments.			
(a) High (+1)	(b) Neutral (0)	(c) Low (−1)	(d) Unknown (0)

POP 10: (Conceptual Framework) What is the level of knowledge (tools, processes, methods, techniques) to involve end-users in conceptual steps of the software development?			
Explanation/Example: Requirements' analysis and elicitation can be executed with participation through brainstorming techniques and interviews.			
(a) High (+1)	(b) None (0)	(c) Bad (−1)	(d) Unknown (0)

POP 11: (Technical Framework) What is the level of knowledge (tools, processes, methods, techniques) to involve end-users in technical steps of the software development?			
Explanation/Example: Multimedia elements of the software can be created with participation of end-users thought audio recordings, photographs, drawings, etc. Authoring tools can enable participation in codification. Interaction tests and questionnaires can be used during tests and evaluations.			
(a) High (+1)	(b) None (0)	(c) Low (−1)	(d) Unknown (0)

References

1. Preece, J., Rogers, Y., Sharp, H.: Interaction Design: Beyond Human-Computer Interaction. Wiley, New York (2011)
2. Abras, C., Maloney-Krichmar, D., Preece, J.: User-centered design. In: Bainbridge, W.S. (ed.) Berkshire Encyclopedia of Human-Computer Interaction. Berkshire, Great Barrington (2004)
3. Chin, G.: A case study in the participatory design of a collaborative science-based learning environment. Virginia Polytechnic Institute and State University, Blacksburg (2004)
4. Muller, M.J.: Participatory practices in the software lifecycle. In: Helander, M.G., Landauer, T.K., Prabhu, P.V. (eds.) Handbook of Human-Computer Interaction, 2nd edn. Elsevier, Amsterdam (1997)
5. Bratteteig, T., Wagner, I.: Disentangling power and decision-making in participatory design. In: Proceedings of the 12th Participatory Design Conference: Research Papers, vol. 1, pp. 41–50 (2012)
6. Slegers, K., Duysburgh, P., Hendriks, N.: Participatory design with people living with cognitive or sensory impairments. In: CHI 2014 Extended Abstracts on Human Factors in Computing Systems, pp. 49–52 (2014)
7. Greenbaum, J., Halskov, K.: PD a personal statement. Commun. ACM **36**(6), 47 (1993)
8. Bergvall-Kåreborn, B., Ståhlbrost, A.: Participatory design: one step back or two steps forward?. In: Proceedings of the Tenth Anniversary Conference on Participatory Design, pp. 102–111 (2008)

PATHY: Using Empathy with Personas to Design Applications that Meet the Users' Needs

Bruna Moraes Ferreira[1(✉)], Simone D.J. Barbosa[2], and Tayana Conte[1]

[1] USES Research Group, Instituto de Computação, Universidade Federal do Amazonas, Manaus, Amazonas, Brazil
{bmf, tayana}@icomp.ufam.edu.br

[2] Semiotic Engineering Research Group, Department of Informatics, PUC-Rio, Rio de Janeiro, Brazil
simone@inf.puc-rio.br

Abstract. The importance of User Experience has been increasingly recognized in the context of developing interactive applications. The Personas technique aims to help designers to better understand users' needs. However, various Personas techniques use too much information and the textual description template does not explicitly guide designers in identifying functionality and features of the applications. Therefore, some designers have questioned the usefulness of the technique, limiting its acceptance and adoption. In this context, we proposed the PATHY technique, combining Personas and Empathy Maps in a novel approach. We conducted an empirical study to determine the participants' perception about the usefulness and ease of use of the technique. We analyzed the participants' quantitative and qualitative answers. The study showed that PATHY was considered both easy to use and useful. Furthermore, the results of the study offer insights for further improvements of the technique.

Keywords: Users' needs · Empathy · Personas · User experience · Empathy map

1 Introduction

Considering users' needs and emotions when interacting with a product is a key factor to software product success [23]. The importance of UX has steadily increased in the context of developing products that meet human expectations, by exploring these needs [1, 20]. A deep understanding about the users who will interact with the application is essential to develop and deliver useful systems [3]. The Personas technique aims to help software engineers to better understand the users' needs.

The Personas technique consists of gathering data about users, in order to provide the development team with an understanding about users' characteristics; defining personas based on this understanding; and keeping focus on these personas throughout software development [3]. Personas can instigate teams to think about users and their needs during the design process, supporting efficient design decisions while avoiding

M. Kurosu (Ed.): HCI 2016, Part I, LNCS 9731, pp. 153–165, 2016.
DOI: 10.1007/978-3-319-39510-4_15

incorrect generalizations, and communicating knowledge about users to various stakeholders [15].

Despite those benefits, the technique is mainly criticized for being hard to implement [16]. Personas can be freely created; no guidance is given to software engineers about what should be described. Therefore, personas may contain information that is useless for the application being developed. A perception of low utility reduces the acceptance of a technique by designers.

We can use Empathy Maps (EM) to guide the personas creation with real user groups and to promote innovative ideas generation [17], supporting the design of business models based on the clients' perspectives [17]. EM proposes checklist questions to create customer segment profiles and a visual template to simplify its implementation. In our work, we adapted EM for personas creation.

We created the PATHY technique based on both Empathy Maps and Personas, aiming to help software engineers to reflect on the users' needs. To support application design, PATHY includes a template based on an EM template to cover both personas and software characteristics. Therefore, the PATHY technique provides better guidance for software engineers in thinking about the application features based on personas.

To evaluate PATHY, we conducted an empirical study to determine the participants' perception about the technique's usefulness and ease of use. During this study, we used the PATHY technique to help understand characteristics of the users and of the application being designed. Besides using the technique, participants answered a questionnaire about their perception of PATHY. We analyzed the participants' quantitative and qualitative answers. The study showed that the PATHY technique was considered easy to use and useful. Furthermore, the results of the study offer insights for further improvements of the technique.

This paper is organized as follows. In Sect. 2 we present some concepts about User Experience, Personas and Empathy Map. In Sect. 3 we present the PATHY technique. In Sect. 4 we describe the study, followed by results in Sect. 5. Finally, conclusions and comments about future work are provided in Sect. 6.

2 Background

2.1 User Experience

According to ISO 9241-210 [11], User eXperience (UX) is defined as: 'a person's perceptions and responses that result from the use and/or anticipated use of a product, system or service'. Such definition can be complemented by other interpretations, such as 'User experience explores how a person feels about using a product, i.e., the experiential, effective, meaningful and valuable aspects of product use' [22].

Modeling users is essential to understand, predict and reason about UX processes, and cause consequences to software design [14]. A product that meets or exceeds users' needs and expectations results in a positive user experience. However, a product that fails to satisfy users' needs and expectations results in a negative user experience [15].

2.2 Personas

A Persona is a hypothetical archetype of a real user [17], which describes a user's goals, skills, and interests [4]. Personas should be employed during technology design and development phases to avoid the 'elastic user' problem, i.e., a user description that can be modified to meet designers', developers', or stakeholders' needs, [15], but not the real users'.

In order to describe Personas, some of their characteristics should be detailed, such as: name, image, clothes, occupation, family, friends, pets, age, sex, ethnicity, education, socioeconomic status, life story, goals, and tasks [10]. Software engineers may choose different ways to represent personas, but they are usually represented in textual form, enhanced by a picture.

Some techniques to describe personas have been proposed to involve users in the software development process. Castro et al. [3] proposed the Personas* technique based on Cooper's version, including new steps to adapt personas to the software development process. In one of the stages use cases are built, based on both generated personas and on obtained knowledge about users after the personas creation process. Javahery and Ahmed [12] proposed the P2P technique, using the concept of personas to document and model user experiences. In this technique, design patterns are derived from personas to build the application user interface. Most Personas techniques make use of text with lots of information to describe personas [3, 6, 7, 12, 18]. However, a vast part of this information may not be useful to develop the application. Having too much information can cause personas to be considered as a tiring technique and this may lead to resistance in using the personas technique in software development. In addition, the textual description template does not explicitly give directions to designers about how to identify functionality and features of the applications. Inexperienced software engineers cannot stay focused on the application while creating personas and then the created personas will not be used. Therefore, some designers have questioned the usefulness of the technique, limiting its acceptance and adoption.

Among the benefits of using Personas, Cooper [4] mentions: (1) Provides support to the development team on understanding characteristics of a user group; (2) Proposes solutions related to major users' needs; and (3) Provides a human face as a way to bring potential users closer to the development team and represent them in a demographic context. Software designers use personas in two ways: in creating them and in communicating knowledge about users to other stakeholders [10]. However, the use of Personas is controversial. Personas creation can involve a lot of creativity, distancing them from real users. Moreover, verifying whether the described personas reflect relevant aspects of the application which is about to be developed is considered a hard task.

2.3 Empathy Map

Empathy Map (EM) is a technique that assists in designing business models according to customers' perspectives. It goes beyond demographic characteristics and develops a better understanding of a customer's environment, behavior, aspirations and concerns

[17]. The EM goal is to create a degree of empathy for a specific person (or group of people) [9]. An empathy map reveals the rationale underlying users' actions, decisions and choices; therefore it helps in designing for users' real needs [1].

Matthews [9] proposed four different areas that should be covered when creating an empathy map: What does the person hear? think and feel? see? say and do? Bland [2] mentioned Pain and Gain as important areas to look for, resulting in the template depicted in Fig. 1.

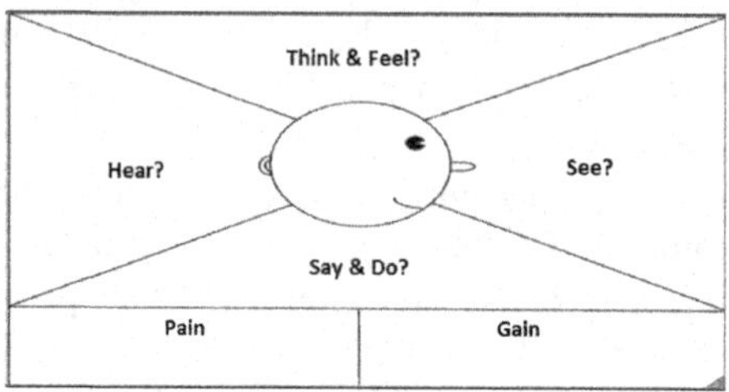

Fig. 1. Empathy map template [17]

3 The PATHY Technique

We developed the PATHY (Personas EmpATHY) technique to help to design for the users' needs, with the goal of improving the quality of the designed application and thus provide a better user experience. PATHY uses the Personas technique to create empathy with the users so as to identify their characteristics and problems.

The PATHY Technique unites Personas and Empathy Map. We adapted the EM template to present a persona's characteristics that can influence the application development. In addition to those characteristics, the technique also deals with the features that a persona would like in the application. The PATHY template is divided in six fields: (a) Do; (b) Feel/Think/Believe; (c) Experience with technology; (d) Problems; (e) Needs, and (f) Existing Solutions. Each field has a set of questions to guide the creation of the persona (see Figs. 2 and 3). The PATHY technique fields were adapted from the EM fields based on the results of a previous study where the structure of the EM was evaluated [8]. From the data analysis of this previous study using the EM it was possible to obtain suggestions for improvements, and from that, the PATHY technique was generated. Furthermore, to improve the support to software development, we added a second part in the PATHY technique, to deal with issues related to identifying the application features and characteristics. PATHY provides better guidance for software developers in thinking about application's features based on a persona's description.

Figure 2 shows the first part of the PATHY template, where the characteristics regarding the persona are described, and its guide questions. Figure 3 shows the second part of the template, where the persona's problems and existing solutions to those problems are described, and its guide questions. The fields that form the PATHY technique template are described in the following.

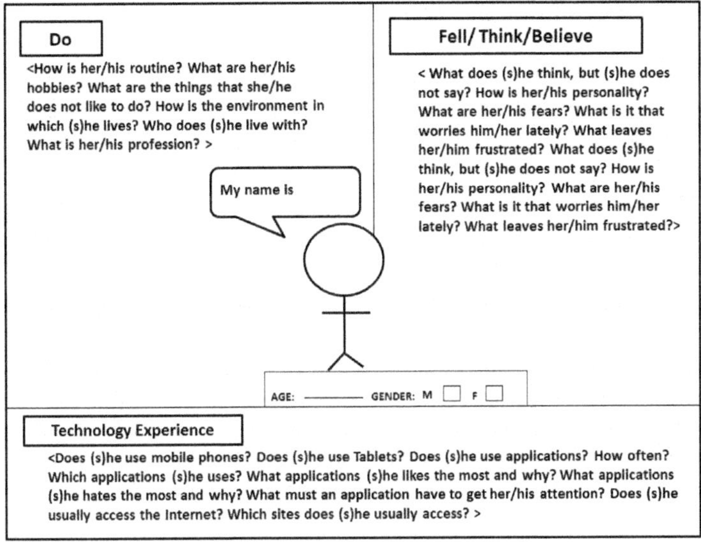

Fig. 2. First part of the PATHYs' template

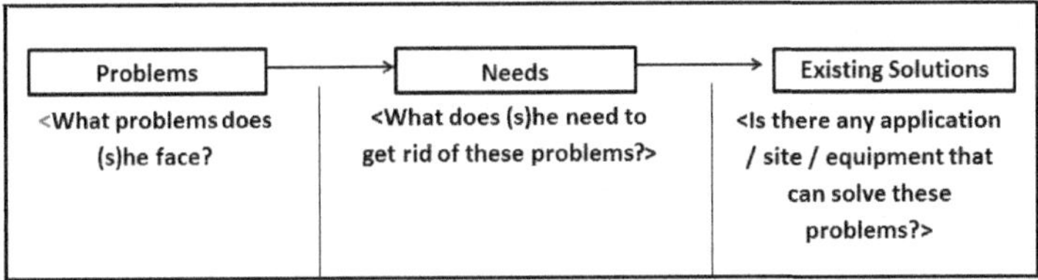

Fig. 3. Second part of the PATHYs' template

- **Do:** the characteristics of the persona's routine, including his hobbies, relevant aspects of the environment in which he lives and a description of the people with whom he lives.
- **Feel/Think/Believe:** subjective characteristics of the persona, including his ideas, aspects of his personality, his fears, and frustrations.
- **Experience with Technology:** the experiences that the persona had with other technologies, as well as application characteristics that please and displease the persona. The goal of this field is to get a better understanding of the user's preferences.
- **Problems:** the problems the persona faces, which can be resolved by the application being designed. The goal of this field is to get a better understanding of the user's problems.
- **Needs:** what is needed to solve the problems described in the previous field.
- **Existing Solutions:** existing solutions to solve the problems, as well as ideas to improve them or to include them in the application to be designed.

4 Designing Personas Using PATHY

In order to evaluate PATHY, we conducted an empirical study to determine the participants' perception about the usefulness and ease of use of the technique. During this study, we applied PATHY to generate personas and to identify the applications requirements from the information in the personas. The study was carried out with 23 third-year Computer Science students. They had already taken classes on Human-Computer Interaction (HCI) and Software Engineering and had designed and developed more than one application.

The study was carried out in two parts. First, the participants created personas based on the textual description provided. Second, the participants formed groups of four people. Each group should write the description of an application that they would like to develop. After choosing the application, the participants had one 1-hour lesson on how to use the PATHY technique. Furthermore, examples of how to use the technique were presented. Each group created the persona for their previously chosen application. Table 1 presents examples of some characteristics filled in the fields of the PATHY template regarding two applications chosen by the participants. One application is to denounce pedophilia. The second application is to help people solve mechanical car problems.

In this study, we used the factors defined within the Technology Acceptance Model (TAM) [5] to investigate the participants' perception of the PATHY technique. The TAM model is based on two factors [13]:

- *Perceived Usefulness*, defined as 'the degree to which a person believes that using a particular technology would improve their job performance';
- *Perceived Ease of use*, defined as 'the degree to which a person believes that using a particular technology would be free of effort' [13].

On the questionnaire we employed a six-point scale with the items: totally agree, strongly agree, partially agree, partially disagree, strongly disagree and totally disagree. We did not use an intermediate level as suggested by Laitenberger and Dreyer [13], since this neutral level does not provide information regarding the side to which the participants are inclined (either positive or negative).

Besides the items regarding usefulness and ease of use of PATHY, to which the participants had to indicate their degree of agreement, we added the following three questions to the questionnaire to obtain some qualitative feedback:

- If you had to use personas again, would you choose the textual description or the PATHY technique? Why?
- What aspects of the PATHY technique do you consider positive?
- What aspects of the PATHY technique do you consider negative?

Table 1. Examples of filled-in PATHY fields

Field	Persona 1 (denouncing pedophilia)	Persona 2 (car problems)
Do	'I live with my husband and my two children: one is 7 years old and the other one is 9 years old.'	'I am a college student; I study psychology at night and work during the day. I just bought my first car and I do not quite understand how it works.'
Feel/think/ believes	'Violence is increasing in our days, which is what worries me. I'm afraid that something might happen to my family.'	'Because I am new in town and I do not understand the car mechanics I feel afraid to hire an unreliable mechanical service.'
Technology experience	'I use a smartphone as a tool' 'I use applications to support communication (e.g. whatsapp)'	'I make frequent use of the phone.' 'I like applications that facilitate my daily life'
Problems	'I worry about what my children access on the Internet.' 'I am concerned with who my children, who are minors, are chatting with on the internet.'	'She doesn't know where the places in the city are.' 'She has no ability to solve mechanical problems.'
Needs	'Identifying the content of the conversations in order to prevent pedophilia.' 'Monitor the child's behavior on the web'	'Find someone of trust to solve her problem.' 'Having qualified help available to meet her at the location of an unexpected problem/accident.'
Existing solutions	'There is a site in England that tracks pedophiles surfing the internet.'	'Google maps' 'Foursquare' 'Ask acquaintances'

5 Results

5.1 Quantitative Analysis

For the analysis of the quantitative results, we considered the participants' answers regarding the empathy map on usefulness and ease of use. Table 2 shows the answers to each statement related to the perceived usefulness of the PATHY. The statements were 'Using PATHY would…'

- U1 enable me to create Personas more quickly.
- U2 improve my performance when creating personas.
- U3 increase my productivity when creating personas.
- U4 enhance my effectiveness when creating personas.
- U5 make it easier to create personas.
- U6 be useful for creating personas in my projects.

Table 2. Number of participants who agreed or disagreed with each statement related to the perceived usefulness, together with a sample quotation

Item	Disagree	Agree	Quotation
U1	2	21	*'The need to incorporate a persona makes the process very subjective and time consuming.'* – P15
U2	0	23	*'The performance has greatly improved due to the fact that there are guides on how to fill out the template.'* – P09
U3	0	23	*'The process was more quickly and productive.'* – P10
U4	0	23	*'With PATHY the persona was richer in details.'* – P05
U5	1	22	*'(...) It has many fields with details'* – P16
U6	1	22	*'PATHY helps me get useful information (...)'* – P13

The results regarding usefulness showed that most of the participants considered PATHY useful for creating Personas. Table 3 shows the answers regarding the perceived ease of use of the PATHY technique. The statements were:

- E1 Learning how to use the PATHY would be easy for me.
- E2 I understood what I had to provide in every part of PATHY.
- E3 It is easy to remember how to create personas using PATHY.
- E4 Using PATHY it was easy to create the persona that I wanted.
- E5 It was easy to become skillful in creating personas using PATHY.
- E6 I find PATHY easy to use.

5.2 Qualitative Analysis

We have also conducted a qualitative analysis of the participants' textual answers. Qualitative methods support a better comprehension of the issues that need a more specific and detailed analysis, allowing the researcher to consider human behavior and thoroughly understand the studied object [19]. The qualitative analysis performed in this work is based on procedures from Grounded Theory, namely *coding*, i.e., the process of assigning meaning to the data [21].

While we analyzed the data contained within the questionnaire, we created codes associated with text fragments. Another researcher reviewed the codes related with the citations in each questionnaire transcription. This researcher verified the codes and categories in order to audit the coding process and therefore to mitigate the bias eventually caused by the participation of a single researcher in the coding process.

After the open coding, we initiated the axial coding phase, creating relationship codes. We identified three main groupings: (a) Ease of use of PATHY; (b) Benefit for the creation of Personas by using PATHY; and (c) PATHY's limitations. Table 4 shows the codes regarding ease of use and benefits of use of the PATHY technique.

Through the qualitative analysis, we identified that the technique helps to:

- understand what should be designed (see quotation from P04 and P03 below);

  '(...) it makes it easy to elicit the features that can be used in the software.' – P04

Table 3. Number of participants who agreed or disagreed with each statement related to the perceived ease of use, together with a sample quotation

Item	Disagree	Agree	Quotation
E1	0	23	*'(...) it is easy to learn how to use it.'* – P23
E2	1	22	*'it is more simple to understand the filled fields (...)'* – P09
E3	1	22	The participant who disagreed did not explain why.
E4	1	22	The participant who disagreed did not explain why.
E5	1	22	The participant who disagreed did not explain why.
E6	0	23	*'I could understand how to use it in a short time and is very simple and easy to use.'* – P18

Table 4. Comments about Ease of Use and Benefits of use

Group	Quotations
Ease of use	It is easy to learn how to use PATHY: *'PATHY has practical ways to create personas; it is also easy to learn how to use it.'* – P23
	It is easy to fill out: *'Fields are simple to understand, that is why there is an improvement in the efficiency'* – P09
	The approach is simple: *'The approach is simple and has a broad scope (needs, existing products, experiences that he already has)'* – P17
	The guiding questions are easy to understand: *'The guides/guidelines are easy to understand, in simple language.'* – P18
Benefit of use	It helps to create persona more accurately: *'The persona was created quickly and accurately.'* – P13
	It helps to create personas with richer details: *'With PATHY the persona becomes richer in detail'* – P05
	It helps to think about the users' needs: *'(...) All the guide questions helped identifying the real needs of the target user of the application.'* – P07
	It helps to think about the subjective characteristics of the persona: *'(...) With the technique I was able to describe the persona in several situations, as well as his states of mind and humor.'* – P03

'(..)Description of problems/needs and solutions, it is essential to better understand what needs to be designed.' – P03

- think in the important characteristics for the application (see quotation from P18 and P12 below). This is a very relevant result, once PATHY's main aim is to help designers describe personas according to the desired features for the software.

  'I found many other things that our app can do, beyond what was proposed before.' – P18

  'Somehow it makes you focus on the important features for application.' – P12

The discovery of relevant characteristics can help in the design of an application that meets the users' needs. Since this was the motivation for proposing PATHY, we carried on an additional analysis aiming at discovering which characteristics for the software applications were identified using the technique. Table 5 presents the features

Table 5. Identified characteristics for the applications

Application description	Identified characteristics
To hitch a ride	Option to request ride Option to call a taxi
To combine sounds and create ring tone	Application should be quick and simple List the audio files that are on mobile
To control calories	Indicate places where the diet products are sold Indicate the prices of diet products

described in the PATHY's template for the different software applications. These features formed the basis for some requirements of the software applications.

In addition to helping to identify application characteristics, PATHY helps to think about similar characteristics in other applications. These characteristics were collected in the field "Existing Solutions". Table 6 presents some examples of characteristics of other applications that can be improved or reused on the application to be designed.

Table 6. Identified similar characteristics of other applications

Application description	Similar characteristics
To hitch a ride	There are applications that inform bus routes in the city.
To combine sounds and create music	There is similar software for creating music but there is not a mobile version.
To control calories	There is an application that shows restaurants but does not show the nutritional information of the dishes served.

From the qualitative analysis, we identified some limitations in the technique:

- <u>The choice of the technique depends on the type of project</u>: '*(...) I consider that the variety of elicited details provides a broad view. On the other hand, this variety may not be useful, depending on the scope of the application.*' – P04
- <u>It does not show relationships between the persona and environment</u>: '*the relationship between the persona and its environment/society is missing*' – *P03*
- <u>It limits the description of the persona</u>: '*(...) sometimes it limits the designer because he only follows the guidelines set in the form.*' – P18

Despite P18's opinion that PATHY restricts the description of the persona, some participants stated the contrary, i.e., the technique helps create a more detailed persona:

'(...) it has, in detail, all the necessary information that helps me develop the personas for my project.' – P14

Furthermore, the technique was also described as broad:

'The description was more consistent and broad.' – P10

To overcome those limitations and improve the technique, we propose the following:

- **Scenario Integration**: In addition to describing the persona and the characteristics of the application, the designers will be able to describe a scenario representing the context of use of the application.
- **Fields Choice**: From the description of the fields, the designer can choose which fields he wants to use in order to make the description of the persona. The fields can be chosen according to the needs of each project.

In this section, we noted that the qualitative research helped us identify the categories and relationships of factors that influence the use of PATHY. Furthermore, we also identified limitations that can help us to improve the technique in the future.

6 Conclusions

This paper proposed PATHY, a novel technique for creating personas. The proposed technique is based on Empathy Maps. The technique aims not only at describing the personas characteristics, but also at providing the designer with an overview of the features that the application should have. In this way, the designer can think of the application characteristics according to the identified users' needs.

To verify the perception of the participants regarding the use of PATHY for the creation of personas, we conducted an empirical study, in which the participants used PATHY to create personas of an application to be designed. After using the technique, the participants answered a questionnaire to evaluate their perception about the usefulness and the ease of use of the technique, as well as their intention to use it, together with positive and negative features of the technique.

The study showed that the PATHY technique was considered easy to use and useful. Our next steps involve evaluating the revised version of PATHY with professional software developers.

Acknowledgment. We thank all the students who participated in the empirical study. And we would like to acknowledge the financial support granted by CAPES (Coordination for the Improvement of Higher Education Personnel); the financial support granted by FAPEAM (Foundation for Research Support of the Amazonas State) through processes numbers: 062.00600/2014; 062.00578/2014; CNPq processes 309828/2015-5, 453996/2014-0, 460627/2014-7; and CAPES process 175956/2013.

References

1. Adikari, S., McDonald, C., Campbell, J.: Reframed contexts: design thinking for agile user experience design. In: Marcus, A. (ed.) DUXU 2013, Part I. LNCS, vol. 8012, pp. 3–12. Springer, Heidelberg (2013)
2. Bratsberg, H.M.: Empathy maps of the FourSight preferences. In: Creative Studies Graduate Student Master's Project. Buffalo State College. Paper 176 (2012)

3. Castro, J.W., Acuña, S.T., Juristo, N.: Enriching requirements analysis with the personas technique. In: Proceedings of the International Workshop on: Interplay Between Usability Evaluation and Software Development (I-USED 2008), pp. 13–18 (2008)
4. Cooper, A.: The Inmates are Running the Asylum: Why High-Tech Products Drive us Crazy and How to Restore the Sanity. Sams Publishers, Indianapolis (1999)
5. Davis, F.: Perceived usefulness, perceived ease of use, and user acceptance of information technology. MIS Q. **13**(3), 319–339 (1989)
6. Faily, S., Fléchais, I.: Finding and resolving security misusability with misusability cases. J. Requirements Eng. **21**(80), 1–15 (2014)
7. Faily, S., Fléchais, I.: Persona cases: a technique for grounding personas. In: Proceedings of the SIGCHI Conference on Human Factors in Computing Systems, pp. 2267–2270. ACM (2011)
8. Ferreira, B.M., Silva, W.A.F., Oliveira, E., Conte, T.U.: Designing personas with empathy map. In: 27th International Conference on Software Engineering and Knowledge Engineering (SEKE 2015), Pittsburgh, vol. 1. pp. 501–506 (2015)
9. Gray, D., Brown, S., Macanufo, J.: Gamestorming – A playbook for innovators, rulebreakers and changemakers. O'Reilly Media, Inc., Sebastopol (2010)
10. Grudin, J., Pruitt, J.: Personas, participatory design and product development: an infrastructure for engagement. In: PDC 2002, pp. 144–152 (2002)
11. ISO DIS 9241-210:2010. Ergonomics of human system interaction - Part 210: Human-centred design for interactive systems (formerly known as 13407). International Standardization Organization (ISO)
12. Javahery, H., Ahmed, S.: P2P mapper: from user experiences to pattern-based design. AIS Trans. Hum. Comput. Interact. **4**(2), 107–128 (2012)
13. Laitenberger, O., Dreyer, H.M.: Evaluating the usefulness and the ease of use of a web-based section data collection tool. In: Proceedings of the 5th International Symposium on Software Metrics, pp. 122–132 (1998)
14. Law, E.L.C., Abrahão, S., Vermeeren, A.P., Hvannberg, E.T.: Interplay between user experience evaluation and system development: state of the art. In: International Workshop on the Interplay between UX Evaluation and System Development, pp. 14–17 (2012)
15. Mashapa, J., Chelule, E., Van Greunen, D., Veldsman, A.: Managing user experience – managing change. In: Kotzé, P., Marsden, G., Lindgaard, G., Wesson, J., Winckler, M. (eds.) INTERACT 2013, Part II. LNCS, vol. 8118, pp. 660–677. Springer, Heidelberg (2013)
16. Nielsen, L., Nielsen, K.S., Stage, J., Billestrup, J.: Going global with personas. In: Kotzé, P., Marsden, G., Lindgaard, G., Wesson, J., Winckler, M. (eds.) INTERACT 2013, Part IV. LNCS, vol. 8120, pp. 350–357. Springer, Heidelberg (2013)
17. Osterwalder, A., Pigneur, Y.: Business Model Generation. Alta Books Editora, Rio de Janeiro (2013)
18. Pruitt, J., Adlin, T.: The Persona Lifecycle: Keeping People in Mind Throughout the Product Design. Morgan Kaufman, San Francisco (2006)
19. Seaman, C.B.: Qualitative methods. In: Shull, F., Singer, J., Sjøberg, D.I.K. (eds.) Guide to Advanced Empirical Software Engineering, pp. 35–62. Springer, Heidelberg (2008)
20. Sproll, S., Peissner, M., Sturm, C.: From product concept to user experience: exploring UX potentials at early product stages. In: Proceedings of the 6th Nordic Conference on Human-Computer Interaction: Extending Boundaries, pp. 473–482. ACM (2010)
21. Strauss, A., Corbin, J.: Basics of Qualitative Research: Techniques and Procedures for Developing Grounded Theory. SAGE publications, Thousand Oaks (1998)

22. Vermeeren, A.P., Law, E.L.C., Roto, V., Obrist, M., Hoonhout, J., Väänänen-Vainio-Mattila, K.: User experience evaluation methods: current state and development needs. In: Proceedings of the 6th Nordic Conference on Human-Computer Interaction: Extending Boundaries, pp. 521–530. ACM (2010)
23. Väänänen-Vainio-Mattila, K., Roto, V., Hassenzahl, M.: Towards practical user experience evaluation methods. In: Law, E.L.C., Bevan, N., Christou, G., Springett, M., Lárusdóttir, M., (eds.) Meaningful Measures: Valid Useful User Experience Measurement (VUUM), pp. 19–22 (2008)

Designing Functional Specifications for Complex Systems

Olga Goubali[1,2(✉)], Patrick Girard[1], Laurent Guittet[1], Alain Bignon[2], Djamal Kesraoui[2], Pascal Berruet[3], and Jean-Frédéric Bouillon[4]

[1] LIAS/ENSMA, 1 avenue Clément Ader, 86961 Chasseneuil, France
{Olga.goubali,girard,laurent.guittet}@ensma.fr
[2] SEGULA Technologies, BP 50256, 56602 Lanester cedex, France
{alain.bignon,djamal.kesraoui}@segula.fr
[3] Lab-STICC, BP 92116, 56321 Lorient cedex, France
pascal.berruet@univ-ubs.fr
[4] ENSM, 38 rue Gabriel Péri, 44100 Nantes, France
Jean-frederic.bouillon@supmaritime.fr

Abstract. For designing complex and sociotechnical (System that strongly interact with humans (e.g., a ship is a large sociotechnical system).) systems, designers are in charge of the functional specification because they have an operational expert knowledge. However, these experts do not usually master the programming knowledge of those who design supervision systems. Complex and sociotechnical systems include supervision systems which comprise monitoring interfaces and associated control codes. In this paper we propose an approach that facilitates functional specification of supervision systems. This approach aims at exploiting Example Based Programming (EBP) to propose a specification tool, which contains a generalization module and an interface generation module. Our tool allows experts who are acting as non-professional software developers to describe high level system functional services from elementary services. These functional services contain elementary interactions and configuration data. Thus, the expert, involved in coding, avoids a lot of errors related to the interpretation of the functional specifications. Our aim is to capture expert knowledge on the system being designed in order to have verified and validated functional specifications, without having to train experts in formal methods.

Keywords: Industrial supervision · Functional specification · Example based programming · Model driven engineering

1 Introduction

Since the 80's, the V-model [21] has become the industry standard designing model. However, it is sometimes difficult to strictly implement this model especially when there are significant changes in specifications, for example new features added by the customer in an advanced project phase. There is a high risk that these changes will affect the system so that it no longer matches the initial requirements as they progress over time. Moreover, it is during the coding phase one often realizes that initial specifications were incomplete, inconsistent, false or unfeasible. The late identification of these defects affects development costs and application evolution.

M. Kurosu (Ed.): HCI 2016, Part I, LNCS 9731, pp. 166–177, 2016.
DOI: 10.1007/978-3-319-39510-4_16

Other approaches such as agile software development methods are proposed to facilitate changes of the initial design. The word "agile" refers to the ability to adapt to changes in contexts and in specifications that might occur during the development process. However, agile software development is mostly used by small teams, adding value to direct communication in a changing environments. Thus these practices are not suitable for all contexts [20].

In the context of large-scale projects such as the design of sociotechnical and complex systems, the number of stakeholders and the diversity of required expertise lead to overall consistency problems and specification misinterpretation. Indeed, errors from misunderstandings are only detected during the system testing phase. In fact, 79 % of failures come from design and implementation services [28], while 72 % of failures are only detected during operational testing [26].

Mixing together Model Driven Engineering (MDE) and the component approach has helped to overcome these problems. This approach aims at raising programming activity abstraction level by using models at the very beginning of the software development process. It introduces models, metamodels and transformations notions as well as representation, "conformity" and "based on" relationships. These terms are detailed in [25]. As for the component approach, it improves the transmission of knowledge through libraries or collections [4]. These two approaches are supported by our Anaxagore tool [4, 12] that enables to automatically generate applications corresponding to a business model, from standard elements libraries and business models. To validate the combination of both approaches, Anaxagore was applied to a concrete case.

The chosen example is a system for the production, storage and distribution of fresh water, onboard a ship, called EdS (Eau douce Sanitaire *in English Sanitary freshwater*). To date, Anaxagore enables to generate a control code and a monitoring interface for this system. The generated monitoring interface only allows basic commands such as "Open" or "Close" a valve. Elaborating high-level functions from this interface leads to element-by-element interactions between the system and the user. Controlling such a system onboard requires triggers (widgets) for high-level control and monitoring, allowing functions to be run more easily. To implement these widgets, we need to describe functional specifications. These specifications are user's sequences of actions on the system, required for performing functions taking into account all possibilities (configurations). The task of the expert in system design is to define these functional specifications. S/he writes these latter in natural language, and then provides them to the designers of the supervision interface and the control-command code. The designers' job is to implement and integrate these specifications into the system. Specification interpretation errors come from the difference of technical knowledge between prescribers (mechanic engineers) and designers (computer system engineers and/or control-command engineers).

We propose in this article a specification tool that facilitates functional specification and automatically generates the widgets for high level functions of complex and sociotechnical systems. To validate our proposition, we evaluate the usability of the system with expert users. Results are analyzed and detailed in this paper.

2 State of the Art

Designing widgets for high-level control and monitoring leads to implement control code and function interfaces. These implementations are based on functional specifications and come to be tedious depending on the complexity of the system. Some works propose automatic generation of the control code, and others, automatic generation of the user interface. Various approaches used for generating control code are surveyed in [5]. Despite their many advantages, these approaches are inadequate for the control laws used to design industrial monitoring for embedded systems on ships. In fact, the generated control code needs to be transformed into normalized language before used in design phase.

In recent years, several works have explored the idea of automatically generating user interface from detailed models of program functionalities, user knowledge, presentation environment etc. This simplified the user interface implementation process by integrating it with the implementation of application logic. Systems proposed by these works came to be known as model-based systems and are surveyed in [23]. The common property of all these systems is that the user interface is automatically generated from a specification. In the literature, several works has been focused on automatic user interface generation from abstract specification. Some model-based systems such as ERGO-CONCEPTOR [22] enable graphical views specification based on detailed description of the appliance. However, this description is tedious and prone to interrogations and omissions. The performance of system degrades as the complexity of user interfaces increases. Other models such as Jade or PUC include no specific detail about graphical references, which keeps each specification small [23]. The generated user interface is rarely sufficient for the entire application because the works focusses on only one aspect of the system design. To address this, for example, ERGO-CONCEPTOR+ [22] combines the knowledge-based system with the formal specification of the application.

Most of the time, describing requirements in natural language to establish specifications is the first step in the development of embedded systems. Specification is a communication base between customers and design teams [7]. Specification documents should be as explicit as possible because they are the reference point for designers of system functional axis [13]. A good functional specification must be correct, unambiguous, complete and consistent. Some formal or semi-formal methods have been proposed to help with respect to these properties.

Formal methods enable expression of specifications with notations and semantics based on mathematical concepts. Baresi gives a survey of formal notations [2], models and techniques for specifying user interface and a lot of researches was published [9, 13]. Formal or semi-formal methods are known for analyzing and validating the specifications, so that the interpretation errors are limited. However, in some industrial sectors, such as shipbuilding, specifications are typically written in natural language [30] as designers of specifications do not have the required technical knowledge for using other languages. Although there are defects detection techniques in the specifications [10], they require a lot of efforts and do not necessarily detect all defects. Despite the use of some of these techniques, undetected errors are still found in specification documents [29].

Usually, the design of control and monitoring applications is difficult because many errors in applications can be traced to defects in their specifications. A main aspect of user-interface development is the specification of exactly what the user interface has to do. The automatic interfaces generation is a difficult problem because it requires to determine what abstract application specification is needed, how to formalize specifications and to build an interface generator that can design usable interface from those abstract specifications.

In our case, the business model can be considered as low level formal specification because it is a standardized structuro-functional diagram which is used systematically and earlier in the project, and follows system designing lifecycle [4]. However, this specification is not enough to implement high-level application functions. To generate a high-level application, it is important to know what functional information about the application is necessary to create a usable interface. Business experts have this knowledge about applications but they do not have any training to express them in formal languages. They can only describe them in natural language by using business model. The issue is how can we help them to express the specification correctly?

Our goal is therefore to facilitate functional specification of complex systems by proposing a tool that enables business expert without training in programming to create program for system specification using a suitable interface.

3 Proposition

In interactive system design, the functional specification phase is preceded by task analysis. Functional specifications contain a list of the major system functions (high-level requirements) and scenarios of operations. They describe what the system needs to do, from all of its user's viewpoints. However, the clear expression of needs and requirements, and their translation into functional specifications are not easy tasks, despite the importance of the latter step in the design phase [17]. Task analysis enables to have a set of functional requirements expressed by the designer that can be used in design approaches but this model does not avoid errors related to the interpretation of the functional specifications. We define a process for obtaining specifications by using an original approach based on task models and the paradigm of Example Based Programming (EBP) [19].

Expression of functional requirements by the designer follows an iterative process which first step is the formalization of functional specifications. This formulation is based firstly on a review and analysis of the literature [1], and secondly on lessons learnt by analyzing specifications established in past real projects and by interviewing design experts. This formalization helps to identify the necessary information in specifications and which must therefore be expressed by the designer for designing task models.

EBP is an extension of the concept of macro recorders, which allows users to record and replay sequences of actions. However, replaying macros is reduced only to replaying the recorded actions, whereas in the case of EBP, the system provides a generalization of recorded actions to generate actual programs. Systems including EBP techniques record, generalize and replay user's actions through specific interfaces that keep the functional aim of the application. Therefore, EBP systems allow non-computer scientists/engineers to build programs. EBP techniques enable users to automate repetitive tasks [11], to adapt an application to their specific needs [8] and to integrate applications for developing a solution made to measure [27]. Systems including EBP techniques record, generalize and replay user's actions. An EBP system must provide specific interfaces that can naturally integrate EBP techniques while maintaining the functional goal of the application. A detailed state of the art of this paradigm [19] shows that its implementation takes place in three phases. A first phase of recording enables the designer to specify the behavior expected by the system interactively by using an interface template of the monitoring system. Then, the system creates generalized programs and configurations from the recorded actions. The generalization remains a central and complex problem of EBP. Although various generalization techniques exist, they are not suited to the generalization of configurations in the designing of industrial complex monitoring systems. For example, designing the base of knowledge to use inference methods to generalize configurations can be a time consuming task. The generalization configuration application proposed here is based on graph theory. Firstly the use of a combination of algorithms enables to propose the user with all possible paths that a system can use to achieve the functional purpose requested. These possible paths are validated by business experts, then we combined them using a solver and a configuration algorithm. The goal is to provide an exhaustive list of possible configurations to run the specified functions. A last phase of replay enables the designer to validate the generalized functions.

The described process is then implemented through a proof of concept, which is a specification tool that consists of a specification interface, a generalization module based on graph theory and a module for interface functions generation that exploits the task model data. Figure 1 describes this process in detail with its phases. During the first phase, the expert uses the specification interface to demonstrate examples of sequences execution for all functions (examples of functional specifications). Two types of generalizations are made during the second phase: the generalization of programs and the generalization of configurations. The third phase enables the use of generalized configurations and tasks models to provide interface models for launching the system functions. The generated possible

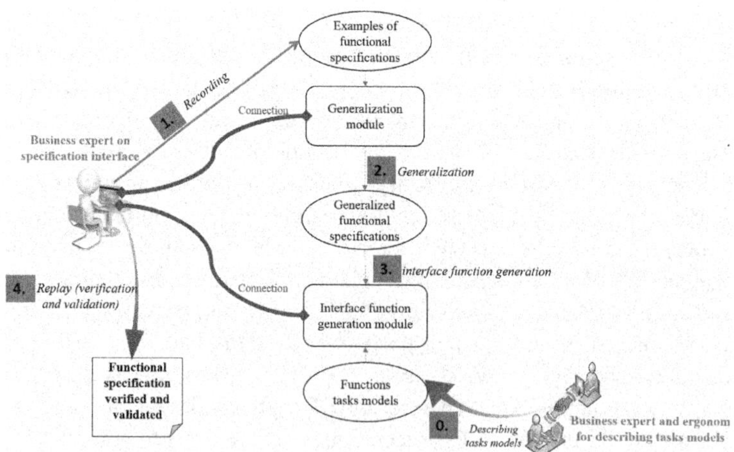

Fig. 1. Specification tool

configurations and functions interface models must then be verified and validated by the expert, in the last phase (4. Replay: verification and validation).

The specification interface is well-known by the expert and integrates the described techniques. This interface has been used for specifying functions of the EdS system taken as example here.

4 Case Study

For our case study, 7 functions need to be specified (transfer, treatment, embedded distribution, distribution from quay, production, loading and unloading) and this implies the description of a total of 73 unit configurations. In fact, given the architecture of the system, each function can be performed according to several configurations. Furthermore these configurations do not take into account the possibility of performing several functions simultaneously. The expert's task is to define these 73 functional specifications as well as simultaneous executions. S/He provides them to the designers of the supervision interface and the control-command code. The designer's job is then to implement and integrate these specifications into the system.

Figure 2 shows an extract of the business model (synoptic diagram) of the considered system. The described system is composed of several elements: tanks, 2-ways valves, water pumps, 3-ways valves, and a chlorination module for water treatment, respectively numbered from 1 to 5. For example, we can consider the function that can transfer water from a tank (St1) to another (St2) via one of the pumps (H1, H2 or H3). Each pump is isolated from the tank St1 by 2-ways valves (V2VM03, V2VM05 and V2VM07). The water transferred is sent to the tank St2 via 3-ways valves (V3VM01, V3VM02 and V3VM03), the chlorination module (TRCH) and V2VM02 valve. The implementation of this function requires the definition of sequences of actions made by the user on the circuit for achieving the function. These are the "functional specifications".

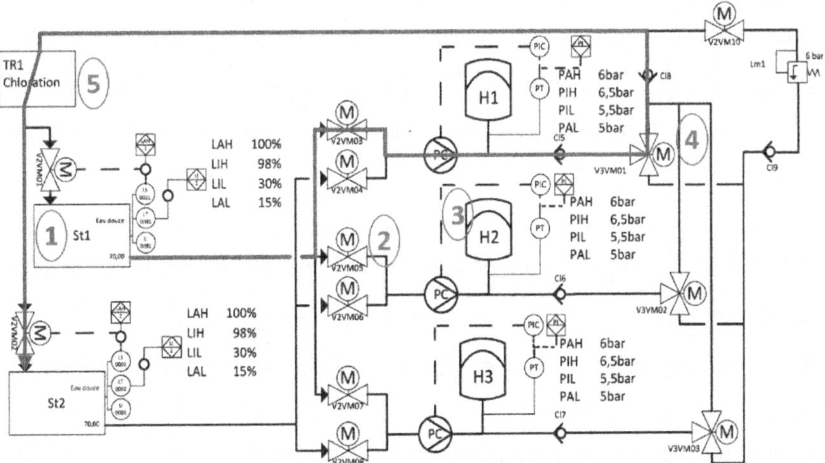

Fig. 2. A function on an extract of synoptic diagram of EdS system

The proposed solution aims at offering the opportunity to the expert to express the functional specifications through an interface that contains elements of the system and integrates EBP techniques.

To test the feasibility of our approach we applied it to the specification of EdS' system functions. The design of the specification interface (Fig. 3) is based on a recorder/replaying (RR) generic model adapted with information from task models, and on graphical views of system components to design, as stored in the standard elements library of Anaxagore.

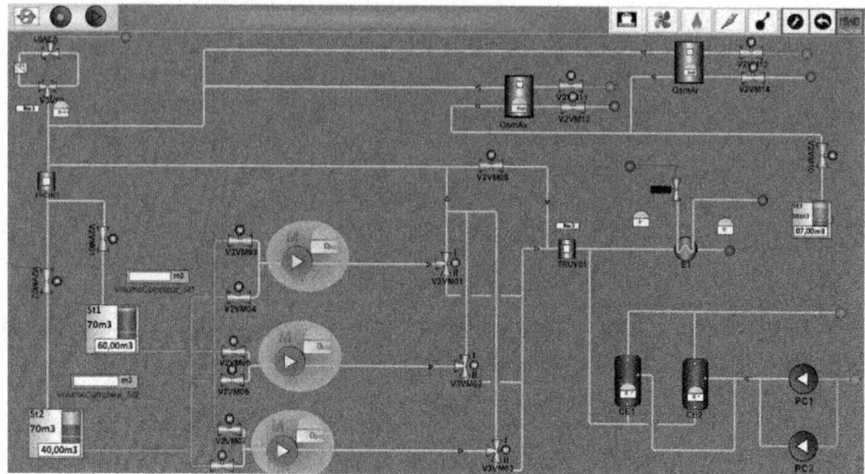

Fig. 3. Specification interface designed for EdS system

4.1 A Recording Model for Specification Interface

EBP techniques (recording, generalization and replay) are implemented through a RR (Recorder Replaying) model present on specification interface. This model is designed with Panorama E2 SCADA software [12] in the form of views. These views show the recorder and the replaying commands (at the top left of Fig. 3).

The recorder command put the system into recording mode and memorize all the expert's actions. It is used for recording examples of sequences of execution for all functions. The system generalizes the recorded examples to generate an executable program in a different context. The replaying command can then replay the recorded examples and their variants. The generic nature of this model allows its integration into any monitoring system. However, setting the adequate parameters is required with the information from the task models of the system to conceive.

4.2 Using the Specification Interface for Describing Functional Specifications

Obtaining functional specifications of a system from the implemented specification interface follows the three steps of EBP: recording, generalization and replay. During the recording step, the system records the whole sequence of actions made by the expert and the state of the elements manipulated to perform the functions. For it to be generalized, two examples must be recorded. A generalization system, integrated to the specification interface, uses these two examples to produce a generic program and all other possible configurations for the function. Verification and validation of these configurations has to be performed during the replaying phase. Validated configurations and generic programs are then used to generate the monitoring interface and the control-command code that contain high-level system functions.

The implementation of the interface specification enabled us to validate our approach of using EBP to describe functional specifications of a system. To validate the proposed interface, we have evaluated the usability of the system with real users to identify required modifications, to verify our choice a posteriori, to analyze behavioral data, critics and feedbacks on the interface and to involve users (system designers) who have an expert knowledge of the system in designing the specification interface.

5 Evaluation

The evaluation method used is semi-structured interviews, aimed to collect specific and qualitative information. This technique is often used for conducting exploratory studies to improve knowledge of a field of study which main themes are familiar to experts but present aspects requiring in-depth study.

The semi-structured interview was centered on the theme of the functional specification of complex systems. The interview guide used for our experiment is articulated around questions related to three main themes. They have been defined on one hand with respect to the knowledge that we had and wanted to acquire about the subject and on the other hand with respect to the use and the improvement of our tool. The experimental protocol and results analysis are described in this section.

5.1 The Protocol

The experiment took place with 5 participants at ENSM[1], all with navigation experience and functional knowledge of the involved type of systems. The equipment used for the experiment included a 23-inch screen to display the specification interface, a mouse and a keyboard. First, the synoptic diagram of the EdS system was presented and explained to them. To verify that they have a good knowledge of this kind of system, it was asked them to verbally describe the diagram (what is this diagram, how it works…). They were also asked to describe the steps to achieve the Transfer from a tank to another, using the same diagram. Next, we simulated with them task models (two task models describe how to achieve the transfer with and without high-level command) through the Prototask tool [18]. The objective of this part of the test was to check whether the method used to define (specify) the transfer function, and then to launch (in use) is correct. Participants were trained for about 15 min with the use of the specification interface (the part of the interface they do not know); then they were required to use this interface to specify the

[1] ENSM: École Nationale Supérieure Maritime – French Maritime College.

"Transfer" function they had previously described verbally. Finally, when they had finished using the interface, they answered a questionnaire that enabled us to get their feedback in order to improve the interface.

5.2 Presentation and Interpretation of Results

Semi-structured interviews enabled participants to give their perceptions of functional specification process. Most often, their remarks were general and not necessarily specific to the application case; this allowed us to obtain a general feedback on the functional specification approach. Describing and analyzing of the transcripts of the voice recordings during the experiment gave us an initial response. The described tasks for performing transfer by using a command were all validated unanimously. We were able to verify compliance of task models which were used in specification interface designing. The various steps proposed in the interface to achieve the specification of a function have been validated. For each step, a widget is proposed to begin the actions. Each widget is named according to the expert tasks at the phase. The action intuitiveness related to the employed themes for the tasks of each phase is summarized in Fig. 4.

On a scale of 1 to 10, with 1 for "very easy" to 10 for "very complicated", the difficulty of using the specification interface is 4. All participants reported that the use of interface became much easier after specifying the first function.

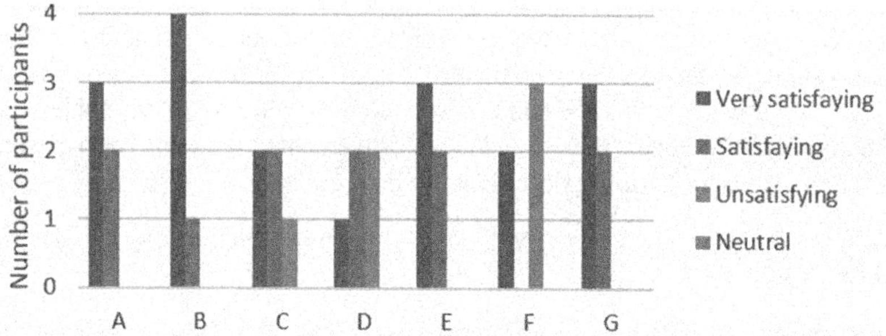

Legend (matching the steps of the function recording approach): **A**: Recording of specifications; **B**: Selecting of origin/destination; **C**: Designation of required passage point; **D**: Grid configuration; **E**: Specifying of end conditions; **F**: Stopping of grid elements; **G**: end of recording specifications

Fig. 4. Evaluation of widgets

The analysis of the experimental results enabled to confirm that our approach is an original solution welcomed by all participants. The use of the interface has been more or less intuitive for all. To complete our analysis, ergonomic expertise was carried out based on the Jacob Nielsen's ten heuristic principles [24] and the criteria of Bastien and Scapin [3]. The information from this analysis will be used to improve the interface and make it more intuitive for the user. Then, the specification interface will be submitted to more stringent tests based on a SUS (System Usability Scale) questionnaire.

6 Conclusion and Future Work

The presented work provides additional support in the process of a system functional specification. Our goal is to reduce specifications effort while getting verified and validated functional specifications through an interface familiar to designers. The introduction of EBP techniques in a specification tool empowers the expert to express functional specifications of the system s/he is designing by simple clicks on an interface; in the same way s/he would describe the system verbally.

The use of this interface by experts in design, but not in software development, solves communication and interpretation problems, which can significantly reduce functional specification design time of a system, hence the project timeline and costs. However, designing specification interface can be time consuming depending on the complexity of system. Current works aim at reducing this design effort by offering methods and tools to automatically generate the specification interface.

Although the specification interface has not yet been generated, its implementation has enabled us to validate our approach of using EBP for describing functional specification of a system. Usability (ISO 9241-11 and ISO-13407) of the specification tool was demonstrated during the semi-structured interviews with users.

In future work, the various defined models will be used to generate the specification interface. From the business model previously used, the library, tasks models and a RR model, information association methods and derivation models will enable to generate gradually, in addition to existing models, the specification interface. Specification interface generation will follow the same steps as those of the low-level interface [4]. We define a design flow based on the principles of MDE, which will enable us to implement our entire approach to generate operational models. The enhanced specification interface with tests results and ergonomic expertise, as well as high level interface generated from these specifications will be evaluated.

Acknowledgements. We would like to thank teachers of the ENSM for their participation. We are grateful to Eric Le Bris, Line Poinel and Davy Rodier for their help.

References

1. AFNOR NF X50-151, Management par la valeur et ses outils, analyse fonctionnelle, analyse de la valeur, conception a objectif designe. French National Standards
2. Baresi, L., Orso, A., Pezzè, M.: Introducing formal specification methods in industrial practice. In: Proceedings of the 19th International Conference on Software Engineering, pp. 56–66. ACM, May 1997
3. Bastien, J.M.C., Scapin, D.: Ergonomic Criteria for the Evaluation of Human-Computer interfaces. Institut National de recherche en informatique et en automatique, France (1993)
4. Bignon, A., Rossi, A., Berruet, P.: An integrated design flow for the joint generation of control and interfaces from a business model. Comput. Ind. **64**, 634–649 (2013)
5. Bévan, R.: Approche composant pour la commande multi-versions des systèmes transitiques reconfigurables (Doctoral dissertation, Lorient) (2013)

6. Bollin, A., Rauner-Reithmayer, D.: Formal specification comprehension: the art of reading and writing Z. In: Proceedings of the 2nd FME Workshop on Formal Methods in Software Engineering, pp. 3–9. ACM, June 2014
7. Clarke, E.M., Wing, J.M.: Formal methods: state of the art and future directions. ACM Comput. Surv. (CSUR) **28**(4), 626–643 (1996)
8. Coutaz, J., Calvary, G., Demeure, A., Balme, L.: Interactive systems and user-centered adaptation: the plasticity of user interfaces. In: Computer Science and Ambient Intelligence, pp. 147–202 (2012)
9. Dix, A.: Formal Methods for Interactive Systems. Academic Press, London (1991)
10. Fagan, M.E.: Design and code inspections to reduce errors in program development. IBM Syst. J. **15**(3), 182–211 (1976)
11. Girard, P., Patry, G., Pierra, G., Potier, J.-C.: Deux exemples d'utilisation de la programmation par démonstration en conception assistée par ordinateur. In: Revue Internationale de CFAO et D'informatique Graphique, vol. 12, no. 1-2, pp. 169–188 (1997)
12. Goubali, O., Bignon, A., Berruet, P., Girard, P., Guittet, L.: Anaxagore, an example of model-driven engineering for industrial supervision. In: Proceedings of the 2014 Ergonomie et Informatique Avancée Conference-Design, Ergonomie et IHM: quelle articulation pour la co-conception de l'interaction, pp. 58–65. ACM, October 2014
13. Harrison, M., Thimbleby, H.: Formal Methods in Human-Computer Interaction. Cambridge University Press, Cambridge (1990)
14. IEEE Guide for Information Technology - System Definition - Concept of Operations (ConOps) Document. IEEE Std 1362-1998. The Institute of Electrical and Electronics Engineers, New York, p. 21
15. Jacobson, I., Booch, G., Rumbaugh, J.: The Unified Software Development Process, vol. 1. Addison Wesley, Reading (1999)
16. Khalil, C., Fernandez, V.: Agile management practices in a "lightweight" organization: a case study analysis. J. Modern Proj. Manage. 1(1) (2013)
17. Knight, J.C., Brilliant, S.S.: Preliminary evaluation of a formal approach to user interface specification. In: Till, D., Bowen, J.P., Hinchey, M.G. (eds.) ZUM 1997. LNCS, vol. 1212. Springer, Heidelberg (1997)
18. Lachaume, T., Patrick, G., Laurent, G., Allan, F.: ProtoTask, new task model simulator. In: Winckler, M., Forbrig, P., Bernhaupt, R. (eds.) HCSE 2012. LNCS, vol. 7623, pp. 323–330. Springer, Heidelberg (2012)
19. Lieberman, H., Paternò, F., Klann, M., Wulf, V.: End-User Development: An Emerging Paradigm, pp. 1–8. Springer, Netherlands (2006)
20. Martin, R.C.: Agile Software Development: Principles, Patterns, and Practices. Prentice Hall PTR, Upper Saddle River (2003)
21. Mathur, S., Malik, S.: Advancements in the V-model. Int. J. Comput. Appl. **1**(12), 30–35 (2010)
22. Moussa, F., Riahi, M., Kolski, C., Moalla, M.: Interpreted petri nets used for human-machine dialogue specification. Integr. Comput. Aided Eng. **9**(1), 87–98 (2002)
23. Nichols, J.: Automatically generating high-quality user interfaces for appliances (Doctoral dissertation, Hewlett-Packard) (2006)
24. Nielson, J.: Heuristic evaluation. In: Usability Inspection Methods, 17 (1), pp. 25–62 (1994)
25. OMG. MDA Guide version 1.0.1. OMG (2003)
26. Pham, H.: System Software Reality (Spring Series in Reality Engineering). Springer-Verlag, New York (2005)
27. Piernot, P.P., Yvon, M.P.: A model for incremental construction of command trees. In: HCI 1995, pp. 169–179. Huddersfield, England (1995)

28. Sourisse, C., Boudillon, L.: La sécurité des machines automatisées: Techniques et moyens de prévention opératifs, systèmes de commandes, utilisation des machines. Institut Schneider Formation (1997)
29. Trudel, S.: Using the COSMIC functional size measurement method (ISO 19761) as a software requierements improvement mechanism. Université du Québec (2012)
30. Weigers, K.E.: Software Requirements, 2nd edn, p. 350. Microsoft Press, Redmond (2003)

A Theoretical Model for the Design of Aesthetic Interaction

Hsiu Ching Laura Hsieh(✉) and Nine Chun Cheng

Department of Creative Design, National Yunlin University of Science and Technology, 123 Section 3, University Road, Douliou 64002, Yunlin, Taiwan
laurarun@gmail.com

Abstract. This study attempts to acquire creative concepts in the field of "new media art interactive creation" from the research on "arts as experience aesthetics", "practical aesthetics", the hypothesis of "somaesthetics", the usability of "human-computer interaction", and the users' experiences to the integration of the design and aesthetic interaction principles required for the experiences of aesthetic interaction so as to make up the past shortcomings. The study aims 1. to shape a theoretical model for the design of aesthetic interaction and 2. to analyze and explain pleasant experiences enhanced by aesthetic interaction with interactive products. The current situations, thorough relevant theories and research are first discussed to further formulate the theoretical model for the design of aesthetic interaction, and then the attributes of aesthetic interaction are analyzed with interactive products. The research outcomes could provide the design of interaction with a point of view different from the past cognition theory and present the originality and the aesthetic interaction in interdisciplinary research.

Keywords: Aesthetic interaction · Somaesthetics · Human-computer interaction

1 Introduction

Different from the past visual field of high technology, cognition theory, and usability emulation, the recent development trend of "human-computer interaction" attempts to pursue the experiences and value of human nature from the derivation from aesthetic field of view and the discussion of interaction. In regard to human expectation of aesthetics, different levels of needs in life are in agreement with Maslow's theory, where aesthetic experiences are necessary in human life to satisfy higher spiritual needs. Unfortunately, past discussion of aesthetics for human-computer interaction stays on appearance aesthetics of user interface. The deeper and latest aesthetic interaction needs to be further explored (Hashim, Noor, Adnan) [7]. Aesthetics has long been applied to art creation and aesthetics to reflect beauty and pleasure; the aesthetics in such art creation presents the relationship between personal mastery and works from the creation of poetry to the murals in chapels. Based on such inference, Tractinsky et al. [21] proposed a new field of view that user interface could also present aesthetics, induce pleasant design of interaction, and assist users in perceiving the experiences in the use of such interactive interface. The early design of "human-computer interaction" used to be compromised between aesthetics and functions, where aesthetics was not emphasized as much as functions. Bardzell [3] indicated that research on aesthetic interaction was

M. Kurosu (Ed.): HCI 2016, Part I, LNCS 9731, pp. 178–187, 2016.
DOI: 10.1007/978-3-319-39510-4_17

shallow and stressed merely on the decoration of visual elements in the interactive interface and emphasized the needs for deeper discussion. Responding to the above users' "inner aesthetic needs", Löwgren [12] emphasized that aesthetics interaction was not simply good and pleasant, but observed and concerned about higher levels, which stressed on the energy and expression of system interface.

It is necessary to comprehend the field of "human-computer interaction" to further satisfy the higher psychological needs of global users from the emphasis of the appearance of interactive interface to "it looks beautiful" and "wonderful use experiences". For this reason, designers and researchers of interaction should realize that the design of interaction is not simply the visual creation but also plays a higher level role of a user being induced the aesthetic experiences when interacting with the interface (system). Such aesthetic experiences (perception) is a mutual interaction (communication) between the system and the user and does not simply rely on the appearance aesthetics of the interface, but requires a designer designing an "experience" for people's perception. This research aims 1. to shape a theoretical model for the design of aesthetic interaction and 2. to analyze and explain pleasant experiences enhanced by aesthetic interaction with interactive products. The current situations, thorough relevant theories and research are first discussed to further shape the theoretical model for the design of aesthetic interaction, and then the characteristics of aesthetic interaction are analyzed with interactive products.

2 The Correlation Between New Media Interactive Art and Human-Computer Interaction

2.1 New Media Interactive Art and Human Computer Interaction

Manovich [14] mentioned that new media interactive art was the confluence of computer history and media technology. Murphie and Potts [18] mentioned that new media art initiated in the mid-19th century when Babbage, a British mathematician, invented an analyzer, the predecessor of computers, and Daguerre invented photography. The appearance of microprocessors in the mid-20th century reduced the production cost of computers and founded the popularization. The production of Macintosh computers later on had computers become personal products. Not until the late 20th century, when various software and hardware efficacy was advanced by leaps and bounds, were computers broadly applied to professional image and sound processing. New media art integrates and digitalizes dynamic images, drawings, modeling, sound, space, and texts. According to Manovich's research [14], new media art presents five features. (1). Numerical representation, all media could become programmable. All works created by computers, despite of the imagery complexity, are the explanation and interpretation of digital information with 0 and 1. (2). Modularity. For instance, A webpage is composed of several independent text, image, video, and program files. (3). Automation. In the production process of new media art, automation is first applied and then programming languages. The work content can even be automated by following the logic procedure, time, input, viewers' physical dynamics to present the changes of works. (4). Variability. New media art is the data and information with diverse forms where the same element could generate distinct appearances through different programming or application. (5). Cultural transcoding. Two levels are discussed for new media art. One is the culture level, which concerns whether the application of media could deliver the creator's deep experiences, observation, and criticism of the society and the culture, i.e. the decoding and messaging of cultural connotation. The other involves in computers, including the above numerical representation, modularity, automation, and variability.

Human-computer interaction is an interdisciplinary subject, the combination of computer science and cognitive engineering. Human-computer interaction involves in the application of language processing, artificial intelligence, multimedia, human factor engineering, linguistics, and sociology. The human-computer interaction model conforming to "simple, easy, friendly, and pleasant" becomes the primary rule to design a user interface. The constant update of human-computer interaction models, the voice recognition and synthesis, the recognition of handwriting and gestures, and virtual reality are the channels for human-computer interaction. The application broadly covers traditional computers, PDA, ATM, and mobile phones.

Interaction qualities are the key in new media art, which relies on the roles of computer interaction. It is similar to the role of interaction in human-computer interaction. Baljko and Tenhaaf [2] indicated that interactive media art presented an interface, through which the users interacted with art work systems; the operation and participation processes depended on digital operation in which the participants operated the data in the interactive interface. Interactivity is a primary quality in new media art, and the interaction model and connotation are constantly deducing. Manovich [14], an important researcher on new media art, mentioned that it was the funniest and the most difficult part to define interactivity, and it was still under processing. It is considered in this study that the development and application of interaction qualities are the most challenging, inspirational, and necessarily discussed and developed issue for designers.

According to the experts of human-computer interaction, Mayer [15] and Morse [16], an interactive device was designed to invite the users investing in the development and changes of social experiences, and interactivity could encourage the users to participate in the exchange and communication of social experiences. The difference between interactive art creation and traditional art work is that the former guides the audience to join in a purposive, inclusive, and mediated process. The past art forms stressed on the creators as the authors that the audience were merely the passive readers and the authors as creators that the audience were the negative readers. Interactive art, on the other hand, gives the users the rights of author and participation so that the audience could participate in the interactive process and become a part of the art creation.

2.2 The Correlation Between New Media Interactive Art and Human-Computer-Interaction

Combining the interaction qualities of human-computer interaction with Dewey's aesthetic view of Art as Experience [5], Petersen et al. [20] proposed pragmatic aesthetic experiences and indicated that the correlation between new media art and human-computer interaction appeared on both emphasizing and stressing on the integration of aesthetics with daily interaction. Aesthetics was shaped in a part of daily life, and the aesthetic feeling came from the relationship between users and interactive devices. Aesthetic interaction integrated two points of (1) aesthetic being pragmatic and (2) artifacts being properly used. Pragmatic aesthetics emphasized the purposive role of aesthetics in an interactive design system, and the aesthetic feeling appeared in the use process and would be the integration between the understanding of the interactive system and the use potential. According to Manovich' research, interactive products (such as smart phones and tablets) largely enter people's daily life and change the lifestyles due to the popularity of personal computers and the Internet so that the reception of information and the styles to exchange with people are greatly changed. It is inferred in this study that such a style reveals great influence on current designers, as creators also use interactive products, which would infiltrate in the thinking and living models, in the daily life; designers would extend more interesting and interactive performance styles through the application and cognition of human-computer interaction in the daily life; and, art creators are the observers and practitioners of life to naturally blend the interaction experiences in the daily life (the use of interactive products) and integrate them into the creation.

Nowadays, interactive products have become the important media for the exchange of production, consumption, and cultural data. For instance, various interactive product interfaces (such as ipod, ipad, and iphone) ubiquitously exist in people's daily life for browsing on the Internet, playing computer games, sending and receiving e-mails, and collecting information through the Internet. In new media art, an interface is the platform for the exchange of information, ideas, and concepts designed and arranged by the users and creators. In human-computer interaction, an interface is the media for presenting aesthetic feeling, inducing pleasure, and assisting the users in the operation. In fact, current artists or designers encounter the challenge to design an interface and experience design. Such experiences have to be able to induce effective responses and feedback of the participants in order to become effective interactive device design. Such a problem could be solved by the theories, technologies, methods, and procedures in human-computer interaction.

3 Discussing Human-Computer Interaction from the Aspect of Art as Experience

Dewey's Art as Experience [5] reveals that the existence of aesthetics is really perceived when a person experiences aesthetic experiences. Aesthetic feeling is an integrated perception covering the entire experiences, rather than a single part or detail of perception, and integrates the relationship between doing and undergoing. Each action and the successively induced results are associated. People could experience the aesthetic properties through doing and undergoing processes; that is, aesthetics is perceived by doing and undergoing. Petersen derived Pragmatic Aesthetic from Dewey's aesthetics theory but stressed on the mutual relationship between psychology and body; meanwhile, he claimed that the aesthetic feeling in aesthetic interaction was not on the art work but appeared on human-system and human-human interaction processes and the perceived experiences in the interaction. Irvin [9] also applied Dewey's aesthetics of Art as

Experience and further explained that people could perceive more satisfaction, elegance, pleasure, and abundance when pay the attention to daily life experiences (e.g. online purchase, searching data on the Internet, and sending and receiving e-mails).

Summing up the above researchers' statements, it is found that aesthetic interaction does not exist in art work but appears on the movement in the interaction and after the interaction between participants and art work. Some experiences are perceived in the process from doing to undergoing. Such experiences are experienced in the process and present aesthetic feeling. As a matter of fact, people could acquire aesthetic experiences from the daily life; the experiences in such daily behaviors (e.g. browsing the Internet, sending e-mails, using interactive products) could be satisfactory, pleasant, and abundant. Generally speaking, daily behaviors are involved in body rhythm (movement). In the experimental research, Moen and Sandsjö [17] indicated that the aesthetic physiological experiences were the feelings or inner images based on different body movement; such imagination was related to personal imagination or the expression in mind about beautiful rhythm (movement). Accordingly, it is inferred that daily life experiences, including the interaction between browsing the Internet and interfaces, e.g. online shopping or searching information on the Internet, could result in aesthetic experiences, as such interaction with interfaces contains the experiences in aesthetic through body rhythm. The correlation between body rhythm theory and interaction and the application are discussed in the following section.

4 Somaesthetics and Human-Computer Interaction

Laban's body rhythm principles [10] are broadly applied by researchers, educators, psychologists, physiologists, professional therapists, and dancers. The body rhythm principles reflect the inner emotion of people and the way they exist in the world. Referring to Leban's body rhythm principles, the effort elements made by a participant refer to Body, Time, Space, and Information, which could be used for analyzing and integrating the application of interaction design, allowing the interactive interface being easy to use, close, and user-friendly. Movement qualities are also permanently applied to the interaction design in human-computer interaction. Four movement qualities were studied by Bacigalupi [1], including Rhythm, Tempo, Sequence, and Direction. Rhythm referred to the tension between dynamics and statics; tempo referred to the rhythm space being fast or slow; sequence referred to the time sequence of an event and the following event; and, direction could be applied to interface design to induce the dynamic model in the interaction between the user and the creation. Loke et al. [13] applied Leban's body rhythm principles in the research on interactive media and proposed different methods and principles to apply body rhythm principles to interaction design and to create a new point of view for applying body rhythm principles to interaction design. Apparently, Leban's body rhythm principles are worth adopting and implementing in practical creation. Nevertheless, it is inefficient to simply analyze the effort elements and movement qualities of body rhythm principles. A medium, an interface for the human-computer interaction system, is necessary for shaping human-computer interaction. In the following section, the interface design strategies and considerations for human-computer interaction are discussed.

5 Aesthetic Interaction and Human-Computer Interaction

Norman [19] proposed the aesthetic experiences in human-computer interaction, where the perception of interactive aesthetic experiences contained the sensory and visceral level, the behavioral level, and the thinking and reflective level. The sensory level was the lowest stage, in which the perception was connected with the sensory cognition of humans. The perception in the behavioral level was the perceived aesthetic feeling after the cognition based on operation and behaviors. The perception in the thinking level referred to the deep emotion; the perception at this stage was far beyond the instantly perceived aesthetic feeling and was the deep aesthetic experiences created by rational judgment. Hassenzahl [6] also found out the correlation between use and aesthetic feeling. Zhang and Li [22] claimed that effective and useful interface system efficacy could affect a user's overall perception of the creation. They defined that effective quality existed in people's experiences in using the system. Such research could help designers think of different degrees of effects and perception, when the audience or participants interacted with the work, in the design interaction. Besides, such research could also assist designers in understanding the close relationship between different levels of perception, work efficacy and aesthetic feeling.

6 Shaping a Model for the Design of Aesthetic Interaction

By analyzing Dewey's aesthetics of Art as Experience and Petersen' Pragmatic aesthetic, it is discovered in this study that aesthetic experiences not only present great correlation with inner perception, but the participation of body movement also deeply affects aesthetic experiences. In this case, Leban's Body Rhythm theory is also integrated. The aesthetic feeling perceived in the interaction covers the practicability of aesthetic feeling and the proper use of creation, and aesthetic experiences are acquired through the actual operation of body rhythm. By integrating the above theories, it is believed that aesthetic experiences would gradually emerge from the process of the participating audience using and operating the interactive interface to further shape an aesthetic interaction module. The composition of the aesthetic interaction module is explained from three stages. First, the major context considered before designing the aesthetic interaction is demonstrated from the use context, the user experiences, and the interactive artifact interface. Second, the dynamic dimensions of body movement, time, space, and information in the real operation of interaction through a participant's body rhythm are interpreted. Third, the movement qualities of rhythm, tempo, sequence, and direction in the interaction are explained. Finally, a theoretical aesthetic interaction model is organized (Fig. 1). Interface component includes:Text, Images, Icons, Layout, Navigation, Buttons. Interaction characteristics are shown in the following. (1) Orderliness (random-to-orderly):The level of orderliness of either artifacts' showing information, or users' searching or manipulating information through an interactive products. (2) Accordance (independent-to-chained):The rank of connectivity among various information elements accessible through interactive artifacts or those artifacts themselves. (3) Continuity (detached-to-continuous):The level of continuity of users' controlling toward interface components. (4) Directness (indirect-to-direct):The level of directness of what is shown through an interactive products or its information components. (5) Proximity (specific-to-proximate):The level of juxtaposition of managing information. (6) Movement (inactive-to-dynamic):The level of movement dynamics for both participants' managing interface components and artifacts' showing information elements.

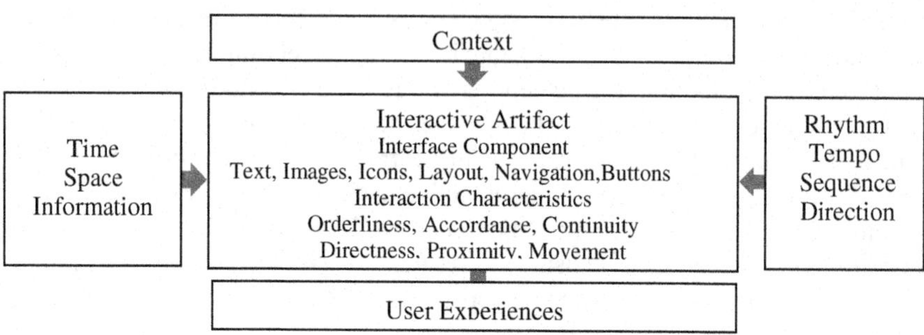

Fig. 1. A theoretical model for the design of aesthetic interaction

6.1 Three Considerations Before Aesthetic Interaction Design: Use Context, User Experiences, and Interactive Artifact Interface

Pragmatic Aesthetic is applied in this study because the viewpoint of Pragmatic Aesthetic would not attach to a single creator or a designer, but concerns about the interaction experiences between human and creation and the background context of interaction. The rationality of system experiences would be multi-dimensionally and completely considered in pragmatic aesthetic. In fact, a user and the existing environment are not independent, but would extend the consideration to the integration and the mutual relationship between the participant and the existing environment. In this case, integrating use situations and user experiences in this study to create aesthetic experiences is the process to invite people enthusiastically participating in and interacting with the creation interface, which could induce the perception, and allow the audience perceiving and understanding the meaning. Aesthetic interaction, related to inducing imagination, focuses on stimulating and encouraging people to present the autonomic thoughts and perception after the real-time interaction and having them operate and use the interactive artifact interface with individual methods. Consequently, a creator has to think of three dimensions of Use Context, User Experiences, and Interactive Artifact Interface when intending to design aesthetic interaction, so as to generate more efficient interaction and allow the audience or participants experiencing the cultural connotation and deep meaning behind an art creator's creation. The relations among use situations, participants, and interactive artifact interface are described as following.

6.2 Dynamic Dimensions of Aesthetic Interaction: Body, Time, Space, Information

By integrating Human-Computer Interaction theories and Body Rhythm principles, it is proposed in this study that four dynamic dimensions of body, time, space, and information in the interaction process are worth noticing when a creator produces the interaction design. Moen and Sandsjö [17], Human-Computer Interaction researchers, emphasized that the dynamic of interactivity appeared on a user operating the creation with body movement speed. Davis [4] and Petersen et al. [20] discussed the importance of time, which could affect a user experiencing aesthetics, in interaction, and then space. The space idea formed in interaction was different from the space formed by other creation. Physical space and virtual space were the basic differentiation. When a virtual element in interaction was placed in the concept of time, it became the movement and created the virtual space cognition. Information, which allows interactive products present the unique properties, is another core in interaction. Here, information refers to digital information which presents flexibility, abundance, and pervasiveness to have interactive products show the uniqueness. Research on Human-Computer Interaction reveals exhaustive and exquisite analyses; the above dynamic analysis of a user's body movement (body movement, time, space, information) is worth the reference for an art creator proceeding interactive creation (Fig. 1).

6.3 Movement Qualities of Aesthetic Interaction: Rhythm, Tempo, Sequence, Direction

Movement qualities contain four items of rhythm, tempo, sequence, and direction. The variation of rhythm often results from a rhythm to the next rhythm. Such a moving process is related to the tension between statics and dynamics. The interaction between continuity and variation creates activity and rest and even controls people's demands for balancing consistence and diversification. Tempo is often defined as the termination of rhythm or speed, meaning the proportional and sonorous interactivity and the play with faster speed. In visual art performance, fast tempo often associates with smaller, narrower, and thinner object shapes or possible a large force on an object. Slow tempo, on the other hand, associates with larger, wider, and fatter object shapes, which are regarded as easier, more powerless, and larger obstruction. Sequence explains that an event occurs following the sequence in the time axis. The visual performance of sequence is often used for displaying cause and effect and revealing the relationship between an event and the next event. The application of sequence to interactive media would present distinct appearances because of the sequence of an event. The application of sequence to interactive media could offer the audience (users) a reminder (direction), set the audience expectation, and support the information structure on the interface. Direction is related to the step in sequence. An object shows the sequence of an event by following the time axis and further presents with steps. The above-mentioned rhythm, tempo, sequence, and direction are applicable to shape efficient and perceived pleasant experiences of the viewers (users).

It is suggested in this study that the above rhythm, tempo, sequence, and direction could be applied to the design of visual interface in an interaction system in order to attract and stimulate the users in the interaction. The visual interface design refers to the presentation of an interface and the visual communication, covering images, texts, symbols, composition, roaming and buttons. The design of such interface elements aims to induce a user's interests, guide the user to touch the interface, and drive the dynamic to induce the exchange of user experiences. When a user presses the interactive interface button, some functions are presented, or more media effects (such as films, animation, and dynamic texts) are added. The entire experiences would present interactivity and could enhance the users' experiences in willingness expression and aesthetic interaction.

7 Conclusion

In short, the relationship among use background, user experiences, and interactive artifact interface is the major context in the aesthetic interaction design. A creator would consider the production of different interactive dynamics through the interactive dynamic dimensions (body movement, time, space, and information), allowing the participants operating the interaction system through body movement and achieving the possibilities of roaming, perceiving, and exchanging. Eventually, movement qualities (rhythm, tempo, sequence, and direction), which could control interaction, are used as the context for constructing the visual interface. It is anticipated that the theoretical aesthetic interaction design module derived in this study could help the human-computer interaction design present aesthetic characteristics and assist the participants in acquiring new vision and new opinions through the use of interactive products. The deductive module, aiming to comprehend and design aesthetic interaction, could be applied to the aesthetic interaction design in interactive interfaces and provide structural knowledge and mutual correlation ideas for comprehending aesthetic interaction. By discussing and integrating the multi-dimensional theories of user experiences, Rhythm Theory, Pragmatic Aesthetic, and Human-Computer Interaction, it is expected that the theoretical model would inspire the future research on aesthetic interaction design.

References

1. Bacigalupi, M.: The craft of movement in interaction design. In: Proceedings of ACM AVI 1998, pp. 174–184 (1998)
2. Baljko, M., Tenhaaf, N.: The aesthetics of emergence: co-constructed interactions. ACM Trans. Comput. Hum. Interact. **15**(3), 1–27 (2008)
3. Bardzell, J.: Interaction criticism and aesthetics. In: Proceedings of the SIGCHI Conference on Human Factors in Computing Systems (CHI 2009), pp. 2357–2366. ACM (2009)
4. Davis, M.: Theoretical foundations for experiential systems design. In: Proceedings of SIGMM 2003, pp. 45–52. ACM, New York (2003)
5. Dewey, J.: Art as Experience. Southern Illinois University Press, Carbondale (1987)
6. Hassenzahl, M.: The interplay of beauty, goodness, and usability in interactive products. Hum. Comput. Interact. **19**(4), 319–349 (2004)

7. Hashim, W.N.W., Noor, N.L.M., Adnan, W.A.W.: The design of aesthetic interaction:towards a graceful interaction framework. In: ICIS 2009, 24-26 November, Seoul, Korea, pp. 69–75. ACM (2009)
8. Heller, D.: Aesthetics and interaction design: some preliminary thoughts. Interactions **12**, 48–50 (2005)
9. Irvin, S.: The pervasiveness of the aesthetic in ordinary experience. Br. J. Aesthet. **48**(1), 29–44 (2008)
10. Laban, R.: The Mastery of Movement. Macdonald & Evans, London (1971)
11. Lim, Y.-K., et al.: Interaction gestalt and the design of aesthetic interactions. In: DPPI 2007 Proceedings of the 2007 Conference on Designing Pleasurable Products and Interfaces, pp. 239–254. ACM (2007)
12. Löwgren, J.: Toward an articulation of interaction esthetics. New Rev. Hypermedia Multimed. **15**(2), 129–146 (2009)
13. Loke, L., et al.: Understanding movement for interaction design frameworks and approaches. J. Pers. Ubiquit. Comput. **11**(8), 691–702 (2007)
14. Manovich, L.: The Language of New Media. The MIT Press, Cambridge (2001)
15. Mayer, P.A.: Computer-mediated interactivity: a social semiotic perspective. Convergence Int. J. Res. New Media Tech. **4**(3), 40–58 (1998)
16. Morse, M.: The Poetics of Interactivity. In: Malloy, J. (ed.) Women, Art, and Technology, pp. 16–33. The MIT Press, London (2003)
17. Moen, J., Sandsjö, J.: BodyBug - Design of KinAesthetic Interaction. In: Digital Proceedings of NORDES in the Making. Copenhagen, Denmark (2005)
18. Murphie, A., Potts, J.: Culture and Technology. Palgrave Macmillan, New York (2003)
19. Norman, D.: Introduction to this special section on beauty, goodness, and usability. Hum. Comput. Interact. **19**(4), 311–318 (2004)
20. Petersen, M., Iversen, O.S., Krog, P.G., Ludvigsen, M.: Aesthetic interaction: a pragmatist's aesthetics of interactive systems. In: Proceedings of DIS 2004, pp. 269–276. ACM, New York (2004)
21. Tractinsky, N., Shoval-Katz, A., Ikar, D.: What is beautiful is usable. Interact. Comput. **13**, 127–145 (2000)
22. Zhang, P., Li, N.: The importance of affective quality. Commun. ACM **48**(9), 105–118 (2005)

Optimization of Complex Structure Based on Human-Computer Interaction Method

Lei Liu(✉), Aijun Ma, Hongying Liu, Xuemei Feng, and Meng Shi

China Astronaut Research and Training Center, Beijing, China
imwindancer@163.com

Abstract. To solve the problem of structural optimization of complex structure under dynamic response constraints, a human-computer interaction method was proposed combined with advantages of human and computer in structural optimization, and being used in structural optimization of an aerospace assembly to verify its practicability and effectiveness. The method was mainly based on two steps: topology optimization by human-computer interaction and size optimization by computer. The aerospace assembly after structural optimization based on the method could satisfy the dynamic environment requirement and the results showed that first integral vibration frequency raised 41.1 % and magnification of acceleration dropped 25.2 % while the mass remained essentially unchanged. Also the experimental results compared with the simulation results showed that the relative error was less than 5 %, which proved the effectiveness of the simulation design. The human-computer interaction method might provide a reference for similar products not limited to aerospace field.

Keywords: Structure optimization · Human-computer interaction method · Aerospace assembly · Dynamic response constraints · Topology optimization by human-computer interaction · Size optimization by computer

1 Introduction

Spacecraft will experience complex mechanics environment in the process of launching, and vibration is one of most important factors to be considered in the development phase of space products. Also spacecraft is strict to quality characteristics because the cost can decrease 10000 dollars as the weight reduces 1 kg [1], and one of the most important factors that limit human to explore space is the weight. For these many reasons, people often choose to use structural optimization technology to find the minimum mass and cost under the given constraints [2].

Although people wish the structure can be the most suitable in the initial process of the development, the space products either may not satisfy the constraints or have large useless material allowance constantly at the beginning. There are two methods to solve the problem; one is traditional means by manual work that the designer can modify the structure by experience again and again. The advantage of this way is that the direction is clear so the designer can adjust the project at any time to find the better structure. Also in the design process, the designer can consider the manufacturing and installing constraints adequately. However, the disadvantage also exists that this way may just

M. Kurosu (Ed.): HCI 2016, Part I, LNCS 9731, pp. 188–197, 2016.
DOI: 10.1007/978-3-319-39510-4_18

find a good scheme but not the best structure. On the contrary, structural optimization by computer can find the best solutions through numerical iteration, but the disadvantage is that computing amount is too large for complex problem such as topology optimization for complex structure under dynamic response constraints.

Researching structural optimization problem under dynamic environment is of great importance [3], but the issue is difficult to solve because of complexity of the sensitivity analysis [4] and hugeness of the computing amount, and remain some theoretical problems to research [5], especially for the topology optimization [6, 7]. For this reason, people often translate the dynamic problems to the static problems according to the given principles. But the static method cannot reflect the influence of the free vibration item and damping, hence the situation often happens that static equivalent condition can satisfy the requirement but the dynamic condition cannot. Considering all above factors, a human-computer interaction method is proposed to solve the optimization of complex structure under dynamic response constraints.

2 The Human-Computer Interaction Method

There are frequency constraints, dynamic response constraints including dynamic response displacement constraints, dynamic response acceleration constraints, and dynamic response stress constraints and so on in dynamic environment structural optimization [8, 9]. And structural optimization has three levels, which are size optimization, shape optimization, and topology optimization. Topology optimization is often used in the concept phase in the optimization progress, and can make significant impact for the improvement of mechanical performance [10]. In consideration of the complexity of topology optimization by computer, we choose to take advantage of the manual work to modify the topology structure, in other words, this stage is topology optimization by human-computer interaction style. Then we can use size optimization to find the best size of the structure under the dynamic response constraints by guidelines method or mathematical programming approach methods.

Human-computer interaction method makes use of advantages of human and computer in structural optimization adequately [11, 12]. Its process concludes the following stages. Firstly, the finite element model can be created by finite element software and the model can be updated by some ways such as modal test to achieve a relatively accurate model. And modal analysis and vibration response analysis can be carried out based on the finite element model. From analysis of the above simulation results, we can get the weak parts of the structure and modify the topology structure to improve the mechanics characteristics. By some cycles of topology optimization by human-computer interaction, the structure will be better performed under the dynamic environment. Secondly, after the topology optimization by human-computer interaction, size optimization by computer is executed to find the best size for the structure to reach the best objective under the constraints. Thirdly, we will check the dynamic stress and other parameters to make sure that it can satisfy the requirement under the dynamic environment.

As the above mentioned, we separate the constraints to three phases to consider including frequency constraints, dynamic response acceleration constraints, and dynamic response stress constraints [13]. In the topology optimization stage by human-computer interaction, frequency constraints are the main constraint condition while the dynamic response acceleration constraints are used to prove the effectiveness of the topology modify. In the size optimization stage by computer, dynamic response acceleration constraints and frequency constraints are the constraints while the mass of the structure is the objective. In the check stage, dynamic response stress constraints are the constraint condition, we can use the shape optimization to reduce the concentrated stress if the stress is too large to satisfy the requirement. Human work not only plays a part in the topology optimization phase, but also in the decisions of whether or not the results are satisfied with the optimum scheme [14]. Figure 1 is the flow chart of the human-computer interaction structural optimization method under dynamic response constraints.

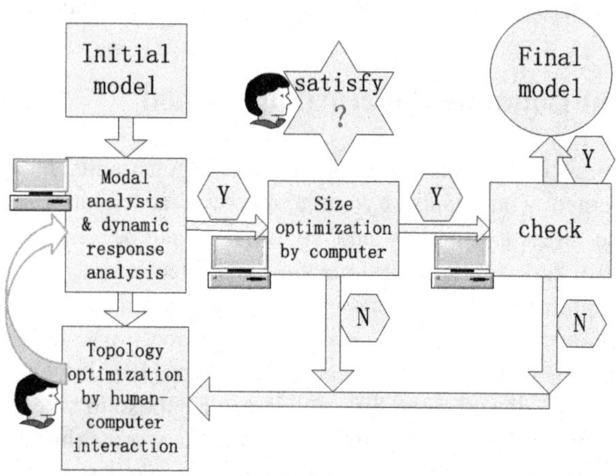

Fig. 1. Flow chart of human-computer interaction structural optimization method

3 Structural Optimization of an Aerospace Assembly Using the Human-Computer Interaction Method

3.1 Problem Description

The aerospace assembly was including external framework and internal function products. As the internal function products was hard to modify, then the optimization concerned on the external framework which was consist of thin-walled beams. So the finite model of the frame was divided by two dimension grids while the internal function products were divided by three dimension grids. The design variable was the topology variable and the size variable, and the objective of the optimization was minimizing the mass under the dynamic response constraints, which included stiffness requirements and strength requirement. The stiffness requirement was that the first integral vibration frequency of the assembly was not less than 60 Hz and the acceleration magnification of the cared nodes was less than 5, while the strength requirement

Table 1. Sine test conditions of the aerospace assembly

Parameters (identification level)	Frequency(Hz)			
	4 ~ 10	10 ~ 17	17 ~ 75	75 ~ 100
Amplitude 0 ~ p	13.09 mm	3.22 g	6.86 g	4.13 g
Loading direction	Three directions			

was that the stress of the assembly was lower than the yield limit of the material (2Al2, 280 MPa) under given sine test conditions. The problem could be described as Eq. (1). The sine test conditions could be described as Table 1.

$$\begin{cases} \text{find best(topo,size)} \\ \text{min Mass} \\ \text{s.t. freq} \geq f_0 \\ \quad \text{freq\_acce(out)/freq\_acce(in)} \leq a \\ \quad \text{freq\_stress} \leq \tau_0 \end{cases} \tag{1}$$

In this model, first integral vibration frequency (f_0) was set as 60 Hz, and magnification of dynamic response acceleration (a) was set as 5, yield limit of the material (τ_0) was 280 MPa.

3.2 Topology Optimization by Human-Computer Interaction

The finite element model was created by HyperMesh software while the mesh size was set as 5 mm, the external frame was meshed to 2d grid, while the internal functions products were meshed to 3d grid and finally the finite element model could be described in Fig. 2. Once the finite element model was created, and then modal analysis and vibration response analysis was being carried out based on the finite element model. From analysis of the above simulation results, we got the weak parts of the structure and modified the topology structure by human-computer interaction work to improve the mechanics characteristics. By some cycles of topology optimization by human-computer interaction, the structure was better performed under the dynamic environment. Figure 3 was the first vibration feature of the four topology structure by human-computer interaction topology optimization. The initial model was structure a, the first integral vibration frequency of a was 42.3 Hz, which was less than the objective that was 60 Hz. Worse still, the vibration feature of cared function products was too bad to satisfy the requirements. So the cared function products position was transferred to other location based on human-computer interaction style as structure b and the first integral vibration frequency increased from 42.3 Hz to 44.2 Hz, and the vibration feature improved a lot. However, it still could not satisfy the final requirements. So we added structure b a beam to structure c, and the first integral vibration frequency of the aerospace model increased from 44.2 Hz to 45.8 Hz. Finally, we added structure c some braces to structure d by human-computer interaction topology optimization, and the first integral vibration frequency improved from 45.8 Hz to 58.2 Hz.

Fig. 2. The finite element model of the initial aerospace assembly

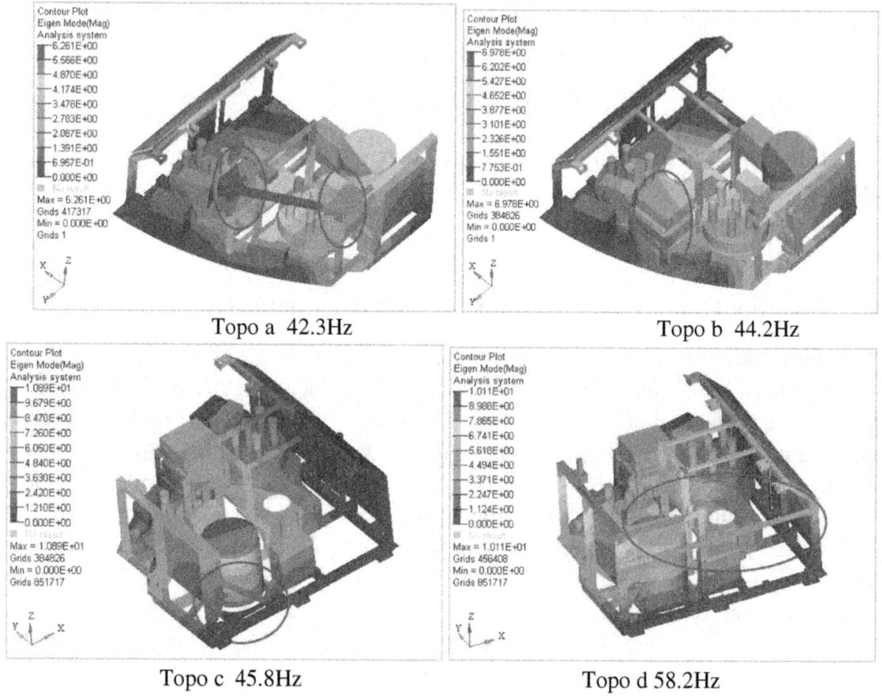

Fig. 3. The first vibration feature of the four topology structure

To get a better look at the effect of the topology optimization by human-computer interaction style, Table 2 listed the parameters change of four topology structure by human-computer interaction topology optimization. And Fig. 4 provided the graph of acceleration magnification (node 516535) of four topology structure by human-computer interaction topology optimization. The first integral vibration of the assembly changed from 42.3 Hz (topology structure a) to 58.2 (topology structure d), while the magnification acceleration of node 516535 changed from 6.18 to 4.91, and the mass of

Table 2. Parameters change chart of four topology structure

Parameters	Topo a	Topo b	Topo c	Topo d	Rate change a & d
First integral vibration frequency/Hz	42.3	44.2	45.8	58.2	+37.6 %
Magnification of acceleration (node 516535)	6.18	6.00	5.12	4.91	−20.6 %
Mass of the frame/kg	17.49	17.25	17.57	17.93	+4.7 %

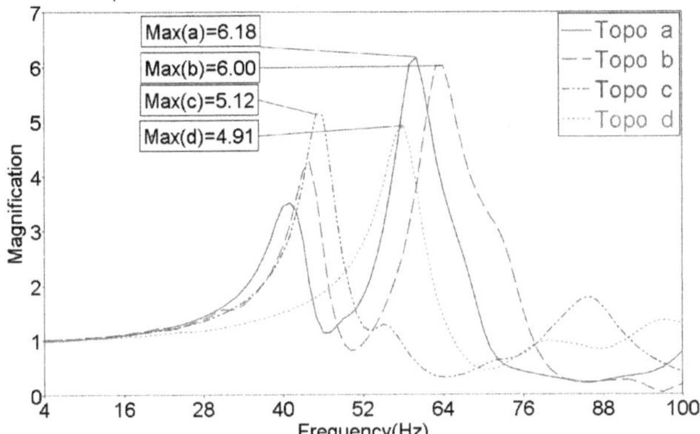

Fig. 4. Acceleration magnification of four topology structure (node 516535)

the frame changed from 17.49 kg to 17.93 kg. The vibration feature improved a lot from topology structure a to topology structure d. However, the mass of the frame increased, which was not what we want.

3.3 Size Optimization by Computer

Size optimization by computer was executed to find the best size for the structure to reach the best objective under the dynamic environment constraints [15, 16]. The objective of the optimization was minimizing the mass under the dynamic response constraints and the design variable in this phase was size variable. Considering of all factors, we chose the following ten size variable and every variable had its maximum limit and minimum limit. After 16 iterations, the results tent to be convergent. Table 3 was the initial value and the final value, the maximum limit and minimum limit. Figures 5 and 6 were respectively iteration graph of the objective function and constraints.

The first integral vibration frequency increased from 58.2 to 59.7 after size optimization by computer, and acceleration magnification of node 516535 dropped from 4.91 to 4.62, while the mass of the frame dropped from 17.93 kg to 17.44 kg. Combined the topology optimization by human-computer interaction and size optimization by computer, the simulation results can be drawn as follows. After the human-computer interaction optimization, the change of cared parameters by simulation results could be described as Table 4. From Table 4 we could see, the first integral vibration of the aerospace assembly increased as much as 41.1 %, and acceleration magnification of cared node dropped as much as 25.2 %, and the mass of the frame also dropped as we expected before.

Table 3. Initial value and final value, maximum and minimum limit of size variable

Number	**1**	**2**	**3**	**4**	**5**	**6**	**7**	**8**	**9**	**10**
Initial value/mm	5	4	4.3	8	9	4.4	10	2	6	3
Max and min limit /mm	6	5	5	10	12	5	15	3	8	4
	4	3	3	6	6	3	5	1	4	2
Final value/mm	5.66	3.81	3	7.72	6	3	5	1.66	4	2

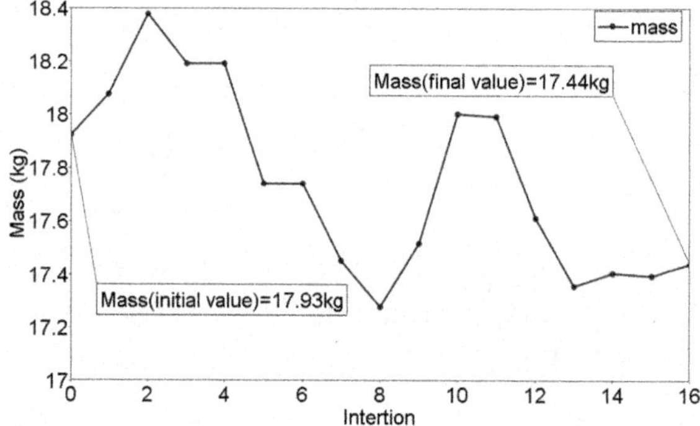

Fig. 5. Iteration graph of objective function

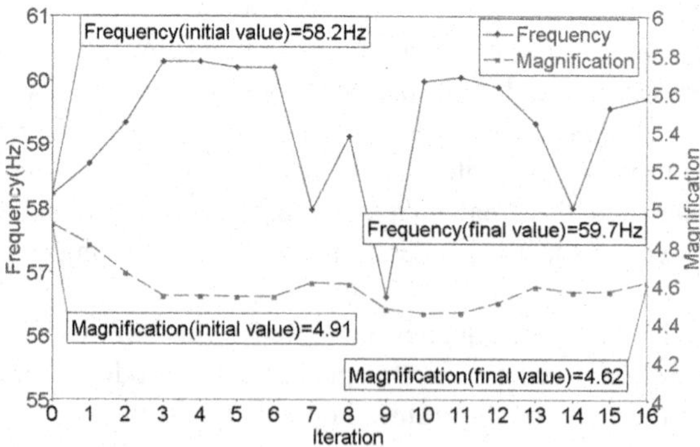

Fig. 6. Iteration graph of constraints

Table 4. Changes of cared parameters by simulations results after human-computer interaction optimization.

Parameters	Initial value	Optimization results	Rate change
First integral vibration frequency/Hz	42.3	59.7	+41.1 %
Magnification of acceleration(node 516535)	6.18	4.62	−25.2 %
Mass of the frame/kg	17.49	19.44	−0.3 %

3.4 Check of Dynamic Response Stress

To make sure that the structure after optimization can satisfy the requirement under dynamic response constraints, especially for the dynamic response stress, we made vibration response analysis based on the given dynamic load condition and the stress cloud of the assembly on given dynamic loads could be described as Fig. 7. The results showed that the maximum of the Von Mises was located in the installation holes of the assembly and the maximum value was 171.2 MPa, which was less than the yield limit of the material (280 MPa). The results indicated that the dynamic response stress could satisfy the requirements.

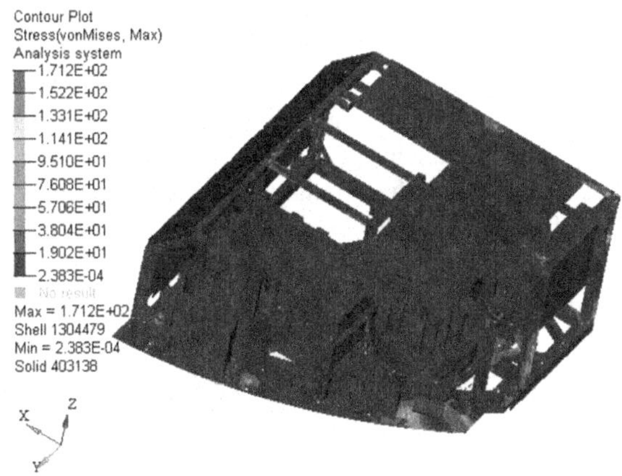

Fig. 7. The stress cloud of the assembly on given dynamic loads (60 Hz)

3.5 Experimental Verification

The final product was produced based on the final simulation optimization results. And vibration environment experiment was established on the 10t platform vibrator. In considering of keeping secret, the figure of experimental design will not be given. From the vibration experiment, the following data could be achieved that the first vibration frequency experimental result of the aerospace assembly was 60.2 Hz, while the simulation result was 59.7 Hz. The magnification acceleration of node 516535 was 4.50, while the simulation result was 4.62. And the mass of the frame was 19.35 kg,

Table 5. Comparison of the simulation results with the experimental results

Parameters	Simulation results	Experimental results	Relative error
First integral vibration frequency/Hz	59.7	60.2	0.8 %
Magnification of acceleration(node 516535)	4.62	4.50	2.7 %
Mass of the frame/kg	19.44	19.35	0.5 %

while the optimization result was 19.44 kg. Also experimental design proved that the dynamic response stress could satisfy the requirements. Table 5 listed the comparison of the simulation results with the experimental results.

4 Conclusion

Combining with the advantages of human and computer in complex structural optimization, the proposed human-computer interaction method could make a good performance in complex assembly's optimization. It also provided new ideas for structural optimization under dynamic response constraints to solve practical problems. In this paper the aerospace assembly could not satisfy the requirement under the dynamic response constraints primitively. But after the human-computer interaction structural optimization, the final structure could satisfy the dynamic environment requirement and results showed that first integral vibration frequency raised 41.1 % (from 42.3 Hz to 59.7 Hz) and magnification of acceleration dropped 25.2 % (from 6.12 to 4.62) while the mass remained essentially unchanged (from 17.49 kg to 17.44 kg). Also the experimental results compared with the simulation results showed that the relative error was less than 5 %, which proved the effectiveness of the simulation design. The human-computer interaction method might provide a reference for similar products that are not limited to aerospace field.

Acknowledgements. Funded by the manned space engineering of China is gratefully acknowledged. Besides, we are very grateful for prof. Qinghua Hu for providing the initial aerospace assembly model.

References

1. Tibert, G.: Deployable tensegrity structures for space applications. Royal Institute of Technology (2002)
2. Christensen, P.W., Klarbring, A.: An Introduction to Structural Optimization. Springer Science & Business Media, Heidelberg (2008)
3. Rong, J.H., Xie, Y.M., Yang, X.Y., Liang, Q.Q.: Topology optimization of structures under dynamic response constraints. J. Sound Vib. **234**(2), 177–189 (2000)
4. Choi, K.K., Kim, N.H.: Structural Sensitivity Analysis and Optimization 1: Linear Systems. Springer Science & Business Media, Heidelberg (2006)

5. Nugen, T.T., Yang, S., Brake, J.: Evolutionary dynamic optimization: a survey of the state of the art. Swarm Evol. Comput. **6**, 1–24 (2012)
6. Stolpe, M., Svanberg, K.: An alternative interpolation scheme for minimum compliance topology optimization. Struct. Multidiscipline Optim. **22**(2), 116–124 (2001)
7. Bendsoe, M.P., Sigmund, O.: Topology Optimization: Theory, Methods and Application. Springer, New York (2003)
8. Schlegel, M., Marquardt, W.: Detection and exploitation of the control switching structure in the solution of dynamic optimization problems. J. Process Control **16**(3), 275–290 (2006)
9. Akesson, J., Arzen, K.E., Gafvert, M., Bergdahl, T., Tummescheit, H.: Modeling and optimization with optimica and JModelica.org-languages and tools for solving large-scale dynamic optimization problems. Comput. Chem. Eng. **34**(11), 1737–1749 (2010)
10. Krog, L., Tucker, A., Rollema, G.: Application of topology, sizing and shape optimization methods to optimal design of aircraft components. In: Proceedings 3rd Altair UK HyperWorks Users Conference (2012)
11. Sobieszczanski-Sobieski, J., Haftka, R.T.: Multidisciplinary aerospace design optimization: survey of recent developments. Struct. Optim. **14**(1), 1–23 (1997)
12. Xie, Y.M., Steven, G.P.: A simple evolutionary procedure for structural optimization. Comput. Struct. **49**(5), 885–896 (1993)
13. Lee, K.S., Geem, Z.W.: A new structural optimization method based on the harmony search algorithm. Comput. Struct. **82**(9), 781–798 (2004)
14. Durgun, İ., Yildiz, A.R.: Structural design optimization of vehicle components using cuckoo search algorithm. Mater. Test. **54**(3), 185–188 (2012)
15. Lambe, A.B., Martins, J.R.: Extensions to the design structure matrix for the description of multidisciplinary design, analysis, and optimization processes. Struct. Multidisciplinary Optim. **46**(2), 273–284 (2012)
16. Deaton, J.D., Grandhi, R.V.: A survey of structural and multidisciplinary continuum topology optimization: post 2000. Struct. Multidisciplinary Optim. **49**(1), 1–38 (2014)

Personalization in the User Interaction Design

Isn't Personalization Just the Adjustment According to Defined User Preferences?

Miroslav Sili[1(✉)], Markus Garschall[2], Martin Morandell[1], Sten Hanke[1], and Christopher Mayer[1]

[1] Health and Environment Department, Biomedical Systems, AIT Austrian Institute of Technology GmbH, Vienna, Austria
miroslav.sili@ait.ac.at
[2] Innovation Systems, Technology Experience, AIT Austrian Institute of Technology GmbH, Vienna, Austria

Abstract. User diversity plays an essential role in the design of modern Human Computer Interaction (HCI) systems. Users differ among their perception and utilization of technology. Thus, designers of modern Information and Communication Technologies (ICT) systems are asked to consider these aspects and to build interaction systems which are able to support and react to changing user wishes and needs. This work focuses on the identification and elaboration of this additional user-related and contextual information and facilitates to structure the design process of new user-adaptive systems. Based on a comprehensive literature review this work presents methods, tools and systems used to pre and post process user- and context-related information as well as different approaches for the adaption decision process. Additionally, based on a set of selected systems the work illustrates the adaption process.

Keywords: Personalization · User · Modeling · Preferences · Context-aware · Adaptivity · Adaption · Decision · Process

1 Introduction

The adaption to the user is a fundamental requirement in the HCI field. Considering the mobile and global working economy, the classical approach "one application fits every user in all situations" is not appropriate anymore. In order to achieve the greatest usability and accessibility for the majority of users and especially for various situations, applications also need to take additional user-related and contextual information into account. Using these parameters, applications can better adapt to the user and the current situation, and thus become more appropriate, accurate and satisfiable. This work targets the identification and the elaboration of these important aspects towards the design of personalized user interaction.

Before starting to elaborate criteria, methods and possibilities for the design of personalizable applications, it is important to provide a basic understanding about what the term "personalization" means in the context of HCI. In [1] personalization is defined

M. Kurosu (Ed.): HCI 2016, Part I, LNCS 9731, pp. 198–207, 2016.
DOI: 10.1007/978-3-319-39510-4_19

as follows: "Personalization is the task of providing adapted capabilities to the user of a system on the basis of implicitly gathered user information". The definition emphasizes two crucial components: first, "providing adapted capabilities to the user", and second, "on the basis of implicitly gathered user information". In this section, we focus on the former component, namely the adapted capabilities, the latter is discussed separately in Sect. 2.3. According to [1] personalization primary aims at the adaption of the system to the needs and wishes of the user. In contrast, Anthony Jameson argues in [2] that personalization encompasses other features besides adaptation to individual user. In his definitions personalization is conducted of several overlapping aspects, namely adaptability, adaption and anthropomorphism. Figure 1 illustrates these overlapping aspects.

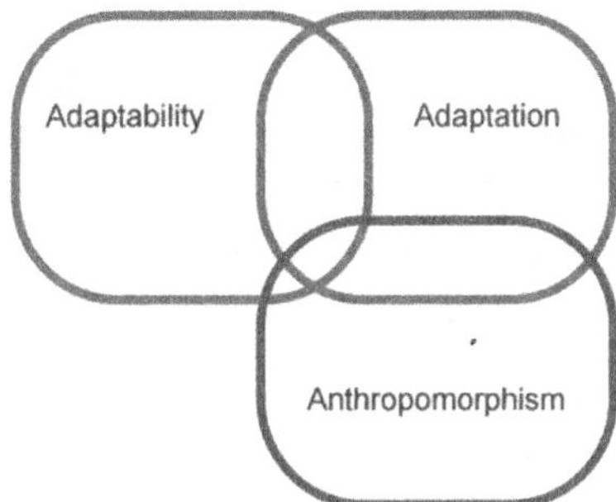

Fig. 1. Illustration of overlapping aspects of personalization as defined in [2]

This definition raises a new question - what are the differences between adaptability, adaption and anthropomorphism? Anthony Jameson [2] uses the following definitions:

- Adaptability: The user is able to modify aspects of a system to suit her own preferences.
- Adaption: The system modifies its own behavior at least partly independently of specifications by the system.
- Anthropomorphism: The system exhibits human-like features e.g., depicted face and/or body, natural language for input or output and lifelike behaviors like eye-blinking and head scratching.

Others [3, 4] distinguish mainly between adaptability (sometimes also called customizability) and adaption, whereas the naming and the meaning of the former remain the same and the naming and the meaning of the later is more concrete. Today, in this context the more popular term "adaptivity" or "user-adaptive system" is used. In [2], a user-adaptive system is defined as follows: "A user-adaptive system is an interactive system which adapts its behavior to each individual user on the basis of nontrivial inferences from information about that user."

Admittedly, this reduction of personalization to adaptability and adaptivity may be suitable for many user interfaces and applications, but especially for modern avatar-based user interfaces (UIs) e.g., as introduced in [5], it makes sense to consider the anthropomorphism aspect in the personalization process.

In summary, personalization aims to adapt a system (**the adaption process**) according to concrete decisions (**adaption decision**) that are influenced by users' wishes, needs, requirements and external circumstances (**the acquisition and preprocessing of applicable information**). The following sections will outline these facets starting from the adaption process, over the acquisition and preprocessing of applicable information to the adaption decision.

2 The Adaption Process

In general, there are numerous ways to adapt a system according to user's wishes, needs and requirements. According to [6], approaches for adaption can be classified into two categories: customization and automatic adaption. Coutand argues in [1] that the first category pertains to systems that offer their users the capability to select some alternative presentations or interaction characteristics. He notes that these systems are able to alleviate some constraints due to the "one-fit-all" paradigm, but that customization does not really improve the usability. For the second category, there are at least two possibilities: (a) One can, e.g., use its own service, system and/or application and implement personalization mechanisms on one or several layers as described in the 3-layer user interface model [4] or (b) one can utilize existing and available frameworks such as [7–9] or [10] to develop an adaptable and adaptive application or service. However, the automatic adaption process on itself involves a wide range of aspects and a detailed elaboration and listing of these aspects would go beyond the scope of this work. This work focuses primary on the question - "What is needed for the adaption decision and how is this decision taken?" rather than on the question – "How is the automatic adaption process implemented or realized?"

3 Acquisition and Preprocessing of Applicable Information

As already mentioned, the adaption decision is influenced by several overlapping aspects like users' wishes, needs, requirements and external circumstances. Thus, in the first step one has to think about how to provide these different information to the system. In order to reach this goal, the following consecutive stages are required:

(a) the definition of the application field, followed by (b) the definition of the user (modeling of the user model), and finally (c) the definition of (additional) contextual parameters (e.g., lightning, user's location, user-task, etc.). The following sections discuss these three stages along a few key requirements relevant for the practical implementation.

3.1 Selection of the Application Field

The first stage tries to limit the amount of potential parameters to those which are useful for the user and the concrete application. It is evident that applications of different fields require very often different parameters. As an example, a system that supports collaborative work requires other parameters as a system that recommends products for a user during an online shopping tour. The former would probably use parameters like "the number of co-workers", whereas the later would probably use parameters like "the search history ". Thus, it is important to identify the primary field of the application before one can start to elaborate additional adaptivity aspects.

In [1], the following application fields have been defined:

- Adapting an interface
- Giving help
- Helping the user to find information (adaptive hypermedia)
- Recommending products, items and services
- Supporting learning (user adaptive tutoring systems)

In [3], the additional two fields have been identified:

- Conduct a dialog
- Support collaboration

Such a list is not meant to be exhaustive, but it provides a good overview about the diversity of systems and applications. The following sections focus mainly on the "adapting an interface" application field.

3.2 The Definition of the User

The user plays the leading role in user-adaptive-systems. Thus, the second stage focuses on user-related information and on building, maintaining and utilizing user models. But what does the term "user model" mean? At this point it is necessary to provide a concrete definition of the term.

User Model. According to [11] "user models are defined as models that systems have of users that reside inside a computational environment". Analogues to this, in [12] the user model is defined as "a representation of information about an individual user that is essential for an adaptive system to provide the adaptation effect, i.e., to behave differently for different users". According to these definitions the user model can be seen as a concrete snapshot representation of the user, which is needed by the user-adaptive-system. The generation of such a snapshot representations is done in the user modeling process.

User Modeling Process. In [12], the user modeling process is defined as: "To create and maintain an up-to-date user model, an adaptive system collects data for the user model from various sources that may include **implicitly observing** user interaction and **explicitly requesting** direct input from the user. This process is known as user modeling". A similar definition was provided by [13], "The aim of user modeling is to capture user information such as preferences, beliefs, goals, and intentions to construct a user model". Both definitions confirm that the aim of the modeling process is to acquire user related data/information in order to update the user model. This information is stored in the **user profile** [1]. Furthermore, the first definition has additionally two interesting aspects, user information is implicitly observed and/or explicitly requested. This conclusion is also drawn by [14]. The most common method for explicit user information collection are simple questionnaires. However, drawbacks of explicit methods are that they place additional burden on the user [15] and create potential privacy concerns towards providing personal data. Methods for implicit user information collection on the other hand do not require any intervention by the user during the process of acquiring user preferences. Widely applied sources for implicit user information collection are browsing activity, web logs and search logs [16].

There are a number of common challenges related to the user modeling process [26]: The so called **cold-start problem** refers to the situation, when a system is lacking implicitly gathered user information, because it is used for the first time. More generally **profile sparseness** can also occur in systems that strongly rely on explicit gathering of user information, in case users provide incomplete feedback on the user preferences questionnaire. Another challenge to address in the user modeling process is to reflect the impact of different contexts, that a system might be used in (**user profile personae**) - e.g., it could make a difference, if an application is used at home or when being on the move. Although considered as a promising approach to address the aforementioned problems [27], sharing user information among different applications (i.e., using **out-of-band data**) might be restricted due to business reasons and requires that both user profiles are based on a common taxonomy.

User Profile. As already mentioned, user models are usually stored in the so called user profile. There are several methods to realize a user profile repository. Starting from scratch one can use, e.g., (a) widely used a key-value model or (b) a markup scheme model (hierarchical data structure consisting of markup tags such as XML tags) or (c) ontology based models expressed in markup languages such as Web Ontology Language (OWL) [17] or Resource Description Framework (RDF) [18]. Alternatively one can utilize existing approaches like [19] or [20].

In [19] the focus is not only on a specific user model, but the solution accepts different techniques in order to address multiple user models. Each user model may address different needs of various domains. Analogous to [19], the solution provided by the Global Public Inclusive Infrastructure (GPII) [20] focuses not only on the description of user preferences, but also on the description of the platform and environmental characteristics. The remaining question is where are the differences between user related data like user preferences and other contextual data like environmental conditions? Are there any differences from the perspective of the persistence? These questions are discussed in the next section.

3.3 Considering Additional Contextual Parameters

In the previous sections, we discussed the modelling of the user and the persistence of the user model within the user profile. However, user-adaptive-systems require very often additional and not directly user-related information in order to adapt the user-system interaction and/or its behavior in an optimal manner. Moreover, these parameters are very often live or at least transient [12]. Concrete practical examples of such short-living parameters are (a) the current lighting or the noise level the user is surrounded by (b) user's location, direction or motion speed or (c) user's task or the goal of the current user-system interaction. In general, this information can be summarized as contextual information and these parameters differ from the user model or the user profile, respectively. In [21] context is defined as follows: "Context is any information that can be used to characterize the situation of an entry. An entry is a person, place, or object that is considered relevant to the interaction between a user and an application, including the user and the application themselves". The emphasis in this definition is on the term "situation" and reflects the previously mentioned transience. Admittedly, the description of a situation can be multilayered and quite complex. There is no definite agreement about what should be included into the area of context. In [12, 13], this issue is tackled by providing the following classifications for context information:

- The **spatio-temporal context** addresses aspects that are related to time and space like the current time, user's current position, his or her direction, speed or track.
- The **environmental context** captures the entities that surround the user such as, the temperature, lighting, noise or physical objects and obstacles.
- The **personal context** represents the user's physiological and mental state. The physiological part consists of parameters like the pulse, weight, age and the mental state consist of parameters like user mood, expertise, anger and stress.
- The **task context** describes the user's intention and may be described with explicit goals or the task breakdown structure.
- The **social context** characterizes the social aspects, e.g., information about friends, neighbors, co-workers, and relatives.
- The **information context** is the information space that is available at a given time.

Following the list, one can see that there are numerous context aspects which may be considered during the design of user-adaptive systems. Depending on the application field designers very often need to pay attention just to one context class or at least to a combination of some context classes. Systems that are able to provide such information are called context-aware systems. In [1], a context-aware system is defined as follows: "A system is context-aware if it uses context to provide relevant information and/or service to the user, where relevancy depends on the user's task". From the designers' point of view a personalization in a limited setting (e.g., using spatio-temporal context information in conjunction with a mobile phone application) it would make sense to develop the own context-aware system to achieve this goal. In a broader setting (e.g., in an environmental setting with different users and various devices) it would make sense to utilize existing approaches and systems. A good overview about existing approaches and systems is given in [22, 23].

4 The Adaption Decision

The last missing step towards personalization is the adaption decision. As argued before, the adaption decision is influenced by the applicable information (presented in Sect. 3) and serves as the main factor for the adaption process (presented in Sect. 2). Again, there are various approaches to realize a concrete adaption decision but at the same time an appropriate approach is very often determined by the nature of the available information. As an example, quantitative values (e.g., a range from 0 to 100) may be applicable by rule-based adaption decision systems whereas probability distribution values may rather be applicable for uncertainty-based adaption decisions. The following section outlines a few selected adaption decision approaches and provides practical examples of applicable input values for the decision making.

4.1 Rule-Based Systems

A very practical and easy way to realize an adaption decision is to use a rule-based decision making process. As mentioned before, rule-based systems use quantitative input values which can be evaluated using simple algebraic methods [12] and comparative operators. In the context of adaptive mobile user interaction, a rule-based decision example could look like the following pseudo code snippet:

```
if illuminance > an overcast summer's day then
|   render high contrast user interface;
else
|   render default user interface;
end
```

4.2 Case-Based Reasoning Systems

In [24], case-based reasoning is described as follows: "Case-Based Reasoning means to retrieve former, already solved problems similar to the current one and to attempt to modify their solutions to fit for the current problem". Applied on the previous example of an adaptive mobile user interaction a case-based reasoning decision could look like the following pseudo code snippet:

```
on illuminance change do
|   retrieve former illuminance adaption decisions;
|   perform a nearest neighbor search algorithm to obtain a similar case;
|   if similar case slightly differs from the current case then
|   |   use the similar adaption decision;
|   else
|   |   modify similar adaption decision (e.g., using interpolation);
|   end
|   retain the modified adaption decision for future purpose;
end
```

The case-based reasoning consists of two processing steps. The first step is the retrieval of former and similar cases and the second step is the concrete usage or the modification of this former case. Case-based reasoning systems rely on a set of former decisions. However, if such a set is not available, one can build a set from scratch by involving the user into the decision process (e.g., by questioning the user if the current adaption decision fits his or her needs) and the learning of these decisions for future purpose.

4.3 Fuzzy Decision Making Systems

Informally, a fuzzy set is a class of objects in which there is no sharp boundary between those objects that belong to the class and those that do not [25]. The basic idea is to allow truth values to take values between 0 and 1, with 0 representing absolute falseness and 1 absolute truth [12]. Applied to the example of an adaptive mobile user interaction, a fuzzy decision making system could use the following three fuzzy functions to define "dark", "bright" and "glary" environments.

$$\mu_{x1} := \textit{dark environment, illuminance between } 0 \textit{ and } 500\ lx$$

$$\mu_{x2} := \textit{bright environment, illuminance between } 50 \textit{ and } 20.000\ lx$$

$$\mu_{x3} := \textit{glary environment, illuminance at least } 7.000\ lx$$

In Fig. 2 the three fuzzy functions are illustrated. The x axis represents the illuminance in lux and the y axis the degree of truth. In this example one can use the maximum operator and a concrete illuminance value e.g., 300 lx to elaborate the maximum degree of membership. This is depicted in the following equation:

$$\mu_{max}(x) = max[\mu_{x1}(x); \mu_{x2}(x); \mu_{x3}(x)] \Rightarrow \mu_{max}(300) = max[0.05; 0.9; 0] = 0.9 = \mu_{x2}(300)$$

Thus, for a concrete illumination value of 300 lx the system would adapt the user interface in order to satisfy the bright environment. The following pseudo code illustrates this decision rule:

```
on illuminance change do
    x:= current illuminance value;
    if max[μx1(x); μx2(x); μx3(x)] == μx1(x) then
    |  render low contrast user interface;
    else if max[μx1(x); μx2(x); μx3(x)] == μx2(x) then
    |  render default user interface;
    else
    |  render high contrast user interface;
    end
end
```

As mentioned previously, examples presented in sections are very simplified and represent just three possibilities one can utilize to realize adaption decisions. For the sake of completeness, it should be noted that there are other approaches like the Bayesian network, neuro-fuzzy approach, machine learning approach or the combination of these [3, 12].

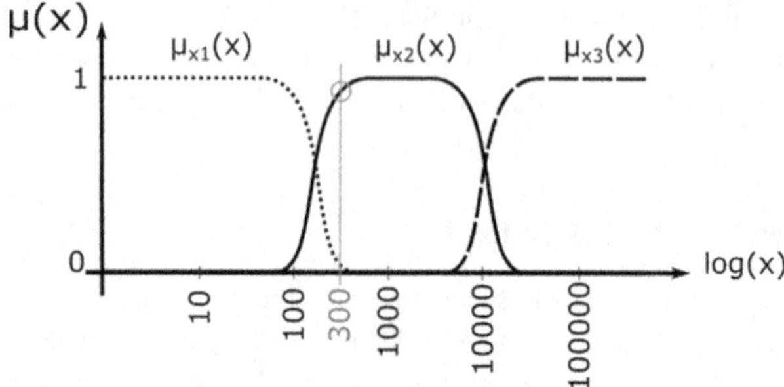

Fig. 2. Illustration of overlapping fuzzy functions defining “dark”, “bright” and “glary” environments.

5 Conclusion

In this paper, we have surveyed the field of the personalization process within modern HCI systems. We clarified the difference between the ordinary customization process, which does not really increase the usability, and the automatic adaption process which in contrast targets this goal. We outlined tree major working processes towards personalization in user-adaptive systems, namely (a) the acquisition and preprocessing of applicable information, (b) the adaption decision and finally (c) the adaption process. The main focus of this work was on the first two working processes, whereas the last one was just briefly sketched. More concrete details regarding the adaption process can be obtained from the referred literature. This survey in not meant to be exhaustive, but it provides a good summary and a quick overview about different aspects which developers have to keep in mind during the design of personalizing applications, services and systems.

Acknowledgements. Much of the work reported here was within the international project YouDo which is co-funded by the AAL Joint Programme (REF. AAL-2012-5-155) and the following National Authorities and R&D programs in Austria, Germany and Switzerland: BMVIT, program benefit, FFG (AT), BMBF (DE) and SERI (CH).

References

1. Coutand, O.: A Framework for Contextual Personalised Applications. Diss Kassel University Press GmbH, Kassel (2009)
2. Jameson, A.: Systems that adapt to their users. Decis. Making **2**, 23 (2011)
3. Weibelzahl, S.: Evaluation of Adaptive Systems. Springer, Heidelberg (2001)
4. Mayer, C., et al.: A comparative study of systems for the design of flexible user interfaces. J. Ambient Intell. Smart Environ. (2015). (in press)
5. Sili, M., Bobeth, J., Sandner, E., Hanke, S., Schwarz, S., Mayer, C.: Talking faces in lab and field trials. In: Zhou, J., Salvendy, G. (eds.) ITAP 2015. LNCS, vol. 9193, pp. 134–144. Springer, Heidelberg (2015)
6. Fink, J., et al.: A review and analysis of commercial user modeling servers for personalization on the world wide web. User Model. User-Adap. Interact. **10**(2-3), 209–249 (2000)

7. Mayer, C., Morandell, M., Gira, M., Hackbarth, K., Petzold, M., Fagel, S.: AALuis, a user interface layer that brings device independence to users of AAL systems. In: Miesenberger, K., Karshmer, A., Penaz, P., Zagler, W. (eds.) ICCHP 2012, Part I. LNCS, vol. 7382, pp. 650–657. Springer, Heidelberg (2012)
8. ISO/IEC, ISO/IEC 24752, Information technology – user interfaces – universal remote console, Part 1: Framework, First edition, Technical report (2008)
9. Vanderheiden, G., et al.: Use of user interface sockets to create naturally evolving intelligent environments. In: Proceedings of the 11th International Conference on Human-Computer Interaction (2005)
10. Hanke, S., Mayer, C., Hoeftberger, O., Boos, H., Wichert, R., Tazari, M.-R., Wolf, P., Furfari, F.: universAAL – An Open and Consolidated AAL Platform. In: Wichert, R., Eberhardt, B. (eds.) Ambient Assisted Living. Non-series, vol. 63, pp. 127–140. Springer, Heidelberg (2011)
11. Fischer, G.: User modeling in human–computer interaction. User Model. User-Adap. Interact. **11**(1-2), 65–86 (2001)
12. Brusilovsky, P., Millán, E.: User models for adaptive hypermedia and adaptive educational systems. In: Brusilovsky, P., Kobsa, A., Nejdl, W. (eds.) Adaptive Web 2007. LNCS, vol. 4321, pp. 3–53. Springer, Heidelberg (2007)
13. Muhammad, A., et al.: Research issues in personalization of mobile services. Int. J. Inf. Eng. Electron. Bus. **4**(4) (2012)
14. Gauch, S., Speretta, M., Chandramouli, A., Micarelli, A.: User profiles for personalized information access. In: Brusilovsky, P., Kobsa, A., Nejdl, W. (eds.) Adaptive Web 2007. LNCS, vol. 4321, pp. 54–89. Springer, Heidelberg (2007)
15. Bozdag, E.: Bias in algorithmic filtering and personalization. Ethics Inf. Technol. **15**(3), 209–227 (2013)
16. Kelly, D., et al.: Implicit feedback for inferring user preference: a bibliography. ACM SIGIR Forum **37**(2), 18–28 (2003)
17. OWL – Semantic Web Standards, W3C (2013). https://www.w3.org/2001/sw/wiki/OWL Web. 03 Feb 2016
18. RDF – Semantic Web Standards, W3C (2014). http://www.w3.org/RDF/ Web. 03 Feb 2016
19. Nurmi, P., et al.: A system for context-dependent user modeling. In: Meersman, R., Tari, Z., Herrero, P. (eds.) OTM 2006 Workshops. LNCS, vol. 4278, pp. 1894–1903. Springer, Heidelberg (2006)
20. Vanderheiden, G., et al.: The global public inclusive infrastructure, Cloud4all and Prosperity4all. Assistive Technol. Res. Pract. **33**, 417–422 (2013)
21. Dey, A.K.: Providing architectural support for building context-aware applications. Diss. Georgia Institute of Technology (2000)
22. Jong-yi, H., et al.: Context-aware systems: a literature review and classification. Expert Syst. Appl. **36**(4), 8509–8522 (2009)
23. Baldauf, M., et al.: A survey on context-aware systems. Int. J. Ad Hoc Ubiquitous Comput. **2**(4), 263–277 (2007)
24. Schmidt, R., et al.: Cased-based reasoning for medical knowledge-based systems. Int. J. Med. Inf. **64**(2), 355–367 (2001)
25. Bellman, R.E., et al.: Decision-making in a fuzzy environment. Manage. Sci. **17**, 141–164 (1970)
26. Ghosh, R., et al.: Discovering user profiles. In: Proceedings of the 18th International Conference on World Wide Web, pp. 1233–1234 (2009)
27. Ghosh, R., et al.: Mashups for semantic user profiles. In: Proceedingd 17th International World Wide Web Conference, Beijing (2008)

Designing Activity Diagrams Aiming at Achieving Usability in Interactive Applications: An Empirical Study

Williamson Silva(✉), Natasha M. Costa Valentim, and Tayana Conte

USES Research Group, Institute of Computing (IComp), Federal University of Amazonas (UFAM), Manaus, Brazil
{williamson.silva,natashavalentim, tayana}@icomp.ufam.edu.br

Abstract. With the increasing use of interactive applications, it is necessary that software companies produce applications providing a good quality of use for end users. It is important to assist designers in elaborating of design models, aiming at achieving usability of the interactive applications. We proposed a technique, called UDRT-AD (Usability Design Reading Technique for Activity Diagrams) that helps designers in modeling Activity Diagrams aiming at achieving usability in interactive applications. The goal of this paper is to present an empirical study carried out to verify the feasibility of using the UDRT-AD technique. The analysis of the results showed that the UDRT-AD technique could be employed to help in both creating the activity diagrams and early prevention of usability problems. Furthermore, we identified some issues that need to be improved in the UDRT-AD technique to further facilitate its use for industry.

Keywords: Usability · Design · Activity diagram · Empirical study

1 Introduction

The success of the interactive applications is related to the quality they provide to their end users. Among the quality attributes, usability is one of the most important quality attributes [4], because it influences in the acceptability of interactive applications [1]. Several techniques have been proposed to help improving usability into the development process of interactive applications. Most of these techniques only evaluate usability through the artifacts designed on early stages or in final version of the application [7]. However, few techniques are created to assist designers in artifacts designing aiming at improving the usability of the application [12]. Therefore, assisting designers in this process ensures that user interactions are efficient, functionally correct and error tolerant [1]. Considering designing for usability in the early stages of the development process (e.g., Design phase), can help preventing early usability problems, improving the quality of use, and reducing project costs [8].

One of the artifacts created in the early stages of the development process is the Activity Diagram (AD) [14]. AD's shows the logic of the activities that can be carried in an interactive application. In addition, this diagram is used as complement for others

M. Kurosu (Ed.): HCI 2016, Part I, LNCS 9731, pp. 208–219, 2016.
DOI: 10.1007/978-3-319-39510-4_20

artifacts into the development process (e.g., scenarios, mockups and others). Therefore, it is important to help designers create these diagrams aiming at developing an application with an acceptable level of usability.

In order to support designers in this direction, we proposed the Usability Design Reading Technique for Activity Diagrams (UDRT-AD) technique. In order to propose this technique, we considered two main principles: (1) to use procedures of reading techniques, because they guide the designers in the creation process of the artifacts [13]; and, (2) to use empirical studies to assess, improve and assist in the evolution of the technique. The UDRT-AD technique assists designers in the prevention of usability problems that may influence the quality of the final application. UDRT-AD provides a set of steps that can be followed by designers. Each step consists of four elements that support the AD modeling, and improve the usability of the final application during the modeling of that AD. Moreover, the technique has application examples to help designers with little experience in both AD modeling and usability principles.

In this paper, we present an empirical study performed that aimed at analysing if the UDRT-AD is feasible when compared to the conventional approach. To do so, we verified through this empirical study: (a) the effectiveness; (b) the time spent for the modeling process of a diagram; (c) the degree of correctness of the designed diagrams; and (d) the number of possible usability problems found through the designed diagrams and that could influence the quality of the final application.

The remainder of this paper is organized as follows: Sect. 2 present the work related to this research. Section 3 provides an overview of the UDRT-AD technique proposed. Section 4 describes the planning and the execution of the empirical study. Section 5 present the results of the study. Finally, Sect. 6 presents our conclusions and future work.

2 Related Works

One of the artifacts used in the early stages of the development process is the Activity Diagram (AD) [2]. The diagram is employed to capture the dynamics of an application, without being limited to the behavior description of a particular functionality [5]. Designing an AD, thinking in the usability of the application, can support the correctness and conformity, as well as increasing the quality of the designed application by this diagram [5, 11]. Therefore, several studies have been proposed in order to ensure usability as well as verify the completeness and correctness of these diagrams [3, 5, 14]. The following are some of the proposed methods to improve the usability of interactive applications through ADs.

Valentim *et al.* [14] proposed the MIT 3, which is part of a set of techniques called MIT (Model Inspection Technique for Usability Evaluation). The MIT's aims auxiliary the usability inspection through design models. Specifically, MIT 3 evaluates the usability through activity diagrams and, to do so, it provides 14 verification items that guide the inspectors during the inspection process.

Silva e Silveira [3] proposed a set of guidelines that aim at evaluating the usability in the design stage of interactive applications, using design models of the areas of Human-Computer Interaction and Software Engineering. Among the guidelines, there are those focused on evaluating the usability through activity diagrams. The technique has 16 items that assist the identification of usability defects.

However, the cited techniques only evaluate the usability of the application through activity diagrams, in other words, when these diagrams have been modeled. Therefore, it is necessary to develop techniques to assist designers in elaborating this artifact, in order to improve the quality of the final application. These techniques should enable designers to be guided in a proactive way to design and to improve the usability of interactive applications, through this diagram. Based on this, we proposed a design technique, which will be shown below.

3 Usability Design Reading Technique for Activity Diagrams - UDRT-AD

The UDRT-AD (Usability Design Reading Technique for Activity Diagrams) technique consists of a reading technique that assists designers in the process of modeling an AD's, aimed at improving usability of the interactive applications [11]. A reading technique is a specific type of technique that provides guidelines that can be employed for assisting in the execution of a specific task [13]. This technique aims to support (or even teach) designers (experienced or not) in building an activity diagram. To do so, the technique helps identifying the diagram elements from a textual description (scenarios or use cases); and, anticipating the usability of the final application, by providing guidelines that suggest improvements of the usability during the construction of the activities diagram.

The phases to use the UDRT-AD technique are shown in Fig. 1. In phase 1, the designers should first try to understand the problem which needs to be solved. In phase 2, the designer uses the UDRT-AD technique for extract the elements, from the textual description and designing the AD. In parallel with the diagram's design, the designers must perform the reading of the usability guidelines presented in UDRT-AD technique. They should also verify what part of the diagram is possible to support the usability of the final application. The UDRT-AD technique has six steps that guide the designers in the designing of diagrams and in anticipation of usability. These steps are: Identification of Actors, Identification of Start Node, Identification of Activities, Grouping of Activities, Transition Activities, and Identification of the End Nodes. Each step consists of: a Heuristic that helps to identify the diagram elements (Fig. 1 element A); the representation of the heuristic Element (Fig. 1 element B); an Instruction that teaches how to insert the elements in diagram (Fig. 1 element C); and, Usability Guidelines that guides how to anticipate the application's usability during the design of the diagram (Fig. 1 Elemento D). To assist in using the technique, each Heuristic and each Instruction has an application example (Fig. 1 Element E), showing how to extract the AD element from the textual description.

As it was exemplified on Fig. 1 element E, the swimlanes identified in the scenario are "User" and "Application". Then, the designers identified that the activities "Execute the Activity A" and "Perform the Activity B" are respectively related to the swimlanes "User" and "Application". In parallel the designers used the usability guidelines to anticipate usability. When using those guidelines, designers can perceive that the

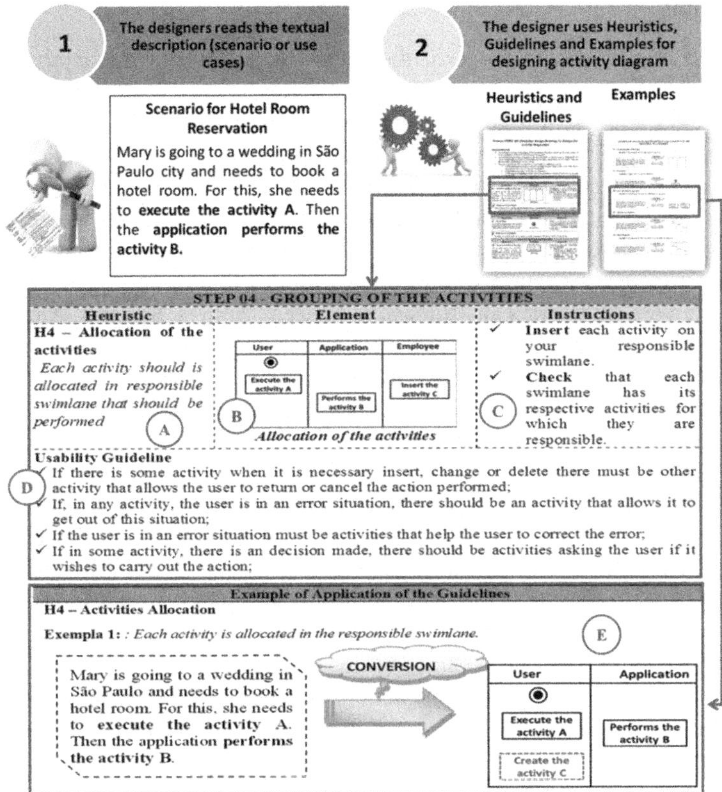

Fig. 1. Example of using the UDRT-AD technique

grouped activity presents an error situation. The designers are instructed to create another activity that allows the user to exit the error situation.

In order to check technique performance compared with the used practice in the software companies (call in this paper of conventional approach), we conducted an empirical study comparing the two approaches (UDRT-AD and conventional approach). The empirical study is described below.

4 Empirical Study

This empirical study was conducted in order to verify the feasibility of the UDRT-AD technique, and to indicate what parts of the technique need improvements. The UDRT-AD technique was compared to a conventional approach, commonly used in software companies. In a conventional approach, first the diagrams are modeled and then, perform a usability inspection through the created diagrams. In this study, the technique applied for inspecting the diagrams was MIT 3, once it was used as a basis for defining the UDRT-AD usability guidelines.

4.1 Planning

In this step, we defined the scope of the study (preparation of the approaches), we prepared the materials which were employed (consent and characterization forms, elaboration of scenarios, instructions for the study, modeling forms, and a worksheet for the annotation of the identified discrepancies for the group that applied the conventional approach), and we selected and trained the subjects. All the activities of this phase were carried out by the study moderator and reviewed by two others researchers. Furthermore, we performed a pilot study for evaluating the study artefacts. The results of the pilot study can be found in our previous work [13].

Subjects were undergraduate student volunteers from a Systems Analysis and Design class in their 5th semester at a course on Information Systems at Federal University of Amazonas. Sixteen undergraduate students consented to participate in the study. They signed a consent form and filled out a characterization form that measured their expertise with Human–Computer Interaction (HCI) Design/Evaluation (HCI) and Software Development (SD).

The characterization data was used to classify subjects into four categories (none, low, medium or high experience). A subject is considered to have: (a) high experience, if (s)he participated in more than 5 projects/evaluations in HCI in the industry; (b) medium experience, if (s)he participated from 1 to 4 projects/evaluations in HCI in the industry; (c) low experience, if (s)he participated in at least one HCI project/evaluation in the classroom; (d) none experience, if (s)he had no prior knowledge on HCI or if (s)he had some notions acquired through readings/lectures, but without practical experience. The data on experience in software development was defined similarly. Third (HCI) and fourth (SD) columns of Table 2, presented in Sect. 5, show each subject's categorization respectively.

To decrease the bias of participants who have more experience than others, the subjects were divided into two groups with the same number of subjects and with equivalent experience. Thus, the subjects were assigned to each group at random and the groups were balanced, according to the subjects' experience, which was reported in the characterization form. Therefore, each group was formed by eight subjects.

4.2 Execution

Before the study, we carried out a training for all study subjects. This training aimed at explaining usability concepts and how to apply an inspection method (Heuristic Evaluation [10]). Then, the subjects were divided into two groups. Each group remained in separate rooms and there was training on each technique. For Group 01, we conducted training on the UDRT-AD technique. For Group 02, we held a training on how to model a diagram and then on how to perform an inspection using the MIT 3. Next, the study artefacts were delivered individually and we did not allow communication between the subjects.

The subjects from each group were given a scenario and, from this scenario, they performed the AD modeling. The scenario employed to model the AD was booking a hotel room. In this scenario, the user carried out the activities from logging in the application to confirming the booking of the hotel room. Furthermore, the subjects in Group 01 (UDRT-AD) received the UDRT-AD technique to assist in the modeling of the activity diagram targeting at improving the usability of the interactive application. On the other hand, subjects in Group 02 (conventional approach) received a document containing instructions, based on literature [2], so that they could consult, in case a difficulty arised during the AD modeling. After performing the modeling of the AD, subjects in Group 02, carried out a usability inspection in the modeled diagram using the MIT 3 technique. During the inspection, after detecting a usability problem using the MIT 3, the subjects wrote down the defect in the discrepancy spreadsheet.

We highlight that throughout the implementation process, the subjects performed their activities individually and received no assistance from the involved researchers.

4.3 Analysis of Results

Finally, we performed the analysis of the results. In this step, the researchers analyzed the diagrams modeled by each subject. In order to perform this process, we removed the name of the participants and a code was inserted to represent them with the goal to avoid causing bias in the analysis of the results. For the analysis of the quantitative data, we employed the following indicators: effectiveness, modeling time, correctness, and usability error prevention.

The Effectiveness indicator was calculated as follows:

$$\text{Effectiveness (Subject X)} = \frac{(\text{NMA} - \text{nAnC})}{(\text{NMA} - \text{nAnC}) + \text{nAO}}, \text{were :}$$

- Subject X is the reference to the study subject;
- NMA is the number of modeled activities by Subject X in the activity diagram;
- nAnC is the number of activities that are not in the context of the scenario employed by Subject X to model the activity diagram;
- nAO is the number of missing activities in the diagram modeled by Subject X, i.e., activities that are present in the scenario but are not present in the diagram modeled by Subject X.

The Modeling Time indicator it was calculated in hours and represents the total time spent by each subject to carry out the modeling of the AD.

The Correctness indicator checks how correct the diagrams were modeled. We classified the defects found by researchers according to the categorization of defects by Travassos *et al.* [13]. This categorization has been employed to classify types of defects found by inspection techniques of design models (e.g., OORTs [13] and ActCheck [5]). In the Table 1 the five categories are presented, these categories were tailored to the specific context of activity diagrams, as suggested by Travassos *et al.* [13].

Finally, the Usability Error Prevention indicator verified if the UDRT-AD technique helps preventing usability problems through the modeled diagrams. To do so, we carried out an inspection with two researchers that using the MIT 3 technique over the

Table 1. Defects Categories (adapted from [13])

Category	General description
Omission	Necessary activities or elements that have been omitted in the activity diagram
Incorrect fact	Activities or elements in the activity diagram that contradict information presented in the employed scenario
Inconsistency	Activities or elements within the activity diagram which are inconsistent with others parts of the activity diagram
Ambiguity	Activities or elements of the activity diagram that are ambiguous, i.e., the designer can interpret the activities or elements in different ways and may not lead to a correct interpretation
Extraneous information	Activities or elements are modeled, but are not needed nor used

activity diagrams modeled by subjects in the group that used UDRT-AD to design the activity diagrams.

5 Results and Discussion

In this section, the quantitative results of the empirical study are presented. The statistical analysis was carried out using the statistical tool SPSS V. 21, and $\alpha = 0.05$. The choice of statistical significance and the Mann-Whitney non parametrical statistic test [9] was motivated by the small sample size used in this study [6], as suggested by Wohlin *et al.* [15]. We used the boxplot graph to facilite visualization of data. The results are shown below.

5.1 Effectiveness

Table 2 shows the overall results per subject and per approach. In this table is shown the number of modeled activities (fifth column), number of activities that were not present in the textual description (sixth column), and number of missing activities (seventh column). Based on that information, we performed the effectiveness calculation for each participant (eighth column). Figure 2 (Item A) shows the boxplots graph with the distribution of effectiveness per approach.

From Fig. 2 (Item A), we can observe that the median of the UDRT-AD Group is a little higher that the median of conventional approach Group. In addition, it is possible to see through the graph that the subjects who employed the UDRT-AD have their effectiveness distributed around the median. The results of the subjects of employing the conventional approach have a greater dispersion. We compared the two samples using the Mann-Whitney test, we found no significant differences between the two groups (p = 0,382). These results suggest that the UDRT-AD and the conventional approach offer similar levels of effectiveness when employed to design an activity diagram.

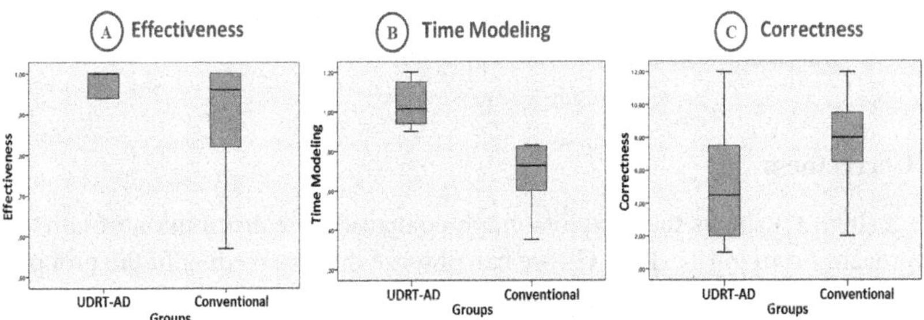

Fig. 2. Boxplots with quantitative results per group

5.2 Time Modeling

Table 2 (ninth column) shows the modeling time in hours per subject. The boxplots graph with the distribution of time modeling per approach (Fig. 2 Item B) suggests that UDRT-AD Group obtained time modeling was much higher than conventional approach Group. Also, the median of the UDRT-AD Group is much higher than the median of the conventional approach Group. This was confirmed by Mann-Whitney test (p = 0,000). Therefore, we can conclude that the modeling time needed for an

Table 2. Results per subjects designing the activity diagram

	#S	HCI	SD	NMA	nAnC	nAO	Effectiveness	Time (h)
Group 01 – UDRT-AD	**01**	L	L	16	01	01	0.94	0.90
	02	L	L	16	-	-	1.00	1.15
	03	M	N	16	-	01	0.94	1.03
	04	N	L	15	-	02	0.88	0.95
	05	N	L	29	04	-	1.00	1.00
	06	N	L	15	-	-	1.00	0.93
	07	N	N	16	-	-	1.00	1.20
	08	N	L	24	-	-	1.00	1.15
Group 02 –Conventional	**09**	N	L	22	02	-	1.00	0.83
	10	N	N	17	-	-	1.00	0.60
	11	L	L	10	-	03	0.77	0.60
	12	L	L	11	-	01	0.92	0.82
	13	M	H	09	01	06	0.57	0.35
	14	L	N	21	-	-	1.00	0.82
	15	N	N	14	-	-	1.00	0.83
	16	N	N	13	-	02	0.87	0.63

Note: #S – Subjects; **HCI -** Experience in **HCI** design / evaluation; **SD –** Experience in **S**oftware **D**evelopment; **N** - None; **H** - High; **M** - Medium; **L** - Low; **NMA –N**umber of **M**odeled **A**ctivities; **nAnC -** **N**umber of **A**ctivities that are **N**ot part of the **C**ontext; **nAO** – **N**umber of **A**ctivities that were **O**mitted in the diagram.

activity diagram to be improved in terms of usability is significantly higher using the UDRT-AD than using the conventional approach.

5.3 Correctness

Figure 2 (Item C) shows the boxplots graph comparing the distribution of correctness per approach. From Fig. 2 (Item C), we can observe that the median of the group using conventional approach is a much higher than the median of the group that used UDRT-AD technique. In other words, we found fewer defects in the diagrams of the participants who used the UDRT-AD than those who used the conventional approach. However, the Mann-Whitney statistical test pointed out that there is no significant difference among the groups (p = 0,161). Therefore, we can be concluded that there is a significant difference between the number of defects found in the modeled diagrams using UDRT-AD and the number of defects found in the modeled diagrams using the conventional approach. However, we can argue that given the small sample used in this study, it is difficult to obtain statistical significance in results obtained.

Table 3. Number of defects found per subjects

Defect types per subject and per group												
	#S	**Om.**		**Inc. Fact.**		**Incons.**		**Ambig.**		**Ext. Inf.**		**TDP**
		At.	**El.**	**At.**	**El.**	**At.**	**El.**	**At.**	**El.**	**At.**	**El.**	
GROUP 01 – UDRT-AD	**01**	01	-	-	01	-	-	-	-	01	-	03
	02	-	-	-	06	-	-	-	-	-	-	06
	03	01	-	-	-	-	-	-	-	-	-	01
	04	02	01	-	-	-	-	-	-	-	-	03
	05	-	-	-	-	-	-	-	-	04	02	06
	06	-	01	-	08	-	-	-	-	-	-	09
	07	-	-	-	12	-	-	-	-	-	-	12
	08	-	01	-	-	-	-	-	-	-	-	01
	TD	04	03	00	27	00	00	00	00	05	02	**TDG=41**
	TTD	**07**		**27**		**00**		**00**		**07**		
GROUP 02 – Conventional	**09**	-	-	-	06	-	-	-	-	02	-	08
	10	-	-	-	06	-	-	-	-	-	-	06
	11	03	-	-	03	-	-	-	-	-	-	10
	12	01	-	-	07	-	-	-	-	-	-	08
	13	06	01	-	01	-	-	-	-	01	-	09
	14	-	03	02	07	-	-	-	-	-	-	12
	15	-	-	-	07	-	-	-	-	-	-	07
	16	02	-	-	-	-	-	-	-	-	-	02
	TD	12	04	02	41	00	00	00	00	03	00	**TDG=62**
	TTD	**16**		**43**		**00**		**00**		**03**		

Note: #S – Subjects; **At.** – Activities; **El.** – Elements; **Om.** – Omission; **Inc. Fact.** – Incorrect Fact; **Incons.** – Inconsistency; **Ambig** – Ambiguity; **Ext. Inf.** – Extraneos Information; **TDP** – Total of Defects per Subject; **TD – T**otal **D**efects per Activities and Elements; **TTD –** Total per Type of Defects; **TDG – T**otal of **D**efects per **G**roup.

Table 3 the number and types of problems identified in the modeled diagrams per subject for each group.

Inconsistency and Ambiguity defects were not found in any of the groups. Regarding the omission defects, Group 01 – UDRT-AD – found fewer defects (07 defects - 04 of activities and 03 of elements) than Group 02 – conventional approach – (16 defects - 12 of activities and 04 of elements). The fact that Group 01 (UDRT-AD) does not have many omission defects may be related to the fact that the UDRT-AD technique uses procedures that guided the subjects to identify the activities and elements of the diagram, from the scenario used.

Group 01 (UDRT-AD) found less Fact Incorrect defects (27 defects – all defects were related to elements) than Group 02 – conventional approach – (43 defects – 02 of activities and 41 of elements). We can observe in Table 3 that most defects were related to the diagram elements. The main reason that caused this type of defect was that the subjects did not use brackets in guard conditions (expressions that decide what the next action to be executed). In Group 02 (conventional approach), since the participants only used a guide containing instructions on how to model of the activity diagram, in almost all diagrams this type of defect was found. However, Group 01 (UDRT-AD) had one heuristic that indicated that the designer had to insert brackets in the guard conditions. Nevertheless, the subjects did not follow this heuristic.

With respect to Extraneous Information defects, in Group 02 (conventional approach) fewer defects were found (03 defects – all were defects related to activities) than in Group 01 (07 defects – 05 of activities and 02 of elements). This may be due to one of the usability guidelines (D9) from the UDRT-AD technique. The D9 guideline suggests the following: "If the user is in an error condition there should be activities that help the user to correct the error". In an attempt to recover from an error condition, the subjects tried to create new activities, which performed the same actions of other activities. One of the suggestions is to improve the guideline so subjects do not get confused.

5.4 Usability Error Prevention

This indicator checked whether the diagram modeled by the subjects from the UDRT-AD group presented potential usability problems that could affect the usability of the application. As the subjects of the Group 02 (conventional approach) had already performed the inspection on their diagrams using the MIT 3 technique, and we wanted to assess the quality of the UDRT-AD, we decided to skip the evaluation of the diagrams designed by this group.

To do this, two researchers with a high degree of industry experience, with 8 and 10 years of experience respectively, were selected to act as the inspectors of the ADs that were modeled using UDRT-AD. To carry out the inspections, the researchers employed the MIT 3 technique. The researchers had already used MIT 3 to conduct inspections in AD of other studies. Table 4 presents the results from the inspection that was held by researchers in the diagrams modeled by the UDRT-AD Group.

From Table 4, we can observe that this group, even though they used the Usability Guidelines present in UDRT-AD, the diagrams showed a high number of potential usability problems that could affect the usability of the application. These problems, if left

Table 4. Number of possible usability problems per subjects of the Group 01 (UDRT-AD)

Subjects of Groups 01	01	02	03	04	05	06	07	08	Total defects
Possible usability problems	05	05	07	03	05	09	01	02	37

untreated, can cause a poor usage experience for end users. Thus, we can see that the Usability Guidelines of the UDRT-AD helped predicting some possible usability problems. However, these Usability Guidelines still need to be improved, in order to assist designers in creating the AD with the least amount of usability problems possible, thus improving the final quality of interactive applications.

6 Conclusion and Future Work

This paper presents an empirical study in order to verify the feasibility of UDRT-AD technique. The UDRT-AD technique is a reading technique that assists designers in modeling activity diagrams aiming at achieving a high degree of the usability during the development of interactive applications. By analyzing the results of the study, we can observe that the UDRT-AD showed a similar effectiveness than the conventional approach. Regarding the time modeling indicator, the group that used the conventional approach had high results than the group that used the UDRT-AD. Thus, the time for modeling an activity diagram predicting usability of the application is increased using the UDRT-AD. Regarding the correctness indicator, we can observe that the UDRT-AD group has a lower number of defects than the conventional approach. Finally, regarding usability errors prevention indicator, in the diagrams designed by subjects yet were identified potential usability problems for application. The study results also showed that the steps present in UDRT-AD technique were important for subjects during diagram design, mainly, the construction examples because these visually aided in the diagram modeling. Furthermore, the UDRT-AD assists in preventing other defects that may influence the quality of the final application. As future work, we intend to implement improvements in UDRT-AD technique and we intend to develop a new version of the UDRT-AD technique. Another objective is to perform further studies to ensure technical quality for future transfer to the software industry.

Acknowledgment. We would like to acknowledge the financial support granted by CAPES (Coordination for Improvement of Higher Education Personnel), and financial support granted by FAPEAM (Foundation for Research Support of the Amazonas State) through processes numbers: 062.00600/2014; 062.00578/2014; and CAPES process 175956/2013. Furthermore, we would like to thank all to the students who participated in the execution of the empirical study.

References

1. Adikari, S., McDonald, C., Collings, P.: A Design Science approach to an HCI research project. In: 18th Australia Conference on Computer-Human Interaction: Design: Activities, Artefacts and Environments, pp. 429–432 (2006)

2. Booch, G., Rumbaugh, J., Jacobson, I.: Modeling Language user Guide. The Addison-Wesley Object Technology Series, 2nd edn., 484 p. (2005)
3. Da Silva, T.S., Silveira, M.S.: Validation of a method for identifying usability problems from UML diagrams. In: IX Brazilian Symposium on Human Factors in Computing Systems (IHC), pp. 179–188 (2010). (in Portuguese)
4. De la Vara, J., Wnuk, K., Berntsson-Svensson, R., Sánchez, J., Regnell, B.: An empirical study on the importance of quality requirements in industry. In: XXIII International Conference on Software Engineering and Knowledge Engineering (SEKE 2011), pp. 438–443 (2011)
5. De Mello, R.M., Pereira, W.M., Travassos, G.H.: Activity diagram inspection on requirements specification. In: XIV Brazilian Symposium on Software Engineering (SBES), pp. 168–177 (2010)
6. Dyba, T., Kampenes, V.B., Sjoberg, D.I.: A systematic review of statistical power in software engineering experiments. Inf. Softw. Technol. **48**(8), 745–755 (2006)
7. Fernandez, A., Insfran, E., Abrahão, S.: Usability evaluation methods for the web: a systematic mapping study. Inf. Softw. Techcol. **53**(8), 789–817 (2011)
8. Juristo, N., Moreno, A.M., Sánchez-Segura, M.-I.: Guidelines for eliciting usability functionalities. IEEE Trans. Softw. Eng. **33**(11), 744–758 (2007)
9. Mann, H.B., Whitney, D.R.: On a test of whether one of two random variables is stochastically larger than the other. Ann. Math. Stat. **18**(1), 50–60 (1947)
10. Nielsen, J.: Heuristic evaluation. In: Nielsen, J., Mack, R.L. (eds.) Usability Inspection Methods. Wiley, New York (1994)
11. Silva, W., Valentim, N.M.C., Conte, T.: Designing activity diagrams aiming at achieving usability in interactive applications. In: XIII Brazilian Symposium on Human Factors in Computing Systems (IHC), vol. A, pp. 349–352 (2014). (in Portuguese)
12. Silva, W., Valentim, N.M.C., Conte, T.: Integrating the usability into the software development process: a systematic mapping study. In: 17th International Conference on Enterprise Information Systems (ICEIS 2015), vol. 3, pp. 105–352 (2015)
13. Travassos, G.H., Shull, F., Fredericks, M., Basili, V.: Detecting defects in object-oriented designs: using reading techniques to increase software quality. In: XIV ACM SIGPLAN Conference on Object-Oriented Programming, Systems, Languages, and Applications, vol. 34(10), pp. 47–56 (1999)
14. Valentim, N.M.C., Silva, T.S., Silveira, M.S., Conte, T.: Comparative study between usability inspection techniques about activity diagrams. In: XII Brazilian Symposium on Human Factors in Computing Systems (IHC 2013), pp. 92–101 (2013). (in Portuguese)
15. Wohlin, C., Runeson, P., Höst, M., Ohlsson, M.C., Regnell, B., Wesslén, A.: Experimentation in Software Engineering: an Introduction, 236 p. Kluwer Academic Publishers, Norwell (2012)

Modeling How to Understand a Target System: Bridging the Gap Between Software Engineers and Usability Experts

Yukiko Tanikawa[1,4](✉), Hideyuki Suzuki[2], Hiroshi Kato[3], Shin'ichi Fukuzumi[1], and Etsuko Harada[4]

[1] NEC Corporation, Kawasaki, Japan
y-tanikawa@cw.jp.nec.com, s-fukuzumi@aj.jp.nec.com
[2] Ibaraki University, Mito, Japan
hideyuki@suzuki-lab.net
[3] The Open University of Japan, Chiba, Japan
Hiroshi@kato.com
[4] University of Tsukuba, Tsukuba, Japan
etharada@human.tsukuba.ac.jp

Abstract. In order to investigate the reasons why software engineers fail in design activities concerning usability, we devised a method to model the features of how to understand a target system. It is the method to visualize differences of system understanding between a software engineer and a usability expert from three aspects, namely qualitative difference, quantitative difference, and difference in recognition to the understanding. Moreover we devised "three layer model diagram" which consists of "system function layer", "task and workflow layer" and "user practice field layer", for describing system understanding. We conducted the experiment and interview for software engineers and analyzed them applying this method. This analysis revealed that software engineers who failed in the activities have a tendency to understand tasks correspond to functions, in addition to understanding an entire system from functions. These suggested that their function-based understandings and little recognition to "system users" and "user practice in the field" in their everyday design activities are included in their failure reason.

Keywords: Design activity · Software engineer · Usability expert · User practice · User task

1 Introduction

Advance in ICT technologies has enabled to realize various functions easily, and it has become more difficult to differentiate an information system in function and performance. Meanwhile, use environment of information systems has become diverse rapidly with the spread of smart devices (smartphones and tablet terminals). The customer of an information system used in work (a business system) has come to emphasize what kind of experience is obtained through the use of the system, more than its function and performance. Usability is one of the central factors of this user experience.

M. Kurosu (Ed.): HCI 2016, Part I, LNCS 9731, pp. 220–232, 2016.
DOI: 10.1007/978-3-319-39510-4_21

In order to make an information system usable and useful, it is necessary to put great importance to the viewpoint of users and to design an entire system, in addition to system development technology [1]. Moreover it is also important to consider cognitive and action process of users and to design interface or interaction between users and a system [1]. Then, design approach (human centered design [2]), design methodologies [3, 4], design principles [1, 5] and tools [6, 7] have been developed, to support software engineers who design a system. These are based on explicit knowledge which is formed through experiences of usability experts. We have worked on developing tools based on explicit knowledge [8, 9], integrating human centered design approach into an existing design process and developing a support method to apply the integrated process [10, 11]. However, even if these are offered, past studies [12, 13] and field trials of our method [14] revealed that there were still a lot of difficulties for software engineers in design activities considering usability.

Through the analysis of our trial results, we found that software engineers have tendencies to fail in specifying tasks to do with a target system, users in charge of the tasks, and workflow to accomplish each task [14]. An appropriate understanding of relations among a system, its users and their tasks is basics for developing a system usable and useful [15]. The activities which software engineers failed are related to this understanding. Thus, in order to investigate the reasons of their failures, it is necessary to clarify the features of how software engineers understand a target system.

Hinds [16] found about cognitive features of software engineers that persons in a system provider with extensive knowledge of a system underestimated novice performance time to complete a complex task using the system. This was revealed through the comparative experiment among experts (persons in the system provider), intermediate users (persons having 3–9 months of experience in using the system) and novice. Seffah [12, 17] and Ferre [13] point out that terminology, concepts, the perception of the role, perspective and emphasis points in system development are different between software engineers and usability experts who assume a role of usability improvement in system development project. They also pointed out that these differences cause miscommunication when software engineers and usability experts collaborate in a system development project [12, 17] as well as disuse of usability improvement techniques by software engineers [13]. However they have not investigated specific cognitive features of software engineers.

In this paper, we focus on the cognitive features of software engineers and investigate especially how software engineers understand the target system in the context of system development. Based on these features clarified, we consider why software engineers fail in design activities concerning usability.

2 Method to Model the Features of How to Understand a System

In order to investigate the features of how software engineers understand a target system in the context of system development, we thought that it is necessary to visualize the following three points through comparing their understandings with those of usability experts being voice of system users.

When a software engineer and a usability expert understand the same system,

(a) What kind of point are both understandings different in?: Qualitative difference of system understanding.
(b) How much are both understandings different?: Quantitative difference of system understanding.
(c) How different are both recognitions to "range to be conscious of and "emphasis point" in system development?: Difference in recognition to system understanding.

Relations of the differences visualized from the aspect of above (a)(b)(c) are analyzed and system understanding peculiar to software engineers is modeled.

2.1 Three Layer Model Diagram to Describe How to Understand a Target System

Before visualizing above (a)(b)(c), it is necessary to visually express how to understand the relations among functions of a target system, its users and their tasks, which are essential to design a system with high usability. There are system visualization expression methods which are commonly employed in software engineering, such as workflow diagram, use case diagram, and activity diagram [18]. However, these expression methods are not enough to describe system understandings or to enable intuitively grasping them through the description. For example, workflow diagram can describe tasks, workflow of each task and a role that perform each work item. However it has difficulty in describing relations between these and functions or users. Use case diagram can describe relations between users (actors) and tasks, while it cannot describe workflow (chronological order). Activity diagram can describe relations between functions, its users and their tasks, while it has difficulty in understanding intuitively the relations among these three.

For solving such problems of existing expression methods, we devised "three layer model diagram" to describe how to understand a target system. It is the diagram build up from "system function layer", "task and workflow layer" and "user practice field layer". This diagram describes the understandings about a target system from viewpoint of system functions, tasks and their workflow, users in the field and relations among them. More precisely, the understandings of relations among system functions, tasks using the system, workflow of each task, a role that perform each work item, and system users in the field are described on this diagram. Figure 1 shows a case of "three layer model diagram" which describes understanding of a usability expert for order subsystem.

2.2 Method to Visualize Qualitative Difference of System Understanding

Using "three layer model diagram", we describe how a software engineer and a usability expert understand the same system. That is, respective understandings of relations among system functions, tasks and each workflow, roles that perform each

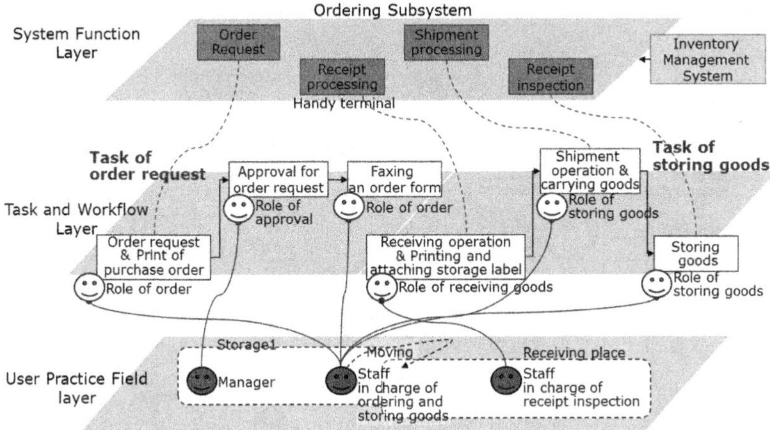

Fig. 1. Three layer model diagram which describes understanding of a usability expert for order subsystem

work item, and system users are described in this diagram. Figure 2 shows a case of "three layer model diagram" which describes understanding of a software engineer for the system identical with the case indicated on Fig. 1. These two diagrams, namely one describes system understanding of a software engineer and the other describes that of a usability expert, are compared and difference between them are extracted. Moreover the differences found in more than one software engineer in common are defined as visualized "qualitative differences of system understanding (a)" between them.

2.3 Method to Visualize Quantitative Difference of System Understanding

We calculate concordance rate between two kinds of "three layer model diagram", namely system understanding of a software engineer and that of a usability expert. Moreover this concordance rate is defined as visualized "quantitative difference of system understanding (b)" between them. The concordance rate is more specifically illustrated below using two cases of Figs. 1 and 2.

The three layer model diagram has elements (e.g. "Order request & Print of purchase order" on "task and workflow layer" in Fig. 1) and relation among elements on each layer. Relation among elements has two types which are order relation (e.g. relation between "Order request & Print of purchase order" and "Approval for order request" on "task and workflow layer" in Fig. 1) and inclusive relation (e.g. relation between "Order request & Print of purchase order" and "Task of order request" on "task and workflow layer" in Fig. 1). Besides, there is relation between elements on neighboring layers (e.g. relation between "Approval for order request" on "task and workflow layer" and "Manager" on "user practice field layer" in Fig. 1. This means relation between a work item and its performer.).

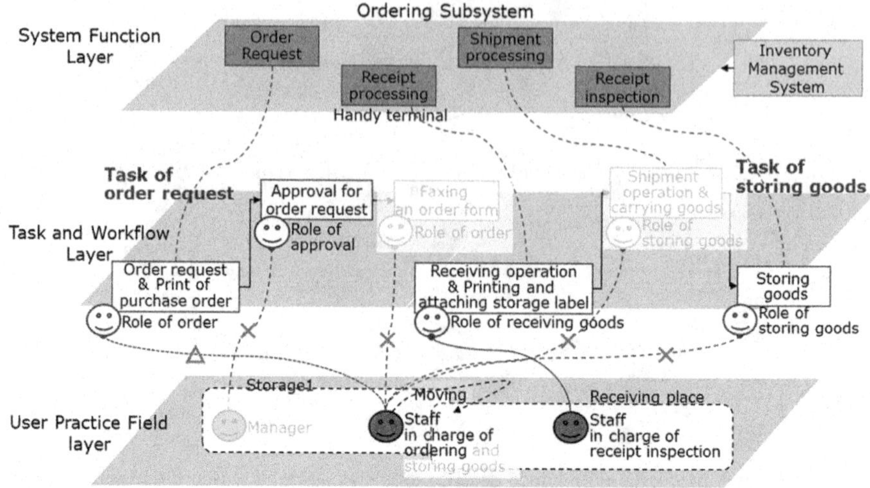

Fig. 2. Three layer model diagram which describes understanding of a software engineer for order subsystem

We compare Fig. 1 which describes understanding of a usability expert with Fig. 2 which describes understanding of a software engineer, focusing on presence and absence of these elements and relations among elements. Comparison patterns defined by presence and absence of these are organized in Table 1.

Table 1. Comparison patterns about an element and relation among elements

		Understanding of a usability expert	
		Presence	Absence
Understanding of a software engineer	Presence	A	B
	Absence	C	–

Meaning of each pattern is illustrated with specific examples in Figs. 1 and 2.

- Pattern A

This pattern means that understanding of a software engineer accords with that of a usability expert. "Order request & Print of purchase order" on "task and workflow layer" in Figs. 1 and 2 is a specific example of this pattern.

- Pattern B

This pattern means that some elements or relations in understanding of a software engineer are missing from that of a usability expert. Relation between "Approval for order request" on "task and workflow layer" and "Manager" on "user practice field layer" in Fig. 1 is a specific example of this pattern.

- Pattern C

This pattern means difference between understanding of a software engineer and that of a usability expert. "Staff in charge of ordering" on "user practice field layer" is a specific example of this pattern.

The number of elements and relations corresponding to each pattern is calculated. Next, ratio of the number of "pattern A" divided by the number of all patterns is calculated. This ratio is defined as concordance rate of system understandings between software engineer and usability expert. Specific math formula is given as follows.

$$\text{Concordance rate of system understandings} = \frac{A}{A+B+C}$$

2.4 Method to Visualize Difference in Recognition to System Understanding

Semi-structured interview is conducted for each of a software engineer and a usability expert to delve into their respective understanding for a target system, using the three layer model diagram which describes understanding of the usability expert. Protocol analysis for this interview is performed focusing on how they understand a target system. Specifically, verbal protocols related to considering order, priority and awareness scope for each layer of the diagram are extracted. These protocols are classified according to their main message. Besides, a label of short sentence representing its essence (e.g. "System function layer is considered first", "Confirming workflow and users together is kept in mind") is given to every classification. Relation between this label and utterer's profession (software engineer or usability expert), is analyzed. Moreover a difference about priority and conscious scope in "three layer model diagram" between them is visualized. This difference is defined as "difference in recognition to system understanding".

3 Experiment for Modeling

The observation experiment was conducted for ten software engineers (seven young engineers who had less than 10 years of practical experience in system development, and three expert engineers) and three usability experts. These research participants were required to try activities representing the approach of human centered design. The specific experiment task was a series of activities to understand relations between a task using the system and its performer (a system user). The activities were,

(1) Specify main task using a system.
(2) Specify workflow of each task and a role that perform each item.
(3) Specify system users and describe the roles of which each user takes charge.

These activities correspond to describe "task and workflow layer" and "user practice field layer" on "three layer model diagram".

The participants were offered the fill-in form made for these activities. They analyzed a system in charge now or in the past and filled out the form. After finishing the task, participants were given in-depth interview about the target system they analyzed, using the completed form. Moreover they were given semi-structured interview about impression and difficulty of the task.

Based on the verbal protocol of a participant in the interview and the completed form by a participant, two usability experts different from the experiment participants (including a experimenter) conducted the same analysis (above-mentioned activities of (1)(2)(3)) about the same system as a participant. Besides, they described the system understanding in "three layer model diagram".

The second semi-structured interview was conducted for the same participant half a year later by using this diagram which described a system understanding of the usability experts to delve into how the participant understand the target system.

The entire process of working on the experiment task and the interview were recorded as video data.

4 Analysis Procedure for Modeling

We correlated the analysis information by the experiment participant to the three layer model diagram which was described understanding of a usability expert for the same system. Besides, we specified points that analysis differed between a participant and usability expert. These points, namely, a difference of element and that of relation among elements (as described in Sect. 2.3) are described on the three layer model diagram.

We compared these two diagrams, namely system understanding of a software engineer and that of a usability expert. The differences found in more than one participant in common were specified as "qualitative differences of system understanding (a)" between a participant and a usability expert.

Concordance rate between these diagrams was calculated as "quantitative difference of system understanding (b)" between them. We calculated this ratio about "task and workflow layer", that of "user practice field layer", and relation between these two layers. The subject of the ratio calculation was the analysis cases of nine participants who finished the second semi-structured interview (seven software engineers and two usability experts). Table 2 shows a list of calculated concordance rate.

Protocol analysis for interview video data of participants was performed focusing on how they understand a target system. We derived the kind of participant's recognition about priority and conscious scope in "three layer model diagram" through analysis. Moreover relation between a kind of recognition and utterer's profession (software engineer or usability expert) was analyzed. We specified this analysis as "difference in recognition to system understanding (c)".

Besids, we analyzed relation among above-mentioned "qualitative differences of system understanding (a)", the concordance rate as "quantitative difference of system understanding (b)", and "difference in recognition to system understanding (c)".

Table 2. Concordance rate of system understanding between an experiment participant and a usability expert

Participant		1	2	3	4	5	6	7	8	9
In a Layer	Tasks and Workflow Layer	0.17	0.50	0.61	0.24	0.42	1.00	0.82	0.53	0.49
	User Practice Field Layer	0.21	0.29	0.10	0.25	0.62	1.00	0.92	0.75	0.67
Between Layers	Tasks and Workflow Layer & User Practice Field Layer	0.15	0.32	0.13	0.18	0.35	1.00	0.73	0.59	0.55

5 Modeling the Features of How to Understand a System

It became clear that system understanding has patterns with a different feature from the following two perspectives.

- Understanding for entire system.
- Understanding for a layer of tasks and workflow.

5.1 Understanding for Entire System

We found that there are two types of understanding for an entire system. One is the understanding that makes the function a starting point, and the other is the under-standing that makes the user's tasks a center.

System Understanding that Makes the Function a Starting Point. This understanding is characterized by considering functions first and putting the highest priority on functions. Persons of such understanding consider by order of "system function layer", "task and workflow layer", and "user practice field layer" on "three layer model diagram", as shown in Table 3. In addition, they are hardly conscious of "user practice field layer", as shown in Tables 4 and 5. Participants who are presumed from their utterance to understand a system from functions are mostly correspond to those whose concordance rate about "user practice field layer" is less than 0.3. We consider that the low consideration for "user practice field layer" is a feature of system understanding that makes the function a starting point.

Table 3. Fragment of protocols about confirmation order in "three layer model diagram"

Participant A:	*First, I watched "task and workflow layer". But it's difficult to understand the description on the diagramr. (Omission) I confirm the diagram from here ("system function layer"), because it seems to be easier for me to understand it if I thought along the actual processing of the system. Then, I relatively can relate a function to workflow*

System Understanding that Makes the User and Their Tasks a Center. This understanding is characterized by putting the highest priority on system users, their

Table 4. Fragment of protocols about scope conscious in everyday work

Participant B:	*I'm rarely conscious about who is a user. I'm not also conscious about how the user works in the field and uses such functions. What I'm conscious about is basically only exchange of data between systems*

Table 5. Fragment of protocols about a "user practice field layer"

Participant C:	*I feel I can test better if I understood the layer ("user practice field layer"). But I have not been conscious about the layer. Still I can test*

tasks, and how they practice work in the field. Persons of such system understanding consider "task and workflow layer" and "user practice field layer" a center, on "three layer model diagram". Besides, they consider "system function layer" based on these two layers, as shown in Table 6. Thus, they are clearly conscious of "user practice field layer", as shown in Table 7. Participant who are presumed from their utterance to understand in the system users and their tasks center are mostly correspond to those whose concordance rate about "user practice field layer" is more than 0.7. We consider that the high consideration for "user practice field layer" is a feature of system understanding that makes the user and their tasks a center.

Table 6. Fragment of protocols about a layer which a participant usually consider first in "three layer model diagram"

Participant E:	*Considering from here (indicating "user practice field layer"), procedure of simultaneous message distribution (one of the function) was not appropriate. So I asked the project members to revise i.*

Table 7. 2nd fragment of protocols about a "user practice field layer"

Participant F:	*I always try to ask who use the system, even though I don't have a chance to contact with end users*

5.2 Understanding of Tasks on "Task and Workflow Layer"

Targets of understanding on "task and workflow layer" are the tasks using a system and workflow of each task. About the tasks, we found that there are two types of understanding. One is the understanding which corresponds to functions, and the other is that from the viewpoint of user practice in the field.

Figure 3 shows a case of "three layer model diagram" which describes understanding of a usability expert about customer information system for sales staff. In this diagram, sales operation utilizing the information provided by the system is defined as the main task. This task is carried out by sales staff who is a primary system user. Figure 4 shows a case of "three layer model diagram" which describes understanding of a participant about the same system. In Fig. 4, sales operation by sales staff is not defined as a task, although the same work items (e.g. "Confirmation of the list of

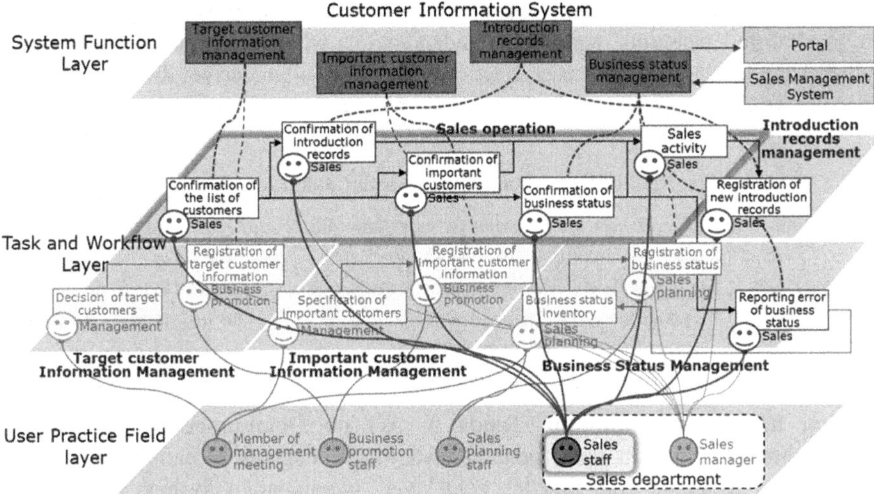

Fig. 3. Three layer model diagram which describes understanding of a usability expert about customer information system for sales staff

customers", "confirmation of business status") is defined as those which sales staff carries out. Tasks defined by the participant are administrative task of various information provided by the system. These tasks correspond to the functions designed according to information type (functions for information life-cycle management) by one to one. The work item carried out by sales staff is located at the end of workflow in this information administrative task. We consider that the participant who analyzes the system of Fig. 4 understands tasks by corresponding to life-cycle management function of information itself, not from the view point of the information users.

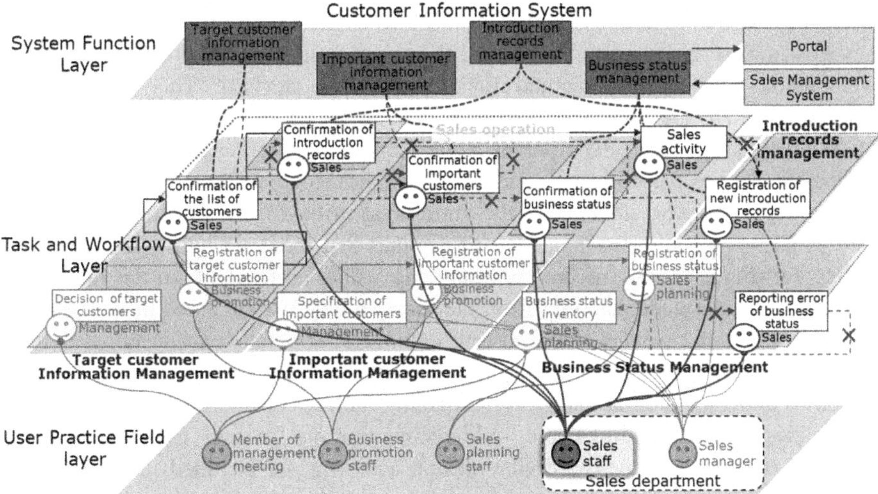

Fig. 4. Three layer model diagram which describes understanding of a software engineer about customer information system for sales staff

The Defined Tasks Differ Between Two Types of Understanding. The gap between two types of understanding, namely the understanding which corresponds to functions and that from the viewpoint of user practice in the field, often derives difference of the defined tasks for the same system. Table 8 shows protocols about this gap.

Table 8. Fragment of interaction protocols about difference of tasks defined

Experimenter:	*They consider the task and its workflow that relates closely to functions for data processing in the system, do they?*
Participant U:	*Yes. About tasks relating to how to process as a system. But a task relates to here (indicating "user practice field layer"), so the task defined by them doesn't agree with ours very much*

Function Based Understanding Tends to Act on Dominance. We found the understanding described above in the three layer model diagrams of participants whose concordance rate about "user practice field layer" is comparatively high (those who understand in the system users and their tasks a center), in addition to participants of the low concordance rate (those who understand a system from functions). This suggests that a participant might give priority to function based understanding in thinking about tasks though they understand "user practice field layer". There were plural experiment participants in which the concordance rate of "task and workflow layer" and that of relation between "task and workflow layer" and "user practice field layer" are quite lower than that of "user practice field layer".

These suggests that function based understanding tends to act on dominance in a software engineer who is in charge of system development.

6 Conclusion

We focused on the cognitive features of software engineers and tried to model especially how software engineers understand the target system in the context of system development, applying the method for modeling we devised. This investigation revealed that there are two types of understanding for an entire system. One is the understanding that makes the function a starting point, and the other is the understanding that makes the user and their tasks a center. Moreover, it was found that the software engineers who understand the entire system based on functions are hardly aware of user practice in the field. We also found that there are two types of understanding for the tasks. One is the understanding which corresponds to the functions, and the other is the understanding from the viewpoint of user practice in the field.

Besides, it was revealed that software engineers who failed in design activities concerning usability have a tendency to understand tasks correspond to functions, in addition to understanding an entire system from functions. These suggested that their function-based understandings and little recognition to "system users" and "user practice in the field" in their everyday design activities are included in their failure reason.

From these, modeling how to understand the target system was found to be effective in specifying the reasons why software engineers fail in design activities concerning usability.

References

1. Norman, D.A.: The psychology of everyday things. Revised and Expanded Edition. Basic Books (2013)
2. IS9241-210: Human-centred design for interactive systems (2010)
3. Metzker, E., Offergeld, M.: An interdisciplinary approach for successfully integrating human-centered design methods into development processes practiced by industrial software development organizations. In: Nigay, L., Little, M. (eds.) EHCI 2001. LNCS, vol. 2254, pp. 19–33. Springer, Heidelberg (2001)
4. Nebe, K., Paelke, V.: Usability-engineering-requirements as a basis for the integration with software engineering. In: Jacko, J.A. (ed.) HCI International 2009, Part I. LNCS, vol. 5610, pp. 652–659. Springer, Heidelberg (2009)
5. Nielsen, J.: Heuristic evaluation. In: Nielsen, J., Mack, R.L. (eds.) Usability Inspection Methods. Wiley, New York (1994)
6. Palanque, P., et al.: A model-based approach for supporting engineering usability evaluation of interaction techniques. In: Proceedings of the 3rd ACM SIGCHI Symposium on Engineering Interactive Computing Systems, EICS 2011, pp. 21–30 (2011)
7. Propp, S., et al.: Integration of usability evaluation and model-based software development. Adv. Eng. Softw. **40**(12), 1223–1230 (2009)
8. Suzuki, S., et al.: Variation in importance of time-on-task with familiarity with mobile phone models. In: Proceedings of the 2011 Annual Conference on Human Factors in Computing Systems, CHI 2011, pp. 2551–2554 (2011)
9. Fukuzumi, S., Ikegami, T., Okada, H.: Development of quantitative usability evaluation method. In: Jacko, J.A. (ed.) HCI International 2009, Part I. LNCS, vol. 5610, pp. 252–258. Springer, Heidelberg (2009)
10. Hiramatsu, T., et al.: Applying human-centered design process to system director enterprise development methodology. NEC Tech. J. **3**(2), 12–16 (2008)
11. Tanikawa, Y., Okubo, R., Fukuzumi, S.: Proposal of human-centered design process support environment for system design and development. In: Proceedings of the 4th Applied Human Factors and Ergonomics (AHFE) International Conference, pp. 7825–7834 (2012)
12. Seffah, A., Metzker, E.: The obstacles and myths of usability and software engineering. Commun. ACM **47**(12), 71–76 (2004)
13. Ferre, X.: Integration of usability techniques into the software development process. In: Proceedings of the ICSE Workshop on Bridging the Gaps between Software Engineering and Human–Computer Interaction, pp. 28–35 (2003)
14. Tanikawa, Y., Suzuki, H., Kato, H., Fukuzumi, S.: Problems in usability improvement activity by software engineers. In: Yamamoto, S. (ed.) HCI 2014, Part I. LNCS, vol. 8521, pp. 641–651. Springer, Heidelberg (2014)
15. Shackel, B.: Usability – context, framework, definition, design and evaluation. In: Shackel, B., Richardson, S. (eds.) Human Factors for Informatics Usability. Cambridge University Press, Cambridge (1991)
16. Hinds, P.: The curse of expertise: the effects of expertise and debiasing methods on predictions of novice performance. J. Exp. Psychol. Appl. **5**, 205–221 (1999)

17. Seffah, A., Gulliksen, J., Desmarais, M.C. (eds.): Human-Centered Software Engineering-Integrating Usability in the Software Development Lifecycle, vol. 8. Springer Science & Business Media, New York (2005)
18. Ambler, S.W.: The Object Primer 3rd Edition: Agile Modeling Driven Development with UML 2. Cambridge University Press (2004)

The Practitioners' Points of View on the Creation and Use of Personas for User Interface Design

Gabriela Viana[1(✉)] and Jean-Marc Robert[2]

[1] Kronos Inc., 3535 Chemin de La Reine Marie Montréal, Québec, Canada
gabiviana@gabiviana.com

[2] Department of Mathematics and Industrial Engineering, Polytechnique Montréal, P.O. 6079, St. Centre-Ville, Montréal, Québec, Canada
jean-marc.robert@polymtl.ca

Abstract. We investigate how practitioners in the field of user interface design create and use personas in order to know the challenges they face with this technique and improve it, if needed. We interviewed 16 practitioners from companies of different sizes in Canada and United States. Main results reveal that designers recommend the use of personas in projects of user interface design. They stress the importance of using real data to define personas so designers and stakeholders can trust them. They validate their personas and consider it is especially important for personas based on assumptions or brainstorming. They report that in most cases, the process of creating personas take several weeks and should involve the whole design team. They often stretch a same persona to different projects but are critical towards this practice. They see that personas are mainly used at the beginning of the project, as a North Star for design. They assert that personas should not replace user testing with real users.

Keywords: Personas · UCD · User interface · Creation and use of personas

1 Introduction

Personas are "hypothetical archetypes of actual users through which designers can develop a precise description of [the] user and what he wishes to accomplish" (Cooper 2004). Numerous designers build personas for projects on user interfaces because they think they will help them to focus on the users and make better design decisions, so they see personas as an effective tool to bring plus-value to their work. Yet, our own professional practice and observations in the field over the years reveal that there are problems and disappointments with personas, which reflect through the sub-use, the misuse, or sometimes the abandonment of personas, and the negative perception of personas. In our opinion the difficulties with personas on the ground deserve more attention if we want to improve their use and make it a more powerful tool for design. So, in this study, we collected data with several practitioners directly involved in the creation and use of personas in different domains, with the goal to understand their successes, failures, and challenges, and draw lessons for a better use. Before presenting our study, let's examine some results from the literature on personas.

M. Kurosu (Ed.): HCI 2016, Part I, LNCS 9731, pp. 233–244, 2016.
DOI: 10.1007/978-3-319-39510-4_22

2 Related Work

In this section we address four main aspects of personas: the benefits, the creation process, the challenges, and the Reasons of failures.

Benefits. Personas facilitate the communication within the teams [15], by providing a common understanding of who the users are and what their goals are. They help to generate and select the best design ideas [2]. They also challenge incorrect organizational assumptions about the users, help to give stronger consumer focus and target the most important consumer segments [4, 5, 13, 15, 16, 19]. Some authors mention that personas can help to create empathy towards the users. For example, putting a human face on the generic user creates this empathy [2, 10]. Personas are also useful for surrogate user testing, evaluate new features, weigh business decisions, conduct task analysis, define use cases, write customer service scripts, facilitate analysis, design, implementation and diffusion, reduce the need to add real users during the design process, and allow the development team to work at a distance [1, 2, 13, 15, 18, 21]. Personas can also be helpful for the development of simulation and training systems, and for making data anonymous.

The Creation Process. Cooper's early personas were rough sketches, but over time his method evolved to include interviews or ethnographic data collection methods to create more detailed characters [18]. In most cases, personas are synthesized from a series of ethnographic interviews with real people and then presented in one or two page descriptions that contain information such as behavior, goals, skills, environment, and some fictional details [6, 11]. For each product or set of tools, a small set of personas is created, in which one persona is the primary focus for the design.

There are several techniques for creating personas. Adlin & Pruitt [1] propose a six-step process organized in two phases: conception and gestation. They also propose a four-step process which only takes a couple of hours when designers are facing important time or budget constraints. Goodwin [12] proposes a nine-step process, which is based on real data. Interestingly enough, the author distinguishes different kinds of user goals (basic human goals, life goals, end goals, experience goals) and defines primary (the best design target) and secondary personas. Nielsen [17] proposes a ten-step approach, which contains four main parts: data collection and data analysis, persona description, scenarios for problem analysis and idea development, and acceptance of the organization and involvement of the design team. It is the first one to introduce the idea of updating the personas. These techniques provide good guidelines to designers. However, they propose a long process that not all companies could afford, or a short process that is not based on real data. The long process addresses the common questions about the creation of personas, but all along the process the designer needs competence and the ability to read the context correctly to make the best decisions (e.g., Develop the persona description, Decide about the final number of personas).

The Challenges of Using Personas. Pruitt & Grudin [19] faced many challenges to create and use personas. Their first project with personas was based on marketing data and did not have much support from the company. In the second project, they needed to involve many more people to have the personas done and they also needed to do a massive campaign to communicate the personas. Dotan et al. [8] had to make extra effort to convince the stakeholders about the use of the personas. Christopher & Blandford [7] encountered some challenges such as a lack of context, the difficulty to differentiate similar personas with different needs, and the difficulty to validate the personas. In the first project of Rönkkö [20], personas were not so important compared to other design aspects, in the second project, they were mainly used as a political tool, and in the third project, the relation between investing in personas efforts and their usefulness was questioned. Some designers resist personas because they are fictional, they can lead to a misunderstanding of who are the real users, and it is not easy to prove that personas are accurate [10, 14, 15]. Many authors also mention the risk of creating stereotypes when creating personas [7, 9, 10, 17–19, 22]. Persona use may raise socio-political issues because each of them has attributes such as age, race, revenue, preferences, etc. [19]. Different levels of trust can affect the use of personas because it is not always clear who organizes and reconciles persona with other data and who interprets them [1, 3]. Furthermore, designers prefer to work with real people rather than with personas [8, 15, 20]. Some authors believe that people need to buy-into the personas and get to know them if they are expected to achieve their goals [8]. Therefore, the designers have to commit themselves and trust in the personas, otherwise it is most likely they will not fully use them.

Failures with Personas. Even well developed personas can result in little or no focus on users in the development process. Moreover, poorly developed personas can keep the development team from investing in other UCD techniques or other efforts that improve product quality. Adlin & Pruitt [1] and Pruit & Grudin [19] mention five reasons that can make the use of personas a failure: (1) The effort was not accepted or supported by the leadership team; (2) The personas were not credible and not associated with methodological rigor and data; (3) The personas were poorly communicated; (4) The product design and development team employing personas did not understand how to use them; (5) The projects had little or no high-level support (not enough people to create and support them and no investment in personas' communication).

3 Methodology

This section on the methodology of our study covers three topics: the participants, the interviews, and the data analysis process.

Participants. Sixteen practitioners in user interface design, aged from 20 to 65 years, female (N = 8) and male (N = 8), from Canada (N = 7) and the United States (N = 8), participated in the study. They were recruited via Linkedin[1] or personal contacts of the two authors of this paper, and thus formed a convenience sample. The main criteria to participate in the study were to be a user interface designer and have previous experience in creating and using personas in either a small, medium or large company. Participants

[1] LinkedIn is a business-oriented social networking service.

were working for companies that developed software in different fields: database, engineering, workforce management, insurance, banking, marketing, healthcare and consultancy. Eleven had experienced working in small companies (1–200 employees), 5 in medium-size companies (201–500), and 15 in large companies (500 employees and more) (N.B.: since some participants have experience in companies of different sizes, the total is superior to 16). In terms of project, nine participants have been involved in more than five projects with personas, and seven have been involved in less than four projects with personas. The participants did not receive any financial compensation for their participation in the study.

Among the 16 participants, 10 were Interaction designers and 6 were Researchers. During the interview, the participants described their role and if their job tasks were more related to Interaction Design, it means being responsible to create the interface, or to Researcher, it means developing research to understand the users and their needs. Among the Interaction designers, three had leadership positions; three had more than 10 years of experience with personas. Among the Researchers, four had leadership positions; four had more than 10 years of experience with personas.

The participants' educational backgrounds were very diversified including industrial design, computer science, information science, human-computer interaction, and industrial engineering. Eleven had a Master's degree in Human Factors.

We classified the participants from their attitudes towards personas, as documented in [15]. We have Persona Champions (fully support the use of personas and are enthusiastic about it - 8 participants), Persona Moderates (focus on the user information and are more moderate about their overall impression about personas - 6 participants), and Persona Pessimist (they may use personas, but they don't really recommend personas - 2 participants).

In terms of training, the participants formed two groups: those who received a long and specific training on personas (more than two days and dedicated to building personas): it includes three participants, all of them were champions; those who only received a short training on personas (a training limited to what they have learned during their Bachelor's or Master's Degree – generally a few hours). The knowledge about personas of this last group is also based on work experience with personas. This group includes 13 participants, five of them were champions, six were moderate and two are pessimists.

Interview. Each participant took part to a semi-structured individual interview during about an hour, through the software GoToMeeting[2]. The first part of the interview was to collect data on the projects of interface design that used personas and wherein the participant was involved (duration: 5–10 min). The second part of the interview was to cover three aspects of personas: the construction, the use, and the effects on the design of interface design (duration: 30–45 min). Participants were asked to report their own activities with personas and also aspects they witnessed with colleagues about the creation and use of personas. The interviews were scheduled according to the best time for

[2] GoToMeeting is a service created by Citrix Systems. It is online meeting software that allows the user to meet with other users via the Internet in real time.

the interviewee, they were conducted from September to November 2015, and they were recorded via GoToMeeting. They were registered and transcribed (approximately three hours per interview).

Data Analysis. The transcriptions of the interviews were imported into the qualitative data analysis software Atlas.ti[3]. Then, all the answers were tagged with codes. In total, 301 codes were created by the researchers. For example, in one paragraph, the researchers could identify that the participant gave answers on different topics (e.g., methods used to collect data on personas, validation, use of personas, problems encountered, etc.) which created many codes. Another participant would give the same answer, but in different parts of the interview. The codes helped to identify the common answers from different participants on the same topic. Once the codes were created, the networks between the codes and participants were created. The results focused on two main points: the participants' perception of how they created and how they used personas.

4 Results

The results cover three topics: the creation of personas, the use of personas, and the evaluation of the impact and the satisfaction towards personas.

4.1 Creation of Personas

The Creation Process. Fourteen participants explained that the process of creating personas starts with the collection of data (mainly by interviewing the target users). Then they compile the data by identifying the common attributes. Once the personas are created, they validate them. Finally, they make a presentation to the team who will use the personas.

Personas Based on Real Data and Aligned with Business Strategy. Most of the participants asserted they start the process of creating personas by interviewing the target users, as personas should be based on real data. However, some participants mentioned that in situations where there is not enough budget or time (because interviews are very time consuming) or it is a new project, it is necessary to find a shortcut. Yet, 12 participants mentioned that they would not use personas if they knew they were not based on real data. Most likely, other stakeholders could be even more hesitant. Another reason why personas should be based on real data is that designers can defend them more easily and avoid stereotypes. For instance, in case a manager has a different opinion about the personas descriptions, the data supporting the persona can be used as a proof that the personas represent real users. The participants also mentioned the importance of having personas aligned with the business strategy. It increases the chance that the stakeholders will accept these personas.

[3] Atlas.ti is a qualitative data analyses software.

Personas Created Through Brainstorming. Two participants, who are champions, mentioned that personas could be created through brainstorming and that these personas could be validated afterwards. When creating personas under severe budget or time constraints, three participants (P10 and P13 are champions, P15 is moderate) suggest to use assumption personas. P10 (champion, has more than 10 years of experience with personas, has a Master's degree and specific training on Personas) mentioned that it is fine to create personas through brainstorming, but after it is necessary to validate them to reflect the reality. P12 (same profile as P10) explains that especially in consultancy, it is common to use brainstorming to create personas, and after validate them with the stakeholders to make sure they are representative of their customers.

How Long It Takes. Seven participants assert that the process of creating persona varies depending on the project. Important factors which impact on the time to create personas are the time to find people to participate in the interviews, to conduct the interviews, to compile the data and to write the report, the quantity of people involved and the time allocated for research. Four participants answered that it takes more than a month and five participants answered that it takes less than a month.

Who Is Involved in the Creation of Personas. To build personas, all the participants believe that it is important to involve the designers (N = 16) and the Product Managers/ Owners (N = 8). Product Owners or Project Managers are people mainly responsible for the project/product and they take decisions about which direction the project/product should take in terms of budget, requirements, priorities, etc. Five participants believe that the whole team should be involved in the process because it facilitates the communication and reduces resistance.

How to Collect Data. To collect data for building personas, the participants mainly referred to interviews (N = 8), pools of users (N = 5), surveys (N = 4), the marketing department of the company (N = 3), and some other methods.

How Many People to Interview. According to the participants (N = 12), the average number of people to interview was 20 with a minimum of 8 and a maximum of 90. Some participants (N = 4) reuse the pool of users from other projects.

Marketing Data. Five participants use marketing data to build personas. These data usually include information about consumers such as demographics and behaviours. However, three participants do not recommend the use of such data because the person who uses the product is not necessarily the one who buys it.

Project-Based Personas. Two participants believe that personas should actually be developed by project, instead of a set of personas for multiple products. Also, if it happens that a persona is related to several projects, then it would be fine to reuse it.

Stretch Personas. Twelve participants experienced to be in a project where they stretched a persona, i.e. use a persona that was originally created for another project and apply it to another project. They believed it was a way to reduce the cost and time to create a new persona and these personas have some items in their description that could also be beneficial to the other project. Two participants would not stretch personas or they would do so depending on the situation.

Data Collection and Personas' Description. When collecting data to build personas, participants ask about the overall demographics (N = 4), followed by the experience level (N = 4), the tasks to execute (N = 3), and the educational level (N = 2). During the interviews 10 participants mentioned what should and should not be included in the personas descriptions. The main items to be included in the personas description were: Big pain points (N = 9), Information related to work (N = 7), Demographics (N = 6), Scenarios (N = 5), and Tasks (N = 5). Items that should not be included, unless they are clearly relevant for a specific project, are extra information such as hobbies, weekend activities, whether the persona has pet or not, and demographics. Adding too much information brings the risk of having personas considered irrelevant by stakeholders and designers. Eleven participants mentioned that they add extra information to personas even if it is not based on real data, and four don't. Adding extra information such as emotions that the persona will feel when using the product, is controversial among the participants. The majority of them would add extra information as a way to give the persona some personification and make it more engaging. Other participants mentioned that they would not add extra information, or if they would do, it should be minimal as there is a risk of wrong interpretation, especially if not based on real data.

Persona Name. All the participants use name in the personas descriptions. However, one participant (P11 - pessimist, has less than 10 years of experience in the field and with personas and has Master's degree) feels like adding a name to persona can be more distracting than useful.

Persona Photo. Fourteen participants also appreciated the use of photo in the personas descriptions and among them, two participants believe that it is very important on the condition that the photos are well selected because they help to personalize the personas. Two participants (P11 - pessimist, P14 - champion) believe that photos are distracting and lead to useless discussions because they could carry stereotypes.

Methods Combined with Personas. Once the data on personas are collected, some participants use affinity diagram (N = 6), task analysis (N = 4) and scenarios (N = 3) to create the personas. The affinity diagram is mainly to organize the data and group the users by user categories. The tasks analysis is useful to describe the tasks and subtasks the user will execute to achieve his/her goals by using the interface and the scenarios help to give better context of use and make richer descriptions.

How Many Personas Are Created per Project. Nine participants reported that they created less than five personas per project, five participants created more than five personas per project (between 5 and 12) and two participants did not answer. Three participants shared their concerns about the number of personas to create, and one participant commented that in a company he worked for, there were so many personas that they became distracting.

Validating Personas. Fifteen participants validated their personas. The way they do it can vary: with customers (N = 6), owners/stakeholders (N = 3), and colleagues/team (N = 3). To validate, most of the participants refer to interviews and user testing. Some of the participants recruit users for user testing based on the personas profile.

Presenting Personas. Once personas are validated and ready to be used, 15 participants made some sort of presentation to the team, especially involving product owners (N = 7), developers (N = 6), and executives (N = 5).

4.2 Use of Personas

Focus on the User. Twelve participants use personas because they think they help to focus on the user. Two participants believe that designers are already user centered, so personas are not necessary for that.

Other Reasons to Use Personas. Nine participants believe that the personas can change the way they work, especially if they are used at the beginning of the project because they serve as a guide, as a reference, they give inspiration to generate ideas. Participants also use personas to educate the stakeholders about the users. Eight participants mentioned that personas are important to help to scope the project by defining if a feature should be added or removed from the product. However, one participant disagrees with the fact that personas can contribute to design decisions because they are too generic and don't provide enough details to help with this kind of decision. Eight participants think that personas are useful for all kinds of projects.

How the Creation Process can Affect the Use of Personas. All the participants said they would trust in the personas even though they would not be involved in their creation, on the condition that they knew the personas were based on real data and what process was used. Two participants also mentioned that the qualification of who did the personas would affect their level of trust. Moreover, some believe that interaction designers could benefit more of the personas if they could participate in their creation.

Update Personas. In case of re-using personas for the same project or a different one, 11 participants mentioned the importance of keeping the personas updated. One of the reasons why designers would not use personas is the fact that they are outdated; since situations change and the context changes, personas need to reflect the new reality.

Personas vs. Real Users. Most of the participants mentioned that they prefer to refer to real people than personas. Two participants (champions) mentioned that it depends on the situation, maybe at the beginning of the project they would refer to personas, but later, it is important to contact real users, do some user testing to validate the design.

Communication. All participants agree that personas are an important tool to communicate and give a common understanding of the persons they will design for. According to the results, the people who use personas are designers, product managers/owners, developers and marketers. However, some participants say that developers and product managers use personas whereas some say they don't. In daily communication about personas, most of the participants mentioned to use posters (N = 11), webpages (N = 7), flyers (N = 3) and cut outs (N = 3) (The cut outs are like big posters in the format of a real person). Four participants have experienced to play the role of personas. Yet, some of the participants (N = 4) who have not experienced to play the role of a persona think that it could be an interesting approach to present personas to the team, as it can help to create empathy. An interesting aspect about the use of the cut outs is that three participants who talked about them said that they can be scary sometimes.

Personas Based on Fake Data. Four participants said they would believe in personas even though they were not based on any research. On the other hand, 12 participants said they would not use these personas. For two participants, personas can be distracting because some stakeholders would pay more attention to small details, such as name and photo's choice than the actual design problem that needs to be solved.

Personas May be Too Generic. Five participants referred to the fact that personas can be too generic, with not enough information, consequently they would not help in the design process. One participant pointed out that some designers don't necessarily know how to use personas. Sometimes it is only the name, but not the personas description. Ten participants agreed that personas are not the tool to validate the design because they do not provide the proper the level of detail to review the design.

Personas Can Lead to Wrong Design Decisions. Four participants said that when personas are not well based, do not include enough information, they could lead to wrong design solutions. Seven participants mentioned the risk of stereotype when using personas. There is risk of interpretation of the personas meaning, therefore some participants highlight the importance of basing the personas on research.

The Lack of Support. Seven participants mentioned that they were somehow discouraged to build personas, as other people in the company would not believe in personas and would not offer appropriate support.

4.3 Evaluation of the Impact and Satisfaction About Personas

Evaluate the Impact on Design. Eight participants found difficult to explain how it would be possible to evaluate the impact of using personas in their projects in terms of numbers, or they could not tell how would be a project with or without personas. Five participants mentioned that they could evaluate the impact of personas as they believe personas improve the design and if the rest of the team adopts them.

Satisfaction About Personas. Even though eight participants mentioned that it is difficult to measure the impact of personas on design, most of them said they were satisfied with the personas they created.

5 Conclusion

This interview-based study showed the points of view of 16 experienced practitioners in the field of user interface design on their practice about the creation and use of personas, and the challenges they faced with personas. Our observations are about four principal issues that need improvements for a better use of personas. First: The practitioners involved in our study received different trainings about personas, they have different levels of knowledge and experience with this technique, and they operate in different work contexts (e.g., small, medium-size and large companies) with different constraints of time and budget. So, despite several common opinions, it is not surprising to see different attitudes and standpoints about specific issues of personas. Some standardized training program (with content, duration, readings, exercises,…) would be welcome to guide the trainers and improve the general level of knowledge on personas. Second: there are several techniques to create personas and at first sight, they have enviable qualities: they are detailed, well explained, freely available, and trustable since they are proposed by well-established authors. Yet they are not fully put into practice, and their application requires much competence and judgment from the professionals who attempt to use them because they have to deal with open questions and the specific contexts of their projects and their organizations. The following activities are good examples of that: Collect (relevant and sufficient) data on the users, develop the persona description (how much extra information?), validate, decide about the final number of personas, align the personas with the business value. Third: the practitioners have difficulty to evaluate the impact of the use of personas on design projects in terms of numbers. So they may lack arguments to convince colleagues or the hierarchy to adopt personas and to provide adequate support to create and use personas. This is a promising avenue for the research community. Fourth: once the personas are created, they should be fully exploited during the different phases of the project and their use should be well coordinated with the use of real users. Our study revealed that most designers prefer to use real users. Actually there is room for both personas and real users in projects because they satisfy different needs. Research results show that personas help designers to select functionalities and qualities of their products, and it is clear that design validation should be done with real users through usability tests. The contribution and advantages of adopting real users and personas should be clarified for each phase of the project.

Acknowledgments. We would like to thank the participants for their collaboration and Kronos for its support.

References

1. Adlin, T., Pruitt, J.: The Persona Lifecycle: Keeping People in Mind Throughout Product Design, 1st edn. Morgan Kaufmann, San Francisco (2006)
2. Bornet, C., Brangier, E.: The effects of personas on creative co-design of work equipment: an exploratory study in a real setting. CoDesign, pp. 1–14 (2015). doi:10.1080/15710882.2015.1112814

3. Chapman, C., Milham, R.P.: The Persona's new clothes: methodological and practical arguments against a popular method. In: Proceedings of the Human Factors and Ergonomics Society 50th Annual Meeting, vol. 50, no. 5, pp. 634–636 (2006). http://citeseerx.ist.psu.edu/viewdoc/download?doi=10.1.1.564.5808&rep=rep1&type=pdf
4. Cooper, A.: The Inmates Are Running the Asylum: Why High-Tech Products Drive Us Crazy and How to Restore the Sanity, 2nd edn. Sams, Indianapolis (2004)
5. Cooper, A., Reimann, R.: About Face 2.0. Wiley, Indianapolis (2003)
6. Cooper, A., Cronin, D., Reimann, R.: About Face 3: The Essentials of Interaction Design. Wiley, Indianapolis (2007)
7. Christopher, J.V., Blandford, A.: The challenges of delivering validated personas for medical equipment design. Appl. Ergonomics **45**(4), 1097–1105 (2014). doi:10.1016/j.apergo.2014.01.010
8. Dotan, A., Maiden, N., Lichtner, V., Germanovich, L.: Designing with only four people in mind? – a case study of using Personas to redesign a work-integrated learning support system. In: Gross, T., Gulliksen, J., Kotzé, P., Oestreicher, L., Palanque, P., Prates, R.O., Winckler, M. (eds.) INTERACT 2009. LNCS, vol. 5727, pp. 497–509. Springer, Heidelberg (2009)
9. Floyd, R., Jones, C., Twidale, B.: Resolving incommensurable debates: a preliminary identification of persona kinds, attributes, and characteristics. Artifact **2**(1), 12–26 (2008). http://hdl.handle.net/2142/9807
10. Friess, E.: Personas and decision making in the design process: an ethnographic case study. In: Proceedings of the SIGCHI Conference on Human Factors in Computing Systems, New York pp. 1209–1218 (2012). doi:10.1145/2207676.2208572
11. Goodwin, K.: Perfecting your personas (2008). http://www.cooper.com/journal/2008/5/perfecting_your_personas
12. Goodwin, K.: Designing for the Digital Age: How to Create Human Centered Products and Services. Wiley, NewYork (2009)
13. LeRouge, C., Ma, J., Sneha, S., Tolle, K.: User profiles and personas in the design and development of consumer health technologies. Int. J. Medical Inf. **82**, 251–268 (2013). doi: 10.1016/j.ijmedinf.2011.03.006
14. Massanari, A.: Designing for imaginary friends: information architecture, personas and the politics of user-centered design. New Media Soc. **12**, 401–416 (2010)
15. Matthews, T., Judge, T., Whittake, S.: How do designers and user experience professionals actually perceive and use personas? In: Proceedings of the SIGCHI Conference on Human Factors in Computing Systems, pp. 1219–122. ACM New York (2012). doi: 10.1145/2207676.2208573
16. Miaskiewicza, T., Kozarb, K.: Personas and user-centered design: how can personas benefit product design processes? Des. Stud. **32**, 417–430 (2011). doi:10.1016/j.destud.2011.03.003
17. Nielsen, L.: Personas - User Focused Design. Aarhus University Press, Copenhagen, Denmark (2011). doi:10.1145/2556288.2557080
18. Nielsen, L., Hansen, K.: Personas are applicable: a study on the use of personas in Denmark. In: Proceedings of the SIGCHI Conference on Human Factors in Computing Systems, pp. 1665–1674. ACM, New York (2014)
19. Pruitt, J., Grudin, J.: Personas: practice and theory. In: DUX 2003 Proceedings of the 2003 Conference on Designing for User Experiences, pp. 1–15. ACM, New York (2003). doi: 10.1145/997078.997089
20. Rönkkö, K.: an empirical study demonstrating how different design constraints, project organization and contexts limited the utility of Personas. In: the 38th Hawaii International Conference on System Sciences (2005). doi:10.1109/HICSS.2005.85

21. Salmi, A., Poyry-Lassila, P., Kronqvist, J.: Supporting empathetic boundary spanning in participatory workshops with scenarios and personas. Int. J. Ambient Comput. Intell. (IJACI) **4**, 21–39 (2012)
22. Turner, P., Turner, S.: Is stereotyping inevitable when designing with Personas? Des. Stud. **32**, 30–44 (2011)

Usability and User Experience Evaluation Methods and Techniques

User Experience (UX) of Heritage Journeys: Design Taxonomy for Quality Measurement

Nada Nasser Al Subhi[1(✉)], David Bell[1], and Paul Lashmar[2]

[1] Department of Computer Science, Brunel University, London, UK
{Nada.al-subhi,david.bell}@brunel.ac.uk
[2] School of Media and Film, University of Sussex, Brighton, UK
p.Lashmar@sussex.ac.uk

Abstract. User experience (UX) design is unsurprisingly challenging, specifically the classification of experience within a customer journey. It is vital that personal sentiment is described using practical quality measures. An experience journey is too broad a term to be easily used. However it is easier to measure the influence of various elements of experience design on a user's opinion across a wider journey.

In this paper, a taxonomy of heritage experience design will be presented wherein improved quality measurement can be developed for user experience journey design. This paper draws on primary and secondary data to propose a taxonomy of user experience for quality measurement. The primary purpose of this framework is to guide experienced designers on choices to initiate high-quality user experience in a heritage context. Included are journey goals, organizational atmosphere, and technological, behavioral or economic biases. The taxonomy is also valuable to experience designers in specifying the scope of quality measurement and further to researchers in creating proposals for further study.

Empirical data was collected from a historical organization (Dorset County Museum) in the UK using semi-structured interviews. It was then analyzed using grounded theory techniques. The importance of user experience was highlighted and prioritized with respect to the journey design process.

Keywords: User experience · Taxonomy · Quality measurement · Quality of experience · Heritage museum

1 Introduction

Understanding the elements of user experience is necessary before undertaking a fuller user experience design. Included in this is the interaction between the user and the system, devices and contents. User experience is often the satisfaction a user gets from interacting with a product or digital tool. It can also encompass all experiences (physical, sensory, emotional and mental) a person has when interacting with a digital tool [14].

However, how do we know if the experience is of high-quality? This research argues that there is a need for high-quality design experiences specifically in heritage landscapes and interlinked museums. Though technology mediation has advanced rapidly in all aspect of human life, there is still a missing element when producing tailored designs

M. Kurosu (Ed.): HCI 2016, Part I, LNCS 9731, pp. 247–256, 2016.
DOI: 10.1007/978-3-319-39510-4_23

for a mobile device that is based on user needs and interests. What are the triggers of so called good and amazing experiences to a visitor and how do we define a good experience, when visitors differ in a myriad of ways. Hence, a study and critical review of available user experience design is required to uncover an appropriate theory. This then needs to be encapsulated within a framework that can be used to guide designers of heritage experience and make use of advancing technology.

While digital heritage experiences are significant, it is important to have an interactive experience with all museum objects, stories and interlinked locations. Nevertheless, this could result in small changes in the interaction process; which then may have a major impact on the experience process. In order to mitigate these effects, higher-quality experience design is expected to provide a way to motivate and interact with visitors to enhance their heritage experience.

The heritage sector is a complex environment and it is changing dramatically in terms of rapid technological developments. The significant increase of the internet of things, big data and digital heritage has affected the way of presenting the experience to visitors. By observing the related literature, it is clear that many authors have focused on motivation of digital interactive heritage experience, while there was a lack of literature on considering user experience design as a tactic in the wider digital heritage environment. Exploring and understanding how museum workers and interested parties think about the digital interactive heritage environment may provide a basis upon which to develop more common approaches to design processes of user experiences. The research question in this paper is, what are the elements of user experience design in the heritage sector? Therefore, the nature of this study is not to confirm and test an established theory; rather, it proposes to identify and categorize the environment of the digital Interactive heritage experience. In other words, an initial set of constructs and a taxonomy model is built in this paper.

The paper is organized as follows. In Sect. 2, a general experience design is illustrated briefly followed by quality of experience (QoE) models that affect the QoE. Section 4 discusses the challenges in heritage experience design and Sect. 6 presents the analysis of the conducted interviews. Finally, Sect. 7 presents the design taxonomy for quality measurement followed by a conclusion articulated in Sect. 8.

2 User Experience Design

User experience is the first and foundational step of an effective digital asset [14].

The table below (Table 1) illustrate the six qualities that makes up a good UX: However, these user experience qualities are more of a technical user experience design which are generally embedded as part of quality of experience models. Hence, more detailed discussion of QoE is presented in the following section.

Table 1. User experience qualities [14]

Findability	Can I find it easily? Does it appear high up in the search results?
Accessibility	Can I use it when I need it? Does it work on my mobile phone, or on a slow Internet connection? Can I use it as a disabled person?
Desirability	Do I want to use it? Is it a pleasant experience, or do I dread logging in?
Usability	Is it easy to use? Are the tools I need intuitive and easy to find?
Credibility	Do I trust it? Is this website legitimate?
Usefulness	Does it add value to me? Will I get something out of the time I spend interacting with it?

3 Quality of Experience

A number of authors (including [9, 12]) identified the key components of all human-computer-, or user-interfaces: Metaphors, mental models, navigation, interaction and appearance as well as information visualization. Taking into consideration User-centered design (UCD) which links the process of developing software, hardware, the user-interface (UI) and the total user-experience (UX) to the people who will use a product or service [4, 8]. The user experience as defined by Hartson and Pyla is the "totality of the [….] effects felt by a user as a result of interaction with, and the usage context of, a system, device, or product, including the influence of usability, usefulness, and emotional impact during interaction, and savoring the memory after interaction [4]. In this paper the focus is mainly on the user experience and its perspectives. In order to design a high quality user experience, it is significant to study state-of-the-art models of Quality of Experience.

There are many models of Quality of Experience (QoE) which introduce different elements that affect the QoE. Examples of these models included in [6, 11, 13]. The main elements are Human, System, Context, Business and Interaction but only three of them introduces interaction as a factor for QoE. However, another study introduced a new layered model for QoE by taking into consideration four main layers; Components,

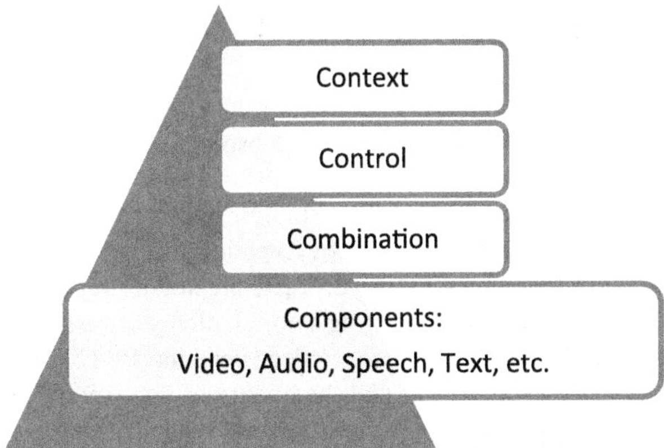

Fig. 1. QoE model adopted from Floris and colleagues [3]

Combination, Control and Context. This model combines all the factors introduced in the state-of-the-art QoE models. However, the human influence elements are assumed to contribute to each layer according to the subjective perceived quality of the end-users [3]. Taking into consideration the elements introduced in Floria and colleagues, the basis of this paper was built. In order to achieve an effective QoE; evaluation should include different domains: Human, system, context, interaction, and business which all considered in this model (Fig. 1). The structure (from bottom to top) is as follows: layer one is the media quality, layer two is for multimedia quality, layer three is for interactivity and action, and last but not least is the layer for device, environment, business and community evaluation.

The lower layer is concentrated on media quality, which is related to Quality of Service (QoS) and system parameters of each single media. The combination layer is focused on how single media qualities are combined to get the multimedia quality. This layer is related to (QoS) as well. The interaction features and user actions on multimedia contents are considered in the control layer. The higher layer is dedicated for the context of use of multimedia services and the context influence elements are device, environment, business and community. As mentioned earlier, human influence elements are affected by all layers.

This earlier work is important and relevant, in that it categorizes QoE elements and evolution activities in the networking field. In this paper, a complementary view of the heritage domain will be taken by focusing more on the design for heritage experiences, specifically, the how, when, what and where, of the design process. This focus here is to propose a taxonomy of characteristics (or element) of heritage experience design and the elements that influence these experience designs. This taxonomy can be used as a system for naming and organizing experience design into groups which share similar journeys. By experience designs, we refer to the techniques and tools used to achieve high-quality experience. The purposes of this taxonomy are: (1) to identify relevant design tactics given a specific experience context; (2) to allow evaluation of an experience design or techniques for a particular experience; (3) to provide an overview of the heritage domain of experience quality.

4 Challenges in Heritage Experience Design

The significant increase of the internet of things, big data and digital heritage has affected the way of presenting the experience to visitors. Despite there being is a lot of research within museum and cultural heritage research focusing on the visitor experience, behaviors and educational goals, there is a lack of studies focusing on the design process of heritage journeys concentrating in Quality of Experience (QoE) as measurements for the design of heritage experiences. However, there are studies highlighting the design process of interactive exhibits and presenting some challenges like funding and external expertise for new technology despite the recognized benefits [10, 12]. Another challenge is based on the audience expectations and the quality of the experience [10, 12]. The rapid change of technology and keeping up to date with user expectation is another vital challenge confronted by museums and cultural heritage [10, 15].

As part of this study a prototype was built under the iSEE project at Brunel University London in coordination with the DCM to explore expected visitor's experience. The prototype was based on a quantitative research study conducted with visitors to DCM and Maiden Castle [1]. This prototype was tested in the field as an example of how physical heritage can be sited (in digital form) within the physical landscape – accessed from experience based on the location based modeling. In other words, the visitor is able to see the map using a smartphone and based on a specific GPS location a pop-up of information including video, photo or audio about a specific fact/scenario/incident related to that location would be presented on the smartphone apps (Fig. 2). However, one of the main obstacle to make this experience was to be able to ensure that such experience is of a high quality experience and how can that be measured. Hence, the need for a taxonomy was crucial.

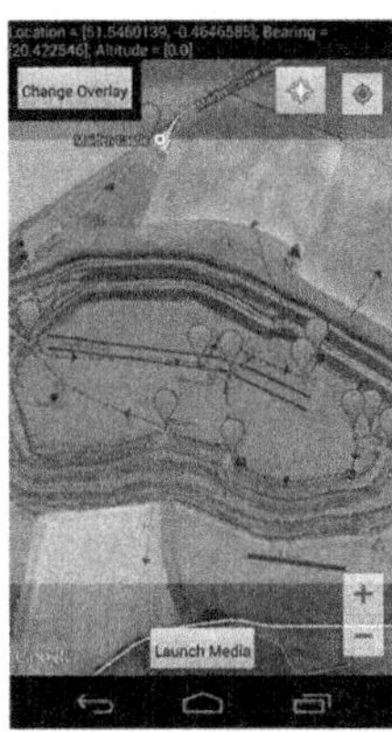

Fig. 2. Snapshot of the smartphone app

All of these challenges were taken into consideration in this research in order to represent a design process that could reduce these challenges and obstacles and epitomize embedded QoE measurements. In the next section, a representation of the methodology will be discussed.

An inclusive range of factors must be focused on the interaction design process including the following elements: the user of the product, how these products will be used and where they will be used. More importantly, creating engaging user experiences by understanding how emotions work and what is meant by aesthetics and desirability [2].

5 Methodology

Empirical data was collected from a historical organization (DCM) in the UK using semi-structured interviews. It was analyzed using grounded theory techniques. The importance of user experience was highlighted and prioritized with respect to journey design process. While grounded theory is traditionally associated with sociology, nursing and health and organizational studies, it has in recent years, started to enter the repertoire of marketing and consumer research. In contrast to other traditional experimental research methods, grounded theory starts from a set of empirical observations or data aiming to develop a well-grounded theory from data [7].

The aim is to develop a robust framework that can be used by designers to create an interactive heritage experience. Thus, grounded theory is suitable as we are not starting with a pre-defined hypothesis; instead we aim at building the theory from the analyzed data itself.

The data used for implementing the theory are the interviews conducted earlier with around five key workers at a heritage museum (DCM). Using NVivo tool (Fig. 3), the interview outcomes were fed into the tool where the analysis took place. In brief, each interviewee feedback was grouped into nodes that represent the main elements that affect the user design experience (e.g. types of visitors, age group, multimedia visual ads).

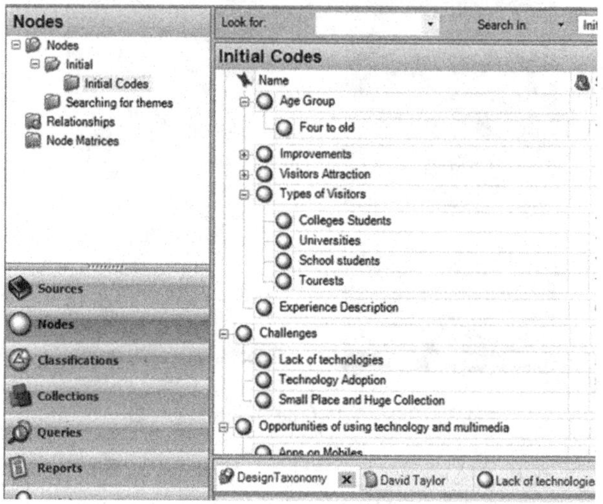

Fig. 3. NVivo tool - open coding phase

Then each of these elements is grouped by the number of sources that was referenced throughout the interviews conducted for all the five workers. As per the grounded theory this represents the internal coding stage (Open coding as per Strauss and Corbin). These elements were then grouped into a smaller clusters (Axial coding). The clusters are then refined further into a more meaningful and close to a detailed development stage (Selective coding) [5, 7]. Finally, the taxonomy is born as a result of the grounded theory technique.

6 Interviews Analysis

The iSEE project aims to engage the visitors within museums and more specifically the nearby heritage locations. Consequently, it aims to enhance visitor experience with a variety of multimedia (sound, image, videos and others) and to increase visitor numbers in local museums. The enhancement of experience requires the input of heritage experts (as well as the visitor). This section gives a summary of information collected from five interviewees and who work for Dorset County museum (DCM). Analysis of interview data helps in understanding the facilities and records available within the museum as well as the technologies used to guide visitors, which are the basis of the design taxonomy.

From the interviews it can be concluded that there are a number of interesting resources available, but staff lack the technical resources to deliver them. They have many objects in collections that are not displayed, as the space is limited and some objects are too delicate to be displayed. Articles and website content are not connected with current databases. They have also used multimedia in rolling images, handset (handhelds) and touchscreens to guide a tour but tech is often broken and needing maintenance. Consequently, they could be replaced with smartphones.

In order to shape the prototype and specify the requirements, it is important to know the most attractive parts of DCM. Interesting responses were received. For example, one specifically mentioned that it depends on visitors' interests, personality and who they are; family, kids or old visitors. Others state that Thomas Hardy, Dinosaurs, skeletons, fossils and Roman corner are the most attractive part. The visitor ages are very important to develop the right application. Many DCM visitors are families, school trips and retired people. However, they want to attract more teenagers. The museum is trying to be child friendly by having more interactive material. Possible features in a smart phone application included enriched video enriched - with sound, color and smell. Other features include a map of Maiden Castle (MC) and the visitor could tap a corner for information. In addition, it is interesting to show time movement in the area and how the sun lights moves through the day, seasons as well as utilize the benefits of google earth 2D/3D views. To design experience it would be useful to show specific stories during MC walk but it is better not to control visitors. Walk need not be restricted to certain points, allowing visitors to choose their experience and stories. It is useful to show the historical link between MC and DCM. The County Council is trying to provide basic links between locations and distributes leaflets to visitors. It is fascinating to bring the historical experience to Maiden Castle and display stories in video or sound, and invest in visual branding by showing artifacts from MC allowing the visitor to choose from different stories and multimedia they prefer.

There are some challenges understanding how, what and why people use phones? As older people use it typically to receive and make call, others use it for communication, games and education. Opportunities exist to use the smartphone. However, it also depends on the technology available and multimedia format. There are so many technologies applied in museums and in other sectors. Other ideas for the future could include applying radio competitions into a mobile phone where group of people play together virtually. The China exhibition (in Cardiff) uses voices talking about their environments. 5D cinema in Korea used a set of projectors in all dimensions, allowing visitors to experience history as if they are in an adventure. However, these approaches have a significant cost implication.

7 Heritage Experience Design (HXD) Taxonomy

This section discusses the components that heritage experience designs (HXD) typically apply to design high-quality experience from the perspective of stakeholders and based on QoE model presented earlier [3]. It is important to change from the traditional quality model which deliberates a fixed context, simple interactivity and one or two media, to a new model which takes into account multi-parameters contexts, complex interaction and real multimedia [3]. To allow for high-quality heritage experience, designers should choose components depending on both the objectives and the visitors. To guide this process, a presentation of a taxonomy will be illustrated which is resulted from the interviews analysis using grounded theory technique. There are five main components in the taxonomy; (1) journey experience which presents abstract guidelines for the design process; (2) journey goal which shows possible means of interaction between visitor and experience,(3) journey control, (4) multimedia of journey and (5) media of journey. The last three components represent the building blocks to implement experience. Figure 4, below reflect an overview of the taxonomy.

Journey experience accounts for the context of the experience which the designer should reflect. For example, in order to design a journey, designer should consider which device (e.g. smartphones, tablets) to use along with study of the environment, business

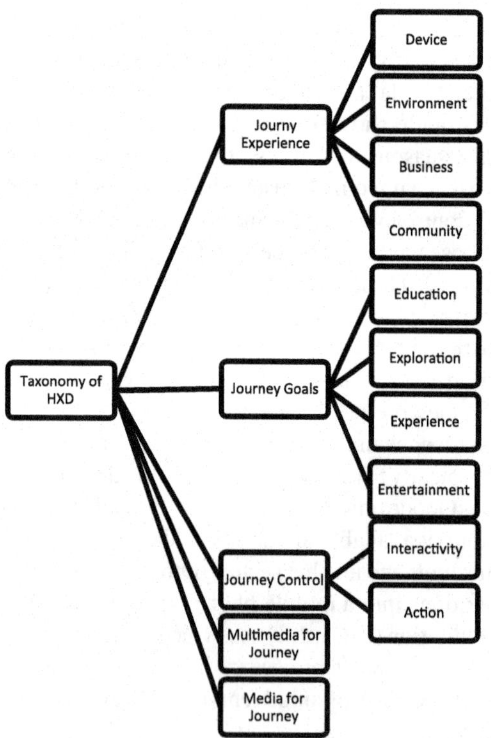

Fig. 4. Taxonomy of heritage experience design

and community. Secondly, it is significant to consider the different goals of the visit as well as taking into account personalizing the journey. The third component is very important as it contain significant elements which are interactivity and action. The last two components accounts for media, as the experience designer should focus on the media qualities composing the multimedia quality and the integration functions for multimedia [3]. As discussed earlier, human elements were not included in the taxonomy, since they influence and are influenced by all components.

The main outcomes from this study are: (1) That in order to enhance the visitor experience we need to assess our services from the visitors' point of view and (2) prioritize our service development, at a time of financial constraint (restriction), by collecting appropriate information from within the museums existing collections and archives in order to sustain a high quality design. Therefore, the paper proposes an evaluation process to assess the presented taxonomy. In a similar contexts discussed in [3] each element focuses on influencing factors belonging to a specific quality domain. Thus, the evaluation of the relevant impact can be conducted individually from that related to others quality domains. This allows conducting independent experiments in different times and places. By combining the individual quality results, the estimation of the overall QoE will be more reliable.

With reference prototype in Sect. 4, the taxonomy can be used as part of an experiment to assess its overall quality. For example, elements such as, interactivity under the journey control (Fig. 4) can be assessed using the video that pops up in the maps and how does the visitor interact with it according to his/her location. That can be assessed with and without the interactive feature on the smartphone apps. Accordingly, the subjective results can be analyzed in order to define the objective quality model to estimate the video quality. Similarly, the same can be applied for the other elements (e.g. entertainment, educational, action) independently. However, this paper is focusing on building the taxonomy and the actual evaluation process will be presented in other future paper.

8 Conclusion

This paper presents a taxonomy that was built in part to evaluate heritage experiences. Interviews were conducted with museum staff and interested parties to uncover specific elements of heritage experience. Employing grounded theory techniques to analysis the interviews resulted in the taxonomy, a basis for heritage journey design. That is by introducing a taxonomy of heritage experience design in order to help the designer to design higher-quality experiences that are embedded in the physical landscape. The results have shown the need to design journeys to suite each visitor's requirements.

Therefore, the importance of carrying out further empirical research is clear, exploiting and building further on the initial taxonomy model. This observation highlighted the need to further investigate how heritage experiences can be articulated as part of a wider co-design process.

Acknowledgement. This paper was supported by the iSEE project funded by Innovate UK. The participation of Dorset County Museum and contributions are sincerely appreciated and gratefully acknowledged.

References

1. Al Subhi, N., Bell, D. Lashmar, P.: Location based modelling for heritage mobile applications. In: UK Academy for Information Systems Conference (2015)
2. Ardito, C., Buono, P., Costabile, M.F., Lanzilotti, R., Piccinno, A.: Enabling interactive exploration of cultural heritage: an experience of designing systems for mobile devices. Knowl. Technol. Policy **22**(1), 79–86 (2009)
3. Floris, A., Atzori, L., Ginesu, G.: Addressing un-interoperability issues in QoE models: is a layered modelling effective? Communications workshops (ICC), In: IEEE international conference on IEEE, p. 563 (2014)
4. Hartson, R., Pyla, P.S.: The UX Book: Process and Guidelines for Ensuring a Quality User Experience. Elsevier, Waltham (2012)
5. Heath, H., Cowley, S.: Developing a grounded theory approach: a comparison of glaser and strauss. Int. J. Nurs. Stud. **41**(2), 141–150 (2004)
6. Laghari, K., Connelly, K.: Toward total quality of experience: a QoE model in a communication ecosystem. IEEE Commun. Magazine **50**(4), 58–65 (2012)
7. Lee, N., Saunders, J., Goulding, C.: Grounded theory, ethnography and phenomenology: a comparative analysis of three qualitative strategies for marketing research. Eur. J. Mark. **39**(3/4), 294–308 (2005)
8. Marcus, A.: Cross-cultural user-experience design. In: Barker-Plummer, D., Cox, R., Swoboda, N. (eds.) Diagrams 2006. LNCS (LNAI), vol. 4045, pp. 16–24. Springer, Heidelberg (2006)
9. Marcus, A., Baradit, S.: Chinese user-experience design: an initial analysis. In: Marcus, A. (ed.) DUXU 2015. LNCS, vol. 9187, pp. 107–117. Springer, Heidelberg (2015)
10. McDermott, F., Clarke, L., Hornecker, E., Avram, G.: The challenges and opportunities faced by cultural heritage professionals in designing interactive exhibits. In: Proceeding NODEM (2013)
11. Möller, S., Engelbrecht, K., Kühnel, C., Wechsung, I., Weiss, B.: A taxonomy of quality of service and quality of experience of multimodal human-machine interaction. Quality of multimedia experience. In: QoMEx. International workshop on IEEE, p. 7 (2009)
12. Parry, R.: Museums in a Digital Age. Leicester Readers in Museum Studies. Routledge, London (2010)
13. Perkis, A.: A QoE cross layer approach to model media experiences. IEEE COMSOC MMTC E-Lett. **8**(2), 6–8 (2013)
14. Stokes, R.: E-marketing: The Essential Guide to Marketing in a Digital World. Fifth edn. Quirk eMarketing (Pty) (2015)
15. Thomas, S., Mintz, A.: Virtual and the real: media in the museum. American Association of Museums, Washington, D.C. (1998)

An Analysis of a Heuristic to Assist Sociability Evaluation in Online Communities

Larissa Albano Lopes, Daniela Freitas Guilhermino(✉), Thiago Adriano Coleti, Roberto Elero Jr., Ederson Marcos Sgarbi, Guilherme Corredato Guerino, Paulo Roberto Anastacio, and Carlos Eduardo Ribeiro

Center of Technological Sciences, State University of Paraná, Bandeirantes, PR, Brazil
{danielaf,thiago.coleti,sgarbi,biluka}@uenp.edu.br,
larii.albano@gmail.com, robertoelerojunior@gmail.com,
guilherme.guerinoSI@gmail.com, paulinho.r.a@gmail.com

Abstract. Online Communities could be defined as environments that allow the interaction and information exchange between their members. An inherent aspect of Online Communities is the sociability, that regards social rules, privacy forms, freedom of speech, confidence, among other relations that may arise from the interaction between people. In this context, a heuristic, named SVCoP was proposed in order to analyze the sociability in Virtual Communities of Practice. As the potential of the aforementioned heuristic towards evaluating other types of online community was being noticed, in the present paper, an analysis of its application in VLEs and on Social Networks is performed. The SVCoP is composed by 46 questions that evaluate sociability aspects of the community related to the purpose, policies, members, knowledge, abilities, behavior, communication, coordination, cooperation, perception and decision-making. From the evaluation performed, the heuristic aspects were classified according to their occurrence and application for each type of community.

Keywords: Heuristic · Online communities · Virtual comunities of practice · Virtual Learning Environments · Social Networks · Sociability

1 Introduction

The evolution of knowledge may take place individually, however, not as much as in groups. The reason why it occurs is that people interaction, namely sharing ideas and opinions, results in enhanced knowledge [26]. [12] states that "collaboration completes individual capacity, knowledge, and efforts".

In a collaboration environment, the interaction elements should offer resources to instigate group activities in order to mitigate difficulties and facilitate people interaction [7]. Online communities may be defined as tools that allow people to interact and exchange information between users via computers connected to the Internet [10]. According to [21], people in online communities, sharing a sole purpose, access a computer's system with policies. [21] also states that in online communities, users are able to socially interact with people, which satisfies their needs, performing roles,

M. Kurosu (Ed.): HCI 2016, Part I, LNCS 9731, pp. 257–267, 2016.
DOI: 10.1007/978-3-319-39510-4_24

sharing information and interests through pre-established rules which guide interpersonal relationship along with support and leverage of computers.

Therefore, a concern regarding sociability, intrinsic to online communities, takes place. Sociability refers to the gathering of people, which generates purposes and practices in which individuals share a sole interest and establish several relations (harmonic and conflicting), thus, individuals always acquire knowledge on capabilities and contributions one another [23].

In this context, this paper presents the classification of a heuristic, initially proposed to an evaluation of sociability within virtual communities of practice (VCoPs), though presenting potential for evaluating other types of online communities. The aspects of the heuristic were classified in accordance with their importance and occurrence in each type of community. In this research, the following online communities were taken into account for heuristic classification: Virtual Learning Environments (VLEs), Social Networks and VCoPs.

2 Online Communities and Sociability

Collaborative systems are places that may provide learning, which could be understood as the possibility of building knowledge not only in group, but also democratically, along with cognitive autonomy [2].

Online communities, which is seen as a taxonomy in collaborative systems, are tools which provide interaction and collaboration. [22] states that the goal of online tools is to engage people to communicate and interact with other people as they were physically present. [22] also affirms that the coordination happen when people work together, and talk between one another sounding commands, so others are aware of the way they are progressing.

In this line, [12] developed the 3C model, which is based on the following premise: aiming the collaboration, individuals should exchange information (communication), organize themselves (coordination), and operate in ground within a shared space (cooperation). The perception is generated by interactions which take place in the group, leveraging all the collaboration. [22] stresses that the perception is essential to the independent tasks, in which the activity result of a person is necessary in order to others to be able to perform their tasks. [1] defines perception as the a person's "knowledge" about the state of a shared computational environment, for instance, the knowledge on other people that share their interactions with the workspace, worked concepts, tasks and status of shared artifacts.

[13] describes that the social interaction is considered the main factor which influence in the collaboration in groups and in learning performances to such groups. According to [8], the collaborative learning is provided through the interaction which pushes involved people to act jointly and thus, a sharing feeling is created, which favors the continuous change and the improvement of group knowledge. [7] states that, in order to support the interaction and the collaboration, several tools become necessary. The main tools are: chat, e-mail, discussion lists, forums, instant messages, audio conference, video conference, and multi user editor.

Facing the online communities' scenario, sociability is a theme which deserves great attention by the software designers. According to [4], verifying and characterizing as the software designers deal with sociability on their interfaces has become a relevant research question in order to not only improve existing systems, but also to develop solutions that leverage social interaction [4]. According to [21], sociability refers to social rules, privacy, freedom of speech, trust, among other aspects which rise along with interaction.

Online communities need to present satisfactory sociability in order to ensure that their goals are reached. [20] stresses that social softwares which present satisfactory sociability are those containing established policies, people, and rules, in which: the purpose refers to the interests, needs, information and shared services by the social software users; people are members whose goals is to interact between one another, approaching the purpose that motivates themselves; and finally, the rules regards the language and protocols which govern people interaction.

There are some types of online communities, among them: Virtual Learning Environments (VLEs), Social Networks and Virtual Communities of Practice (VCoPs). The aforementioned communities are described in the following section:

2.1 Sociability and VLEs

VLEs are cyberspaces where communication between participants could happen anywhere, anytime, one to one, one to many, and many to many [17]. In such spaces, collaborative learning may occur, which in the opinion of [8], is provided through the interaction that drives involved individuals to act jointly and thus, a sharing feeling is created, which favors constant change and improvement of the group knowledge.

Learning environments are strongly interactive and hold a synchronicity aspect of what happens in real time. Interaction between different knowledge levels, decision-making in groups, and the accomplishment of joint tasks not only facilitate learning, but also the knowledge development [16]. EVAs enable people to cohabit along with diversity of view points, to dialogue, decision making and to produce knowledge, moreover, to express thoughts and feelings [19]. An EVA is a space where an individual, interacting with knowledge objects, becomes the learning process core.

Knowledge is seen as a social construct, and therefore, the educational process is favored by the social participation in such environments, that encourages interaction, collaboration and evaluation. According to [16], the basic elements of the collaborative learning are:

- Group interdependence: students aim to proceed and should work efficiently in group in order to achieve it;
- Interaction: improve students competency when working in teams;
- Conflicting opinions: activities should be elaborated in order to encourage collaboration, instead of competition;
- Evaluation: methods of independent evaluation are based on question games, exercises, observations regarding the group interaction and ***hetero-evaluation.

An EVA is an open and flexible environment, thus, its expansion takes place due to the high production of information and knowledge built by individual and groups distributed geographically. Such environment develop and socialize knowledge in several ways, not only via software, but also interfaces, hypertexts, and other media [24].

Sociability in EVAs is given as the professor's capacity of making social bonds with other professors and especially with students through synchronous interaction and communication (chats, instant messages) and asynchronous (mail, discussion forum) [9].

The cyberculture has promoted new possibilities of socialization and learning via EVAs. [3] reports that it is not possible to implement programs which allow interactivity, autonomy, learning to learn and the sociability promotion. According to [3], several strategies are utilized to reach the learning objective. For instance, the perception and sociability strategies, which are disposed through the content of a certain group.

2.2 Sociability in Social Networks

Online social networks allow people grouping who hold common interests [5]. According to [23], such spaces are composed by two elements: actors and relationships which actors develop between one another. There are several types of social networks, however, a similarity among them is the fact that the user has a profile, so it is possible to visualize their friends' network [5].

Online relationships networks aim to encourage human relations through technology [15]. Such networks gather people who wish to communicate and interact, namely, they look for shared purposes. Each network has a set of policies and rules [21]. Social networks are big flow channels in the circulation of information, links, values and social speeches, which has been enlarging, delimiting, and merging territories [15]. Interaction is a condition for the social construction of such networks. The most important elements for the relationship to be kept in such networks are: motivation, available time and involvement of people around these discussions, permanency, and technical grasp aiming the utilization of resources and communication establishments [15].

2.3 Sociability in VCoPs

The expression "Community of Practice" is defined as a group of people who share an interest or passion towards a subject and aim to interact regularly in order to improve their knowledge about the aforementioned subject [28]. VCoP regards a group of people sharing common interests via a virtual environment. In a VCoP, through the practice and exchange of experiences, not only acquiring knowledge becomes achievable, but also finding and reaching problems' solutions in a shorter amount of time compared to regular individual processes.

The main goal of Communities of Practices (CoPs) is the sociability promotion, participants' competency development, and the generation and exchange of knowledge [6]. According to [27], a CoP characterizes itself by the following aspects: community, members, competency, collaboration, decision-making, and CoP's resources.

[28] states that a CoP is a group of people who share an interest or passion by a certain subject and aim to interact regularly in order to improve their knowledge about

the aforementioned subject. The construction of knowledge occurs during the collaboration within these communities, via the exchange of experiences, observations and simulation of specific skills, which are intrinsic to every participant.

3 Heuristics Application Methodology

The heuristic of the sociability evaluation is titled SVCoP and is composed by 46 questions, structured in five axes: (i) Community - Purpose and Policies; (ii) Members; (iii) Competency - Knowledge, Skills and Behavior; (iv) Collaboration - Communication, Coordination, Cooperation and Perception and (v) Decision Making. The SVCoP was structured based on the following researches: [22], which describe directives towards guiding the development of heuristics focusing on the sociability aspect; [27], who presents a series of concepts of a CoP, including main elements and their inter-relations; and [11], who includes in their research the 3C Collaboration Model. In [14] the SVCoP is described with more details. Figure 1 presents the conceptual structure of the SVCoP heuristic.

Fig. 1. Conceptual structure of the SVCoP heuristic

The SVCoP is organized as follows:

- "Community" refers to the domain, objective, composition, and cultural diversity of the CoP. It connects to the concepts of [21], in the second level. "Purpose" regards the reason why a member pertains to the VCoP and "Policies" are records and codes which guide interpersonal within VCoP.

- "Members" are people of the CoP holding their personal roles and characteristics. "Members" refers to characteristics of the people in the community and their roles.
- "Competency" is defined as a set of resources provided to be acquired by an actor, in the second level of the tree. The resources to acquire the competency are "knowledge", which refers to acquiring theoretical information on a certain subject, "skills" regards the capacity of an actor to perform in practice and behavior conceptualizes in the fashion an actor behaves in a group or in certain situation.
- "Collaboration" groups concepts of "communication", "coordination", "cooperation" and "perception" cited by [11] and the 3C Collaboration Model, which is present in the second level. This model is based on the following premise: in order to establish collaboration, a junction of communication, coordination, cooperation and perception is required.
- "Decision making" refers to the available resources for such, involved actors and utilized strategies.

The heuristic presents parameters to the verification of aspects' occurrence in the community. The parameters vary from −1 to 2 as follows: (−1) Do not apply; (0) No occurrence, the aspect is not identified in the community; (1) Partial occurrence, the aspect is identified in an unsatisfactory way in the community; (2) Satisfactory occurrence, the aspect occurs satisfactorily in the community.

The classification of the heuristic involved four steps: (i) Selection of online communities which would be evaluated; (ii) Selection of evaluators according to the required profile (online community users and specialists in IHC); (iii) Application of the heuristic in the evaluation of online communities (EVAs and Social Networks), performed in an individual fashion by each one of the evaluators; (iv) Outcome analysis aiming the heuristic classification.

Two EVAs and three social networks were chosen for evaluation. Information Systems and Computer Science students and professors of the State University of Southern Parana, totalizing sixty-two people, distributed according to their familiarity towards online communities.

After performing the evaluations, by sixty-two evaluators, the aspects that does not apply to certain types of online communities were identified. For the classification, not only the parameters "Do not apply" and "No occurrence" demonstrated evidence of the aspect not being pertinent to such type of online community. However, the aspect "No occurrence" may also indicate that the community could not present satisfactory sociability. Thus, the study on the characteristics of each type of online community was added to the evaluation in order to better identify the not pertinent aspects.

3.1 Results and Discussion

From the evaluations performed on the SVCoP, the heuristic aspects that would not apply to certain type of online community may be noticed. In addition, another important observation was the identification of the sociability aspects that are not satisfactorily present in the evaluated communities.

The evaluators are users, who were chosen by their availability and familiarity with the online communities. There were 31 evaluators regarding the VLEs, and 31 regarding Social Networks. As the SVCoP was firstly developed towards VCoPs, such is not evaluation again, once their aspects were already validated in [14].

Table 1. Most outstanding SVCoP heuristic aspects in the evaluation of VLEs

Axes	Aspects	NA	NO	OP	% NA e NO	% NO e OP
Purpose	The title and content communicate satisfactorily the purpose of the community, thus, people are willing to participate of the community?	1	3	17	12,9	64,5
Policies	If there are commercial transactions in the community, is there a declaration that assures the safety of the user's' credit card data?	20	9	2	93,5	35,5
	Is there any way of complaint regarding the cases in which the community is incorrectly used?	15	10	5	80,6	48,4
	Is it established any type of punishment in case the community is incorrectly used?	13	13	4	83,9	54,8
Behavior	Does the community allow the evaluation of members' satisfaction?	10	12	3	71,0	48,4
Communication	Can I express myself the way I wish in the community?	12	13	3	80,6	51,6
	Is there a protocol (rules) towards the communication in the community?	15	6	8	67,7	45,2
Cooperation	Is there disclosure of events that encourage people to cooperate and return regularly to the community?	11	10	7	67,7	54,8
Perception	Are people able to view what other people are doing in the community?	9	13	8	71,0	67,7
Decision making	Does the community promote mechanisms regarding decision-making?	13	13	3	83,9	51,6

Tables 1 and 2 show the most outstanding heuristic aspects to the VLEs and Social Networks. The NA column represents the number of answers "Do not apply", the NO

Table 2. SVCoP heuristic aspects of more featured on Social Networks evaluation

Axes	Aspects	NA	NO	OP	% NA e NO	% NO e OP
Politicies	Are the policies of use largely published?	0	6	19	19,4	80,6
	In professional groups of discussion, are there copy-rights' statement?	10	13	6	74,2	61,3
Cooperation	Does the community allow the use of pre-elaborate messages in order to users to be able to exchange during the conversation?	3	19	5	71,0	77,4
Perception	Are people able to visualize what other people are doing in the community?	0	6	16	19,4	71,0
	Does the community present the user's function?	10	11	5	67,7	51,6
Decision making	Does the community promote mechanisms regarding decision-making?	10	9	4	61,3	41,9
	Is there any specialist with specific knowledge towards decision-making?	15	9	5	77,4	45,2

column represents the number of answers "No occurrence", the OP column represents the number of answers "Partial occurrence", the % NA and NO column represents the percentage of the sum of the columns NA and NO, finally, the % NO and OP column indicates the percentage of the sum of the columns NO and OP.

The present analysis has taken into account that in case a evaluated heuristic aspect does not occur in the community, such aspect may not apply to the respective type of community, or the respective community may present a sociability problem. Therefore, understanding that the answers "No occurrence" may also point out that the evaluation aspect do not apply for such type of community, these answers were summed to the answers "Do not apply" and the percentage regarding the total of evaluations (column % NA and NO) was obtained. Likewise, in order to analyze the aspects presenting bigger sociability problems, the answers "No occurrence" and "Partial occurrence" (column % NO and OP) were summed.

Table 1 demonstrates the heuristic aspects that shows more percentage for the %NA e NO column or for the % NO and OP column to the VLEs.

Once all the answers were compiled, it was observed that, to the VLEs (Table 1), the heuristic aspect that could present the biggest evidence of not applying to the community was related to the commercial transaction. Other aspects that do not apply to this community, to the answers, are related to the ways of complaint and punishment for the incorrect use of the community; the possible ways of expression in the community; and the mechanisms of decision making. However, analyzing the characteristics of VLEs, it is observed that commercial transactions may occur, once events are promoted in such environments, several materials are provided, among others. The VLEs could establish types of decision making (which learners opine towards the event type, evaluation, research, among others) and also protocols, including rules, punishments and types of complaint regarding the incorrect use of the community in order to reach its goal.

The compilation of answers also allowed identifying bigger problems regarding sociability within such environments. The aspects that may not occur satisfactorily in VLEs are related to: lack of identification to the purpose of community; absence of ways to punish the incorrect use of community; absence of events which stimulate cooperation; and lack of perception towards other peoples' actions in the environment.

Table 2 shows, to Social Networks, heuristic aspects which presented the biggest percentages to the %NA and NO column or to the %NO and OP column.

To Social Networks (Table 2), the heuristic aspects point out the most of not applying to such type of community are related to: declaring copyright; users' roles and decision making. Regarding the amplitude and features of Social Networks, it appears that it is hard to provide mechanisms to the declaration of copyrights in case of disclosure of contents. Furthermore, the fact that users may not hold different roles and an explicit coordination on the network may not exist is observed, which decharacterizes the existence of a specialist moderator for the decision-making in the environment.

However, regarding sociability, it appears that the aspects presenting the biggest problems were associated to: concealment of policies of use; unavailability of pre-elaborated messages for conversation and the unsatisfactory perception of action that are being conducted by people.

4 Conclusion

In the present paper an analysis on the SVCoP heuristic (first developed in order to evaluate the sociability in VCoPs) as your application in other types of online community, the VLEs and the Social Networks was conducted.

The SVCoP containing 46 questions, organized in five aspects (Community, Members, Competency, Collaboration and Decision Making) was applied by 62 users who evaluated three Social Networks and two VLEs.

Once the answers analysis and the verification of characteristics of online communities were concluded, we found that the SVCoP heuristic also applies to VLEs and to Social Networks, once, of 46 evaluation aspects, the majority are pertinents to such environments.

Based on the evaluators' answers regarding "Do not apply" and "No occurrence", only five elements pointed out evidences of not applying to VLEs. However, none was considered not applicable by the majority evaluators. The item that obtained the biggest number of answers "Do not apply", referring to commercial transactions in the community, reached 64,5 %. On the other hand, to social networks, only three elements pointed out evidences of not applying to such environments, taking into account that the answer which obtained the biggest percentage of "Do not apply", referring to decision making, reached 48,4 %.

From the application of the heuristic, the sociability aspects that are not satisfactory within such communities are verified. In the VLEs, a lack of attractively took place as the community purpose was given; lack of punishment forms towards the incorrect use of users within the community; absence of events which stimulate cooperation; and finally, lack of perception towards other peoples' actions in the environment. On the other hand, in Social Networks, the weakest points were the lack of disclosure of policies of use; the unavailability of pre-elaborated messages for the conversation between members and the unsatisfactory perception towards actions performed by other users in the community.

As future work, we aim to perform new evaluations in order to reinforce the results hereby achieved and also to verify the application of the heuristic on other types of online communities.

References

1. Alves, S.V.L., Alves, E.C.M., Gomes, A.S.: Percepção em groupware educacionais. Revista Brasileira de Informática na Educação (2008)
2. Amarante, D.P.M.: Utilização do design instrucional em curso ead: Análise do Ambiente Virtual de Aprendizagem de curso técnico à distância de uma instituição pública de ensino. Universidade FUMEC, Belo Horizonte, MG (2015)
3. Arbex, D.F., Bittencourt, D.F.: Estratégias para o desenvolvimento de um ambiente virtual de aprendizagem: um estudo de caso realizado na unisul virtual, Revista Brasileira de Aprendizagem Aberta e a Distância, São Paulo, Dez. (2007)
4. Barbosa, G.A.R., Santos, G.E., Pereira, V.M.O.: Caracterização Qualitativa da Sociabilidade no Facebook. In: IHC (2013) Proceedings - Full Papers
5. Batista, H.: Aplicativo de comunidade virtual para a prática de esportes voltada para dispositivos móveis (2014)
6. Benghozi, P.: Les Communautés Virtuelles: Structuration Sociale ou Outil de Gestion? Entreprises et Histoire **43**, 67–81 (2006). France
7. Brito, R.F., E Pereira, A.T.: Um estudo para ambientes colaborativos e suas ferramentas. Universidade Federal de Santa Catarina (2004)
8. Chagas, C.G., Freitas, C.S.C.: O Uso Das Redes Sociais No Ensino A Distância Como Ferramenta De Aprendizagem, Revista Cesuca Virtual: Conhecimento Sem Fronteiras 2(3), Ago (2015). ISSN: 2318–4221
9. Cunha, F.O., Silva, J.M.C.: Análise das Dimensões Afetivas do Tutor em Turmas de EaD no Ambiente Virtual Moodle (2009)
10. Forato, B.B.A.: Heurísticas para a criação de uma comunidade online (2011)
11. Fuks, H., Raposo, A.B., Gerosa, M.A.: Engenharia de Groupware: Desenvolvimento de Aplicações Colaborativas. In XXI Jornada de Atualização em Informática, Anais do XXII Congresso da Sociedade Brasileira de Computação, vol. 2, Chap. 3 (2002). ISBN: 85-88442-24-8
12. Fuks, H., Raposo, A.B., Gerosa, M.A.: Do modelo de colaboração 3c à engenharia de groupware. In: Simpósio brasileiro de sistemas multimídia e web - web-mídia 2003, 9, 2003. Anais… [S. l.: s. n.], pp. 445–452 (2003)
13. Kreijns, K., et al.: Measuring perceived sociability of computer-supported collaborative learning environments (2007)

14. Lopes, L.A., Guilhermino, D.F., Coleti, T.A., Sgarbi, E.M., de Oliveira, T.F.: Heuristic to support the sociability evaluation in virtual communities of practices. In: Kurosu, M. (ed.) Human-Computer Interaction, Part III, HCII 2015. LNCS, vol. 9171, pp. 3–14. Springer, Heidelberg (2015)
15. Machado, J.R., Tijiboy, A.V.: Redes Sociais Virtuais: um espaço para efetivação da aprendizagem cooperative, 3(1), Maio (2005)
16. Martins, J.G.: Aprendizagem baseada em problemas aplicada a ambiente virtual de aprendizagem, Universidade Federal de Santa Catarina, Programa de Pós-Graduação em Engenharia de Produção (2002)
17. Moraes, M.: A monitoria como serviços de apoio ao aluno na educação a distância
18. Florianópolis: Tese (Doutorado em Engenharia de Produção) pelo Departamento de Engenharia de Produção da UFSC. Florianópolis (2004)
19. Obregon R.F.A.: O padrão arquetípico da alteridade e o compartilhamento de conhecimento em ambiente virtual de aprendizagem inclusivo (2011)
20. Pereira, R., Baranauskas, M.C.C., da Silva, S.R.P.: Softwares sociais: uma visão orientada a valores. In: Proceedings of the IX Symposium on Human Factors in Computing Systems, IHC 2010, pp. 149–158 (2010)
21. Preece, J.: Online Communities: Designing Usability, Supporting Sociability. Wiley, NewYork (2000)
22. Preece, J.: Online Communities: Designing Usabiliy, Supporting Sociability. Preece, Rogers, Sharp Design de Interação, 3ª ed. (2013)
23. Recuero, R.: Facebook x Orkut no Brasil: alguns apontamentos. Social Media, 24 Ago. (2009)
24. Santos, E.O.: Educação online: cibercultura e pesquisa-formação na prática docente, Capitulo II - A educação online para além da educação a distância: um evento da cibercultura (2005)
25. Silva, S.: Sociabilidades juvenis online (2007)
26. Terra, J.C.C., Gordon, C.: Portais Corporativos: A Revolução na Gestão do Conhecimento. São Paulo, SP: Negócio, 480 p. (2002)
27. Tifous, A., Ghali, A.E., Dieng-Kuntz, R., Giboin, A., Evangelou, C., Vidou, G.: Na ontology for supporting communities of practice. In K-CAP 39-4 (2007)
28. Wenger, E.: Communities of practice and social learning systems: the career of a concept. Social Learning Systems and Communities of Practice. Chap. 11 in Blackmore, p. 179. Springer, Dordrecht (2010)

New ISO Standards for Usability, Usability Reports and Usability Measures

Nigel Bevan[1(✉)], Jim Carter[2], Jonathan Earthy[3], Thomas Geis[4], and Susan Harker[5]

[1] Professional UX Services, 12 King Edwards Gardens, London W3 9RG, UK
mail@nigelbevan.com
[2] Computer Science Department, University of Saskatchewan, Saskatoon S7N 5C9, Canada
carter@cs.usask.ca
[3] Lloyd's Register EMEA, 1 Grosvenor Square, Southampton SO15 2JU, UK
Jonathan.Earthy@lr.org
[4] ProContext Consulting GmbH, Unter Käster 14-16, 50667 Cologne, Germany
Thomas.Geis@procontext.de
[5] Loughborough Design School, Loughborough University, Loughborough LE11 3TU, UK
S.D.Harker@lboro.ac.uk

Abstract. Several new and revised ISO standards will be published in 2016/17 that define the basic terms and concepts of usability (ISO 9241-11), give guidance on processes and outcomes of human-centred design (ISO 9241-220), provide examples of measures that can be used in usability evaluation (ISO/IEC 25022 and 25023) and define what should be included in usability evaluation reports for usability tests, inspections and surveys (ISO/IEC 25066). The paper explains some of the new content and how it can be used.

Keywords: Standards · Usability · User experience

1 New ISO Standards for Usability

Standards from the International Organization for Standardization (ISO) are produced by international groups of experts after a rigorous review process, and represent a consensus on the current state-of-the art. Because of the number of international experts involved in their development they provide a more balanced perspective than is typically found in textbooks or individual publications. Several new and revised standards relating to usability will be published in 2016/7:

- ISO 9241-11: *Usability: Definitions and concepts* [6], replacing the 1988 version of ISO 9241-11.
- ISO 9241-220: *Processes for enabling, executing and assessing human-centred design within organizations* [9], replacing the earlier ISO TR 18529.
- ISO/IEC 25066: *Common industry Format for Usability — Evaluation Reports* [17].

M. Kurosu (Ed.): HCI 2016, Part I, LNCS 9731, pp. 268–278, 2016.
DOI: 10.1007/978-3-319-39510-4_25

- ISO/IEC 25022: *Measurement of quality in use* [11], (includes measures of effectiveness, efficiency and satisfaction), replacing ISO TR 9126-4.
- ISO/IEC 25023: M*easurement of system and software product quality* [12], (includes measures for usability attributes), replacing ISO/IEC TR 9126-2 and ISO/IEC TR 9126-3.

The paper summarises some of the new content included in these standards.

2 ISO 9241-11: Usability: Definitions and Concepts

The new version of ISO 9241-11 retains and elaborates on the concepts in the 1988 version of the standard, with the original definition of usability extended to apply to systems and services: "the extent to which a system, product or service can be used by specified users to achieve specified goals with effectiveness, efficiency and satisfaction in a specified context of use". The content has been extended to include current approaches to usability and user experience [2]. Some examples are given below.

Goals. Historically, usability has been associated with achieving predetermined practical goals, but the concept has been widened in the new version of ISO 9241-11 to include achieving personal outcomes such as entertainment or personal development. It is also recognised that users can have several interrelated goals. For example the goal of completing a report could include the potentially conflicting sub-goals to (a) please the client by sending the report today, (b) ensure a quality of content that indicates professional expertise, and (c) finish the report in time to get home for a family event.

Absence of Negative Consequences. Effectiveness has been associated with completing a task completely and accurately, but it is also important to take account of the potential negative consequences if the task is not achieved correctly. The new definition of effectiveness: "accuracy, completeness and lack of negative consequences with which users achieved specified goals" takes account of negative consequences such as:

- economic harm
  e.g. high costs for accidently selected the roaming option on a mobile phone
- harm to health
  e.g. injury of a patient resulting from use errors with a medical device
- harm to the environment
  e.g. unnecessary use of energy through inability to set central heating controls appropriately

Objectively Achieved Outcomes and Subjectively Perceived Outcomes. For a successful outcome of interaction with an interactive system (effectiveness) both objective and perceived success is typically necessary. There can be negative consequences if objective success is perceived as failure, for example, if you book a flight but don't get a confirmation, so assume the booking was not made, and book again. Now you have two reservations! Perceiving objective failure as success can also have negative consequences, for example, you use a voting machine to make your vote. You think it was made, but it is not counted because you did not press hard enough. If you had realised it was not successful, you would have tried again.

Satisfaction. Satisfaction has been redefined to take account of the wider range of concerns that are now recognised as important for user experience: "positive attitudes, emotions and/or comfort resulting from use of a system, product or service". These three aspects relate to the cognitive, affective and psychomotor responses of an individual.

Wide Applicability. The new draft makes it clear that usability applies to all aspects of use, including:

- Learnability, to enable new users to be effective, efficient and satisfied when learning to use a new system.
- Regular use, to enable users to achieve their goals effectively, efficiently and with satisfaction.
- Accessibility, so that the system if effective, efficient and satisfying for users with the widest range of capabilities.
- Maintainability, to enable maintenance tasks to be completed effectively, efficiently and with satisfaction.

3 ISO 9241-220: Processes for Enabling, Executing and Assessing Human-Centred Design Within Organizations

According to ISO 9241-210, human-centred design is an "approach to systems design and development that aims to make interactive systems more usable by focusing on the use of the system and applying human factors/ergonomics and usability knowledge and techniques".

ISO 9241-220 elaborates on ISO 9241-210 to provide a comprehensive description of the processes that support the activities that are required as part of human-centred design. Figure 1 (adapted from ISO 9241-220) summarises the processes that need to be in place in each area of an organisation that has some responsibility for human centred design. The groups of processes related to these levels are called "Human Centred Process categories" (HCP). HCP.1 addresses what organizations need to do to enable human-centred design on a corporate level. HCP.2 describes the required infrastructure and management of human-centred design across projects and systems, and HCP.3 details the project-specific aspects of human-centred design during development or change of a system. HCP.4 covers the specific processes during introduction and operation of a system. Together the implementation of these four sets of processes ensures that the systems produced, acquired and operated by an organization have appropriate levels of usability, accessibility, user experience and mitigation of risks that could arise from use. This combined objective is referred to as human-centred quality, the: "extent to which requirements relating to usability, accessibility, user experience and minimizing risks arising from use are met".

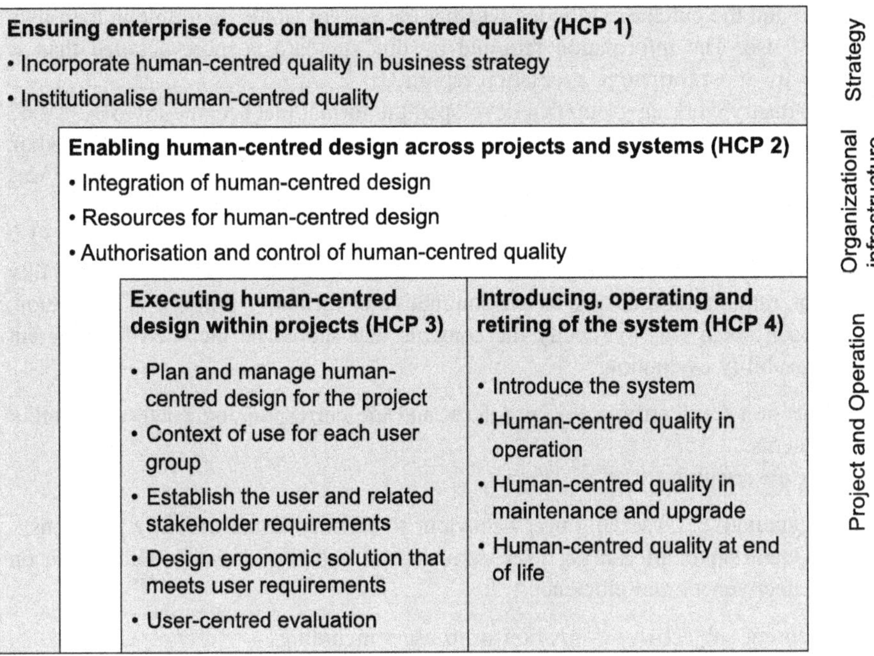

Fig. 1. Human centred design process categories and contents

The current draft of the standard proposes a broadened definition of user experience to take account of the way the term is commonly used: "a person's perceptions and responses resulting from the use and/or anticipated use of an interactive system, and from the user's interaction with the organization that supplies or delivers the interactive system; from discovering the system, adopting and using it, through to final use".

ISO 9241-220 can be used for:

- implementing human-centred design based on the process outcomes needed to achieve human centred quality as part of a system development or procurement process and/or support lifecycle;
- assessing an enterprise's existing capability to carry out the human-centred processes;
- improving the effectiveness of human-centred design as part of an existing system development process;
- specification and development of necessary competence in human-centred design.

4 ISO/IEC 25066: Usability Evaluation Reports

ISO/IEC 25062 *Common Industry Format (CIF) for usability test reports,* published in 2008, specifies the information to be included in a summative test report that is intended to enable a supplier to demonstrate the usability of their system to a potential purchaser, and the purchaser to judge whether the system would be usable in their own context of use. The information required by this standard is more detailed than is necessary for most formative evaluation reports.

The industry working group that developed the format that became ISO/IEC 25062 [1] worked on the production of guidance for the content of a formative report based on user testing [18] but concluded that the extent of the variation needed in practice was too great to support the development of a single recommended format.

When the new ISO/IEC 25066 *Common Industry Format for usability (CIF) – Evaluation reports* was developed to cover a wider range of approaches to usability evaluation, rather than focusing on the summative or formative purpose of evaluation, the approach taken was to specify the contents that should be included for different types of usability evaluation:

(a) Inspection to identify usability defects and the corresponding potential usability problems.
(b) User observation
    - Qualitative: Observing user behaviour to identify actual usability problems.
    - Quantitative: Measuring user performance and responses to obtain data on effectiveness and efficiency.
(c) Obtaining subjective information from users including:
    - Qualitative: Problems, opinions and impressions given during or after a usability evaluation.
    - Quantitative: Measures of user satisfaction or perception.

The potential content items for a report that included each of these types of evaluation is categorised under the headings:

1. Executive summary (if used)
2. Description of the object of evaluation
3. Purpose of the evaluation
4. Method
    a. General
    b. Evaluators/participants
    c. Tasks (if used in the evaluation)
    d. Evaluation environment
5. Procedure
    a. Design of the evaluation
    b. Data to be collected
6. Results
    a. Data analysis
    b. Presentation of the results
7. Interpretation of results and recommendations

For each type of content, the standard lists the potential content items relevant to each type of usability evaluation, indicating whether they are required, recommended or optional. Table 1 is an example of some of the items for the evaluation environment.

Table 1. Evaluation environment

Type of evaluation: Content elements to be included in the report:	Inspection	User observation		Information from users
		Observing user behaviour	Measuring user performance and response	
(a) Physical environment and facilities	N/A	Required	Required	Optional
(b) Technical environment (if applicable)	Required	Required	Required	Recommended
(c) Evaluation administration tools (if used)	Recommended	Recommended	Recommended	Recommended

The 64 content items in the standard can be used as a checklist to ensure that for each type of evaluation that is reported, all the required content and appropriate recommended items are included.

5 ISO/IEC 25022: Measurement of Quality in Use

Quality in use which is defined in ISO/IEC 25010 *System and software quality models* includes: effectiveness, efficiency, satisfaction, freedom from risk and context coverage. The measures for quality in use in ISO/IEC 25022 include measures for the components of usability that are defined in ISO 9241-11: effectiveness, efficiency and satisfaction (Table 2).

Table 2. Measures of effectiveness, efficiency and satisfaction

Effectiveness	Efficiency	Satisfaction
Tasks completed	Task time	Overall satisfaction
Objectives achieved	Time efficiency	Satisfaction with features
Errors in a task	Cost-effectiveness	Discretionary usage
Tasks with errors	Productive time ratio	Feature utilisation
Task error intensity	Unnecessary actions	Proportion of users complaining
	Fatigue	Proportion of user complaints about a particular feature
		User trust
		User pleasure
		Physical comfort

ISO/IEC 25022 provides suggested measures for freedom from risk, which is defines as the: "degree to which the quality of a product or system mitigates or avoids potential risk to the user, organisation or project, including risks to economic status, human life, health, or the environment" (Table 3). This recognises that it is not sufficient simply to consider successful interaction, it is also important to minimise the possibility of any adverse consequences that could arise from poor usability (such as an individual failing to purchase the correct transport ticket, adverse economic consequences for a company, or environmental consequences resulting from poor usability of home-heating controls). The importance of the risk of negative consequences that can result from poor quality was first introduced in the ISO/IEC 9126-1 standard in 2001, and was updated in ISO/IEC 25010 in 2011. The concept of the risk of negative consequences that can result from use is being incorporated into ISO 9241-220 and is addressed in the revised version of ISO 9241-11 as part of effectiveness.

Table 3. Measures of risk

Economic risk	Health and safety risk	Environmental risk
Return on investment (ROI)	User health reporting frequency	Environmental impact
Time to achieve return on investment	User health and safety impact	
Business performance	Safety of people affected by use of the system	
Benefits of IT Investment		
Service to customers		
Website visitors converted to customers		
Revenue from each customer		
Errors with economic consequences		

An example measure is: "Proportion of usage situations where there are human or system errors with economic consequences". Although it is usually not possible to control other factors in the context of use that could influence freedom from risk, it is often possible to provide evidence for the potential risks that could result from poor usability or poor product quality, and to suggest target values for usability that would mitigate these risks.

ISO/IEC 25022 also provides measures for context coverage: "the degree to which a product or system can be used with effectiveness, efficiency, satisfaction and freedom from risk in both specified contexts of use and in contexts beyond those initially explicitly identified" (Table 4). Context coverage was introduced into ISO/IEC 25010 to support specification and evaluation of usability in all defined and anticipated contexts of use. The measure of context completeness is defined as: "The proportion of the intended contexts of use in which a product or system can be used with acceptable usability and risk". It could for example be measured by the proportion of the intended contexts of use for which there are measures showing that the product can used with acceptable usability and risk.

Table 4. Measures of context coverage

Context completeness	Flexibility
Context completeness	Flexible context of use
	Product flexibility
	Proficiency independence

Flexibility measures are used to assess the degree to which a product or system can be used with acceptable levels of effectiveness, efficiency, satisfaction and freedom from risk in contexts beyond those initially specified in the requirements for the system. Flexibility enables products to take account of circumstances, opportunities and individual preferences that might not have been anticipated in advance. Flexibility can be measured by analysing the characteristics of the product and the context of use to assess the extent to which a product can be used by additional types of users to achieve additional goals with effectiveness, efficiency, satisfaction and freedom from risk in additional contexts of use, or by testing the product with users in these additional contexts of use, or by the capability of the product to be modified to support adaptation for new types of users, tasks and environments by means of suitability for individualization as defined in ISO 9241-110.

Proficiency independence assesses the extent to which the product can be used by people who do not have specific knowledge, skills or experience. The product could be primarily intended for a user group with specific knowledge, skills or experience, but potentially usable by a wider range of types of user.

6 ISO/IEC 25023: Measurement of System and Software Product Quality

ISO/IEC 25023 contains measures for system and software product quality, including measures of usability as a product attribute (Tables 5 and 6). The main reason for including the usability measures was to complement the better-established measures for

Table 5. Measures of usability attributes

Appropriateness recognisability	Learnability	Operability
Description completeness	User guidance completeness	Operational consistency
Demonstration coverage	Entry fields defaults	Message clarity
Entry point self-descriptiveness	Error message understandability	Functional customizability
	Self-explanatory user interface	User interface customizability
		Monitoring capability
		Undo capability
		Understandable categorization of information
		Appearance consistency
		Input device support

Table 6. Measures of usability attributes (continued)

User error protection	User interface aesthetics	Accessibility
Avoidance of user operation error	Appearance aesthetics of user interfaces	Accessibility for users with disability
User entry error correction		Supported languages adequacy
User error recoverability		

software qualities such as system performance, reliability, security and maintainability. Measures such as response time, system availability, fault tolerance and data integrity are widely used for specifying, evaluating and monitoring software quality. Without equivalent measures for usability that can be used in early systems development, usability is likely to be ignored in favour of the hard software qualities.

This creates a problem, as usability in early systems development typically focuses on identifying and fixing usability defects, and it is not clear whether detailed measures of usability properties would be of any benefit to a usability engineer. So the initial audience for detailed usability measures is likely to be the software testers who will only be able to use quite simple measures in a restricted context of use, but at least it will flag usability as an important issue in systems development.

In principle the evaluation of almost any usability guideline (of which there are hundreds in the literature) could be treated as a measure, which caused a problem deciding which usability measures to include in ISO/IEC 25023. Eventually it was decided to use selected examples of "dialogue principles" in ISO 9241-110 as a source.

7 Conclusions

The ISO 9241-11, ISO 9241-220 and ISO/IEC 25066 standards provide rich resources for usability practitioners and researchers, who may also find the measures in ISO/IEC 25022 and 25023 useful. ISO/IEC 25023 is primarily intended for use in a software development environment, and cross-references the ISO 9241 series of standards for additional information.

The standards described are part of the ISO 9241 series developed by the ISO Ergonomics subcommittee TC159/SC4 and the ISO 25000 series developed by the Systems and software engineering committee ISO/IEC JTC1/SC7. The ISO/IEC 2506x Common Industry Format standards are developed jointly by the two committees and also include:

- ISO/IEC 25063: Context of use description
- ISO/IEC 25064: User needs report
- ISO/IEC 25065: User Requirements Specification [in preparation]

If you would like to contribute to the development of future standards related to usability, or to comment on drafts, you can either do this via your national standards body [3], or if you are a member of one of the ISO TC159/SC4 liaison organisations [4] such as UXPA [19] you can participate through the liaison organisation.

Acknowledgements. These ISO standards were developed by their editors (which include the authors of this paper) supported by the other members of ISO TC159/SC4/WG6, ISO/IEC JTC1/SC7/WG6 and the joint working group (WG28) between ISO TC159/SC4 and ISO/IEC JTC1/SC7.

References

1. Bevan, N.: Industry standard usability tests. In: Brewster, S., Cawsey, A., Cockton, G. (eds.) Human-Computer Interaction – INTERACT 1999, vol. II, pp. 107–108. British Computer Society (1999)
2. Bevan, N., Carter, J., Harker, S.: ISO 9241-11 revised: what have we learnt about usability since 1998? In: Kurosu, Masaaki (ed.) HCII 2015. LNCS, vol. 9169, pp. 143–151. Springer, Heidelberg (2015)
3. ISO: Members. www.iso.org/iso/home/about/iso_members.htm
4. ISO: TC159/SC4 Ergonomics of human-system interaction. www.iso.org/iso/home/standards_development/list_of_iso_technical_committees/iso_technical_committee.htm?commid=53372
5. ISO 9241-11: Ergonomic requirements for office work with visual display terminals (VDTs) — Part 11 Guidance on usability (1998)
6. ISO DIS 9241-11: Ergonomics of human-system interaction — Part 11: Usability: Definitions and concepts (2015)
7. ISO 9241-110: Ergonomics of human-system interaction — Part 110: Dialogue principles (2006)
8. ISO 9241-210: Ergonomics of human-system interaction — Part 210: Human-centred design for interactive systems (2010)
9. ISO DIS 9241-220: Ergonomics of human-system interaction — Part 220: Processes for enabling, executing and assessing human-centred design within organizations (2016)
10. ISO/IEC 25010: Systems and software engineering — Systems and software product Quality Requirements and Evaluation (SQuaRE) — System and software quality models (2011)
11. ISO/IEC FDIS 25022: Systems and software engineering — Systems and software Quality Requirements and Evaluation (SQuaRE) - Measurement of quality in use (2016)
12. ISO/IEC FDIS 25023: Systems and software engineering — Systems and software Quality Requirements and Evaluation (SQuaRE) - Measurement of system and software product quality (2016)
13. ISO/IEC 25062: Software engineering — Software product Quality Requirements and Evaluation (SQuaRE) — Common Industry Format (CIF) for usability test reports (2006)
14. ISO/IEC 25063: Systems and software engineering — Systems and software Quality Requirements and Evaluation (SQuaRE) — Common Industry Format (CIF) for usability: Context of use description (2014)
15. ISO/IEC 25064: Systems and software engineering — Software product Quality Requirements and Evaluation (SQuaRE) — Common Industry Format (CIF) for usability: User needs report (2013)
16. ISO/IEC NP 25065: Systems and software engineering — Systems and software Quality Requirements and Evaluation (SQuaRE) — Common industry Format for Usability — User Requirements Specification (2014)

17. ISO/IEC FDIS 25066: Systems and software engineering — Software product Quality Requirements and Evaluation (SQuaRE) — Common Industry Format (CIF) for usability: Evaluation report (2016)
18. Theofanos, M., Quesenbery, W.: Towards the design of effective formative test reports. J. Usability Stud. **1**(1), 28–45 (2005)
19. UXPA: User Experience Professionals Association liaison with ISO. www.uxpa.org/standards

Evaluation of UX Methods: Lessons Learned When Evaluating a Multi-user Mobile Application

Bruna Moraes Ferreira[1(✉)], Luís Rivero[1], Natasha M. Costa Valentim[1], Renata Zilse[2], Andrew Koster[2], and Tayana Conte[1]

[1] USES Research Group, Federal University of Amazonas, Manaus, Brazil
{bmf,luisrivero,natashavalentim,tayana}@icomp.ufam.edu.br
[2] Samsung Research Institute Brazil, Campinas, Brazil
{renata.borges,andrew.k}@samsung.com

Abstract. The User Experience (UX) of a software product is influenced by pragmatic and hedonic aspects, and it is necessary to choose a UX evaluation method that takes both of these aspects into account. In this paper, we report on the lessons learned from applying different UX evaluation methods (3E, 3E*, SAM, MAX, EM, Think Aloud, and Observation) in prototyping a multi-user mobile application. We analyzed the different methods in terms of: (i) the type of problems they identified, (ii) their contribution to improve the prototype in each development phase, (iii) encountered difficulties when applying the method, and (iv) encountered difficulties when analyzing the results of the method. We found that SAM and MAX were the easiest methods to apply and also to analyze their results. They are best used to identify hedonic problems, as is EM, whereas Think Aloud, EM and 3E* best identify pragmatic ones.

Keywords: User Experience · Usability · Evaluation method · Lessons learned

1 Introduction

The number of methods for evaluating the User Experience (UX) and Usability in all phases of the software development process is growing [2]. We know that experiences are influenced not only by the system features (e.g. complexity, usability and functionality), but also by the user's psychological state (e.g. motivation, expectations, needs, humor, others) and the context in which the interaction takes place [1]. Due to the increasing attention of the HCI field for usability engineering, features such as UX, user emotions, influences, motivations and values are getting as much attention as features such as ease of use, learning and subjective satisfaction [10].

While usability evaluation emphasizes effectiveness and efficiency, UX evaluation explores hedonic aspects. That is, UX evaluation explores how a person feels after using an application, as well as the experience, affection and significant and valuable aspects of such use. Therefore, through UX and Usability evaluations it is possible to measure both the understanding of how users feel and their satisfaction with the application (UX) and the time required to carry out certain activities in the application and the success rate of such activities (usability) [15].

M. Kurosu (Ed.): HCI 2016, Part I, LNCS 9731, pp. 279–290, 2016.
DOI: 10.1007/978-3-319-39510-4_26

This paper presents the result of applying some methods for evaluating UX and usability. These methods were employed during the development process of a distributed mobile application that helps a team of caregivers in a home care situation (involving both family members as well as professionals) to plan and organize the day-to-day tasks that are necessary in order to care for a senior citizen.

We discuss the types of UX and usability problems encountered by each method, which were analyzed and classified into hedonic and pragmatic. This classification was chosen since, according Hassenzahl [4], interactive systems are perceived through these two dimensions. We also verified which methods better contributed to improving the evaluated prototype, what difficulties we encountered when applying each method and when analyzing its results. Finally, we documented how some of the modification of UX and usability methods that we used contributed to enhancing the evaluation results. Through the results of the assessments, this paper provides information that may encourage software development teams to carry out cost-effective UX and usability evaluations. Also, we hope to support the choice of the most appropriate methods, according to the needs of each software development project, improving software quality in the process.

In the next section, we present the concepts of User Experience and Usability, and present some existing evaluation methods and motivate our selection. Section 3 presents the project context in which the methods were used and how the project was executed. In Sect. 4 we describe how the Usability and User Experience evaluations were performed. Next, in Sect. 5 we present the analysis of the results from the methods that were used during the evaluation. Finally, in Sect. 6 we conclude the paper and present possible future work.

2 Background

2.1 User Experience and Usability

The international standard ISO 9241-210 [6] defines User Experience as "a person's perceptions and responses that result from the use or anticipated use of a product, system or service". People perceive UX through two dimensions: pragmatic and hedonic quality [4]. Pragmatic quality refers to the perception of the product with regards to the fulfillment of its purpose [5]. It focuses on aspects of usefulness and usability regarding the tasks to be carried out. Hedonic quality is more focused on the human needs and expectations someone has for using a particular product [5].

By the ISO/IEC 25010 norm [7], usability is "the capability of the software product to be understood, learned, operated, attractive to the user, and compliant to standards/guidelines, when used under specific conditions". Thus, usability subsumes the aspects of how easy the system is to use, such as learnability, operability, aesthetics, and also the extent to which usability affects the user's choice to accept a product or not [1].

As Vermeeren et al. [16] point out, we see that the relationship between usability and UX is intertwined. While usability focuses on task performance (e.g. measuring task execution time, number of clicks or errors), UX focuses on experiences by analyzing peoples' emotions while they interact with the software product. In that context, usability is related to UX. Furthermore, because UX is subjective, objective usability measures are not sufficient for measuring UX. For a complete evaluation, it is also necessary to analyze how the user feels about the software application while performing tasks on it.

2.2 UX and Usability Evaluation Methods

Usability and UX evaluation is a fundamental activity in any development process that seeks to produce an interactive system with high-quality use. It helps the evaluator make a value judgment about the quality of use of the proposed solution, and identify problems that affect the user experience while using the system [11].

The methods for UX evaluation that were employed during the project were 3E (Expressing Experiences and Emotions) [13], MAX (Method for the Assessment of eXperience) [3] and SAM (Self-Assessment Manikin) [9]. These methods can gather insightful information on the UX of a product in sessions lasting less than an hour per participating user [3]. Additionally, the designer does not need to be an expert in UX since the selected methods are easy to apply. We also employed modifications of these methods to collect information that the original methods did not allow to obtain: the modified methods are 3E* (modified 3E) and Empathy Map (EM) to evaluate UX. Finally, to evaluate the pragmatic aspects, we employed the Think Aloud [14] and Observation [8] methods. We briefly summarize each method below.

SAM. SAM allows the evaluation of the affective quality of an interface. Through the SAM scale, it is possible to assess three dimensions: (a) pleasure (pleasure/displeasure); (b) dominance (control of the situation/dominated by the situation); and (c) arousal (calm/excited). The method was designed to collect information on subjective feelings. When applying SAM, the user marks on each of the scales the image that corresponds to his/her emotional response after using the application.

3E. 3E is a self-report method in which the user can express his/her emotions and experiences through drawings or by writing. The template of the method has a human body outline. The user can draw a face on the picture to express his/her emotional state. Beside the human figure there are two balloons. One of the balloons is used to represent inner thoughts and the other one for representing oral expression.

MAX. The MAX method [3] uses a board and cards. During the use of the prototype of the developed software, the evoked emotions and experiences are collected through the answers to the questions that are written on the MAX board. In that context, the board has four questions: (a) "What did you feel when using it?"; (b) "Was it easy to use it?"; (c) "Was it useful?"; and (d) "Do you intend to use it?". To answer the questions the MAX cards are used. The cards contain words that allowed the user to express his/her opinion regarding the application. While the users choose a card for each of the questions on the board, they report the reasons for choosing that card.

3E*. We modified was in the 3E method to allow a more in-depth evaluation of different activities in the application. We name this modification 3E*. Using the original 3E method, a subject can only describe a general view of the application's use. Our modification allows a subject to describe his/her experiences for each performed activity. In this modification, the method is applied for each of the tasks performed by the subjects. We also added bubbles where the user describes his/her thoughts and opinions regarding the application.

EM. Another method that we modified was the Empathy Map (EM) [12]. This method is not originally employed for evaluating the UX. It is a method that helps to design business models according to the clients' perspectives. The original method is divided into fields, in which the client describes what he/she thinks, feels, hears, does and speaks, together with his/her problems and needs. In the context of the UX evaluation, the template of the EM method was modified so that the subject can describe what tasks he/she managed to successfully complete, what he/she thought of the application and whether the application met his/her needs.

Think Aloud. In the Think Aloud (TA) method, users are asked to literally think out loud; and report their interaction with the application, the tasks they are performing and what difficulties they are having. Thus, it is possible to obtain data about the users' reasoning during the performed tasks.

Observation. In this method, moderators observe the user interacting with the software and take notes about the observed difficulties. Unlike the other methods, this requires an observer with experience in UX evaluation.

3 The Home Care Development Project

The Home Care development project is intended to deal with a growing problem worldwide. It is motivated by the aging population in many countries. In the scenario we study, a senior citizen is cared for by a team composed of family members and professional caregivers. The problem we address is how to coordinate the many tasks that caring for a senior citizen entails. In this context, the scope of this work is to evaluate the UX and usability of the application being developed.

There were two distributed teams working on this project. One team was responsible for technical details regarding the underlying multi-agent based task allocation system. Our team was responsible for the design and evaluation of the user interface of the system. Our team was composed of six members, a team manager and five UX designers and evaluators. The evaluators had previous experience in applying UX and Usability evaluation methods, and they all applied the methods listed in Sect. 2.2. Also, our team had access to 8 mobile devices, in which users performed the UX and usability evaluations. In total, the project lasted for 6 months and adopted an iterative process lifecycle. For each month of the project there was an Iteration.

During that six-month period, we developed and evaluated more than a hundred low-fidelity prototypes, which were derived from 10 use cases implementing more than 20 functionalities. The overall process is shown in (Fig. 1).

In Iteration 1, we developed a total of eight personas in order to identify the different user profiles, their features and needs. After that, we specified the functionalities and use cases that would meet the needs of these users through activity diagrams. Also, we created 10 detailed scenarios describing each use case and its relationship with the personas and devices of the project. In Iteration 2, we developed the first set of prototypes of the application and interaction models to represent the interaction possibilities between the application and the users. In Iterations 3, 4 and 5, while developing the set of prototypes of the other prioritized use cases; we also evaluated and redesigned the set of prototypes that were developed in previous iterations. Finally, in Iteration 6, we carried out a complete UX evaluation of all of the redesigned prototypes to assess the impact of the modifications we made on the overall UX of the software system.

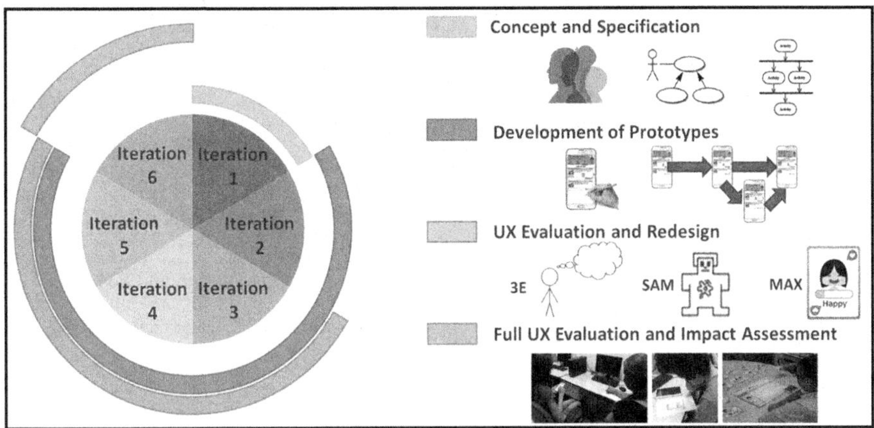

Fig. 1. Process for the design, evaluation and redesign of the prototypes

4 Project Execution: UX and Usability Evaluations

During the development of the project interface, four UX and Usability evaluations were performed. In each iteration from 2–5, the prototype was developed to fulfill the functionality of a specific use case for the application, according to the project's initial prioritization in iteration 1. Thus, each evaluation in iteration 3–5 was performed over the developed prototypes from the previous iteration. In the fourth evaluation of iteration 6, the complete prototype was evaluated since this was the last evaluation and no further mockups were developed.

The four evaluations were conducted with students as users. Most of the study participants were living with elderly or thought that the application could be useful to look after their parents when they become elderly. In each assessment we used different methods (see Table 1). For the evaluations, the participants had to carry out some tasks using the prototype application on a mobile device. The evaluation was guided by three moderators, who explained to the subjects what tasks they needed to perform. Also, the moderators explained to the subjects how they had to employ the UX methods in order to express their opinion regarding their interaction with the prototype. Table 1 shows an overview of the participants and methods for each evaluation.

After each evaluation, the project team classified the identified defects. The classification process was composed of two activities: (1) removal of duplicates and (2) a meeting for the classification of problems. After the removal of the duplicated problems, the project team carried out a meeting where they reviewed the problems. The team discussed which classification was the best for each of the problems (cosmetic defect, relevant defect or not defect). Based on this classification, we verified which problems were to be modified in the application's interface.

Table 1. Overview of the performed evaluations

Evaluation/iteration	Participants	Used method
First/Iteration 3	14 undergraduate and graduate students in a Computer Science course	3E and 3E*
Second/Iteration 4	11 participants: 9 graduate students in Computer Science, 1 Physics undergraduate student and 1 Social Science undergraduate student	SAM, MAX and Think Aloud
Third/Iteration 5	6 participants: 1 graduate and 5 undergraduate in Computer Science	3E and Think Aloud
Fourth/Iteration 6	18 undergraduate students from the Computer Science course	Observation and EM

5 Analysis of the Evaluation Methods

5.1 Type of Identified Problems (Hedonic or Pragmatic)

We verified the defects that were previously classified after the evaluations (as described in Sect. 4). In this analysis, we counted how many defects were identified by each method. All the defects were further classified as Hedonic (H) or Pragmatic (P). Such classification differs from the classification presented in Sect. 4. The goal of the first classification was to classify what needed to be modified in the user interface in order to improve the application. This new classification, on the other hand, aimed at analyzing what UX and usability methods can best be employed to find hedonic or pragmatic defects.

For the defects classification, the team based their decision on the proposal by Hassenzahl [4] regarding hedonic and pragmatic qualities (see Sect. 2). From this classification, we verified how many defects of each type the UX methods identified. We also conducted an analysis over the type of employed evaluation, i.e. if the method evaluates specific tasks or if the method provides an overview of the application. The use of some methods allowed the users to evaluate specific functionalities of the application (SF). Other methods allowed the users to express their general view of the application (GV). Table 2 presents the analysis of the UX and usability methods.

Table 2. Analysis of the evaluation methods

Evaluation	Users	Method	Quantity of Defects			Type of evaluation
			H	P	Total	
First	14	3E*	9	15	24	SF
		3E	9	5	14	GV
Second	11	MAX	10	2	12	GV
		SAM	14	8	22	SF
		TA	7	21	28	SF
Third	6	TA	6	9	15	SF
		3E	2	3	05	GV
Fourth	18	OBS	10	9	19	SF
		EM	12	21	33	SF and GV

Legend: H - Hedonic; P - Pragmatic; SF – Specific Functionality; GV – General View.

In the first evaluation, regarding the classification of hedonic and pragmatic problems, both methods identified 9 hedonic problems. However, 3E* found a higher number of pragmatic problems when compared to the 3E method. These results can be explained by the fact that the 3E* method allows the subject to express his/her opinion towards each individually performed task, whereas the 3E method allows the subjects only to provide a general view of the application.

In the second evaluation, the SAM method found more hedonic problems than the other methods. Think Aloud identified a higher number of pragmatic problems. A possible reason for these results could be that the SAM method is more focused on the hedonic attributes of UX, evaluating features such as emotions. On the other hand, the TA method focuses more on the functionalities of the application. In this evaluation context, the TA method was employed in order to support a usability test. Similar to SAM, MAX identified a high number of hedonic problems, but very few pragmatic ones. We suspect the same cause: MAX focuses more on evaluating aspects related to experience and emotions and less on evaluating usability.

In the third evaluation, we employed the Think Aloud and 3E methods. The TA method found more hedonic and pragmatic problems than the 3E method. TA found 6 hedonic and 9 pragmatic problems. The 3E method found 2 hedonic problems and 3 pragmatic problems. In the last evaluation regarding the pragmatic and hedonic defect classification, the EM method identified a higher number of hedonic (12 problems) and pragmatic (21 problems) problems than the observation method.

5.2 How the Methods Contributed to Improve the Evaluated Prototypes

Table 3 presents some examples of problems that were identified using the employed methods in each of the four evaluations from this project. In the following paragraphs, we explain how each method contributed to identifying improvement opportunities in the evaluated prototype.

Table 3. Examples of problems found in each evaluation

Evaluation	Methods	Problems
First	3E	The user found it unnecessary to keep notifying him/her about updates
	3E*	The user found that the details in the notification screen were the same as in the details screen.
Second	Think Aloud	The user thought that there should be an option to refuse the appointment after it was accepted - user perspective
	MAX	The user thought that it was possible to learn how to use the application, and that it was not difficult to use it.
	SAM	The notification message has a lot of text.
Third	3E	The application does not support taking care of more than one elderly.
	Think Aloud	When a user selects the "maintain appointment", the application should give the same confirmation message as when asking if he/she wishes to maintain the appointment.
Fourth	EM	The application exhibits too much information and therefore, it takes too much time to carry out the tasks.
	OBS	Users have difficulty in finding the notified option in the appointments menu.

In the first evaluation, through the 3E method, it was possible to gather a general view of what the users thought about the application. By using the 3E* method, it was possible to gather a specific view of each of the performed tasks during the interaction with the application's prototype. The modified method identified 24 defects in comparison to the only 14 defects identified by the original 3E method.

In the second evaluation, through the MAX method, it was possible to gain a general view of what the users thought about the developed prototypes. Through the SAM method, it was possible to gather the users' opinions regarding the screens and messages of the prototypes. We also managed to collect further information about the usability and opinions of the users through the Think Aloud method. In that context, the MAX method identified 12 problems, the SAM method identified 22 problems, and the Think Aloud method allowed identified 28 problems to improve the application. The MAX method was employed similarly to the 3E in the previous evaluation, gathering the general view of the subject regarding the application. The SAM and Think Aloud methods collected information on the specific tasks of the application. In the SAM methods, several screens and messages from the application were evaluated, while in the Think Aloud method, all the interaction from the user with the application was evaluated.

In the third evaluation, we employed 3E and Think Aloud. During the execution of the tasks, the Think Aloud method was employed the same way it was employed in the second evaluation. Through the use of this method it was possible to identify usability problems and the user's opinion during the use of the application. When using the Think Aloud method, the subject could orally express him/herself. Furthermore, we employed the 3E method again, because in the first performed evaluation we collected relevant information for the improvement of the application with this method. Through the 3E technique, it was possible to obtain a general view of what the users thought about the developed application. When employed together in the third evaluation, the 3E method found 5 problems while the Think Aloud method identified 15 problems to improve the application. Also, the 3E method allowed the subject to express a general view of the application, while the Think Aloud method allowed the subject to express his/her opinion on each performed task.

In the fourth evaluation we employed two methods. EM was employed for the UX evaluation. Also, observation (OBS) was employed as a way of supporting the usability evaluation during the execution of specific tasks. In this evaluation, the UX evaluation method identified a higher number of problems in the application than the usability evaluation method.

5.3 Difficulties in the Application of the Methods

Although the application of the methods was easy, the users that applied the methods encountered some difficulties. 3E, 3E* and Empathy Map were tiring for users as they required a lot of writing from users to allow them to express their opinions. As in these methods it is needed to draw a face to express the users' emotion, some participants found them difficult to use or disliked the method as they did not like to draw.

The difficulties regarding the application of Think Aloud and Observation were related to the collection of the data. These methods require notes or records about the interaction of the participant with the application. Some information can be missed during this process. Furthermore, some participants do not like to speak while interacting with the application, which can be distracting but is mandatory while using the Think Aloud method. In the Observation method, some participants feel uncomfortable with the presence of the evaluator during their interaction with application.

The simplest methods were SAM and MAX. In the SAM method the participants had some difficulties in understanding the emotions they could choose in the scale. In the MAX method, the participants had some difficulties in understanding the meaning of some cards. Still, this method was the most fun because of its entertaining features and the dynamics between the cards and the board.

5.4 Difficulties When Analyzing the Results Generated by the Methods

Most of the used methods collect qualitative data. This makes the analysis more complex. The obtained information is relevant to the application, but a lot of time is spent on its analysis. It is necessary to organize the data, classify the problems and prepare the report with the results.

In the first evaluation we spent about 8 h analyzing the collected data with the 3E and the 3E* methods, because the methods obtained a large amount of feedback from the participants. The 3E* obtained more data than the 3E method. Therefore, more time was required for the analysis. In the second evaluation, the Think Aloud Method demands more time to analysis than SAM or MAX. We spent 6 h analyzing the data from the Think Aloud method. The data collected from the SAM and MAX methods was faster to analyze and we only spent about 5 h on this analysis.

In the third evaluation, we spent about 4 h analyzing the data and preparing the report, because in this evaluation the application was only used by six participants. In the last evaluation, we spent about 9 h analyzing the data since the Empathy Map method collects more information and this evaluation was performed with 18 participants. The observation method used in this evaluation did not return much data, and its analysis spent less time (about 2 h).

The main difficulties in carrying out such an analysis are in the categorization of the problems: the removal of duplicated problems, classifying problems as hedonic or pragmatic, and identifying their correction priority. Sometimes, a problem may refer to an interface component, and at other times it may refer to an interaction step, or specific features/looks that the user would like the application to provide. As users have difficulties in explaining what the cause of the problem is, or different users may have different ideas about when an issue affects their experience, it is necessary to carefully verify the cause of the problem and its effect in order to make the correct decisions when dealing with the identified issue. Thus, it is necessary to pay attention and consider the context of use of the application when analyzing the gathered information after an evaluation.

5.5 Benefits of the Modifications in the Application of the Methods

The 3E* was one of the modified methods, and it allowed the user to provide his/her opinion on each executed task, besides expressing him/herself in a written way. Thus, we were able to verify that the written form finds more problems. Also, it was possible to verify whether a method that evaluates each of the performed identifies a higher number of problems when compared to a method that evaluates the application as a whole. This modified method was used in the first evaluation and uncovered more issues than the original 3E method. This method found more problems because it evaluated specific functionalities of the application and the original method evaluated the application in general.

The Empathy Map was adapted to evaluate UX and was used in the last performed evaluation. The Empathy Map allowed the subject to express his/her opinion in a specific way (i.e., the subject expresses his/her opinion for each performed task) and also in a general way. The method found more problems than the Observation method. We collected problems in specific functionalities of the application and opinions of the participants about general characteristics of the application.

6 Conclusions

In this paper we applied six different methods for evaluating UX and usability. We employed three already applied UX evaluation methods: 3E, SAM and MAX, and we proposed changes in existing methods to gain further information on the users' needs: EM and 3E*. Also, to complement the results from applying UX evaluation methods, we employed OBS and TA to find out about features that could be improved in order to enhance the quality of the application in terms of ease of use.

We identified that SAM, MAX and EM are better to identify hedonic problems, while Think Aloud, EM and 3E* are better to identify pragmatic problems. According to the evaluators who applied the methods, when applying UX methods that focus on evaluating the hedonic aspects of UX such as SAM or MAX, it is also useful to apply methods that can support the evaluation of usability features (e.g.: Observation and Think Aloud), which are more related to the pragmatic aspects of UX. Another point to consider is whether the method evaluates specific tasks of the application or if it allows describing a generic view of the application. Methods that evaluate specific tasks (i.e.: 3E*, SAM, TA, OBS) may identify a higher number of problems, however they can be more demanding for users, as they require that the user spends more time and effort evaluating each task. Through these lessons learned, we intend to encourage software companies to carry out cost-effective UX evaluations.

The categorization of the methods in terms of type of evaluated tasks can be a guide for software development teams willing to choose a method that suits their needs. However, we still need to verify how these methods perform in other conditions, such as being employed by users from different profiles, in the evaluation of other types of applications, and when applied in different environments. As future work, we intend to extend this research by testing these and other UX and usability evaluation methods under different circumstances to enhance the generalization of our results. That way, we can provide further information on scenarios in which each method is more suitable, advancing the research in UX and usability evaluation; and providing practitioners with a guide on when and why to apply existing and proposed UX and usability evaluation methods.

Acknowledgment. We thank Professors Rafael Bordini, Felipe Meneguzzi, Renata Vieira, and all their team. We also thank all the participants in the evaluations. We would like to acknowledge the financial support granted by "Large Scale Qualification PROgram on MOBILE Technologies", which is supported by Samsung Eletrônica da Amazônia Ltda, under the terms of the Informatics Law number 8387/91; CAPES; and FAPEAM through processes numbers: 062.00600/2014; 062.00578/2014.

References

1. Balasubramoniam, V., Tungatkar, N.: Study of user experience (UX) and UX evaluation methods. Int. J. Adv. Res. Comput. Eng. Technol. (IJARCET) **2**(3), 1214–1219 (2013)
2. Bernhaupt, R., Pirker, M.: Evaluating user experience for interactive television: towards the development of a domain-specific user experience questionnaire. In: Kotzé, P., Marsden, G., Lindgaard, G., Wesson, J., Winckler, M. (eds.) INTERACT 2013, Part II. LNCS, vol. 8118, pp. 642–659. Springer, Heidelberg (2013)
3. Cavalcante, E., Rivero, L., Conte, T.: MAX: a method for evaluating the post-use user eXperience through cards and a board. In: 27th International Conference on Software Engineering and Knowledge Engineering, pp. 495–500 (2015)

4. Hassenzahl, M.: User experience (UX): towards an experiential perspective on product quality. In: Proceedings of the 20th International Conference of the Association Francophone d'Interaction Homme-Machine, pp. 11–15. ACM (2008)
5. Hassenzahl, M., Diefenbach, S., Göritz, A.: Needs, affect, and interactive products–facets of user experience. Int. Comput. **22**(5), 353–362 (2010)
6. ISO 9241-210. International Standardization Organization (ISO). Ergonomics of human system interaction -Part 210: Human-centred design for interactive systems. Switzerland (2010)
7. ISO/IEC 25010, International Organization for Standardization, ISO, Systems and software engineering – SquaRE – Software product Quality Requirements and Evaluation – System and Software Quality Models (2011)
8. Jordan, P.W.: Designing Pleasurable Products: An Introduction to the New Human Factors. CRC Press, Boca Raton (2002)
9. Lang, P.J.: Behavioral treatment and bio-behavioral assessment: computer applications. In: Sidowski, J.B., Johnson, J.H., Williams, T.A. (eds.) Technology in mental health care delivery systems. Ablex, Norwood, NJ (1980)
10. Law, E.L., Abrahão, S., Vermeeren, A.P., Hvannberg, E.T.: Interplay between user experience evaluation and system development: state of the art. In: International Workshop on the Interplay between User Experience (UX) Evaluation and System Development (I-UxSED 2012), pp. 14–17 (2012)
11. Lizano, F., Sandoval, M.M., Bruun, A., Stage, J.: Usability evaluation in a digitally emerging country: a survey study. In: Kotzé, P., Marsden, G., Lindgaard, G., Wesson, J., Winckler, M. (eds.) INTERACT 2013, Part IV. LNCS, vol. 8120, pp. 298–305. Springer, Heidelberg (2013)
12. Osterwalder, A., Pigneur, Y.: Business Model Generation. Alta Books Editora (2013)
13. Tähti, M., Marketta, N.: 3E–expressing emotions and experiences. In: Proceedings of the WP9 Workshop on Innovative Approaches for Evaluating Affective Systems, HUMAINE (Human-Machine Interaction Network on Emotion), pp. 15–19 (2006)
14. Van Someren, M.W., Barnard, Y.F., Sandberg, J.A.: The Think Aloud Method: A Practical Guide to Modelling Cognitive Processes. Academic Press, London (1994)
15. Väätäjä, H., Koponen, T., Roto, V.: Developing practical tools for user experience evaluation: a case from mobile news journalism. In: European Conference on Cognitive Ergonomics, pp. 23–30 (2009)
16. Vermeeren, A., Law, E., Roto, V., Obrist, M., Hoonhout, J., Väänänen-Vainio-Mattila, K.: User experience evaluation methods: current state and development needs. In: Proceedings of the 6th Nordic Conference on Human-Computer Interaction: Extending Boundaries, pp. 521–530 (2010)

Impact of Performance and Subjective Appraisal of Performance on the Assessment of Technical Systems

Matthias Haase[1(✉)], Martin Krippl[2], Mathias Wahl[1], Swantje Ferchow[1], and Jörg Frommer[1]

[1] Department of Psychosomatic Medicine and Psychotherapy, Medical Faculty, Otto-von-Guericke University Magdeburg, Magdeburg, Germany
matthias.haase@med.ovgu.de

[2] Institute for Psychology, Department Methodology, Psychodiagnostics and Evaluation Research, Otto-von-Guericke University Magdeburg, Magdeburg, Germany

Abstract. Technical systems of the future are companion systems. These systems should be individualized, adaptive and accommodating. In order to create this technology, detailed evidence about users' behavior is needed. In this study, user-specific factors (user performance, subjective appraisal of user performance and user characteristics) are examined in terms of their impact on user satisfaction. In the WOZ experiment "last minute", 130 subjects interacted with a simulated speech-controlled technical system and had to complete a specific task. Over the course of the experiment, the subjects had to cope with different challenging situations. Using bivariate and point-biserial correlations, significant correlations for age and NEO-FFI personality dimension extraversion on a user's assessment of the simulated system were determined. Consequently, the postulated model could not be empirically proven, but provides important information for future studies .

Keywords: Companion system · User characteristics · Personality traits · Wizard of oz experiment · User experience · User satisfaction

1 Introduction

"Technical systems of the future are companion systems - cognitive technical systems, with their functionality completely individually adapted to each user" [1]. To gain this functionality, systems should be able to adapt to the individual abilities, preferences and needs of their users. This level of adaptiveness requires a recognition of users' situative contexts and their particular conditions. Creating such so-called cognitive technical systems is more than just a process of technical realization. It is also necessary to analyze the behavior of users when interacting with technical systems [2], the ascriptions users make to the system [3] and user characteristics that influence their interactions with technical systems [4].

Research efforts regarding user satisfaction, which is an important aspect of companion technology, are also relevant to other approaches, like usability or user experience (UX). In the present empirical study, we analyzed the impact of user-specific variables (user performance, subjective appraisal of performance and user characteristics) on satisfaction with a simulated speech-based system. First, we will give an overview of the relevance of user satisfaction in the context of interaction with technical systems.

M. Kurosu (Ed.): HCI 2016, Part I, LNCS 9731, pp. 291–301, 2016.
DOI: 10.1007/978-3-319-39510-4_27

1.1 Satisfaction

User satisfaction surveys are an established and reliable method of the quantitatively assessing technical systems [5, 6]. Taking user satisfaction into account not only serves to systematically eliminate undesired weaknesses or faults, as seen in the development of applications for mobile devices [7, 8], it also represents an essential element of several theoretical models and constructs, like the Information System (IS) Success Model [e.g. 9] or User Experience (UX) [10]. Indeed, although the IS Success Model according to DeLone and McLean [11] focused primarily on the efficiency and economy of information systems, user satisfaction still has an important function. DeLone and McClean [11] postulated that the success of an information system depends on system quality, information, quality, use, user satisfaction, individual impact and organizational impact. During the revision of the IS Success Model [9], the revision of the category "use" to "intention to use" represents a further step towards a user-oriented perspective. Intension to use is affected by user satisfaction, among other variables. According to some authors, the term usability has started to become replaced by the concept of UX [e.g. 12]. Accordingly, user satisfaction has come into the spotlight because it is part of one the most significant influencing factors of UX.

Whether in UX or the IS Success Model, the evaluation of user satisfaction generally occurs with the help of questionnaires. The frequently-used End User Computing Satisfaction (EUCS) questionnaire can be viewed as exemplary for the IS Success Model; it consists of the scales content, accuracy, format, ease of use and timeliness.

In contrast, the AttrakDiff [13] focuses on different aspects like pragmatic or hedonic quality. However, in most assessment systems, or rather in the methods they apply, variables that influence the assessment process, like user characteristics, performance or subjective appraisal of performance [8], are not considered. This is astonishing, at least for UX, where several reports verify influences of the technical system as well as influences of users [e.g. 14].

1.2 Performance and Subjective Appraisal of Performance

As mentioned before, UX considers several factors related to both the product (e.g. technical systems) and the user (e.g. user characteristics). Winter and colleagues [14] extracted in a literature review 21 important factors influencing UX (e.g. adaptability, efficiency, originality, timeliness, transparency, identity, intuitive operation, usefulness, trust). This large number of variables is not surprising, because a common definition of UX and its factors does not exist. Usually, UX is defined as the "relationship between the product and the user" [15, S.27], "interaction between a user and a product, including the degree to which all our senses are gratified" [16, S. 57] or "primarily evaluative feeling (good-bad) while interacting with a product" [12, S. 12]. All of these descriptions focus primarily on interaction as well as well-being and disposition on the user side. However, Tullis and Albert [10] define UX as follows: "there are two main aspects of the user experience: performance and satisfaction" [10, S.44]. Satisfaction is defined similarly to the introduced concepts but performance is described as "all about what the user actually does in interacting with the product. It includes measuring the degree to which users can accomplish a task or set of tasks successfully" [10, S.44]. In this sense, performance is based on measurements like the amount of effort, the number of mistakes or failed attempts as well as the time that was required. Thus, performance tends to be recognized in a work-related context [e.g. 17, 18]. Including user performance, the authors' [10] perspective on UX is quite different from the general view that UX is characterized mainly by the performance of the system (e.g. adaptability, efficiency, originality). When it comes to the subjective appraisal of performance, user's ability self-concept seems to be an important factor. Humans actively try to explain their own performance, which leads to very differential causal attributions [19]. Hence, users may refer to good or bad performance as accidental, as caused by external conditions or as a reflection of their own competence or deficits. These are exclusively cognitive processes. Szalma and Hancock [8] postulate that user characteristics influence their subjective appraisal of their performance. In turn, this appraisal of performance can influence satisfaction with a technical system. Therefore, measuring disposition or performance alone seems to be insufficient.

1.3 User Characteristics

Besides the already mentioned connection between subjective appraisal and performance, user characteristics are also associated with user performance.

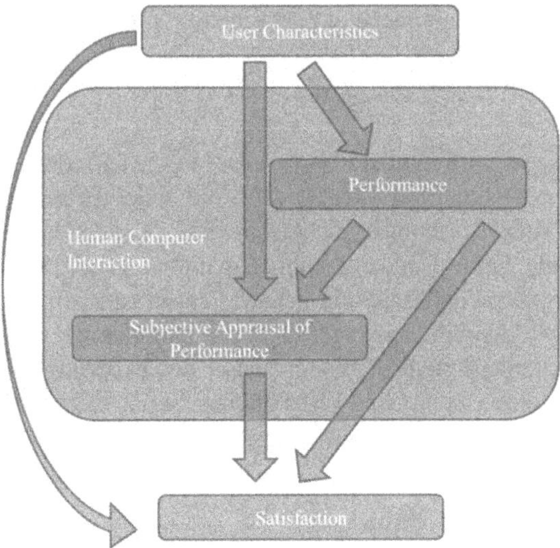

Fig. 1. Schematic illustration of user-specific factors (user characteristics, performance, subjective appraisal of performance) that influence user satisfaction.

Motowidlo and van Scooter [20] report an influence of experience and personality on performance as well. In addition, Rösner and colleagues [2] as well as Haase und colleagues [4] were able to empirically demonstrate the impact of user characteristics on performance with a technical system. More precisely, these empirical studies looked at differences in user performance in terms of the user characteristics age, experience with computer systems as well as the NEO-FFI personality dimensions [Costa] neuroticism and agreeableness over the course of time [2, 4]. Participants with higher performance on average were younger, more experienced with technical systems and showed lower levels of neuroticism as well as higher levels of agreeableness. Due to a lack of previous empirical research, this study analyzes the interconnections between user characteristics, performance (realized as dialog success) and subjective appraisal of performance and how these influence user satisfaction, and the assessment of technical systems (Fig. 1).

2 Method

2.1 Research Questions

After examining the aforementioned findings from previous research, we generated and examined the following research questions: What impact do user characteristics and performance have on participants' subjective appraisal of performance? What impact do user characteristics, performance and subjective appraisal of performance have on the assessment of the simulated system? For statistical analysis, bivariate correlation (Spearman's rho for ordinal variables) and point-biserial correlation (rpb coefficient when one variable is dichotomous) has been used. If significant correlations are shown, multiple linear regression models will be used to explore the effect of user characteristics, performance and subjective appraisal of performance on the AttrakDiff subscales.

2.2 Sample

Basically, the sample was differentiated with regard to age and educational level. Participants were between 18 and 29 or over 60 years old and were equal distributed into a "lower educational level" (secondary school or modern secondary school certificate, apprenticeship as the highest educational/occupational qualification) and a "higher educational level" (general matriculation standard, studies at a university or a university of applied sciences). Altogether, we recruited 135 participants; three participants did not fill out the psychometric questionnaires and at two experiments we had recording problems. The final sample comprised 130 participants, one of which could not be properly assigned to a level of education.

2.3 WoZ Experiment Last Minute

We developed a Wizard of Oz experiment (WoZ) where participants had to interact with a simulated speech-controlled cognitive technical system [21]. The speech output runs via a text-to-speech system (TTS). The participants only got the information that they "are talking to a prototype of a computer program designed to assist users in dealing with everyday tasks. What is unique about this program is that it adapts itself individually to its users. For this purpose, you will be run through some tasks and test situations in the course of this session." [21, S. 19]. The interaction with the simulated system was similar to an exploration task, because participants had to first test the skills and constraints of the system. Then, they received the task of packing luggage for a vacation with the help of the system. They could choose clothes and other pieces of luggage out of 12 categories (e.g. tops, trousers, shoes, accessories). It is suggested that they will be going on a summer vacation. Participants collect their luggage with the aid of the system. This stage is called baseline (BSL). After finishing the eighth category, the system gives the information that the luggage has exceeded the weight limit. Participants have to remove items before they can add new items. This limitation wasn't announced, and every participant got this information at the same point during the experiment. This stage is called the weight limit barrier (WLB). After the tenth category, participants are faced with another challenge situation. The system specifies that it has received delayed weather information and the participants will be going to a place with winter weather. This is called the weather information barrier (WIB). At this point, participants need to adapt their task-solving strategy under increased time pressure. Subsequent to this challenge situation, a randomized sample of participants receives an intervention focused on general psychotherapeutic factors (resource activation, problem actualization, accomplishment and clarification) [22]. After completing all categories, participants get the chance to unpack some items and replace them with more appropriate items (revision stage (RES)). In cooperation with the simulated system, participants had to solve a mundane task (packing luggage for a holiday trip) that necessitates planning, problem solving and strategy change. In the experiment, participants need to handle a large amount of interacting variables. WIB, especially, presents a complex set of problems, according to Funke [23]. This means that the problems are complex, enmeshed, dynamic and nontransparent and therefore not so easy to resolve.

2.4 Independent Variables

User Characteristics: We collected data regarding sociobiographic variables such as age, level of education and aspects like experience with computer devices. Participants also completed different questionnaires such as the NEO-FFI (regarding Big Five Personality Traits) [24].

Performance (Dialog Success): Performance was assessed by measuring the dialog success, which is operationalized as systems' reactions to users' verbal expressions [25]. "During the experiment, all contributions of speech output of the computer system, including their exact times, were logged. Afterwards, those outputs were chosen which represented a reaction of participants' interaction-contributions (e.g. phrases, single words or longer silence). This allowed a categorization of interaction-contributions of participants without regards to contents of transcripts: system is able to process a contribution (positive logs) and system is not able to process a contribution (negative logs). …. The positive logs represent all contributions of participants which could be processed by the system" [4]. Negative logs can be the result of a synonym failure (e.g. participant said shorts instead of jeans) or utterances that are not implemented [21].

"By using the experimental values, it is possible to generate a 'log quotient' ($Quotient_{logs} = \frac{N_{positiv\ logs}}{N_{all\ logs}}$) for each participant. The log quotient permits for an intra- and inter-individual comparison of different time stages during the experiment. A high value indicates that a participant succeeded more in adaption to the conditions" [4]. For the following analyses, participants' performance was considered over the course of the entire experiment (BSL, WLB, WIB and RES).

Subjective Appraisal of Performance: At the end of the experiment, participants were asked for their satisfaction with the results. Participants' statements were evaluated and divided into five categories (5. satisfied, 4. relatively satisfied, 3. neither, 2. relatively unsatisfied and 1. unsatisfied). This categorization allowed for statistical analysis.

Rating of the System (User Satisfaction): After finishing the experimental part, participants rated the simulated system with the standardized AttrakDiff [13], which means that they assessed its hedonic and pragmatically quality with the help of 28 pairs of adjectives (e.g., simple or complicated) over four subscales (pragmatic quality (PQ), hedonic quality identification (HQI) and stimulation (HQS) and the overall appeal or attraction (ATT)). A high value on a subscale means users' requirements are met for this specific area.

3 Results

3.1 Subjective Appraisal of Performance

The bivariate correlation between user characteristics (age, gender, experiences with technical systems and NEO-FFI personality dimensions neuroticism and agreeableness), dialog success and subjective appraisal of performance revealed just a statistically significant correlation between subjective appraisal of performance and experience with technical system (Spearmans rho = 0.244, $p < 0.007$). Mentionable dialog success and subjective appraisal of performance did not correlate (Spearmans rho = 0.000, $p < 0.998$). The NEO-FFI personality dimension neuroticism and subjective appraisal of performance showed a trend toward negative correlation (Spearmans rho = −0.161, $p < 0.08$).

The findings support the view that participants with more technical experience (Fig. 2) and lower scores in NEO-FFI subscale neuroticism (Fig. 3) stated that they were more satisfied with their performance.

3.2 Assessment of a Simulated Technical System

First, a bivariate correlation between independent variables dialog success, subjective appraisal of performance and user characteristics a well as the AttrakDiff scales was examined. Age and the AttrakDiff scale HQS showing a correlation (rpb = 0.180, $p < 0.041$) and the NEO-FFI extraversion and also the AttrakDiff scale HQS showing a negative correlation (Spearmans rho = −0.180, $p < 0.040$).

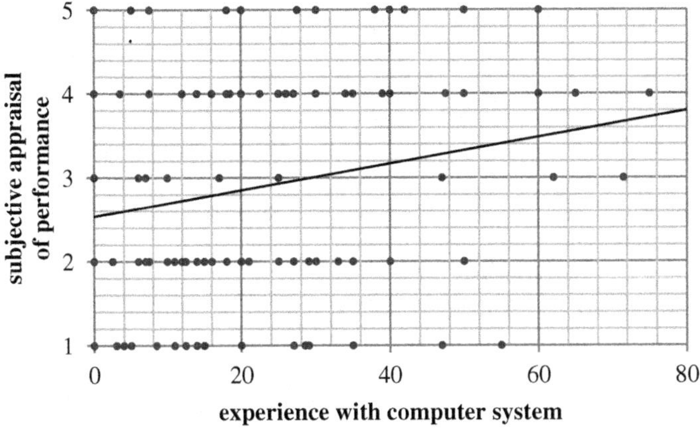

Fig. 2. Experience with computer systems (hours working with computer systems per week) and appraisal of performance (1 = not satisfied, …, 5 = satisfied).

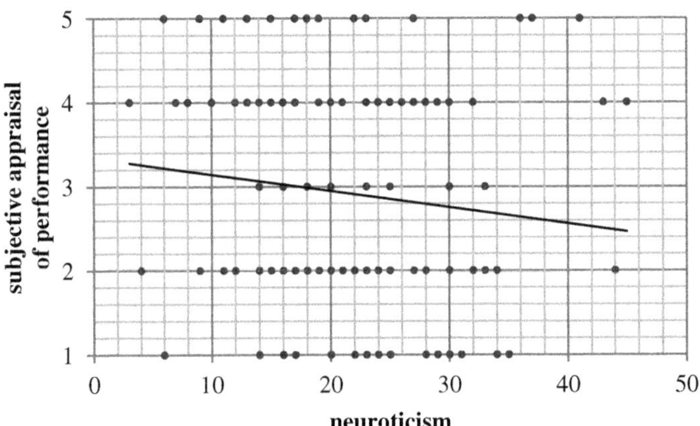

Fig. 3. NEO-FFI subscale neuroticism (high value = high level of neuroticism, low value = low level of neuroticism) and subjective appraisal of performance (1 = not satisfied, …, 5 = satisfied)

The descriptive account showed that older participants (Fig. 4) as well as participants with lower scores in NEO-FFI subscale extraversion (Fig. 5) rated higher quality of stimulation (HQS). Due to the small number of significant correlations no linear regression models are executed.

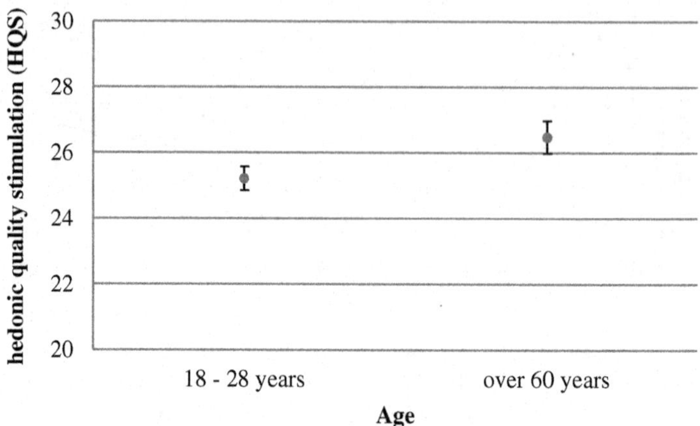

Fig. 4. Age (dichotomous, younger vs. older participants) and AttrakDiff subscale HQS (high value = high quality of stimulation, low value = low quality of stimulation).

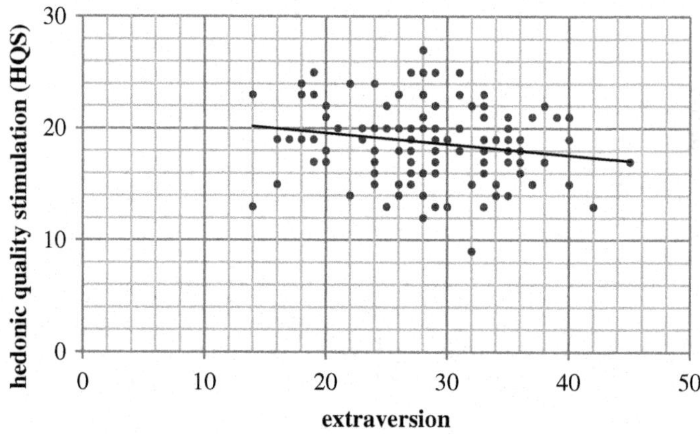

Fig. 5. NEO-FFI subscale extraversion (high value = high level of extraversion, low value = low level of extraversion) and AttrakDiff subscale HQS (high value = high quality of stimulation, low value = low quality of stimulation).

4 Conclusion

The further development of technical systems will primarily rely on characteristics such as availability, functionality, and adaptability to individual preferences, weaknesses and needs. User satisfaction represents a central aspect not only of the development of so-called companion technologies but also of other models (e.g. UX and the IS Success Model [11, 12]). Previous studies have not sufficiently considered user-specific factors that influence satisfaction with technical systems [8]. On the basis of an interdisciplinary review of the literature and of previous empirical findings [2, 4], a predominantly user-oriented model of satisfaction was developed. Both Rösner and Haase and colleagues

[2, 4] were able to find statistically significant effects of sociobiographical factors such as age and experience with computer systems as well as the NEO-FFI personality dimensions of neuroticism and agreeableness on performance (dialog success).

The present study first investigated whether user characteristics and performance influence users' appraisals of their own performance. However, statistically significant correlation could only be found with regard to experience with computer systems. Significant trends could only be found at the Big Five personality dimension neuroticism. At first glance, this is surprising, since with regard to gender, for example, Dickhäuser and Stiensmeier-Pelster [26] note that women tend to attribute failure in their work with technical systems to their own deficits, while men attribute failure to the technical system itself. This study was not able to confirm these results. With regard to satisfaction with the technical system, measured on the basis of participants' evaluations of the simulated technical system (AttrakDiff), only statistically significant correlations be found with regard to the age and Big-Five personality dimension extraversion (NEO-FFI). Nevertheless, the results of this study should not lead to a rejection of the model presented here.

Limitations: The first "last minute" experimental setup had some methodological vulnerabilities. For example, self-report (e.g. affective state, satisfaction) and assessing the simulated system in different stages of the experiment were missing. It also had been neglected to request participants' motivation and locus of control with regard to computer systems. In a revision of the "last minute" experiment these aspects have been taken into account [27].

Acknowledgements. The presented study is performed in the framework of the Transregional Collaborative Research Centre SFB/TRR 62\A Companion-Technology for Cognitive Technical Systems" funded by the German Research Foundation (DFG). The responsibility for the content of this paper remains with the authors.

References

1. Wendemuth, A., Biundo, S.: A companion technology for cognitive technical systems. In: Esposito, A., Esposito, A.M., Vinciarelli, A., Hoffmann, R., Müller, V.C. (eds.) COST 2102. LNCS, vol. 7403, pp. 89–103. Springer, Heidelberg (2012)
2. Rösner, D., Haase, M., Bauer, T., Günther, S., Krüger, J., Frommer, J.: Desiderata for the design of companion systems. KI - Künstliche Intelligenz **30**(1), 53–61 (2016)
3. Krüger, J., Wahl, M., Frommer, J.: Making the system a relational partner: users' ascriptions in individualization-focused interactions with companion-systems. In: Berntzen, L.: Böhm, S. (eds.) Proceedings of the 8th International Conference on Advances in Human-oriented and Personalized Mechanisms, Technologies, and Services (CENTRIC 2015), pp. 48–54. IARIA XPS Press (2015)
4. Haase, M., Krippl, M., Ferchow, S., Otto, M., Frommer, J.: Influence of user characteristics on coping with stress. In: Human-Computer Interaction. LNCS. Springer, Berlin (2016). Submission ID: 611
5. Bailey, J.E., Pearson, S.W.: Development of a tool for measuring and analyzing computer user satisfaction. Manage. Sci. **29**(5), 530–545 (1983)

6. Hassenzahl, M.: The thing and I: understanding the relationship between user and product. In: Blythe, M., Overbeeke, C., Monk, A.F., Wright, P.C. (eds.) Funology: From Usability to Enjoyment, pp. 31–42. Kluwer Academic Publishers, Dordrecht (2003)
7. Lin, C., He, Y., Pedrinaci, C., Domingue, J.: Feature LDA: a supervised topic model for automatic detection of web API documentations from the web. In: Cudré-Mauroux, P., Heflin, J., Sirin, E., Tudorache, T., Euzenat, J., Hauswirth, M., Parreira, J.X., Hendler, J., Schreiber, G., Bernstein, A., Blomqvist, E. (eds.) ISWC 2012, Part I. LNCS, vol. 7649, pp. 328–343. Springer, Heidelberg (2012)
8. Szalma, J.L., Hancock, P.: Task loading and stress in human-computer interaction: theoretical frameworks and mitigation strategies. In: Sears, A., Jacko, J.A. (eds.) Human Factors and Ergonomics. The Human-Computer Interaction Handbook: Fundamentals, Evolving Technologies, and Emerging Applications, pp. 115–132. Lawrence Erlbaum Associates, New York (2007)
9. DeLone, W.H., McLean, E.R.: Information system success: the quest for the dependent variable. Inf. Syst. Res. **3**(1), 60–95 (1992)
10. Tullis, T., Albert, B.: Measuring the User Experience: Collecting, Analyzing, and Presenting Usability Metrics. Elsevier, Amsterdam (2013)
11. DeLone, W.H., McLean, E.R.: The DeLone and McLean model of information systems success: a ten-year update. J. Manag. Inf. Syst. **19**(4), 9–30 (2003)
12. Hassenzahl, M.: User experience (UX): toward an experiential perspective on product quality. In: Brangier, É., Michel, G., Bastien, J.M.C., Carbonell, N. (eds.) IHM 2008 Proceedings of the 20th International Conference of the Association Francophone d'Interaction Homme-Machine, pp. 11–15. ACM, New York (2008)
13. Hassenzahl, M., Burmester, M., Koller, F.: AttrakDiff: Ein Fragebogen zur Messung wahrgenommener hedonischer und pragmatischer Qualität. In: Szwillus, G., Ziegler, J. (eds.) Berichte des German Chapter of the ACM. Mensch & Computer 2003, pp. 187–196. Vieweg + Teubner Verlag, Wiesbaden (2003)
14. Winter, D., Schrepp, M., Thomaschewski, J.: Faktoren der User Experience: Systematische Übersicht über produktrelevante UX-Qualitätsaspekte. In: Fischer, H., Endmann, A., Krökel, M. (eds.) Mensch und Computer 2015 - Usability Professionals, pp. 33–41. De Gruyter, Berlin (2015)
15. McNamara, N., Kirakowski, J.: Functionality, usability, and user experience. Interactions, 13(6), 26–28 (2006)
16. Desmet, P., Hekkert, P.: Framework of product experience. Int. J. Des. **1**(1), 57–66 (2007)
17. LePine, J.A., van Dyne, L.: Voice and cooperative behavior as contrasting forms of contextual performance: evidence of differential relationships with big five personality characteristics and cognitive ability. J. Appl. Psychol. **86**(2), 326–336 (2001)
18. Borman, W.C., Motowidlo, S.J.: Task performance and contextual performance: the meaning for personnel selection research. Hum. Perform. **10**(2), 99–109 (1997)
19. Stiensmeier-Pelster, J., Schöne, C.: Fähigkeitsselbstkonzept. In:. Handbuch der Psychologie, Handbuch der Pädagogischen Psychologie, vol. 10, pp. 62–73. Hogrefe, Göttingen (2008)
20. Motowidlo, S.J., van Scotter, J.R.: Evidence that task performance should be distinguished from contextual performance. J. Appl. Psychol. **79**(4), 475–480 (1994)
21. Frommer, J., Rösner, D., Haase, M., Lange, J., Friesen, R., Otto, M.: Project A3 - Detection and Avoidance of Failures in Dialogues. Pabst Science Publisher, Lengerich (2012)
22. Grawe, K.: Grundriß einer allgemeinen psychotherapie. Psychotherapeut **40**, 130–145 (1995)
23. Funke, J.: Complex problem solving: a case for complex cognition? Cogn. Process. **11**(2), 133–142 (2010)

24. McCrae, R.R., Costa, P.T.: A contemplated revision of the NEO five-factor inventory. Pers. Individ. Differ. **36**(3), 587–596 (2004)
25. Rösner, D., Frommer, J., Friesen, R., Haase, M., Lange, J., Otto, M.: LAST MINUTE: a multimodal corpus of speech-based user-companion interactions. In: Workshop Abstracts, LREC 2012, Istanbul, Turkey, pp. 2559–2566. ELRA, Istanbul (2012)
26. Dickhäuser, O., Stiensmeier-Pelster, J.: Erlernte hilflosigkeit am computer? geschlechtsunterschiede in computerspezifischen attributionen. Psychologie in Erziehung und Unterricht **27**, 486–496 (2002)
27. Ferchow, S., Haase, M., Krüger, J., Vogel, M., Wahl, M., Frommer, J.: Speech matters – psychological aspects of artificial versus anthropomorphic system voices in user-companion interaction. In: Human-Computer Interaction. LNCS. Springer, Berlin (2016). Submission ID: 1110

Tool-Supported Usability Engineering for Continuous User Analysis

Anna Hüttig(✉) and Michael Herczeg

Institute for Multimedia and Interactive Systems, University of Luebeck, Luebeck, Germany
{huettig,herczeg}@imis.uni-luebeck.de

Abstract. There is a large set of methods and measures to strengthen the usability of interactive products; however the practical application of usability engineering still seems to be difficult and is not practiced widely. As main problems we identified a low level of guidance, insufficient flexibility of methods and lack of awareness of results within the project team. We will discuss these problems and present a new approach of performing usability engineering in practice as collection of easy to handle tools that can be combined and integrated throughout the whole development process. The contribution places particular attention to the area of user analysis and how to support this important aspect of software development within our system Usability Engineering Repository (UsER).

Keywords: Persona · Software engineering · Tooling · Usability engineering · User-centered design · User analysis · User class

1 Challenges of Performing Usability Engineering

In theory, there are plenty of methods, processes and measures to analyze and strengthen the usability of interactive products [1, 3, 13, 16, 19, 26]. However, the practical application of usability engineering still seems to be difficult and is therefore often neglected or practiced insufficiently [8, 17, 23, 25, 27, 29]. We identified three main problems that can be seen as obstacles for the practice of usability engineering within authentic project contexts: no or low level of guidance, insufficient flexibility of methods and lack of awareness of results within the project team (Table 1).

1.1 Guidance in Method Application

The first point, the low level of guidance, refers to the question, how software analysts, designers, programmers and testers can be enabled or supported to apply methods of user analysis. This often starts with a lack of understanding of the methods, the difficulty of finding a reasonable starting point or the challenge of a meaningful adaption of methods chosen for the particular project or domain [17].

The efforts of method application depend on the specific methods used. Within certain application domains or under certain project management conditions, some methods are better suited though being more labor-intensive and expensive. Methods with low thresholds or efforts often provide weaker results. Another important factor is the experience and

M. Kurosu (Ed.): HCI 2016, Part I, LNCS 9731, pp. 302–312, 2016.
DOI: 10.1007/978-3-319-39510-4_28

routine of the persons performing the usability engineering processes. Human-centered design skills are not trained in most software development enterprises [25, 29].

Table 1. Main challenges of practical application of usability engineering (UE) methods

Challenge	Implied obstacles for the user who may not know how to	Frame conditions
The user of UE methods receives little *guidance* for the application	… understand the method itself … find a suitable starting point … adapt the methods for the needs	• (special) requirements of UE method • experiences of executing persons/project team • existing and habitual software engineering processes • budget • available time
The UE methods do not seem to be flexibly *integrable*	… integrate the measures into existing processes … combine the methods to foster the linkage of developed results	
Developed results and models lose their potential since they are not *perceived* by the team	… communicate the results … achieve acceptance for the results … foster the utilizing of results	

1.2 Flexibility in Method Application

The second problem addresses insufficient flexibility and the question how usability methods can be integrated into existing processes. Companies often are not able or willing to change their development processes. Others seem to be quite helpless, how to change existing development workflows for usability methods or how to see interfaces between usability engineering activities and standard software engineering procedures [17].

Fading results are a related problem, meaning that the potentially expensive application of usability engineering methods becomes worthless in later phases of the process because of deficient integration of the results in ongoing or following development phases. This is related to the issue that the results of the analyses need to be merged and cross-referenced to provide a coherent overview of the project and problem scope. A set of single, self-contained methods without bringing the results together cannot reveal all relevant aspects.

1.3 Awareness for Developed Results

The third problem area, the lack of awareness, stresses the point, that especially small or medium sized enterprises do not have the resources to hire their own usability experts [29]. But even if they have a team or person responsible for this, the efforts become useless if the results are not communicated to all project members or if they are not accepted by them. Especially user analysis and user modeling become rarely interweaved with standard system development processes. In practice, even when flexible and low-threshold methods like personas have been applied, the outcome is ignored, neglected or simply gets lost during the further process [17].

The classical split of roles within software project teams that can be found in conventional as well as in more agile software engineering approaches implies certain communication paths and processes. These require the frequent exchange of information between domain experts or team members with various backgrounds. A typical project team could consist of a consultant who is in contact with relevant stakeholders and end users of the software product that has to be developed. The consultant discusses his or her insights with product designers who incorporate the findings in the conceptual design of the application. These concepts have to be implemented later by a team of software developers. Along this communication path through groups with different perspectives on the problem domain, the typically quite unstructured, but authentic statements of end users have to be transformed into technical implementation specifications. This process demands the need for a common and shared understanding of the project's scope. The exchange and alignment of information has to be supported often among teams that do not consist of members that are particularly educated in mediating usability ideas.

1.4 Novel Approach to Usability Engineering in Practice

The above mentioned challenges can be approached by making usability engineering methods more practical to use and more capable to be integrated and combined. They shall not appear as particular procedures that have to be performed at some point in the process, but as manageable activities that can be integrated flexibly and that can be used and extended at any time throughout the development process. To achieve this a strong *tool support* for usability engineering methods is needed. Well-designed tools can decrease the threshold of method application and give sufficient guidance in method execution. Therefore, they have to be easy to use and flexible enough to be integrated into existing project settings. Additionally, they can help to create a holistic view of the application domain and the target group of end users if the results are combinable. By this, a more understandable and more appropriate model of the application project can be spread out over all software development processes in order to support the common understanding among all project members. We found this tool approach to be a promising way to foster *manageability* and *extensibility* of methods and to strengthen *embedment* of usability results in major contexts.

2 Continuous User Analysis

Concerning the analysis of users, specialized tools and their combination with instruments for other usability engineering methods can support all phases of user analysis and foster a *Continuous User Analysis* throughout the project and its phases with steady user focus among the project team. The term *continuous* shall emphasize that user analysis should not be seen as a closed method within some temporary phase. In the sense of user-centered design processes, the user has to stay in focus throughout the whole development and all design decisions should be based on or at least be balanced against user needs.

Figure 1 shows a possible structure of the different steps of user analysis measures in terms of usability engineering. The first step ("Data collection as starting point for analyses") is the main foundation for further analyses. This covers the huge set of field study techniques and methods from simple third party research over user interviews to complex supervision studies [6, 15, 18]. Collected data has to be reviewed, evaluated and prepared for further usage and integration in follow-up processes ("Data evaluation").

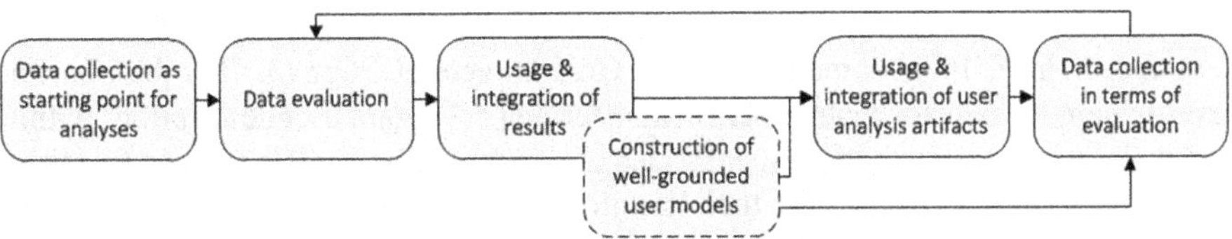

Fig. 1. Possible division of phases of user analysis for usability engineering. The usage of user models is one suitable method within this process of *Continuous User Analysis*.

User data can be abstracted into user models which are a basic concept of user analysis and the realization of steady focus on user needs in all project phases. User models are well-suited to be utilized and applied in all following conception and development phases in many ways. Serving as independent artifacts, they can be used for discussions and reviews and be combined with other usability methods. Problems that have to be faced – besides the quite common complete lack of user models in general – are the creation of unsuitable and ill-defined models and the insufficient transfer of user models into the ongoing system development process.

Concerning the modeling of users, several techniques have been developed: While in usage-centered design more abstract models like actors or role descriptions have been used to analyze usage patterns [2], user-centered design aims for more realistic models. An obvious first step to handle the diversity of users is their division into user classes [30]. Main distinctive features can be – depending on the product's context – the user's goals concerning the target system, the technical or use-oriented level of experience or the organizational role of the users [10, 22]. Latter shows the tight interplay between role descriptions and user classes. Class descriptions can reach from simple, often assumption-based category depictions to detailed, well-grounded user profiles [9]. However, user classes remain abstract and are often not telling enough about the real user needs. More vivid are user descriptions that depict a single concrete, fictive person as a representative for a specific group of users. Popular methods are the modeling of different types of personas [3]. They consist of detailed, mainly narrative descriptions of fictive persons often based on extensive studies and data of real people [22]. The potential and handling of personas has been described extensively in literature [20].

Another form of modeling is the archetype (e.g. "the blind user of a vending machine") or – with rather negative connotation – the stereotype (e.g. "the helpless elderly user of a vending machine"). Here, the archetype shall be understood as a denomination for a putative precisely defined class of persons with specific characteristics that is – at least along general lines – interindividually valid. The delimitation to user classes and to concrete user descriptions is smooth and often unclear. Archetypes represent, like user classes, a type of users, though archetypes are more precisely and demonstratively defined. They are suited to mediate specific characters of a category, but also tend to caricatures so that the values of these descriptions are often quite limited [10]. However, an advantage of archetypes is their simple creation since only few or even no user data has to be collected [7, 28]. Furthermore, so-called Extreme Characters are described as narrative, extreme personalities with exaggerated emotional attitudes [5].

User models only unfold their entire potential when being integrated in the ongoing development process during and after their creation and refinement. Especially personas seem to be helpful. Process models like the Goal-Directed Design [3, 4] or the Concept Development Process for requirements engineering [27] regard user descriptions within the development process and pursue the idea of not letting the models become fixed and more or less dead artifacts after their creation. Instead, they should permanently be present, accompany and support the development process and teams together with other usability methods and also be evolved and enhanced during the design and implementation phases of product development.

The necessity for continuous consideration of user data is obvious since the software product is intended to address the observed user needs – and will likely fail if not fulfilled. So, steady extensions of user focused analyses – not necessarily in form of user models – and combinations with analysis methods concerning other usability engineering artifacts as tasks and requirements are obviously meaningful. Especially, stronger interweaving of requirements and user needs seems promising. The systematic, transparent and comprehensible coupling of usability engineering and requirements engineering is currently not sufficiently practiced ("Usage & integration of user analysis artifacts"). For reviews of first prototypes or in context of formative evaluations of the software product ("Data collection in terms of evaluation"), the created user models can be consulted, too. Several techniques are named in literature [22].

3 The Usability Engineering Repository (UsER)

We have implemented the ideas described above within our Usability Engineering Repository (UsER). UsER is a web-based system supporting classic as well as agile software development processes by providing modules representing usability engineering methods (Fig. 2). All information gathered is modeled in form of entities by one

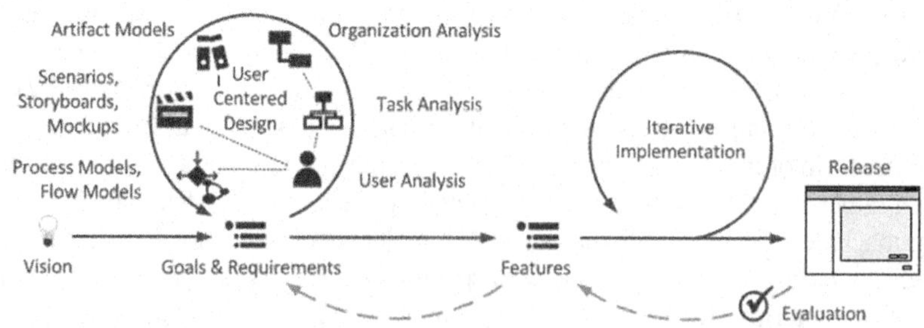

Fig. 2. Possible usability engineering process supported by UsER modules

of the UsER modules and may be interlinked with entities from the same as well as other modules. Besides the versatile cross-references between entities, the development teams may select and combine the modules as needed [11, 15, 21].

Usually a project will be organized in a classical linear structure as in conventional development documents. Standard development processes therefore will be supported more easily. Every "chapter" in "a UsER document" provides the functionality of a specific method module. They can be dragged into the linear organized administration area of the current development document (Fig. 3). By this, hierarchically structured specification documents can be constructed and the development document itself becomes a starting and anchor point for the different development tools. This is an important change of paradigm, leading from classical text- or table-centered specifications into active and semantically modeled living documents with a classical linear outer structure and an inner structure of semantic networks for holistic analysis, design and evaluation of interactive systems. Apart from the user analysis module that will be described more detailed, UsER offers a variety of other modules, e.g. for collecting and managing requirements, analyzing organizational structures or describing scenarios. Modules can be used in several phases within an engineering process.

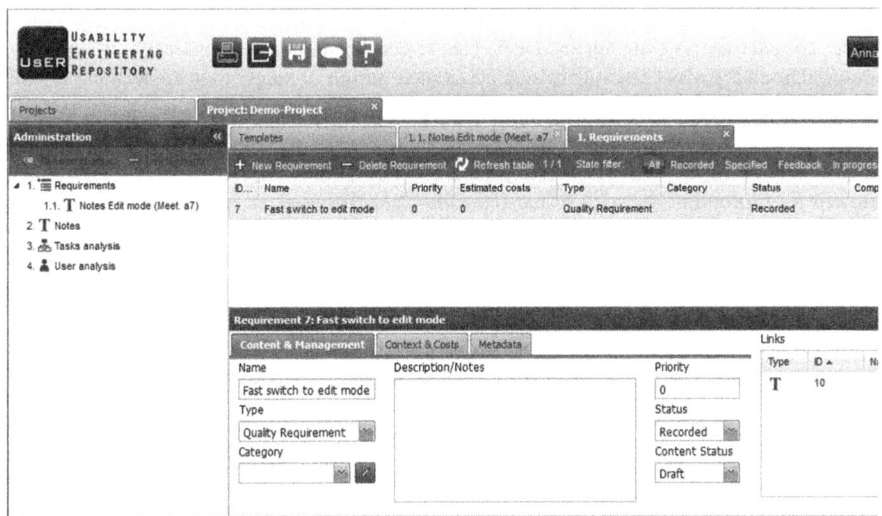

Fig. 3. This screenshot of UsER shows the opened Requirements Module next to the document management panel (on the left). The detail area of each module includes the linking widget (on the bottom right) offering the functionality to define links between UsER entities.

4 Integration of Continuous User Analysis Within UsER

As discussed, user analysis is a central aspect of user-centered design processes and user models act as helpful instruments to support all phases of software development. Therefore, tool support for user analysis and user modeling should be a substantial component within frameworks for the development of interactive systems. UsER in particular –

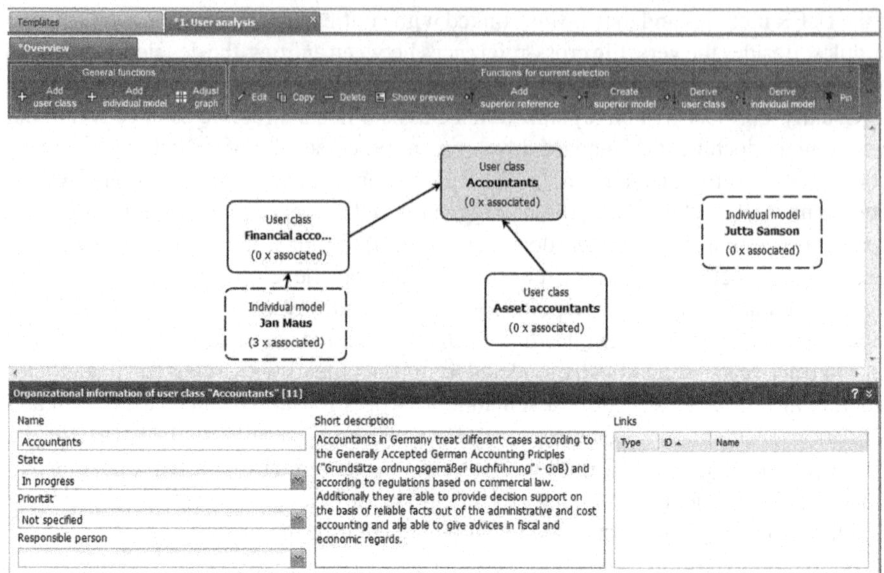

Fig. 4. The user analysis module in UsER. This screenshot shows the graphical user landscape editor. Additional views exist for the content-related design of single user models and for the definition of user model templates.

with its collection of several usability engineering instruments – offers a suited environment to implement the idea of *Continuous User Analysis*.

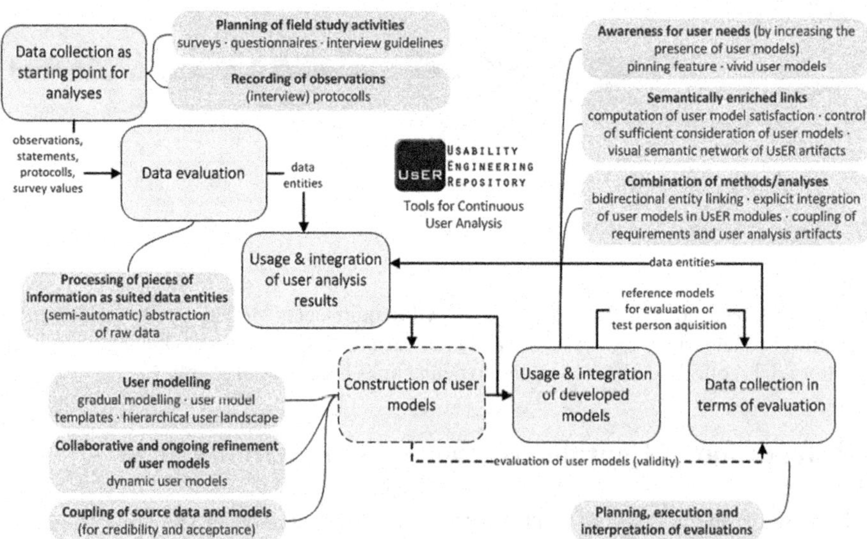

Fig. 5. Tools for *Continuous User Analysis* within UsER as a platform for usability engineering instruments. The tools shall support all phases of user analysis as named above.

The development of the User Analysis Module (Fig. 4) in UsER [12, 24] was the first step for a systematic integration of user analysis artifacts within the system. At the beginning, the focus lay mainly on building user models, so that after several iterations the instrument supported software designers in creating and improving user models by providing a systematic approach of gradual two-stage user modeling. This allows constructing e.g. abstract user classes or more detailed stereotypes and quite individual descriptions like concrete personas – means user models on different levels of abstraction.

Utilizing the potential of UsER as a platform and toolbox for usability engineering methods, we then fostered the integration of user models into other modules next to the user analysis tool and into the UsER core system (Fig. 5). We now enable the explicit integration of modeled users as performers of tasks in task analyses, as vivid actors in scenario descriptions or we let the models be built in into flow models or organigrams as representatives for organizational entities.

As a central feature, UsER allows the definition of arbitrary bidirectional links between any two UsER entities. So, each user model can be associated with any defined usability engineering artifact, like for example requirements. Beyond, as one of the next steps, we will address a closer combination of requirements and user analysis artifacts. This shall include referencing user models as origin of a requirement and the introduction of user needs as new type of requirements.

Another aspect is the extension of the UsER linking concept itself: The bidirectional links (cross-references) between UsER entities shall be complemented with additional semantic annotations and attributes. These named links offer the potential for semi-automatic evaluations of analysis artifacts and their relationships. Within the scope of user analysis, one aim is the introduction of a kind of user (model) satisfaction: By semantically enriched links, we expect to be able to define validated rules and functions that process the status of entities linked to a user model and return cues for the satisfaction level of modeled users. One simple scenario could be described like this: A highly prioritized personas is linked to several requirements. Additional semantic annotations specify the links further – determining the linked requirements as must-have features for this certain persona. Now, if many of those requirements are marked as rejected (within the requirements module) or are not in advanced implementation stages, the project situation seems not beneficial for the persona's satisfaction. This can be reported within the system.

Furthermore, semantically enriched links offer more possibilities to control the sufficient consideration of relevant user models within all analyses and design activities.

In addition, we want to depict most links between UsER entities graphically. Especially after the introduction of semantic link attributes, a graphical overview on all UsER artifacts and their relationships among each other can serve as a suited entry point for the system. It enables a visual network of knowledge about the problem domain and fosters the clarification of the project scope.

To further foster the awareness for user needs and strengthen the focus on users throughout the entire project phase we are looking for methods to increase the presence of the models created within the system like integrating the models within different modules, as described above, and by integrating the models into the core system components of UsER. By a special feature, the Pin-Function (Fig. 6), selected user models can be placed on the always visible project header within the UsER screen. An icon shows the most important facts about the modeled user and offers quick access to further information. This feature can be extended by letting the model become more alive by actively communicating to the current users of the system. For example, a persona could tell about its satisfaction level, i.e. how well its requirements have been addressed.

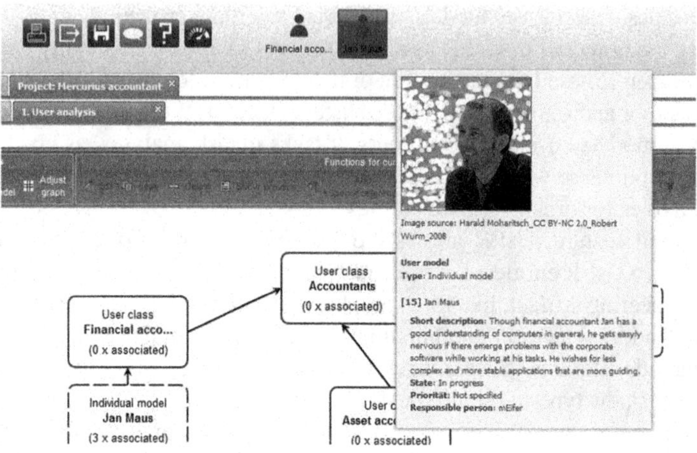

Fig. 6. The Pin-Function in UsER

User modeling and the propagation of the user models into the development process are just two steps within the process of a comprehensive user analysis. To get a well-founded basis for models, the overall process should start with data collection. To support this initial phase, we want to integrate modules for interview preparation and interview protocols as well as tools that support other field study activities such as contextual inquiries [1]. Furthermore, a tool for the construction of surveys has already been implemented and will be extended. Important collected pieces of information such as relevant user statements or evaluated survey items shall be integrated in the UsER system as entities that are connectable like all other UsER objects. By this, all collected facts can be referenced and used as credible pieces of justification for further analyses and user model design decisions.

To support the evaluation phase, tools for the planning, execution and interpretation of evaluations are modeled to be integrated as appropriate UsER instruments. User models can be involved within this phase as fictive reference users for the evaluations themselves or by consulting them for test person acquisition. Furthermore, UsER should offer the option to evaluate the user models themselves. Thereby, the compatibility of the modeled users towards the real user landscape can be validated.

5 Conclusions and Future Work

We discussed the demand for better tool support for usability engineering methods to overcome central problems of the weak usability engineering in practice. By introducing flexible and easy to use instruments, we raise manageability of methods and the extensibility of analyses whose entities shall be easily embeddable in larger project contexts.

Especially, we consider user analysis activities as a central aspect of user-centered design processes that are quite often neglected. Our concept of Continuous User Analysis has already been established inside our Usability Engineering Repository UsER. It fosters steady focus on user needs and enables extensions of all findings. Further concepts and ideas are planned to be integrated to support all phases of user analysis. In the long term, this also includes expanding the systematic participation of real users within all project phases. They shall become active participants of the system UsER and shall be allowed to inspect and manipulate certain UsER artifacts by themselves. For that, more sophisticated user rights management and further collaboration features have already been planned. On the other hand, we like to take a closer look at the concept of Evidence-Based Usability Engineering as introduced by Metzker et al. [17] to support the sustainability of usability engineering experiences and knowledge.

UsER can be seen as a research platform for our concepts of *Tool-Supported Usability Engineering*. By integrating the idea of *Continuous User Analysis* into the system we like to contribute to more user-centered design and development processes that can be applied and controlled by teams within realistic project contexts. Positive evaluations of system components indicate that more representative evaluations of the overall system will verify our ideas.

References

1. Beyer, H., Holtzblatt, K.: Contextual Design: Defining Customer-Centered Systems (Interactive Technologies). Morgan Kaufmann Publishers Inc, San Francisco (1998)
2. Constantine, L.: Users, roles, and personas. In: Pruitt, J., Adlin, T. (eds.) The Persona Lifecycle, pp. 499–519. Morgan Kaufmann/Elsevier, Amsterdam (2006)
3. Cooper, A.: The Inmates are Running the Asylum. SAMS, Indianapolis (1999)
4. Cooper, A., Reimann, R., Cronin, D.: About Face 3: The Essentials of Interaction Design, 3rd edn. Wiley, Indianapolis (2007)
5. Djajadiningrat, J.P., Gaver, W., Fres, J.W.: Interaction relabelling and extreme characters: methods for exploring aesthetic interactions. In: Proceedings of the 3rd Conference on Designing Interactive Systems: Processes, Practices, Methods, and Techniques, pp. 66–71. ACM, New York (2000)
6. Goodman, E., Kuniavsky, M., Moed, A.: Observing the User Experience: A Practitioner's Guide to User Research. Elsevier, Waltham (2012)
7. Grudin, J.: Why Personas work: the psychological evidence. In: Pruitt, J., Adlin, T. (eds.) The Persona Lifecycle, pp. 643–663. Morgan Kaufmann/Elsevier, Amsterdam (2006)
8. Grudin, J., Poltrock, S.E.: User interface design in large corporations: coordination and communication across disciplines. In: Bice, K., Lewis, C. (eds.) Proceedings of the SIGCHI Conference on Human Factors in Computing Systems (CHI 1989), pp. 197–203. ACM, New York (1989)
9. Helander, M.G., Landauer, T.K., Prabhu, P.V.: Handbook of Human-Computer Interaction, 2nd edn. Elsevier Science Inc., New York (1997)
10. Herczeg, M.: Software-Ergonomie. Theorien, Modelle und Kriterien für gebrauchstaugliche interaktive Computersysteme, 3rd edn. Oldenbourg, München (2009)

11. Herczeg, M., Kammler, M., Mentler, T., Roenspieß, A.: The usability engineering repository UsER for the development of task- and event-based human-machine-interfaces. In: Narayanan, S. (eds.) 12th IFAC, IFIP, IFORS, IEA Symposium on Analysis, Design, and Evaluation of Human-Machine Systems. International Federation of Automatic Control, pp. 483–490. Las Vegas (2013)
12. Hüttig A., Herczeg M.: Tool-based gradual user modeling for usability engineering. In: Proceedings of the European Conference on Cognitive Ergonomics ECCE 2015 (2015)
13. ISO/DIN 9241-210: Ergonomics of human-system interaction - Part 210: human-centred design for interactive systems. Beuth, Berlin (2008)
14. Kammler, M., Roenspieß, A., Herczeg, M: UsER: Ein modulares usability-engineering-repository. In: Mensch & Computer 2012: interaktiv informiert – allgegenwärtig und allumfassend, pp. 333–336. Oldenbourg, Munich (2012)
15. Lazar, J., Feng, J., Hochheiser, H.: Research Methods in Human-Computer Interaction. Wiley, Indianapolis (2010)
16. Mayhew, D.J.: The Usability Engineering Lifecycle: A Practitioner's Handbook for User Interface Design. Morgan Kaufmann, San Francisco (1999)
17. Metzker, E., Reiterer, H.: Use and reuse of HCI knowledge in the software development lifecycle – existing approaches and what developers think. In: Hammond, J., Gross, T., Wesson, J. (eds.) Usability: Gaining a Competitive Edge/IFIP 17th World Computer Congress, Montréal, Québec, Canada, pp. 39–55 (2002)
18. Mulder, S., Yaar, Z.: The User is Always Right: A Practical Guide to Creating and Using Personas for the Web, 1st edn. New Riders Publishing, Thousand Oaks (2006)
19. Nielsen, J.: Usability Engineering. Morgan Kaufmann Publishers Inc., San Francisco (1993)
20. Nielsen, L.: Personas – User Focused Design. Springer, London (2013)
21. Paul, M., Roenspieß, A., Herczeg, M.: UsER – Ein prozessorientiertes Entwicklungssystem für Usability-Engineering. In: Boll, S., Maaß, S., Malaka, R. (eds.) Mensch & Computer 2013: Interaktive Vielfalt, pp. 181–190. Oldenbourg, Munich (2013)
22. Pruitt, J., Adlin, T.: The Persona Lifecycle: Keeping People in Mind throughout Product Design. Morgan Kaufmann, San Francisco (2006)
23. Richter, M., Flückiger, M.D.: Usability Engineering kompakt. Springer, Berlin (2013)
24. Roenspieß, A., Paul, M., Mentler, T., Herczeg, M.: Levels of abstraction for user modeling in the usability engineering repository UsER. In: Ahram, T., Karwowski, W., Marek, T. (eds.) Proceedings of the 5th International Conference on Applied Human Factors and Ergonomics, AHFE, pp. 390–400. AHFE, Krakow (2014)
25. Seffah, A.: Learning the ropes: human-centered design skills and patterns for software engineers' education. Interactions **10**(5), 36–45 (2003). ACM, New York
26. Sharp, H., Rogers, Y., Preece, J.: Interaction Design: Beyond Human-Computer Interaction, 2nd edn. Wiley, New York (2011)
27. Sim, W., Brouse, P.: Empowering requirements engineering activities with Personas. Procedia Comput. Sci. **28**, 237–246 (2014)
28. Turner, P., Turner, S.: Is stereotyping inevitable when designing with personas? Des. Stud. **32**(1), 30–44 (2011)
29. Vukelja, L., Müller, L., Opwis, K.: Are engineers condemned to design? A survey on software engineering and UI design in Switzerland. In: Baranauskas, C., Abascal, J., Barbosa, S.D.J. (eds.) INTERACT 2007. LNCS, vol. 4663, pp. 555–568. Springer, Heidelberg (2007)
30. Wang, X., (n.d).: Personas in the User Interface Design, Alberta, Canada (2011). http://pages.cpsc.ucalgary.ca/~saul/wiki/uploads/CPSC681/topic-wan-personas.pdf

Smiling in a Wizard of Oz Experiment: Emotional vs. Social Smiles, General Effects and Sex Differences

Martin Krippl[1(✉)], Matthias Haase[2], Julia Krüger[2], and Jörg Frommer[2]

[1] Institute for Psychology, Department Methodology, Psychodiagnostics and Evaluation Research, Otto-von-Guericke University of Magdeburg, Magdeburg, Germany
martin.krippl@ovgu.de
[2] Department of Psychosomatic Medicine and Psychotherapy, Medical Faculty, Otto-von-Guericke University Magdeburg, Magdeburg, Germany

Abstract. Derks et al. (2008) showed the similarity of user's emotional involvement in human-human-interaction compared to human-computer-interaction. This implies display rules and gender norms on display rules. In a Wizard of Oz Experiment users had to overcome two challenging situations, were emotions should be induced. Emotional smiles and social smiles were categorized after facial movements were coded with the Facial Action Coding System (Ekman and Friesen 1978). Emotional smiles were more frequent during one of the challenges compared to the baseline, showing that emotion induction was successful. Social smiles were more frequent at the start of the experiment compared to the challenges, but only for woman. This supports the assumption of Derks et al. (2008) that the display rule "smile at the start of on interaction" is only valid for woman. Together the results back the idea that computers are seen as human-like counterparts.

Keywords: Smiling · Emotional smile · Social smile · FACS · Sex differences · Display rules · Gender norms

1 Introduction

1.1 Social Versus Emotional Smiles

Derks et al. (2008) show that the users' emotional involvement in computer-mediated interaction is comparable to that in face-to-face interaction. Thus, it might be suggested that the computer/technical system is perceived as a virtual person by the user and therefore he/she behaves as if the computer/technical system would be a human-like counterpart.

This implies the usage of display rules (Ekman and Friesen 1982; Ekman et al. 1969). One of these display rules is to smile at the start of a communication with a new interaction partner. Such an intentional smile is a social smile (Ekman and Friesen 1982), telling the other person that one will not harm him/her.

M. Kurosu (Ed.): HCI 2016, Part I, LNCS 9731, pp. 313–320, 2016.
DOI: 10.1007/978-3-319-39510-4_29

To be able to distinguish between different kinds of smiles and facial actions in general, one needs a coding system, which objectively describes facial movements. The gold standard here is the Facial Action Coding System (FACS, Ekman and Friesen 1978; Ekman et al. 2002), where movements are anatomically defined as so called Action Units (AUs). According FACS the social smile involves only the zygomaticus major muscle pulling the lip corners up (AU 12), whereas the emotional smile also involves the orbicularis oris muscle (AU 6), which induces crow feet wrinkles (Fig. 1). Besides such initial interaction situation, it could furthermore be expected that emotional smiles also occur during events which induce negative emotions. This could be because events that induce negative emotions could the same time also induce positive emotions. Additionally as mentioned above smiling is not only a sign of joy, but also one of a mere social signal. This could be shown for human-human-interaction (Ekman et al. 1969) and for human-computer interaction (HCI) contexts (Hoque and Picard 2011).

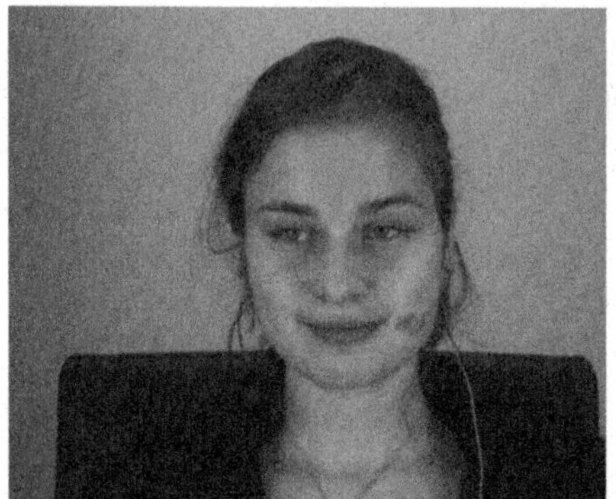

Fig. 1. Social smile (left) and emotional smile (right)

Another interesting research question in HCI and in emotion research is whether and which differences in social and emotional smiling occur between genders. In a meta-analysis, LaFrance et al. (2003) showed that in general woman smile more often than men. We want to check whether this difference can also be found in HCI, suggesting the assumption that the technical system is treated like a person, and whether the sex difference in smiling frequency is based on social or emotional smiles.

1.2 Current Experiment

In the current Wizard-of-Oz (WOz) experiment (Rösner et al. 2012), a speech based system was simulated. The user had to create a solution for a time sensitive task. During the task the users were had to overcome challenges. The subjects got to know the simulated system by a system's self-introduction at the beginning (*baseline*). Afterwards, they had to pack their baggage for a holiday trip. At one moment the weight of their baggage transgressed a not defined amount (*Weight limit barrier*) and subjects had to change their baggage. Another challenge appeared when participants were told that the holidays were not summer, but winter holidays (*Waiuku barrier*). The German participants thought they would pack for summer holidays as suggested in the cover story of the experiment. During the experiment, they got the information that their holiday's destination will be Waiuku, a city in New Zealand, where the temperature is obviously lower than in Germany at the travel time. Accordingly, participants had to change the clothes in their baggage to adapt to the new situation. Therefore, they were given only a few minutes.

Regarding facial activity, both challenge situations (*weight limit barrier* as well as *Waiuku barrier*) were interesting regarding a comparison to the facial activity during the *baseline* (system's self-introduction).

1.3 Questions

1. Does social smiling frequency differ between baseline and challenge situations?
2. Does emotional smiling frequency differ between baseline and challenge situations?
3. Is there a sex difference in social smiling frequency in general or in only a part of the conditions?
4. Is there a sex difference in emotional smiling frequency in general or in only a part of the conditions?

2 Methods

2.1 Sample

We gathered participants from two different age groups (aged between 19 and 29 as well as above 60). Efforts were made to achieve an equal distribution of participants with regard to age group, gender and level of education. We acquired a total of 135 participants. Data from five participants was excluded due to technical problems regarding the records and/or absence from the second appointment despite several attempts to establish contact. Therefore, the total sample consisted of 130 participants.

The facial activity data of 80 participants in the total sample were used for FACS coding and statistical analysis. Two participants were used to check interrater agreement. The rest of the total sample could not be used because of technical problems with regard to the synchronization of videos with sound stimuli and time markers. The final sample consisted of 37 men and 43 women (see Table 1). The age range was from 18 to 81 with a mean of 49.23 (SD = 22.78). Participants were part of either the younger (18 to 28) or the older group (60 to 81).

2.2 Design and Procedure

Implementing a fully automated technical system is difficult, however simulating one by the use of the WOz experiments allows examining research questions and provide a

Table 1. Sample parameters

	N	Women	Age mean	Age SD
Young	34	20	23.06	2.806
Old	46	23	68.28	5.06
All	80	43	49.06	22.89

deeper understanding regarding the interaction between users and computer systems. In such experiments an interface is controlled by a human operator which simulates the computer system.

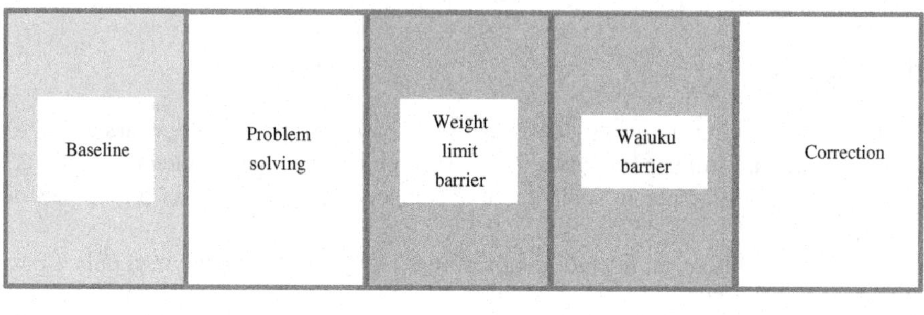

Fig. 2. Design

Participants were instructed to communicate with the computer system via speech input and output. The simulated system asked for personal information from users under the pretext of needing to conduct an individual calibration. This served the underlying purpose of having participants adjust to the speech control and functionality of the simulated system. This section was defined as baseline (Fig. 2). Subsequently, participants were told to prepare baggage for a trip with the aid of the system and were informed about the time limit for this task. In the following, participants worked through twelve categories (e.g., jackets, tops, trousers, shoes, etc.) to gather items for their baggage.

It was suggested that participants pack for a summer vacation. They began by choosing items out of each category. This section was defined as the baseline. The first limitation was introduced after solving the eighth category. Participants were informed that they had exceeded the weight limit for their baggage, independently of the number of items they had gathered so far. This required the removal of some items in order to add more. The system advised participants to change their strategy. This section was called weight limit barrier. During the third section (Waiuku barrier), which also represented a challenge, it was disclosed that participant's holiday destination is a summer location but a winter one. At this point, a randomly pre-selected subsample received a system-initiated intervention based on psychotherapeutic objectives. The intervention focused on problem actualization and the activation of resources.

System-initiated communication shifted to a more interpersonal level. All participants had to re-adapt their strategy without clearly defined time limitations. Finally, they all had the opportunity to modulate their choices under time restrictions. This section simultaneously represented the last challenge as well as the experimental part of the WOz trial.

Self-report measures of emotions were not used in the experiment because they bring users out of the flow of the experience, changing the physiological features of and the experience of emotion (Kassam and Mendes 2013). More complete information with regard to the resulting data corpus are presented in Frommer et al. (2012) and Rösner et al. (2012).

2.3 FACS Coding

FACS (Ekman and Friesen 1978; Ekman et al. 2002) has been the gold standard of facial movement categorization ever since its publication. FACS describes every facial movement independently of emotion categorization.

Four certified FACS coders coded the videos in groups of two, meaning that each video was coded by two coders. In the case of disagreement, the coders discussed their codes until they arrived at a joint decision. Data from two participants who were not part of the statistical analysis formed the basis of the interrater agreement computation. Agreement was computed via a formula by Wexler (Ekman and Friesen 1978). Agreement scores between the group of two standard coders and an additional fifth coder (first author) were between .71 and .89 for all AUs.

For each experimental condition, the five seconds immediately following the conveyance of the relevant information (in the baseline at the start of the experiment) were coded. The frequency of each emotion served as the dependent variable.

Although AUs were classified into several emotion categories, we concentrated on emotional and social smiles in this paper.

3 Results

In order to answer the research questions, we conducted a mixed ANOVA with the experimental conditions as repeated measurement factor and sex as between-subjects factor for both, the 'social smile' (Fig. 3) and the 'emotional' smile (Fig. 3b).

Whereas for the dependant variable 'social smile' no main effect on the experimental conditions ($p = .10$) and the main effect sex ($p = .797$) showed up, the interaction of experimental conditions with sex was significant ($p = .026$).

For the dependant variable 'emotional smile' the main effect on experimental conditions was significant ($p = .030$), whereas no main effect sex ($p = .907$) and no interaction effect ($p = .567$) showed up.

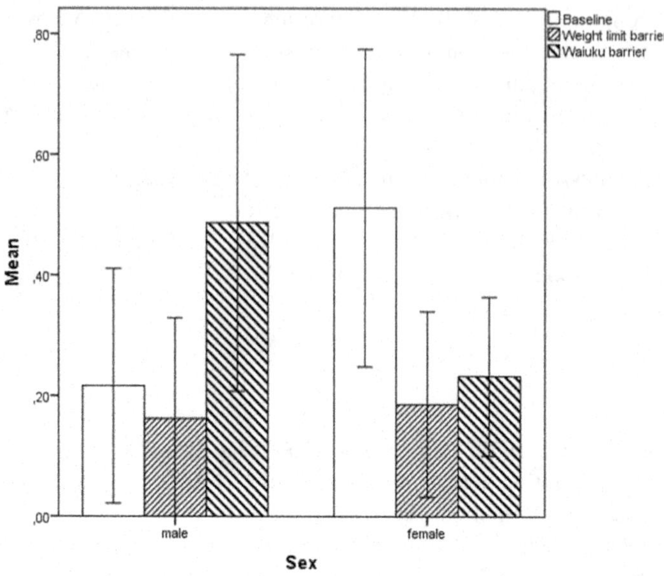

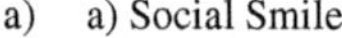
a) a) Social Smile

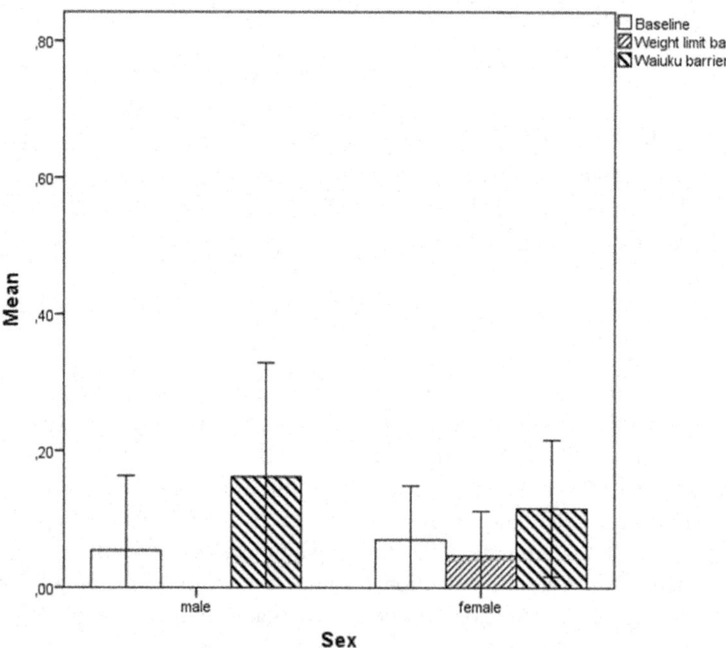

b) Emotional Smile

Fig. 3. Mean frequencies of social (a) and emotional (b) smile during the three conditions, separated by sex

4 Discussion

As assumed, a considerable amount of participants showed smiling, especially social smiling during the *baseline* condition. Furthermore, we also found out that woman showed more social smiling during *baseline* but less during the *Waiuku barrier*, whereas in men it was the opposite.

This supports the idea that social smiling during baseline is based on display rules. The social smile during baseline probably represents a greeting sign, signaling to the computer that one will not harm him. The higher frequency of the social smiles in woman maybe based on gender norms LaFrance et al. (2003), a specific form of display rules, indicating that woman should smile and men need not. The application of display rules and gender norms suggests that users attribute human-like characteristics to the technical system.

Results on emotional smiles support the findings by Hoque and Picard (2011) in a way that emotional smiles can even be induced by negative events. As described by Papa and Bonanno (2008), this could be understood as a kind of self-regulation, which is part of a dissociating reaction for being fooled. By dissociating from the situation (which implies a reduction of ego-involvement), users feel amused about being fooled by the technical system.

All in all, results on social and emotional smiles indicate that users interact with a technical system as if it would be a human-like counterpart. This is in line with findings based on semi-structured interviews with the users after the experiment (Krüger et al. 2015). The results show a phenomenon called anthropomorphism. It means the tendency to imbue the real or imagined behavior of nonhuman agents with humanlike characteristics, motivations, intentions, or emotions" (p. 864, Epley et al. 2007). As Epley et al. (2007) point out, three components are important for anthropomorphism: "the accessibility and applicability of anthropocentric knowledge (elicited agent knowledge), the motivation to explain and understand the behavior of other agents (effectance motivation), and the desire for social contact and affiliation (sociality motivation)" (p. 864, Epley et al. 2007). Although we did not measure these aspects, they should have been relevant in our experimental situation. This should be the case especially for the desire for social contact and affiliation, because participants were alone with the computer.

References

Derks, D., Fischer, A.H., Bos, A.E.R.: The role of communication in computer-mediated communication: A review. Comput. Hum. Behav. **24**, 766–785 (2008)

Ekman, P., Friesen, W.V.: Facial Action Coding System. Consulting Psychologists Press, Palo Alto (1978)

Ekman, P., Friesen, W.V.: Felt, false, and miserable smiles. J. Nonverbal Behav. **6**, 238–258 (1982)

Ekman, P., Friesen, W.V., Hager, J.C.: Facial Action Coding System - The Manual on CD ROM. Prentice-Hall, Englewood Cliffs (2002)

Ekman, P., Sorensen, E.R., Friesen, W.V.: Pan-cultural elements in facial displays of emotion. Science **164**(3875), 86–88 (1969)

Epley, N., Waytz, A., Cacioppo, J.T.: On seeing human: a three-factor theory of anthropomorphism. Psychol. Rev. **114**(4), 864–886 (2007)

Frommer, J., Michaelis, B., Rösner, D., Wendemuth, A., Friesen, R., Haase, M., Siegert, I.: Towards emotion and affect detection in the multimodal LAST MINUTE corpus. In: Paper Presented at the LREC, Eighth International Conference on Language Resources and Evaluation, Istanbul (2012)

Hoque, M., Picard, R.W.: Acted vs. natural frustration and delight: many people smile in natural frustration. In: Paper Presented at the 2011 IEEE International Conference on Automatic Face & Gesture Recognition and Workshops (FG 2011) (2011)

Kassam, K.S., Mendes, W.B.: The effects of measuring emotion: physiological reactions to emotional situations depend on whether someone is asking. PLoS ONE **8**(6), e64959 (2013). doi:10.1371/journal.pone.0064959

Krüger, J., Wahl, M., Frommer, J.: Making the system a relational partner: users' ascriptions in individualization focused interactions with companion-systems. In: Paper Presented at the CENTRIC 2015: The Eighth International Conference on Advances in Human-Oriented and Personalized Mechanisms, Technologies, and Services, Barcelona (2015)

LaFrance, M., Hecht, M.A., Paluck, E.L.: The contingent smile: a meta-analysis of sex differences in smiling. Psychol. Bull. **129**, 305–334 (2003)

Papa, A., Bonanno, G.A.: Smiling in the face of adversity: The interpersonal and intrapersonal functions of smiling. Emotion **8**(1), 1–12 (2008)

Rösner, D., Frommer, J., Friesen, R., Haase, M., Lange, J., Otto, M.: LAST MINUTE: a multimodal corpus of speech-based user-companion interactions. In: Paper Presented at the Proceedings of the Eighth International Conference on Language Resources and Evaluation (LREC 2012), ELRA. http://lrec.elra.info/proceedings/lrec2012/pdf/550_Paper.pdf (2012). Accessed Sept 2015

Knowledge-Oriented Selection of Usability Engineering Methods for Mobility Scenarios

Luise Künnemann, Stephan Hörold, and Heidi Krömker(✉)

Technische Universität Ilmenau, Ilmenau, Germany
{luise.kuennemann,stephan.hoerold,heidi.kroemker}@tu-ilmenau.de

Abstract. Different areas of application and scenarios necessitate different sets of usability engineering methods. The selection of these methods depends on a variety of conditions. This paper presents a new approach for selecting and combining usability engineering methods, dependent on individual conditions of the corresponding method, company-based and product-specific measures as well as an analysis of the knowledge in the area of application. The approach is exemplarily presented for the mobility and transportation sector, focusing on the knowledge-based selection of methods for mobility scenarios.

Keywords: Usability engineering methods · Framework · Mobility scenarios

1 Introduction

Nowadays, user-centered quality criteria become more and more important, even in areas of application which have focused on technical and organizational quality criteria before. Therefore, the value of usability engineering methods rises as well, even though the stakeholders often do not know the set of different usability engineering methods. In this context, the mobility and transportation sector represents a typical area of application, where a change to a stronger user orientation can be observed. Mainly driven by the introduction of new communication technologies and mobility offerings, the user has become the center of attention.

In addition to this circumstance, the mobility and transportation sector possesses comprehensive knowledge, e.g. ticket and travel statistics, platform capabilities and restrictions, as well as common problems of travelers. This knowledge can be integrated into user-centered development and evaluation procedures. Nevertheless, this process is complicated by the extent of usability engineering methods and the low accessibility for experts from other areas of application. This paper describes an approach of how the selection of usability engineering methods can be based on an analysis of the existing knowledge of a defined area of application. The mobility and transportation sector serves as an example for this approach, as it provides a heterogeneous and complex context of use [1] and the described change towards the user. In addition, different case studies have shown the value of combining existing transportation knowledge and usability engineering activities [2, 3].

M. Kurosu (Ed.): HCI 2016, Part I, LNCS 9731, pp. 321–330, 2016.
DOI: 10.1007/978-3-319-39510-4_30

2 State of the Art

There are different approaches for the classification of usability engineering methods, e.g. by their position in the usability engineering process, the type of data collected, their form and the approach used. This way of classification can be shown exemplarily for usability evaluation methods:

- Nielsen [4] describes a differentiation between formative and summative evaluation. Formative evaluation aims to improve an interface's usability in an iterative evaluation procedure, while summative evaluation is mainly used for the assessment of existing, that is, finished interfaces, and for quality assurance. Summative evaluation can also be used for the decision "between two alternatives or as a part of competitive analysis to learn how good the competitor really is" [4]. Formative evaluations are used during the design process; summative evaluations take place at the end of product development and, hence, assess the (almost) final product [5].
- A distinction can also be made between the types of data collected. Summative evaluations provide quantitative data [6], i.e. data that are collected through the measurement of certain relevant things that represent facts and can be analyzed through statistical inferences and comparisons of numbers. The counterpart of quantitative data are qualitative data, which deal with understanding certain behavior from the perspective of people observed or interviewed. These data cannot be measured; however, they provide an insight into the informant's point of view [7].
- Another distinguishing characteristic is the form of the evaluation. Usability evaluation methods can be either formal or informal. Formal testing is also called traditional laboratory-based testing, while informal testing can also be named naturalistic usability, or, in an extreme form, field usability [8]. This differentiation applies to both the method itself and the evaluation environment. Formal evaluations take place in an artificial environment, embedded in a usability lab. They are expensive, time-consuming and characterized by a limited degree of realism with regard to their ecological validity, that is, the authenticity of the scenarios resorted to during the evaluation. Informal tests, on the other hand, are reduced versions of formal tests, hence, they necessitate less effort and cost, but also provide a more realistic evaluation environment. They are also called quick and dirty tests and may require compromising with regard to efficiency measures or the recruitment of test participants. The advantage of informal tests is that they allow unique results, concerning user satisfaction. In addition, full usability testing may not be affordable in very early development stages. Informal testing should be combined with expert assessments in order to increase the quality of results collected [9].
- One of the most substantial distinguishing marks is the one between the analytical and the empirical approach. Analytical usability methods, also called usability inspection methods, encompass drawing on experts that empathize with real users when assessing the system evaluated, whereas empirical methods, also called usability testing methods, are based on observing and surveying real users as they use the system [10]. Several authors categorize in that sense [5, 11], specifying analytical methods as expert-oriented and empirical methods as user-based [5].

This distinction goes back to Schriver who developed a model that classified different forms of evaluation by their degree of user target group involvement [12]. In addition to usability inspection and usability testing methods, there are also survey methods. These are characterized by the use of standardized questionnaires for evaluating a system [13].

Criticism of the various different terms and forms used for categorizing usability methods, among others, comes from Dumas and Fox, stating that what the aforementioned notions "denote is not always clear. They add to the ambiguity about what a usability test is" [14]. They recommend classifying methods making use of a combination of the purpose of the test, the scope of the system evaluated, the location of the test sessions, the presence or absence of a moderator and the functionality level the product has [14].

Despite the disparity and diversity of present classifications for usability evaluation methods, the necessity of a differentiation by itself is undoubted. For example, if it is inevitable to have real users evaluate the system, the choice is, hence, limited to usability testing methods, that is, methods that involve real users as part of the evaluation. It is also possible to combine different categorizations in order to make an informed decision regarding which method would be best suited for the evaluation planned [5]. In addition, e.g. for usability evaluation, nowadays, using a combination of different corresponding methods is recommended in order to combine strengths and marginalize weaknesses of specific methods [15].

The aforementioned suggests that all of the classifications outlined matter in the decision-making process stated above. However, there is no clear and generally valid approach as to how to choose and combine the right methods for the specific context of use and area of application. Such an approach has to include not only the characteristics of different usability engineering methods, but also the special characteristics of the area of application, especially the existing knowledge. This leads to the approach introduced as follows.

3 Approach

3.1 Framework

For reaching the aim of providing a framework that allows for a context-based selection and combination of methods suited for predetermined circumstances, a new approach is used, which is currently being developed within the scope of a PhD thesis. This approach combines (1) considering the individual preset conditions of each usability method used with (2) factoring in company-based and product-specific measures and (3) regarding a knowledge-oriented analysis of the existing knowledge and knowledge gaps in the specific area of application.

- With regard to (1), the approach makes use of exhaustively researched, detailed descriptions and critical analyses of each usability method. Based on the critical evaluation of each method, criteria for a categorization of methods in the form of a method catalog will be developed and used for defining conditions specific to each method.

- Referring to (2), users of the framework will be requested to provide basic information relevant for assessing the situation of the corresponding enterprise.
- With reference to (3), there will be an analysis of knowledge which is assumed to be existent. As a consequence, gaps needing to be filled will be identified. It will then be evaluated which and how specific usability methods may allow for filling these gaps.

The combination of these three aspects will enable a comprehensive and easy-to-use methodology for choosing and combining usability methods.

3.2 Analysis of the Expertise in the Area of Application

This paper focuses on the third aspect mentioned in the framework, the analysis of the knowledge in the specific area of application in which the selected usability method(s) are supposed to be applied. Thus, a new application-oriented access to usability engineering methods, based on the existing knowledge, is provided to ease the dissemination of the methods in different areas of application. The approach is derived from the results of different projects in the mobility and transportation sector and combines analytical and empirical case studies. Figure 1 shows the basic procedure.

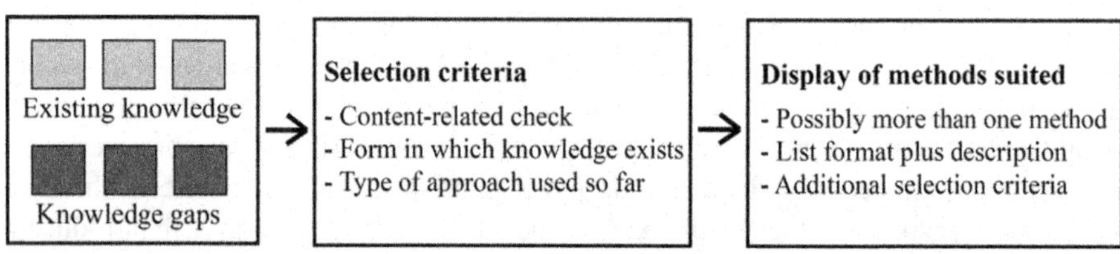

Fig. 1. Schematic description of the procedure for defining suitable methods

First of all, the existing knowledge and knowledge gaps have to be identified using either an internal or an external analysis of the area of application and related documents. To reduce the effort of using the final framework, a question-based procedure will be developed to extract the relevant information for the selection process. Subsequently, the relevant information will be categorized and analyzed with regard to the selection criteria. The selection will cover a detailed analysis of the following criteria:

- Content of the existing knowledge, e.g. user, task, system and design information
- Form of the existing knowledge, e.g. implicit or explicit knowledge
- Type of approaches used so far, e.g. quantitative or qualitative approaches

The combination of the selection criteria provides a deeper understanding of the existing knowledge as well as knowledge gaps and allows for the final selection of suitable methods. The result of this step will include one or more methods, which can be used to close the identified knowledge gaps, and enables the user of the framework to select methods, based on short descriptions.

Additionally, steps (1) and (2) of the framework support a detailed assessment and selection process, if special restrictions, e.g. budget or technical conditions, have to be considered.

4 Utilization of the Approach: Case Study Mobility Scenarios

In the following, a simplified version of the approach for this analysis and first results will be applied exemplarily to the mobility and transportation sector as a case study. As previously described, the mobility and transportation sector provides high complexity in regard to the context of use and the existing knowledge. Therefore, the mobility and transportation sector allows for a detailed evaluation of the approach and its applicability in complex areas of application.

4.1 Characteristics of the Mobility and Transportation Sector

The mobility and transportation sector is characterized by heterogeneous users, a combination of physical and cognitive tasks, different mobility offerings and information systems and a dynamic physical and social context [1, 2]. Even though it appears evident, the application of usability engineering methods as well as the user-oriented development of information and mobility systems is nevertheless rare. Furthermore, the base for usability engineering methods, from requirements analysis to evaluation, is insufficient, although different activities and results from requirements engineering activities can be used in the usability engineering process.

Content of the Existing Knowledge. The mobility and transportation sector has extensive knowledge in different areas. The knowledge covers e.g.:

- Travel behavior, e.g. distances, usage times, means of transport [16, 17],
- Ticket sales, e.g. percentage of different tickets sold [17],
- Technical regulations, e.g. communication interface standards.

However, knowledge gaps include e.g. descriptions of mobility users, including expectations and experiences, as well as tasks and concrete information needs along the journey.

Form of the Existing Knowledge. Some of this knowledge, especially travel behavior, ticket sales and technical regulations, is documented extensively. Regular publications of statistical reports include this knowledge. Knowledge about mobility users, tasks and user interface design is present among some experts from mobility companies but a consistent documentation of this knowledge is missing, and therefore, this knowledge cannot be accessed or easily used.

Type of Approaches Used So Far. The set of methods used in the mobility sector comprises mainly quantitative methods. Analysis of travel behavior, derived from large questionnaires and statistical analysis of system data, are typical representatives within this set.

Based on this first analysis of the mobility and transportation sector, Tables 1 and 2 exemplarily show the results for the requirements analysis and evaluation phase, which are the base for the described selection process.

Table 1. Exemplary characteristics for requirements analysis

Criteria	Analysis result
Content	User descriptions are mainly related to ticket statistics. A deeper description of expectations and experiences is missing.
	Task analyses are related to basic tasks along the travel chain. An analysis of user specific subtasks is missing.
	Platform capabilities and restrictions are widely known and documented in detail.
	Context analyses cover different basic classifications of e.g. stop points but lack a non-technical perspective.
Form	Explicit statistical data
	Implicit expert knowledge
Approaches	Quantitative approaches

Table 2. Exemplary characteristics for evaluation

Criteria	Analysis result
Content	Evaluations have a technical focus and users are integrated into that process while the system is running. Evaluations with users, prior to the implementation, are rare.
Form	The technical knowledge is documented and often introduced by experts from specialized companies.
Approaches	Quantitative approaches

4.2 Requirements Analysis

Requirements analysis, with respect to Mayhew's usability engineering lifecycle, is an integral aspect of usability engineering. It consists of several different activities to be carried out, e.g. generating user profiles, conducting task analysis and applying general design principles. Finally, usability goals are achieved, which are then transferred into a style guide, forming the basis of the actions in the following steps [18].

Given the considerations displayed in Table 1, the framework supports the identification of suitable methods. A method that meets the identified knowledge gaps is the personas design tool. Personas were developed by Cooper in the late 1990ies, quickly becoming a popular method used in the software industry [19]. Personas consist of a variety of user-oriented data, e.g. user goals, professions, tasks and responsibilities, user knowledge and expertise, behavioral patterns and strategies as well as user expectations regarding a new design solution [20]. A detailed description of the method's functionality can be found in [21].

As personas represent user needs [20], they are perfectly suited for requirements analysis. But there are more methods that may well be applied in this phase of the usability engineering lifecycle. For example, the user needs analysis, defining goals as well as limitations of the target audience and their use of the design, could be useful in this regard [22]. Another option would be resorting to scenarios that can be used to exemplarily describe the future interaction of users with the system developed. In this way, scenarios can fill the gap between gathering requirements and drafting respective solutions [20].

In order to decide which method(s) would be best to use in the actual context, the first and second phase of the framework introduced earlier should be consulted. Factoring in both the specific conditions of each of the suitable methods and the company-related and product-based measures will help to refine the first selection of methods.

Different studies in German public transport, e.g. [1, 2], have shown that the persona method provides the necessary insights to reduce qualitative knowledge gaps in the mobility sector. In combination with e.g. focus groups and expert interviews, the implicit knowledge in the mobility sector can be derived and documented for different stakeholders.

4.3 Evaluation Phase

The evaluation phase described in Mayhew's usability engineering lifecycle is part of what follows the requirements analysis and, among others, is characterized by iterative testing [18]. The primary benefit of iterative testing is that the design can be constantly refined and usability problems, arising during the iterations, can be removed in between iterations [4]. As the evaluation procedure per se is one of the crucial aspects of usability optimization [23], the evaluation phase deserves a particular emphasis as follows.

Based on Table 2, usability field tests appear to be recommendable, considering the lack of actual user testing in the mobility and transportation sector. Field tests are rather informal variations of usability testing [8], in which representative users conduct predefined tasks within the real context of use [24]. Hence, there is no artificial imitation of the system's actual context of use [25]. On the other hand, field usability testing is considered expensive, time-consuming and hardly controllable, compared to laboratory testing [26].

It seems natural that, as an alternative to usability testing in the field, usability testing in a lab-based environment could also be applied in the evaluation phase. Testing in laboratories eases recording the sessions and provides a more structured, controllable environment. Yet, because of the artificially created environment, results tend to not be as relevant for the actual context of use [26]. In addition to lab-based testing, evaluations based on heuristics would also be conceivable. Heuristic evaluations are based on a set of well-established usability principles and involve a few expert evaluators that examine the system with regard to their compliance with these principles, which are called the heuristics [27]. As has been highlighted in Table 2, user data are especially rare. Hence, it may be preferable to resort to usability testing methods involving real users. Also, further analyzing the situation on hand, making use of the first and second aspect of the framework explained earlier, could potentially lead to further insight as to which method(s) may be used best for the actual context.

Field usability tests in public transport have already proven their value in the mobility sector [3, 28]. Knowledge gaps can be closed and user feedback can be incorporated into the evaluation of technical systems. A combination of field and lab-based tests seems suitable for the different tasks and the existing expertise, throughout the course of the iterative testing process.

5 Discussion

The described approach combines the selection of usability engineering methods along the development and evaluation process with an analysis of the existing expertise and knowledge in a specified area of application. While this analysis, prior to the selection of methods, is challenging, it provides new access to user-centered development and usability engineering methods for different stakeholders in different areas of application.

An issue that arises is the necessity of transferring the analysis, described exemplarily with regard to the mobility and transportation sector above, to a generally applicable process that can be used to identify knowledge gaps in a particular area of application. It is not yet decided how to design this process. There are two options to approach this issue: The first one would require consulting usability engineering experts every time knowledge gaps are to be identified and ask them to analyze the intended area of application prior to a usability engineering activity. The second option would be a generic procedure that, based on information provided by the user of the framework, is able to give competent support in selecting methods.

At this point, the second option, i.e. the generic approach, seems to be more suited when it comes to achieving the overall aim of providing a comprehensive, easy-to-use framework for selecting usability engineering methods. Deciding in favor of the first approach would mean introducing an additional barrier created by involving another service provider. It would lead to more effort and costs and, hence, might be a hindrance for using the framework altogether.

6 Conclusion

First results from the mobility sector show that the expertise-based approach provides new insights and a more systematic approach for the selection of methods. The analysis of existing knowledge and knowledge gaps is challenging, but the approach holds great potential to overcome the limitations of other approaches, that focus on method characteristics and economical factors only.

This paper does not provide a ready-made solution but rather an approach to be discussed, in order to obtain more stimuli and possibly derive new solutions. The approach to be refined was applied to one area of application only and should be broadened, in order to be able to factor in more fields of use. With this aim, focus groups with experts in the field of usability engineering are being conducted, in order to derive insights into which significant criteria could form the basis of the framework needed.

Acknowledgements. This paper has been prepared within the scope of a PhD thesis which is funded by the Thüringer Graduiertenförderung, in the form of a doctoral scholarship.

References

1. Hörold, S., Mayas, C., Krömker, H.: User-oriented development of information systems in public transport. In: Anderson, M. (ed.) Contemporary Ergonomics and Human Factors. CRC Press, Boca Raton (2013)
2. Mayas, C., Hörold, S., Krömker, H.: Meeting the challenges of individual passenger information with personas. In: Stanton, N.A. (ed.) Advances in Human Aspects of Road and Rail Transportation, pp. 822–831. CRC Press, Boca Raton (2012)
3. Hörold, S., Mayas, C., Krömker, H.: Passenger needs on mobile information systems – field evaluation in public transport. In: Stanton, N.A. (ed.) Advances in Human Aspects of Transportation Part III, AHFE Conference Proceedings, pp. 115–124 (2014)
4. Nielsen, J.: Usability Engineering. Academic Press, San Diego/London (1993)
5. Schweibenz, W., Thissen, F.: Qualität im Web: Benutzerfreundliche Webseiten durch Usability Evaluation. Springer, Heidelberg (2003)
6. Haas, R.: Usability Engineering in der E-Collaboration: Ein managementorientierter Ansatz für virtuelle Teams (Habilitationsschrift). Deutscher Universitäts-Verlag/GWV Fachverlage GmbH, Wiesbaden (2004)
7. Minichiello, V., Aroni, R., Timewell, E., Alexander, L.: In-Depth Interviewing: Researching people. Longman Cheshire, Melbourne (1990)
8. Siegel, D.: Usability for engaged users: the naturalistic approach to evaluation. In: Jacko, J.A. (ed.) The Human-Computer Interaction Handbook: Fundamentals, Evolving Technologies, and Emerging Applications, 3rd edn, pp. 1243–1257. CRC Press, Boca Raton (2012)
9. Thomas, B.: 'Quick and dirty' usability tests. In: Jordan, P.W., Thomas, B., Weerdmeester, B.A., McClelland, I.L. (eds.) Usability Evaluation in Industry, pp. 107–114. Taylor & Francis Ltd., London (1996)
10. Sarodnick, F., Brau, H.: Methoden der Usability Evaluation: Wissenschaftliche Grundlagen und praktische Anwendung (2., überarb. u. aktual. Aufl.). Bern, Verlag Hans Huber (2011)
11. Karat, C.-M.: A comparison of user interface evaluation methods. In: Nielsen, J., Mack, R.L. (eds.) Usability Inspection Methods, pp. 203–233. Wiley, New York (1994)
12. Schriver, K.: Evaluating text quality: the continuum from text-focused to reader-focused methods. IEEE Trans. Prof. Commun. **32**(4), 238–255 (1989). doi:10.1109/47.44536
13. Dumas, J.S., Redish, J.: A Practical Guide to Usability Testing, Revised edn. Intellect Ltd, Exeter/Portland (1999)
14. Dumas, J.S., Fox, J.E.: Usability testing. In: Jacko, J.A. (ed.) The Human-Computer Interaction Handbook: Fundamentals, Evolving Technologies, and Emerging Applications, 3rd edn, pp. 1221–1241. CRC Press, Boca Raton (2012)
15. Backhaus, C.: Usability-Engineering in Der Medizintechnik: Grundlagen – Methoden – Beispiele. Springer-Verlag, Heidelberg (2010)
16. Follmer, R., Gruschwitz, D., Jesske, B., Quandt, S., Lenz, B., Nobis, C., Köhler, K., Mehlin, M.: Mobilität in Deutschland 2008: Ergebnisbericht. Mobility in Germany Website (2010). http://www.mobilitaet-in-deutschland.de
17. Association of German Transport Companies (VDV): VDV-Statistik 2014. https://www.vdv.de/statistik-2014.pdfx
18. Mayhew, D.J.: The Usability Engineering Lifecycle: A Practitioner's Handbook for User Interface Design. Morgan Kaufmann Publishers, San Francisco (1999)

19. Cooper, A.: The origin of personas (2008). http://www.cooper.com/journal/2008/05/the_origin_of_personas
20. Richter, M.: 100 Seiten Spezifikation – und was ist die Konsequenz für uns? In: OBJEKTspektrum (RE/2008) (2008). http://www.michaelrichter.ch/richter_OS_RE_08.pdf
21. Cooper, A.: The Inmates are Running the Asylum: Why High-Tech Products Drive us Crazy and How to Restore the Sanity. Sams Publishing, Indianapolis (1999)
22. Brinck, T., Gergle, D., Wood, S.D.: Designing Web Sites that Work: Usability for the Web. Morgan Kaufmann Publishers, San Francisco (2002)
23. Kappel, K., Wimmer, C., Bachl, S.: Usability engineering in der softwareentwicklung. In: Grechenig, T., Bernhart, M., Breiteneder, R., Kappel, K. (eds.) Softwaretechnik: Mit Fallbeispielen aus realen Entwicklungsprojekten, pp. 519–588. Pearson Studium, München (2010)
24. Kantner, L., Sova, D.H., Rosenbaum, S.: Alternative methods for field usability research. In: Jones, S.B., Novick, D.G., (eds.) Proceedings of the 21st Annual International Conference on Documentation (SIGDOC 2003), 12–15 October 2003, San Francisco, California, USA, pp. 68–72. ACM Press, New York (2003)
25. Nielsen, C.M., Overgaard, M., Pedersen, M.B., Stage, J., Stenild, S.: It's worth the hassle!: the added value of evaluating the usability of mobile systems in the field. In: Proceedings of the 4th Nordic Conference on Human-Computer Interaction: Changing Roles (NordiCHI 2006), pp. 272–280. ACM Press, New York (2006)
26. Kjeldskov, J., Skov, M.B., Als, B.S., Høegh, R.T.: Is it worth the hassle? exploring the added value of evaluating the usability of context-aware mobile systems in the field. In: Brewster, S., Dunlop, M.D. (eds.) Mobile HCI 2004. LNCS, vol. 3160, pp. 61–73. Springer, Heidelberg (2004)
27. Nielsen, J.: How to conduct a heuristic evaluation (1995). https://www.nngroup.com/articles/how-to-conduct-a-heuristic-evaluation/
28. Mayas, C., Hörold, S., Rosenmöller, C., Krömker, H.: Evaluating methods and equipment for usability field tests in public transport. In: Kurosu, M. (ed.) HCI 2014, Part I. LNCS, vol. 8510, pp. 545–553. Springer, Heidelberg (2014)

UX Graph and ERM as Tools for Measuring Kansei Experience

Masaaki Kurosu[1(✉)], Ayako Hashizume[2], Yuuki Ueno[3], Tuyoshi Tomida[3], and Hirotoshi Suzuki[3]

[1] Faculty of Informatics, The Open University of Japan, Chiba, Japan
masaakikurosu@spa.nifty.com
[2] Faculty of System Design, Tokyo Metropolitan University, Tokyo, Japan
hashiaya@tmu.ac.jp
[3] Otsuka Business Service, Tokyo, Japan
uenoyuuki@gmail.com

Abstract. UX graph (Kurosu 2015) is a revised version of UX curve (Kujala et al. 2011) in which the emphasis is not on the curve itself but on the episodes that constitute the graph, hence the graph will be drawn after plotting each episodic events. Furthermore, UX graph expands its temporal scope by including the expectation before purchase and the anticipation for future.

Although the original UX graph was a paper-based method, Hashizume et al. (2016) developed a smartphone/PC application that dynamically shows the graph depending on the input episodic information and allows users to manipulate the event and the curve by finger/mouse. Compared to the original paper-based method, this interactive software facilitates users to change the coordinate of the event point vertically (level of satisfaction) and horizontally (time).

Furthermore, another method is proposed under the name of "ERM" or the experience recollection method. In this method, users are asked not to place the events at exact temporal coordinate on the abscissa but to classify them in the rough time zone. This will make it possible to represent past experience stored in memory more easily and more "correctly".

Keywords: User experience · UX curve · UX graph · ERM

1 Introduction

Based on the idea that various aspects of the user experience (UX) are to be integrated into the concept of satisfaction (Kurosu 2015-1), the authors thought that the temporal dynamism of UX can be represented as the curve of satisfaction, hence developed the idea of UX graph (Kurosu 2015-2, 3).

As can be seen in Fig. 1, quality characteristics are divided to the objective quality characteristics (above) and subjective quality characteristics (below) and they are also divided to the quality in design (left) and the quality in use (right), thus are distinguished in four areas.

As can be seen in Fig. 1, Objective Quality in Design is linked to Objective Quality in Use and Subjective Quality in Use, Objective Quality in Use is linked to Subjective

M. Kurosu (Ed.): HCI 2016, Part I, LNCS 9731, pp. 331–339, 2016.
DOI: 10.1007/978-3-319-39510-4_31

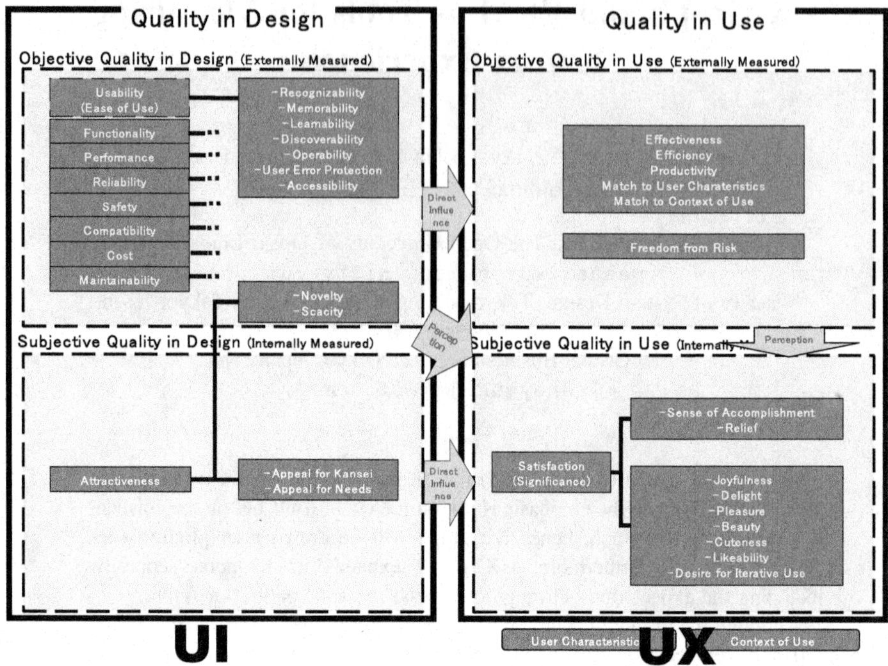

Fig. 1. Quality characteristics in four regions: objective quality characteristics (above) and subjective quality characteristics (below), and quality in design (left) and quality in use (right). (Kurosu 2015-1)

Quality in Use, and Subjective Quality in Design is linked to Subjective Quality in Use. In other words, all quality characteristics other than Subjective Quality in Use influences Subjective Quality in Use. And, in the region of Subjective Quality in Use, the satisfaction is located as the ultimate criterion.

This led us to adopt the satisfaction as the measure for the UX graph. Besides, the satisfaction can be categorized as a part of Kansei quality from another perspective, thus the measurement of satisfaction can be interpreted as the measurement of Kansei as well as the measurement of the UX.

2 UX Graph

Unlike the usability as a part of the design quality, the level of satisfaction is not stable. Compared to the satisfaction, the level of usability can be measured by rather fixed values as the rate of correct recognition, the rate of correct target discovery, and the learning curve. These measures for the usability are usually obtained from a group of people, thus the value is rather stable. Compared to the usability, UX and Kansei are subjective and individualistic as written in the UX White Paper (Roto et al. 2011). Because of its subjectivity and individualistic nature, the level of UX will change on the temporal scale dynamically and no fixed measure can be obtained. Of course, we can ask users to rate the degree of the UX or Kansei at any time, but there is no guarantee that the value measured at an arbitrary time point was constant in the past and will be the same in the future. There are many events in the life of human beings and the degree of satisfaction may go up or down in relation to those events.

With this in mind, there are many challenges to measure the dynamic nature of the UX or Kansei. For example, von Wilamowitz-Moellendorff et al. (2006) proposed CORPUS that is a retrospective interview method to reconstruct the change of UX for more than a year. But this was a qualitative approach and will not bring the quantitative representation of dynamic change in UX.

Ando (2007) proposed the method of collaborative creation of chronological table of usage. This method is based on the interview and the informant and the interviewer discuss and describe major events during the long-term usage and draw a line on the time scale. But what were written on the time scale are just the events and no evaluation, e.g. in terms of satisfaction, was made.

Karapanos et al. (2010) developed an evaluation method using the computer and named it as iScale. The use of computer in this method was to help draw the line automatically on the display.

Kujala et al. 2011 developed UX curve method. Informants are asked to draw a line in terms of the attractiveness, ease of use, functionality and the degree of use. Four aspects to be described as graphs are major components of UX and do not include the satisfaction as a generic measure. At each inflection points, the informant is asked about the event that resulted in the change of the curve. In other words, in UX curve, the curve was first drawn and the points were specified later.

Based on the concept structure described in Fig. 1, Kurosu (2015-1, 2) revised the UX curve regarding following aspects.

1. The graph is only drawn in terms of satisfaction as a generic measure of quality characteristics. It is observed that asking informants to draw more than one graph is time taking and deteriorate the concentration of informant.
2. The order of drawing was reversed, i.e. each event is first written down with the satisfaction rating from 10 to -10, and after that the graph will be drawn considering the coordinate of each point. The name "graph" is derived from this procedure, i.e. usually, the dots are drawn then (regression) line or curve will be drawn in the graph.
3. The abscissa or the time scale was added the phase of expectation before the purchase and the phase of anticipation at present. It is based on the idea that the UX should include such expectation and anticipation.

As a result, the format as shown in Fig. 2 were made.

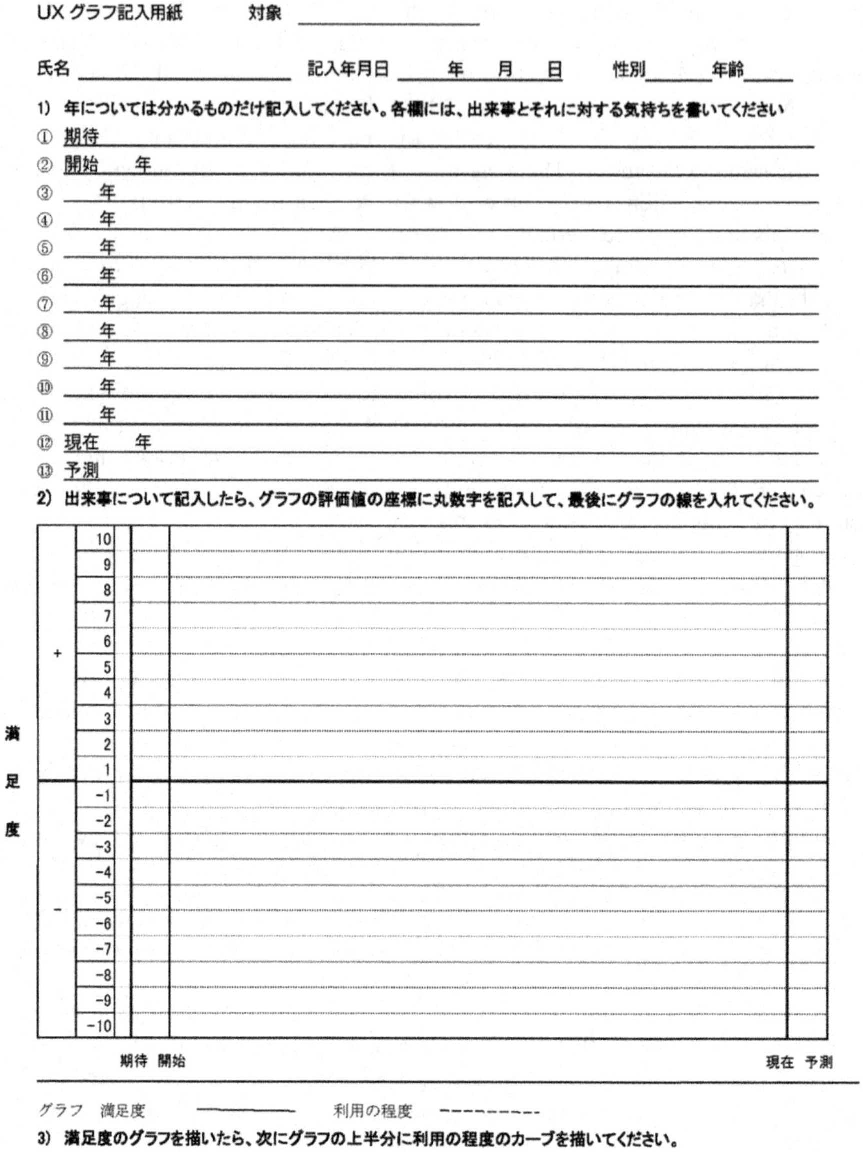

UX グラフ記入用紙　対象 ____________

氏名 ____________ 記入年月日 ____年____月____日 性別____ 年齢____

1) 年については分かるものだけ記入してください。各欄には、出来事とそれに対する気持ちを書いてください

① 期待 ____________

② 開始 年 ____________

③ 年 ____________

④ 年 ____________

⑤ 年 ____________

⑥ 年 ____________

⑦ 年 ____________

⑧ 年 ____________

⑨ 年 ____________

⑩ 年 ____________

⑪ 年 ____________

⑫ 現在 年 ____________

⑬ 予測 ____________

2) 出来事について記入したら、グラフの評価値の座標に丸数字を記入して、最後にグラフの線を入れてください。

満足度

+ 10 9 8 7 6 5 4 3 2 1

− −1 −2 −3 −4 −5 −6 −7 −8 −9 −10

期待 開始 現在 予測

グラフ　満足度 ——————　利用の程度 ----------

3) 満足度のグラフを描いたら、次にグラフの上半分に利用の程度のカーブを描いてください。

Fig. 2. UX graph sheet (in Japanese)

3 Interactive Tool for UX Graph

After collected more than 300 data, it was realized that it should be better that the computer support is introduced. There are some problems to be fixed for UX graph as follows.

1. As it is hand-written on paper, the co-ordinate points and text (experience episodes), once written, can be difficult to correct, and even when corrections are necessary, they may not be made at times due it to being troublesome.
2. If writing is untidy for the same reason, being handwritten, the characters in text can be difficult to read.
3. Some people tend to mix-up the positions of the default horizontal axis co-ordinates (prior expectations, the start of use, current, prediction) and the additional text from the start of use to current, and forget to label the horizontal axis co-ordinates.
4. Even though a text entry area has been provided in the form for creating the UX graphs, some people tend to write the text inside the graph area.

Hashizume et al. (2016) developed a web-based UX graph tool on the PC. The β-version of UX graph tool is available free of charge (on http://ux-graph.com/) from December 11th, 2015, and it can be used by anybody, under the environment of use described later. Renovation of functions and the user interface are currently underway.

The UX graph tool can be used under a PC environment as follows.

- The device allows the mouse operation.
- The device is equipped with an internet environment that allows access to the website.
- The device is equipped with an environment that allows for saving /browsing of PDF files.
- The device is equipped with an environment that allows for use of modern browsers such as the latest version of Firefox or Chrome.

Procedure for using the tool is as follows.

The first step is the entry of information on informant and the targeted experience. The "age" and "sex" of the Informant is selected, and the artifact targeted for evaluation is entered into the "experience" section.

Figure 3 shows the entry screen for the episodes (event). Episode entries are made while imagining the expectations (prior expectations) before acquiring the artifact (the targeted product), impressions at the start (at the start of use), experience episodes from the start until now, current evaluation (current feelings) and future predictions (expectations beyond the current state).

Episodes on prior expectations, start of use, and current and future predictions were regarded as fixed episodes, with their "content of experience" all being regarded as essential. The number of episodes from the start of use to current can be set optionally, and the order of each episode can be switched around by dragging and dropping through mouse operations. Aside from the content of experience, episodes consist of "time of experience" and "satisfaction (−10 to +10)," but the entries concerning the time and satisfaction are optional. When all the content for each of the episodes has been entered, a UX graph chart, drawn according to the episodes, will appear underneath the episodes section (Fig. 4). While all initial values for "satisfaction" on the UX graph charts have been set to "0," the UX graph charts were made to reflect any entries made concerning satisfaction at the same time that episode entries are made.

The axes on the UX graph charts were set to be the time on horizontal axis (past towards the left, future towards the right) and the satisfaction levels on the vertical axis (above the origin being positive, and below the origin being negative), same as with the UX graphs. The episode point created on the UX graph chart after entering the episode details is dragged up and down through mouse operations to control the "satisfaction" levels, in order to create the graph.

The content of experience appears when hovering the mouse cursor over the episode point and it was made possible to edit the content of experience by clicking this display. Furthermore, the order of the "episodes" from the start of use to current, which are not fixed episodes (prior expectations, start of use, current and future predictions), can be switched around by dragging the vertical axis of each episode between the left and right. Whenever the "Satisfaction" levels are controlled, or the episode orders are switched around, the UX graph chart is re-drawn, so as to connect the points.

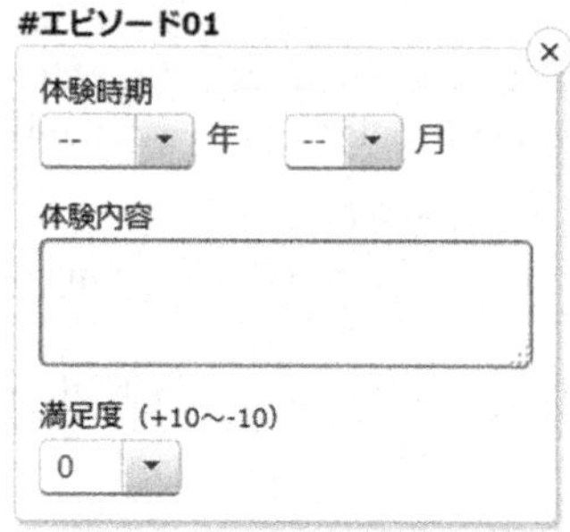

Fig. 3. Data entry screen

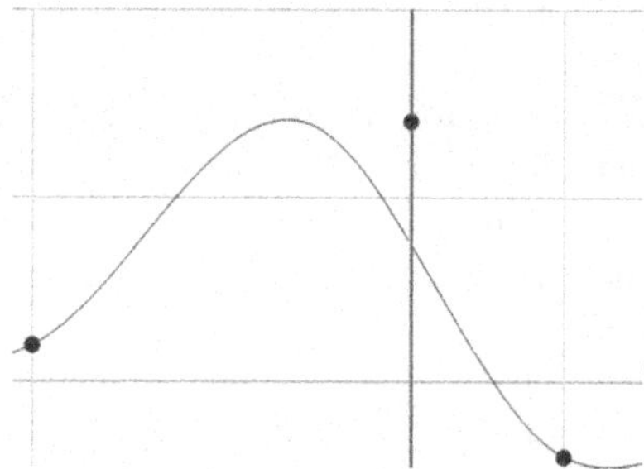

Fig. 4. Graph displayed on the screen

4 ERM (Experience Recollection Method)

Although the usability of UX graph was improved by implementing it to the PC, UX graph has a strong constraint for the user to specify the time of occurrence of each event. As Ross (1989), Oishi and Sullivan (2006) and Norman (2009) wrote, human memory is not much reliable. Some past event might be exaggerated, some others might have been forgotten, etc.

For example, if two adjacent events A and B were wrongly remembered as A after B, the corrected graph with B after A will give us a different impression compared to the graph with A after B. And the gradient of the graph is not so much important. Actually, it was found to be difficult for users to clarify the time when each event actually happened.

Because of this nature of the UX graph, the ERM or the Experience Recollection Method was proposed. In this method, the satisfaction graph was discarded because of uncertainty of the time of each event. Instead, only the rough time sequence is given verbally to the user. As can be seen in Fig. 5, there are 'the evaluation at early days

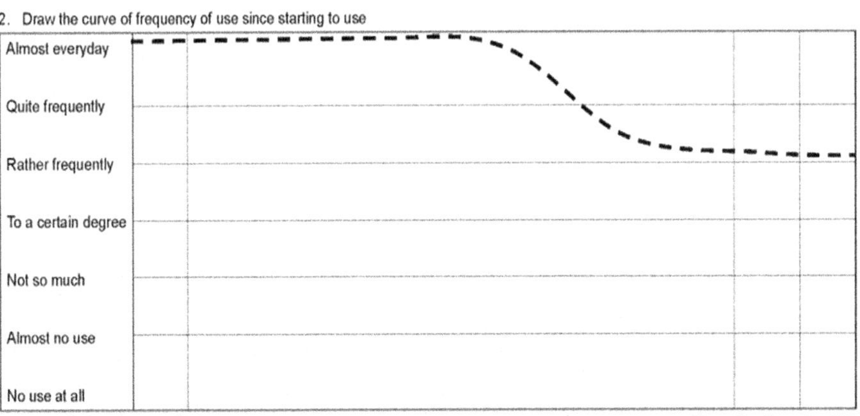
Recording Sheet for ERM: Experience Recollection Method Target Item Smartphone (iPhone 6) Male/Female Age 27

1. Write what you experienced at each phase and fill in the evaluation by +10 to -10 rating.

Phase		What you experienced	Evaluation (+10~−10)
Expectation before purchase		I expected to get the latest model of iPhone on the day of sale.	8
Evaluation at the time of starting to use	Year 2014	I was bewildered for the larger screen compared to my previous model (iPhone5).	5
Evaluation at early days from starting to use		I got used to the large screen soon. And I felt the advantage of large screen for enjoying the game.	10
Evaluation during the use		The body was bent, but was straighten back by pushing it harder.	5
Recent evaluation		The power loss of battery is unexpectedly fast.	-5
Present evaluation	Year 2016	It's now a must to carry the backup battery.	-5
Evaluation in the near future		I will use this until the next model will appear.	-2

2. Draw the curve of frequency of use since starting to use

Fig. 5. Recording sheet of experience recollection method

from starting to use', 'the evaluation during the use' and 'the recent evaluation' are inserted between 'the evaluation at the time of start to use' and 'the present evaluation', because such rough time segmentation was thought to be sufficient. Other features of the UX graph, i.e. the satisfaction rating from +10 to −10 and the curve of frequency of usage are kept.

The satisfaction rating is important as was in the UX graph to realize how much each event recollected from the past experience is evaluated positively or negatively. For the purpose of user research, events that resulted in positively should be maintained in the next version of the product or in the future service activity and events that resulted in negatively should be improved in the near future considering the degree of the rating.

In the example described in Fig. 5, we can see that the big sized screen that astonished the user at the first time was gradually accepted, hence we can think that the size of this smartphone (iPhone 6) can be accepted by (this) user. But the hardware feature or the battery life is a serious issue to be improved in the next version. Fortunately, this user is not leaving the iPhone and is expecting a better new model coming. Because other informants who filled in the ERM format wrote in the same way about the battery life as a big defect as large negative aspect, the manufacturer should take this issue very seriously.

The ERM is a qualitative method and it is recommended to confirm the tendency found in the result by conducting the quantitative method, e.g. the questionnaire for 300 or more informants, based on the hypothesis generated by this method.

5 Conclusion

Based on the UX curve, we first developed the UX graph, then implemented it on the PC. And based on the reflection that the severe temporal constraints are less meaningful, we developed the ERM. We are going to implement ERM on the PC, too.

ERM is a tool to measure the dynamic change of satisfaction, that is, it can be used for measuring the UX and Kansei (or the subjective aspect of UX).

References

Ando, M.: Dynamic change in long-term usability – changes in the context of use and their influence. Sokendai Cultural Stud. **3**, 27–49 (2007)

Hashizume, A., Ueno, Y., Tomida, T., Suzuki, H., Kurosu, M.: Web tool for the UX graph. In: Proceedings of ISASE2016 (2016)

Karapanos, E., Zimmerman, J., Forlizzi, J., Martens, J.B.: Measuring the dynamics of remembered experience over time. Interact. Comput. **22**(5), 328–335 (2010)

Kujala, S., Roto, V., Vaananen-Vainio-Mattila, K., Karapanos, E., Sinnela, A.: UX curve: a method for evaluating long-term user experience. Interact. Comput. **23**, 473–483 (2011)

Kurosu, M.: Usability, quality in use and the model of quality characteristics. In: Proceedings of HCII2015 (2015-1)

Kurosu, M.: Dynamic change of satisfaction among undergraduate students of the Open University of Japan by the UX graph. Annual Report of the Open University of Japan 2015 (2015-2). (in Japanese)

Kurosu, M.: Does the evaluation of satisfaction measured by the ux graph reflect the accumulation or the recency effect? In: Conference of Japan Kansei Engineering Society Proceedings 2015 (2015-3). (in Japanese)

Norman, D.A.: Memory is more important than actuality. Interactions **16**, 24–26 (2009)

Oishi, S., Sullivan, H.W.: The predictive value of daily vs. retrospective well-being judgments in relationship stability. J. Exp. Soc. Psychol. **43**, 460–470 (2006)

Ross, M.: Relation of implicit theories to the construction of personal histories. Psychol. Rev. **96**(2), 341–357 (1989)

Roto, V., Law, E.L.-C., Vermeeren, A., Hoonhout, J. (eds.): User Experience White Paper – Bringing Clarity to the Concept of User Experience (2011). http://www.allaboutux.org/uxwhitepaper/

von Wilamowitz-Moellendorff, M., Hassenzahl, M., Platz, A.: Dynamics of user experience: how the perceived quality of mobile phones changes over time. In: "User Experience – Towards a Unified View", Workshop at the 4th Nordic Conference on Human-Computer Interaction, pp. 74–78 (2006)

Development of a Usability Questionnaire for Automation Systems

Akihiro Maehigashi[1(✉)], Kazuhisa Miwa[1], Kazuaki Kojima[2], and Hitoshi Terai[3]

[1] Graduate School of Information Science, Nagoya University, Nagoya, Japan
mhigashi@cog.human.nagoya-u.ac.jp, miwa@is.nagoya-u.ac.jp
[2] Learning Technology Laboratory, Teikyo University, Tokyo, Japan
kojima@lt-lab.teikyo-u.ac.jp
[3] Faculty of Humanity-Oriented Science and Engineering, Kindai University, Osaka, Japan
terai@fuk.kindai.ac.jp

Abstract. In this study, we positioned automation systems as the third-generation artifacts and developed a generalized usability questionnaire with 18 questions for automation systems as daily used artifacts. This questionnaire could be used to evaluate various types of automation systems and is useful for the development and improvement of automation systems as artifacts used in our everyday life.

Keywords: Automation system · Usability test · Questionnaire

1 Introduction

1.1 Automation System

Today, technological progress offers many opportunities to use automation systems such as cleaning robots and automated driving systems in everyday life. An automation system is a technology that autonomously conducts a task on behalf of humans [1]. Their use is expected to increase further in the near future.

Automation systems provide a completely new interaction between people and artifacts. Classical first-generation artifacts, such as knives and hammers, are used to support users' physical activities. The physical structures of such artifacts are usually simple and their functions are easy to understand. Therefore, in the interaction between people and classical artifacts, the artifacts normally perform along the users' intentions [2]. Furthermore, cognitive artifacts, such as computers and smartphones, are used to support users' cognitive activities by storing, expressing, and manipulating information [3]. Such artifacts are considered second-generation artifacts. As the inner structures of such artifacts are complex, their functions difficult to comprehend. Therefore, in the interaction between people and cognitive artifacts, discrepancies between the users' intentions and the artifacts' performance often occur [4].

M. Kurosu (Ed.): HCI 2016, Part I, LNCS 9731, pp. 340–349, 2016.
DOI: 10.1007/978-3-319-39510-4_32

Automation systems, in contrast, autonomously conduct tasks in the users' physical and cognitive activities. Moreover, when using classical or cognitive artifacts, the central player of each task is the user, and the artifacts support the user. However, when automation systems are employed, the central player of each task is the system, and the users monitor and supervise the systems. Thus, automation systems are considered third-generation artifacts. Additionally, because automation systems conduct far more complex information processing than first- and second- generation artifacts, users generally cannot understand the internal functions of the systems. However, if the discrepancies between the users' intentions and the automation systems' performance occur, they could lead to fatal accidents [1].

1.2 Usability Test

Artifacts used in everyday life are often evaluated through usability tests. Usability is defined as "the extent to which a product can be used by specified users to achieve specified goals with effectiveness, efficiency and satisfaction in a specified context of use" [5]; this is the world standard definition of usability [6]. The evaluation targets are usually cognitive artifacts, mainly computer software systems, to be developed and improved [6].

On the other hand, automation systems are usually evaluated based on the users' trust in the systems or their assigned workload [1]. The evaluation targets, in this case, are automated control systems in nuclear and manufacturing plants and automated operating systems of airplanes and ships. With the increased use of automation systems in daily life, their usability must be evaluated as well. Objective data on the use of automation systems may be obtained in multiple ways. However, automation systems cannot be evaluated using existing usability test questionnaires, such as SUS (system usability scale) [7], SUMI (software usability measurement inventory) [8], and QUIS (questionnaire for user satisfaction) [9], because the features of the automation systems, their autonomy and the complex inner information processes, are not considered in these questionnaires. Therefore, a new evaluation index is required, which will consider the features of automation systems.

In this study, we developed a generalized usability questionnaire for evaluating automation systems, which can be applied under different environmental settings.

2 Questionnaire Design

The usability elements effectiveness, efficiency, and satisfaction defined in ISO [5] were reflected in the usability questionnaire for automation systems. Effectiveness is "the accuracy and completeness with which users achieve specified goals," efficiency is "the resources expended in relation to the accuracy and completeness with which users achieve goals," and satisfaction is "the freedom from discomfort, and positive attitudes towards the user of the product" [5].

We added three new usability elements to the questionnaire to evaluate automation system usability. The first element is understandability the comprehensibility of the intentions of automation systems. Automation systems autonomously conduct tasks; however, as users cannot usually comprehend the internal functions of the systems, it is desirable for users to understand the intentions of the systems without discrepancies [10]. The second element is discomfort the absence of comfort or ease in using automation systems. Because automation systems receive information from the external environment and make decisions using this information, automation systems sometimes achieve tasks with users' unpredicted behaviors [10]. Furthermore, the task-performing process influences users' subjective evaluations of automation systems [11]; users feel comfort or discomfort because of the task-performing process, regardless of the task performance of the systems. The third element is motivation the users' desire to conduct the tasks by themselves. Because automation systems autonomously conduct tasks instead of the users, users tend to significantly depend on the systems [1,12]. Additionally, users' overreliance on the systems reduces their motivation and ability to conduct tasks by themselves [13]. Automation systems should not take away the users' motivation and ability to conduct tasks.

Based on these considerations, we developed a usability questionnaire for automation systems comprising six questions for each element effectiveness, efficiency, satisfaction, understandability, discomfort, and motivation and a total of 36 questions, rated on a five-point scale: 1. Strongly disagree, 2. Disagree, 3. Neither agree nor disagree, 4. Agree, 5. Strongly agree.

3 Experiment

We conducted an experiment using and evaluating automation systems with the designed usability questionnaire to investigate its reliability and validity.

3.1 Experimental Task

Line-Tracing Task. We used a line-tracing task as an experimental task, a modified version of the line task used by Maehigashi et al. [14]. In this task, participants traced a line that scrolls downward past a circular vehicle. When the vehicle veered off the line, the performance score reduced according to the operational error. The participants were allowed to switch to either the auto-tracing mode (operation performed entirely by the system) or the manual mode (operation performed by participants using left and right arrow keys). The circular vehicle in the task had a diameter of 24 pixels. The window scrolling speed was 24 pixels per second. In the line task, the line was five-pixels wide. When operational errors occurred, a flashing red square frame appeared around the task window as error feedback.

Auto-tracing Systems and Task Situations. We set up two types of auto-tracing systems: the operational pathway-displaying system and the non-displaying system (Fig. 1). The operational path-way-displaying system indicated the pathway (light green) along which the system tried to operate the vehicle. The non-displaying system, in contrast, did not indicate the pathway. The participants used and evaluated these systems in various situations: (1) the system accurately traced the line or failed to trace it, (2) the vehicle stably traced the line or unstably snaked along the line in the auto-tracing mode, and (3) pressing a selector on the keyboard or typing a command, switch, when it was necessary to switch from the manual to the auto-tracing mode.

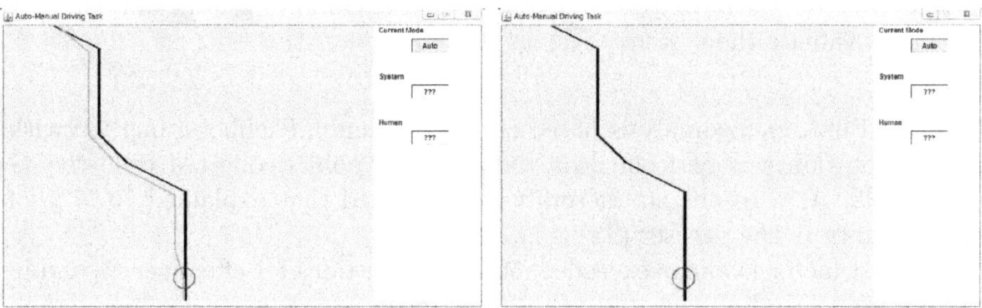

Fig. 1. Two types of auto-tracing systems: operational pathway-displaying system (left) and non-displaying system (right).

The auto-tracing system performance was controlled by the success rate of the operation command. In the experimental task, the system's operation in the auto-tracing mode was generally reflected in the vehicle movements with a 50 Hz sampling frequency. We controlled the percentage of how much the system's operation reflected in actual vehicle movements. In one situation, the system's operation, which was always perfect, was reflected in 100 % of the vehicle's movements. Therefore, the vehicle did not veer off from the line. In another situation, however, the system's operation was reflected in only 40 % of the vehicle's movements. The remaining 60 % of the system's operation was accepted in the experimental task system as no operational command. Therefore, the vehicle did not appropriately trace the line.

Auto-tracing system behavior was controlled by the observed vehicle behavior, independent from the system performance. If the system performed perfectly, the center of the circular vehicle was on the line. In another situation, although the system performed perfectly, the vehicle unstably snaked along the line. However, the circular vehicle was always on the line.

Switching from the manual to the auto-tracing mode was controlled by the command input method. The participants either pressed the spacebar or typed a command to switch from the manual to the auto-tracing mode. Switching back from the auto-tracing to the manual mode was performed by pressing the spacebar.

3.2 Method

Participants. Forty-eight university students participated in the experiment.

Procedure. Half the participants used the operational pathway-displaying system, and the other half used the non-displaying system. Each participant conducted the task in the eight different situations created by combining the task situations mentioned above. Performing the task in each situation took five minutes. After the participants completed the task in each situation, they evaluated the system with the usability questionnaire. After the evaluation, they took a two-minute break. Before they engaged in the task in each situation, they were instructed to achieve as high a score as possible and to use the auto-tracing system to evaluate the system.

Results. First, factor analysis based on the maximum likelihood method with varimax rotation was performed on the 384 data points collected from the 48 participants. As a result, six factors were extracted that explained 73.77 % of the variability in the dataset (Table 1).

The first factor loadings exceeded .50 in six questions for effectiveness and in two questions for efficiency, and were below .50 in one question for motivation. Therefore, the first factor is considered to indicate effectiveness. The second factor loadings exceeded .50 in four questions for efficiency. Consequently, the second factor is considered to indicate efficiency. The third factor loadings exceeded .50 in six questions for satisfaction. Therefore, the third factor is considered to indicate satisfaction. Regarding the fourth factor, the factor loadings exceeded .50 in six questions for understandability and in one question for discomfort. Therefore, the fourth factor is considered to indicate understandability. Regarding the fifth factor, because the factor loadings exceeded .50 in five questions for discomfort, it is considered to indicate discomfort. Finally, the sixth factor loadings exceeded .50 in five questions for motivation; thus, the sixth factor is considered to indicate motivation.

Next, we selected three questions whose factor loadings were among the three highest for each factor, and we prepared a questionnaire comprising these 18 selected questions. We performed factor analysis using the maximum likelihood method with varimax rotation of the collected data for these 18 questions. As a result, six factors were extracted, and the validity of the questionnaire was confirmed (Table 2). The accumulated proportion of the six factors was 72.30 %. In each factor, the factor loadings exceeded .50 for three questions in each element.

Furthermore, we calculated Cronbach's alpha coefficient among the three questions for each factor. The coefficient was .959 for the first factor, effectiveness; .833 for the second, efficiency; .872 for the third, satisfaction; .836 for the fourth, understandability; .911 for the fifth, discomfort; and .933 for the sixth, motivation. Since the alpha coefficient for each factor exceeded .80, the reliability of the questionnaire was confirmed.

Table 1. Thirty-six questions and factor loadings. Factor loadings greater than .50 are in gray. (R) indicates reverse scored question.

	Factors					
	1	2	3	4	5	6
Effectiveness						
This system did not conduct the task accurately. (R)	.79	.10	.25	.24	.23	-.10
I think that I would not make any mistakes by using this system.	.81	.06	.29	.21	.22	-.15
I was able to perform the task accurately by using this system.	.82	.12	.27	.22	.21	-.17
Using this system incurs errors during the task. (R)	.77	.09	.23	.19	.13	-.15
This system prevented me from committing errors during the task.	.81	.13	.31	.26	.20	-.10
This system decreases the task accuracy. (R)	.76	.13	.32	.29	.19	-.13
Efficiency						
Using this system incurs fatigue. (R)	.40	.58	.26	.26	.30	-.08
This system made the task easier.	.81	.17	.27	.26	.21	-.17
This system let me complete the task with less effort.	.84	.17	.28	.27	.13	-.12
I think that someone's support is necessary to use this system. (R)	.01	.69	.23	.22	.16	-.17
I was able to get used to this system in a short amount of time.	.11	.73	.20	.28	.15	-.11
By using this system, performing the tasks became more difficult. (R)	.44	.61	.28	.30	.19	-.13
Satisfaction						
I would never use this system again. (R)	.30	.20	.81	.16	.06	-.05
I did not feel any anxiety to use this system.	.19	.07	.70	.16	.25	-.24
I am satisfied with this system.	.34	.19	.82	.14	.10	.02
I was worried about using this system. (R)	.31	.14	.82	.14	.12	-.13
I am not satisfied with this system. (R)	.30	.17	.83	.08	.11	-.08
I would like to use this system again.	.40	.18	.78	.16	.03	-.07
Understandability						
I was able to predict the action of the system during the task.	.22	.13	.08	.74	.08	-.02
This system behaved against my expectation. (R)	.27	.13	.15	.72	.38	-.07
I could predict how this system behaved.	.27	.16	.19	.68	.13	.01
This system never behaved against my expectation.	.27	.10	.13	.67	.43	-.01
I think nobody can predict this system. (R)	.12	.20	.08	.76	.03	-.21
I had no idea what this system would do. (R)	.23	.21	.16	.73	.26	-.11
Discomfort						
This system behaved smoothly.	.39	.27	.17	.26	.64	-.02
I did not get used to this system's behavior.	.37	.36	.19	.44	.12	-.11
This system sometimes behaved unnaturally. (R)	.25	.14	.09	.62	.58	-.09
This system behaved naturally.	.38	.19	.17	.38	.65	-.13
I did not feel any discomfort with this system.	.34	.12	.24	.46	.62	-.09
This system behaved awkwardly. (R)	.28	.30	.13	.30	.70	-.14
Motivation						
Based on the experience of using this system, I feel like performing better by myself.	-.02	-.10	.05	-.07	.05	.62
It is more fun to perform the task by myself than relegating the task to the system.	-.13	-.04	-.08	-.03	-.12	.75
Based on the experience of using this system, I feel like performing the task by myself.	-.27	-.08	.-18	-.13	-.06	.84
Based on the experience of using this system, I think I should conduct the task by myself, only when it is necessary.	-.48	-.19	-.22	-.23	-.11	.22
I can perform the task by myself better without using the system.	-.33	-.10	-.16	-.04	-.12	.73
I feel like delegating the task to the system for as long as possible. (R)	-.57	.01	-.22	-.10	-.13	.33

Table 2. Eighteen questions and factor loadings. Factor loadings greater than .50 are in gray. (R) indicates reverse scored question.

	Factors					
	1	2	3	4	5	6
Effectiveness						
I think that I would not make any mistakes by using this system.	.79	.29	.18	.12	.19	-.25
I was able to perform the task accurately by using this system.	.78	.28	.18	.14	.22	-.20
This system prevented me from committing errors during the task.	.76	.29	.27	.08	.19	-.25
Efficiency						
I think that someone's support is necessary to use this system. (R)	.29	.76	.29	.19	.15	-.14
I was able to get used to this system in a short amount of time.	.18	.77	.33	.22	.21	-.10
By using this system, performing the tasks became more difficult. (R)	.32	.68	.33	.23	.26	-.17
Satisfaction						
I am satisfied with this system.	.17	.23	.81	.14	.11	-.19
I was worried about using this system. (R)	.18	.22	.86	.12	.12	-.06
I am not satisfied with this system. (R)	.19	.21	.86	.02	.09	-.15
Understandability						
I was able to predict the action of the system during the task.	.09	.22	.07	.83	.11	-.19
I think nobody can predict this system. (R)	.18	.14	.08	.65	.22	-.02
I had no idea what this system would do. (R)	.20	.23	-.14	.66	.36	-.10
Discomfort						
This system behaved smoothly.	-.11	.19	-.14	.23	.78	-.08
This system behaved naturally.	.10	.26	.10	.22	.80	-.19
This system behaved awkwardly. (R)	.33	.21	-.13	.32	.66	-.18
Motivation						
It is more fun to perform the task by myself than relegating the task to the system.	-.07	-.09	-.07	-.04	-.11	.75
Based on the experience of using this system, I feel like performing the task by myself.	-.18	-.12	.-13	-.15	-.06	.87
I can perform the task by myself better without using the system.	-.23	-.12	-.15	-.09	-.14	.79

4 General Discussion

Based on the conducted experiment, the usability questionnaire with 18 questions was developed, and its reliability and validity were confirmed (Appendix A). In the following, we indicate the relationships between the six usability elements effectiveness, efficiency, satisfaction, understandability, discomfort, and motivation.

We developed a structural equation model to investigate the relationships. The model is based on two assumptions; (1) the users' evaluations of effectiveness, efficiency, discomfort, and understandability directly reflect the automation system behaviors and (2) the users' evaluations of satisfaction and motivation are influenced by their evaluations of the other four elements. Therefore, we separated the usability elements into high-level elements satisfaction and motivation and low-level elements effectiveness, efficiency, discomfort, and understandability to develop the model.

Based on the answer data for the 18 questions in the questionnaire, we performed covariance structure analysis using the proposed model. First, the model fit test results showed that the proposed model is sufficient to explain the data: CFI (goodness of fit) = .93, TLI (Tucker-Lewis index) = .92, RMSEA (root mean square error of approximation) = .09, and SRMR (standardized root mean square residual) = .05. Second, the analysis results showed interactive influences among the low-level elements: effectiveness and efficiency ($r = .78, p < .001$), effectiveness and discomfort ($r = .66, p < .001$), effectiveness and understandability ($r = .58, p < .001$), efficiency and discomfort ($r = .71, p < .001$), efficiency and understandability ($r = .68, p < .001$), and discomfort and understandability ($r = .70, p < .001$).

The analysis results also showed that the four low-level elements influence one of the high-level elements, satisfaction. The path coefficients indicating the influence of effectiveness, efficiency, discomfort, and understandability on satisfaction were .43 ($p < .001$), .53 ($p < .001$), .13 ($p < .001$), and .09 ($p < .001$), respectively. The effects of discomfort and understandability were very weak, but negative. Therefore, negative influence on users' satisfaction was the result of not only their discomfort but also their low understandability. In this experiment, the participants used the operational pathway-displaying system or the non-displaying system to conduct the line-tracing task in various situations. Thus, when the operational pathway-displaying system was used, in particular, in a situation where the auto-tracing system did not trace the line accurately, users' satisfaction prominently reduced because the displayed pathway and the actual traced pathway were obviously different. Consequently, understandability affects satisfaction negatively.

Moreover, the analysis results showed that the low-level elements effectiveness, efficiency, and understandability affect the other high-level element, motivation. The path coefficients indicating the influence of effectiveness, efficiency, and understandability on motivation were .35 ($p < .001$), .22 ($p < .001$), and .06 ($p < .005$), respectively. Discomfort did not affect motivation. Higher effectiveness, efficiency, and understandability of the system reduced users' motivation to conduct tasks by themselves. Additionally, there was no correlation between satisfaction and motivation ($r = -.01, p = .20$).

In summary, we considered automation systems as third-generation artifacts and developed a generalized usability questionnaire for such systems. This questionnaire can be used to evaluate various types of automation systems and is useful for developing and improving automation systems as daily used artifacts.

A Appendix: Usability Questionnaire for Automation Systems

The order of the questions can be randomized, and (R) indicates reverse scored questions.

1. It is more fun to perform the task by myself than relegating the task to the system.

2. I think nobody can predict this system. (R)
3. I was worried about using this system. (R)
4. This system behaved smoothly.
5. I think that someone's support is necessary to use this system. (R)
6. Based on the experience of using this system, I feel like performing the task by myself.
7. I was able to perform the task accurately by using this system.
8. This system behaved naturally.
9. I am satisfied with this system.
10. This system prevented me from committing errors during the task.
11. I was able to get used to this system in a short amount of time.
12. This system behaved awkwardly. (R)
13. I can perform the task by myself better without using the system.
14. I was able to predict the action of the system during the task.
15. I am not satisfied with this system. (R)
16. I think that I would not make any mistakes by using this system.
17. By using this system, performing the tasks became more difficult. (R)
18. I had no idea what this system would do. (R)

References

1. Parasuraman, R., Riley, V.: Humans and automation: use, misuse, disuse. Abuse. Hum. Factors **39**, 230–253 (1997)
2. Rasumussen, J.: Information Processing and Human-Machine Interaction: An Approach to Cognitive Engineering. Elsevier Science Publishing, New York (1996)
3. Norman, D.A.: Cognitive artifacts. In: Carroll, M. (ed.) Designing Interaction, pp. 17–38. Cambridge University Press, Cambridge (1991)
4. Norman, D.A.: The Psychology of Everyday Things. Basic Books, New York (1988)
5. ISO: Ergonomic requirements for office work with visual display terminals (VDTs)-Part 11: Guidance on usability. ISO 9241-11:1998 (1998)
6. Hornbæk, K.: Current practice in measuring usability: challenges to usability studies and research. Int. J. Hum. Comput. Stud. **64**, 79–102 (2006)
7. Brooke, J.: SUS: a quick and dirty usability scale. In: Jordan, P.W., Thomas, B., Weerdmeester, B.A., McClelland, I.L. (eds.) Usability Evaluation in Industry. Taylor and Francois, London (1996)
8. Kirakowski, J., Corbett, M.: SUMI: the software usability measurement inventory. Br. J. Educ. Technol. **24**, 210–212 (1993)
9. Chin, J.P., Diehl, V.A., Norman, K.L.: Development of an instrument for measuring user satisfaction of the human-computer interface. In: Proceedings of the ACM Conference on Human Factors in Computing Systems. pp. 213–218. ACM Press, New York (1988)
10. Lee, J.D., See, K.A.: Trust in automation: designing for appropriate reliance. Hum. Factors **46**, 50–80 (2004)
11. Sarter, N.B., Mumaw, R.D., Wickens, C.D.: Pilots' monitoring strategies and performance on automated flight decks: an empirical study combining behavioral and eye-tracking data. Hum. Factors **49**, 347–357 (2007)
12. Parasuraman, R., Manzey, D.H.: Complacency and bias in human use of automation: an attentional integration. Hum. Factors **52**, 381–410 (2010)

13. Miwa, K., Terai, H.: Theoretical investigation on disuse atrophy resulting from computer support for cognitive tasks. In: Harris, D. (ed.) EPCE 2014. LNCS, vol. 8532, pp. 244–254. Springer, Heidelberg (2014)
14. Maehigashi, A., Miwa, K., Terai, H., Kojima, K., Morita, J.: Experimental investigation of calibration and resolution in human-automation system interaction. IEICE Trans. Fund. Electron. Commun. Comput. Sci. **E96–A**, 1625–1636 (2013)

Validating a Quality Perception Model for Image Compression: The Subjective Evaluation of the Cogisen's Image Compression Plug-in

Maria Laura Mele[1,2,3(✉)], Damon Millar[3], and Christiaan Erik Rijnders[3]

[1] Department of Philosophy, Social and Human Sciences and Education, University of Perugia, Perugia, Italy
marialaura.mele@gmail.com

[2] ECONA, Interuniversity Centre for Research on Cognitive Processing in Natural and Artificial Systems, Sapienza University of Rome, Rome, Italy
marialaura@cogisen.com

[3] COGISEN Engineering Company, Rome, Italy
{damon,chris}@cogisen.com

Abstract. User experience has a fundamental role in determining the effectiveness of image compression methods. This work presents the subjective evaluation of a new compression plug-in for current compression formats developed by Cogisen. The quality of image compression methods is often evaluated by objective metrics based on subjective quality datasets, rather than by using subjective quality evaluation tests. Cogisen's compression method follows an adaptive compression process that evaluates the saliency of any image and calculates the level of compression beyond which viewers shall be aware of image quality degradation. The Single Stimulus Continuous Quality Scale method was used to conduct the subjective quality evaluation of image compression. Pictures compressed by the Facebook Mobile lossy JPEG compression and by the Cogisen plug-in integrated in the Facebook Mobile compression settings were used. The results of the user quality evaluation of pictures show about a 45 % compression improvement, with no loss in perceived image quality, for pictures compressed by the Cogisen plug-in compared to jpeg pictures as compressed by Facebook Mobile.

Keywords: Image compression methods · Image quality assessment · Subjective evaluation methods

1 Introduction

The increase of multimedia applications such as information or entertainment systems is leading the industry to find new solutions related to image storage capacity and transmission bandwidth requirements, especially for smartphones and other mobile technologies. Over the last years, many methods for image compression have been proposed, aiming at efficiently reducing image file size without compromising image quality or changing image format. The compression methods proposed so far in the literature are

M. Kurosu (Ed.): HCI 2016, Part I, LNCS 9731, pp. 350–359, 2016.
DOI: 10.1007/978-3-319-39510-4_33

often based on metrics for image quality measures such as Multi-scale Structural Similarity (MS-SSIM), Mean Square Error (MSE), Peak Signal to Noise Ratio (PSNR), Structural Similarity (SSIM) [1]. Objective measures such as these evaluate the difference between the absolute quality of a distorted picture and a reference picture, therefore, they are fast, easily repeatable and do not require high human resources. However they do not always predict subjective ratings provided by human evaluators in a reliable way [1, 2]. Subjective quality evaluation is still a key process in image or video compression methods because low perceived quality contributes directly to a poor user experience [3, 4].

This paper shows the subjective evaluation of a new compression plug-in for current compression formats. The plug-in has been developed by an engineering company called Cogisen (www.cogisen.com). It follows an adaptive compression process that is able to evaluate the visual saliency of the image and also provide a quality perception model that is able to quickly calculate at which amount of compression a user will perceive a reduction in image quality. In this manner with the quality perception threshold the compression adapts differently for each image. The compression model proposed by Cogisen has been created with a deep learning platform, with algorithms that are able to capture processes that are highly nonlinear, sparse and have a high noise-to-signal. Since the Cogisen filter has no effect on compatibility with other main compression models, using the plug-in the resultant images can be made fully compliant with all formats. Moreover, the solution has a minimal impact on mobile processor usage and already allows for an adaptive JPEG solution, which is the most used image compression standard. The Cogisen compression plug-in does not use any mathematical correlation function between the aforementioned compression quality metrics for its quality perception model. For this reason the subjective evaluation and validation of the Cogisen quality perception model was fundamental.

This work describes the evaluation of the subjective quality perception of pictures compressed separately by the Facebook Mobile and the Cogisen plug-in integrated in the Facebook Mobile compression settings.

2 Methodology

The main aim of this work was to assess the user experience of the perceived quality of color images compressed by the Cogisen's compression plug-in. The assessment procedure was first validated by using a subjective quality dataset (Phase I) and then applied to evaluate the experimental stimuli (Phase II).

Phase I. Implementation and validation of a web-based image quality assessment method. In the first phase of this work, we focused on the design process and the validation of a web-based image quality evaluation tool using a Single Stimulus method. We used an existing image database provided with previously validated subjective quality scores. The subjective data obtained with the new tool was compared to subjective data provided by the reference database.

Phase II. Subjective evaluation of pictures compressed by the Cogisen plug-in. The second phase of this work consists of the subjective evaluation of two kind of compressed color images: (1) pictures compressed by the Facebook Mobile application and (2) pictures compressed by the Cogisen plug-in integrated in the Facebook Mobile compression settings. Both groups of experimental images were compared to the quality scores assigned to corresponding high quality reference pictures. Three compression amounts were used in three different testing sessions: 15 % compression, 30 % compression, and 45 % compression.

3 Phase I. Implementation and Validation of a Web-Based Image Quality Assessment Method

This section describes the design process and the validation of a web-based image quality evaluation tool. We selected a public test image library called LIVE Image Quality Assessment database[1] [5]. In order to build an image quality evaluation tool based on the SurveyGizmo platform[2], we used the same methodology that was used to obtain the image quality scores that accompany the chosen database. The LIVE subjective scores were then compared to the subjective scores obtained with the new testing procedure. The purpose of validation testing is to ensure that the chosen method of test application using a crowdsourcing web platform (SurveyGizmo), produced reliable subjective image quality scores that were consistent with the reference scores obtained with traditional methods of recruiting and test administration, as for the LIVE image dataset.

3.1 Material: Source Database

As reference image set, we selected the LIVE Image Quality database because (1) it offers one the largest subjective image quality databases in the literature; and (2) it has been evaluated by a subjective quality assessment study using a Single Stimulus method, which is the most natural image quality assessment method for home viewing conditions [6]. The LIVE database is based on twenty-nine high-resolution color images, which are compressed in different image distortion types, including JPEG compression [6]. Since for the LIVE test each subject evaluated both the distorted and reference images in each session, the authors calculated a quality difference score for all distorted images and for all subjects. The LIVE experiments were conducted using a web-based interface showing the image to be ranked using a Java scale-and-slider applet for assigning a quality score. The subjective quality DMOS values obtained during the assessment of the LIVE database are publicly available.

In order to create a test model for Cogisen's web-based subjective tests, efforts were made to replicate the LIVE test methodology. A selection of both reference high quality and JPEG distorted images was taken from the LIVE database and used to set up a web-based image quality evaluation test.

1 http://live.ece.utexas.edu/research/quality/subjective.htm (Last access: 25 January 2016).
2 http://www.surveygizmo.com (Last access: 25 January 2016).

3.2 Method

In Single Stimulus (SS) method, a single image or sequence of images is presented and the observer assigns a score to the presentation. This method is generally used as an alternative to the Double Stimulus (DS) method, which asks observers to assess two simultaneously shown versions of each test picture. It was adopted the Single Stimulus Continuous Quality Scale (SSCQS) method [7] instead of a DS method because the former replicates the single stimulus home viewing conditions.

The SSCQS allows continuous measurement of the subjective quality of images, with subjects viewing the material once without a source reference. The technique presents one picture at a time to the viewer. The test pictures or sequences are presented only once in the test session. An example of a high quality image is presented only once at the beginning of the test so the users know what a high quality image looks like and are able to frame their expectation. The reference images are randomly shown during the test as a control condition. At the beginning of the first sessions some stabilization sequences (also called "dummy" sequences) are introduced to stabilize the user's opinion. The sequence presentations are randomized to ensure that the same picture is not presented twice in succession. Observers evaluate the quality of each image using a grading scale as the presentation of each trial ends.

3.3 Procedure

At the beginning of the test, a preliminary questionnaire asks participants' age, gender, visual acuity, contrast sensitivity, color vision, general health conditions, and prior experience with video display systems or devices. Participants are also asked to check the physical dimensions of their display and to regulate it to the maximum brightness. Other information such as operating system, browser and country are directly collected by the web service. If participants meet requirements—i.e., no vision impairments, no desktop device less than 13-inches wide, maximum brightness on—a new page with test instructions is shown before the test begins. The image quality evaluation test is implemented through a web-based platform called SurveGizmo. The test has been translated into both Italian and English to accommodate the participants' mother language.

The presentation of each image lasted 7 s. After that, a quality scale field lasting at least 3 s is shown. The quality scale that was used consisted of integers in the range 1–100. The scale was marked numerically and divided into three equal portions, which were labeled with adjectives: "Bad", "Fair", and "Excellent". Subjects were asked to report their assessment of quality by dragging the slider on the quality scale. The position of the slider was automatically reset after each evaluation.

Following ITU-R BT.500-8 [7], the test consists of 3 different trial sequences: a training sequence (4 trials), a stabilization (also called "dummy") sequence (5 trials) and a testing sequence (25 trials). The training trials was presented only once per subject at the very beginning of the test. The stabilization trial was presented immediately before the test session without any noticeable interruption to the subjects. The stabilization phase consists of pictures ensuring coverage of the full quality range to help observers in stabilizing their opinion. In accordance with the ITU-R standard, the data issued during the stabilization phase is not taken into account in the results of the test, and the stabilization pictures do not appear during the test session.

The trial position in each sequence was randomized to avoid showing the same picture one after the other. The whole session is designed to last no longer than 15 min to avoid errors due to participants' fatigue and loss of attention.

3.4 Subjects

The subjective test was carried out in the participants' home conditions via the Survey-Gizmo web platform. In total, 43 volunteers (44.2 % males, mean age = 35 years old, Italian speakers = 39, English speakers = 4), 23 non-expert viewers (53.3 % males, mean age = 35.4) and 20 expert users (34.7 % males, mean age = 34.5) participated in the study. The validation test was completed between June 17, 2015 and June 20, 2015. A post-screening of the subjective test scores was conducted prior to conducting the data analysis. For each viewer it was first checked that they met the preliminary requirements. The data from 19 participants was discarded from the subjective data set. The final screened subjective data set included scores from a total of 24 viewers.

3.5 Results

Opinion Scores. Mean opinion score (MOS): Opinion scores were integers in the range 1–100. The mean opinion scores (MOS) were calculated for each subject (MOS = 53.3). The raw opinion scores were converted to difference mean opinion score (DMOS):

$$dij = riref(j) - rij$$

where *rij* is the raw score for the *i*-th subject and *j*-th image, and *riref(j)* denotes the raw quality score assigned by the *i*-th subject to the reference image corresponding to the *j*-th distorted image [5, p. 4]. The Difference Mean Opinion Scores (DMOS) were obtained by calculating the difference between the MOS of reference images and the MOS of the related compressed images (DMOS = 18.82).

Scale Assessment. The Cronbach's alpha of opinion scores was calculated in order to evaluate the internal consistency measure on the 34 trials composing the whole experimental session. An index of reliability Alpha = 0.919 (Cronbach's Alpha Based on Standardized Items = 0.924) was obtained.

Comparison Between Subjective Scores. The Pearson linear correlation was calculated between LIVE DMOS and the Test DMOS for measuring prediction accuracy. Results show a coefficient R = 0.541; p = 0.005.

Comparison within Subjects. The effect of the participants' expertise on their performance was investigated using the One-way Analysis of Variance (ANOVA). Results show no effect of expertise on difference mean opinion scores ($F(1,23) = 0.398$; $p > 0.05$).

3.6 Discussion

The analysis of the internal consistency of the proposed subjective evaluation procedure indicates an excellent internal consistency within the evaluation test. Moreover, the subjective quality score comparisons given by 24 subjects to 25 images strongly correlate with the corresponding difference mean opinion scores provided by the LIVE database, with no significant difference between expert and non-expert participants. Therefore, since the subjective image quality assessment tool that was developed is internally consistent, it can be used as a basis model for evaluating the perceived quality of images compressed by the Cogisen method.

4 Phase II. Subjective Evaluation of Pictures Compressed by the Cogisen Plug-in

This section describes subjective tests aimed at evaluating the participants' quality perception of two sets of compressed images: (i) pictures compressed by Facebook Mobile; and (ii) pictures compressed by the Cogisen plug-in integrated in the Facebook Mobile compression settings. Three tests – Test 1, Test 2 and Test 3 – were conducted to respectively evaluate the 15 %, the 30 %, and the 45 % gain of the Cogisen plug-in over the Facebook Mobile compression amount. Participants were recruited through the Prolific Academic platform[3], which is a crowdsourcing platform for psychological research. Participants who completed the whole test were rewarded with a £1.50 payment.

4.1 Material

The images used for all three tests were obtained from high quality pictures selected by the Colourlab Image Database: Image Quality (CIDIQ)[4] [8]. The CIDIQ has 23 images, with varying attributes including hue, saturation, lightness and contrast. The resolution of all images is 800 pixels by 800 pixels.

Fourteen reference stimuli were selected from a group of 23 high-quality pictures. Each picture was compressed by Facebook Mobile and then additionally compressed by the Cogisen plug-in. Each testing session consisted of 8 high-quality reference images, 8 Facebook Mobile compressed pictures and 8 Cogisen compressed pictures. Each test consisted of a total of 37 trials: 4 trials for the testing sequence, 5 trials for the dummy sequence, 24 images for the testing session, and 4 attention checks, i.e., low quality compressed pictures placed twice into the test to check participants' attention level. If participants assigned a significantly different rating to the same attentional picture, they were excluded from data analysis. The sequence presentation was randomized to avoid clustering of the same pictures.

3 http://prolific.ac (Last access: 25 January 2016).

4 www.colourlab.no/cid (Last access: 25 January 2016).

4.2 Procedure

Participants are asked to answer a preliminary questionnaire and follow setting requirements as described in Sect. 3.3. The three tests consisted of assigning a quality rating to pictures by dragging the slider on a 1–100 quality scale, using the same methodology that was designed and validated in Phase I.

4.3 Subjects

Test 1: 15 % Gain Over Facebook Mobile. In Test 1 there were 29 volunteers (mean age = 36.6 years old, 53.3 % males, Italian speakers = 26, English speakers = 3), 16 non-expert viewers (mean age = 33.3, 38.8 % males) and 13 expert users (mean age = 34.6, 69.2 % males) who took part in the subjective tests. All the tests were completed in a single session between June 30, 2015 and July 6, 2015. The post-screening of the subjective test scores consisted of determining if the participants met the preliminary requirements (no vision impairments, only personal computers, maximum brightness on). Viewers who did not correctly pass the training session were discarded. Nine participants' data sets were deleted from the subjective database. Finally, the screened subjective database included the scores provided by a total of 20 subjects.

Test 2: 30 % Gain Over Facebook Mobile. In Test 2, 37 subjects (mean age = 27 years old, 64.8 % male, 100 % English speakers), 31 non-expert viewers (mean age = 27.2, 64.5 % male) and 5 expert users (mean age = 26.4, 80 % male) took part in the tests. All the tests were completed in a single session in October 07, 2015. The screened subjective database included the scores provided by a total of 33 subjects, mean age = 26.5 years old, 69.7 % male, 48.4 % indoor with natural lights; 51.6 % indoor with artificial lights). Four subjects were excluded before data analysis because they did not pass the preliminary requirements. Since 2 outliers were excluded after a descriptive analysis, results refer to 31 subjects' data.

Test 3: 45 % Gain Over Facebook Mobile. Thirty-five subjects (mean age = 28.5 years old, 45.7 % males, 100 % English speakers), 32 non-expert viewers (mean age = 28.2, 46.8 % males) and 3 expert users (mean age = 26.7, 33.3 % males) took part in the tests. All the tests were completed in a single session in October 27, 2015. The screened subjective database included the scores provided by a total of 31 subjects, mean age = 29 years old, 41.9 % males, 45.2 % in-door with natural lights; 54.8 % indoor with artificial lights). Since 4 outliers were excluded after the descriptive analysis, results of Test 3 refer to 27 subjects' data.

4.4 Results

Opinion Scores. The mean opinion scores (MOS) were calculated for each subject. The Difference Mean Opinion Scores (DMOS) were obtained by calculating the difference between the MOS of reference images and the MOS of the related processed images (Table 1).

Table 1. Subjects' mean opinion scores and difference mean opinion scores

	TEST 1: 15 % gain	TEST 2: 30 % gain	TEST 3: 45 % gain
MOS	Tot = 75.81	Tot = 72.51	Tot = 74.94
	Cogisen = 74.04	Cogisen = 72.62	Cogisen = 75.03
	Facebook M = 75.16	Facebook M = 72.41	Facebook M = 74.35
DMOS	Tot = 3.62	Tot = 5.09	Tot = 3.43
	Cogisen = 4.18	Cogisen = 4.98	Cogisen = 2.91
	Facebook M = 3.06	Facebook M = 5.19	Facebook M = 3.94

Cogisen Pictures Compared to Facebook Mobile Pictures: Difference Mean Opinion Scores. The Pearson linear correlation was calculated between the DMOS assigned to Cogisen compressed stimuli and the DMOS assigned to Facebook Mobile compressed stimuli. Results show high correlation coefficients, which means that the Cogisen pictures are greatly correlated with the Facebook Mobile pictures (Test 1: $R = 0.944$; $p = 0.000$; Test 2: $R = 0.943$; $p = 0.000$; Test 3: $R = 0.845$; $p = 0.000$).

Within Subjects Comparisons. For each test, the effects of (i) compression level (ii) expertise (iii) lighting condition on the participants' performance, and of (iv) position of trials into the testing sequence were investigated.

Test 1: 15 % gain over Facebook Mobile

i. *Compression level effect.* The repeated measures ANOVA shows no significant difference in DMOS assigned to Cogisen compressed stimuli compared to the DMOS assigned to Facebook Mobile compressed stimuli ($F(1,19) = 3.551$; $p > 0.05$).
ii. *Expertise effect.* The one-way ANOVA shows no effect of expertise on difference mean opinion scores ($F(1,19) = 0.238$; $p > 0.05$).
iii. *Lighting condition effect.* The one-way ANOVA shows no significant difference in the DMOS assigned in four different lighting conditions (indoors with natural lights, indoors with artificial lights, outdoors with natural lights, outdoors with artificial lights), $F(2,17) = 0.712$; $p > 0.05$.

Test 2: 30 % gain over Facebook Mobile

i. Compression level effect. The repeated measures ANOVA shows a significant difference in DMOS assigned to Cogisen compressed stimuli compared to the DMOS assigned to Facebook Mobile com-pressed stimuli ($F(1, 30) = 0.067$; $p > 0.05$).
ii. Expertise effect. The one-way ANOVA shows no effect of expertise on difference mean opinion scores ($F(1,30) = 0.699$; $p > 0.05$).

iii. Lighting condition effect. The one-way ANOVA shows no significant difference in the DMOS assigned in two different lighting conditions (indoors with natural lights, indoors with artificial lights), ($F(1,30) = 1.36$; $p > 0.05$).
iv. Position effect. In test 2 and 3, it was investigated if the participants' performance has been influenced by the position of the pictures into the testing sequence. Multiple linear regression analysis showed that the position of the stimuli on the test was not able to predict the subjects' answers ($R^2 = 0.151$, $F(1,23) = 0.3.89$, $p > 0.05$; $\beta = -0.388$, $p > 0.05$). Therefore, no differences were found between the answers given in the first half of the study and those assigned in the second half.

Test 3: 45 % gain over Facebook Mobile

i. Compression level effect. The repeated measures ANOVA shows no significant difference in DMOS assigned to Cogisen pictures compared to the DMOS assigned to Facebook Mobile pictures (Wilks' lambda = $F(1, 26) = 2.476$; $p > 0.05$).
ii. Expertise effect. The one-way ANOVA shows no effect of expertise on difference mean opinion scores ($F(1,26) = 1.321$; $p > 0.05$).
iii. Lighting condition effect. The one-way ANOVA shows no significant difference in the DMOS as-signed in two different lighting conditions (indoors with natural lights, indoors with artificial lights), ($F(1,26) = 0.011$; $p > 0.05$).
iv. Position effect. It was investigated the role of trials position into the test following the same methodology as Test 2. Multiple linear regression analysis showed that the position of the stimuli on the test was not able to predict the subjects' answers ($R^2 = 0.039$, $F(1,23) = 0.885$; $p > 0.05$; $\beta = -0.197$; $p > 0.05$).

5 Discussion

No significant difference was found between the opinion scores assigned to Cogisen pictures compared to those assigned to Facebook Mobile pictures, meaning that the difference mean opinion scores assigned to Cogisen pictures were not significantly higher than those assigned to JPEG stimuli. No significant effects of expertise, lighting conditions and stimuli position were found on the image quality assessment performance. Table 2 shows a summary of main results.

Table 2. Summary of the main results obtained in Test 1, 2 and 3

Test	Compression method	DMOS	Std. dev.	N. subj.	Correlation	DMOS difference
(1)	Cogisen	4.18	3.52	20	R = 0.955; p = 000	$F(1,19) = 3.551$; $p > 0.05$
	FB mobile	3.06	3.49			
(2)	Cogisen	4.98	5.07	31	R = 0.867; p = 000	$F(1,30) = 0.067$; $p > 0.05$
	FB mobile	5.19	4.86			
(3)	Cogisen	2.91	2.32	27	R = 0.845; p = .000	$F(1,26) = 2.476$; $p > 0.05$
	FB mobile	3.94	2.93			

6 Conclusion

In this work, it was evaluated the subjective quality perception of pictures compressed by a new plug-in developed by Cogisen which can be integrated into the compression settings of mobile applications such as Facebook Mobile. Three different groups of viewers were asked to assess the quality of both images compressed by the Cogisen plug-in and pictures compressed with the Facebook Mobile application. Since subjective evaluation does not refer to absolute values, participants were asked to assess the quality of high quality reference pictures randomly shown during the test. The experimental design followed the Single Stimulus Continuous Quality Scale (SSCQS) method. The tests were administered by means of a web-platform that was validated by comparing results with subjective data obtained with a traditional method. Findings highlight that web-based solutions can be as reliable as traditional methods for both recruiting participants and administering tests, thus improving efficiency and inexpensiveness of collecting data. The results of this study show that the Cogisen compression plug-in can be applied to JPEG compressed images with no significant impact on the perceived quality up to a gain of 45 % file size reduction compared to Facebook Mobile. This means that the Cogisen quality perception model allows for immediate compression gains by highly reducing transmission bandwidth and storage requirements for mobile systems and, at the same time, avoiding a poor user experience. The next step is to also evaluate the Cogisen plug-in for video compression by applying methods provided by International Recommendations for Subjective Video Quality Assessment [7]. The question of how users subjectively perceive and evaluate the quality of compressed videos is a priority for further investigation.

References

1. Mohammadi, P., Ebrahimi-Moghadam, A., Shirani, S.: Subjective and objective quality assessment of image: a survey. (2014). arXiv preprint arXiv:1406.7799
2. Joshi, M.A., Raval, M.S., Dandawate, Y.H., Joshi, K.R., Metkar, S.P.: Image and Video Compression: Fundamentals, Techniques, and Applications. CRC Press, Boca Raton (2014)
3. Borsci, S., Kurosu, M., Federici, S., Mele, M.L.: Computer Systems Experiences of Users with and without Disabilities: An Evaluation Guide for Professionals. CRC Press, Boca Raton (2013)
4. Borsci, S., Kurosu, M., Federici, S., Mele, M.L.: Systemic User Experience. In: Federici, S., Scherer, M.J. (eds.) Assistive Technology Assessment Handbook, pp. 337–359. CRC Press, Boca Raton (2012)
5. Winkler, S.: Analysis of public image and video databases for quality assessment. IEEE J. Sel. Top. Sig. Process. **6**(6), 616–625 (2012)
6. Sheikh, H.R., Sabir, M.F., Bovik, A.C.: A statistical evaluation of recent full reference quality assessment algorithms. IEEE Trans. Image Process. **15**(11), 3440–3451 (2006)
7. Recommendation, I. T. U. R. B. T.: 500-11: Methodology for the Subjective Assessment of the Quality of Television Pictures, Recommendation ITU-R BT, 500-11. ITU Telecom, Standardization Sector of ITU (2002)
8. Liu, Xinwei, Pedersen, Marius, Hardeberg, Jon Yngve: CID: IQ – a new image quality database. In: Elmoataz, Abderrahim, Lezoray, Olivier, Nouboud, Fathallah, Mammass, Driss (eds.) ICISP 2014. LNCS, vol. 8509, pp. 193–202. Springer, Heidelberg (2014)

Can I Reach that? An Affordance Based Metric of Human-Sensor-Robot System Effectiveness

Taylor Murphy(✉) and Alexander M. Morison

Department of Industrial System Engineering, Ohio State University, Columbus, USA
{murphy.1018,morison.6}@osu.edu

Abstract. A person's ability to perceive and act fluently in a remote environment through teleoperation of a robotic platform is clearly limited when compared to acting directly in an immediate environment. Despite the contrast between teleoperation and direct action, there are few metrics in the human robot interaction literature that are sensitive to these differences. Existing human-robot assessment studies rely on observational accounts and studies that simulate domain tasks, then applying ad hoc metrics to assess performance. These metrics are typically properties of the task like completion time, number of targets found, and operator mental workload. This study introduces a formal method and metric based on the perception of affordances. The study assesses a human-robot systems ability to perceive the reachability of an object using a mechanical arm. Affordance-based metrics are a new tool to quantify the effectiveness of different teleoperated sensor-robot systems designs.

Keywords: Human-Robot interaction · Psychometrics · Psychophysics · Visual perception · Remote perception · Affordance · Human-sensor-robot system · Ecological perception · Teleoperation · Reachability · Simulation

1 Introduction

What constitutes a sensor-robot system is expanding. There are a growing number and variety of systems that allow people to see and act at a distance [1]. Despite the dizzying pace of innovation and deployment of these human-sensor-robot systems, there are few formally derived metrics to facilitate comparison across designs [2]. Researchers have observed the introduction of teleoperated sensor-robot systems in many different work domains [3]. The observations from these studies can be organized into three basic findings [1]:

1. Independent of sensor platform type, practitioners have difficulty understanding and acting in a remote environment once their platform has left their line of sight. They often must stop to consider whether their platform is capable of performing an action in its surrounding environment.
2. In response to this difficulty practitioners develop ad hoc operating procedures or kludges, through trial and error to help them carry out their goals. Practitioners adapt their behavior to fill shortcomings in the platform's design.

M. Kurosu (Ed.): HCI 2016, Part I, LNCS 9731, pp. 360–371, 2016.
DOI: 10.1007/978-3-319-39510-4_34

3. While the kludges operators create are often effective, they are slow, error prone, and require a high degree of concentration to execute.

These findings suggest that operators are unable to perceive the relationship between the sensor-robot platform and the environment when operating at a distance. The uncertainty that operators experience while teleoperating a sensor-robot platform arises from two sources. First, uncertainty grows from a limited ability to understand the layout of the robot's environment through sensors. Second, operators are unable to perceive the action capability of the robot through the robot's sensor feeds. Judgments such as, what is traversable? what is reachable? or what is passable? are effortful and slow, even in ideal visual environments.

In perceptual psychology the concept of a fit between an actor's capability and the surrounding environment is called an affordance. Traversability, reachability, passability are all examples of affordances. The observed difficulties in teleoperation can be framed in terms of difficulties perceiving affordances through the sensor system given current platform designs. Measuring a human-sensor system's ability to perceive affordances should be a useful and diagnostic metric to compare the effectiveness of different platform designs.

The theory of affordances in Ecological Perception holds that organisms understand their physical surroundings in part by how the scale of that environment fits their body's own capabilities [4]. For example, when trying to reach for an object you do not think about whether your arm can reach it. You immediately perceive the reachability of the object. Psychologists have documented humans' ability to perceive the affordances around them and have created well-accepted experimental methods and measures [5–7]. The current study adapts a method from the psychophysics and perception literature [8] to measure a human-robot system's ability to perceive an object's reachability under several different visual conditions representative of current and proposed sensor-robot systems.

Study participants were presented with a camera feed from a simulated explosive ordinance disposal robot and asked whether or not the mechanical arm attached to the robot's chassis could reach a target object. Using a within subjects design, participants were exposed to three conditions. Each condition presented different visual cues roughly simulating different types of operating environment. The data was analyzed by computing psychometric functions for each of the three conditions and using them to compare psychophysical performance across the three conditions.

2 Related Work

The following section will outline previous work on several topics, including previous studies measuring teleoperated sensor-robot system performance, the link between teleoperation and ecological perception, and how the perception of affordances is measured in the ecological perception literature.

2.1 Research on Robotic System Effectiveness

Existing research on the effectiveness of teleoperated systems can be broken into two large categories: observational field studies and staged world studies. Robotics field studies describe the practicalities of operating these platforms outside of the lab. The work of [9] represents the first time Unmanned Ground Vehicles (UGV) were deployed for an Urban Search and Rescue task in the field. This extensive report describes the effectiveness of the physical platforms in the difficult, broken terrain of the collapsed World Trade Center. In addition the report details the challenges operators had in controlling the platform and interacting with other groups of stakeholders. One of the co-authors, Dr. Robin Murphy, has built a large corpus of studies examining the challenges associated with operating robotic platforms in the field [3].

Staged world studies bring robotic platforms into the laboratory, adding a layer of control not available in the field. The National Institute of Standards and Technology (NIST) conducted several studies of unmanned ground vehicle effectiveness in an attempt to establish common metrics for their performance. These studies generally involve expert operators using a teleoperated robot to navigate obstacle courses of varying fidelity. These operators are tasked with finding targets in the environment such as simulated disaster victims [10]. Human-robot performance is gauged by metrics like task completion time, number of targets found, and operator mental workload.

One staged world study asked operators to use robotic platforms outfitted with a manipulator arm to pick up a cylinder and place it into a similarly sized aperture such that the cylinder would not fall back out. While the results of the study were not published, the authors observed expert operators struggling with this simple task. Operators would often spend minutes not moving the manipulator arm, but attempting to understand the position of the arm relative to the surrounding environment (see Fig. 1).

Fig. 1. Operator using a robotic platform with manipulator arm to pick up a cylinder and place it into a similarly sized aperture such that the cylinder would not fall back out in NIST test case. Performance was very poor in general and virtually impossible when the teleoperator could not directly see the robot arm. Note: the two images shown here are of two different robotic platforms.

None of the existing human-robot interaction metrics capture the difficulties observed in teleoperated sensor-robot systems. Perceiving a remote environment through sensors on robotic platforms challenges the teleoperator. Measuring these challenges reveals why current designs are limited and suggests new design directions.

2.2 A Perceptual Model of Human-Sensor System Interaction

The work of [1] has proposed shifting the way we think of teleoperated systems. Rather than designing a platform as an independent technological artifact, one can think of the robot as a stand in for a human operator's own perceptual system in a remote environment. Thus the platform's primary purpose becomes supporting the human's ability to perceive the remote environment as quickly and effortlessly as possible. Any other goals, such as the physical manipulation of, or movement through, the remote environment can only be effective and efficient once this is accomplished. Reframing teleoperated systems as an extended perception opens up new design directions based on how humans perceive their immediate surroundings, and new ways to measure a design's effectiveness.

One relevant perspective on visual perception is Gibson's theory of Ecological Perception [11]. Within Ecological Perception the concept of an affordance describes the fit between the capabilities of an actor and the constraints of the surrounding environment. The theory of affordances also provides a solid theoretical and methodological foundation to anchor the study of human-sensor-robot system perception. Gibson posits that visually guided action in the world requires an understanding of the perceived match between the properties in the environment and the known properties of the acting system, as described by [4, 12]. Organisms navigating an environment apprehend these affordances continuously, accessing perceptually defined attributes of the environment in relation to their own capabilities.

The work of [6] explores the affordance of passability, comparing a participant's shoulder width to the width of an aperture. Participants were highly proficient in judging not the absolute width of the aperture, but the relative fit between their own shoulder width and the width of the aperture. Similarly, several studies have measured the ability of participants to discriminate reachable objects from unreachable objects [7]. These studies show that the participants are quite accurate in making a perceptual judgment about the reachability of an object, but performance begins to degrade when participants are given time to ruminate about the object's distance and its relation to arm length [5].

Many modern studies in the psychometric literature, and specifically the affordance literature, use a psychometric function as a compact was way to describe a participant's performance. The function relates the proportion of positive responses to a stimulus level, with the slope of the function represents the participant's precision and the midpoint, or 50 % point, represents the participant's accuracy [13]. Other parameters can also be estimated including the participant's guessing, or lapse, rate.

2.3 Measuring Affordances in Human-Sensor Systems

Several recent studies have investigated the ability of robotic system operators to perceive affordances in a remote environment. These studies both examined the perception of an aperture's passability, building on the work of [6]. The work of [14] examined the differences in passability perception when operating a platform inside and outside line of sight. Unsurprisingly, participants were more accurate and consistent when operating the platform within line of sight. Additionally, [14] investigated the effects of camera height on passability perception, finding that both camera height and distance to an aperture effected participants' perception of passability.

Inspired by the work of [6, 9, 15] investigated how difficulties in perception can contribute to Murphy's observation that platforms would frequently become stuck in apertures during urban search and rescue. Results showed that comparing solely the width of the platform to the width of the aperture was insufficient to ensure good driving performance. Rather, consistent with [6], the operator needed compare the aperture to the width of the platform plus a safety margin.

3 Experiment

The current study examined participants' ability to perceive the reachability of a target at different distances from a virtual robotic platform featuring a mechanical arm. During each trial participants were shown a feed from the robot's camera and responded with a binary reachable/unreachable answer in an adaptive psychophysical procedure.

3.1 Participants

Twelve participants were recruited to participate in the study, ten males and two female. Each participant attended three 45–60 min data collection sessions within the space of a week. All participants were between 24 and 28 years old and were screened for experience with video games or other interaction with 3D virtual environments (e.g. CAD software).

3.2 Design

The current study used a within subjects design, exposing all participants to three different conditions. The ordering of these conditions was counterbalanced between participants to counter any learning effects. Each condition contained a different number of visual cues to depth. The conditions were labeled low, medium, and high.

The low condition contained only sparse visual cues, including target size, target position within the camera's field of view, and shading. The target object had a solid color with no texture applied. This condition was created to loosely mimic operating a sensor platform underwater, where there is no consistent horizon, indirect lighting and few useful cues to the scale of objects. The medium condition added a ground plane to the environment, providing a landmark with which to judge the height of the target. The ground plane included a texture of random noise. The visual cues in the medium condition resembled a deconstructed environment like a collapsed building, where there is no direct lighting and few useful landmarks. The high condition added a texture to the target and direct lighting, which resulted in a shadow being cast by the target and the mechanical arm. This high condition most closely mimicked operating a robotic platform outdoors in direct sunlight (see Fig. 2).

Fig. 2. A) Three different viewing conditions used in the study based on actual experiences in rescue robotics. B) The robot-sensor in the simulated environment for the reachability task.

In order to remove any confounding effects on distance perception, many aspects of the virtual environment were randomly varied from trial to trial. These aspects included target height above the ground plane, target diameter, target color, orientation of the direct light source, ground plane texture scale and orientation, and the configuration of the mechanical arm. The mechanical arm required additional constraints because it provided an important landmark from which to judge reachability. In order to eliminate the arm as a confound it was important not only to keep it in view for each trial, but to also have it fill roughly the same percentage of the sensor feed. To achieve this consistency 20 arm configurations were predefined prior to the study, which were then selected at random at the beginning of each trial.

In all conditions the distance of the target from the base of the robotic platform was systematically varied using a weighted and transformed staircase procedure [16, 17]. This adaptive method changes the stimulus strength based on the participant's response from the preceding trial. Over numerous trials, the algorithm converges on a threshold along the participant's psychometric function, for example the point at which the participant responds that the target object is reachable 70 % of the time. This point is determined by the algorithm's up/down rule and the weighted distance the target is moved. The up/down rule determines how many consecutive responses must be the same before the target distance or stimulus strength is changed. Each time a participant's answer changes from reachable to unreachable, or unreachable to reachable, the target distance is recorded as a reversal point. The algorithm terminates once it records 18 reversals [17]. During analysis, these reversal points are averaged together to estimate the predetermined threshold point.

While this method has proven accurate at estimating the position of a psychometric function [16] it does not estimate the slope - a measure of a participant's precision. In order to compare the precision between conditions without a slope value, the current study estimated two thresholds on each participant's psychometric function and took the difference. To accomplish this, staircase algorithms were run in interleaved pairs, each pair consisting of one algorithm using a 3:1 up/down rule and another using a 1:3 rule. The use of inverse up/down rules resulted in two points symmetrical around the function's 50 % point, the perceived boundary between what is reachable and unreachable.

3.3 Apparatus

The current study was conducted using a MacBook Pro laptop as a computer workstation for the participant. The screen measured 19 inches on the diagonal, and used a resolution of 1920 × 1080. Participants gave input using a standard three-button mouse. Each participant was run in a area isolating them from outside stimuli.

The testing software was built using a 3D videogame authoring engine, Unity 3D. This engine handled the rendering of the 3D environment and the recording of test data. The software was engineered to maintain a rate of 60 frames per second or higher.

Virtual Robotic Platform. The virtual robotic platform used in the study simulates the Talon built by QinetiQ North America. The platform featured a mechanical arm with four controllable servomotors. The camera was positioned on a stalk above, behind, and slightly to the left of the mechanical arm. The orientation of the camera was such that the chassis of the robot was visible at the bottom of the feed.

3.4 Procedure

Each participant was involved in three data collection sessions. Each session covered one experimental condition, and took approximately 45 min to an hour. Each session took place on a separate day, with all sessions occurring within a seven-day period.

Each session consisted of three phases: familiarization, training, and data collection. The familiarization phase helped the participant become familiar with the capabilities of the mechanical arm by asking participants to use the arm to 'touch' a target object with the mechanical arm's end effector. The familiarization phase provided scaffolding for the participants by structuring which servos could be controlled from trial to trial. The first trial restricted control to a single servo, teaching the participant how to use the interface. The familiarization scaffolding continues during the next three trials where during each of these trials an additional servo. At the end of these four trials all four servos are unlocked. All subsequent trials required the participant to manipulate all four servos in order to touch the target.

The training phase allowed participants to practice the data collection reachability task. During this training phase participants received feedback about the accuracy of their response, correct or incorrect. This phase asked the participant to judge whether or not a target was reachable at different distances. The participant was first presented with a mask screen counting down from 3 to 1. At 1 the mask screen was replaced with the camera feed, along with two buttons labeled "reachable" and "unreachable" at the bottom of the screen. The participant had 3 s [5] to select an answer before the feed was replaced with a black screen. At this point participants had unlimited time to select and answer. Upon selecting an answer a red or green box, labeled with the words "incorrect" or "correct" respectively, appeared, informing the participant of whether they were correct. After 3 s, the mask for the next trial appeared and started to count down.

The procedure of the data collection phase was identical to the training phase, but without the feedback about the participant's correctness. The data collection in each session was divided into three sections, each divided by rest periods up to 2 min. Each session presented target distances based a pair of staircase algorithms. Each trial alternated which algorithm was used so as to obscure the pattern of sampling.

After completing each session the participants were debriefed and asked if they had any questions. Additionally, they were asked not to discuss their experience with anyone until the completion of the study.

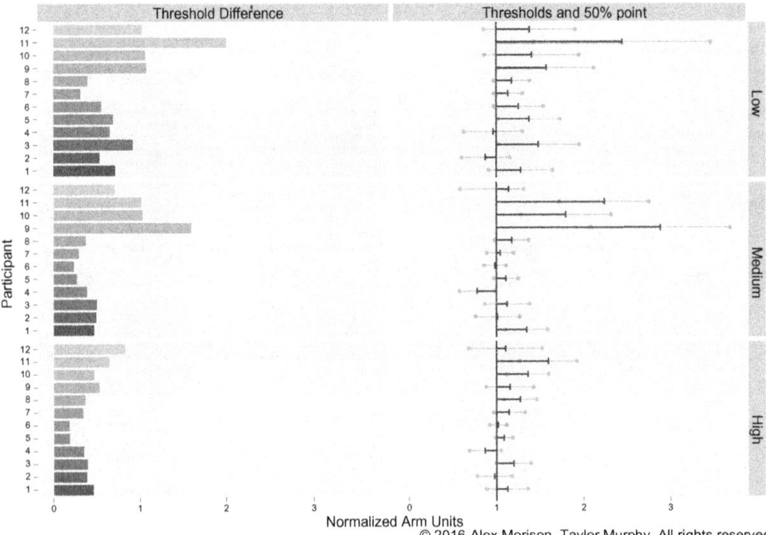

Fig. 3. Individual performance data. The left panels show the difference between each participant's two thresholds in each condition. The right panels show each participant's 50 % point, their perceived reachability boundary, and highlight its displacement from the true reachability boundary. Additionally the right panels show each participant's inner and outer threshold.

4 Analysis and Results

Following similar approaches to assessing affordances, data analysis in the current study involved fitting a sigmoid function to the binomial data using a logistic regression. The sigmoid function measures the human-robot-sensor systems ability to perceive the reachability of a target object. This sigmoid function is the psychometric function of the system. The psychometric function for the current study is defined by position and slope, estimating the participant's accuracy and precision respectively. The analysis first compared each participant's performance across the three conditions. Then, the analysis was performed across all participants and conditions to examine trends.

The first analysis performed a repeated measures ANOVA on the estimated 50 % position. The ANOVA was performed on a logistic regression with a within subjects variable of condition (low, medium, and high). The results are shown in panel A of Table 1. Nine of the 12 participants showed a significant different for either high, low, or all three, while one participant showed a significant difference for medium. The high or low only significantly different conditions might indicate that sources of information for perceiving depth are not sufficiently different across the different conditions.

Table 1. The table on the left (panel A) shows the estimated 50 % thresholds by condition for each participant. The table on the right (panel B) shows the estimated slope values by condition for each participant. The significantly different conditions at the $p < 0.05$ level are noted by an asterisk (*).

50% Threshold for Each Participant Across Conditions

Participant	Condition	Mean	SD	FLSD
participant 1	Low	1.28	0.09	0.13
	Medium	1.34	0.14	0.13
	High*	1.13	0.07	0.13
participant 2	Low*	0.88	0.06	0.08
	Medium	1.01	0.06	0.08
	High	0.98	0.09	0.08
participant 3	Low*	1.48	0.09	0.10
	Medium	1.12	0.05	0.10
	High	1.20	0.07	0.10
participant 4	Low*	0.96	0.04	0.03
	Medium*	0.78	0.05	0.03
	High*	0.87	0.03	0.03
participant 5	Low*	1.37	0.04	0.05
	Medium	1.11	0.03	0.05
	High	1.09	0.03	0.05
participant 6	Low*	1.25	0.10	0.10
	Medium	0.98	0.02	0.10
	High	1.02	0.03	0.10
participant 7	Low	1.13	0.04	0.14
	Medium	1.04	0.06	0.14
	High	1.15	0.16	0.14
participant 8	Low	1.18	0.13	0.11
	Medium	1.18	0.08	0.11
	High	1.27	0.05	0.11
participant 9	Low*	1.57	0.20	0.42
	Medium*	2.88	0.52	0.42
	High*	1.15	0.05	0.42
participant 10	Low	1.41	0.21	0.22
	Medium*	1.80	0.15	0.22
	High	1.36	0.07	0.22
participant 11	Low	2.44	0.42	0.35
	Medium	2.23	0.31	0.35
	High*	1.59	0.08	0.35
participant 12	Low*	1.38	0.07	0.06
	Medium*	0.95	0.06	0.06
	High*	1.10	0.06	0.06

Threshold Differences for Each Participant Across Conditions

Participant	Condition	Mean	SD	FLSD
participant 1	Low*	0.73	0.11	0.16
	Medium	0.48	0.09	0.16
	High	0.47	0.13	0.16
participant 2	Low	0.55	0.06	0.08
	Medium	0.50	0.07	0.08
	High*	0.39	0.04	0.08
participant 3	Low*	0.93	0.19	0.17
	Medium*	0.51	0.06	0.17
	High*	0.40	0.04	0.17
participant 4	Low*	0.66	0.08	0.07
	Medium	0.40	0.08	0.07
	High	0.36	0.01	0.07
participant 5	Low*	0.70	0.07	0.08
	Medium*	0.28	0.05	0.08
	High*	0.19	0.02	0.08
participant 6	Low*	0.57	0.19	0.15
	Medium	0.25	0.05	0.15
	High	0.19	0.05	0.15
participant 7	Low	0.32	0.06	0.10
	Medium	0.31	0.07	0.10
	High	0.35	0.04	0.10
participant 8	Low	0.41	0.07	0.14
	Medium	0.39	0.12	0.14
	High	0.37	0.08	0.14
participant 9	Low*	1.09	0.06	0.41
	Medium*	1.60	0.39	0.41
	High*	0.54	0.19	0.41
participant 10	Low	1.08	0.31	0.37
	Medium	1.04	0.17	0.37
	High*	0.48	0.18	0.37
participant 11	Low*	2.02	0.31	0.46
	Medium	1.03	0.42	0.46
	High	0.65	0.18	0.46
participant 12	Low	1.04	0.16	0.17
	Medium*	0.72	0.06	0.17
	High	0.84	0.05	0.17

A second repeated measures ANOVA was performed on the slope estimates, which are shown in panel B of Table 1. Similar to the previous analysis, the ANOVA was performed on a logistic regression with condition (low, medium, and high) as the within subjects independent variable. Matching the threshold data, both participants 7 and 8 show no difference in their slope estimates. Participant 9 slope estimates are significant but the order does not match the condition with medium being their poorest performing condition followed by low and then high. The remaining 9 participants results matched the predicted ordering, but without significance in some cases. This is potentially due to the visual cues not being different enough across conditions or a possible saturation of the psychophysical performance of the human-sensor-robot system.

The second phase of the analysis examined the threshold positions and the slope estimates for each condition but across all participants. The thresholds were examined individually to more closely examine the effect across all conditions. A repeated measures ANOVA was used to test the within-subjects factors of threshold (inner vs. outer) and condition (low, medium, and high). The analysis revealed a main effect of boundary, $F(1,11) = 52.2$ $p < .0001$, with an effect size of $\eta p^2 = 0.32$ (generalized eta-squared), but not of condition. After correcting the degrees of freedom using a Greenhouse-Geisser estimate of sphericity ($e = 0.54$), an interaction effect between condition and threshold emerged, $F(2,22) = 7.978$, $p < .01$, $\eta p^2 = .03$. Exploring this further, Tukey post-hoc 95 % confidence intervals show a difference between all three outer thresholds. This can be interpreted as a main effect for outer threshold. Tukey 95 % confidence intervals did not reveal a difference between the inner thresholds.

The slope estimates were compared next and were calculated by the difference between in the inner and outer threshold points for each condition across all participants. A repeated measures ANOVA was performed on the slope estimates. Similar to the previous analyses, the ANOVA was performed on a logistic regression with condition (low, medium, and high) as the within subjects independent variable. The results for the slope estimates for the three conditions are low (mean = 0.84, SD = 0.45, FLSD = 0.21), medium (mean = 0.63, SD = 0.41, FLSD = 0.21), and high (mean = 0.44, SD = 0.18, FLSD = 0.21). The repeated measures ANOVA showed a significant difference between the low and high conditions. The medium condition was not significantly different from the low or high conditions. Similar to the results form the per participant analyses, the lack of difference between the medium condition and the high or low conditions is potentially due to scaling, where the selected cues to embed in each condition did not provide a large enough effect.

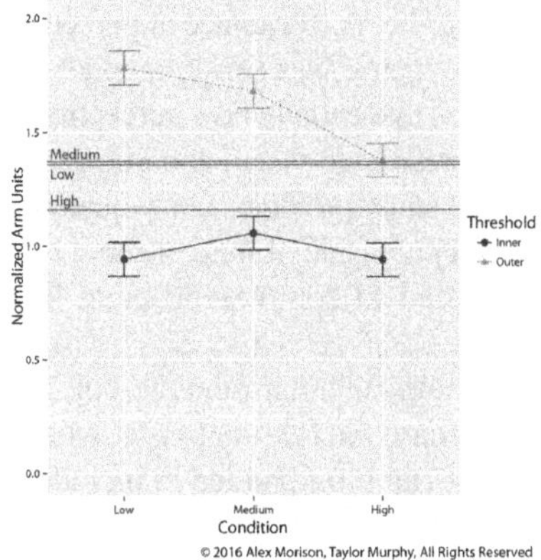

Fig. 4. Inner and outer thresholds averaged over all participants plotted by condition. Black horizontal lines represent the 50 % point for each condition. Note the sharp drop in the outer threshold, this suggests that participants became more precise as more visual cues were added.

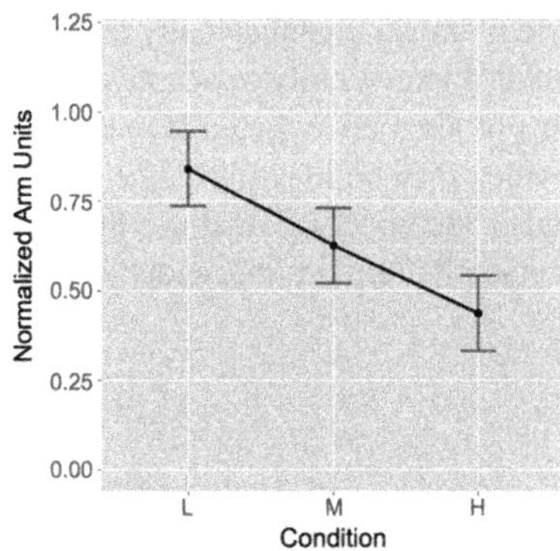

Fig. 5. Distance between thresholds plotted with 95 % confidence intervals by condition. Distance normalized to length of the mechanical arm.

These results demonstrate that the procedure can discriminate performance differences across different human-robot-sensor systems. These differences are based on the ability to estimate psychometric functions for a human-robot-sensor system across environments with different visual cues to depth information. More specifically, the results show that the ability of a human-robot-sensor system to perceive the reachability of a target object degrades as the visual cues to depth in the environment becomes sparser (Figs. 4 and 5).

5 Discussion

This work provides a new metric for assessing quantitatively one performance dimension of human-sensor-robot systems — the ability to perceive affordances. The metric is derived from formal and well-established methods in psychophysics transformed for human-sensor-robot systems. The study shows that the perception of affordances, in this case reachability, can be measured and that performance at perceiving affordances varies with task conditions. In this study, the metric was sensitive to changing visual cues about the structure of the environment – cues that explain how perception of the environment is more difficult and less accurate under restricted visual conditions similar to those encountered in rescue robotics. As a result, the study provides a new quantitative, precise measurement tool for use in assessing the perceptual side of human-robot interaction. Moving forward, this measurement tool can be used to compare different human-robot-sensor systems configurations.

The method presented is a complete measurement tool, however, the method can be expanded in several ways to increase the fidelity to real-world operations. For instance, the simulated robot environment can be expanded to include temporal properties of the target object. In addition, the fidelity of the simulated robot could be expanded. Depending on the objective of the measurement this could include both the dynamics and kinematics of the robot, but could also include a higher fidelity interface to more closely match the operator-robot interaction. The method could also be expanded to include other types of affordances, providing a more holistic assessment.

Future studies can also expand the method to accommodate different psychometric procedures. The psychometric literature contains many methods to estimate participants' psychometric function including a large family of adaptive procedures, and the method of constant stimuli. Comparisons of alternative methods to estimate psychometric functions will allow identification of which method maximizes the ability to discriminate performance reliably. Additional studies are underway that use the current method and metric to compare different sensor-robotic platform designs under different visual conditions.

References

1. Morison, A., Woods, D.D., Murphy, T.B.: Human-robot interaction as extending human perception to new scales. In: Hoffman, R.R., Hancock, P.A., Scerbo, M., Parasuraman, R., Szalma, J.R. (eds.) Handbook of Applied Perception Research, vol. 2, pp. 848–868. Cambridge University Press, New York (2015)

2. Fong, T., Kaber, D., Lewis, M., Scholtz, J., Schultz, A., Steinfeld, A.: Common metrics for human-robot interaction. In: IEEE International Conference on Intelligent Robots and Systems (2004). doi:10.1145/1121241.1121249
3. Burke, J.L., Murphy, R.R., Rogers, E., Lumelsky, V.J., Scholtz, J.: Final report for the DARPA/NSF interdisciplinary study on human – robot interaction. IEEE Trans. Syst. Man Cybern. - Part C: Appl. Rev. **34**(2), 103–112 (2004)
4. Gibson, J.J.: The theory of information pickup and its consequences. In: The Ecological Approach to Visual Perception, pp. 238–263. Houghton Mifflin, Boston (1979)
5. Heft, H.: A methodological note on overestimates of reaching distance: distinguishing between perceptual and analytical judgments. Ecol. Psychol. **5**(3), 255–271 (1993). doi: 10.1207/s15326969eco0503
6. Warren, W.H., Whang, S.: Visual guidance of walking through apertures: body-scaled information for affordances. J. Exp. Psychol. Hum. Percept. Perform. **13**(3), 371–383 (1987). doi:10.1037/0096-1523.13.3.371
7. Mark, L.S., Nemeth, K., Gardner, D., Dainoff, M.J., Paasche, J., Duffy, M., Grandt, K.: Postural dynamics and the preferred critical boundary for visually guided reaching. J. Exp. Psychol. Hum. Percept. Perform. **23**(5), 1365–1379 (1997)
8. Carello, C., Grosofsky, A., Reichel, F.D., Turvey, M.T.: Visually perceiving what is reachable. Ecol. Psychol. **1**(1), 27–54 (1989)
9. Casper, J., Murphy, R.R.: Human-robot interactions during the robot-assisted urban search and rescue response at the world trade center. IEEE Trans. Syst. Man Cybern. - Part B: Cybern. **33**(3), 367–385 (2003)
10. Drury, J., Scholtz, J., Yanco, H.: Awareness in human-robot interactions. In: Proceedings of IEEE International Conference Systems, Man, Cybernetics, vol. 1, pp. 912–918 (2003)
11. Gibson, J.J.: The Ecological Approach to Visual Perception. Lawrence Erlbaum Associates, Hillsdale (1986)
12. Warren, W.H.: Perceiving affordances: visual guidance of stair climbing. J. Exp. Psychol. Hum. Percept. Perform. **10**(5), 683–703 (1984). doi:10.1037/0096-1523.10.5.683
13. Treutwein, B., Strasburger, H.: Fitting the psychometric function. Percept. Psychophys. **61**(1), 87–106 (1999). doi:10.3758/BF03211951
14. Moore, K.S., Gomer, J.A., Pagano, C.C., Moore, D.D.: Perception of robot passability with direct line of sight and teleoperation. Hum. Factors **51**(4), 557–570 (2009). doi: 10.1177/0018720809341959
15. Jones, K.S., Johnson, B.R., Schmidlin, E.A.: Teleoperation through apertures: passability versus driveability. J. Cogn. Eng. Decis. Mak. **5**(1), 10–28 (2011). http://edm.sagepub.com/lookup/doi/10.1177/1555343411399074
16. Levitt, H.: Transformed up-down methods in psychoacoustics. J. Acoust. Soc. Am. **49**, 467–477 (1971)
17. García-Pérez, M.A.: Yes-No staircases with fixed step sizes: psychometric properties and optimal setup. Optom. Vis. Sci. **78**(1), 56–64 (2001)

Userbility: A Technique for the Evaluation of User Experience and Usability on Mobile Applications

Ingrid Nascimento[1,2(✉)], Williamson Silva[1,2], Bruno Gadelha[2], and Tayana Conte[1,2]

[1] USES Research Group – Institute of Computing (IComp), Federal University of Amazonas (UFAM), Manaus, AM, Brazil
{inc, williamson.silva, tayana}@icomp.ufam.edu.br

[2] Institute of Computing (IComp), Federal University of Amazonas (UFAM), Manaus, AM, Brazil
bruno@icomp.ufam.edu.br

Abstract. User eXperience (UX) covers the relationship between usability, context of use, and user emotions regarding an application. Improving the UX and usability of an application, especially mobile applications, can influence their acceptance by end users. Although UX and usability evaluations focus on improving the quality of these applications, the software industry performs these evaluations separately. Based on this, we proposed Userbility, a technique for evaluating UX and usability in mobile applications. This technique is based on two methods: the Heuristic Evaluation and 3E method. In order to evaluate the Userbility technique, we conducted a study through the evaluation of five mobile applications. The results of this study show that it is possible to identify improvements in applications through a UX and usability inspection conducted with Userbility and a new version Userbility.

Keywords: User eXperience (UX) · Usability · Mobile application · Evaluation

1 Introduction

Industry analysts estimate that there are over 250,000 mobile applications available in the various application stores, some of which are available for various types of mobile devices, such as, smartphones and tablets [13]. As a result of this growth, software companies began to investigate the interactions between the user and the product in order to develop applications with higher quality [13].

The characteristics of the interaction and the interface that make an application appropriate are emphasized by the use of quality criteria [10]. One important quality of use criteria is usability [10]. Usability assesses how easy the interface is to use, as well as the user satisfaction as a result of such use [9]. In the definition of usability, the use of an application is affected by the user's characteristics (his/her cognitive perception, his/her ability to act upon the application and how (s)he perceives the response from the application) [10].

M. Kurosu (Ed.): HCI 2016, Part I, LNCS 9731, pp. 372–383, 2016.
DOI: 10.1007/978-3-319-39510-4_35

Just evaluating usability is not enough to improve the quality of an application. Practitioners must also be concerned about the emotions and feelings of users with respect to the applications they use. The quality related to the evaluation of the users' feeling while interacting with a software application is defined as User Experience (UX) [4]. User experience is associated with aspects that go from traditional usability to beauty, hedonic, affective or experiential aspects of the system [3]. In order to achieve a positive UX, it is necessary that the application promotes satisfaction of the human needs of the users [4].

Therefore, usability evaluation focuses on the realization of the task, i.e. it considers user performance while (s)he performs a particular activity [5], while UX evaluation focuses on his/her experiences, emotions, perceptions and judgment in the evaluation of applications [3]. Consequently, both are important for the evaluation of the quality of applications, especially for mobile applications, since these applications have features that make the evaluation difficult [2]. As examples of these features, we have the mobile context, connectivity, small screen size, different display resolution, limited processing capability and power, and data entry methods [2]. In these applications, the dynamism of the mobile scenarios makes the task of evaluating the user experience, context and usability altogether more difficult [6].

Considering the importance to evaluate both, usability as user experience, in mobile applications, we have developed a technique called Userbility. This paper presents an empirical study of Userbility, which was carried out to verify the feasibility of the technique when employed by practitioners without expertise in UX and usability evaluation. It also indicates which parts of the technique need improvement. During evaluation, subjects evaluated the user experience and usability of five developed applications. Furthermore, based on the results found, we made enhancements on the technique.

The paper is organized as follows: Sect. 2 focuses on the works related to this research. Section 3 presents the initial version of the Userbility technique. Section 4 describes the empirical study, the obtained results and a second version of Userbility. Finally, Sect. 5 presents our final remarks.

2 Background

Usability and user experience are important quality attributes for applications. User experience (UX) focuses on hedonic aspects such as, fun and enjoyment [3]. Two main types of quality attributes are perceived by the user when evaluating UX: pragmatic quality (*usability perceived by the user*) and the hedonic quality (*pleasure - producing product quality*) [3]. Even though hedonic aspects can meet universal human needs, they do not necessarily have utilitarian value. This aspect is explored to make the user experience more pleasant [3].

The Expressing Emotions and Experiences (3E) method aims at capturing the experience and feelings of users [11]. It uses an approach in which users draw and write their experiences and emotions about the evaluated application. The model of this method includes: (a) a blank face, where the user can draw his/her emotional state; (b) a speech bubble where the user can verbally express him/herself; and (c) a bubble cloud, in which the user can report what (s)he is thinking [11]. Through this method, users can express themselves more freely, either by writing (through the bubbles), or drawing (through the face expression).

Besides evaluating aspects related to the emotions, experience and feelings of the users, it is also necessary to evaluate the usability. According to the *ISO 9241-11 norm* (1998), usability is defined as the extent to which a product can be used by users to achieve a set of goals with effectiveness, efficiency and satisfaction in a specified context of use [5].

There are different types of usability inspection methods to evaluate the usability of an application. One of the most accepted evaluation methods for diagnosing usability problems is the Heuristic Evaluation [1], due to its simplicity and low application costs. The Heuristic Evaluation is summarized in ten *"golden rules"*, developed for the design and evaluation of interactive applications [9].

Furthermore, there are also usability inspection techniques to assess mobile applications. An example is the *Checklist for measuring usability of mobile phone applications* that consists of a questionnaire [12]. This questionnaire is employed to identify usability issues in mobile applications, using a 67 items questionnaire (which identifies a higher number of usability issues) and a 48 items questionnaire (which is less demanding and therefore, requires less time to accomplish an evaluation) [12].

As noted above, the presented studies allow assessing UX and usability separately. Even though it is possible to capture aspects focused on usability, this is not the only focus of the presented UX studies. Therefore, it is important to investigate and propose a technique for mobile applications that allows evaluating UX and usability at the same time.

3 Userbility v 1.0

The Userbility technique (Integration of **User** eXperience and Usa**bility**) aims at helping non-specialist practitioners in HCI to evaluate user experience, considering the usability of mobile applications. The Userbility technique v 1.0 was proposed based on two methods: the Heuristic Evaluation [9], as this is the most employed method to perform usability evaluations [1]; and the Expressing Emotions and Experiences (3E) method, since this is a method that collects rich data on the emotional response of users [11]. Therefore, the Userbility technique aims to integrate the usability evaluation with UX, which is more focused on emotions and user experiences. This integration is important in order to improve the evaluation process, especially for less experienced evaluators.

Based on heuristics from the Heuristic Evaluation, we defined ten aspects to evaluate applications using questions related to UX. These aspects were included in the Userbility technique, as shown in Table 1. We've simplified the ten aspects of the heuristics from the Heuristic Evaluation to make it possible for non-specialists in HCI to apply a UX and usability technique. Our technique consists on a questionnaire that assesses the usability of the application and the user experience on mobile devices after using the mobile application.

From the 3E model, where users draw and write their experiences and emotions [11], we selected two questions (Q1 and Q2) in each aspect that evaluates the usability

Table 1. Usability aspects based on the Heuristic Evaluation

Usability aspects
A1. The user understands the system state, feedback and alert message.
A2. The user can understand all communication with the system in its context. That is, the system uses a terminology that is understandable by the user.
A3. The user can exit, cancel and redo an action on the application at any time.
A4. The user can more easily identify actions and standard terms (buttons, terminology, symbols and messages). That is, it treats similar items in the same way.
A5.The user receives enough information to avoid making mistakes
A6. The user manages to use the system without the need to remember any options, just by recognizing the options within the system. That is, the system guides the user.
A7. Shortcuts are a simpler way to perform an action. More experienced users can use shortcuts to perform tasks.
A8. The dialogs between the user and the system are simples, direct and without unnecessary information.
A9. The user can recognize, diagnose and recover from mistakes made while using the system.
A10. If the user has a question, (s)he can access the documentation (optional). The documentation must be visible, easy to access and contain a search tool in the help option.

of the application: (Q1) *"What did you feel regarding this aspect in the application?"*; and (Q2) *"What do you think or would improve regarding this aspect in the application?"*.

The selected questions aim to assist in capturing the experience and emotions of non-specialist evaluators about the application. Furthermore these issues are simple and easy to understand by no experts practitioners. In order to answer Q1, the evaluator describes how (s)he feels when observing a certain aspect of the mobile application. For Q2, the evaluator answers by describing what (s)he "*thinks*" of the application, which problems occurred when using this application, what is missing or what could be improved in the application. As an example, let's consider a scenario where an inspector needs to evaluate an e-commerce app. The task (s)he might accomplish is to create a shopping list. In question Q1 regarding aspect A1, a possible answer could be: *"I felt discouraged to find that I did not receive feedback when making a purchase"*. In this case, the user experience was negative, because the user did not manage to receive *feedback* from the application. In addition, there is a possible usability problem, as suggested in aspect A1. Also, considering the same application to answer question Q2, a possible answer could be *"I think that the application has failed in the A1 aspect, because I did not identify that I was in the products evaluation page"*. In this case the evaluator can indicate what (s) he is thinking made A1 fail and why.

In addition, an item related to the satisfaction of the evaluator for the usability aspects was also included. This item was included so the evaluators could provide their degrees of satisfaction about the aspects of the technique. This item is composed of a five-point scale (unsatisfied, little satisfied, moderately satisfied, very satisfied and extremely satisfied) and represented by a face. These five points were chosen in order to provide richer information about the user satisfaction on every usability aspect.

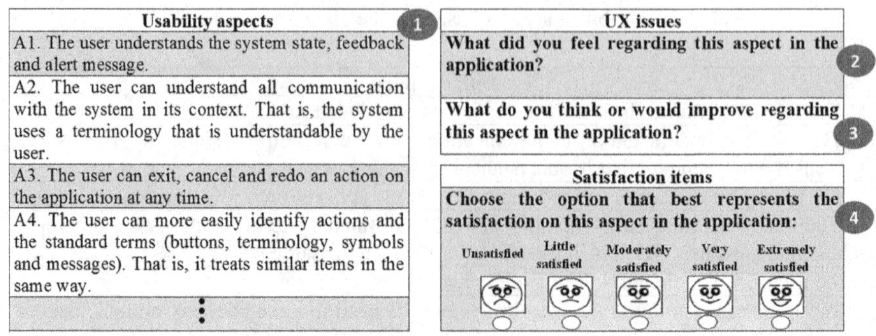

Fig. 1. Userbility technique v 1.0

Figure 1 shows the Userbility v 1.0 technique and also shows its organization: usability aspects (1), the UX questions (2 and 3) and the satisfaction items on the usability aspects (4).

4 Empirical Study

We conducted an empirical study with the Userbility v 1.0 technique using five mobile applications, in order to verify the feasibility of the technique and indicate what parts of the technique need improvements. The evaluated applications were: (1) *Simbora, which* provides means for university students to collaboratively get a ride; (2) *GRUM,* which provides the location of events inside the university; (3) *PartyNote,* which informs what festivals and events are taking place on a date or month; (4) *Personal Diet,* which helps or to motivates people to keep diets when they are out-of-home; and (5) *Book-zone, which* helps users find and sell their books.

The subjects of this study were student volunteers of a class on Collaborative Mobile Systems. There were 09 undergraduate students of the Engineering and Computer Science courses at Federal University of Amazonas (UFAM). The subjects were also the developers of the evaluated mobile applications. However, each subject did not evaluate his/her own applications, but another application developed by students from other groups. All students signed a consent form. Figure 2 shows the process of applying the Userbility technique.

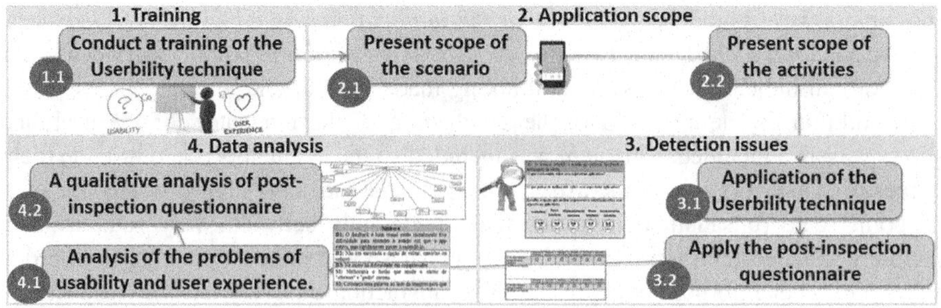

Fig. 2. Study's execution phases

The process depicted in Fig. 2 was executed following the phases in Table 2.

Table 2. Description of the study phases

Phases	Activity	Description
1. Training	1.1. Conducting training on the Userbility technique	First, we carried out a training, introducing the concepts and usability examples, Heuristic Evaluation, user experience and Userbility Technique to balance the knowledge of the subjects.
2. Application Scope of the activities	2.1. Present scope of the scenario	We introduced the applications scope to describe their user and their needs. For example, for the Simbora application, the scope was: "*Simbora is an application for searching and sharing rides within UFAM. Simbora shows which users are available to request and offer a ride to a particular passenger within UFAM. This application also allows the driver to define routes in order to offer rides to other students. Furthermore, the application provides a chat where passengers and drivers may interact*".
	2.2. Present scope of the activities	In this activity, we offered details of the activities to be made in the application. For example, for the Simbora application the following activities were presented: *(1) log in to the app; (2) change the app status to "available"; (3) select the option to "take a ride"; (4) view the source of the route (where it starts); (5) choose destination of the route; (6) define the route; (7) view the route; (8) select the "ask for a ride" option.*
3. Detection issues	3.1. Application of the Userbility technique	We conducted the inspection process using the Userbility technique to evaluate the applications.
	3.2. Apply the post-inspection	A post-inspection questionnaire was applied in order to collect the perceptions of the use
	questionnaire	regarding the Userbility technique.
4. Data analysis	4.1. Analysis of the problems of usability and user experience	We analyzed the collected data on the usability and user experience evaluation to assess the applications.
	4.2. A qualitative analysis of post-inspection questionnaire	We analyzed the collected data on post-inspection questionnaire in order to evaluate the ease of use and adoption of the Userbility technique.

Table 3 shows the usability problems found in the applications and the suggested improvements indicated by the subjects to mitigate these problems. We classified the possible usability problems and the related improvements suggested. Moreover, it was possible to see suggestions related to the hedonic quality attributes of user experience. Some of these improvements were related to expectations and user experience of the subjects, such as: *"One could add favorite rides"* (Simbora app); *"There could be an option to trace a route on the map."* (Grum app); "*I expected more, since there should be an incentive from the system as it is a diet*" (Personal Diet app); and "*The use of words such as healthy is an attraction for the younger audience. But I do not know if there would be an acceptance from the general public*" (Personal Diet app).

Table 3. Main problems and suggestions/improvements that the subjects made regarding the applications using the Userbility v 1.0 technique.

Usability Problems (I) and Suggestions (S)
Simbora
I1: Feedback is very visual so, initially, I had trouble understanding the state where the app was, but quickly started to understand it.
I2: The app did not show the option to return, cancel and redo.
S1: I would change the button that changes the status of "offering" and "requesting" ride.
S2: There could be a message to "click the map to set path".
GRUM
I3: The user can leave, cancel and redo, but not login in which, after registering with an e-mail account, there is no way to logout and log in as it has no password and the login screen requires a password.
I4: The dialogues are simple but not so intuitive.
S3: Guiding messages could be added.
S4: I would add more objective messages in response to a user request.
Personal Diet
I5: It is confusing. It mixes buttons, symbols and messages and one guesses it is the same thing.
I6: In the registration, there was no information that all fields are required, only after the user tries using the option (if there were asterisks, they were hardly visible).
S5: Messages could take longer to disappear.
S6: There are only the standards commands and tabs in the application; it could improve with the use of icons and shortcut buttons.
BOOKZONE
I7: When errors occur, the application is not always warns to the user.
S7: The application could provide more feedback to the user.
S8: The application could provide some buttons at specific locations to become even more intuitive.
PartyNote
I8: In the login, I had to remember the email and password to enter.
S9: There should be more information in case there is no internet connection.
S10: There should be more symbols, to reduce the amount of text in application.

After applying the questionnaire of the Userbility technique, we conducted the collection activity. We generated a list of all the problems and suggestions without duplicates (problems or suggestions identified by more than one inspector). A researcher with high experience in usability and user experience evaluations grouped the problems, and we perform the removal of duplicates. Then one researcher revised these problems, and, finally, we conducted the discrimination activity with the participation of two researchers.

Table 4 shows the time for evaluation, the number of duplicated usability problems, suggestions and improvements indicated in each application. Two subjects did not count the time spent for the inspection (P3 and P9). Furthermore, only one subject evaluated the *PartyNote* application, therefore, there are no duplicated problems (DP) and suggestions (DS) for this application.

Table 4. Inspection results: number of defects/suggestions and duplicates per application

App	S	T (min.)	NP	DP	NS	DS
Simbora	P1	15	06	02	08	03
	P2	15				
Grum	P3	-	06	01	08	01
	P4	31				
Personal Diet	P5	48	09	03	12	02
	P6	41				
Bookzone	P7	30	09	01	12	00
	P8	25				
Partynote	P9	-	07	-	13	-

Legend: S: Subject; **T:** Time spent in the evaluation; **NP:** Number of problem; **DP:** Number of Duplicated problems; **NS:** Number of suggestions and **DS:** Number of Duplicated suggestions.

Figure 3 shows the level of satisfaction of the subjects, on the scale set, for the applications. We determined the level of user satisfaction, item 4 in Fig. 1, according to every aspect of the application (A1, A2 ...) identified in Table 1. In the evaluation of the *Simbora* application, two subjects (P1 and P2) were satisfied with 9 out of 10 evaluated aspects. Considering the aspect A3, subject P1 was little satisfied. The most and least satisfactory aspects are shown for each application. This analysis of the level of satisfaction is interesting for researchers because it makes it possible to identify which aspects satisfy or dissatisfied the evaluators.

In order to evaluate the ease of use and adoption of the Userbility technique, a post-inspection questionnaire was applied with the inspectors. This questionnaire had questions related to the ease of use, usefulness, positive and negative points of the Userbility technique. For the analysis of the post-inspection questionnaire we adopted procedures of the *Grounded Theory* method [8] to perform data coding. A researcher performed the coding procedure. Then, two experts reviewed the coding.

During the coding process, three categories and 25 codes emerged. The categories were: Benefits of the use of the technique (14 codes), Difficulties in understanding

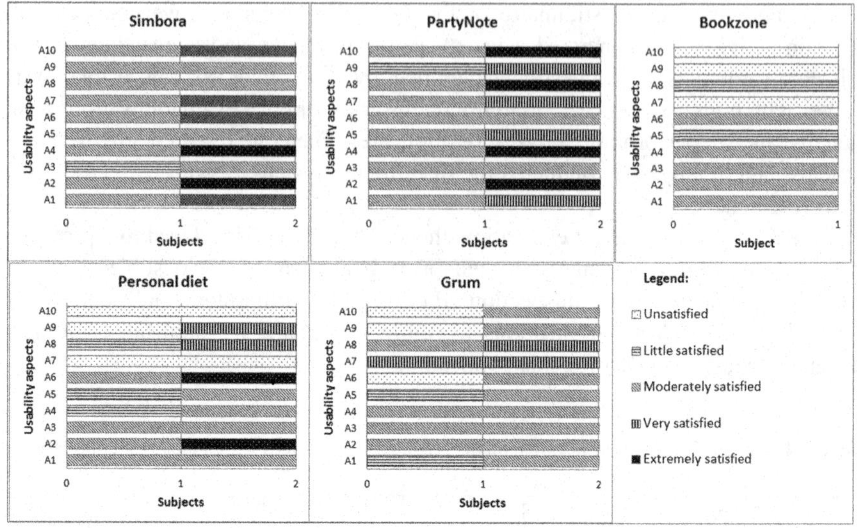

Fig. 3. The level of satisfaction of subjects per application

(4 codes) and Suggestions for improvements of the technique (7 codes). These categories are described as follows:

Benefits of the use of the technique: this category highlights the benefits perceived by subjects in the use of the technique. Some of the codes were: The Technique characterizes the usability of the application ("Easy characterization of usability features" - P6); It guides what aspects need to be inspected ("I would not notice things like menu navigation feedback" - P2); The technique is intuitive ("The technique is very intuitive" - P6); The questions helped in the evaluation ("The questions raised helped in this evaluation" - P4); The justification fields allow the evaluators to express themselves ("And the justification fields let us expressed ourselves in more detail" - P6). In this category, we perceived that the technique helps and guides inspectors during the evaluation. Also, inspectors pointed out that the questions and the fields were positive factors in the use of the technique.

Difficulties in understanding: this category highlights the difficulties in understanding that were perceived by the subjects in the use of the technique. Some of the codes were: The aspects of shortcuts are subjective ("Not the shortcuts, which is something very subjective" - P7); Some aspects of the technique are similar and confusing ("Some sections are similar: the system messages, communication with the user… It just confused me" - P2); It generates repetition of information ("I felt that once or twice I said the same thing. I gave the same answer" - P1); The item related to satisfaction is hard to understand ("Most of them are easy to understand, but the part of the technique that was difficult to understand was the part of symbols" - P8). In this category, we perceived that the technique caused confusion in some aspects that are similar and generated repetition of information. Also, the inspectors pointed out that the shortcuts and items related to satisfaction were difficult to understand. These points should be improved in the technique.

Suggestions for improvements in the technique: this category highlights improvement suggestions cited by the subjects in the use of the technique. Some of the codes were as follows: Making the technique less tiring, reducing the analysis ("Being less tiring" - P8); Allow users to comment freely ("One should be able to comment freely on other themes, letting the user make suggestions" - P7); The technique should provide multiple choice questions ("More options (multiple choice questions)" - P5); Prioritize the app context in the technique ("Directly approaching what is a priority in the context of an application" - P9). In this category, we perceived that the technique analysis is tiring and that the subjects prefer more multiple-choice questions. Consequently, we included sub-items with yes/no questions, to report problems through the sub-items with less cognitive effort. Also, it was pointed out that we could guide the technique regarding the app context, but it is preferred that the technique is generic to allow evaluating different types of mobile applications.

Finally, the qualitative analysis revealed some issues that needed to be reviewed in the technique. Taking into account the comments of the subjects, we also make improvements in the Userbility technique based on a questionnaire to support the usability evaluation on mobile applications [12]. This questionnaire was chosen because, although it does not evaluate UX, it evaluated the usability in mobile applications. This new version includes usability items, example for the usability items, UX questions and item related to the satisfaction of the evaluator.

After empirical study, we identified that some of the usability problems had not been clearly indicated. In some circumstances, subjects did not know how describe the problem, but gave suggestions and improvements (identified in Table 3). In these cases, the subjects did not indicate where exactly the problem was. Therefore, we decided to detail each aspect with sub-questions. These sub-questions have been created in order to make the aspects easier to understand, and to be more helpful in the process of identifying usability and UX problems in mobile applications.

A1. Visibility of system status		
I1. The application provides system status, feedbacks and alert messages immediately? Example: After a task, such as user deletion, confirmation occurs.	☐Yes	☐No
I2. The selected interactive components stand out from others? Example: the pressed buttons or tabs menus being displayed.	☐Yes	☐No
I3. The slowest operations offer feedback? Example: An activity is 50% complete.	☐Yes	☐No
What did you feel regarding this aspect in the application? What feelings were awakened?		
What do you think or would improve regarding this aspect in the application?		
Choose the option that best represented their satisfaction on this aspect in the application: Unsatisfied ◯ / Little satisfied ◯ / Moderately satisfied ◯ / Very satisfied ◯ / Extremely satisfied ◯		

Fig. 4. Exemple of the Userbility technique v 2.0

We also propose to improve usability and UX questions adding new sub-questions related to specific aspect of mobile applications, based on *Checklist Heuristic Evaluation for Smartphones Applications* [7]. This new version of Userbility was evaluated and reviewed by another researcher with high knowledge of usability and UX, which was not directly involved in this research.

Figure 4 shows part of the new version of the Userbility v 2.0 technique. The usability aspects are composed of items including an issue and an example to facilitate the understanding of the evaluator.

5 Conclusion

This paper presents an empirical study that was conducted in order to evaluate the feasibility of using the Userbility technique with five applications under development. Userbility is a technique that helps designers to evaluate the usability and user experience of mobile applications. Applying the technique makes it possible to verify two different quality criteria: usability and user experience. Aspects of usability of the Userbility assist the inspectors in describing usability problems, guiding subjects to think about the experience that each of these aspects evoked. Although the technique is not specific to identify usability problems, it leads the user to describe various problems given that the usability aspects are based on the Heuristic Evaluation. The UX aspects on Userbility are expectations and experiences, i.e. the aspects that the subjects described they wish were in the application in order to improve the experience of the end users. However, we found out that subjects were focused more on pointing out the usability problems they encountered instead of describing what they felt regarding each aspect.

Based on the results found in this empirical study, it was possible to identify various usability problems in the applications and several improvements suggested by the study subjects. Furthermore, it was observed that the Userbility v 1.0 technique found usability problems without specifying their location. Also, it was possible to perceive though the qualitative analysis that various issues still needed to be reviewed in the Userbility v 1.0. Based on the performed analysis, we proposed a new version of the technique, where verification items have been added to every usability aspect in order to obtain more detailed results from the inspection. Thus, as future work, we intend to execute a study with the Userbility v 2.0 and to analyze their effectiveness and efficiency. Consequently, we expect that Userbility v 2.0 allows identifying more specific usability problems in order to help designers when they are performing the correction of these problems. We also hope that the inspectors report more of their experiences and feelings when using the application that is being evaluated. In this way, we intend to encourage the use of Userbility in the industry for rapid assessments.

Acknowledgments. We thank the financial support granted by CAPES (Coordination for the Improvement of Higher Education Personnel) and FAPEAM (Foundation for Research Support of the Amazonas State). And the financial support granted by CAPES through process number 175956/2013 and FAPEAM through processes numbers: 062.00600/2014; 062.00578/2014. And all the students volunteers who participated in the study.

References

1. Baker, K., Greenberg, S., Gutwin, C.: Empirical development of a heuristic evaluation methodology for shared workspace groupware. In: Proceedings of the 2002 ACM Conference on Computer Supported Cooperative Work, pp. 96–105. ACM (2002)
2. Harrison, R., Flood, D., Duce, D.: Usability of mobile applications: literature review and rationale for a new usability model. J. Interact. Sci. (JoIS) **1**(1), 1–16 (2013)
3. Hassenzahl, M., Tractinsky, N.: User experience-a research agenda. Behav. Inf. Technol. **25**(2), 91–97 (2006)
4. Hassenzah, M.: User experience (UX): towards an experiential perspective on product quality. In: Proceedings of the 20th International Conference of the Association Francophone d'Interaction Homme-Machine, pp. 11–15. ACM, New York (2008)
5. ISO 9241-11: Ergonomic requirements for office work with visual display terminals (VDTs) – Part 11: Guidance on usability (1998)
6. Kronbauer, A.H.; Santos, C.A., Vieira, V.: An experimental study of user experience evaluation of mobile application from the automatic capturing of contextual data and interaction (in Portuguese). In: Proceedings of the 11th Brazilian Symposium on Human Factors in Computing Systems, pp. 305–314. Brazilian Computer Society (2012)
7. Krone, C.: Validation the usability heuristic for touchscreen mobile (in Portuguese). Technical report. Grupo de Qualidade de Software/INCoD/UFSC. Florianópolis, SC (2013)
8. Muller, M.: Curiosity, creativity, and surprise as analytic tools: grounded theory method. In: Olson, J.S., Kellogg, W.A. (eds.) Ways of Knowing in HCI, pp. 25–48. Springer, New York (2014)
9. Nielsen, J.: Usability inspection methods. In: Conference Companion on Human Factors in Computing Systems, pp. 413–414. ACM (1994)
10. Seffah, A., Donyaee, M., Kline, R.B., Padd, H.K.: Usability measurement and metrics: a consolidated model. Softw. Qual. J. **14**(2), 159–178 (2006)
11. Tähti, M., Niemelä, M.: 3e–expressing emotions and experiences. In: Proceedings of the Workshop on Innovative Approaches for Evaluating Affective Systems (WP9), HUMAINE, pp. 15–19 (2006)
12. Von Wangenheim, C.G., Witt, T.A., Borgatto, A.F., Nunes, J.V., Lacerda, T.C., Krone, C., de Oliveira Souza, L.: A usability score for mobile phone applications based on heuristics. Int. J. Mob. Hum. Comput. Interact. (IJMHCI) **8**(1), 23–58 (2016)
13. Wasserman, A.I.: Software engineering issues for mobile application development. In: Proceedings of the Workshop on Future of Software Engineering Research (FSE/SDP), pp. 397–400. ACM (2010)

City Usability: A Proposal for Evaluating the Perceived Usability of a City on the Basis of the Website Quality Models

Antonio Opromolla[1,2(✉)], Valentina Volpi[1,2], Roberta Grimaldi[1,2], and Carlo Maria Medaglia[1]

[1] Link Campus University, Rome, Italy
{a.opromolla,v.volpi,r.grimaldi,c.medaglia}@unilink.it
[2] ISIA Roma Design, Rome, Italy

Abstract. The assumption at the basis of this work is that people are an essential part of the city and that its different elements are adapted to the desires of citizens who live in. In order to do that it is important to apply adequate methodologies and tools that help to identify the user needs and to design solutions with people. In this paper we propose to apply the c oncept of "usability", borrowed from the Human-Computer Interaction field, to the city environment in order to adopt a user perspective about the interaction with a specific territory. So, we identify the equivalences between the main features of the website quality models and those present at the city level, through a usability framework composed by a series of elements to consider for trying to create a human-centered city.

Keywords: Usability · Smart city · User perspective · Website quality model

1 Introduction

People are an essential part of the city, since they consciously or unconsciously influence the definition of its structures and services. Even into the smart city paradigm, people are a fundamental component of the smartness of the city, together with technologies and institution. Indeed, in the academic literature many approaches focus on people as the central element to realize a "smart city", considering their needs as the most important reference for defining and implementing really effective city services. In the end, this approach allows creating cities on a human scale [1].

However, in order to obtain this outcome it is important to rethink all the touchpoints between people and the city, transforming them according to this vision. These touchpoints mainly concern public spaces and public services, and in particular the different tools that define them. In the case of spaces, we are talking for example of public infrastructures (e.g. a street, a square, etc.) and public furniture (e.g. a bench, a bus shelter, etc.), while in the case of public services we are talking for example of digital services (e.g. mobile applications, websites, etc.) or physical touchpoints (e.g. an information desk). Therefore, the human smart city vision focuses on the importance of adapting

M. Kurosu (Ed.): HCI 2016, Part I, LNCS 9731, pp. 384–395, 2016.
DOI: 10.1007/978-3-319-39510-4_36

these listed elements not only to the general user needs, but also to the specific human desires of people who live in a specific territory.

In this paper, we intend to apply the concept of "usability", borrowed from the Human-Computer Interaction field, to the city environment. In effect, the city represents an interface between people and the different processes occurring in the urban context. The different urban places and infrastructures provide specific functions and information, inviting citizens to adopt specific behaviours. However, when the city elements do not anymore suit people's needs and requirements, they are gradually transformed and adapted to the new requests. In fact, it might happen that the city, with whatever it has to offer, do not exactly match with the current citizens requirements. This inconsistency between what the city offers and what people really need negatively influences the modes of use the city, leading to a diffused uneasiness, ineffectiveness, and inefficiency. Then, in so far as the city is used by citizens to accomplish their needs, in this paper we draw a parallel between city and website usability. In detail, in the next section we report a general overview concerning the citizen centrality in the urban issues, then focusing on the pertinence of applying the "usability" concept for the evaluation of the city elements. In the third section we deeply analyse this concept, as applied in the Human-Computer Interaction field, and its main characteristics. In the fourth section in order to make clear the parallelism between city and websites usability we show through some examples how these characteristics can be identified in the city environment. Finally, the conclusions, with the proposal of a framework which aims to really apply the "usability" concept for the evaluation of the city environment from the citizen perspective.

2 An Overview on the Evaluation of the City from a City User Perspective

Generally, in the academic literature citizens are increasingly regarded as an important element to be considered during the design process of services and applications. In effect, Public Administration should involve people in their realization, since this involvement would produce more satisfied citizens. This process can follow different levels of people engagement. The basic level consists in the user-centered design approach, that Norman [2] defines as the design process that focus on people's wants and needs in all its stages, while, the most engaging approach is the co-design, that lets people play an active role during all the design process [3]. Both these approaches are increasingly applied in the city context in order to foster the process of innovation of the territory [4]. However, if the involvement of the city users in the design and redesign of new services, spaces, and products has been strongly boosting, a low consideration has been given to people's ease of use and satisfaction. So, little importance has been given to the evaluation of the actual city services, spaces, and products from a city user perspective.

Otherwise, the academic literature (and not only) has focused on the evaluation of the city from a point of view that goes beyond the people scale. In effect, a lot of frameworks and models have been elaborated in order to evaluate the cities performances. According to these models, cities can be measured through indicators and indices concerning their different characteristics that are not related to the city user perspective, as in most cases they are extracted from statistical sources or from data collected through monitoring technologies and sensors. On this basis "smart city" rankings are elaborated. One of the most important smart city ranking is the work of Giffinger et al. [5], where the six general areas of a smart city are described (smart economy, smart mobility, smart governance, smart environment, smart living, smart people), each of them is defined by 31 factors (e.g. "Touristic attractivity") and 74 indicators (e.g. "Overnights per year per resident"). This work focuses on the performances of the different analysed elements of the city, comparing them with those of the other cities. On the basis of the study of Giffinger et al. many other works have been conducted [6, 7]. However, a specific position in a ranking only points out the general strengths and weaknesses of a city and the areas in which it should improve through urban interventions, but no indications about the lacks of the city from the city user point of view are provided. In fact, these rankings do not let emerge how citizens live and consequently what their needs are.

On the contrary, a user perception approach to the city is necessary for evaluating the city smartness. One of the few proposal about a possible mechanism for measuring the level of citizen's centrality in city policies and local governance, and consequently their suitability to citizen's needs, is based on the city indicators on social sustainability elaborated by Marsal-Llacuna [8], which monitor the performance of cities in positively impacting the citizen life. Indeed, standards are suitable tools for the evaluation of the city performance from a city-user perspective, as they are fundamental parts in building evaluation models. In the case of the smart city, the first standard provided is the *ISO 37120:2014 Sustainable development of communities. Indicators for city services and quality of life*. Another standard, still under development, that is suitable to be applied to the smart city is the *ISO/DIS 37101 Sustainable development in communities. Management systems. General principles and requirements*. Both these standards highlight the importance of the human component, i.e. the community, in defining and measuring the city performance, but they still remain mostly focused on the environmental and economic aspects of sustainability, and less on the social ones [8]. The social sustainability certainly needs to undergo in wider standardization process.

However, in evaluating the capacity of the city in meeting the citizens' needs from a user perspective, we believe that it is adequate to also consider the concept of quality of use applied to the city, since it can be seen as an interactive system "used" by people. The concept of quality of use is strictly connected to the design and evaluation of interactive digital systems, assuming the human experience as the central element of the process. In this regard, the main reference standards are *ISO 9241 Ergonomics of human-system interaction* (especially *Part 210:2010 Human-centred design for interactive systems*, *Part 110:2006 Dialogue principles*, and *Part 11:1998 Guidance on usability*), *ISO/TR 16982:2002 Ergonomics of human-system interaction. Usability methods supporting human-centred design*, and *ISO/IEC 25010:2011 Systems and software engineering. Systems and software Quality Requirements and Evaluation (SQuaRE). System and software quality models*. All these standards provide requirements, recommendations, models, and methodologies to design and evaluate interactive and human-computer systems. They also show the centrality of the ease of use of these systems by a user-centered perspective. The concept of quality of use is a key point of this work. In fact, in this paper we apply to the city the concept of usability, derived from the Human-Computer Interaction field, creating a parallelism between the structure and organization of cities and websites. In effect, some websites evolve during the time as cities do, with a continuous change and overlap of elements that produces the peculiar structure of the sites. This process of transformation risks to not be consistent with what people need, consequently making websites and cities unusable. So, it is necessary to safeguard their quality of use. In general, the evaluation of the quality of use of a certain website is determined from its usability as the capacity to let a certain target of user to satisfy a certain objective or need into a certain context. In our work the target is represented by the city users, the context by the city, and the objective by the quality of life. The concept of usability as a qualitative research method applied to the city can be connected to the Lynch' work [9], and in detail to his book "The image of the city" [10], where he identified the key elements of cognitive maps as being landmarks, nodes, paths, districts, and edges, and looked at how people build a mental representations of environmental spaces, then elaborating the concept of wayfinding. This work has been of inspiration for several authors [11–14] in supporting the design and evaluation of virtual environments and websites. On this basis, in this paper we adopt a website quality model to support interventions on the urban environment assuming the parallelism between cities and websites as a useful instrument to meet the city user's needs.

3 The Website Quality Models

As stated above, the approach we have adopted for the evaluation of the quality of use of the urban environment derives from the principles of the *ISO 9241-11:1998 Guidance on usability*, where the concept of usability is defined as: "extent to which a product can be used by specified users to achieve specified goals with effectiveness, efficiency and satisfaction in a specified context of use".

On the basis of this standard, a lot of practical models for the evaluation of the website's usability (i.e. the website quality models) have been elaborated. In general, it has been approached from three perspective: machine, experts, and users. About machine perspective, the quality evaluation of a website is generally made through a specific software that tests a set of established parameters [15]. For the experts' side, there are different techniques applied to predict usability problems, such as the heuristic evaluation or the cognitive walkthrough. The first is a usability inspection technique in which experts apply their knowledge of typical users, on the basis of a set of broad rules known as "heuristics", to evaluate user-interface elements (e.g. the ten heuristics of Nielsen [16]). Cognitive walkthrough technique consists in simulating the user interaction with the system, checking if the user's goals and actions can lead to a successful interaction in completing the tasks [17]. The evaluations executed by machine or experts have several benefits, as the possibility to focus on technical aspects, but they do not reveal the user perception on the quality of the website. Since the websites are designed for the end-user and their success is determined only by the end-user, it is a contradiction that their perception of quality and usability is not measured. Lastly, concerning the user perspective, a lot of website quality evaluation models have been elaborated. To name a few: the QUIS (Questionnaire for User Interaction Satisfaction) [18] is one of the most used questionnaire for evaluating the user interfaces; the Website Quality Model of Polillo [19] based on seven macro-features, useful not only for the evaluation, but also to adequately manage the website design process; the Framework for a Global Quality Evaluation [20], based on a website quality concept made up of three main dimensions (i.e. content, service, and technical quality). In addition, several quality models are designed for a specific kind of website, e.g. the e-commerce site. In this case, the user quality perception influences the customer satisfaction, encouraging the purchase.

Considered the above-cited ISO and several website quality models, we opt for the seven macro-features identified by Polillo's model for evaluating the usability of the city. In effect, this model constitutes a clear and well-organized framework for a general and complete evaluation of the website quality of use. Moreover, it highlights the importance of the user needs satisfactions in determined the success of a website. Following, we describe the macro-features highlighting the main issues to consider in the evaluation and detailing the related sub-features.

1. *Architecture.* It identifies the general information architecture of the website with its surfing paths, evaluating if it is suitable for the website content. In fact, a website has a good architecture if its organization in pages is content-coherent and allows an easy to understand navigation. The sub-features of architecture are: structure, site map, navigation.
2. *Communication.* It concerns how clearly and coherently the website communicates its aim through its visual identity. Referring to the sub-features (i.e. home page, brand identity, graphic design), they allow to evaluate how and if the website reached its communication aims through the brand identity hallmarks and the choice of graphic design (from layout, colours, fonts, etc.).
3. *Features.* It examines in detail the set of functionalities offered by the website and how the users could perform them. From this point of view, a good site must: have appropriate features supporting the user in finding information; prevent and help to reduce errors or malfunctioning; ensure the security of data entered. Indeed, the sub-features are: suitability, reliability, privacy, security.
4. *Content.* It identifies the reliability, the adequacy, the level of update, and the understanding of the information present on the website. The sub-features are: taxonomy/labelling, content style, information, translation, localization.
5. *Management.* It concerns the workability of the website and measures the overall quality of the website management. It is essential a continuous work to ensure proper workability for the whole time: technical supervision, software upgrade and data update, aids and supports to users. In fact the sub-features are: availability, monitoring, update and upgrade, relations with the users.
6. *Accessibility.* It deals with the aspects that allow everyone to quickly and easily access to the website. This feature examines fundamentally if the website is easy to access for all, regardless of the age and the ability and the hardware and the software (e.g. browser, search engine). The sub-features are: time's access, easy to find, browser independence, accessibility for all.

The Polillo's model includes another feature to evaluate, i.e. usability. We choose to leave it out from our city evaluation framework as it concerns everything making the website easy and pleasant to use and it does not arise from a specific aspect, but from all the above-illustrated features. In fact, usability can be intended as the result of the evaluation of all of them.

4 Discussion

As we said, the focus of this work is the application of a usability evaluation model to the urban environment. In order to do that, in this section we intend to investigate the matching points between the main features of the Polillo's website quality model and the main characteristics of the city environment. In detail, we specify how the peculiar aspects of the six features emerged in the previous section find some equivalences at the city level. For each feature some examples related to the city of Rome are provided. The human perspective at the basis of this approach should guarantee that in this case it is measured and evaluated how the city is perceived by the city users.

4.1 Architecture

In the urban environment, this level might correspond to the physical level, that is to say the organization of the city, the relationship between the different elements that constitute it (for example the urban and the mobility infrastructures), and the correspondence of the city composition (and elements) to the main city users' needs. The architecture also includes the tools useful for travelling within the city (e.g. road signs and directions) and the elements for the representation of the city structure (e.g. maps).

In order to evaluate the suitability of the city architecture to the user needs, it is mainly important to identify the general structure and composition of the city and the main objectives of its users, by pointing out the variance between these two elements. It is also important to evaluate the efficacy and the effectiveness of the tools that help people moving within the city, identifying both the real correspondence between the real structures of the city and how it is represented, and if these tools really help people during their travel. An important element to focus on is the user understanding of the city structure and of the different levels of the city. In this sense, just think how a traditional tool to "navigate a city", the map, can communicate several aspects of the city, such as the touristic one, the administrative one and so on. As an example, many different maps illustrate the city of Rome mostly referring to a single aspect (especially the touristic points of interest and the government buildings) and without integrating each other. These redundancy might contribute to create information fragmentation and to add confusion to the city user mind, impeding him/her to find the right information when needed. So the current tools may not adequately communicate the different aspects of Rome, as they represent a disjointed structure. This way to communicate the city of Rome might influence the way Rome is lived by its users, i.e. enjoying a single aspect at a time (as tourists, residents, workers, etc.).

4.2 Communication

In the urban context, this level might refer to the entire identity of the city (official and not) concerning its values and visual elements. In fact, different cities have different messages and give different suggestions. So, evaluating the communication of a city means focusing on how it communicates these contents towards the outside and on how it emphasizes their distinctive characteristics. In detail, it is important to identify how the city matches its visual identity with its real identity aspects, as well as if these characteristics are consistently present in the different city elements. It is also important to focus on the evaluation of the effectiveness of the communication system in helping people to use the city for reaching their goals.

Regarding that, we can focus on a specific similarity between the banners of the websites and the advertising signs of the city. In fact, as well as the banners cannot be perfectly integrated with the graphic elements of a website, by disturbing the user, also the billboards can clash with the general city elements and they can distract the city user, as shown in Fig. 1.

Fig. 1. Advertising panels of the city of Rome that can distract people, also impeding a clear visibility.

In order to avoid this negative citizen experience, in 2014 the Municipality of Rome prepared a plan that regulates the advertising panels of the city, both protecting its cultural heritage (that is a strong point of the city of Rome) and bringing the user to focus only on his/her activity, with no elements that could distract him/her.

4.3 Features

In the urban environment, this level might regard the delivery of public utility services and spaces offered by the Public Administration. So, the evaluation of the city features focuses on how services and spaces adequately meet the city users' needs and how they work. In detail, it is important to evaluate if these services (with their specific sub-functions) or spaces (with their specific characteristics) are consistent with what people want and with their objectives, if people always have the correct and necessary contextual information when he/she accesses to them, and if people can access to services and spaces and to the related information in an easy way. Moreover, the concrete performances of the different services and spaces should be evaluated.

As an example, in 2012 the citizens of Rome complained about the low quality of the public transport service by doing "ticket crossing" actions that consist in giving the unexpired bus ticket to the next bus passenger. This is an example that shows what a service that does not meet the people needs can produce. Considering the high number of protest by the city users, nowadays the public transport service of Rome is providing them with many value-added services, in order to improve their experience within the city, such as: promotion and discount for accessing to the services offered by the affiliated museums, theatres, restaurants, shops, and other kind of entertainments.

About the city spaces, we observe how human behaviours has been continually changing and influencing the urban structures. However, in general, the physical aspect of the city is mostly shaped on the basis of well-defined plans that take time to be effectively implemented, while behaviours change in a more quick and liquid way. So it is very probable that the city spaces often show some elements that do not adequately meet the current needs of citizens. This is made evident in the transformation of urban furniture in respect of the effective use made of them by the citizens. Figure 2 shows an example of a bottom up process of adjustment of the features offered by a public space in accordance with the real needs of people.

Fig. 2. Seats added by citizens in a square of the city of Rome to supply to the shortage and unsuitable arrangement of public benches.

4.4 Content

In the urban environment, this level might correspond to the information of the city, concerning both the physical and the digital environment. In detail, in this case it is important to evaluate how the information is "grouped" and organized. For example, we could evaluate how the different levels of the city (e.g. the political structures, the shopping streets, etc.) are present within the urban environment (if they create different areas, each dedicated to a specific level of the city, or if these levels are disseminated into different areas) and how people consider the related configuration. Moreover, we should evaluate the "labelling" of places and services (e.g. if the name of a specific space is appropriate and clear), if the used language (not only the verbal language) is suitable for the people aims, and if the provided information is appropriate and reliable. One of the important elements to focus on nowadays is also the direction of the information, since it is produced not only by the Public Administration that addresses it to the city users (top-down processes), but more and more by the city users themselves that address it to the Public Administration (bottom-up processes) or to other city users (peer-to-peer processes). Figure 3 shows an example related to the suitability of the label to the people aims and to the reliability of the information. In the city of Rome digital screens "as that illustrated into the picture below" give information concerning the limited traffic zones, and in particular if in a specific moment drivers can go in or not. If drivers can go in the message on the screen is "Active gate" (tr. "Varco attivo"); if not, the message is "Inactive gate" (tr. "Varco non attivo"), as reported in the picture below. These labels are generally considered not clear and people are confused when they read these messages. The reason is that usually people associate the adjective "active" to something that they

Fig. 3. The message "Varco non attivo" ("Inactive gate") confuses people. It communicates that drivers can access to a limited traffic zone by using an adjective ("inactive") usually associated to the impossibility to do something.

can do, and the "inactive" with something that they cannot do. In the given example, this association is inverted, inducing many users to make mistakes.

4.5 Management

In the urban environment, this characteristic might concern the management of the city by the Public Administration. The evaluation of the management focuses on: the availability of the city services and spaces; the city user perception of the duration of the possible services suspensions and the way in which they are communicated; who are the city users that use the different spaces and services of the city and how they enjoy them; how people see the possible maintenances of the city.

An example: the city of Rome had different problems related to the public works, mainly concerning the road maintenance. The most important problems have been: the lack of transparency regarding the duration of public works; the overlapping of the public interventions on the same urban area; the security of citizens; etc. In 2015 specific measures were adopted in order to facilitate the life of the city users, even in this sense. Among them: the use of electronic signage providing real-time updates for the work in progress the sharing of a map of the work on the road surface through which the city users can be informed and decide how moving; and the preparation of a plan which defines the different interventions avoiding the overlapping of works in the same urban area.

4.6 Accessibility

In the urban context, this feature (truthfully already applied in the city context) might mainly be referred to the accessibility to the physical and digital infrastructures of the

Fig. 4. One of the architectural barriers of the city of Rome

city. In detail, this characteristic evaluates if all the people categories can access, in any way, to the city services and structures. Moreover, this level of usability also focuses on the times of access to the different services or structures (e.g. public buses) and on the findability of the different places of the city (also through different means of transportation and not only through one mean).

One of the main problems related to this feature is the presence of the architectural barriers that impede to people with physical impairments the movement or the use of services. Figure 4 is an example of this issue related to the city of Rome.

5 Conclusion and Future Work

This work focuses on the application of the usability concept to the urban environment as a possible way to understand and evaluate the city from a user-centered perspective. In effect, the assumption is that as the application of the usability concept in evaluating interactive systems allows users to interact with them with efficiency, effectiveness, and satisfaction, as the application of the same concept in evaluating a city allows the city users to interact with the different elements of the urban environment in an effective (i.e. assuring the achievement of city users objectives), efficient (i.e. assuring the appropriate use of resources in achieving city users objectives), and satisfactory (i.e. assuring the comfort in "using" the city) way.

Moreover, the concept of usability has been made arise from the interaction among six specific features: architecture, communication, features, contents, management, and accessibility. In fact, each of them should be considered as linked to the others.

Lastly, this work does not intend to provide specific solutions to the city issues, but only to focus on the citizen perception and satisfaction of the city, an aim that the concept of usability can contribute to better explore. However, both for website and city environments, the usability concept is not only based on the point of view of the real final users, but also on some general solutions applicable in different contexts. In this paper we apply these characteristics to the city of Rome with the aim to better illustrate them. However this work aims to create a usability framework that can be used by different cities. Moreover, it does not intend to overlook the peculiarities of a single city, since it only provides general elements for investigating the city from the user point of view. Indeed, the identified problems and needs should be solved by each city in a context-based and specific way. In the future work, we intend to test it with different Italian cities.

References

1. Oliveira, Á., Campolargo, M.: From smart cities to human smart cities. In: 48th Hawaii International Conference on System Sciences, pp. 2336–2344. IEEE Computer Science, Washington (2015)
2. Norman, D.A.: The Psychology of Everyday Things. Basic books, New York (1988)
3. Sanders, E.B.N., Stappers, P.J.: Co-creation and the new landscapes of design. Co-Design **4**(1), 5–18 (2008)

4. Schuurman, D., Baccarne, B., De Marez, L., Mechant, P.: Smart ideas for smart cities: investigating crowdsourcing for generating and selecting ideas for ICT innovation in a city context. J. Theor. Appl. Electron. Commer. Res. **7**(3), 49–62 (2012)
5. Giffinger R., Fertner C., Kramar H., Kalasek R., Pichler-Milanović N., Meijers E.: Smart Cities: Ranking of European Medium-Sized Cities. Centre of Regional Science at the Vienna University of Technology, Department of Geography at University of Ljubljana and the OTB Research Institute for Housing, Urban and Mobility Studies at the Delft University of Technology (2007). http://www.smart-cities.eu/download/smart_cities_final_report.pdf
6. Cohen B.: What exactly is a smart city? Fast Co.Exist (2012). http://www.fastcoexist.com/1680538/what-exactly-is-a-smart-city
7. Lombardi P., Giordano S., Farouh H., Wael Y.: An analytic network model for smart cities. In: 11th International Symposium on the Analytic Hierarchy Process for Multicriteria Decision Making, pp. 1–6. AHP Academy (2011)
8. Marsal-Llacuna, M.L.: City indicators on social sustainability as standardization technologies for smarter (citizen-centered) governance of cities. Soc. Indic. Res., 1–24 (2015)
9. Tuters, M., de Lange, M.: Executable urbanisms: messing with Ubicomp's singular future. In: Buschauer R., Willis K.S. (eds.): Locative Media: Multidisciplinary Perspectives on Media and Locality, pp. 49–70. Transcript, Bielefeld (2013)
10. Lynch, K.: The Image of the City. MIT Press, Cambridge (1960)
11. Tan, G.W., Wei, K.K.: An empirical study of web browsing behaviour: towards an effective website design. Electron. Commer. Res. Appl. **5**(4), 261–271 (2006)
12. Dieberger, A., Frank, A.U.: A city metaphor to support navigation in complex information spaces. J. Vis. Lang. Comput. **9**(6), 597–622 (1998)
13. Cato, J.: User-Centered Web Design. Addison Wesley, Boston (2001)
14. Hinton, A.: Understanding Context: Environment, Language, and Information Architecture. O'Reilly Media, Sebastopol (2014)
15. Bauer, C., Scharl, A.: Quantitive evaluation of web site content and structure. Internet Res. **10**(1), 31–44 (2000)
16. Nielsen, J., Molich, R.: Heuristic evaluation of user interfaces. In: Carrasco Chew, J., Whiteside, J. (eds.) SIGCHI Conference on Human Factors in Computing Systems, pp. 249–256. ACM, New York (1990)
17. Wharton, C., Rieman, J., Lewis, C., Polson, P.: The cognitive walkthrough method: a practitioner's guide. In: Usability Inspection Methods, pp. 105–140. Wiley, New York (1994)
18. Chin, J.P., Diehl, V.A., Norman, K.L.: Development of an instrument measuring user satisfaction of the human-computer interface. In: O'Hare, J.J. (ed.) SIGCHI Conference on Human Factors in Computing Systems, pp. 213–218. ACM, New York (1988)
19. Polillo, R.: Il Check-up dei Siti Web. Valutare la Qualità per Migliorarla. Edizioni Apogeo, Milano (2004)
20. Rocha, Á.: Framework for a global quality evaluation of a website. Online Inf. Rev. **36**(3), 374–382 (2012)

Identifying Relevant Dimensions for the Quality of Web Mashups: An Empirical Study

Tihomir Orehovački[1(✉)], Cinzia Cappiello[2], and Maristella Matera[2]

[1] Department of Information and Communication Technologies, Juraj Dobrila University of Pula, Zagrebačka 30, 52100 Pula, Croatia
tihomir.orehovacki@unipu.hr

[2] Dipartimento di Elettronica, Informazione e Bioingegneria, Politecnico di Milano, Via Ponzio 34/5, 20133 Milan, Italy
{cinzia.cappiello,maristella.matera}@polimi.it

Abstract. Web mashups available online today are very often characterized by a poor quality. Several researchers justify this aspect by considering the situational, short-living nature of these applications. We instead believe such a low quality is also due to the lack of suitable quality models. This paper presents a quality model that tries to capture the nature of Web mashups by focusing on their component-based nature and the added value that they are required to introduce with respect to their single constituents. A finite set of indicators and attributes was first determined by reviewing the literature. An analysis of data collected from domain experts revealed a relevance of performance variables at different levels of granularity. An empirical study was then carried out to assess which dimensions are the most relevant with respect to the mashup quality as perceived by users.

Keywords: Web mashups · Quality evaluation · Model validation · Relevance identification · Empirical study

1 Introduction

Web mashups are composite applications that integrate reusable data, application logic and/or user interfaces typically - but not mandatorily, sourced from the Web [11]. After several years of research and development experiences on this class of applications, it is still difficult to find high-quality, useful mashups on the Web. On the one hand, it is true that still there are not stable development practices and tools. On the other hand, Web mashups are meant to satisfy situational, short-living needs and in this scenario quality might not be a primary concern. Moreover, suitable quality models, able to capture mashup peculiarities, are still lacking. If adequate models would be available, developers and final users as well would reach an increased awareness of how mashups could (and should) be.

We first observed a lack of adequate quality models when we conducted a study on the mashups published on programmableweb.com [5], the reference Web site for the community of API and Web mashup developers. To evaluate a subset of about 100

M. Kurosu (Ed.): HCI 2016, Part I, LNCS 9731, pp. 396–407, 2016.
DOI: 10.1007/978-3-319-39510-4_37

mashups available on that site we adopted quality metrics generally valid for Web applications. We compared the objective results achieved by computing such metrics with the findings of a heuristic evaluation conducted by a pool of independent evaluators acquainted with Web technologies and mashup development. The result was a sharp discrepancy between the two assessments, highlighting that mashup quality requires revised models able to capture the specifics of such applications. Certainly, traditional quality principles for Web applications must not be neglected but, even for simple Web mashups, generic Web models need to be repurposed.

Given the previous observations, this paper investigates the relevance of traditional quality factors with respect to the nature of mashups and what additional factors can be further considered to focus especially on the added value that such composite applications can introduce with respect to exploiting their single components. Drawing on an extensive literature review, we determined a finite set of indicators and attributes that contribute to the quality of mashups and employed them to design a conceptual model in the form of a quality requirements tree. An analysis of data collected from domain experts revealed a relevance of performance variables at different levels of granularity in a quality requirements tree. With the objective to examine the validity of the introduced conceptual model, an empirical study was then carried out. During the study, participants accomplished predefined scenarios of interaction with a representative sample of mashups and assessed them by exploiting the quality model. Study findings helped us determine which dimensions, among those identified in the quality requirements tree, are considered as relevant with respect to the mashup perceived quality.

The paper is organized as follows. Section 2 reviews the most relevant related works discussing the quality of mashups. Section 3 then illustrates the model that we defined. Section 4 describes how we validated the model and the main implications deriving from the conducted empirical study. Section 5 finally draws our conclusions.

2 Related Work

A quality model consists of a selection of quality characteristics that are relevant for a given class of software applications and/or for a given assessment process [13]. In the Web scenario, the first quality models focused on static Web sites [17, 39], then some authors started addressing more complex Web applications [25, 29]. Recently, quality models for Web 2.0 applications have been proposed [35, 38, 41]. In the more restricted mashup context, the quality dimensions suggested by all these works, as well as the one proposed in Software Engineering [15, 19] and Web Engineering [4, 27] may be partly appropriate to measure the internal quality of a mashup (e.g., code readability), as well as its external quality in-use (e.g., usability). However, Rio and Brito e Abreu [39] showed that, in order to effectively support system development and evaluation, quality model must be domain-dependent, as there is a strong impact of the application domain on the usefulness of quality dimensions. In line with these findings, this paper aims to assess the relevance of some quality dimensions with respect to the mashup peculiarities. This research is motivated by some past experience of some authors of this paper that showed that quality models that generally work well for traditional Web applications do not help identify even sever problems when applied to the evaluation of mashups [5].

Other works also tried to explore diverse aspects of the mashup quality and usability. Drawing on recent standards [16] and usability guidelines for Web design, Insfran et al. [14] proposed the Mashup Usability Model that decomposes usability into appropriateness, recognisability, learnability, operability, user error protection, user interface aesthetics, and accessibility. Koschmider et al. [20] then emphasized that the selection of quality metrics also depends on the type of mashups. For example, UI mashup should be evaluated especially in terms of consistent graphical representation, while data and function mashups are required to fulfill criteria that address more the integration and the orchestration of the involved resources.

Quality of the mashup can be also observed from the perspective of heterogeneous components that constitute it [6] as well as from the aspect of the final composition [43]. In that respect, Cappiello et al. [5] developed a model which addresses: data quality (accuracy, timeliness, completeness, availability, and consistency), presentation quality (usability and accessibility), and composition quality (added value, component suitability, component usage, consistency, and availability). Nevertheless, results of a systematic mapping study [9] suggest that there is still a need for empirical research addressing the assessment of the proposed quality dimensions.

In this paper we capitalize on all the previous works. The quality dimensions that we investigated were selected by carefully reviewing all such works. In addition, as illustrated in the next sections, we experimentally show how some dimensions are more relevant than others. We believe this effort to validate the model is original and introduces a valuable contribution in the Web mashup domain.

3 A Quality Model for Web Mashups

Drawing on a comprehensive literature review that included prior studies on the assessment of mashups [5, 9, 11], mashup components [6], mashup tools [37], and Web 2.0 applications designed for collaborative writing [30, 31, 33], mind mapping [33, 35, 36], and diagramming [31, 35], an initial pool of 165 items meant for measuring diverse facets of quality in the context of mashups was designed. To ensure content validity at all levels of granularity in the model, the relevance of items was examined by two independent mashup experts on a three-point scale (1- mandatory, 2 - desired, 3 - not relevant). Data collected from experts were examined with two criteria: content validity ratio (CVR) and average value of assigned relevance ($\bar{x}$). A total of 62 items which have not met the cut-off values of the aforementioned criteria (CVR = 0.99, $\bar{x} \geq 2.00$) [22, 23] were omitted from further analysis. This procedure resulted in a quality model for Web mashups which consists of 6 categories and 24 attributes.

System quality is composed of four quality attributes: efficiency, effectiveness, response time, and compatibility. *Efficiency* refers to the degree to which the employment of a Web mashup saves resources in a specified context. In that respect, Web mashups should be implemented in a way so that users can complete intended tasks in the shortest time possible and with minimal number of steps. *Effectiveness* is the extent to which users can, by means of a Web mashup, realize intended tasks completely and accurately. Perceived effectiveness can be evaluated with two objective metrics: proportion of tasks completed and proportion of tasks that are completed correctly [15]. Keeping that in mind, the interface of a Web mashup should provide all functionalities needed for task completion. *Response time* reflects the degree to which a Web mashup efficiently reacts to users' actions. Considering that users have very low tolerance threshold related to the response time, this quality attribute plays an important role in a success of every Web application, including mashups [31]. Therefore, a Web mashup and its components need to be quickly loaded in a Web browser whereas execution of selected interface functionalities should take very little time. *Compatibility* represents a level to which a Web mashup operates properly with different types of devices and among different environments. Taking into account that Web mashups are commonly referred to as one of the representatives of Web 2.0 applications [34], they also have to meet the aforementioned compatibility criteria.

Service quality deals with attributes measuring the quality of interaction between a Web mashup and users. It includes three quality attributes: availability, reliability, and feedback. *Availability* denotes the extent to which a Web mashup and its components can be accessed at any time. *Reliability* refers to the degree to which a Web mashup is dependable, stable, and bug-free. Since this attribute belongs to a set of essential predictors of the quality and satisfaction of users [45], a Web mashup has to perform as intended, without errors or operational interruptions. *Feedback* is related to the extent to which a Web mashup returns appropriate messages and notifies users about its status or progress of displaying the content in its components. It originates from Nielsen's ten usability heuristics [26], and according to Seffah et al. [42] it can be used as a metric which indicates to what level a piece of software congruously responds to users' actions by supplying them with convenient messages. In that respect, a Web mashup should timely inform users with messages that are clear, understandable, precise, and useful.

Content Quality refers to the perception or the assessment of the suitability of the content that the mashup provides for a specific goal in a defined context. In this category, we consider five dimensions that analyze the provided data from different perspectives: content accuracy, content completeness, content credibility, content timeliness, and content added value. *Content accuracy* refers to the correctness of the content that is displayed as output in the mashup. Correctness is usually assessed as the similarity between the considered value and the correct one [40]. *Content completeness* refers to the ability of mashup components to produce all expected data values [7]. Usually completeness is evaluated on the basis of the query submitted by the user. In fact, it can be defined as the ratio between the number of values obtained and the expected one. *Content credibility* is related to the trustworthiness of the mashup components and thus to the related data sources. Trustworthiness is an important aspect to consider especially when accuracy is not precisely assessable: if data are gathered from a certificated source, their correctness is guaranteed. *Content timeliness* refers to the fact that data have to be accessed at the right time. Data should be temporally valid. This dimension can be assessed as the ratio between currency (the data's "age" from the time of component creation or last update) and volatility (the average period of data validity in a specific context) [3]. *Content added value* refers to the possibility to gather more information and thus value from integration of different components. It refers the possibility to perform additional queries due to the fact that data are integrated or to acquire more knowledge simply for the fact that data are visualized together (and not necessarily integrated [5]).

Composition Quality aims to evaluate the orchestration among components and the way in which the mashup provides the desired features [5]. This category includes three dimensions: component suitability, composition added value and effectiveness of integrated visualization. *Component suitability* refers to the suitability of the offered component functionalities and data with respect to the output that the mashup is supposed to provide. *Composition added value* refers to the functionalities and data offered by the mashup. In particular, the added value is generated by the new functionalities enabled by the integration of components. In fact, effective mashups exploit and combine the functionalities offered by the components in order to provide new and advanced operations. *Effectiveness of integrated visualization* refers to the cohesiveness of the visualization that is the opportunity to visualize in the same screen data coming from different sources [8]. Users benefit from the fact that heterogeneous data are aggregated into a unified visualization.

Effort stands for attributes, which measure the effortlessness of the Web mashup use. The following five attributes constitute this dimension: minimal memory load, accessibility, ease of use, learnability, and understandability. *Minimal memory load* refers to the amount of mental and perceptive activity needed for completing an intended task by means of the Web mashup. It is commonly employed for measuring the amount of information user needs to memorize to complete a particular task [42]. *Accessibility* denotes the extent to which the Web mashup is usable to people with the widest range of characteristics and capabilities. In order to achieve this goal, Web mashups have to comply with as many guidelines suggested in [46]. For instance, both interface functionalities and content returned by the Web mashup should be of sufficient size to be readable to visually impaired people. *Ease of use* presents the degree to which the use of the Web mashup is free of effort. Considering that ease of use significantly contributes to the perceived usefulness, and users' satisfaction [32], the Web mashup should be easy to operate in a way that users have no need to seek assistance of any kind when using it. *Learnability* refers to the extent to which it is easy to learn how to use the Web mashup. *Understandability* is the degree to which functionalities of the mashup interface are clear and unambiguous to users.

User experience concerns the quality attributes such as usefulness, playfulness, satisfaction, and loyalty which directly contribute to the adoption of the Web mashup by users. *Usefulness* refers to the extent to which the employment of the Web mashup enhances users' performance in completing intended tasks. Findings of prior study indicate that usefulness has significant influence on users' satisfaction and loyalty [32]. Taking this into account, features provided by the Web mashup should be advantageous compared to those offered by any other alternative. *Playfulness* is the degree to which the use of the Web mashup successfully holds users' attention. *Satisfaction* is the level to which users like to have an interaction with the Web mashup. It is of a great importance that Web mashup meet users' expectations. *Loyalty* refers to the extent to which users are willing to continue to use the Web mashups and recommend it to others. The Web mashup should be able to turn occasional visitors into regular users that are willing to spread a good word among their families, friends, and colleagues.

4 Quality Model Validation

4.1 Research Design

We conducted an empirical study adopting a within-subjects research design contrasting four Web mashups ("Gaiagi 3D Driver" (http://www.gaiagi.com/driving-simulator), "Health Map" (http://www.healthmap.org), "Leeds Travel Info" (http://www.leedstravel.info), and "This is Now" (http://now.jit.su)) that are heterogeneous with respect to their purpose. At the beginning of the study, details on the architecture of mashups, their taxonomy, and practical usefulness were presented to participants. In the next step, predefined scenarios with representative steps of interaction with mashups were given to each student. After finishing scenarios with all four mashups, students were asked to complete an online post-use questionnaire. It was composed of 6 items related to participants' demography and 103 items meant for measuring 24 diverse facets of mashups' quality as deriving from the model illustrated in the previous section. Responses to the questionnaire items were modulated on a four-point Likert scale (1 – strongly agree, 4 – strongly disagree). Each attribute was measured with between two and seven items. For the purpose of data analysis, attributes and categories were operationalized as composite subjective measures. Values for quality attributes were estimated as a sum of responses to items that are assigned to them. The same holds for quality categories and overall perceived quality of evaluated mashups.

The assumption that data was sampled from a Gaussian distribution was examined with the Shapiro-Wilk Test. Considering that in all comparisons the Shapiro-Wilk statistic for at least one variable significantly deviated from a normal distribution ($p < .05$), the analysis of collected data was conducted with non-parametric tests. With the goal to explore differences among evaluated mashups, the Friedman's ANOVA expressed as chi-square ($\chi 2$) value was applied as the non-parametric counterpart to the one-way ANOVA with repeated measures. By employing separate Wilcoxon Signed-Rank Test (Z) on all possible pairs of evaluated mashups, actual differences existing among them were identified. In order to avoid a Type I error and declare results of pairwise comparisons significant, a Bonferroni correction was applied to the results of Wilcoxon Signed-Rank Tests. It was calculated by dividing the significance level of .05 by number of comparisons. The effect size (r) is an objective measure that reflects the relevance of difference between a pair of evaluated mashups. It represents a quotient of Z-value and a square root of the number of observations. Values of .10, .30, or .50 for the effect size can be, as a rule of thumb, interpreted as small, medium, or large, respectively [10].

As regards participants, 43 subjects took part in the empirical study. They ranged in age from 19 to 45 years ($M = 20.93$, $SD = 3.900$). The sample was composed of 83.72 % male and 16.28 % female students. At the time when the study took place, they were all in the second year of an undergraduate programme in Information Systems. Up to the implementation of the study, 51.16 % of participants had never used mashups before. Remaining 48.84 % of students are using mashups at least once a week where majority of them (85.71 %) is spending less than an hour on interaction with mashups. On the other hand, study participants are loyal users of popular Web 2.0 applications such as Facebook, Twitter and Instagram. Majority of students (53.49 %) are using those social Web applications three or more times a day. When frequency in use expressed in hours is considered, majority of study participants (69.76 %) are spending between four and ten hours a week on interaction with the aforementioned Web 2.0 applications.

4.2 Findings

Since another instrument for measuring the perceived quality of mashups does not exist in literature, it was not possible to conduct benchmarking thus obtain a quantitative measure of validity. As an alternative, Lewis [23] proposes the assessment of sensitivity which affects the validity of the measuring instrument. The sensitivity of the introduced model and employed post-use questionnaire was examined by exploring differences among evaluated mashups.

Friedman's ANOVA revealed a significant difference ($\chi 2(3) = 19.866$, $p = .000$) among the four mashups in the overall quality perceived by study participants. Drawing on this finding, a post-hoc analysis with the significance level set at $p < .0125$ was applied. It was discovered that significant difference in perceived quality exists between This is Now and Health Map ($Z = -4.302$, $p = .000$, $r = -.46$), This is Now and Gaiagi 3D Driver ($Z = -2.839$, $p = .005$, $r = -.31$), Health Map and Gaiagi 3D Driver ($Z = -2.494$, $p = .013$, $r = -.27$), and between Leeds Travel Info and Health Map ($Z = -2.476$, $p = .013$, $r = -.27$).

When categories of quality are considered, *composition quality* is associated with the highest level of relevance. This resulted from two large in size (.53 and .51) and two medium in size (both .39) differences among evaluated mashups. It is followed by quality categories *user experience* that uncovered three medium in size (in range from .47 to .40) differences, *effort* which demonstrated one large (.50) and three medium in size (in range from .48 to .37) differences, and *content quality* which has shown one large (.50), one medium (.37), and one small (.27) in size difference among four mashups. Finally, it appeared that *system quality* and *service quality* have the lowest degree of relevance among identified categories meant for measuring quality of mashups. Namely, system quality revealed one medium in size (.34) difference whereas service quality uncovered two small in size (.28 and .26) differences among mashups that took part in the study. The aforementioned findings are summarized in Table 1.

Table 1. Taxonomy of proposed categories with respect to their relevance in evaluating the quality of Web mashups

Quality categories for Web mashups	$\chi 2$	Effects in size (r)		
		Large	Medium	Small
Composition quality	37.899	.53[c], .51[e]	.39[d], .39[b]	-
User experience	33.393	-	.47[e], .45[c], .40[f]	-
Effort	28.520	.50[f]	.48[c], .38[a], .37[d]	-
Content quality	22.584	.50[e]	.37[c]	.27[d]
System quality	8.198	-	.34[a]	-
Service quality	7.950	-	-	.28[e], .26[d]

[a] Gaiagi 3D Driver vs. Health Map, [b] Gaiagi 3D Driver vs. Leeds Travel Info,
[c] Gaiagi 3D Driver vs. This is Now, [d] Health Map vs. Leeds Travel Info,
[e] Health Map vs. This is Now, [f] Leeds Travel Info vs. This is Now

Table 2. Taxonomy of proposed attributes with respect to their relevance in evaluating the quality of Web mashups

Quality attributes for Web mashups	χ2	Effects in size (r)		
		Large	Medium	Small
Mandatory				
Content added value	51.618	.57[e], .50[c]	.49[f]	-
Response time	43.793	-	.49[c], .41[b], .38[f], .37[e]	.29[a]
Ease of use	43.387	-	.48[e], .44[c], .37[f], .32[d]	-
Playfulness	42.135	-	.46[b], .44[d], .38[c], .38[e]	-
Effect. of Int. Visualizations	40.958	.52[c], .52[e]	.42[f], .36[b], .34[d]	-
Satisfaction	40.500	.54[f]	.44[b], .42[e], .37[c]	-
Sufficient				
Compatibility	37.358	-	.40[a], .40[f], .38[b]	-
Loyalty	36.951	-	.42[b], .41[d], .40[e], .35[c]	-
Usefulness	31.190	-	.44[e], .37[c]	.27[d]
Effectiveness	30.404	-	.48[e], .38[c], .34[d]	-
Content Timeliness	28.657	-	.46[c], .43[a], .38[b]	-
Composition Added Value	24.467	-	.39[c], .38[d], .35[e], .34[b]	-
Content Credibility	24.076	-	.41[c], .40[e], .31[b]	-
Desired				
Reliability	22.941	-	.38[c], .37[b]	.28[a]
Learnability	22.106	-	.39[f], .33[c]	.28[d]
Minimal Memory Load	21.995	-	.37[f], .33[c]	.27[e]
Feedback	20.610	-	.40[c], .39[e]	.28[f]
Content Completeness	20.334	-	.48[e], .37[c], .33[d], .32[b]	-
Composition Suitability	20.213	-	.40[e], .34[c]	-
Optional				
Accessibility	12.895	-	.33[f], .31[a]	.29[c], .28[d]
Content Accuracy	8.385	-	.34[d]	-
Efficiency	8.075	-	.34[e]	-
Availability	8.006	-	.30[f]	-
Not relevant				
Understandability	5.140	-	-	-

[a] Gaiagi 3D Driver vs. Health Map, [b] Gaiagi 3D Driver vs. Leeds Travel Info,
[c] Gaiagi 3D Driver vs. This is Now, [d] Health Map vs. Leeds Travel Info,
[e] Health Map vs. This is Now, [f] Leeds Travel Info vs. This is Now

Taking into account results related to attributes, they can be classified into five groups (mandatory, sufficient, desired, optional, and not relevant) of relevance with respect to the quality of mashups, as presented in Table 2. If the Web mashup does not comply with requirements specified by mandatory attributes its quality will be significantly reduced. Sufficient attributes are also very important, but failing to meet requirements defined by them will affect the overall perceived quality to a lesser extent than in the case of mandatory attributes. If requirements that constitute desired attributes are not satisfied, the overall perceived quality will be penalized to some extent but users will not reject the Web mashup. Optional attributes have similar role as desired attributes, but their impact on overall perceived quality is lower than the impact of desired attributes. Not relevant attributes are the ones that might be important in the case of other types of software, but not in the context of Web mashups.

4.3 Discussion

The reported findings indicate several contributions and implications for academic scholars and practitioners. First, the concept of quality that is introduced in recent international standard on quality of software [15], was reworked and adapted to the context of mashups. More specifically, the proposed model is composed of attributes which originate from theories related to the acceptance of technology [2, 24, 43, 44], success of information systems [12], models and guidelines aimed for evaluating quality [4, 6, 15, 16, 28, 35, 38, 41], user experience [18, 21, 26], and usability [1, 42] thus reflecting pragmatic and hedonic facets of quality. Next, the relevance of the dimensions considered in the proposed model was empirically identified. Considering the results of data analysis, all dimensions of the model, except the understandability, demonstrated the significant differences among mashups and can be consequently used for the quality evaluation purposes in this context. All quality attributes together with the composite measure of overall quality that have met the criteria of sensitivity have shown between small (.26 in the case of the category which deals with the assessment of service quality) and large (.57 in the case of an attribute which measures the extent to which content returned by mashups adds value to users) effects in size (as specified by Cohen [10]) which additionally confirms their suitability in assessing the quality of mashups.

Third, for all attributes and categories that have proven to fulfill the criteria of sensitivity, the practical relevance for evaluating the quality of mashups was determined. The set forth relevance is based on the amount of differences that were discovered as well as on the effect size of each difference. It should be noted that when two or more attributes had similar number of differences identified, their level of relevance in evaluating the quality of Web mashups sequence was determined by the value of their overall effect size.

Given that introduced quality model and measuring instrument add to the extant body of knowledge, academic scholars can use them as a foundation for future advances in the field. Practitioners can employ the post-use questionnaire in order to examine quality of existing mashups. In addition, the reported findings can be used by practitioners as guidelines for the development of novel mashups.

As with majority of empirical studies, the work presented in this paper has several limitations. The first one is related to the homogeneity of study participants since heterogeneous sample of users may have different attitude towards facets of quality in the context of mashups. Keeping that in mind, results of the conducted study should be interpreted carefully. The second limitation concerns the sample of mashups that were involved in the study. Although reported findings have shown significant difference among heterogeneous mashups, it would be worth to investigate if introduced framework would yield significant differences among mashups that have similar purpose. Since each type of mashups has its specific features which may affect dimensions of perceived quality, the last limitation indicates that reported findings cannot be generalized to all types of mashups. Taking the aforementioned into account, further studies should be carried out in order to draw sound conclusions and examine the robustness of study results.

5 Conclusions

This paper represents one of the few attempts to define a quality model capturing the peculiarities of mashups. Driven by the results of some past studies, we took a better look at the characteristics of mashups and identified some relevant dimensions that reflect the quality of such applications as perceived by the end users. Differently from other contributions, we experimentally assessed the relevance of the considered quality dimensions. Taking into account the overall difference that was found among evaluated Web mashups together with the number and strength of differences in pairwise comparisons, the proposed set of attributes was classified into five different groups. We in particular found that attributes such as content added value, response time, ease of use, playfulness, effectiveness of integrated visualizations and satisfaction strongly contribute to the overall perceived quality of Web mashups. On the other hand, it appeared that attributes like accessibility, content accuracy, efficiency, and availability, which have proven to be important for assessing other breeds of software, are less important in the context of evaluating the quality of Web mashups.

We recognize that many of the quality dimensions introduced in this paper are not easy to turn into operative metrics and to be automatically assessed, yet we also recognize that quality assessment to a large degree will always be a qualitative process. Our future work will be however devoted to the development of a measuring instrument as an extension of a quality-aware composition paradigm already implemented in mashup platform [8].

References

1. Alonso-Ríos, D., Vázquez-García, A., Mosqueira-Rey, E., Moret-Bonillo, V.: Usability: a critical analysis and a taxonomy. Int. J. Hum. Comput. Interact. **26**(1), 53–74 (2010)
2. Bhattacherjee, A.: Understanding information systems continuance: an expectation-confirmation model. MIS Quart. **25**(3), 351–370 (2001)
3. Bovee, M., Srivastava, R., Mak, B.: A conceptual framework and belief-function approach to assessing overall information quality. Int. J. Intel. Syst. **18**(1), 51–74 (2001)
4. Calero, C., Ruiz, J., Piattini, M.: Classifying Web metrics using the Web quality model. Online Inf. Rev. **29**(3), 227–248 (2005)
5. Cappiello, C., Daniel, F., Koschmider, A., Matera, M., Picozzi, M.: A quality model for mashups. In: Auer, S., Díaz, O., Papadopoulos, G.A. (eds.) ICWE 2011. LNCS, vol. 6757, pp. 137–151. Springer, Heidelberg (2011)
6. Cappiello, C., Daniel, F., Matera, M.: A quality model for mashup components. In: Gaedke, M., Grossniklaus, M., Díaz, O. (eds.) ICWE 2009. LNCS, vol. 5648, pp. 236–250. Springer, Heidelberg (2009)

7. Cappiello, C., Daniel, F., Matera, M., Pautasso, C.: Information quality in mashups. IEEE Internet Comput. **14**(4), 14–22 (2010)
8. Cappiello, C., Matera, M., Picozzi, M., Daniel, F., Fernandez, A.: Quality-aware mashup composition: issues, techniques and tools. In: Proceedings of the 8th International Conference on the Quality of Information and Communications Technology, pp. 10–19. IEEE, Lisbon (2012)
9. Cedillo, P., Fernandez, A., Insfran, E., Abrahão, S.: Quality of Web mashups: a systematic mapping study. In: Sheng, Q.Z., Kjeldskov, J. (eds.) ICWE Workshops 2013. LNCS, vol. 8295, pp. 66–78. Springer, Heidelberg (2013)
10. Cohen, J.: A power primer. Psychol. Bull. **112**(1), 155–159 (1992)
11. Daniel, F., Matera, M.: Mashups: Concepts, Models, and Architectures. Data-Centric Systems and Applications. Springer, Heidelberg (2014)
12. DeLone, W.H., McLean, E.R.: The DeLone and McLean model of information systems success: a ten-year update. J. Manag. Inf. Syst. **19**(4), 9–30 (2003)
13. Fenton, N.E., Peeger, S.L.: Software Metrics: A Rigorous and Practical Approach. PWS Publishing, Boston (1997)
14. Insfran, E., Cedillo, P., Fernández, A., Abrahão, S., Matera, M.: Evaluating the usability of mashups applications. In: Proceedings of the 8th International Conference on the Quality of Information and Communications Technology, pp. 323–326. IEEE, Lisbon (2012)
15. ISO/IEC 25010: Systems and software engineering - Systems and software Quality Requirements and Evaluation (SQuaRE) - System and software quality models (2011)
16. ISO/IEC 25012: Systems and software engineering - Systems and software Quality Requirements and Evaluation (SQuaRE) – Data quality model (2008)
17. Ivory, M.Y., Megraw, R.: Evolution of Web site design patterns. ACM Trans. Inf. Syst. **23**, 463–497 (2005)
18. Hassenzahl, M., Tractinsky, N.: User experience - a research agenda. Behav. Inf. Technol. **25**(2), 91–97 (2006)
19. Kan, S.H.: Metrics and Models in Software Quality Engineering. Addison-Wesley Longman Publishing Co., Boston (2002)
20. Koschmider, A., Hoyer, V., Giessmann, A.: Quality metrics for mashups. In: Proceedings of the Annual Research Conference of the South African Institute of Computer Scientists and Information Technologists, pp. 376–380. ACM, Bela-Bela (2010)
21. Law, E.L.-C., Van Schaik, P.: Modelling user experience – an agenda for research and practice. Interact. Comput. **22**(5), 313–322 (2010)
22. Lawshe, C.H.: A quantitative approach to content validity. Pers. Psychol. **28**(4), 563–575 (1975)
23. Lewis, J.R.: IBM computer usability satisfaction questionnaires: psychometric evaluation and instructions for use. Int. J. Hum. Comput. Inter. **7**(1), 57–78 (1995)
24. Liao, C., Palvia, P., Chen, J.-L.: Information technology adoption behavior life cycle: toward a Technology Continuance Theory (TCT). Int. J. Inf. Manage. **29**(4), 309–320 (2009)
25. Mavromoustakos, S., Andreou, A.S.: WAQE: a Web Application Quality Evaluation model. Int. J. Web Eng. Technol. **3**, 96–120 (2007)
26. Nielsen, J., Mack, R.L.: Usability Inspection Methods. Wiley, New York (1994)
27. Olsina, L., Covella, G., Rossi, G.: Web quality. In: Mendes, E., Mosley, N. (eds.) Web Engineering: Theory and Practice of Metrics and Measurement for Web Development, pp. 109–142. Springer, Heidelberg (2005)
28. Olsina, L., Lew, P., Dieser, A., Rivera, B.: Updating quality models for evaluating new generation Web applications. J. Web Eng. **11**(3), 209–246 (2012)
29. Olsina, L., Rossi, G.: Measuring Web application quality with WebQEM. IEEE Multimedia **9**, 20–29 (2002)

30. Orehovački, T.: Perceived quality of cloud based applications for collaborative writing. In: Pokorny, J., et al. (eds.) Information Systems Development – Business Systems and Services: Modeling and Development, pp. 575–586. Springer, Heidelberg (2011)
31. Orehovački, T.: Proposal for a set of quality attributes relevant for Web 2.0 application success. In: Proceedings of the 32nd International Conference on Information Technology Interfaces, pp. 319–326. IEEE Press, Cavtat (2010)
32. Orehovački, T., Babić, S.: Predicting students' continuance intention related to the use of collaborative Web 2.0 applications. In: Proceedings of the 23rd International Conference on Information Systems Development, pp. 112–122. Faculty of Organization and Informatics, Varaždin (2014)
33. Orehovački, T., Babić, S., Jadrić, M.: Exploring the validity of an instrument to measure the perceived quality in use of Web 2.0 applications with educational potential. In: Zaphiris, P., Ioannou, A. (eds.) LCT 2014, Part I. LNCS, vol. 8523, pp. 192–203. Springer, Heidelberg (2014)
34. Orehovački, T., Bubaš, G., Kovačić, A.: Taxonomy of Web 2.0 applications with educational potential. In: Cheal, C., Coughlin, J., Moore, S. (eds.) Transformation in Teaching: Social Media Strategies in Higher Education, pp. 43–72. Informing Science Press, Santa Rosa (2012)
35. Orehovački, T., Granić, A., Kermek, D.: Evaluating the perceived and estimated quality in use of Web 2.0 applications. J. Syst. Softw. **86**(12), 3039–3059 (2013)
36. Orehovački, T., Granić, A., Kermek, D.: Exploring the quality in use of Web 2.0 applications: the case of mind mapping services. In: Harth, A., Koch, N. (eds.) ICWE 2011. LNCS, vol. 7059, pp. 266–277. Springer, Heidelberg (2012)
37. Orehovački, T., Granollers, T.: Subjective and objective assessment of mashup tools. In: Marcus, A. (ed.) DUXU 2014, Part I. LNCS, vol. 8517, pp. 340–351. Springer, Heidelberg (2014)
38. Pang, M., Suh, W., Hong, J., Kim, J., Lee, H.: A new Web site quality assessment model for the Web 2.0 Era. In: Murugesan, S. (ed.) Handbook of Research on Web 2.0, 3.0, and X.0: Technologies, Business, and Social Applications, pp. 387–410. IGI Global, Hershey (2010)
39. Rio, A., Brito e Abreu, F: Websites quality: Does it depend on the application domain? In: Proceedings of the 7th International Conference on the Quality of Information and Communications Technology, pp. 493–498. IEEE, Porto (2010)
40. Redman, T.C.: Data Quality for the Information Age. Artech House, Norwood (1996)
41. Sassano, R., Olsina, L., Mich, L.: Modeling content quality for the Web 2.0 and follow-on applications. In: Murugesan, S. (ed.) Handbook of Research on Web 2.0, 3.0, and X.0: Technologies, Business, and Social Applications, pp. 371–386. IGI Global, Hershey (2010)
42. Seffah, A., Donyaee, M., Kline, R.B., Padda, H.K.: Usability measurement and metrics: a consolidated model. Software Qual. J. **14**(2), 159–178 (2006)
43. Venkatesh, V., Bala, H.: Technology acceptance model 3 and a research agenda on interventions. Decis. Sci. **39**(2), 273–315 (2008)
44. Venkatesh, V., Thong, J.Y.L., Xu, X.: Consumer acceptance and use of information technology: extending the unified theory of acceptance and use of technology. MIS Q. **36**(1), 157–178 (2012)
45. Webb, H.W., Webb, L.A.: SiteQual: an integrated measure of Web site quality. J. Enterp. Inf. Manage. **17**(6), 430–440 (2004)
46. World Wide Web Consortium: Web Content Accessibility Guidelines (WCAG) 2.0 (2008). http://www.w3.org/TR/WCAG20/

Heuristics for Grid and Typography Evaluation of Art Magazines Websites

Ana Paula Retore(✉), Cayley Guimarães, and Marta Karina Leite

Federal Technological University – Parana, Curitiba, Brazil
aretore@alunos.utfpr.edu.br, {cayleyg,martaleite}@utfpr.edu.br

Abstract. This article proposes a set of heuristics to inform web designers and developers in the evaluation of online art magazines. The authors compiled the heuristics from judicious literature reviews and analysis of websites from five art magazines. The set focuses on two graphic design elements, grid and typography, that are applied to online material. A heuristic evaluation was performed per the proposed heuristic, which validated the set for effective application as a web design tool.

Keywords: Heuristics · Grid · Typography · Guidelines · Web design

1 Introduction

The presence of new outlets and art magazines that are either online or digital is ever increasing. Unfortunately, a great part of such digital objects lack adequate design when it comes to the use of grid and typography. This is akin to the trend that occurred when the first “bricks & mortars” stores created their websites, and designers initially tried to transpose some design principles (such as the use of color, grid, typography, images etc.) from paper to the digital media. Most of the initial sites failed, just like the e-commerce websites did, simply because they did not take full advantage of the innovative new media available to them. When it comes to magazines, graphic design has long studied grid and typography. But there is a lack of studies for digital artifacts, which require different solutions [1]. A grid organizes the space in planes giving it structure, hierarchy and consistency [2]. On the web, they differ vastly from the paper [3]. Typography is “[…] the means by which a visual form is given for a written idea […] a visual language that enhances power and clarity” [4]. Both grid and typography greatly define the final usability of a digital artifact [5], and should be adapted to the new digital media. This article proposes a set of heuristics to evaluate online art magazines for grid and typography adequacy. Also, this paper presents the methodology used to implement the heuristics. It then presents the set of heuristics and the results of an qualitative evaluation conducted to validate them. They can be a tool to be used by designers and developers of online objects.

M. Kurosu (Ed.): HCI 2016, Part I, LNCS 9731, pp. 408–416, 2016.
DOI: 10.1007/978-3-319-39510-4_38

2 Methodology

The heuristics were derived from a study of grid and typography variables. For grid the variables are: structure, hierarchy, and constancy and variation; for typography the variables are: legibility, hierarchy, and identity. These variables were chosen in order to give this research more focus. They were also the basis for the state of the art literature review regarding the use of grid and typography for the development of good websites.

Five art magazines were analyzed according to the parameters established by the literature review. If the site of the magazine met these parameters, they were classified as best practices (e.g. good care regarding ergonomic principles as to the font used to enhance legibility). If the parameters weren't met, they were classified as worst practices (e.g. the logo identity is not identifiable– the typography is generic to the extent that it does not support a logo: it is recommended that a more solid reference should be used in the construction of the identity). After best and worst practices were determined, their recurrence and severity were analyzed. Figure 1 shows the complete methodology used for generating the heuristics[1].

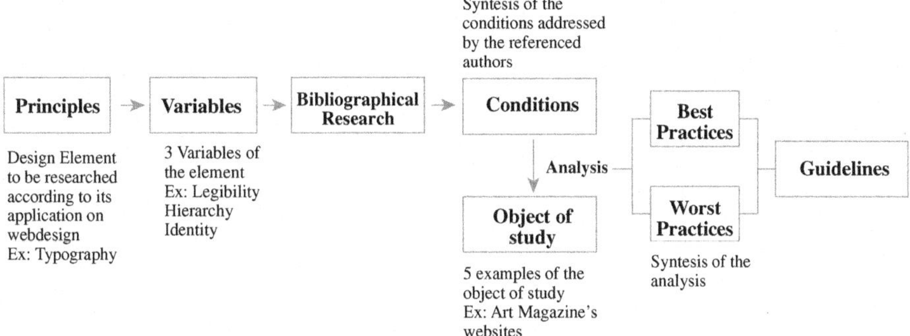

Fig. 1. Screenshot showing the top of the home page

3 Elaboration

3.1 Heuristics

Guidelines for grid and typography were originated from the analyzed data. The authors studied a total of 30 entries: five art magazines times six requirements (parameters). Crossing this information yielded 15 heuristics – eight for grid and seven for typography.

Heuristics for grid.

Subjected to the Content. Every kind of content has its own limitations and needs, and all of them have to be met by the grid. If the content has more text, then it requires a different grid (than if it had more images, for instance).

[1] The reference for applied methodology and the process to determine the heuristics can be found at [9].

Emphasis to What is Important. Important elements are noteworthy and should be highlighted, but auxiliary information shouldn't. Avoid having secondary information as a primary role. The hierarchy is an important factor in the content organization and grids are directly connected to it.

Coherent Alignments. Display the items in an adequate way; random placements can damage your layout. Shuffled or lost elements on the page mean that either the grid is not being well used or it has to be changed. A good grid offers place for all elements of the composition and maintains the hierarchy at the same time.

Visible Navigation. Easy navigation is a basic requirement. The grid needs to have a place where the user can have constant access to the menu, regardless of screen roll. A proper back navigation may also be considered. It is important for the reader to easily know where he is and how to get back to where he came from.

Visual Elements Arrangement. Images, videos, tables and graphics, in most cases, need to be shown fully on the screen. However, they cannot be downsized in a way that it will compromise its visibility or legibility.

Variation According to Each Page. Different products require different structures. It is natural that pages of any website have different styles of content. For this reason, the grid should be adequate to the specific content of each page.

Logical Constancy. Constancy is as important as variety. Repeated elements throughout the pages (such as the menu, the footer and margins) should be static. It helps to create a consistency and helps the user to develop references inside the website. It is possible to maintain constancy in other ways, such as color patterns and typography for example, which are also associated with the construction of identity.

Responsive Web Design. It means that it has to be designed to work across devices. The website needs to work well in any device and adapt itself to all screen sizes.

Heuristics of Typography.

Respect the Function of the Text. Employ the typeface according to the text's function. Texts used to call the attention of the reader can have more elaborated typefaces. Texts whose function is to inform should be designed for readability and legibility.

Typography has Identity. The typography can communicate subjective meanings and it is important that type identity is coherent with its purpose's identity. This should also be considered when choosing a typeface. When using ordinary or generic font, the site should rely on other elements to keep the identity (through color and graphics, for instance).

Balance. Combination of typefaces needs to be balanced. The excess of different fonts in a project can break the identity's reference. On the other hand, one single typeface with few variations can be monotonous. Once again, it's the content that will determine these choices.

Hierarchy for Organization. The hierarchy tells the reader which information needs to be read first and what is the sequence thereof. Important texts need to be highlighted while less significant texts can receive less emphasis. But making a big title that is lost in the middle of images and advertisements doesn't work. It is essential that not only legible the text should also be noticeable.

Value Legibility and Readability. The aim of a website is usually to communicate some kind of information. And if this information is in a text, it's important to make it legible to the user. No matter how interesting, fun or exciting is your text, if it is difficult to read; the reader might give up reading halfway. A typeface choice has to be a careful decision.

Consider Type Size According to the Medium. The font size will depend on two factors. The first is the typeface itself. For example, if it has a small x-height it may be necessary to increase its size. The second factor is the device. In her book "Type on Screen" Ellen Lupton explains that computers are usually further from the user's face than handheld devices, such as books or mobile phones. Letterforms appear fuzzy because of low pixel densities and backlighting, do not mix these problems by adding a very small typography [7].

Adequate Spacing. The text must maintain a balance between lines, words, and letter spacing because the excess is as harmful as the shortage. The line length might also prioritize the ideal number of characters. Lengthy lines makes reading tiresome because they allow for few pauses. Typefaces with short spacing between letters and words may appear truncated. The space between lines should also be carefully thought. If it's scarce, it may cause problems to the user to find the next line, and if it's in excess it isolates the lines so that they can't seem related.

3.2 Evaluation

In order to validate the proposed set, the criteria were used following the heuristic evaluation proposed by Nielsen [8] where multiple evaluators are able to find problems on an interface based on recognized principles – the heuristics. Three specialists with Graphic Design and Computer Science background conducted the evaluation. The evaluators worked parallel in order to find the problems. Then, they met to consolidate the findings.

The succeeding topic is a summary of the evaluations. The results are divided by the heuristics followed by the problems – elements that are not according to the criteria. Sometimes, a problem is related to more than one heuristic and is reported only once (in order to avoid repeating information). Logos and names of the analyzed magazine were blurred in the images. Analyzed contents are marked and numbered.

1. Subjected to the content.

The left column mixed different kinds of content in the same area (number 1 in the highlighted area in Fig. 2). For example, links to social media are on the same level and in the same grid as external art bulletins. Thereafter, there is a navigation menu. One solution could be to organize these contents in modules and to bring the menu to the top.

2. Emphasis to what is important.

The left and the right grids are distracting from the main content (1 and 2 in the highlighted area in Fig. 2). The ads and posts occupy two main positions and, since they are colorful and animated they can distract the reader from the main content. These areas should not have this much emphasis, or should be placed in a less important position inside the grid.

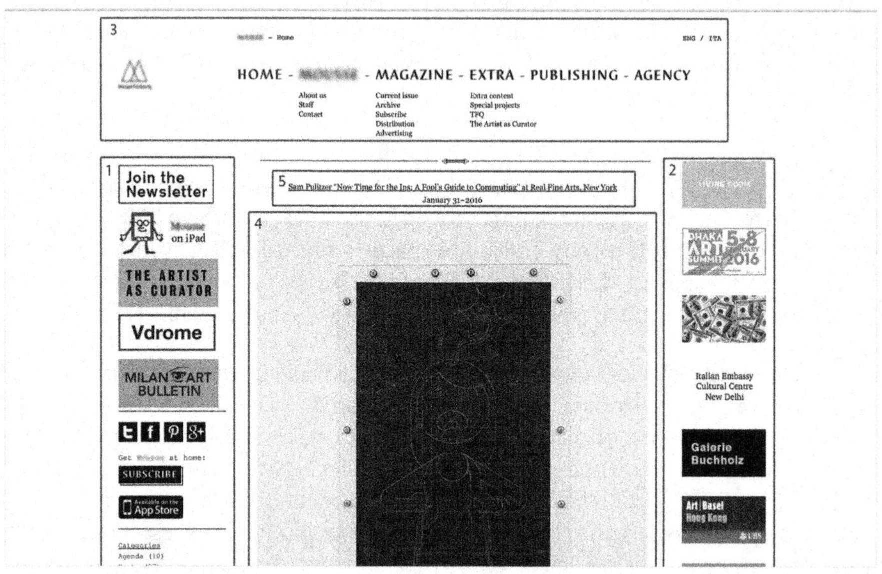

Fig. 2. Screenshot showing the midpoint of the home page

3. Coherent alignments.

The header has random placement of the menus and links (3 in the highlighted area in Fig. 2). The language links are not aligned to anything and the logo on the left of the menus looks arbitrarily placed on the upper-left part of the page. The grid should offer a proper position for all the elements and should make them look cohesive.

4. Visible Navigation.

The Categories menu in the left-hand side is not completely visible at the home page (Fig. 2). Subsequently, once the reader scrolls down, the top menu is hidden (Fig. 3). To have access to the menu again, it is necessary to scroll up the page. The solution in this case would be fixed menus.

5. Visual elements arrangement.

Portrait images of news entries do not fit on the same page (4 in the highlighted area in Fig. 2). It isn't possible to see the entire image at once even scrolling down the page. Long images should be resized in a way to fit in the screen.

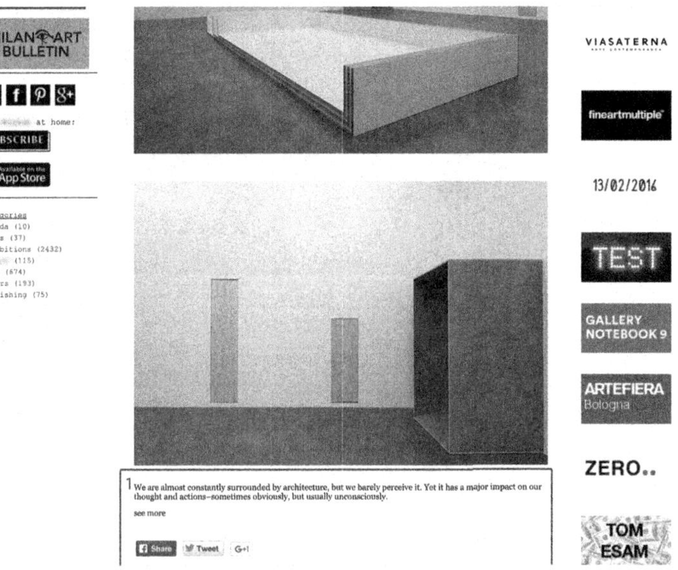

Fig. 3. Screenshot of home page

6. Variation according to each page.

The grid is exactly the same through the pages. It affects text content, making the line length extensive (Fig. 4). Different grids for different pages would allow for a better text fit.

7. Logical constancy.

No problems were found relating to this criterion.

8. Responsiveness.

The website isn't responsive. Images, texts, menus, and so on are not replaced or resized in order to better adapt to mobile devices. It is complicated to read, navigate, and use the website on a phone. Responsive layout, with grids according to the screen size would improve the usability.

9. Respect text's function.

On the menu, items that are links look pretty much the same as items that are not (3 in the highlighted area at Fig. 2). That can confuse the user because there is no marking telling if the items are clickable or not. Texts that are links should be marked as such.

The text at the end of the article has the same highlighting as the title (1 at Fig. 4 and 5 at Fig. 2). Since they have different functions they should look different, otherwise they can mislead the user.

The "see more" link (1 at Fig. 3) looks exactly the same as the body text. Once again, the typography does not clearly indicate the text role.

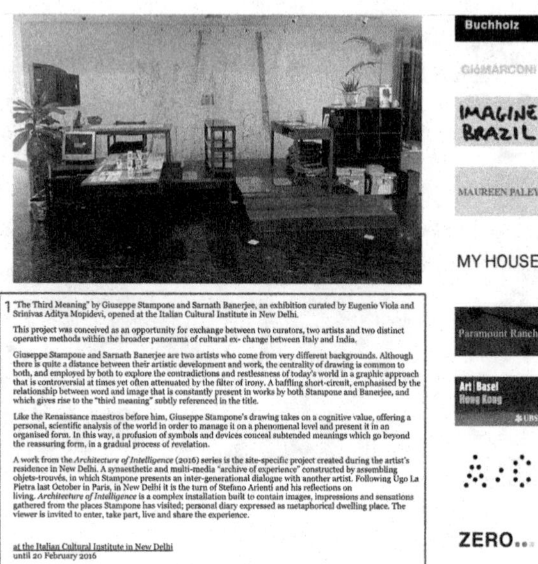

Fig. 4. Screenshot of an article page

10. Typography has identity.

    No problems were found relating to this criterion.

11. Balance.

    No problems were found relating to this criterion.

12. Hierarchy for organization.

The titles aren't quite noticeable (5 at Fig. 2). They have the same size as the body text and are next to an image that demands more attention. Perhaps they should receive more emphasis because they are the first things to be read and are helpful to the user to find information at a glance.

13. Value Legibility and Readability.

The magazine's name, under the logo (3 at Fig. 2) is too small and difficult to read. It becomes an issue first because the logo is the core of the identity of the website and second because it could be used as a navigation item, redirecting the user to the home page.

14. Consider type size according to the medium.

The font size is too small on mobile devices due to the lack of responsiveness. After opening the website on a phone, it is necessary to zoom-in in order to be able to read the content.

15. Adequate spacing.

The body font is hard to read (1 at Fig. 4). The tracking and kerning are tight, the line height is short, and the line length is extensive. It makes the readability slower and can compromise the legibility as well. The solution on this case would be adjusting spacing and the column width.

4 Results

It was found that the analyzed website didn't meet 12 of the 15 proposed requirements. The evaluators related 19 problems in total. Some of them appeared in more than one evaluation, for example: the type size under the logo, the lack of emphasis on titles and links, and the fact that the side columns were distracting.

The heuristic that presented more problems was "Respect text's function". It was evaluated as one of the major problems of the object of study, because it is directly related to other factors such as navigation, hierarchy and legibility.

The analyzed magazine also presented several problems related to usability. The magazine does not have a mobile version, fixed menus, and good readability: all serious problems, as they limit the accessibility of the website.

The evaluators considered that the use of the heuristics helped them to find serious problems in the studied magazine, thus validating its use as an evaluation tool.

In order to contribute with future studies and meet web designers and web developers needs, these heuristics are also freely available online, on the following address: http://annaretore.wix.com/guideline#!home/c1dmp.

5 Conclusion

Graphic design has a long history of providing best practices for visual content. Unfortunately, those guidelines are not always adequate for online devices. Little to no studies deal directly with such issues – most of them are concerned with usability in general. Thus, there is a need for studies to help designers to find and avoid errors caused by inadequate use of grid and typography in digital objects.

This research proposes a set of heuristics aimed to help anyone to evaluate a website when it comes to grid and typography. The proposed set was pivotal in finding severe problems in an evaluation of an art magazine – ranging from navigation and responsive layout to good legibility and readability issues. It was shown that the heuristics deal with parameters that are more impacting than just the visual aspects of the page.

Further research, with other digital objects, should be conducted, in order allow for generalization. The research methodology should be applied to other graphic design elements – color – or to other object of study – online newspapers for instance.

References

1. Lynch, P.J., Horton, S.: Web Style Guide, 2nd edn. Yale University, New Haven (2002)
2. Franz, L.: Typographic Web Design: How to Think Like a Typographer in HTML and CSS. John Wiley & Sons, Chichester, West Sussex (2012)
3. Vinh, K.: Ordering Disorder: Grid Principles for Web Design. New Riders, Berkeley (2011)
4. Ambrose, G., Harris, P.: The Fundamentals of Typography. G. Ambrose paperback. (2011)
5. Spiekermann, E.: The Invisible Language of Typography. Blucher, São Paulo (2011)
6. Sriven, M.: The Methodology of Evaluation. Indiana University, Bloomington (1965)
7. Lupton, E.: Type on Screen: a Guide for Designers, Developers, Writers, and Students. Princenton Architectural Press, New York (2014)
8. Nielsen, J.: How to conduct a Heuristic Evaluation. In: Nielsen Normam Group. Web, 01 January 1995, 03 February 2015
9. Retore, A.: Proposal of guidelines elaborated after research on grid and typography applied to art magazines websites' design. Completion of course work – Degree of Technology in Graphic Design, Federal University of Technology – Parana. Curitiba (2015)

Interface Aesthetics Effect on Usability: A Comparison of Two Screen Designs

Liang Zhao(✉) and Mihaela Vorvoreanu

Computer Graphics Technology, Purdue University, West Lafayette, IN, USA
{zhao334,mihaela}@purdue.edu

Abstract. An empirical study was conducted to examine whether the redesigned version of an online interactive visual analytics platform has a positive effect on perceived usability. 8 participants took part in the experiment, completed 8 tasks and answered follow-up interviews. The results show that the effect on perceived usability is positive, and it provides insights of participants' attitude toward the correlation between aesthetics and usability. Limitations and future work are addressed after the discussion.

Keywords: Interface · Aesthetics · Usability · Comparison

1 Introduction

In recent years, the correlation of interface aesthetics with usability has become of major interest within the field of human-computer interaction, especially in the context of user experience research [2]. Abundant research indicates that there is a strong connection between interface aesthetics and perceived usability, however, with further experiment, the significant relationship between interface aesthetics and perceived usability appears to be questioned [13, 18, 24].

In spite of existing debates on whether interface aesthetics is strongly tied to perceived usability, this condition is variable because different circumstances alter different cases. Thus, in this research, we tend to focus on how users perform in two different screen designs applied to not only the same content, but also the same function.

Due to the argument focusing on the correlation of aesthetics and usability, it's important to test whether aesthetics can make a positive effect on usability. The investigation of this topic will not only provide insights to researchers for further reference, but also provide design requirements and design guidelines for designers.

For this study, we chose the tool page of DIA2 as the research tool. DIA2 (Deep Insights Anytime, Anywhere) is a web-based visual analytics platform [11]. One of DIA2's target groups are professors in STEM (science, technology, engineering, and mathematics). Moreover, the tool page is where users perform their tasks, and a refined design for the tool page has just been finished. Conveniently, two different designs for the tool page are suitable for this study.

M. Kurosu (Ed.): HCI 2016, Part I, LNCS 9731, pp. 417–430, 2016.
DOI: 10.1007/978-3-319-39510-4_39

In the next section, we summarize related literatures in order to provide an impression of what is the attitude of the academy and industry toward the relationship of aesthetics and usability.

2 Literature Review

In the industry, [22] found that good interface design can have a positive effect on usability, and this kind of relationship still stands even after actual use of the system [23]. [6] supported the importance of aesthetics and further suggested a theoretical framework for future practice. In the product design area, aesthetics for vehicle interiors has been examined and the author indicated that the impact of aesthetics cannot be ignored [7]. In the meanwhile, aesthetics of different forms of products have also been studied, concluding that the positive effect of product aesthetics is obvious [17]. In the field of human-computer interaction, the correlation of aesthetics and usability has been studied for a long time, and numerous results showed support for the principle "what is beautiful is usable" [15, 16, 20, 21, 27]. Studies related to web user interface agreed with the correlation between perceived usability and aesthetics [4, 5, 9]. The tight aesthetics-usability relation became widely accepted within several academic areas. The overall attitude toward the correlation of aesthetics and usability is positive and supportive.

However, with further experiments, the significant relationship between interface aesthetics and perceived usability appears to be questioned. [13] brought up the conclusion that though web page aesthetics has positive effect on usability, but the effect is small. [24] argued that the inclusion of the visual attractiveness construct contributes more on enjoyment but less on usefulness. [18] concluded that the type of aesthetics that is relevant to users' perceptions appears to depend on the application domain. [14] indicated that multiple mechanisms could be responsible for the relationship between attractiveness and usability. Moreover, some of the findings showed that, although the essential result supported the correlation of aesthetics and usability, differences between objective usability in reported problems and subjective usability ratings have been affected by multiple factors such as halo effect and provided content [5, 25, 26]. The existing controversy in the area of Web design and usability points to the need for further research. We explore this topic in the context of an online visual analytics platform. As opposed to a regular website, a visual analytics platform's main role is functional. Its goal is to provide clear information to users. It does not have hedonic or entertainment purposes. Thus, we can think of such a platform as a critical case: if aesthetics has an effect on perceived usability for this utilitarian product, it will likely have an effect on other products that have broader purposes.

In terms of testing the correlation between aesthetics and usability, we bring up the research question: does the refined design of the tool page of DIA2 have a positive effect on the usability of professors in STEM?

In the following section, we explain the method we used in this study, including sampling strategy, participants and the procedure of data gathering.

3 Methodology

3.1 Design

Two screen designs for DIA2 tool page were chosen for this study (See Fig. 1.). The only difference between these two screens is the design of two parts of the interface. For the dashboard area on the left side of the screen, we reduced the spaces between each dashboard. We added a blue bar to indicate the active status of the dashboard. "Add a dashboard" button changed, too. The refined version emphasized the button by adding a blue background. For the tool bar area on the top side of the screen, we moved all the icons toward to the right side of the screen in order to let users notice them easily. Participants were manually assigned to use one of the screens to perform provided tasks.

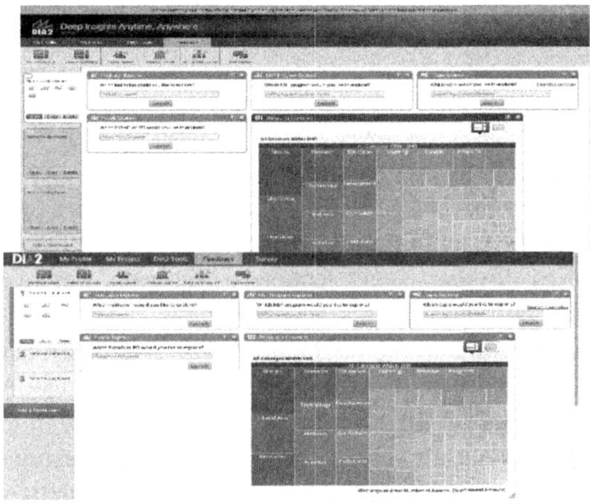

Fig. 1. Current version (left) and Refined version of DIA2 tool page

3.2 Sampling Strategy

The participants were professors within areas of science, technology, engineering, and mathematics (STEM), and have been awarded, are seeking or have sought funding from the National Science Foundation (NSF). This is because the visual analytics platform presents data from the NSF. The sampling strategy we used is a mix of criterion sampling and snowball sampling (one participant helped with finding another participant) [10]. These sampling strategies are advantageous to study participants that meet some criterion [12], but also with special experiences [3], and participants may be able to recommend useful candidates for study [8].

3.3 Participants

The sample of this study consisted of 8 participants, including 2 females and 6 males. All of them were professors at Purdue University. Previous knowledge shows that they all have experience with trying to get funded by the National Science Foundation. Some of them own projects that have successfully gotten funded by National Science Foundation. They had never experienced with DIA2 before this study.

3.4 Measures

Perceived Interface Attractiveness. Participants were asked to choose the screen design they like more between two difference screens designs.

User Performance. Both quantitative and qualitative measures of user performance were recorded. For quantitate measures, task completion time referred to the time needed to accomplish the task. For qualitative measure, verbal expression and non-verbal expression were recorded during the task.

3.5 Procedure

The study was conducted in participants' offices. A laptop was provided. The whole process lasted for approximately half an hour.

There are four sections for data gathering. The first section is a pre-task, semi-structured interview, asking demographic information and previous experience regarding activities related to NSF. In the second section, participants were asked to perform 8 tasks using computer provided by researcher. These tasks were selected because performing these tasks requires more interactions with dashboard and tool bar, which are the two main areas that differs the two versions of the tool page. After finishing the tasks, participants were asked to fill out a questionnaire regarding of the usability of the tool page. Finally, participants answered a list of open-ended questions in terms of their experience with the tool page. The process has been recorded with the permission of the participants. Participants' facial expression and screen activities during the second section were recorded with a software called Silverback with the permission of the participants. Please see Appendix A for interview questions and task list.

3.6 Data Analysis

The researcher calculated the time each participant spent on individual tasks. Participants' performance of each task was summarized and compared. Verbal and non-verbal expressions were categorized into three categories (positive, neutral and negative expressions) based on the scale provided by [1]. Answers to follow-up interviews were summarized based on each question.

4 Results

4.1 Perceived Website Attractiveness

The result of the attractiveness evaluation of two screen designs is presented in Table 1.

5 out of 8 participants chose the refined version as their preference design. 2 out of 8 thought the current version was better. One participant couldn't choose between two designs. She explained:

> *I like the consistency of this bar (the current version). The "add a dashboard" really fits into the whole screen. The top banner tells me what this site is about. But on the other hand, here (the refined version) has more room. This white space. The dashboard looks better in here. Oh I didn't notice "my project" in here (the refined version). Sorry, I...I can't choose between. They all seem fine to me.*

Representing an aesthetics preference, the result supported the hypothesis that the refined version of the tool page is more attractive to participants than the current version.

Table 1. The result of website attractiveness

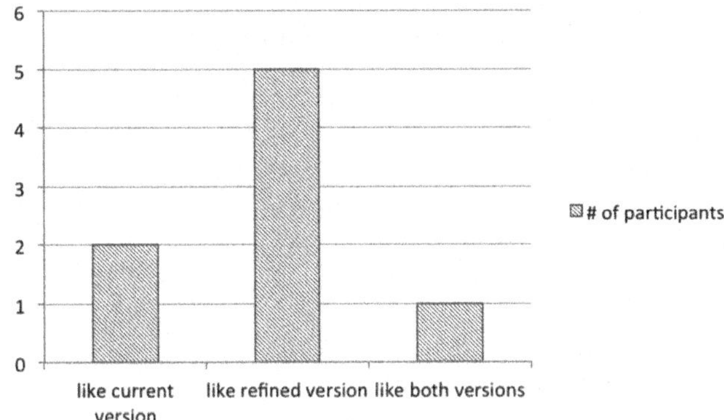

4.2 Time Spent on Tasks

Time Spent on Completing 8 Tasks. The comparison of how much time in average participants spent on different screens is showed in Table 2. It's obvious that the time spent on the refined version of the tool page is shorter that the time spent on the current version.

Table 2. Comparisons of time spent on 8 tasks

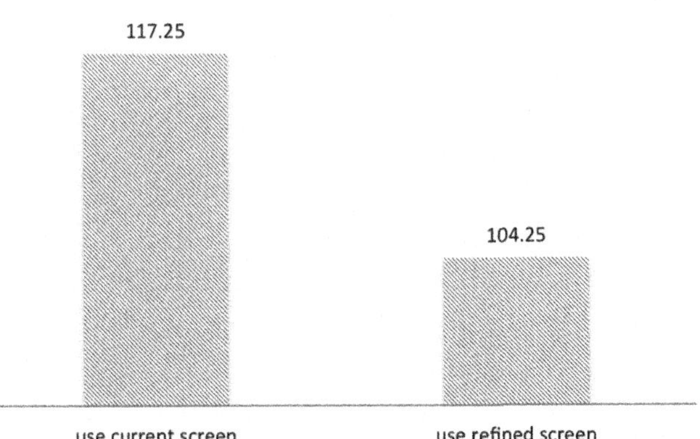

Table 3. Comparison of time spent on each task

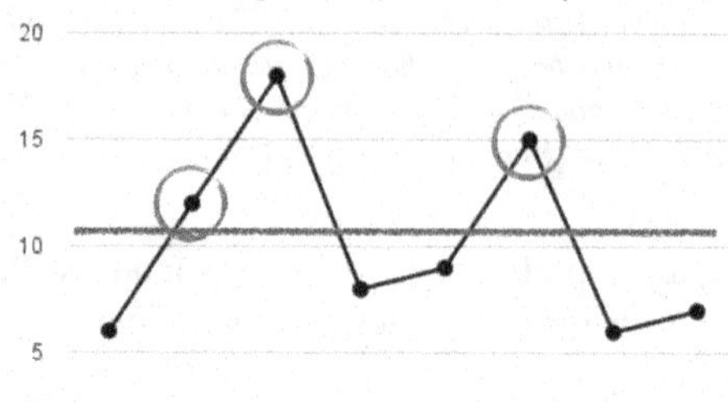

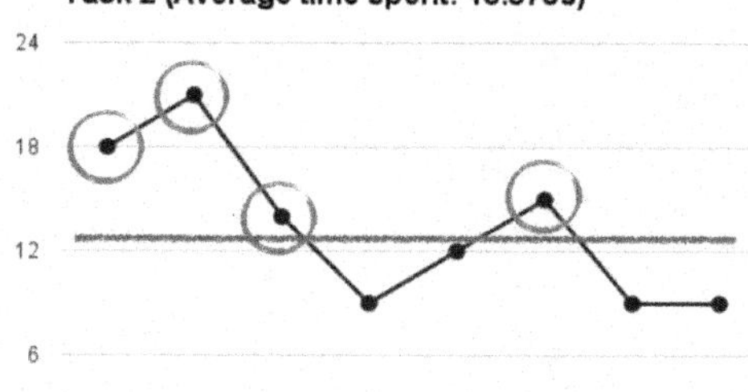

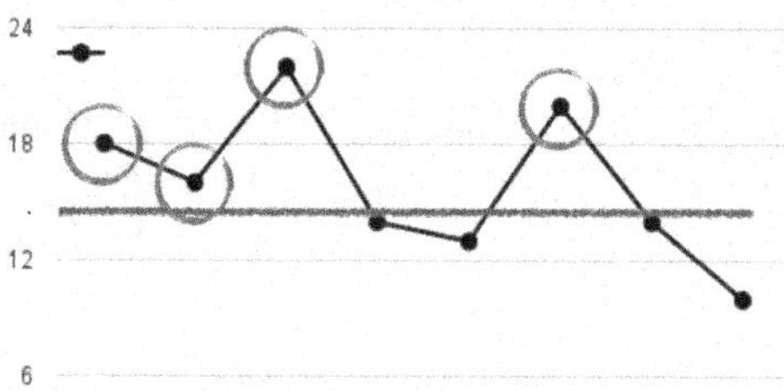

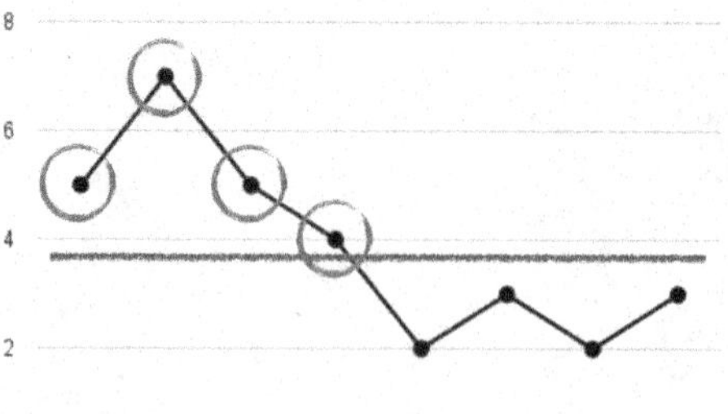

Time Spent on Each Task. Table 3 shows tasks that have significant difference among eight performances. 4 left dots present participants using current version while performing tasks, and 4 right dots means participants using refined version. Green lines represent the average time spent on each task. It's obvious that most of the performance that involving current version took longer time than using refined version.

4.3 Website Credibility

The result of website credibility is presented in Table 4. 4 of the participants didn't consider the possibility that aesthetics will affect their judgment toward such website. One participant described:

Table 4. Website credibility

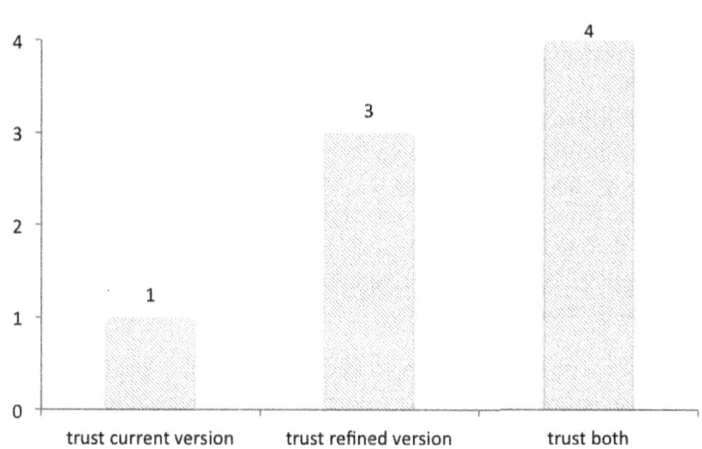

I know it's a NSF website. I won't question it, because I already know the organization behind it is NSF.

3 participants chose to trust the refined version more due to the "clear look" of the design. Two of them admitted the aesthetics is one of the main reasons that affect their judgment. Only one participant chose to trust the current version. He described:

This (the current version) is a more, how can I say, academic look to me? Yes, I feel that this (the current version) is an academic website, instead, this one (the refined version) is too clean.

4.4 Attitude Toward Aesthetics Before Task Performance

During the pre-task interview section, we asked participants what were their attitudes toward aesthetics versus function, in other words, do they consider function as the only factor that will affect usability, or do they think aesthetics can make a difference to usability performance. Surprisingly, 7 out of 8 participants thought only function matters. One participant said:

> *I don't think myself sensitive to, you know, design? I can't really tell which design is better. And personally I don't care. To this system, because there are a lot of data involved, if it is easy to use, I can't see how many difference aesthetics can help with me using this system.*

Another participant explained his opinion from another perspective:

> *I mean, aesthetics is not the main focus of this website, right? All I need is to find the right information. No matter how beautiful, how nice this website is, as long as I can find the information, it's useful. Aesthetics? Aesthetics can't help me find the information, right?*

As a conclusion, participants believed aesthetics would not affect usability, which contradicts the task performance data.

4.5 Task Performance

Below presents participants' performance for each task.

Task One. For task one, participants were asked to change the first dashboard's name to "My first dashboard". This task is designed for the purpose of testing whether participants can interact with the features of dashboard easily. To this purpose, all the participants shared the same process of naming the first dashboard: they hovered the mouse over the text that says "name the dashboard". After a grey shadow appeared, participants clicked on the text. After an input box appeared, they typed "my first dashboard" into the correct input box and clicked the "save" button. Three participants asked if they should rename the dashboard before beginning the task. One used the current version, the other two used the refined version.

Task Two. Task two asked participants to find the profile of a specific individual who is currently working at the University of Michigan. We designed this task based on the fact that in order to finish this task, participants need to interact with the tool bar. The individual to be found was chosen because (1) the name of the individual is within a reasonable length, (2) the spelling of the name is comparatively easy, and (3) the name can be found within the "people explorer" tool. Similar to the first task, all the participants shared the same process and completed the task successfully. First, participants clicked on the "people explorer" tool icon, and then input the name of the individual. However, two participants using the current version experienced a noticeable usability issue. When they clicked the "people explorer," they didn't click right on the icon. Instead, they chose to click the area around the icon. Since for the current version, the tool will be active only if the icon itself has been clicked, this design caused one participant to click the "people explorer" twice and the other to click three times before the tool showed up. This action indicated that participants ideally thought the entire area between the separators should be clickable.

Task Three. For task three, participants were asked to choose a different dashboard and name it "my second dashboard". All the participants completed this task by simply clicking on another dashboard and then repeating the process performed for the first task. Yet, before starting this task, two participants using the refined version asked which dashboard they should choose. We responded by asking why they had asked this question. One participant answered me by saying:

> *The dashboard looks like a three-step process. You see, with all these numbers and, yeah, like this is step one, step two, and step three. They are too close, maybe.*

The other one provided a similar explanation:

> *I firstly thought these tabs here, I don't know why, but these seem like steps, you know, like you need to finish these tabs then you can find what you want.*

Task Four. Participants were asked to find the graph that shows the collaboration within Purdue University. The task requires interactions with the tool bar but with a different tool. All the participants followed the same process and successfully finished the task. The usability issue here, however, was the same as during task two. Two participants clicked the empty area around the icon instead of clicking right on the icon itself.

Task Five. Task five asked participants to find a specific program categorized by the National Science Foundation. To finish this task, participants had to understand the definition of "program" and know which tool was the correct one. All the participants clicked the "NSF program explorer" tool without hesitating. However, the same issue that occurred during tasks two and four also occurred during this task. One participant using the current version clicked the tool area twice and showed a little bit of impatience. On the other hand, one participant who also used the current version chose to move the mouse comparatively carefully toward the icon when choosing the tool.

Task Six. Participants were asked to add two more dashboards in this task. The feature they needed to interact with was the "add dashboard" button placed in the dashboard area. What participants did was simply clicked the "add dashboard" button twice.

Task Seven. For this task, participants needed to delete the fifth dashboard, which is the dashboard with a "5" on the top-left corner. All the participants deleted the assigned dashboard by clicking the "delete" button placed on the bottom-right corner of the fifth dashboard. However, all of the participants using the current version either scrolled the screen or dragged it to the bottom in order to delete the fifth dashboard. The reason for this action is that for the current version, the browser window isn't long enough to accommodate all the five dashboards at once.

Task Eight. Participants were asked to find the profile of another specific individual at Purdue University. Unlike with task two, this profile can't be found through the "people explorer"; instead, the "institution explorer" is the correct tool for searching for such information. Thus, this task requires more constant interactions with the tool bar. All the participants first clicked on the "people explorer" and typed the name of the individual into the input box. After receiving incorrect information, they clicked the "institution explorer" icon, found the profile for Purdue University, and typed the name into the collaborator search bar.

4.6 Expressions During the Task Performance

Due to the design of data gathering process, not many comments were gathered. However, several noticeable negative verbal and non-verbal expressions were captured during the process, and a comparatively large amount of neutral verbal comments were recorded. Next section will start with neutral expressions, following with negative expressions.

Neutral Expressions. During task performance, interjections and short confirmations have been used constantly for indicating a finish of one task. “ok.” “oh, I see.” “let’s see.” “Done.” were highly used. Other than these expressions, participants merely said or behaved anything that could be categorized into “neutral expression” category.

Negative Expressions. Several noticeable verbal comments were captured during task performance. During task 4, two participants using current version of the tool page said “come on!” after clicking one icon twice but nothing happened. During task 7, all 4 participants slightly muttered when they couldn’t find the fifth dashboard on the screen.

Obvious facial expressions were also recorded during task performance. During task 4, one participant using current version of the tool page slightly frowned when clicking twice was not triggering anything. And during task 5, all four participants using current version of the tool page slightly frowned when the same situation happened.

4.7 Attitude Toward the Website After Task Performance

After showing two screen designs to participants, most of the feedback to the refined version is positive.

I like the clean look of this one (refined version) rather the other website.

For this website (refined version), I have a bigger space to put this small windows.

Cool, I like this one better. The tabs are more concise.

Suggestions were also brought up. One participant said that the dashboard looks like “a three-step process instead of individual dashboard because they are too close to each other”. Another suggestion is that the tab “add a dashboard” is not consistent with the dashboard above.

Though there were two participants that prefer the current version, they didn’t provide negative feedback to the refined version. When being asked why they prefer the current version, one participant said that the current version looks like an academic website to him. Another participant couldn’t explain why. In his word, he was used to the dark blue color, which might affect his judgment in some ways.

5 Discussion

The finding shows aesthetics has a positive effect on usability of DIA2, which supports the hypothesis. There are significant differences between the performance using two different screen designs. It's obvious that participants using the refined version of tool page performed better than the participants using the current version. Moreover, due to the design difference, two usability problems were solved in the refined version. Although there were not many verbal or non-verbal expressions, negative expressions were mainly concentrated in the performance that was related to current version of tool page, which indicated that the enjoyment of using current version was not as pleasing as using refined version. It is confirmed that in this particular case, aesthetics helps with usability.

On the other hand, based on the pre-task interview and feedback from participants after task performance, though most of the participants didn't think aesthetics could help with usability, the result shows the opposite. The refined version, which is considered as more well-designed, has a better performance than the current version. Faced with this conflict, it is not surprising that a majority of arguments are focusing on discussing whether aesthetics matter. People don't realize the fact until they perform. They tend to trust their own experience or knowledge and are used to judge certain unknown perception based on their consciousness. In spite of existing conclusions that it depends on the circumstance whether aesthetics help with usability, in this case, aesthetics does have a positive effect on usability. Specifically, this study's results suggest that, even for a very functional product, and even when participants claim that aesthetics would not influence usability, aesthetics does improve both actual and perceived usability.

In addition, this study is subject to a number of limitations. The number of participants is not ideal. 8 is not a suitable number for quantitative data gathering. The environment of conducting this study is not ideal. Though we were staying in each participant's office, researcher provided the device they used for performing the task. Unfamiliarity of the device may affect task performance. Besides, one of the participants has just done an eye surgery, such situation seemed to affect his performance in a noticeable way.

6 Conclusion

Although it is widely accepted by several academic areas that aesthetics has positive effects on perceived usability, we consider different circumstances alter different cases. Thus, for DIA2, this particular web platform, we conducted a study in order to find out whether the refined version of DIA2 tool page has a positive effect on usability. Eight participants were involved in this study by being interviewed and asked to perform 8 tasks. The result demonstrated that the refined version has a positive effect on usability, which support the hypothesis that aesthetics helps with perceived usability when using DIA2. Future work can focus on identifying specific aspects of aesthetics and their individual influence on usability, in order to produce a deeper understanding of how aesthetics affect usability.

Appendix A: Pre-task Questionnaire, Task List, and Pro-task Questionnaire

Pre-task questionnaire

1. What are the department and school you are in right now?
2. Have you tried to get funded by NSF?
3. What are the most painful things for you to do while working on proposal?
4. What's your regular procedure of finding the information you want?
5. Have you ever used any systematical system for data gathering?
6. Before using DIA2, how will you image the screen will be like?

Task list

1. Name the first dashboard "my first dashboard".
2. Find the profile of Nancy Love who works in the University of Michigan.
3. Choose another empty dashboard and name it "my second dashboard".
4. Find the graph that shows the collaboration within Purdue University.
5. Find out a program called "MATHEMATICAL SCIENCES".
6. Add 2 more dashboards.
7. Find the fifth dashboard and delete it.
8. Find professor Thomas Hacker who is a professor at Purdue University.

Can't find Thomas hacker in the people explorer and then click institution.

Pro-task questionnaire

1. What's your overall impression of the screen of DIA2?
2. Does this screen meet your expectation? Why is that?
3. Is there any specific part you like? Why?
4. Is there any specific part you think needs more improvement? And why?
5. What is your opinion towards continuing using DIA2 after this interview?
6. By comparing with the other screen, do you think the information in this website is worthy trusting or not? Which one will you trust more? And why?

References

1. Albert, W., Tullis, T.: Measuring the User Experience: Collecting, Analyzing, and Presenting Usability Metrics. Morgan Kaufmann, Newnes (2013)
2. Bargas-Avila, J.A., Hornbæk, K.: Old wine in new bottles or novel challenges: a critical analysis of empirical studies of user experience. In: Proceedings of the SIGCHI Conference on Human Factors in Computing Systems, pp. 2689–2698. ACM, May 2011
3. Bradley, C.P.: Turning anecdotes into data—the critical incident technique. Fam. Pract. **9**(1), 98–103 (1992)
4. David, A., Glore, P.R.: The impact of design and aesthetics on usability, credibility, and learning in an online environment. Online J. Distance Learn. Adm. **13**(4), X (2010)

5. Hartmann, J., Sutcliffe, A., De Angeli, A.: Investigating attractiveness in web user interfaces. In: Proceedings of the SIGCHI Conference on Human Factors in Computing Systems, pp. 387–396. ACM, April 2007
6. Kallio, T.: Why we choose the more attractive looking objects - somatic markers and somaesthetics in user experience. In: Proceedings of the DPPI 2003, pp. 142–143. ACM Press (2003)
7. Lin, Y., Zhang, W.J.: Integrated design of function, usability, and aesthetics for automobile interiors: state of the art, challenges, and solutions. Proc. Inst. Mech. Eng., Part I: J. Syst. Control Eng. **220**, 697–708 (2006)
8. Marshall, M.N.: Sampling for qualitative research. Family Pract. **13**(6), 522–526 (1996). Sage, Park, CA
9. Miller, M., Choi, G., Chell, L.: Comparison of three digital library interfaces: open library, Google books, and Hathi Trust. In: Proceedings of the ACM/IEEE Joint Conference on Digital Libraries, pp. 367–368 (2012)
10. Patton, M.Q.: Qualitative Evaluation and Research Methods, 2nd edn. Sage, Newbury (1990)
11. Madhavan, K., Elmqvist, N., Vorvoreanu, M., Chen, X., Wong, Y., Xian, H., Johri, A.: DIA2: Web-based Cyberinfrastructure for Visual Analysis of Funding Portfolios (2014)
12. Patton, M.Q.: Designing qualitative studies. Qual. Res. Eval. Methods **3**, 230–246 (2002)
13. Purchase, H.C., Hamer, J., Jamieson, A., Ryan, O.: Investigating objective measures of web page aesthetics and usability. In: Conferences in Research and Practice in Information Technology Series, vol. 117, pp. 19–28 (2011)
14. Quinn, J.M., Tran, T.Q.: Attractive phones don't have to work better: independent effects of attractiveness, effectiveness, and efficiency on perceived usability. In: Proceedings of the SIGCHI Conference on Human Factors in Computing Systems, CHI 2010, pp. 353–362 (2010)
15. Reinecke, K., Yeh, T., Miratrix, L., Mardiko, R., Zhao, Y., Liu, J., Gajos, K.Z.: Predicting users' first impressions of website aesthetics with a quantification of perceived visual complexity and colorfulness. In: Proceedings of the SIGCHI Conference on Human Factors in Computing Systems - CHI 2013, pp. 2049–2058 (2013). http://dl.acm.org/citation.cfm?doid=2470654.2481281. (Retrieved)
16. Sauer, J., Sonderegger, A.: The influence of prototype fidelity and aesthetics of design in usability tests: effects on user behaviour, subjective evaluation and emotion. Appl. Ergonomics **40**(4), 670–677 (2009)
17. Sauer, J., Sonderegger, A.: The influence of product aesthetics and user state in usability testing. Behav. Inf. Technol. **30**(6), 787–796 (2011)
18. van Schaik, P., Ling, J.: The role of context in perceptions of the aesthetics of web pages over time. Int. J. Hum Comput Stud. **67**(1), 79–89 (2009)
19. Sonderegger, A., Sauer, J.: The influence of design aesthetics in usability testing: effects on user performance and perceived usability. Appl. Ergonomics **41**(3), 403–410 (2010)
20. Strebe, R.: Visual aesthetics of websites: the visceral level of perception and its influence on user behaviour. In: Gradmann, S., Borri, F., Meghini, C., Schuldt, H. (eds.) TPDL 2011. LNCS, vol. 6966, pp. 523–526. Springer, Heidelberg (2011)
21. Thüring, M., Mahlke, S.: Usability, aesthetics and emotions in human–technology interaction. Int. J. Psychol. **42**(4), 253–264 (2007)
22. Tractinsky, N.: Aesthetics and apparent usability: empirically assessing cultural and methodological issues. In: Proceedings of the ACM SIGCHI Conference on Human Factors in Computing Systems, pp. 115–122. ACM, March 1997
23. Tractinsky, N., Katz, A.S., Ikar, D.: What is beautiful is usable. Interact. Comput. **13**(2), 127–145 (2000)

24. Van der Heijden, H.: Factors influencing the usage of websites: the case of a generic portal in The Netherlands. Inf. Manag. **40**(6), 541–549 (2003)
25. van Schaik, P., Ling, K.M., Kashimura, K.: Apparent usability vs. inherent usability: experimental analysis on the determinants of the apparent usability. In: Conference Companion on Human Factors in Computing Systems, pp. 292–293. ACM, May 1995
26. van Schaik, P., Ling, J.: The role of context in perceptions of the aesthetics of web pages over time. Int. J. Hum.-Comput. Stud. **67**(1), 79–89 (2009)
27. Wang, Y.J., Hernandez, M.D., Minor, M.S.: Web aesthetics effects on perceived online service quality and satisfaction in an e-tail environment: the moderating role of purchase task. J. Bus. Res. **63**(9–10), 935–942 (2010)

Models and Patterns in HCI

Agile Usability Patterns for User-Centered Design Final Stages

Ana Paula O. Bertholdo(✉), Fabio Kon, and Marco Aurélio Gerosa

Department of Computer Science, University of São Paulo, São Paulo, Brazil
{ana,fabio.kon,gerosa}@ime.usp.br

Abstract. The integration between Agile Methods and User-Centered Design (UCD) has been addressed by several authors in recent years. Nevertheless, a gap remains regarding a systematically consolidated description of agile usability practices for the final stages of UCD. Our aim is to describe agile usability practices based on the literature in the form of patterns, focusing on the UCD final stages, namely "Create Design Solutions" and "Evaluate Designs". A literature review was conducted to identify patterns of use of agile usability practices. The major results of the study presented here are the selection and classification of the usability practices for the UCD final stages within the agile community and their structured presentation in the form of patterns (Name, Context, Problem, Solution, and Examples). Presenting agile usability practices as patterns can increase their applicability; it facilitates the visualization of the similarities between the communities of UCD and Agile Methods and also presents the ideas more clearly to other communities that can benefit from using these patterns in their specific development contexts.

Keywords: Agile usability · Agile UCD · Agile UX · Best practices · Patterns

1 Introduction

The integration between agile methods and UCD has been addressed by several authors in recent years [1–6]. The challenge in combining these two methodologies focuses on finding the best way to carry out all the activities related to usability improvement, meeting users' real needs, designing and evaluating interfaces within agile environments, and having typical users involved in the activities.

There are several agile usability practices defined in the literature with different names, representing small variations of the same practice. The description of agile usability practices, in a common form, help to organize similar practices in a standardized way. It can also facilitate the visualization of similarities between the communities of UCD and Agile Methods.

In this context, we carried out earlier research leading to a description of usage patterns of agile usability practices in the early stages of UCD, namely

M. Kurosu (Ed.): HCI 2016, Part I, LNCS 9731, pp. 433–444, 2016.
DOI: 10.1007/978-3-319-39510-4_40

Identify Needs for Human-Centered Design, Specify Context of Use, and Specify Requirements [7]. However, a gap remains regarding a description of usage patterns of agile usability practices in the final stages of UCD.

This study aims to describe usability practices based on the literature using the patterns format, focusing on the UCD final stages, namely Create Design Solutions and Evaluate Designs, within agile environments. This paper complements our previous work [7] by answering the research question: What are the agile usability practices related to the final stages of UCD used?

2 Background

Sy [6] suggests that the aim of integrating UCD and agile methods [8,9] is breaking UCD stages down into the agile cycles size. To do so, UCD should be performed aiming at applying all the activities of the UCD cycle for each feature subset in agile iterations. The basis for many UCD methods is described in an international standard (ISO 13407: Human-Centered Design Process), which defines a general process for including human-centered activities in a development life-cycle, but does not specify specific methods. In this standard, when necessary to use a human-centered design process, four activities form the main cycle of work: (*i*) Specifying Context of Use; (*ii*) Specifying Requirements; (*iii*) Producing Design Solutions; (*iv*) Evaluating Designs.

In 2011, the systematic literature review on UCD and agile methods conducted by Silva et al. [4] presented 58 studies addressing this topic. Some of them depict an overall picture for integrating UCD and agile methods, such as Fox et al. [5] and Sy [6]. In 2014, the systematic literature review for agile processes and UCD integration conducted by Salah et al. [2] identified challenging factors that restrict Agile and UCD integration, exploring the proposed practices to solve them. This study included a total of 71 papers. In 2015, Brhel et al. [1] analyzed 83 relevant publications. The analysis resulted in five principles for user-centered agile software development.

With a more specific focus on practices related to the final stages of UCD, Silva et al. [10] noticed that it is difficult to perform traditional user testing sessions due to the tight schedules inherent to Agile. They described a set of practices used to evaluate software product usability. This paper aims at organizing the similar practices described in the literature in a pattern format and at providing a categorization for the patterns according to the UCD final stages.

3 Method

A literature review was conducted to find the usability practices used by the agile community. The search criterion was defined as follows:

- ((“usability” OR “usability methods” OR “User Centered Design” OR “User eXperience” OR “Human-Computer Interaction” OR “Computer-Human Interaction”) AND (“agile methods” OR “agile development” OR “eXtreme Programming” OR “Scrum” OR “agile”)).

The filtering process consisted of: (*i*) Reading the title, (*ii*) Reading the summary, and (*iii*) Reading the complete study. Studies were included if they met the following criteria: (1) The study reported how usability practices were applied to agile communities in order to raise at least one of the following pieces of information for each practice: context, problem, or solution; (2) For separate studies using the same data, for example, dissertation and a paper, only the study with the most comprehensive report was included to avoid overloading a particular data set; (3) Studies written in English. For each phase, the studies that were not in accordance to the inclusion criteria were excluded.

4 Agile Usability Patterns for UCD Final Stages

The agile usability practices identified in our literature review were described in the following format: (*i*) Name; (*ii*) Context; (*iii*) Problem; (*iv*) Solution; and (*v*) Example, according to the definition of a pattern [11]. Following Alexander's definition [11], a pattern is a structured method of describing good design practices within a field of expertise. The selection of practices to become patterns considered only the practices used by at least three different cases.

The patterns were divided into categories according to the UCD stage [12] in which they are present, which facilitates understanding the goal of each pattern described. The selection and classification of the usability practices for UCD final stages within the agile community and presentation in the aforementioned format represent the major results of this research. This paper focuses only on the usability practices comprising the following steps of the UCD: (1) Create Design Solutions; and (2) Evaluate Designs.

4.1 Create Design Solutions

Pattern: *Low Fidelity Prototyping*

Context: Need to communicate and to validate an idea, with customers and team members, which is developed and refined quickly in agile environments. This communication is performed during the initial stage of an agile iteration and in meetings with team members and/or customers while the project development evolves.

Problem: Low fidelity prototyping for the key features of the entire system prior to development is common in traditional usability practices. This practice is incompatible with agile environments, in which the development cycle comprises a series of small incremental releases. Therefore, the problem is to get feedback from customers and typical users on the interface of a subset of features within an iteration and not for the entire system prior to the development. The main forces involved are:

- **Force 1**: Getting feedback from customers and users on the interface and the interaction flow in the early stages of the development cycle, when the features are not implemented.

- **Force 2**: Creating the interface design according to the features within an iteration and not for the key features of the entire system prior to the development, taking the "big picture" into account.

Solution: Low fidelity prototyping during the initial stage of an iteration and in meetings with team members and/or customers. The main difference between traditional low fidelity prototyping techniques and the ones used within agile environments is that prototypes are built for a subset of features of an iteration and not for the entire system prior to the development. The subset of features contains the key features of an iteration, for which improving understanding is necessary. Team members having boards with screen prototypes at the workplace. To specify the visual layout, teams that have interface design specialists create low fidelity prototypes as the basis for implementation.

Examples: For several authors, prototyping happens during the initial stages of the development and is used to evaluate usability both for inquiries and user testing [13,14]. Patton [15] defines the practice Prototype in low fidelity, informing that the prototypes only need to be good enough to understand, to learn, and to communicate quickly. After that, he says, they can be thrown away, since they are consumable and not deliverable for agile development.

Pattern: ***High Fidelity Prototyping***

Context: Need to evaluate the interface and the interaction flow of a system during the development cycle, when the features have been implemented.

Problem: High fidelity prototyping for the key features of the entire system prior to development is common in traditional usability practices. This practice is incompatible to agile environments, in which the development cycle comprises a series of small incremental releases. Therefore, the problem is to get feedback from customers and users on the interfaces of features that have been implemented in each agile iteration and not for the key features of the entire system prior to the development. The main forces involved are:

- **Force 1**: Getting feedback from customers and users on the interface and on the interaction flow during the development cycle, when the features have been implemented.
- **Force 2**: Creating the interface design according to the features of an iteration and not for the key features of the entire system prior to the development, taking the "big picture" into account.

Solution: High fidelity prototypes are part of the system under development, which is evolving at each iteration, already with the working code. When the features have been implemented, they are evaluated as high fidelity prototypes which evolve depending on the development of iteration requirements. Online techniques such as sharing access to prototype versions on the Web are used. In an iteration, teams create the interface design and, at the subsequent iteration, the team of developers writes the code implementing the design proposed in the previous iteration.

Examples: For Williams and Ferguson [16], prototypes evolve for high fidelity prototypes. Hussain [17] cites the use of high fidelity prototypes to conduct inquiries and usability tests with the customer. Six [18] states that: "... a user experience team that includes front-end Web developers can prototype or even build an application's actual user interface rather than writing detailed user experience design specifications".

Pattern: *Design Studio*

Context: After some UCD tasks for gathering requirements are performed, usually in the format of user interviews or observations, there is the need to create and to explore design versions that meet the users goals.

Problem: Creating alternative design versions for the key features of the entire system prior to development is a way to allow the innovation to be part of the development of traditional usability practices. However, in agile environments, the short time of each iteration prevents exploiting several design options. The main forces involved are:

- **Force 1**: Proposing innovative solutions within agile iterations, with less time to build different interface design ideas and interaction flows.
- **Force 2**: Proposing innovative solutions for features of the next iteration and not for the key features of the entire system prior to the development, taking the "big picture" into account.

Solution: Participants come up with several alternative design solutions for an interface during a pre-established time. When time is over, a discussion is performed to select a design for the system interface. In the Design Studio, each design sketch is presented to the team, which can involve developers and UCD specialists. Then, the team has some time for reflection and criticism. At the end of the studio, a design concept is defined and developed. The chosen design reflects the good parts of the ideas presented during the studio. After the studio, the user experience team creates usage scenarios from the results. Since the design studio makes it easier to understand what the system needs are, the development work may proceed immediately [19]. Members of the development team might be allocated for user interface design activities. Usually, design studio tasks are performed face-to-face with members gathered in a room to create design versions.

Examples: Dubakov [20] describes the Design Studio methodology as a simple and efficient way of having agile meetings. The author reports that there are several variations for the Design Studio, but he used a simple group containing the following 5 steps: (1) defining a problem; (2) individually brainstorming 5 ideas without exceeding 5 min per idea; (3) presenting and divide the ideas into categories for the team; (4) discussing positive and negative characteristics of the ideas; and (5) selecting the interesting ideas and creating two versions for each final solution. According to Ungar et al. [19], design studio has four main points: (1) Research: Design Studio is guided by user research; (2) Design: also known as pre-work, where many projects and ideas are quickly created; (3) Studio: a one-day workshop to evaluate alternatives, make decisions and consolidate design and (4) Participants: a team composed of designers or user experience professionals who are willing to learn and to grow within the design process. Evans and Gothelf [21] describe that a design studio might generate several iterations about the design and that there are several variations of the studio which might be employed with good effects within agile processes.

Pattern: ***Collaborative and Participative Design***

Context: After some UCD tasks for gathering requirements are performed, usually in the format of user interviews or observations, it is necessary to put the perspective of each participant involved with the development cycle, to include typical users in the interface design process, for improvement and refinement of systems requirements.

Problem: In traditional usability practices, the UCD team creates alternative design versions for the key features of the entire system prior to development such that the perspective of users and customers can be incorporated. However, when just the UCD team is involved with creating design solutions, the understanding is not complete for the entire team to build only what has the higher value for the business and for the end user. The main forces involved are:

- **Force 1**: Gathering the perspective of each participant for a design problem into agile iterations, with less time for each session.
- **Force 2**: Proposing design solutions for features of the next iteration and not for the key features of the entire system prior to the development, taking the "big picture" into account.

Solution: Sessions for creating design versions in a collaborative way, i.e., different stakeholders create designs together, showing their views in relation to the needs that have to be met by the user interface, and in a participative way, by involving system real users. The objective is to put the point of view of each participant to solve a design problem based on their needs in relation to the system and their own understanding of it. As in the Design Studio, this activity stimulates innovation. Also, it allows new requirements to be suggested and gathered during the sessions. The involvement of developers is very beneficial to the quality of the system, both internal and external. Additionally, it allows all team members to become involved with the stage of defining requirements. Collaborative design also contributes to creating a shared view among participants.

Examples: Govella [22] includes collaborative design in his list of strategies for the user experience, in which members of the design team may sketch, talk, and iterate to achieve a consensual idea of the design. Details only need to be recorded if they might be forgotten. The same happens if there is an error, but all members understand the general view since they have worked together. For Beltrame [23], collaborative design is all about leaving developers do part of the ideation process and designers do part of the development process. Developers might help proposing good solutions, which are technically suitable, and avoiding conceptual failures due to technical limitations. Tyne [24] describes participative design in three main tasks: (1) sketching ideas, (2) presenting ideas to the team, and (3) criticizing presentation based on solutions. The process is repeated three times and the fidelity of scopes increases at each cycle.

4.2 Evaluate Designs

Pattern: *Tests with Users*

Context: Need to obtain a spontaneous impression from the user about a version of the system.

Problem: Evaluating the system with real users is an essential practice in traditional usability practices. However, is not a trivial task to perform tests with users for each agile iteration with less time to run evaluations. The main forces involved are:

- **Force 1**: Evaluating the system with its real users from the early stages of the development process.
- **Force 2**: Conducting usability tests according to the functionalities developed in an iteration or agile sprint, taking the "big picture" into account.

Solution: Conducting usability tests with users employing the Think aloud protocol. The central idea is to provide tasks for the users to perform while using the system, aiming at evaluating if the tasks are easily performed or if they encounter difficulties discovering the right path, or even if they are unable to do the required task. The Think Aloud protocol aims at requesting users to say what they intend to do to complete the task, what they think about the interface, and what they thought about the steps they had to follow to accomplish the task successfully. While users are using the system, their impressions are gathered so as to analyze the results in relation to the accomplishment of the task. Usually, in agile teams, tests with users are conducted with the presence of project customers and involve usability specialists. When real users are involved, usability specialists also participate as test mediators. However, there are reports of projects that involved several members of the team as observers and they noticed that the developers' view benefited from watching how real users understand the system. Tests with users in agile teams are mostly laboratory-based, although there are reports of successful remote tests. Normally, developers incorporate results from tests with users into the system during the following iteration.

Examples: Expero [25] reports that when tests with users are conducted as part of the agile process, the tests should occur before or during the development and should have user tasks that take the "big picture" into account more than the limited scope of the next release. Another unique aspect of tests with users within agile environments is to make sure that the changes recommended from user studies find a solution in an appropriate release. It might be the case of planning a release for the following months. Frequently, the development team changes characteristics and functionalities. There are several reports on tests with users functioning as the main tool for refining user interface prototype for the next iteration [4,5,16].

Pattern: ***Evaluation by Inspection***

Context: Need to evaluate the interface even at the initial stages of the system without exposing serious issues to the real users.

Problem: In traditional usability practices, inspecting interface is an important task to refine the system before introducing the features for customers or real users. However, in agile environments, the interface refinement should be performed for each agile iteration, in which time is shorter to execute inspection and to correct problems. The main forces involved are:

- **Force 1**: Evaluating system usage scenarios from the very beginning and frequently during development.
- **Force 2**: Not showing serious problems to real users.
- **Force 3**: Evaluating the usability of features of the current agile iteration.

Solution: Inspecting user interfaces, of low- or high-fidelity prototypes, through usability scenarios, rules, or heuristics. Usability specialists perform evaluation by inspection to verify whether the user interface under test meets the rules or follows expected paths for the given scenarios. Normally, two or three specialists execute it. First, each specialist individually analyzes and then what was found to consolidate results is discussed by all. This way, tests with users are conducted in interfaces that were already evaluated internally, without exposing (ideally) serious issues to the real users of the product. Specialists share results with the development team so that problems found may be corrected. Some teams report the involvement of developers and, in this case, they describe such participation as positive, since it facilitates the process of sharing usability knowledge with the team. Also, meetings for consolidating results found in each individual analysis are mostly laboratory-based. Usually, developers solve problems found during the evaluation by inspection in the same iteration or sprint.

Examples: Similar to what occurs during tests with users, the systematic review by Silva et al. [4] also raised user interface refinement as the main goal of evaluation by inspection, according to [13,16,19]. Obendorf and Finck [26] state it is possible to use scenarios to guide evaluation by inspection of paper prototypes.

Pattern: ***RITE Method***

Context: Need to identify and to solve as many problems as possible and to check the efficacy of solutions as soon as possible.

Problem: In agile environments, there is not enough time for usability tests and correction of problems, for each iteration, using traditional usability methods, which leads to rare usability tests and the correction of few bugs. The main forces involved are:

- **Force 1**: Receiving feedback from corrections as close as possible to tests conduction.
- **Force 2**: Shortening the distance between finding usability problems and correcting them in the system.
- **Force 3**: Evaluating features within agile iterations, with less time to run tests and to correct bugs.

Solution: Identifying and solving problems found, by using tests with typical users of the system and checking how efficient the solutions are as soon as possible. Rapid Interactive Testing and Evaluation (RITE) emphasizes changes and quick verifications of their efficacy. Usability testing and the quickest correction of errors. Usually, usability specialists perform RITE and its results are shared with other team members to be evaluated.

Examples: This practice is present in the list of best practices published by the User eXperience Magazine, focusing on changes and verifications of their efficiency quickly [27]. For Patton [15], RITE is used to iterate the user interface before the development. In [28], RITE is defined as a variation of traditional usability tests, documented by Microsoft researchers in 2002, being credited to Medlock. In sum, by testing a design with five users on the first day, on the second day, the design is improved based on the feedback; it is tested again on the third day; on the fourth day, another iteration is conducted, and then the final design is tested on the fifth day with eight users. The authors also state that RITE is not always appropriate (if there are too many tasks, for example). However, whenever possible, it is highly recommended by them since it saves time, promotes collaboration within the team besides customer satisfaction.

Pattern: ***Acceptance Tests***

Context: Need to check if the goals of real users and customers were met in a version of the system already with the working code.

Problem: Validating whether the needs of customers and typical users are being met by the features prior to development is common in traditional usability practices, which is incompatible with agile environments, which entail adaptive planning and iterative processes. In agile environments, this task should be performed keeping the documentation updated in relation to features that successfully or unsuccessfully meet the needs of users. The main forces involved are:

- **Force 1**: Making the validation of the system by customers and typical users from the very beginning and frequently during development.
- **Force 2**: Keeping the documentation updated according to already-implemented user needs.
- **Force 3**: Evaluating features within agile iterations, with less time to run tests.

Solution: Creating automatic acceptance tests using Test Driven Development (TDD), which is already part of agile methods. Tests are created with the customers or typical user participation by using standard formats similar to natural language, such that non-experts on programming are capable of describing user needs. By conducting automatic tests based on TDD, a report is generated showing the status of the defined tests. This practice helps validating the user needs and creates an updated documentation of everything the system does, which functionalities already have tests, and whether the tests are executed successfully.

Examples: Dyba et al. [29] describe automatic acceptance testing as a good practice to validate user interface design. The agile community acknowledged the importance of acceptance tests and built tools such as the Framework for Integrated Test (fit.c2.com), JBehave (jbehave.org), and Cucumber (cucumber.io) to help automate them. Automated testing is performed frequently, at least every day or several times a day. Manual tests with users, on the other hand, are normally conducted one iteration ahead. At the end of an iteration, many agile teams implement a system functioning in a testing environment, where automated tests of the system and tests with users are conducted. The team continues to develop version N+1 of the system while gathering reports on version N. Failure reports are treated as any other requirement: they are estimated, prioritized, and put into a requirement list to be treated in the future [30]. According to Rice [31], these tests should not be treated as "functional tests based solely on user requirements", since you are "likely to miss the same things in testing that were missed in defining the requirements".

5 Conclusion

According to Sy [6], all the activities of the UCD cycle should be performed for each subset of features in agile iterations. The patterns presented organize the practices described in the literature in a common format. Therefore, it is possible to select the patterns of each phase of the UCD cycle that best fit specific development environments and apply them within an agile iteration.

In addition, the patterns presented here can help understand how to integrate the practices of UCD and agile methods, allowing developers to visualize the similarities shared, and also the commonalities among other communities that could use the patterns in their contexts of development. We described a set of patterns of agile usability practices for UCD final stages extracted from the literature. The presentation of patterns in a format including name, context, problem, solution, and examples can increase their applicability.

Overall, the patterns described for the UCD stage - Create design solutions - have in common the fact of seeking knowledge sharing in order to facilitate understanding the requirements and the user interaction flow with the system. For the patterns described for the UCD stage - Evaluate designs - there is the need of user interface refinement for the following iteration. The goal is to evaluate designs during the development process, from early stages with prototypes in low fidelity. This work complements our previous study on the early stages of UCD [7]. Future studies may define an order of application of the patterns according to the stage of development in an agile environment while maintaining the DCU cycle for each agile iteration.

Acknowledgements. This research was supported by FAPESP, Brazil, proc. 2012/24409-2, and the European Comission, proc. 034763.

References

1. Brhel, M., Meth, H., Maedcher, A.: Exploring principles of user-centered agile software development: a literature review. Inf. Softw. Technol. **61**(C), 163–181 (2015)
2. Salah, D., Paige, R.F., Cairns, P.: A systematic literature review for agile development processes and user centred design integration. In: Proceedings of the 18th International Conference on Evaluation and Assessment in Software Engineering, 13–14 May 2014
3. Silva da Silva, T., Silveira, M., Maurer, F., Hellmann, T.: User experience design and agile development: from theory to practice. J. Softw. Eng. Appl. **5**, 743–751 (2012)
4. Silva da Silva, T., Martin, A., Maurer, F., Silveira, M.: User-centered design and agile methods: a systematic review. In: Imperial College Robotics Society (ed.) Agile Conference (Agile) 2011, pp. 77–86 (2011)
5. Fox, D., Sillito, J., Maurer, F.: Agile methods and user-centered design: how these two methodologies are being successfully integrated in industry. In: Agile 2008, AGILE 2008 Conference, pp. 63–72 (2008)
6. Sy, D.: Adapting usability investigations for agile user-centered design. J. Usability Stud. **2**(3), 112–132 (2007)
7. Bertholdo, A.P.O., da Silva, T.S., de O. Melo, C., Kon, F., Silveira, M.S.: Agile usability patterns for UCD early stages. In: Marcus, A. (ed.) DUXU 2014, Part I. LNCS, vol. 8517, pp. 33–44. Springer, Heidelberg (2014)
8. Beck, K., Andres, C.: Extreme Programming Explained Embrace Change. Addison-Wesley Professional, Reading (2004)
9. Schwaber, K., Beedle, M.: Agile Software Development with Scrum, 1st edn. Prentice Hall PTR, Upper Saddle River (2001)
10. Silva Da Silva, T., Selbach Silveira, M., Maurer, F.: Usability evaluation practices within agile development. In: 2015 48th Hawaii International Conference on System Sciences (HICSS), pp. 5133–5142. IEEE (2015)
11. Alexander, C., Ishikawa, S., Silverstein, M., Jacobson, M., King, I.F., Angel, S.: A Pattern Language: Towns, Buildings, Construction. Center for Environmental Structure Series. Oxford University Press, New York (1977)
12. Association, U.E.P.: What is user-centered design? January 2014

13. Fox, D., Sillito, J., Maurer, F.: Agile methods and user-centered design: how these two methodologies are being successfully integrated in industry. In: Proceedings of the Agile 2008, pp. 63–72 (2008)
14. Detweiler, M.: Managing ucd within agile projects. Interactions **14**, 40–42 (2007)
15. Patton, J.: Emerging best agile ux practice (2008). http://agileproductdesign.com/blog/emerging_best_agile_ux_practice.html
16. Williams, H., Ferguson, A.: The ucd perspective: before and after agile. In: AGILE 2007, pp. 285–290 (2007)
17. Hussain, Z., Milchrahm, H., Shahzad, S., Slany, W., Tscheligi, M., Wolkerstorfer, P.: Integration of extreme programming and user-centered design: lessons learned. In: Abrahamsson, P., Marchesi, M., Maurer, F. (eds.) Agile Processes in Software Engineering and Extreme Programming. LNBIP, vol. 31, pp. 174–179. Springer, Heidelberg (2009)
18. Six, J.M.: Integrating ux into agile development, April 2011. http://www.uxmatters.com/mt/archives/2011/04/integrating-ux-into-agile-development.php. Accessed Dec 2011
19. Ungar, J., White, J.: Agile user centered design: enter the design studio - a case study. In: CHI 2008 Extended Abstracts on Human Factors in Computing Systems. CHI EA 2008, pp. 2167–2178. ACM, New York (2008)
20. Dubakov, M.: Ux meets agile: design studio methodology, May 2011. http://www.targetprocess.com/blog/2011/05/ux-meets-agile-design-studio-methodology.html. Accessed Dec 2011
21. Evans, W., Gothelf, J.: Design studio and agile ux: process and pitfalls, November 2011. http://uxmag.com/articles/design-studio-and-agile-ux-process-and-pitfalls. Accessed Dec 2011
22. Govella, A.: Agile + ux: six strategies for more agile user experience (2008). http://www.thinkingandmaking.com/view/agile-ux-six
23. Beltrame, M.: Just married: user centered design and agile, May 2011. http://www.memibeltrame.ch/slides/. Accessed Dec 2011
24. Tyne, S.V.: User experience design in agile development (2011). http://www.slideshare.net/sdeconf/sdec-2011-uxagilesvt. Accessed Dec 2011
25. Enterprise E: Incorporating user-centered design into an agile development process, December 2011. http://experoinc.com/incorporating-user-centered-design-into-an-agile-development-process/. Accessed Dec 2011
26. Obendorf, H., Finck, M.: Scenario-based usability engineering techniques in agile development processes. In: CHI 2008 Extended Abstracts on Human Factors in Computing Systems, pp. 2159–2166. ACM, New York (2008)
27. Lu, C., Rauch, T., Miller, L.: Agile teams: best practices for agile development. vol. 9, no. 1, pp. 6–10 (2010)
28. Leggett, N.: User research findings - analyzing the user research segment - the power of doing it rite, July 2008. http://www.userresearchfindings.com/2008/07/power-of-doing-it-rite.html. Accessed Dec 2011
29. Dingsoyr, T., Dybå, T., Moe, N.B.: Agile Software Development - Current Research and Future Directions, 1st edn. Springer, Heidelberg (2010)
30. Ambler, S.W.: Introduction to agile usability user experience activities on agile development projects - user testing on an agile project (2009). http://www.agilemodeling.com/essays/agileUsability.htm#AcceptanceTesting. Accessed Dec 2011
31. Rice, R.W.: What is user acceptance testing? (2009). http://www.riceconsulting.com/articles/what-is-UAT.htm. Accessed Dec 2011

A Unified Pattern Specification Formalism to Support User Interface Generation

Jürgen Engel[1,2(✉)], Christian Märtin[1], and Peter Forbrig[2]

[1] Faculty of Computer Science, Augsburg University of Applied Sciences, An der Hochschule 1, 86161 Augsburg, Germany
{Juergen.Engel,Christian.Maertin}@hs-augsburg.de
[2] Institute of Computer Science, University of Rostock, Albert-Einstein-Straße 21, 18059 Rostock, Germany
{Juergen.Engel,Peter.Forbrig}@uni-rostock.de

Abstract. The development of interactive software typically requires the combined skills of software developers, HCI, platform and marketing specialists in order to create applications with good software quality, usability, and user experience. The combination of model-based user interface development practices with pattern-based approaches that specify HCI- and software-patterns in a formalized way and respect emerging standards, has the potential to facilitate and automate the software development process, reduce development costs, and provide solutions that can easily be adapted to varying contexts of use. To satisfy these goals we have developed a framework for Pattern-based Modeling and Generation of Interactive Systems (PaMGIS). The paper at hand describes the topical version of the PaMGIS Pattern Specification Language (PPSL) which is designed to accomplish both, capturing all information required to support model-based user interface generation and offering the highest level of compatibility to existing pattern description languages.

Keywords: Model-based user interface development · Pattern-based development · User interface modeling · User interface generation · HCI patterns · Formal pattern specification

1 Introduction

The model-driven part of the PaMGIS framework is designed in the style of the CAMELEON Reference Framework [1]. Particularly, the ontological domain and context-of-use models are used as proposed by the CRF. However, we decided to split the CRF platform model into a device model and a user interface (UI) toolkit model. While the former comprises all relevant characteristics of the respective end-user device, the latter holds information about the user interface elements that are available on the respective underlying software development platform. This avoids redundancies especially in cases where the same software basis supports significantly different devices, e.g. Android on smartphones and tablet computers. On the basis of the domain model a dialog model is prepared that, in turn, helps to derive an abstract user interface model which is subsequently transformed into a concrete and lastly into the final user

M. Kurosu (Ed.): HCI 2016, Part I, LNCS 9731, pp. 445–456, 2016.
DOI: 10.1007/978-3-319-39510-4_41

interface model. The various UI model transformations are affected by the information which is deposited within the context-of-use model. An overview of the PaMGIS models and their interrelations is illustrated in (Fig. 1).

However, the construction of the required models is a time-consuming and

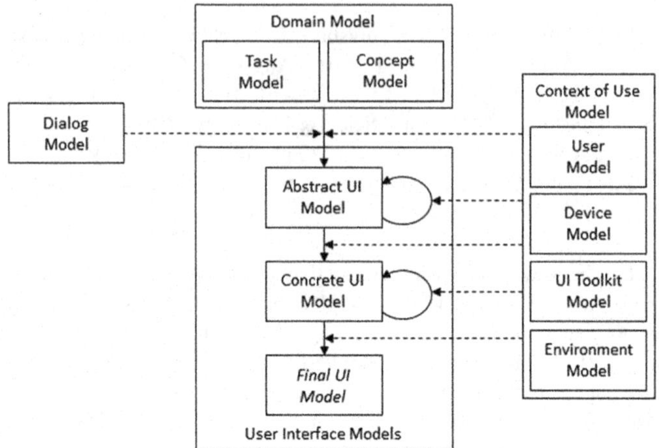

Fig. 1. Overview of the PaMGIS models and their interrelations

error-prone task. Hence, our combined user interface development approach uses patterns as means to alleviate the complexity of the model-driven design and transformation process. The basic idea is to equip patterns with pre-assembled model fragments which can be used as building blocks for the construction of the domain and UI models. In addition, certain patterns could also provide valuable input for the various model transformation steps as highlighted in (Fig. 1) .

For this purpose, we have developed the pattern specification language PPSL which allows us both, to particularize patterns in a formal and machine-readable way and to coevally incorporate any kind of information required to support the PaMGIS model-driven mechanisms. Beyond that, the design of PPSL was driven by two further major requirements. On the one hand, we aimed at the possibility to easily adopt already existing patterns from popular and well-accepted sources, such as the pattern collections of van Duyne [4], Tidwell [11], and van Welie [12]. On the other hand, we intended to raise the acceptability of PPSL by offering the highest level of compatibility to existing pattern description languages, i.e. the *Pattern Language Markup Language* (PLML) 1.1 [7], PLML 1.2 [3], and the *Extended Pattern Language Markup Language* (PLMLx) [1]. We also considered the *Pattern and Component Markup Language* (PCML) [9] and the *Task Pattern Markup Language* (TPML) [10]. However, these two languages are not elaborated within the paper at hand due to space restrictions. They can be translated to PPSL in an analogous manner.

We already have demonstrated in [5] that patterns from [4, 11, 12] can be mapped to PLML 1.1 in at least in a semi-automatic manner. Therefore, we now emphasize on the aforementioned pattern description languages and how respective pattern definitions can be translated into PPSL-based specifications.

2 Existing Pattern Description Languages

Within the context of the *CHI 2003 Conference on Human Factors in Computing Systems* a workshop was held named *Perspectives on HCI Patterns: Concepts and Tools*. One of the goals was the definition of a uniform description language for Human-Computer Interaction (HCI) patterns. Result was the XML-compliant *Pattern Language Markup Language* (PLML) version 1.1 which was intended to standardize pattern specifications and hence allow automatic pattern processing by means of standardized tools. PLML comprises several description elements resp. attributes, which are listed in Table 5 [7]. Brief descriptions can be found in Sect. 3.

PLML 1.2 is a further improved refinement of PLML 1.1 and was defined in 2006 within the context of the implementation of a pattern tool called *Management of User Interface Patterns* (MUIP). Major changes have been made in terms of the PLML 1.1 elements <forces>, <examples>, and <management>. Here, <forces> consists of a sub-element <force> which allows to specify particular influence factors separately and hence make them individually searchable and reusable. The same applies to the <example> element. In addition, individual examples are structured by means of the sub-elements <example-name>, <example-diagram>, <description>, and <known-uses>. The <management> element is enriched by the additional <change-log> sub-element which, in turn, is composed of <log-creation-date> and <log-content>. The entirety of amendments in PLML 1.2 compared to PLML 1.1 is illustrated in (Table 6) [3].

The primary goal of PLMLx is to describe patterns in a presentable, human- and machine-readable article-like format. Like PLML 1.2, PLMLx is based on PLML 1.1. PLMLx introduced three anew description elements, i.e. <acknowledgements>, <resulting-context>, and <organization>. Here, <acknowledgements> provides information on persons who were involved in the definition of the pattern and <resulting-context> contains a description of the context which is effective after the application of the pattern. This might include one or more new problems that need to be resolved. The <organization> element is intended to hold pattern-related metadata and comprises of three sub-elements, i.e. <category>, <collection> und <classification>. Additionally, the <management> element was supplemented by three further sub-elements, i.e. <copyright>, <license>, and <change-log>. The complete list of differences between PLMLx and PLML 1.1 can be found in (Table 7).

3 Introduction of the PaMGIS Pattern Specification Language

In order to appropriately support the modeling and UI generation process the patterns are described according to a particular markup language named *PaMGIS Pattern Specification Language* (PPSL). It incorporates the original expressiveness of PLML 1.1 and remedies some of PLML's inherent weaknesses, notably in terms of pattern relation modeling and provision of details required for automated pattern processing [6]. In addition, PPSL is designed to allow straight forward mapping of patterns defined in existing description formats, i.e. PLML 1.1, PLML 1.2, PLMLx, PCML, and TPML. According to our terminology, the current version is called PPSL 3.0.

Generally, PPSL pattern specifications are structured by means of four top level description elements, i.e. <Head>, <Body>, <Relationship>, and <Deployment>.

Here, the <Head> element incorporates pattern metadata, including information on pattern identification, names, work status, synopsis, originators, change history, further sources and literature, and legal aspects. Amongst others, pattern metadata is exploited

Table 1. PPSL description elements within the top level element <Head>

Element	Brief Description
<UniquePatternID>	Unique pattern identifier
<UPID_PatternCompilationID>	Identifier of the respective pattern collection
<UPID_PatternID>	Identifier of the pattern
<UPID_VersionNumber>	Version number of the pattern (major changes)
<UPID_RevisionNumber>	Revision number of the pattern (minor changes)
<Classification>	Information on classification of the pattern
<CLSS_PatternCompilationName>	Name of the respective pattern collection
<CLSS_Domain>	Name of the domain the pattern belongs to
<CLSS_PatternType>	Type of the pattern, e.g., "HCI pattern"
<CLSS_AbstractionLevel>	Abstraction level of the pattern
<CLSS_Category>	Category within the pattern collection
<CLSS_Subcategory>	Sub-category within the pattern collection
<CLSS_SubSubCategory>	Sub-sub-category within the pattern collection
<CLSS_Keywords>	List of keywords characterizing the pattern
<CLSS_Keyword>	Individual keyword
<Names>	Names of the pattern
<Name>	Preferred name of the pattern
<Aliases>	List of alternative names
<Alias>	Individual alternative name
<Status>	Work status, e.g., "draft" or "released"
<Synopsis>	Concise summary of the pattern's relevance
<Contribution>	Information on contributions to the pattern
<Authors>	List of pattern authors
<Author>	Information on an individual author
<ATHR_AuthorID>	Identifier of the author
<ATHR_FirstName>	Author's first name

<ATHR_LastName>	Author's last name
<ATHR_Organization>	Organization the author works for
<ATHR_PersonalDate>	Further information, e.g., a CV
<ATHR_ContactInformation>	Contact details
<ATHR_Link>	Link to a personal website
<ATHR_LinkDisplayName>	Name of the website
<ATHR_URL>	Actual URL
<Credits>	Information on contributing persons not mentioned within the list of authors
<History>	Development of the pattern specification over time
<Ancestry>	Information on the origin of the pattern
<ANCS_PatternCompilationName>	Name of the original pattern collection
<ANCS_PatternName>	Original name of the pattern within this collection
<ANCS_PatternID>	Identifier of the pattern in this collection
<ANCS_Category>	Name of the respective category in this collection
<ANCS_VersionNumber>	Version number within this collcection
<ANCS_RevisionNumber>	Revision number within this collection
<ANCS_Link>	Link to a website providing more information
<ANCS_LinkDisplayName>	Name of the Website
<ANCS_URL>	Actual URL
<CreationDate>	Date of pattern creation in PPSL format
<LastModified>	Date of latest change to the pattern specification
<Changes>	List of changes which were applied to the pattern
<Change>	Information on an individual change
<CHNG_ChangeID>	Identifier of the change
<CHNG_Date>	Date of change
<CHNG_VersionNumber>	Version number before the change
<CHNG_RevisionNumber>	Revision number before the change
<CHNG_Originator>	Name(s) or ID(s) of author(s)
<CHNG_Description>	Description of the change
<CHNG_Reason>	Reason for the change
<CHNG_Link>	Link to a website with further information
<CHNG_Link DisplayName>	Name of the Website
<CHNG_URL>	Actual URL
<References>	List of related sources and literature
<Reference>	Information on an individual source
<RFNC_Type>	Type of source, e.g., "book" or "website"
<RFNC_Title>	Titel or name of the source
<RFNC_Author>	Name(s) or ID(s) of author(s)
<RFNC_Description>	Summary in terms of purpose and contents
<RFNC_Reference>	Unique identifier, e.g., ISBN or URL
<LegalFoundation>	Legel foundation regarding the usage of the pattern
<Copyright>	Information on copyright restrictions
<License>	License-related information
<LCNS_Description>	Description of the licensing
<LCNS_Type>	Type of license, e.g., "GNU"
<LCNS_Agreement>	License agreement or link to it
<FurtherInformation>	Further information not yet mentioned in <Head>

to retrieve particular patterns within a pattern repository. An overview of the description elements of <Head> are listed in (Table 1).

The PPSL top level element <Body> represents the description of the actual pattern and is divided into the two sub-elements <Theory> and <Practice>. The former holds theoretical background information, including descriptions of the problem to be solved, the application context, and the solution for the given problem. The latter provides practical examples and known uses as well as results of usability activities, e.g. user testing. Details of the <Body> element are provided in (Table 2).

Relations between patterns can be defined by the <Relationship> top level element of PPSL. Compared to PLML 1.1 the identification of related patterns is more precise. Hence, relations between particular pattern versions resp. revisions of patterns can be expressed. (Table 3) shows the structure of the <Relations> element.

Finally, the <Deployment> top level element is a further development of the PLML 1.1 element <Implementation> and incorporates, amongst others, the information required for automatic processing and model construction within the PaMGIS framework.

It is designed to hold fragments of PaMGIS's fundamental models, including task model, concept model, dialog model, abstract UI (AUI) model, concrete UI (CUI) model, and final UI (FUI) model fragments. These model fragments are intended to be automatically integrated into the overall PaMGIS models as soon as the framework user selects and applies them. They can be regarded as building blocks for the PaMGIS models which have the potential to speed up the model design process, feature reuse of design work, and positively contribute to high usability and acceptable user experience of the final user interface. The structure of the PPSL top level element <Deployment> is depicted in (Table 4).

4 Mapping Existing Pattern Description Languages to PPSL

The mapping of PLML 1.1 description elements to PPSL is shown in Table 5. The left column contains the PLML 1.1 source elements while the right column specifies the respective PPSL target elements.

In a similar way, the correlation between PLML 1.2 and PPSL is illustrated in (Table 6) Due to space limits solely the differences between PLML 1.1 and PLML 1.2 are listed.

Finally, (Table 7) outlines the relation between PLMLx and PPSL. Like before, only the differences to PLML 1.1 are listed.

Duc to lack of space we do not elaborate on the relationship between PCML resp. TPML and PPSL. However, the mapping is feasible analogously in both cases.

Table 2. PPSL description elements within the top level element < Body>

Element	Brief Description
<Theory>	Theoretical aspects regarding the pattern
<Problem>	Description of the problem to be solved
<PRBL_Digest>	Summary
<PRBL_Elaboration>	Detailed description
<Context>	Situations in which the pattern can be applied
<CNTX_Digest>	Summary
<CNTX_Elaboration>	Detailed description
<Solution>	Description of how to resolve the problem
<SLTN_Digest>	Summary
<SLTN_Elaboration>	Detailed description
<Forces>	List of forces in the environment
<Force>	Force that the pattern will resolve
<FRCE_Digest>	Summary
<FRCE_Elaboration>	Detailed description
<Rationale>	Discussion and any principled reasons
<Confidence>	Rating of how likely the pattern provides an invariant solution for the given problem
<ResultingContext>	Context after the application of the pattern
<Diagrams>	List of schematic visualization of the pattern
<Diagram>	Individual schematic visualization
<Practice>	Pratical aspects regarding the pattern
<Examples>	List of application examples (within PaMGIS)
<Example>	Information on one individual example
<XMPL_Type>	Example type, i.e., (counter)example
<XMPL_ExampleID>	Identifier of the example
<XMPL_Label>	Name of the example
<XMPL_Description>	Textutal description of the example
<XMPL_Diagram>	Schematic visualization of the example
<XMPL_Images>	List of relevant images
<XMPL_Image>	Individual image, e.g., a screenshot
<XMPL_Realizations>	List of links to implementations
<XMPL_Realization>	Individual link to an implementation
<XMPL_Modelings>	List of modelings
<XMPL_Modeling>	Individual modeling (list of links)
<XMPL_ModelFragmentID>	Link to model fragments within the PPSL description element <Deployment>
<Known Uses>	List of known uses (outside of PaMGIS)
<KnownUse>	Information on one individual known use
<KNWN_CreationDate>	Date of creation
<KNWN_KnownUseID>	Identifier of the known use
<KNWN_Label>	Name of the known use
<KNWN_Description>	Textual description
<KNWN_Originator>	Name of the originator
<KNWN_Link>	Link to a website using the pattern
<KNWN_LinkDisplayName>	Name of the website
<KNWN_URL>	Actual URL
<KNWN_Images>	List of relevant images
<KNWN_Image>	Individual image, e.g., a screenshot
<UsabilityFeedback>	Results of usability activities, e.g., user testing

Table 3. PPSL description elements within the top level element < Relationship>

Element	Brief Description
<RLTN_Information>	Textual description of relations to other patterns
<Relations>	List of relations to other patterns
<Relation>	Information on an individual relation
<RLTN_RelationID>	Identifier of the relation
<RLTN_Label>	Name of the relation
<RLTN_Nature>	Nature of relation (within PaMGIS or external)
<RLTN_Type>	Type of relation, e.g., "aggregation"
<RLTN_Reference>	Identity of the related pattern
<RLTN_PatternCompilationID	Identifier of the respective pattern collection
<RLTN_PatternCompilationName>	Name of the respective pattern collection
<RLTN_PatternID	Identifier of the related pattern
<RLTN_PatternName>	Name of the related pattern
<RLTN_VersionNumber>	Version number of the related pattern
<RLTN_RevisionNumber>	Revision number of the related pattern
<RLTN_Description>	Textual description, comments, and hints

Table 4. PPSL description elements within the top level element < Deployment>

Element	Brief Description
<Implementations>	List of possible implementations
<Implementation>	Information on an individual implementation
<IMPL_ImplementationID>	Identifier of the implementation
<IMPL_Label>	Name of the implementation
<IMPL_Description>	Textual description of the implementation
<IMPL_Code>	Code fragments
<EmbeddingLinks>	List of links to OOA and/or OOD models (see [8])
<EmbeddingLink>	Information on an individual link
<EMBL_EmbeddedLinkID>	Identifier of the link
<EMBL_Label>	Name of the link
<EMBL_ReferenceClassID>	Class within the OO model being referenced
<EMBL_UMLRelationshipType>	UML type of relationship
<PaMGIS>	Information for processing with PaMGIS
<ModelFragments>	List of model fragments
<ModelFragment>	Information on an individual model fragment
<MDFR_Type>	Type of model fragment, e.g., task model
<MDFR_FragmentID>	Identifier of model fragment
<MDFR_Label>	Name of model fragment
<MDFR_Purpose>	Description of the purpose of the fragment
<MDFR_Fragment>	Actual model fragment
<MDFR_Base>	List of references to model fragments from which the current fragment has been derived
<MDFR_BaseReference>	ID of an individual model fragment
<MDFR_Annotation>	Comments and annotations in textual format

Table 5. Mapping of PLML 1.1 to PPSL

PLML 1.1 Element	Corresponding PPSL Element
<patternID>	<Head> <UniquePatternID> <UPID_PatternID>
<name>	<Head> <Names> <Name>
<alias>	<Head> <Names> <Aliases>
<illustration>	<Body> <Practice> <Examples> <Example>
<problem>	<Body> <Theory> <Problem>
<context>	<Body> <Theory> <Context>
<forces>	<Body> <Theory> <Forces> <Force>
<solution>	<Body> <Theory> <Solution>
<synopsis>	<Head> <Synopsis>
<diagram>	<Body> <Theory> <Diagrams> <Diagram>
<evidence>	Merely used for structuring purposes; not required in PPSL
<example>	<Body> <Practice> <Examples> <Example>
<rationale>	<Body> <Theory> <Rationale>
<confidence>	<Body> <Theory> <Confidence>
<literature>	<Head> <References> <Reference>
<implementation>	<Deployment> <Implementations> <Implementation>
<related-patterns>	<Relationship> <RLTN_Information>
<pattern-link>	<Relationship> <Relations> <Relation>
<type>	<RLTN_Type>
<patternID>	<RLTN_Reference> <RLTN_PatternID>
<collection>	<RLTN_Reference> <RLTN_PatternCompilationName>
<label>	<RLTN_Label>
<management>	Merely used for structuring purposes; not required in PPSL
<author>	<Head> <Contribution> <Authors> <Author>
<credits>	<Head> <Contribution> <Credits>
<creation-date>	<Head> <History> <CreationDate>
<last-modified>	<Head> <History> <LastModified>
<revision-number>	<Head> <UniquePatternID> <UPID_RevisionNumber>

5 Conclusion and Outlook

Within the present paper we introduced the topical version of the PaMGIS Pattern Specification Language (PPSL). On the one hand, it is designed to equip patterns with all information required to use them as building blocks for model construction in the context of the PaMGIS framework. On the other hand, PPSL strives for best possible compatibility to existing pattern description languages in order to enable the reutilization of already available patterns without major efforts. To this effect, we demonstrated how PLML 1.1, PLML 1.2, and PLMLx can be mapped to PPSL. Mapping of PCML and TPML is also possible, but not elaborated in the paper due to space limits.

Table 6. Mapping of PLML 1.2 PPSL (differences of PLML 1.2 compared to PLML 1.1)

PLML 1.2 Element	Corresponding PPSL Element
<collection>	<Head> <Classification> <CLSS_PatternCompilationName>
<forces>	<Body> <Theory> <Forces>
<force>	<Force>
<example>	<Body> <Practice> <Examples> <Example>
<example-name>	<XMPL_Label>
<example-diagram>	<XMPL_Diagram>
<description>	<XMPL_Description>
<known-uses>	<Body> <Practice> <KnownUses>
<literature>	Merely used for structuring purposes; not required in PPSL
<work-name>	<Head> <References> <Reference> <RFNC_Title>
<reference>	<Head> <References> <Reference> <RFNC_Reference>
<implementation>	<Deployment> <Implementations> <Implementation>
<implementation-name>	<IMPL_Label>
<code>	<IMPL_Code>
<other-details>	<IMPL_Description>
<pattern-link>	<Relationship> <Relations> <Relation>
<revision-number>	<RLTN_Reference> <RLTN_RevisionNumber>
<management>	Merely used for structuring purposes; not required in PPSL
<change-log>	<Head> <History> <Changes>
<log-creation-date>	<Change> <CHNG_Date>
<log-content>	<Change> <CHNG_Description>

To fulfill the aforementioned requirements PPSL consists of a multitude of description elements. In order to preserve manageability of the pattern specifications we semantically grouped them into the four top level elements <Head>, <Body>, <Relationship>, and <Deployment>. In addition, the patterns are created, managed, retrieved, and applied with the aid of a set of tools included in the PaMGIS framework.

Our upcoming activities will target on the augmentation of our pattern repository. For this, we will focus on both, the translation and enrichment of existing patterns and the development of new domain-specific patterns, e.g. for electronic vending and commerce. Further, we intend to intensify our research on how results of usability activities, e.g. user testing, can be exploited to improve the quality of our patterns and hence also of the user interfaces being generated by PaMGIS. As a consequence, this will entail more substance and structure of the PPSL description element <Body> <Practice> <UsabilityFeedback>.

Table 7. Mapping of PLMLx to PPSL (differences of PLMLx compared to PLML 1.1)

PLMLx Element	Corresponding PPSL Element
<acknowledgements>	<Head> <Contribution> <Credits>
<evidence>	Merely used for structuring purposes; not required in PPSL
<example>	<Body> <Practice> <Examples> <Example>
<rationale>	<Body> <Theory> <Rationale>
<organization>	<Head> <Classification>
<category>	<CLSS_Category>
<collection>	<CLSS_PatternCompilationName>
<classification>	<CLSS_PatternType>
<resulting-context>	<Body> <Theory> <ResultingContext>
<management>	Merely used for structuring purposes; not required in PPSL
<author>	<Head> <Contribution> <Authors> <Author>
<change-log>	<Head> <History> <Changes>
<change>	<Change>
<author>	<CHNG_Originator>
<description>	<CHNG_Description>
<version>	Merely for structuring purposes; not required in PPSL
<date>	<CHNG_Date>
<majorNo>	<CHNG_VersionNumber>
<minorNo>	<CHNG_RevisionNumber>
<copyright>	<Head> <LegalFoundation> <Copyright>
<creation-date>	<Head> <History> <CreationDate>
<credits>	<Head> <Contribution> <Credits>
<last-modified>	<Head> <History> <LastModified>
<license>	<Head> <LegalFoundation> <License>
<license-type>	<LCNS_Type>
<ulink>	<LCNS_Agreement>
<revision-number>	<Head> <UniquePatternID> <UPID_RevisionNumber>

References

1. Bienhaus, D.: PLMLx Doc (2004). http://www.cs.kent.ac.uk/people/staff/saf/patterns/plml.html. Accessed 6 Jan 2016
2. Calvary, G., et al.: The CAMELEON reference framework. Document D1.1 of the CAMELEON R&D Project IST-2000-30104 (2002)
3. Deng, J., et al.: Focusing on a standard pattern form: the development and evaluation of MUIP. In: Proceedings of the 6th ACM SIGCHI New Zealand Chapter's International Conference on Computer-Human Interaction: Design Centered HCI (2006)
4. van Duyne, D., et al.: The Design of Sites: Patterns for Creating Winning Websites, 2nd edn. Prentice Hall International, Upper Saddle River (2006). ISBN 0-13-134555-9
5. Engel, J., et al.: Exploiting HCI pattern collections for user interface generation. In: Proceedings of Patterns 2012 (Nice, France), IARIA 2012, pp. 36–44 (2012)

6. Engel, J., et al.: Pattern-based modeling and development of interactive information systems. In: Frotschnig, A., Raffaseder, H. (eds.) Forum Medientechnik – Next Generation, New Ideas, pp. 155–167. vwh Hülsbusch, Glückstadt (2012)
7. Fincher, S., et al.: Perspectives on HCI patterns: concepts and tools (introducing PLML). In: CHI 2003 Workshop Report (2003)
8. Märtin, C., Herdin, C., Engel, J.: Patterns and models for automated user interface construction – in search of the missing links. In: Kurosu, M. (ed.) HCII/HCI 2013, Part I. LNCS, vol. 8004, pp. 401–410. Springer, Heidelberg (2013)
9. ObjectVenture Inc.: Pattern and Component Markup Language (PCML), Draft 3 (2002). http://www.cryer.co.uk/glossary/p/pcml/PCMLSpecification.pdf. Accessed 6 Jan 2016
10. Sinnig, D.: The complicity of patterns and model-based UI development. Master thesis, Concordia University, Montreal, Québec, Canada (2004)
11. Tidwell, J.: Designing Interfaces: Patterns for Effective Interaction Design, 2nd edn. O'Reilly Media Inc., Sebastopol (2011). ISBN 978-1-449-37970-4
12. van Welie, M.: Patterns in Interaction Design. http://www.welie.com. Accessed 6 Jan 2016

Pattern-Based Engineering of Systems-of-Systems for Process Execution Support

Albert Fleischmann[1], Werner Schmidt[2(✉)], Christian Stary[3], and Christian Fichtenbauer[4]

[1] Interaktiv Expert, Pfaffenhofen, Germany
Albert.fleischmann@interatkiv.expert
[2] Technische Hochschule Ingolstadt, Ingolstadt, Germany
Werner.schmidt@thi.de
[3] Johannes Kepler University, Linz, Austria
Christian.stary@jku.at
[4] C-FC, Mortsel, Belgium
Fichtenbauer@icloud.com

Abstract. Globalization and digital transformation increasingly drives agility requirements of business processes, hand-in-hand with execution support by highly flexible, interactive and distributed socio-technical systems. The design of such systems spans the conceptual level of business process models and the implementation level with regard to the organizational environment (assignment of tasks to units/people) and the IT environment (assignment of tasks to applications or services). The organizational and IT environment are often quite heterogeneous, particularly in large, globally operating organizations. The latter may also face specific regulations in different countries, which impacts the way of doing business there. As a consequence, multiple business process variants are developed, both with respect to the organization of work, and IT support. However, such a business reality limits the desirable homogeneity of solutions. It rather requires design concepts allowing for technical and organizational flexibility while keeping mutual coherence. We present ideas for a pattern-based concept ensuring both. It combines System of Systems (SoS) thinking and Subject oriented BPM (S-BPM).

Keywords: System of systems · BPM · S-BPM · Process variants

1 Introduction

Globally operating enterprises are doing business in many countries. While following the same objective, like selling cars, operations at different locations usually vary depending on the organizational environment, he IT support for accomplishing tasks, and other factors, e.g., legal regulations.

Business Process Management (BPM) is a widely accepted approach to align different operational aspects. It comprises several activities like process discovery, design, implementation and execution. One way to capture the different business realities is to identify process variants embedded in a specific target environment.

M. Kurosu (Ed.): HCI 2016, Part I, LNCS 9731, pp. 457–466, 2016.
DOI: 10.1007/978-3-319-39510-4_42

Thereby, tasks specified in a process model are assigned to units/members of the organization and their IT support is realized by integrating existing with newly implemented applications and services.

The result is a set of Locally Executable Business Processes (LEBP), being considered as combinations of work procedure descriptions (process models) and their embedding into the local organization and IT infrastructure.

This perspective in many ways refers to the notion of System of Systems (SoS) as 'a set or arrangement of systems that results when independent and useful systems are integrated into a larger system that delivers unique capabilities' [16]. As systems of systems in the mentioned context can be seen:

- the overall structural organization as the sum of all local, subsidiary parts of the organization, in the end representing the human resources (e.g., departments, teams, places, people)
- the overall process organization as the sum of (partial) process models
- the overall IT infrastructure as the sum of all distributed IT resources, which can be integrated in order to support operation (e.g., workflow engines, enterprise resource planning systems, enterprise content management systems, enterprise service bus etc.)
- the overall operational business system of the enterprise as the sum of all LEBPs, representing the enterprise architecture. Each LEBP itself can also be seen as an SoS, as a whole providing a particular solution for running the respective business process.

The major challenge for practical use is to effectively and efficiently design and maintain those systems of systems. Here some of the characteristics of SoS come into play as there are operational and managerial independence of elements, evolutionary development, emergent behavior and geographic distribution. The exchange of messages and the agreements upon their content facilitate the interconnection and interoperability of the SoS parts. They are a prerequisite for the contribution of the single, autonomous systems to the achievement of higher-level goals, like jointly accomplishing business process instances, as well as for emergent behavior of the SoS. The independence of the single systems and their lose coupling to a SoS allow changing, replacing and adding pieces without affecting other parts. This is exactly what agile behavior of an enterprise requires.

Following the System of Systems notion we present a pattern-based process framework for specifying building blocks of highly flexible yet consistent and coherent process execution support systems. This is of particular interest not only for engineering internal but also cross-enterprise systems-of-systems, e.g., along supply chains or networks. The framework is based on the subject-oriented approach to Business Process Management (S-BPM), which puts the communication of active entities and their individual behavior in a business process in the center of interest. This perspective on work procedure level finds its analogy on IT level with the concept of communicating micro-services, which, however, is not part of this paper.

The remainder of the article is structured as follows: After this introduction we look at related work. In Sect. 3 we present our concept for a Subject-oriented Process System of Systems, before we conclude in Sect. 4.

2 Related Work

Subject-Oriented Business Process Management (S-BPM). S-BPM is a communication-oriented paradigm focusing on subjects as acting parties in business processes (people, systems) [7]. These parties are loosely coupled and synchronize their work on the common goal of executing process instances by exchanging messages. Each subject has a behavior defining the work procedure to accomplish its contribution to the process result. Subject representatives can model subject behaviors independently as long as the messages (interfaces) remain untouched or are agreed upon newly. This behavior encapsulation allows highly flexible self-organization, with the communication structure assuring overall coordination. It also facilitates exchanging behavior descriptions without affecting other parts of the process model. On the implementation level the notion of subjects decouples their occurrence in a process model from people or systems executing their behavior at runtime. This feature fosters implementation and execution flexibility, e.g., identical process activities can be performed by different organizational units and supported by different IT solutions at various locations (e.g., headquarter and subsidiaries).

Systems of Systems. [3] in their recent report introduce 'platform' to abstract from concrete elements, such as vehicles, in a universe of discourse depending on a certain context. A 'platform architecture', consequently, 'may reflect the separation of payload from platform' (p. 3). Extending the traditional notion of industry platform they identify a SoS platform as provider of 'common information models (semantics) and common communication mechanism (ibid.) It may also prescribe patterns or sequences of interaction for certain SoS functions' (ibid.). In analogy to that understanding, S-BPM as a SoS platform supports interoperation among systems, as its subject diagrams scope business-relevant information models that can be shared and mutually interact based on a common communication mechanism, namely exchanging messages.

With respect to designing an SoS architecture from scratch [3] identified top-down decomposition as one way to accomplish interoperability. Their empirical findings indicate that developers recognize the claim for architectural 'purity' which cannot be achieved in a straightforward way. As a consequence not all systems of SoS are changeable. In those cases, rather than rethinking modularity based on a common communication mechanism, only interfaces can be managed. From DoD's SoS experience, the developers concluded the focus of design should be on runtime with an integrator for the infrastructure and the constituent systems. They warn from the effort to integrate differently architected systems for autonomous operations to collaborate without a common information exchange pattern (p. 15f.)

[8] recognized decomposition and bottom-up construction to be complementary along spiral development of SoS, as it reflects the dynamics of accomplishing change. In addition, constituent systems of SoS should be self-aware, at least on the goal level, in order to meet challenges on a level of single systems (cf. [2]). Explicit representation of goals could help to adjust a system in operation during build time in the sense of identifying a 'best fit' for each component handling a global task before actually executing a SoS. However, such a perspective needs revisiting Requirements

Engineering and the embodiment of fundamental SoS categories, such as directness, acknowledged objectives, collaboration, and virtuality with respect to control (cf. [14]).

Recognizing the resulting need of structured tool support [4] have developed COMPASS aiming for collaborative SoS development (see also [10]). In that context, they came up with a modeling language representing the particularities of SoS. However, they were focusing on abstract SoS modeling concepts rather than a particular execution logic controlling SoS behavior, as e.g., the hypergraph approach for constraint satisfaction [11].

The COMPASS language abstracts from SoS as a collection of constituent systems. They are specified by SoS behavior which is very likely to be incomplete (as emergence hinders capturing all cases). However, in line with S-BPM, each constituent system has

- to have a specification of its behavior relevant to the SoS
- to provide sufficient state information to allow the constituent system to be verified and executed
- to represent a consistent abstraction of the specification, however, its internal state need not be exactly the same as the actual system specification
- to have a specification, that is completely independent of the overall SoS. If it is not possible to create such a specification, then it may not be a system in its own right.

In order to capture operation of SoS, a SoS model should include an infrastructure specification, modelled as constituent systems. 'These parts of the overall specification are used to either bind the component systems into the SoS, or to provide a bit of extra functionality beyond what is provided by any of the constituent systems. Full specifications of these constituent systems must be provided in detail to all members of the SoS' [4, p. 452].

From a managerial perspective, SoS projects benefit from a layered approach to define dynamic behavior capabilities in the course of analysis, e.g., as provided by [19]. Their Base Level addresses networked actors in terms of human agents. They utilize information and resources to perform (project) activities. The Activity Level contains networked activities abstracted from the actions (including interaction) of the networked actors on the Base Level. The Process Level networks processes as aggregates of Activity Level's activities. Finally, the Project Level captures all emerging properties from the network on the Process Level.

Modelling Process Variants. This topic has been investigated for quite a while. Approaches range from the so-called fragmented- or multi-model concept to the consolidated- or single-model concept [5, 9]. However, [13] state 'Striking a trade-off between modelling each process variant separately versus collectively in a consolidated manner is still an open research question.' We do not discuss this question in more detail, but rather resolve this issue pragmatically.

3 Subject-Oriented Process System of Systems

3.1 Drivers for Locally Executable Business Processes

The number of various Locally Executable Business Processes necessary to cover operation on all markets depends on the diversity of the respective environment. To identify LBEPs we suggest a three-dimensional model, inspired by [1, 6, 12]. It comprises the following, partially interdependent dimensions:

- **Market.** This dimension represents variation caused by the location where a process is executed, and its consequences. Factors like differing legal regulation or habits can limit standardization of business logic or let it seem not reasonable.
- **Organization.** Organization refers to the question of whether tasks of a process being operated in different markets are executed by similar organizational units or roles.
- **IT.** The IT dimension serves to differentiate applications and services in place to support processes at various locations.

As each dimension can comprise an arbitrary number of characteristics and therefore can be split differently, the resulting body is a cuboid. It can be partitioned repeatedly into sub-cuboids, all of which represent an LEBP, suitable for the particular combination (see Fig. 1). Process variants not necessarily differ in all dimensions, allowing for standardization with patterns wherever possible and reasonable. On the other hand, not all combinations may actually occur, meaning there can exist empty sub-elements. Nevertheless, the cuboid covers all enterprise operations.

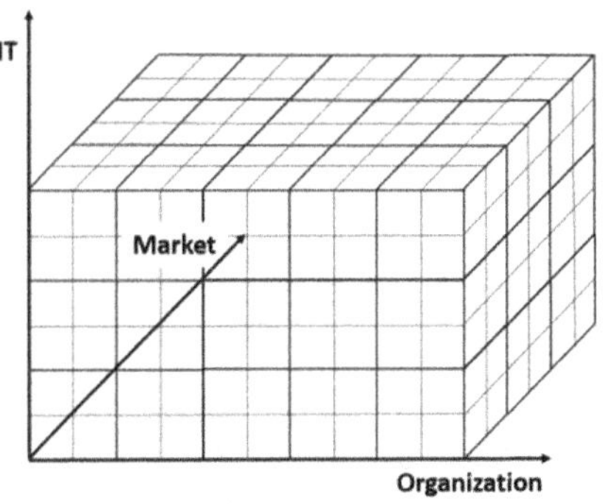

Fig. 1. Dimensions of LBEPs

An example from the automotive industry shows how IT infrastructure causes variants and LBEPs. The following scenario is about arranging an appointment for car maintenance in a garage, which is part of the overall car service process. The way the process works for the garage, belonging to a dealership, and the car manufacturer, mainly depends on whether the dealership has an own Dealer Management System (DMS) or not. Figure 2 depicts the resulting variants with the effect on the distribution of the business logic.

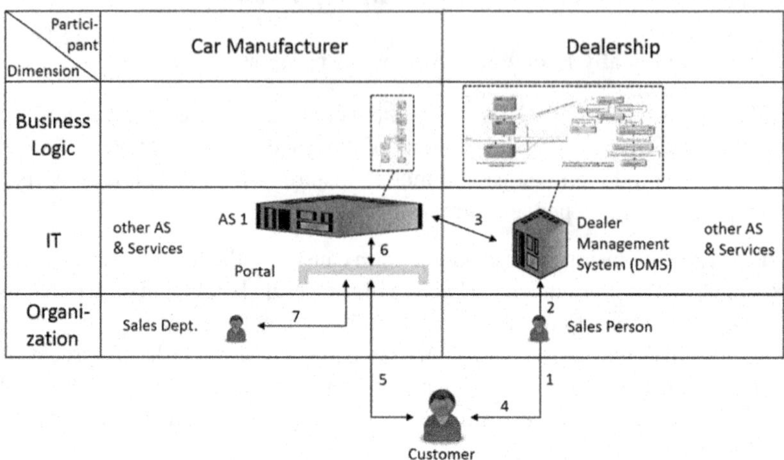

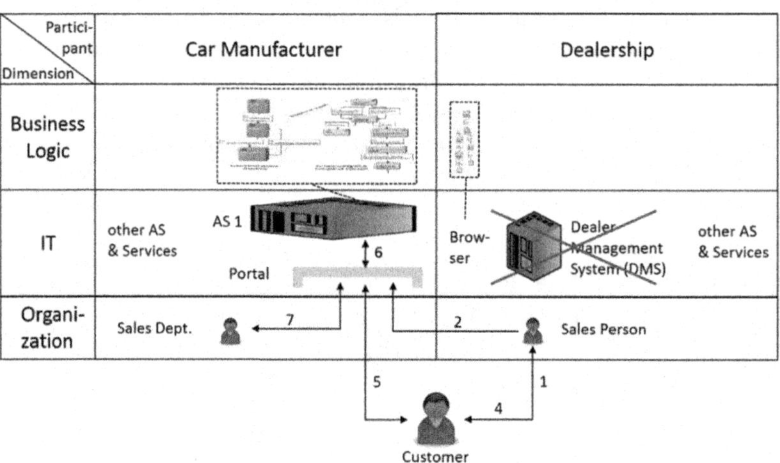

Fig. 2. Process variants

In variant 1 the customer articulates an appointment request to the dealer (1). There, an employee there uses the DMS to manage customer data, dates etc. (2), to connect to an application system AS 1 of the car manufacturer (3), to synchronize data, and to get access credentials to be passed on to the customer (4). Then, the customer can access this system via a portal (5, 6). Data in AS 1 is also maintained by the sales department on the manufacturer's side (7, 6). In this variant main parts of the business logic is represented in the DMS, only a few steps for handling the data access are executed in AS1.

In case of variant 2 the customer either directly accesses AS1 through the portal (if registered before) (5, 6), or the sales person at the Dealer's does that by proxy, using a browser (1, 2, 4). The overall business logic is different, the processes on both sides need to be designed accordingly.

3.2 Concept of the Process Framework

To cope with the sketched variety, the objective is to model process fragments, i.e. subsystems, ensuring their maximal independence and interoperability, as well as constructing largely generic patterns where these systems can be plugged in. As mentioned in the previous sections the System of Systems philosophy and the S-BPM approach as an SoS platform seem to provide conceptual ground for a process framework meeting these requirements.

S-BPM considers humans and systems as subjects, having an encapsulated behavior and exchanging messages in order to coordinate their activities. Systems in this context can be processes, IT applications or services, robots etc. This notion allows building SoS solutions for process execution support, both decomposing top-down and constructing bottom-up as suggested by [3, 8], in any case consisting of elements loosely coupled by message exchange in order to accomplish interoperability.

While decomposition splits processes from the business perspective horizontally and vertically (hierarchically) into pieces or phases linked by messages, construction based on behavior of distinct systems lets the communication structure evolve, when they need to be linked in order to accomplish a (sub) process.

Any of the dimensions in Sect. 3.1 can give evidence for how to crop process parts during initial design and when changes occur over time. They also determine whether independent building blocks need to be modified, replaced, added etc.

Figure 3 depicts the frame of the already mentioned car service process, being decomposed in subsystems representing phases of the overall process. Subject orientation considers a business process to be a system of communicating entities. They produce results that add to accomplishing the task of the overall process system. Following this notion, each subsystem contains the involved subjects, their interaction and their individual behavior. Messages between subjects in different phases connect the parts loosely, however, deliver results. Although linear with a back loop in the example, the communication pattern can be networked. The figure also shows three variants of the ‘Arrange Appointment’ phase, each of which can be plugged in the frame depending on their fit to the concrete situation. The only constraint is to assure compatibility or adaptation of the connecting messages.

The coupling by messages facilitates easy variation both horizontally regarding the phases, and vertically over multiple levels of detail. This allows situative design of LBEPs, where business and system architects can select or develop the variant fitting to each phase or, within phases, the relevant subjects (i.e., their encapsulated behavior). This is not only valid for initial design, but also for maintenance.

Architects can create patterns with identical building blocks for situations with similar characteristics of the cuboid dimensions, and add or replace only those with deviating facts. In our sample, variant 1 of ‘Arrange Appointment’ can be applied as a pattern for all cases (countries, markets, etc.) where the dealership has a DMS, assuming there are no differences with respect to the other dimensions. In cases without DMS, the same process frame (pattern) is used, but with variant 2 another pattern is plugged in, specifying different subjects, communication structure and behavior (see Fig. 3).

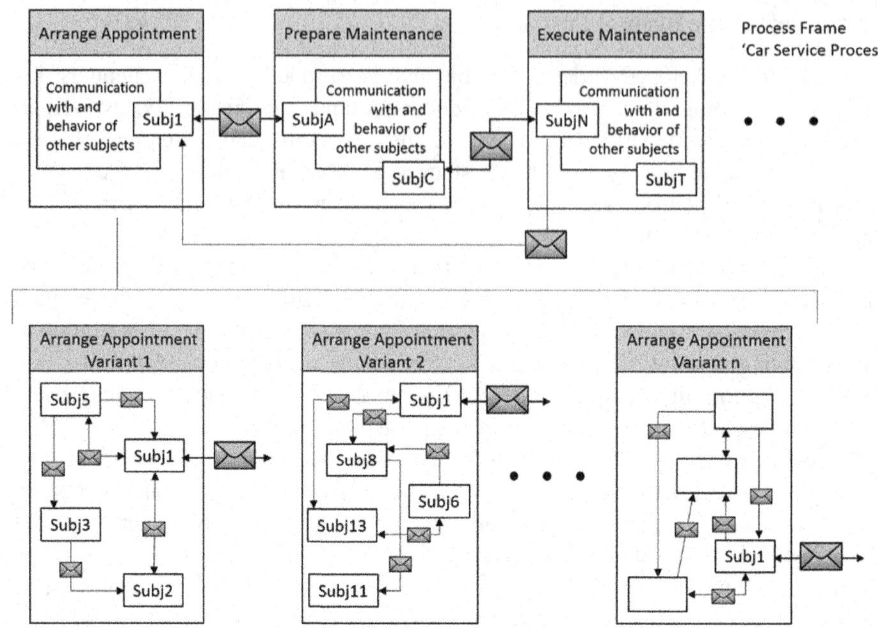

Fig. 3. Process frame and variants

Case-specific design and plugging building blocks into the frame on demand is a compromise of existing ways to generate process variants, as there are behavior-based and structural configurations [17]. The first starts with a comprehensive model covering all known aspects. Subsequently, variants are derived by hiding and blocking model parts. Structural configuration uses a base model and pre-specified changes (e.g., insert, delete, move activities) to be applied at adjustment points. In case of many variants, both approaches may cause extensive effort.

Major benefits from our concept can be expected w.r.t. reducing complexity while increasing flexibility, due to encapsulating and loosely coupling of building blocks. Replacing elements is possible with minimal effect on other parts, either at design time or in the course of deployment. Such straightforward reconfiguration facilitates emergence of new behavior.

4 Conclusion and Further Research

We combined the SoS philosophy and the S-BPM approach to a concept for engineering comprehensive yet flexible process execution support systems. The concept particularly aims for globally acting enterprises requiring many different Locally Executable Business Processes.

The concept is in an early stage of development. It is currently tested, revised and detailed in a practical setting in industry. Revisions will undergo evaluation efforts in future. For instance, detailing processes refers to IT implementation in terms of LBEPs using micro-services. This is a logical consequence as the presented concept is their counterpart on the level of business process models. Micro-services as small, decoupled pieces of software, implemented in different programming languages, and representing certain encapsulated capabilities are correspond to the representatives of the IT dimension of the cuboid in Fig. 1 [15]. By communicating via language-independent interfaces, they allow building complex applications following a modular LBEP architecture whose elements can easily be replaced. Strategic alignment of business process variants (e.g., see [18]) is another topic to be investigated to see how the presented approach can be related to business strategies.

References

1. Abbott, M.L., Fischer, M.T.: The Art of Scalability. Addison-Wesley, Boston (2015)
2. Cavalcante, E., Batista, T., Bencomo, N., Sawyer, P.: Revisiting goal-oriented models for self-aware systems-of-systems. In: 2015 International Conference on Autonomic Computing (ICAC), pp. 231–234. IEEE Press, New York (2015)
3. Cohen, S., Klein, J.: State of practice report: essential technical and nontechnical issues related to designing SoS platform architectures. Technical report CMU/SEI-2015-TR-007 (2015)
4. Coleman, J.W., Malmos, A.K., Larsen, P.G., Peleska, J., et al.: COMPASS tool vision for a system of systems collaborative development environment. In: 7th International Conference on System of Systems Engineering (SoSE), pp. 451–456. IEEE Press, New York (2012)
5. Dumas, M.: Consolidated management of business process variants. In: Daniel, F., Barkaoui, K., Dustdar, S. (eds.) BPM Workshops 2011, Part II. LNBIP, vol. 100, p. 1. Springer, Heidelberg (2012)
6. Fichtenbauer, C., Fleischmann, A.: Three dimensions of process models regarding their execution. In: Proceedings of S-BPM ONE 2016. ACM DL (in print)
7. Fleischmann, A., Schmidt, W., Stary, C., Obermeier, S., Börger, E.: Subject-Oriented Business Process Management. Springer, Heidelberg (2012)
8. Gomez, A., Fonck, B., Ayoun, A., Inzerillo, G.: Concurrent system engineering in air traffic management: steering the SESAR program. In: Proceedings of the Posters Workshop at CSD&M, p. 25 (2013). http://ceur-ws.org/Vol-1085/04-paper.pdf
9. Hallerbach, A., Bauer, T., Reichert, M.: Configuration and management of process variants. In: Brocke, J., Rosemann, M. (eds.) Handbook of Business Process Management, pp. 237–255. Springer, Heidelberg (2010)
10. Hallerstede, S., Hansen, F.O., Holt, J., Lauritsen, R., Lorenzen, L., Peleska, J.: Technical challenges of SoS requirements engineering. In: 7th International Conference on System of Systems Engineering (SoSE), pp. 573–578. IEEE Press, New York (2012)
11. Khalil, W., Koubeissi, A., Merzouki, R., Conrard, B., Ould-Bouamama, B.: Contribution to system of systems modeling. In: 10th System of Systems Engineering Conference (SoSE), pp. 182–186. IEEE Press, New York (2015)
12. Milani, F., Dumas, M., Matulevičius, R.: Identifying and classifying variations in business processes. In: Bider, I., Halpin, T., Krogstie, J., Nurcan, S., Proper, E., Schmidt, R., Soffer, P., Wrycza, S. (eds.) EMMSAD 2012 and BPMDS 2012. LNBIP, vol. 113, pp. 136–150. Springer, Heidelberg (2012)
13. Milani, F., Dumas, M., Matulevičius, R.: Decomposition driven consolidation of process models. In: Salinesi, C., Norrie, M.C., Pastor, Ó. (eds.) CAiSE 2013. LNCS, vol. 7908, pp. 193–207. Springer, Heidelberg (2013)

14. Ncube, C., Lim, S.L., Dogan, H.: Identifying top challenges for international research on requirements engineering for systems of systems engineering. In: 21st International Requirements Engineering Conference (RE), pp. 342–344. IEEE Press, New York (2013)
15. Newman, S.: Building Microservices. O'Reilly, Sebastopol (2015)
16. Office of the Deputy Assistant Seceratry of Defense: SoS Systems Engineering. http://www.acq.osd.mil/se/initiatives/init_sos-se.html. Accessed 9 Feb 2016
17. Reichert, M., Weber, B.: Enabling Flexibility in Process-Aware Information Systems. Springer, Heidelberg (2012)
18. Zellner, P., Laumann, M., Appenfeller, W.: Towards managing business process variants within organizations - an action research study. In: Proceedings of the 2015 48th Hawaii International Conference on System Sciences, pp. 4130–4139. IEEE Press, New York (2015)
19. Zhu, J., Mostafavi, A.: Towards a new paradigm for management of complex engineering projects: a system-of-systems framework. In: 8th Annual IEEE Systems Conference (SysCon), pp. 213–219. IEEE Press, New York (2014)

Elaboration on Terms and Techniques for Reuse of Submodels for Task and Workflow Specifications

Peter Forbrig[1(✉)] and Christian Märtin[2]

[1] Department of Computer Science, University of Rostock, Albert-Einstein-Str. 22, 18059 Rostock, Germany
Peter.Forbrig@uni-rostock.de
[2] Faculty of Computer Science, Augsburg University of Applied Sciences, An der Hochschule 1, 86161 Augsburg, Germany
Christian.Maertin@hs-augsburg.de

Abstract. In this paper, terms and techniques are revisited to discuss a terminology for different kinds of reuse. It identifies problems of currently used terminology and suggests using the term generic submodel. An ontology for terms like template, component, subroutine, pattern, and generic submodel is provided.

Keywords: Patterns · Components · Templates · Task models · Business process models · BPMN · Generic components · Patterns · Generic submodel

1 Introduction

Model-based approaches have proven to be useful for developing interactive systems [12]. However, creating models is still challenging. Even with tool support modeling of real world problems is still time consuming an error prone.

The number of errors can be reduced if existing building blocks can be assembled that have proven to be useful in other projects. This phenomenon is well known from programming. The reuse of already tested code fragments is very helpful to improve the quality of software. For programming subroutines, templates, macros, components, and patterns are known concepts to reuse already specified knowledge.

There have been attempts to apply similar ideas to specifications describing the activities of humans in form of task models or workflow specifications. We will have a look at such approaches and try to harmonize the terminology.

The paper is structured in such a way that reuse of task models and reuse of workflow specifications are revisited and discussed separately. Afterwards, it is tried to find a common terminology in a kind of ontology. The paper ends with a summary and an outlook.

2 Reuse of Models

From our point of view, the reuse of models in general is best supported by Design Patterns [11]. They allow the reuse of modeling knowledge on an abstract level.

M. Kurosu (Ed.): HCI 2016, Part I, LNCS 9731, pp. 467–475, 2016.
DOI: 10.1007/978-3-319-39510-4_43

First, a submodel has to be identified that is a candidate for a pattern application. After a pattern was identified that is appropriate, the solution has to be adapted to the context provided by the submodel. An instance of the pattern is created that is ready for integration (application). The four application steps of design patterns can be formalized in the following way.

1. **Identification**: A subset M' of the original model M is selected for pattern application $\mathbf{M'} \subseteq \mathbf{M}$
2. **Selection**: A pattern P is selected that can be usefully applied to M'
3. **Adaptation**: The pattern P is adapted to the current context C of M'. As a result a pattern instance I is delivered. $\mathbf{A}\,(\mathbf{P}, \mathbf{C}) = \mathbf{I}$
4. **Integration**: The instance I is integrated into M' $\mathbf{F}\,(\mathbf{M'}, \mathbf{I}) = \mathbf{M'^{*}}$ (which also changes M to M*)

Design patterns are generic solutions for reoccurring problems. UML provides a notation for applying design patterns. Figure 1 provides an example for that.

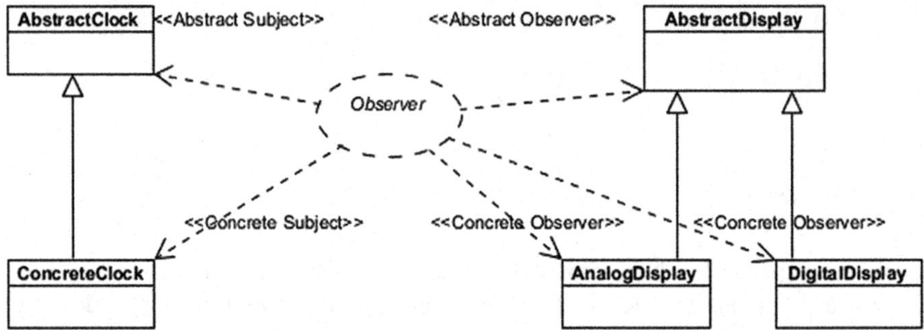

Fig. 1. Application of the GoF patterns observer

Identification was performed by selecting the appropriate classes. Selection was done manually to insert the pattern symbol with the name observer. Adaptation is represented by the connecting arcs. In the above example, there are e.g. two concrete observers. Integration is not represented. The consequences of the pattern application have to be done manually. However, tool support is provided for pattern application in a different way by some case tools.

Additionally to the application of patterns, UML has a notion for generic classes. However, tool support is missing for presenting the resulting models in all case tools we know.

In the following two paragraphs, we will have a look at approaches applying ideas of patterns and genericity for models able to describe activities of humans.

2.1 Reuse for Task Models

In [3] the term task pattern was discussed the first time. However, it was defined as sub-tree only. Within the HAMSTERS environment ([9, 10]) this kind of reuse is called submodel.

The usage of generic task patterns was suggested in [7]. Tool support for task patterns was discussed in [13]. It was shown how generic task patterns were adapted to the context of use and inserted into a larger model. However, in both cases the substitution of parameter values was considered to be performed during design time only. In [5] the runtime substitution of parameter values was discussed the first time for such models. For those patterns, the notation of HAMSTERS was used that allows submodels, procedures, and conditional sub-trees.

To get an impression of the notation, we will specify an example that was given as introduction to BPMN modeling [1]. It originally specifies that it is noticed that somebody recognizes to be hungry. Groceries have to be acquired to be able to prepare the meal. After preparing the meal, it can be eaten. Afterwards, hunger is satisfied. Pre- and post-conditions are not visually represented in Hamsters. Therefore, the task model looks like the graphics presented in Fig. 2.

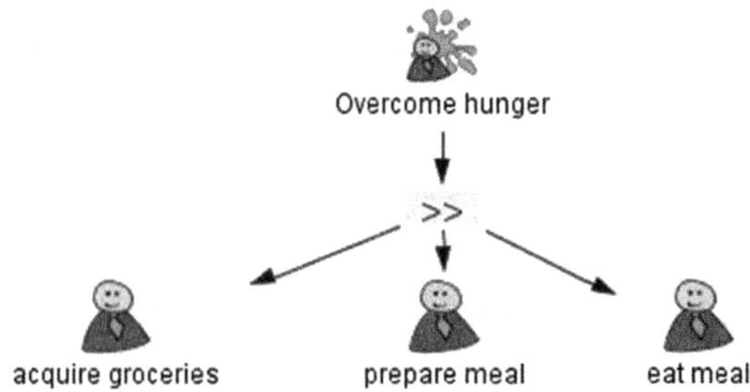

Fig. 2. Task model for overcoming hunger

The presented model can be generalized in such a way that activities of thirsty people can be covered as well. The following generic task model component fulfills the mentioned requirements. It can be instantiated to models for hungry and thirsty people (Fig. 3).

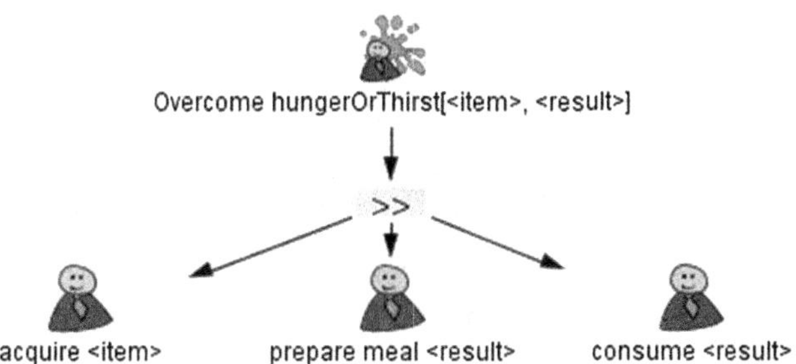

Fig. 3. Generic component to overcome hunger or thirst

Two parameters are used. The first one is called item and can have the values "groceries" for meals and "ingredients" for drinks. The second parameter result can have the values "meal" and "drink". Instantiating the task component with "groceries" and "meal" results nearly in the original model. The only difference is the task eat meal that is generalized to consume meal to abstract eat and drink to consume. A further parameter could have been introduced to deliver exactly the original model.

Additional, to simply propagating values it is possible to make decisions based on these values during design time as well as during runtime. Within runtime, it can be decided, whether values for parameters are used at instantiation time or at decision time.

2.2 Reuse of Workflow Models

Van der Aalst et al. introduced 20 workflow patterns in [15]. Most of these patterns are discussed on a low level of abstraction (see also [16, 17]). They describe solutions for workflow patterns on the level of language features like sequences, alternatives, procedure, metaphors etc.

They are not on the level of describing something like buying or managing something. In [6] we introduced the concept of generic components for BPMN specifications. The hungry people example that was already used for task models [1] was generalized to a generic component. Figure 4 provides this example.

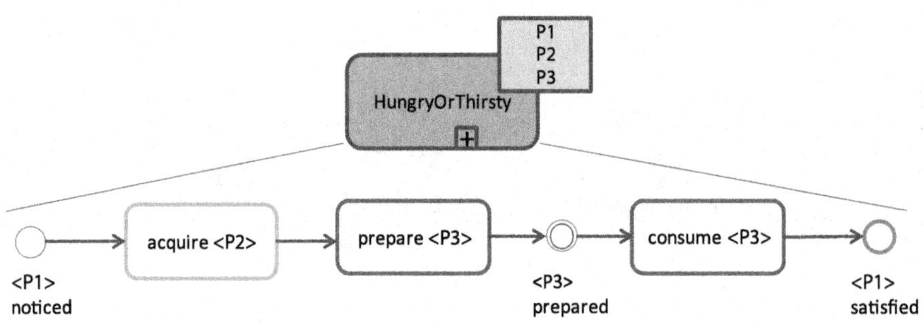

Fig. 4. Generic workflow component for supporting hungry or thirsty people

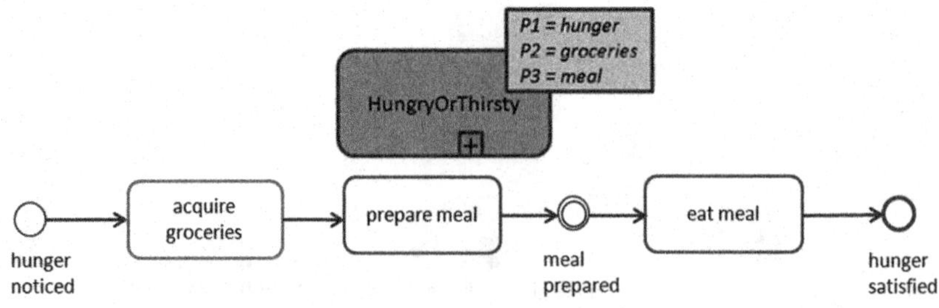

Fig. 5. Instantiation and instance of a generic workflow component

Parameter P1 is expected to have the values “thirsty” or “hungry”. The second parameter P2 specifies the required resources. It can have the values “groceries” or “ingredients”. The third parameter P3 specifies the wanted final result. The values could be “drink“ or “meal”. Figure 5 presents the component with parameter values “hunger”, “groceries”, and “meal” and the corresponding instance of the pattern with substituted parameters.

Hopefully, the selected example allows a good understanding of the idea and a good comparison of task models and workflow specifications. However, it might be too tiny to show the advantages of reuse of existing generic component.

Therefore, an example for ordering a pizza is recalled and generalized. The pizza that is ordered is represented by parameter <sthg> which stays for something. The term “Hungry for Pizza” is generalized to “Keen on <sthg>”. Correspondingly, “Hunger satisfied” is replaced by “Satisfied with <sthg>. Additionally, the roles “pizza customer”, “pizza vendor” and “pizza chief” are replaced by “<sthg> customer”, “<sthg> vendor” and “<sthg> creator” respectively. The resulting generic workflow component is presented in the following Fig. 6.

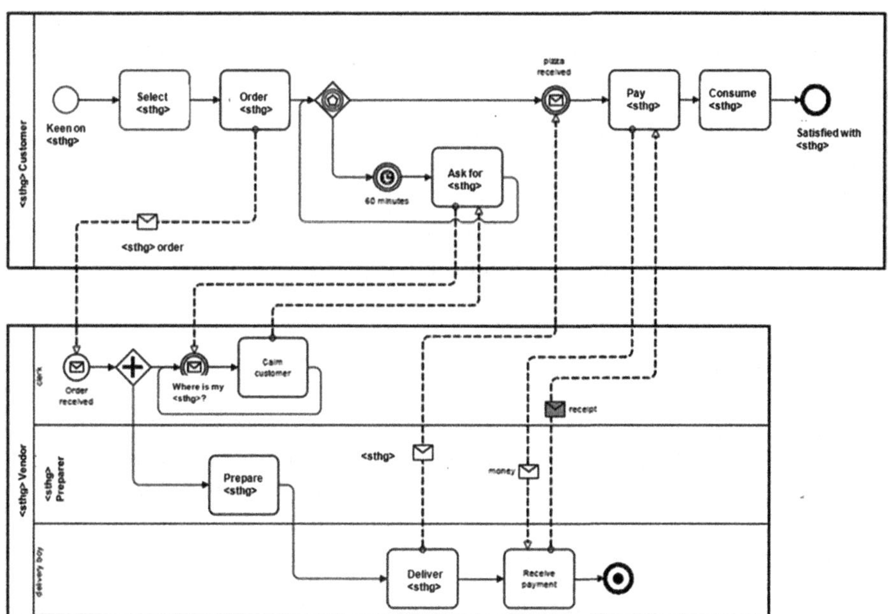

Fig. 6. Generic workflow component based on the pizza ordering example from [2]

The generic workflow component allows not only the specification of ordering pizzas but also of sandwiches in a simple way.

Analysts or business process modelers have simply to instantiate the generic submodel accordingly by providing appropriate parameter values.

2.3 Discussion

Currently, generic components are implemented only for task models for the HAMSTERS case tool [8]. In a case study existing task models describing tasks for a ground segment application was reengineered.

The application is used to monitor and to control the Picard satellite that was launched in 2010 for solar observation. More details about the system are discussed in [5, 9, 10].

The task models became smaller and better readable. The identification of possible component applications allowed even to correct an existing modeling mistake.

Some statistical data are recalled in the following Table 1.

Table 1. Quantitative comparison of the approach (from [5])

Structuring methods	Number of tasks	Number of operators	Reduction percentage
Flat model (without composition mech-anisms)	59	13	Reference model for calculus
Structuring with sub-models, subrou-tines and compo-nents	35	7	41 % less tasks and 46 % less operators than in flat model

Using structuring mechanisms allowed to reduce the size of the specification by nearly 50 %. This makes us hope that workflow specifications can benefit in the same way. Their similarity was already discussed in [4].

The wording for the different technologies is quite difficult to follow. The term pattern e.g. is used quite differently. Within the context of workflow specifications, it is used quite specific. In the context of workflows, a sequence of actions is called a pattern [15]. This is quite different for task models. In the context of tasks, a pattern is considered to be something more abstract like buying something or running a shop. It is also considered to be generic [7].

While reviewing the models of an existing project we identified our generic task patterns as reusable submodels. They allowed us to model the project in a more compact and better readable way [5]. Our first submission used the term generic patterns.

However, reviewers complained that the identified generic submodels are too specific to be patterns. It was suggested to use the term generic component. Indeed our specified submodels are in no way general patterns that have to be taught to analysts. They are in some way similar to subroutines. In addition to subroutines of Hamsters, task names are not the same all the time. With respect to this aspect, the notion of a template describes the behavior in a better way.

However, templates assume to get all values for generic parameters at the same time. Most of the time this parameter substitution is performed during design time. This could be extended to instantiation time or even runtime. Nevertheless, the combination of value propagation during design time, instantiation time, and runtime is not part of the concept of templates.

Therefore, the term generic component was used in the implementation and in several publications.

Unfortunately, some aspects of the technology we are proposing do not fit to the concept of components. In fact, components support information hiding, which is not true for our ideas. There is one important aspect we want to support. Stakeholders should be able to see the instances of the so called generic component like in Fig. 5. Details of the execution should be visible and not hidden.

Therefore, the term generic submodel seems to be more appropriate than generic component.

Figure 7 provides the suggested ontology for reusable parts of models

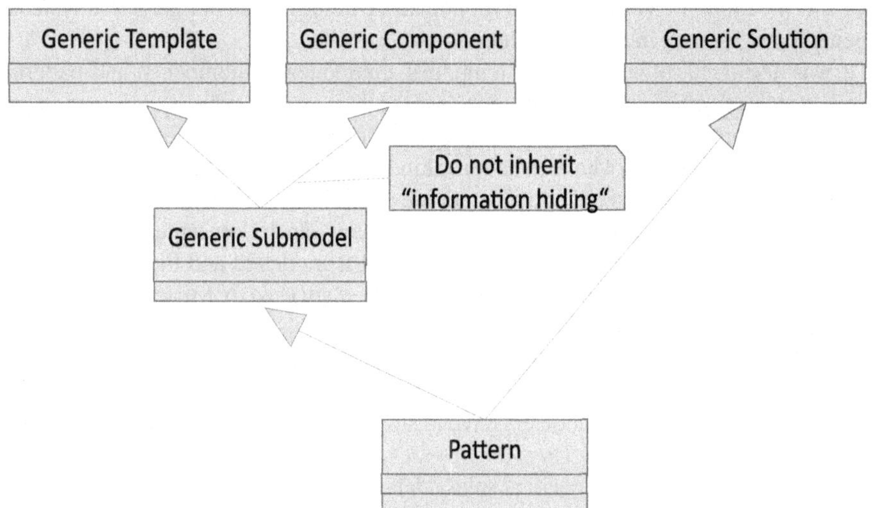

Fig. 7. Suggested ontology

From our point of view, generic submodels inherit all features from templates. Parameters can be used to specify any generic aspect. In this way, names of model elements can be adapted. The same is true for conditions or any expressions.

In addition, generic submodels inherit some features from components. Parameters can be instantiated at several stages of development and execution. However, information hiding is not inherited.

Generic submodels can be patterns. However, not all submodels are patterns. It depends on the level of abstraction and on the importance for general applications. There can be patterns for general solutions and domain-specific patterns that are important for reuse in a specific domain.

Additionally, there might be submodels that are important in a specific project. However, these submodels are not general or abstract enough to be considered as patterns. This is reflected by the inheritance relation from generic submodels to patterns. Specific submodels are patterns but not all of them.

However, patterns do not have to be submodels in the sense of templates and components. They can provide general ideas as well.

This reflected in our suggested ontology by providing inheritance from class generic solution to class pattern.

3 Summary and Outlook

This paper has discussed some strategies of reusing models. It started with the application of design patterns and generic classes for object-oriented class diagrams and continued with task models and workflow specifications describing activities of users. Such specifications are very important for human-centered design of interactive systems in general and for user interfaces in detail.

It was discussed, how terms like templates, components, submodels, and patterns are related to each other. It was suggested to use the term generic submodel in connection with tool support for task models because not all useful model fragments are patterns. Additionally, patterns do not have to be some kind of template, component, or submodel. They can provide more general and abstract ideas as well.

Additionally, it is important to notice, that users can be presented models with appropriate names and terms from the domain, that is modelled and that is familiar to the users. Names and terms are presented in a way they are used to. Models can be easily reused in a way that allows user friendly specifications.

Based on the experience with task models in Hamsters, an implementation of generic submodels is under development for a BPMN editor of an open source projects. Experiments with business process modelers have to show how predefined generic submodels are used.

Later, libraries of already specified submodels have to be created that support a good overview of the generic submodels. Additionally, they have to provide efficient search strategies.

References

1. BPMN: http://www.bpmn.org. Accessed 03 Feb 2016
2. BPMN 2.0 Tutorial: https://camunda.org/bpmn/tutorial/#simple_flow_BPMN. Accessed 03 Feb 2016
3. Breedvelt-Schouten, M., Paternò, F., Severijns, C.: Reusable structures in task models. In: Harrison, M.D., Torres, J.C. (eds.) Proceedings of DSV-IS 1997, pp. 225–239. Springer, Heidelberg (1997)
4. Brüning, J., Dittmar, A., Forbrig, P., Reichart, D.: Getting SW engineers on board: task modelling with activity diagrams. In: Gulliksen, J., Harning, M.B., Palanque, P., van der Veer, G.C., Wesson, J. (eds.) EIS 2007. LNCS, vol. 4940, pp. 175–192. Springer, Heidelberg (2008)
5. Forbrig, P., Martinie, C., Palanque, P., Winckler, M., Fahssi, R.: Rapid task-models development using sub-models, sub-routines and generic components. In: Sauer, S., Bogdan, C., Forbrig, P., Bernhaupt, R., Winckler, M. (eds.) HCSE 2014. LNCS, vol. 8742, pp. 144–163. Springer, Heidelberg (2014)

6. Forbrig, P.: Generic components for BPMN specifications. In: Johansson, B., Andersson, B., Holmberg, N. (eds.) BIR 2014. LNBIP, vol. 194, pp. 202–216. Springer, Heidelberg (2014)
7. Gaffar, A., Sinnig, D., Seffah, A., Forbrig, P.: Modeling patterns for task models. In: Proceedings of the 3rd Annual Conference on Task Models and Diagrams (TAMODIA 2004), pp. 99–104. ACM, New York (2004)
8. HAMSTERS: http://www.irit.fr/ICS/hamsters/
9. Martinie, C., Palanque, P., Winckler, M.: Structuring and composition mechanisms to address scalability issues in task models. In: Campos, P., Graham, N., Jorge, J., Nunes, N., Palanque, P., Winckler, M. (eds.) INTERACT 2011, Part III. LNCS, vol. 6948, pp. 589–609. Springer, Heidelberg (2011)
10. Martinie, C., Palanque, P., Ragosta, M., Fahssi, R.: Extending procedural task models by explicit and systematic integration of objects, knowledge and information. In: Proceedings of ECCE 2013, article no. 23, pp. 1–10 (2013)
11. Gamma, E., et al.: Design Patterns. Elements of Reusable Object-Oriented Software. Addison-Wesley, Boston (1995)
12. Kruschitz, C., Hitz, M.: Human-computer interaction design patterns: structure, methods, and tools. Int. J. Adv. Softw. **3**(1 & 2) (2010)
13. Radeke, F., Forbrig, P.: Patterns in task-based modeling of user interfaces. In: Winckler, M., Johnson, H. (eds.) TAMODIA 2007. LNCS, vol. 4849, pp. 184–197. Springer, Heidelberg (2007)
14. Sinnig, D., Gaffar, A., Reichart, D., Seffah, A., Forbrig, P.: Patterns in model-based engineering. In: Jacob, R.J.K., Limbourg, Q., Vanderdonckt, J. (eds.) Proceedings of CADUI 2004, pp. 197–210. Springer, Heidelberg (2004)
15. Van der Aalst, W.M.P., ter Hofstede, A.H.M., Kiepuszewski, B., Barros, A.P.: Workflow patterns. Distrib. Parallel Databases **14**(3), 5–51 (2003)
16. White, S.A.: Process modeling notations and workflow patterns. BPTrends (2004). http://www.omg.org/bp-corner/bp-files/Process_Modeling_Notations.pdf. Accessed 22 Nov 2015
17. Wohed, P., van der Aalst, W.M., Dumas, M., ter Hofstede, A.H., Russell, N.: On the suitability of BPMN for business process modelling. In: Dustdar, S., Fiadeiro, J.L., Sheth, A.P. (eds.) BPM 2006. LNCS, vol. 4102, pp. 161–176. Springer, Heidelberg (2006)

A Library System to Support Model-Based User Interface Development in Industrial Automation

Matthias Freund(✉), Christopher Martin, and Annerose Braune

Institute of Automation, Technische Universität Dresden, Dresden, Germany
{matthias.freund,christopher.martin,annerose.braune}@tu-dresden.de

Abstract. Conventional visualization systems in industrial automation are equipped with powerful library systems that offer aggregated reusable visualization elements. These represent important domain-specific knowledge and promote the necessary consistent look-and-feel of visualizations. In contrast, modeling languages used in model-based workflows do not offer library systems. This hinders the acceptance of such approaches in industrial automation.

Hence, this paper presents an approach towards a library system for the model-based development of visualizations. We present a generic approach that can be applied to a variety of modeling languages. A case study demonstrates this for one specific modeling language and illustrates the application of the library system.

Keywords: Human-machine interfaces · Library system · Model-based user interface design · Model transformation

1 Introduction

In industrial automation, human-machine interfaces (HMIs) are used to supervise and control technical processes and machines. Developing these HMIs is in general performed manually by an HMI engineer with industrial visualization systems like *Simatic WinCC*[1] or *Wonderware InTouch*[2]. Such visualization systems offer powerful tools and editors, one key asset being their very extensive library systems that offer different domain- and/or company-specific libraries. As illustrated in Fig. 1, such libraries are created by domain experts and contain reusable parameterized elements (called *widgets*, *symbols*, or *faceplates*). These library entries contribute to the supply of built-in elements that can be used by an HMI engineer for the creation of an HMI. Thus, they represent important domain-specific knowledge and promote a consistent look-and-feel of visualizations that is especially important in industrial automation. In order to browse the entries that are available inside a library as well as to retrieve and insert a selected entry into a target HMI, library systems also offer a set of management algorithms (cf. Fig. 1).

[1] http://w3.siemens.com/mcms/human-machine-interface/en/visualization-software/scada/simatic-wincc/.

[2] http://global.wonderware.com/DE/Pages/WonderwareInTouchHMI.aspx.

M. Kurosu (Ed.): HCI 2016, Part I, LNCS 9731, pp. 476–487, 2016.
DOI: 10.1007/978-3-319-39510-4_44

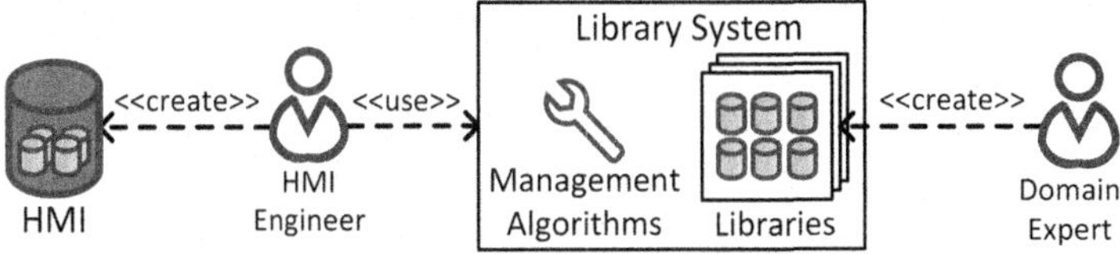

Fig. 1. The role of library systems during the development of HMIs

However, the available industrial visualization systems are committed to a single target technology resp. to a fixed set of target platforms. *Model-based User Interface Development* (MBUID) approaches like *UsiXML* [1] or *MARIA* [2] try to solve this problem by allowing an HMI engineer to specify the functionality of an HMI via declarative models [3] that abstract from implementation details and can ideally be used to generate executable HMIs for different hard- or software platforms. Whereas MBUID has been a hot topic in the research community for many years, acceptance by the industry is according to [3] still a major issue. While most approaches offer more or less powerful graphical editors and limited tool support, one of the main problems compared to industrial visualization systems is usually the missing availability of library systems.

Hence, this paper presents an approach for a model-based library system that supports HMI engineers in the creation of HMI models. As there is a variety of modeling languages currently used in MBUID, a generic solution that can easily be adopted for a specific modeling language or workflow is proposed. Therefore, general requirements are discussed in Sect. 2. Our generic approach towards a model-based library system is presented in Sect. 3 and a specific adaptation for the modeling language *Movisa* is demonstrated in Sect. 4. Section 5 discusses related work in the field of library systems for model-based approaches. Finally, conclusions and future work are presented in Sect. 6.

2 Requirements for Model-Based Library Systems

As library entries usually aggregate multiple HMI elements, their complexity can range from simple (e.g., symbolic representations of switches, valves, or lamps according to [4]) to complex (e.g., faceplates for the visualization of complete silos including multiple sensors). Consequently, a library system has to enable the persisting of such aggregated HMI objects as library entries. In contrast to a *normal* aggregated HMI object, the structure of the child objects inside a *library entry* is treated as immutable: If changes to the structure are to be made, a new library entry has to be created. The same applies to most attribute values, e.g., for the position of a contained object relative to the enclosing entry. Instead, a library entry offers only a dedicated interface that is made up of a set of *parameters*. The types of elements to be stored as library entries as well as the types of parameters that are necessary/useful depend on the concrete structure, capabilities, and semantics of the used HMI meta-model and have to be predefined by the library system to support the definition of new library entries. For example, the library system may state that every entry must define exactly one parameter that allows the customization of the entry's size upon instantiation in an HMI model. Furthermore, every library entry usually can be equipped with additional metadata like a name or an ID, a version, a description, or a thumbnail in order to be identifiable by the user.

Currently, different modeling languages are used for MBUID depending, e.g., on the application domain, on prior knowledge, or on suitable tools [3]. Most of these languages base upon similar concepts and use similar modeling technologies, though. Thus, it is reasonable to define a generic data structure for the persisting of library entries that can easily be adapted to a specific modeling language or workflow.

A library system is also responsible for organizing the otherwise loose collection of various library entries into different (e.g. domain-specific) libraries and enable their integration with HMI tools and editors. Hence, library systems require management functions that allow to browse, add, remove, and instantiate library entries. In summary, a model-based library system has to comply with the following requirements:

1. A data structure has to be provided that allows to define and persist the different parts of a library entry:
   (a) the immutable structure of aggregated HMI objects and attribute values,
   (b) a dedicated parameter interface indicating modifiable elements,
   (c) metadata for the identification by a user or a model transformation
2. Library management algorithms have to enable a user or a model transformation to browse, add, remove, and instantiate library entries

3 Generic Model-Based Library System

This section introduces the concepts necessary for the realization of a generic model-based library system – the *GenLibrary*. Herein, the term generic describes the fact that the concepts presented are not tied to a single implementation for a specific modeling language. Instead, they are designed to be used and easily extended for any HMI modeling language and workflow. In this paper, we focus on the realization of a generic extensible data structure (cf. Sect. 2) – the realization of the management algorithms is not discussed in detail but briefly covered as part of the case study presented in Sect. 4.

HMI library entries consist of reusable parameterized visualization snippets comprising parts of an HMI description. In MBUID, the HMI description exists as an HMI *model*. Consequently, the library entries should be realized as parameterized *model snippets*, i.e. excerpts of an HMI model representing an aggregation of HMI elements. That way, the same tools and frameworks that are also employed for the realization of editors and model transformations for the selected modeling language can be used. We have created the meta-model that defines the data structure for these model snippets by means of the *Eclipse Modeling Framework*[3] (EMF) as it offers powerful tools, editors, and a simple possibility

[3] http://eclipse.org/modeling/emf/.

to store and load models via the XMI[4] standard. EMF-based meta-models may consist of a set of classes (*EClass*) that hold a set of attributes (*EAttribute*) and a set of references (*EReference*) to other classes. References can be either *containment* (meaning that the referenced object is included in the referencing object) or *non-containment* (representing a cross-reference).

3.1 Simple Model Snippets

As every element of an EMF model (except the root element itself) must be a direct or indirect child of the root element via containment references, every model can be displayed as a containment tree with cross references. As described above, a library entry comprises a model snippet (a part of such a containment tree) as illustrated by Fig. 2: It shows a sample model (for a hypothetical HMI meta-model *ABC*) with a root element of type *AContainer*. The snippet in the dashed box shall be stored as library entry. It consists of an element of type *A* and two elements of classes *B* and *C* that are contained in *A* and coupled via a cross-reference. This could, e.g., represent a *text label* (*A*) that contains a *representation* (*B*) as well as an *animation* (*C*) that is referenced by the representation. The additional file *f* could represent an image file used by the representation.

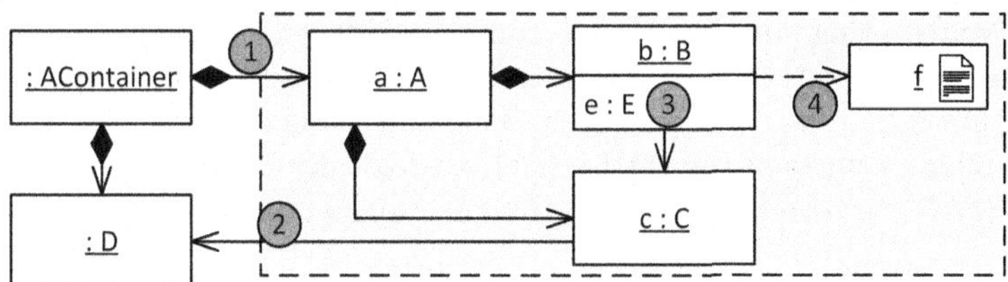

Fig. 2. Hypothetical sample library entry instance (dashed box) as part of a model containment tree

Because of the XMI standard, it is easily possible to create a copy of the element (and its child elements) and persist this model snippet as a library entry. The *GenLibrary* meta-model must however additionally enable the specification of metadata like an ID or a version (cf. Sect. 2). Therefore, it introduces the element *LibraryEntry* that represents one entry inside a library (cf. Fig. 3). In order to persist the actual model elements of a library entry (e.g. the structure presented in Fig. 2), an abstract base class *LibraryItem* has been defined that has to be extended by concrete implementations for a specific HMI meta-model. For the purpose of illustration, a simple example for such an implementation is represented by the hypothetical element *ABCLibraryItem* that allows to store instances of type *A* by directly referencing the respective element (EClass) from

4 *XML Metadata Interchange*, http://www.omg.org/spec/XMI/.

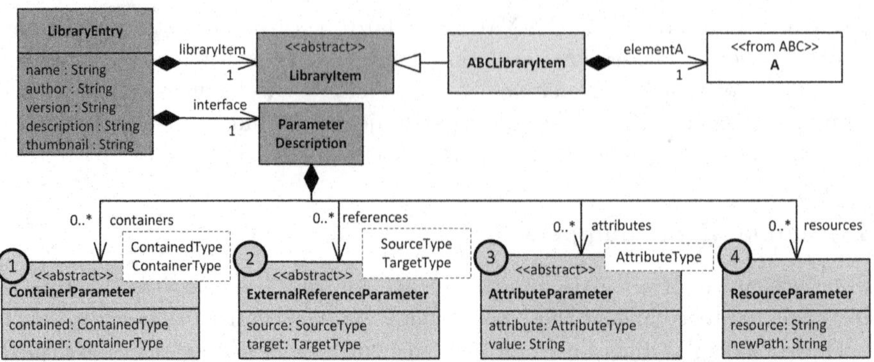

Fig. 3. *GenLibrary* meta-model and hypothetical concrete extension (upper right)

the corresponding HMI meta-model (in the example the EClass *A* from the meta-model *ABC*). Note that all contained elements (e.g. the elements *b* and *c* in case of the structure presented in Fig. 2) are stored as well automatically even if their types are not directly referenced by the *GenLibrary* meta-model.

This mechanism allows specific implementations to declare the type of elements that may be stored as library entries by referencing a specific HMI modeling language with its meta-model. In the case of MBUID, this will usually be elements representing simple widgets, complex widgets, or complete panels (as well as their children). If necessary, even multiple elements that are not contained within each other can be stored. This may be necessary if elements that reside at different parts of the HMI model but logically belong together shall be stored in the library item (e.g. a widget plus information about access rights).

3.2 Parameterized Model Snippets

As described in Sect. 2, a library entry has to provide an explicit specification of the parameters that may resp. have to be specified by the user or by a model transformation. The meta-model elements required for this specification can be abstracted from the tasks that have to be performed during the instantiation of a library entry (i.e. the insertion into a target model). These tasks can also be obtained from Fig. 2 if we consider the dashed box not as entry to be created but as existing entry that has been instantiated in a model.

The first and most obvious task is the insertion into the target model at a specific position in its containment tree. This is equivalent to the creation of a containment reference from an existing element in the target model (the new container object) to a top-level element of the library entry (cf. symbol ① in Fig. 2). If multiple top-level elements exist as described above, a parent element has to be determined for each of these elements. The second task consists in the creation of non-containment references from the inserted library entry to

Table 1. Types of tasks executed during the instantiation of a library item and information necessary for the execution

Type of task	Necessary information/elements to be specified
① Creation of containment references	• Contained element (a top-level element inside the library entry)
	• Container element (part of the target model)
② Creation of external references	• Source element (part of the library entry)
	• Target element (part of the target model)
③ Changing of attribute values	• Attribute to be changed (part of the library entry)
	• New attribute value
④ Copying of resources	• Name of the resource (as stored in the library)
	• New path of the resource

existing elements of the target model (cf. symbol ②)[5]. Third, it can be desirable or necessary to change attribute values of internal elements of the library entry during the insertion process (cf. symbol ③). The last task is responsible for the copying of resources or files that are required by the library entry to a new location (usually inside the project that the target model belongs to) as indicated by the symbol ④ in Fig. 2.

As summed up in Table 1, each of these tasks requires specific information for its execution. Thus, an own parameter type representing each task is required. We have realized this by means of the *ParameterDescription* element (cf. Fig. 3) that is composed of the four abstract parameter types deduced above. The necessary information for each parameter type as of Table 1 is represented by corresponding attributes and references. The references are realized by means of *generic types* (indicated by the dashed boxes on the top-right corner of the parameters) which enabled a generic implementation of the execution of the four tasks as part of the management algorithms. Concrete implementations of these parameters are again dependent on the actual HMI meta-model. They have to be specified by extending one of the abstract parameter types and with that by binding the generic types to concrete types.

4 Case Study: Library System for Movisa

To illustrate a concrete adaptation of the introduced generic library concepts, an implementation for the HMI modeling language *Movisa* [5] is shown in this section. Movisa is a domain-specific language created for the description of HMIs in industrial automation. A simplified subset of its meta-model is shown in the

[5] Non-containment references from the target model to elements of the inserted library item are also possible but not part of the insertion process of the library item.

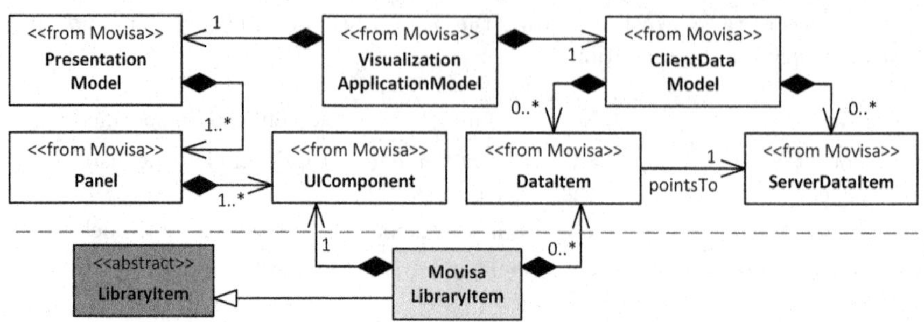

Fig. 4. Top: Simplified subset of the *Movisa* meta-model (cf. [5]); Bottom: Specification of the *MovisaLibraryItem*

top of Fig. 4. The top-level element (*VisualizationApplicationModel*) contains two sub-models: The *PresentationModel* divides the visual aspects of an HMI into *Panels* which consist of multiple HMI elements (*UIComponents*), e.g. containers, buttons, and text labels. The *ClientDataModel* aggregates variables in a collection of *DataItems* (logical viewpoint) that can be used to, e.g., animate the UI components. Therefore, every variable can be updated via a process data server. This is realized by means of the *ServerDataItems* (technical viewpoint).

Information from both sub-models is necessary for a widget to be functional. Therefore, a library implementation for Movisa has to be able to persist library entries containing (1) a UIComponent (that may contain aggregated components) and (2) associated DataItems. Therefore, we have created an extension of the *GenLibrary* meta-model. This Movisa-specific extension introduces a concrete implementation of the abstract *LibraryItem* – the *MovisaLibraryItem* (cf. Fig. 4, bottom). In order to enable the persisting of the two parts described above, the MovisaLibraryItem provides corresponding references to the Movisa meta-model. As the concrete process data server should not be specified in a library entry (because the entry should be independent of a specific communication technology) only the *DataItems* are saved without the associated *ServerDataItems*. Consequently, a parameter has to be created that allows to specify the server information upon instantiation of a library entry. As this is performed via the creation of a *non-containment reference* to a concrete *ServerDataItem* (reference *pointsTo* in Fig. 4), an *ExternalReferenceParameter* (cf. Fig. 3) has to be used. This is implemented by the *ServerDataItemParameter* shown in Fig. 5 which needs to be defined for each DataItem of a library entry. The parameter type therefore binds the *SourceType* to elements of the type *DataItem*. Similarly, the *TargetType* is bound to elements of the type *ServerDataItem* so that only elements of this type can be specified as target of the *pointsTo* reference to be created upon instantiation of the library entry.

Another parameter required for the insertion of a library entry into an existing HMI model is the *UIComponentContainerParameter* (cf. Fig. 5) that allows the container specification for the library entry, i.e. the selection of the panel that the UIComponent inside the entry should be displayed in. In contrast to

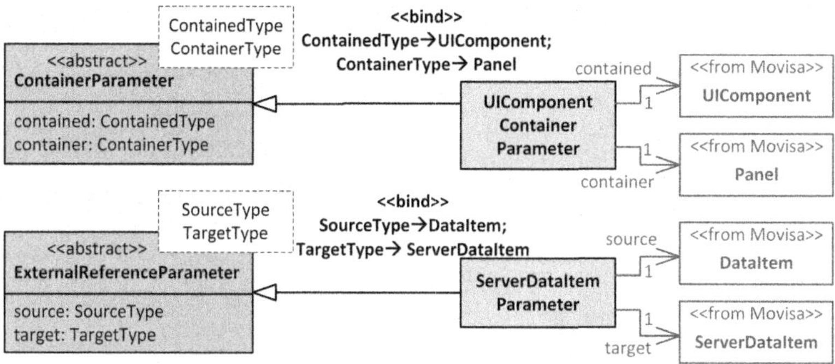

Fig. 5. Subset of the specification of the Movisa-specific parameters (The grayed out references are only shown to emphasize the result of the type binding.)

the UIComponents that can be displayed in one of the multiple panels defined in a Movisa model, the *DataItems* are always located at the same spot in its containment tree (directly below the single instance of *ClientDataModel*). Thus, we have implemented the insertion of the DataItems as part of the specific extension of the library system's management algorithms in order to reduce the number of container parameters necessary for each library entry.

Besides the extension of the meta-model and the management algorithms, we have also integrated the set of generic wizards that is offered by our library system into the existing Movisa editors. These support the user in the manual application of the library system. Figure 6 illustrates the import wizard that supports the user in the insertion of a library entry into an existing Movisa model[6]. Once all parameters have been specified, the instantiation of the selected library entry can be executed. The parameters specified in the wizard are used to insert the library item into the target model, create the non-containment references, and resize and position the UIComponent on the selected Panel. Figure 7 shows the result of this process: The elements inserted during a single instantiation are shown in a tree view of the Movisa model. It can be seen that the UIComponent (represented by a *SimpleContainer*) has been inserted into the panel *NAVTOP* and the DataItems have also been added to the ClientDataModel.

An example for the application of the library system in a more complex MBUID workflow is presented in [6]. It demonstrates the automatic generation of HMI models from a more abstract model via a model-to-model transformation. In such a case, a missing library system requires the specification of the entire target model only with the help of simple built-in elements. All knowledge about aggregated elements has to be implicitly represented in the transformation rules that get unnecessarily complex. The library system enabled a significant simplification of the transformation rules and ensures a consistent look and feel by

[6] Another similar wizard allows to export existing HMI elements as a new library entry but is not shown due to reasons of compactness.

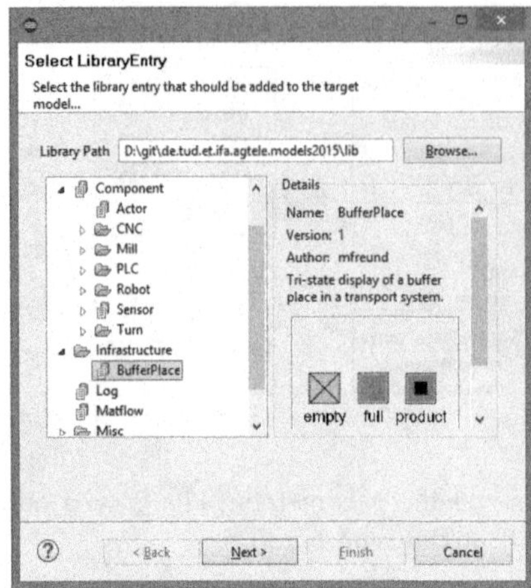

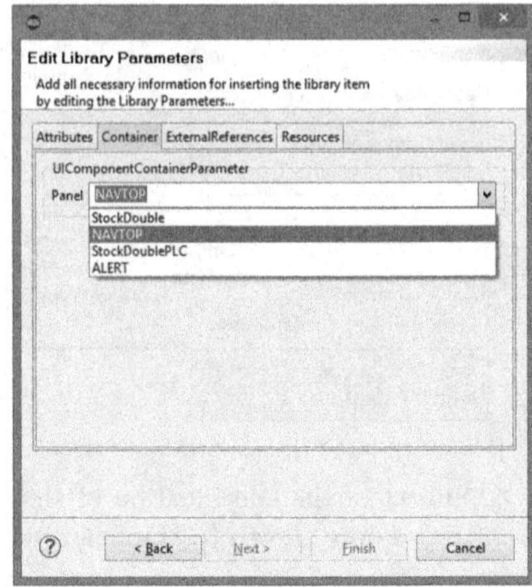

Fig. 6. Specification of the *MovisaParameterDescription*

- Visualization Application Model
  - Client Data Model Client Data Model
    - Logical Data Perspective
      - Data Item DataItem_MATFLOW_ControlElements_Stopper_001_1_Status_LP
      - Data Item DataItem_MATFLOW_ControlElements_Stopper_001_1_CarrierID_CarrierIDATInt_LP
    - Technical Data Perspective
  - Presentation Model Presentation Model
    - Panel NAVTOP
      - Simple Container MATFLOW_ControlElements_Stopper_001_1_0_SimpleContainer

Fig. 7. Result of the insertion of a library entry into a Movisa model displayed in the model containment tree

using the already available domain-specific library entries and the corresponding management algorithms for their insertion.

5 Related Work

As discussed in Sect. 2, a library system has to implement two main functionalities: (1) the provision of a data structure to persist parameterized library entries and (2) library management algorithms. Most modeling languages currently used for MBUID like *UsiXML* [1] or *MARIA* [2] neither offer any possibilities to store parameterized model snippets separate from their enclosing model nor do they provide any library management algorithms. The modeling language *UIML* introduces "a template mechanism that allows defining reusable components" [7] that can be parametrized. However, this constitutes a special implementation for a single HMI meta-model and not a generic solution as targeted by our approach. As UIML does not allow the modeling of process communication because it does not introduce a data model [8], this UIML-specific library concept is not suited very well for industrial automation. Furthermore, the definition of metadata and storage concepts are not discussed.

While generative UI patterns also enable the instantiation of reusable HMI parts, the concrete realization of a pattern differs depending on its problem context and thus for each concrete instance (cf. [9]). Hence, the structure of the HMI parts described by a pattern has to be flexible – e.g. concerning concrete contents of (sub-)elements – in contrast to the immutable structure of a library item. Consequently, generative UI patterns cannot be used for the description of library entries. However, both approaches could be combined, e.g. by using library entries to realize the concrete contents of a pattern upon instantiation.

Apart from the domain of MBUID, there are some approaches to use XML dialects for the realization of data structures that represent library entries including metadata and parameters. The most promising approach is *AutomationML* [10] that is used as an exchange format in industrial automation. Based on the data format *CAEX* [11], it offers a library concept that allows to define some metadata (e.g. an ID, a version, and an author) and an inheritance concept for library entries. However, *AutomationML* covers a very broad domain (including the description of 3D data and PLC logic) but does not incorporate an HMI meta-model. Thus, a distinct implementation for the domain of HMI libraries based on the introduced concepts seems beneficial.

In the context of software engineering, *(model) templates* allow to define parameterizable elements or models (cf., e.g., [12–14]) that could be used for the definition of library entries. However, most of those approaches consider templates only at the meta-model level resp. the level of UML class diagrams [14]. While the application at the *model* level is proposed in [14], specific extensions that are dependent on the used HMI meta-model are not discussed. Thus, the concept cannot be used to enforce the description of an immutable structure or a dedicated parameter interface specific for the used meta-model. Similar to templates applied at the model-level, *declarative transformation languages* like, e.g., *QVT* or approaches based on *graph transformations* (cf. [15] for an overview of both technologies) allow to define mappings that consist of a left-hand side, a right-hand side, and a relation between both sides. Such a mapping could be treated as a library entry where the right-hand side defines the element structure to be created and the mapping including the left-hand side implicitly defines a parameter interface (those elements that need to be present in the source model and that are applied to the right-hand side). However, just like the model templates described above, these approaches do not allow to restrict the structure inside a library entry and its parameter interface as they are dedicated to another application context.

6 Conclusions and Future Work

In this paper, we have presented an approach for a model-based library system for HMI development that allows the definition, management, and instantiation of aggregated, reusable HMI objects. Our proposed generic solution enables an extension for a variety of modeling languages. In order to use the library system with a new modeling language, the following steps have to be performed:

1. Analysis of the used HMI meta-model concerning types of elements to be stored in a library entry and parameters to be influenced by the user
2. Extension of the *GenLibrary* meta-model by realizing a concrete subclass of *LibraryItem* and by defining concrete parameter types
3. Extension of the generic management algorithms and wizards to add HMI language-specific behavior resp. integrate them in existing editors and tools

While the generic approach provides a good starting point for extensions, the steps described above still demand considerable work. We have illustrated this by means of an adaptation for the modeling language *Movisa* that has been evaluated in the *AutoProBe* project (cf. [6]). As the library system can be applied for manual application as well as to model-based workflows, it should promote the acceptance of model-based approaches in industrial automation. In the future, we plan to evaluate our approach by creating extensions for additional modeling languages like UsiXML or MARIA.

An important challenge is the support for both the evolution and the aggregation resp. inheritance of existing library entries. While the presented wizards can help with this challenge (import library entries to a model, change or combine them, and create a new entry via an export), our solution does not allow to directly reference other library entries.

As an instantiated library entry is represented by standard elements of the used HMI meta-model, our approach enables existing model transformations to be applied (e.g., to produce an executable HMI). However, the downside of this is that it becomes hard to distinguish between *normal* and *library-based* elements. This makes it complicated to, e.g., completely remove an inserted library entry. In the future, this could be solved by a tracing mechanism.

Acknowledgments. The authors would like to thank *Christian Petzka* for his contributions.

The IGF proposal 16606 BG of the research association "Gesellschaft zur Förderung angewandter Informatik e.V." (GFaI) is funded via the AiF within the scope of the "Program for the promotion of industrial cooperational research" (IGF) by the German Federal Ministry of Economics and Technology (BMWi) according to a resolution of the German Bundestag.

We gratefully acknowledge funding by the "Deutsche Forschungsgemeinschaft" (DFG).

References

1. Limbourg, Q., Vanderdonckt, J., Michotte, B., Bouillon, L., López-Jaquero, V.: USIXML: a language supporting multi-path development of user interfaces. In: Feige, U., Roth, J. (eds.) DSV-IS 2004 and EHCI 2004. LNCS, vol. 3425, pp. 200–220. Springer, Heidelberg (2005)

2. Paternò, F., Santoro, C., Spano, L.D.: MARIA: a universal, declarative, multiple abstraction-level language for service-oriented applications in ubiquitous environments. ACM Trans. Comput. Hum. Interact. **16**(4), 1–30 (2009)
3. Meixner, G., Paternò, F., Vanderdonckt, J.: Past, present, and future of model-based user interface development. i-com **10**(3), 2–11 (2011)
4. ISO 7000: Graphical symbols for use on equipment (2014)
5. Hennig, S.: Design of Sustainable Solutions for Process Visualization in Industrial Automation with Model-Driven Software Development, 1st edn. Jörg Vogt Verlag, Dresden (2012)
6. Martin, C., Freund, M., Braune, A., Ebert, R.E., Pleow, M., Severin, S., Stern, O.: Integrated design of human-machine interfaces for production plants. In: Proceedings of 20th IEEE International Conference on Emerging Technologies and Factory Automation (ETFA 2015). IEEE (2015)
7. Helms, J., Schaefer, R., Luyten, K., Vermeulen, J., Abrams, M., Coyette, A., Vanderdonckt, J.: Human-centered engineering of interactive systems with the user interface markup language. In: Seffah, A., Vanderdonckt, J., Desmarais, M.C. (eds.) Human-Centered Software Engineering. Human-Computer Interaction Series, pp. 139–171. Springer, London (2009)
8. Trewin, S., Zimmermann, G., Vanderheiden, G.: Abstract user interface representations: how well do they support universal access? In: Proceedings of the 2003 Conference on Universal Usability, CUU 2003, NY, USA, pp. 77–84. ACM, New York (2003)
9. Seissler, M., Breiner, K., Meixner, G.: Towards pattern-driven engineering of run-time adaptive user interfaces for smart production environments. In: Jacko, J.A. (ed.) Human-Computer Interaction, Part I, HCII 2011. LNCS, vol. 6761, pp. 299–308. Springer, Heidelberg (2011)
10. Draht, R. (ed.): Datenaustausch in der Anlagenplanung mit AutomationML. Springer, Heidelberg (2010)
11. IEC 62424: Representation of process control engineering - Requests in P&I diagrams and data exchange between P&ID tools and PCE-CAE tools (2008)
12. Kulkarni, V., Reddy, S.: Separation of concerns in model-driven development. IEEE Softw. **20**(5), 64–69 (2003)
13. Muller, A., Caron, O., Carré, B., Vanwormhoudt, G.: On some properties of parameterized model application. In: Hartman, A., Kreische, D. (eds.) ECMDA-FA 2005. LNCS, vol. 3748, pp. 130–144. Springer, Heidelberg (2005)
14. de Lara, J., Guerra, E.: Generic meta-modelling with concepts, templates and mixin layers. In: Petriu, D.C., Rouquette, N., Haugen, Ø. (eds.) MODELS 2010, Part I. LNCS, vol. 6394, pp. 16–30. Springer, Heidelberg (2010)
15. Taentzer, G., Ehrig, K., Guerra, E., De Lara, J., Lengyel, L., Levendovszky, T., Prange, U., Varro, D., Varro-Gyapay, S.: Model transformation by graph transformation: a comparative study. In: Workshop Model Transformation in Practice at MODELS 2005 (2005)

Task Models in Practice: Are There Special Requirements for the Use in Daily Work?

Marius Koller(✉) and Gerrit Meixner

UniTyLab, Heilbronn University, Heilbronn, Germany
{marius.koller,gerrit.meixner}@hs-heilbronn.de

Abstract. Task models are a well-known and common concept in Human-Computer-Interaction. However, there is no big break-through in the usage in daily work in industry. There are use-cases that use task models and we are interested in their settings. We conducted a pilot-study that evaluated the special needs for task models in daily industrial use. Therefor we interviewed five subjects that are affiliated in two companies. One central matter is the lack of iterative support for the development of task models. We introduce four levels of detail that support the iterative development of task models. The subjects also need defined conditions to use the model in their future work process. We implemented these aspects in the notation of the Useware Markup Language.

Keywords: Task models · Useware markup language · UseML · Industrial practice · Requirements engineering

1 Introduction

Task models have a long history in the research of Human-Computer-Interaction (HCI) and several research groups are using and still developing them. There are notations that have an extended history of development and that are still in use. ConcurTaskTrees (CTT) [10] is one prominent example. However, there is no significant breakthrough in the daily use in industry. Some industrial use cases make the usage of task models necessary and task models are already used in some. The use-cases analyzed could not differ more; one use case aims to ease the communication between different disciplines while the other grounds the product-development on the task models. Our goal was to evaluate if there are special requirements for the use in daily practice that are not implemented by the existing scientific notations. We believe that the scientific use differs from the use in daily practice. Hence, these specific features and requirements may not be implemented.

This paper presents the results of a first pilot-study that evaluates the use of task models in practice. The study takes part in two different industrial settings with five participants that have different backgrounds and professions.

Section 2 gives a brief overview about task models and different notation. In Sect. 3 we describe our methods and the participants that participated. The results of the study are summarized in Sect. 4. Section 5 contains some aspects of the realization in

M. Kurosu (Ed.): HCI 2016, Part I, LNCS 9731, pp. 488–497, 2016.
DOI: 10.1007/978-3-319-39510-4_45

useML. At the end, in Sect. 6 we present our conclusion and Sect. 7 gives an outlook on future work.

2 State of the Art

Task Models are a well-known concept in research; different notation or so-called languages were developed by many research groups. Task models have a long history that goes back to Hierarchical Task Analysis (HTA) that was defined in 1967 by Annett and Duncan [1]. HTA's goal is to analyze the tasks of a worker and structure it hierarchically. Based on HTA [13], Goals, Operators, Methods and Selection Rules (GOMS) [5] was developed to estimate the effort that is necessary to earn the knowledge to perform a task sufficient. For this estimation, a detailed record of the tasks is needed and GOMS offers the possibility. It is not possible to include any temporal information in a GOMS-model. Groupware Task Analysis (GTA) is a method that supports the task-based development of groupware [14]. Groupware supports the work of groups or more users. It is possible with GTA to record and model the tasks in a hierarchical model. GTA has a graphical tool called EUTERPE for the creation of task models [15]. The Méthode Analytique de Description (MAD) is a semi-formal method to record user tasks based on interviews [12]. K-MADe is a tool to structure the tasks and create the model [3]. It has integrated temporal information that can structure the task model. Furthermore, it distinguishes between user- and system tasks. It is not possible to specify interactive tasks that are performed by a human and a system. The ConcurTaskTrees (CTT) is an engineered approach [10]. It supports the creation of hierarchical task models that can be structured with weighted temporal relations. CTT distinguishes between abstract-, interactive-, system- and user-tasks. CTTE is a graphical tool that supports the development with a graphical notation [9, 11]. CTTE enables the user to create a model graphically and analyze it with a simulation. CTTE has received an update that brings now a web-based solution, the tool is now called "Responsive CTT" [2]. Figure 1 shows a comparison between the two versions of the graphical notation that is implemented by the two tools. On the left the left is the syntax of CTTE depicted, the right model shows the icons of Responsive CTT. CTT has further usages, for example HAMSTERS is uses the concept and the notation of the integrated temporal relations [4]. HAMSTERS is an approach that identifies possible human errors and represents them [6].

The Useware Markup Language (useML) is a notation to model the user's tasks within the human-centered development process [7]. UseML defines a "*Usemodel*" that is further structured in "*Useobjects*", in CTT this would be represented by abstract tasks. The "*Useobejcts*" are structured in so-called "*elementary Useobjects*" that are actions that cannot be divided further. The aim of useML is to generate a User Interface by using different models, e.g. DISL and UIML, using transformation processes. Udit, is the graphical tool to develop the task model that allows also to simulate it [8]. As CTT, useML supports a graphical notation but implements it in a different way. To visualize the elements, useML uses colored boxes with text integrated as depicted in Fig. 2.

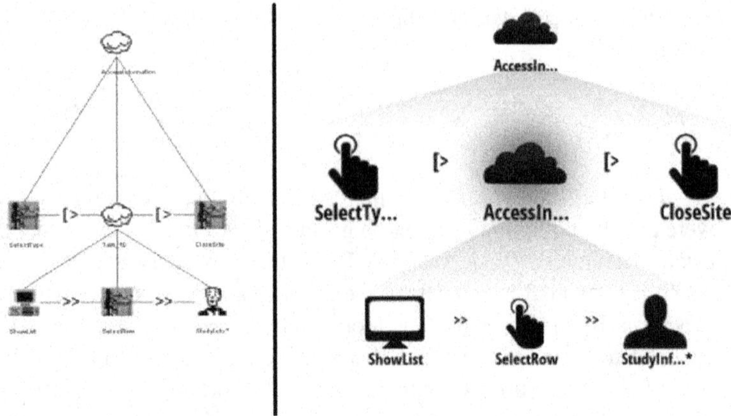

Fig. 1. Graphical CTT syntax, left CTTE and right responsive CTT.

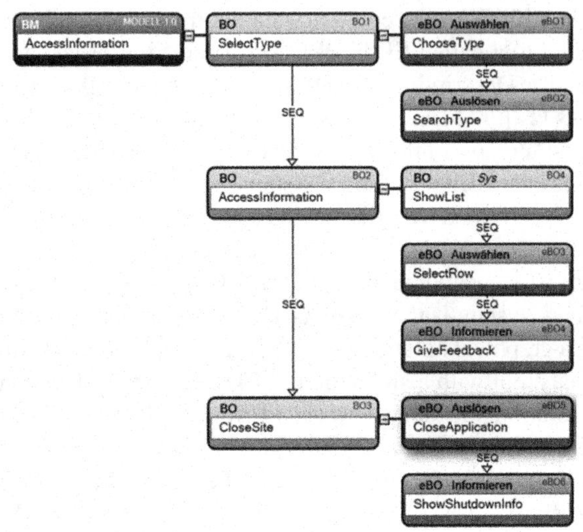

Fig. 2. Graphical notation of useML.

3 Participants and Methods

We got access to two German companies that work in different areas. One located in telecommunication sector, is a large company that has a number of offices all over the world, from now on called "company A". We could talk to three people from this company, one Interaction Designer, one Requirements Engineer and one User Experience Designer. The other company is a German medium sized company that delivers custom-fit solutions for many sectors, we call it "company B". They develop both hard- and software for different products. The products differ from coffee-machines to medical devices. We were able to talk to one Software Developer and one User Interface Designer.

We used semi-structured interviews to get information about their work and the use of task models. To get suitable feedback, we conducted the same interview with each of the participants. After we found the initial requirements, we did two further iterations of unstructured interviews with the participants to evaluate the requirements. The evaluations were necessary because we interviewed people from two different organizations with different background and corporate philosophies.

4 Results of the Study

The company B uses no task models at the time of the interview. The Software Engineer and User Interface Designer similarly mention that they have problems with the interdisciplinary communication. They already tried to solve this using other artifacts like further textual descriptions but did not succeed. They believe that task models could solve this issue or at least ease the communication. The two participants have no special training in the field of task modeling. In addition, the Software Engineer has no Usability-related knowledge. Both worked for the company for more than five years and are working in two different departments.

Right at the beginning of the two interviews it became clear that the requirements and expectations are different. The User Interface Designer emphasized that he does not want a tool that limits him in his creativity. He also expects a less detailed model than the Software Engineer. The User Interface Designer argues that the actions of the user are interesting and that he does not need a detailed model what happens in the "software's background". In his opinion a graphical notation with unambiguous names of tasks as identifiers is the best way to represent the model graphically. He argues that the model will have to iterate to improve its quality and validity. In contrast, the Software Engineer wants task models to be as detailed as possible. For his domain the details give each developer specifications how the software and its User Interface has to be implemented. This makes it easy for colleagues to understand the code since they have a reference that is common for all. As most important we found the need for iterative development in order to give the different discipline the possibility to get access for different levels of detail. We collaboratively worked out four levels of detail that give the users the possibility to choose which details they want to view.

- **First level of detail:** This level of detail allows the user to create the initial structure of the model. It includes the modeling of abstract tasks; the more detailed actions of a user will not be included in this stage.
- **Second level of detail:** In this level the users can enhance the model and add further detail, this includes the integration of the more detailed actions. On this level it will be necessary to enable a simulation of the task model. The simulation will give the opportunity to analyze the model and possibly find some problems.
- **Third level of detail:** Within this level the user can assign attributes to all tasks. One example for such an attribute is the assignment to a user group. Other attributes are the assignment of tasks to a specific platform or device.

- **Fourth level of detail:** The fourth and last level provides the assignment of functions to tasks. Especially Software Developers will be interested in this kind of information.

Both, the User Interface Designer and the Software Developer argue strongly for a graphical representation that is simple and easy to understand for the user. Especially the User Interface Designer mentions that his discipline is dominated by "visual people" and a graphical notation will support their mindset. We compared the icon-based representation (CTT) with a representation that uses boxes (useML). Both subjects feel more comfortable with the representation and syntax of useML.

We interviewed the participants of company A. Again, we interviewed the subjects with the same questions and got similar responses. The greatest difference is that in this company task models are already used in daily work. The used models are different to the in languages presented in Sect. 2. In this company they call task models "*Task Flows*" and they contain for example conditions that are adapted from flowcharts. However, they have the same purpose like task models, they record and structure the tasks that the users fulfil during their work with a system. Figure 3 shows a short extract of such a *Task Flow*. It has similarities with useML and the participants would not like to replace their notation with an icon-based notation like CTT. The Task Flow's conditions can have many outgoing edges and only one can be executed.

The *Task Flows* are an integral artifact in each project and a fair amount of time is spent on their development. The time spent depends on the complexity of the task and the familiarity with the domain. The User Experience Designer came up with the example of "self-care apps" that is for her an easy topic and hence the creation of a task model will take less time than for a "large management system". They use the *Task Flows* as a base for their future development, especially the navigation concept grounds on this artifact. They review the model at first within their department, using the "four-eye-principle". This means that one person develops the *Task Flow* and another person will review it and gives feedback. Once they got a first draft, they give it to other departments like the Software Architects. They will also give feedback and the *Task Flow* evolves. These participants were confronted with the idea of iterative support for the task model development process. The first impression was positive and they believe that this modality will support their process. They told us that the four level of detail look well-considered but we should include the refinement of the task model in the first level of detail.

Figure 3 shows the importance of conditions in their work. The Interaction Designer explains that for her daily work a conditional branch is a central aspect. She thinks that if they use a scientific developed notation, it has to include conditions. To get a better understanding of her expectations, we showed her useML and asked her to comment on the implementation of conditions. She thinks that the existing possibilities are not satisfying. Especially that they are not depicted in some way in the model is criticized by her. She argues that conditions have to be displayed in the graphical model to understand the model and implement the next steps. The Requirements Engineer and User Experience Engineer agree on this. To visualize the condition in a model, two ways are suggested by the three subjects (see Fig. 4). The first version is a simple implementation that was the idea of the User Requirements Engineer. The second possibility is inspired

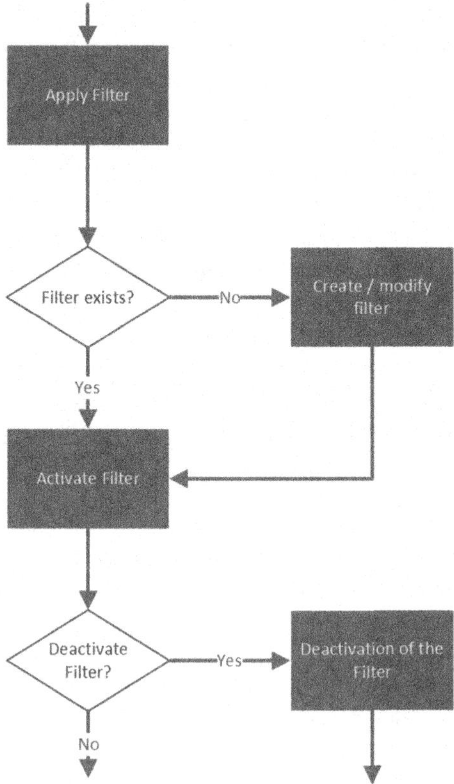

Fig. 3. Example for a used *Task Flow*.

by the flowcharts. This is a representation that Task 2 has a pre-condition and the user is able to view it on detail. The condition could be a delay or a state, for example machine turned on. If the condition could not be satisfied the task model could stop or a jump to another task is possible, depends on how it is implemented.

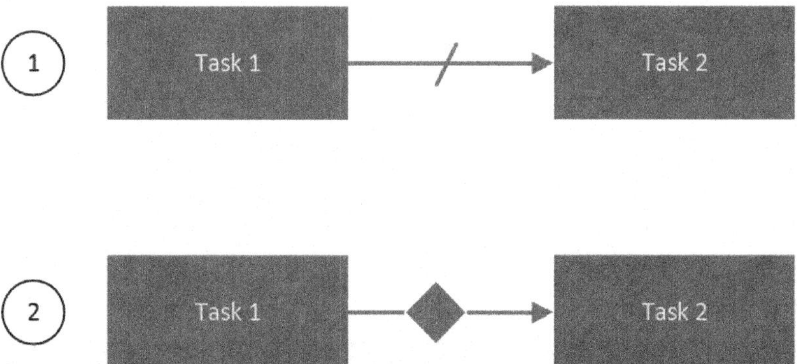

Fig. 4. Possible visualizations of conditions.

The participants of the two companies reviewed the tools CTTE and Udit for possible enhancements of the user interfaces and interactions. The participants mentioned that none of the tools fit to their requirements. However, both of them have strengths and weaknesses. The two tools implement the graphical notation in a different way. While CTTE on the one hand implements small icons as representation, useML on the other hand represents the tasks with boxes and a color-code. Especially the technically trained subjects argue that the colored boxes are sufficient while especially the User Interface Designer argues that the colors confuse him: "*I don't understand why this box is black and the other is orange.*". Furthermore, he thinks that the direct manipulation needs to be introduced. Both tools do not support this interaction. The implementations force the user to choose one element in the model and then using a "right-click" and choose the fitting element or click in the upper part on the fitting element. This indirect interaction, he argues, will interrupt the creation process. The other participants feel also that a direct manipulation is way more intuitive and modern. All participants wish a clear split between the functionalities and their reduction since they believe that they will not use them all.

During the review of the tools with the subjects it became clear that the current implementations do not fulfil the expectations they have. The indirect interaction and arrangement of the User Interface elements do not satisfy them. The human-centered redesign of a task model editor was conducted; the final mockup (developed with Balsamiq Mockup) is depicted in Fig. 5. We used the ribbons, as they are known from other products like Microsoft Office 2010. The subjects believe that the functionalities of the tool need to be separated. Hence, we used the ribbons above. One ribbon consists of the basic functionality for modeling, the other consist of filter and the last one will start the simulation. The central part is the area that will contain the task model, the

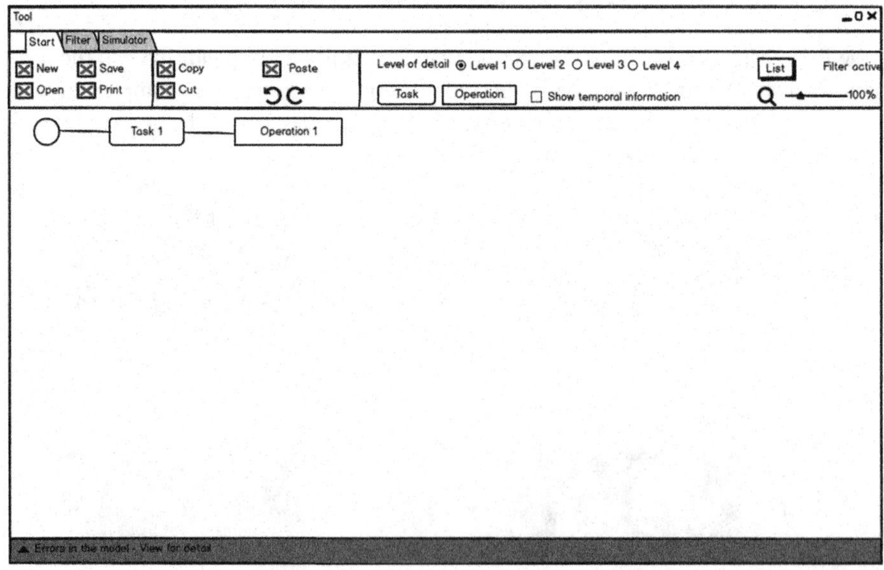

Fig. 5. Final mockup of the task model editor.

elements are consistent depicted in the model and above in the ribbon which is important for the subjects. Depicted is one possible graphical representation that was suggested by the participants. In this mockup it is also possible to choose the "*Level of detail*" in the upper part. The tabs "*Filter*" and "*Simulation*" switch to other views and actions.

To implement the changes that are needed we used useML since the participants believe that this notation only needs some changes to fit the requirements they have. Also, the tool Udit needs to be adapted according to the mockup above.

5 Realization in UseML

UseML is a XML-dialect and defined in a XSD-schema. This schema defines the language and the rules that structure the task model (called "Usemodel") implements but also include the logical definitions. To implement the first and most important improvement, the level of detail, a minor revision in the definition is needed. An attribute that saves the current level is introduced. According to it, the graphical editor will allow or forbid the manipulation according to the definition that is explained above.

To implement the conditions further changes are necessary. The subjects demand two types of conditions:

- **Logic condition:** This condition will have two specifications, pre- and post-conditions. If a logic condition is used, the user could provide a string with the description of the condition.
- **Temporal condition:** To include some waiting time or latency a temporal condition is included as well. Two main characteristics are mentioned by the participants: duration and instant of time. The duration could be for example the startup of a machine. The instant of time is a particular point that is fixed, for example a change of shifts.

A complex type "conditions" is included in the schema and extended by two attributes that define the described types. A tool that implements all the aspects that are evaluated during the first phase is in development.

6 Conclusion

There are special requirements for task models in industrial use that are not implemented in scientific approaches yet. The current scientific implementations of task models do not fit the requirements of the subjects, hence they defined their own notations. To overcome this gap, we proposed an iterative approach that allows the users to create their model in different levels of detail. This offers the user the possibility to show only the relevant information for their work. It includes four levels of detail that begin with the initial creation of a task model. As next step the task model will be enriched by further actions and can be simulated to find possible problems within the model. The third level of detail includes the assignment of user groups or platforms to tasks. This is of special interest if the task model includes tasks that only a special user group can perform. The fourth and last level enables the user to assign functions to the tasks. This is relevant for

Software Developers to get a richer specification of the task model. As well, the participants emphasize the need of conditions and their graphical representation. This is a central matter for the subjects. One subject told us that for her work the conditions are important and a notation without conditions will not be useful.

7 Discussion and Outlook

The results show that the scientific developed notations and languages do not fit to every requirement that is needed for the daily industrial use. However, some already well known concepts are valid and required for the daily use. The most prominent example is the hierarchical structure itself and the graphical representation. But especially the new iterative support could be a step forward to use task models more in a daily practice. The conditions that are introduced have also an effect on the task models. Especially that they have to appear in the model is currently not implemented. However, this is an important aspect but can lead to a model that includes some aspects of flow charts.

As the tool is completed an evaluation will be conducted. The evaluation will include the future users. They will get tasks and will have to solve them using the tool. The feedback they give will be worked in next versions of the tool.

References

1. Annett, J., Duncan, K.D.: Task analysis and training design. Occup. Psychol. **41**, 211–221 (1967)
2. Anzalone, D., et al.: Responsive task modelling. In: Proceedings of the 7th ACM SIGCHI Symposium on Engineering Interactive Computing Systems. pp. 126–131. ACM, New York (2015)
3. Baron, M., et al.: K-MADe: un environnement pour le noyau du modèle de description de l'activité. In: Proceedings of the 18th Conference on L'Interaction Homme-Machine, pp. 287–288. ACM, New York (2006)
4. Basnyat, S., et al.: Extending the boundaries of model-based development to account for errors. In: MDDAUI (2005)
5. Card, S.K., et al.: The Psychology of Human-Computer Interaction. L. Erlbaum Associates Inc., Hillsdale (1983)
6. Fahssi, R., et al.: Enhanced Task Modelling for Systematic Identification and Explicit Representation of Human Errors. In: Abascal, J., Barbosa, S., Fetter, M., Gross, T., Palanque, P., Winckler, M. (eds.) INTERACT 2015, Part IV. LNCS, vol. 9299, pp. 192–212. Springer, Heidelberg (2015)
7. Meixner, G., Seissler, M., Breiner, K.: Model-driven useware engineering. In: Hussmann, H., Meixner, G., Zuehlke, D. (eds.) Model-Driven Development of Advanced User Interfaces. SCI, vol. 340, pp. 1–26. Springer, Heidelberg (2011)
8. Meixner, G., et al.: Udit–a graphical editor for task models. In: Proceedings of the 4th International Workshop on Model-Driven Development of Advanced User Interfaces (MDDAUI), Sanibel Island, USA, CEUR Workshop Proceedings. Citeseer (2009)
9. Mori, G., et al.: CTTE: support for developing and analyzing task models for interactive system design. IEEE Trans. Softw. Eng. **28**(8), 797–813 (2002)

10. Paternò, F.: ConcurTaskTrees: an engineered approach to model-based design of interactive systems. In: The Handbook of Analysis for Human-Computer Interaction, pp. 483–500. Lawrence Erlbaum Associates, Mahwah (2004)
11. Paternò, F., et al.: CTTE: an environment for analysis and development of task models of cooperative applications. In: CHI 2001 Extended Abstracts on Human Factors in Computing Systems, pp. 21–22. ACM, New York (2001)
12. Rodriguez, F.G., Scapin, D.L.: Editing MAD* task descriptions for specifying user interfaces, at both semantic and presentation levels. In: Harrison, M.D., Torres, J.C. (eds.) Design, Specification and Verification of Interactive Systems 1997. Eurographics, pp. 193–208, Springer, Vienna (1997)
13. Tucker, A.B.: Computer Science Handbook, 2nd edn. Chapman & Hall/CRC, Boca Raton (2004)
14. Van Der Veer, G.C., et al.: GTA: groupware task analysis—modeling complexity. Acta Psychol. (Amst.) **91**(3), 297–322 (1996)
15. van Welie, M., et al.: Euterpe-tool support for analyzing cooperative environments. In: Proceedings of the Ninth European Conference on Cognitive Ergonomics, pp. 24–26 (1998)

Avoiding Inaccuracies in Task Models

Thomas Lachaume[1,2], Patrick Girard[1(✉)], Laurent Guittet[1,2], and Allan Fousse[1,2]

[1] LIAS/ISAE-ENSMA/University of Poitiers, 1 Rue Clément Ader, 86961 Chasseneuil, France
{thomas.lachaume, patrick.girard, laurent.guittet, allan.fousse}@ensma.fr
[2] Futuroscope, Chasseneuil-du-Poitou, France

Abstract. In the field of user-centered design of interactive systems, task models play a major role, especially in defining requirements, or during the system validation phase. They lean on precise semantics, based on a set of formal operators. In this article, we demonstrate how the addition of new description tools (pre-conditions, objects) introduced ambiguities in model interpretation, and we propose our solutions to solve this problem.

Keywords: Task models · User-centered design

1 Introduction

Task models come from the wider domain of the analysis of users [3]. Initially oriented towards the human factor studies, they were first used in Computer Science to help structure the description of observable human activities, using more or less technical aspects [5]. Gradually, task modelling explored new avenues, and turned to interactive system design with methods such as MAD [8]. Becoming more and more formal, authors developed tools that support the proposed methodologies, resulting in a significant extension of task model usage, as illustrated by the pair CTT/CTTE [7].

The main strength of task modeling in the field of interactive application design stands in the capacity to distinguish the role played by human operators from the role played by the studied system, and to express prescribed tasks that take into account the completeness of an activity by the way of operators that describe the task dynamics.

Meanwhile, the task models were more and more enriched, in response to the addition of much richer elements such as actors of the activity, or the "world objects" manipulated during the activity. Notions initially somewhat formalized, such as the condition for the execution of tasks, were then clarified. The proposals converged.

However, the evolution of task models is also characterized by a lack of general synthesis, which leads to inaccuracies in the interaction between separate notions proposed by different authors. In this article, we focus on one such elements: consistency between the temporal operators and task associated conditions. The latter, formally developed recently in the methods, have not been specifically linked with the dynamic semantics expressed through temporal operators, which can lead to several inaccuracies.

M. Kurosu (Ed.): HCI 2016, Part I, LNCS 9731, pp. 498–509, 2016.
DOI: 10.1007/978-3-319-39510-4_46

As Caffiau et al. showed [2], only the tools developed to support the models can accurately solve the problem of model interpretation. We therefore restricted our study to only maintained and widely available tools only, which illustrate by example the semantic models, namely the tools including a simulator.

First, we study, illustrated by examples, basic concepts manipulated by the task models. Then, we present some limitations to the interpretation of the task models currently offered through a case study. Finally, we offer some clarification of the semantics in order to lead to unambiguous semantics, before concluding with some perspectives.

2 Task Model Key Concepts

Despite their diversity (tens of task models have been proposed within the past thirty years), the majority of developed task models offer similar principles, based on a breakdown of tasks inspired by hierarchical planning [9]. This is the case of historical models such as [3, 8], but also of all those currently supported by a maintained tool (CTT [7], K-MAD [1], eCOM, HAMSTERS [6]). Beyond this structural semantics, they have a dynamic semantics, informally described in the first models, then formalized through a set of attributes attached to tasks and temporal operators governing relations between tasks. In the remainder of this article, we will focus on three formalisms, CTT, K-MAD and HAMSTERS, which include a powerful simulation tool.

2.1 Common Features in Most Models

Over the years, especially because of the increasingly important use of task models in the field of interactive system design, the different models have incorporated identical or quite similar notions.

To illustrate these concepts, we use an example, which represents the activity of exchanging an amount of money between two currencies as follows: the user determines the amount he/she wishes to convert, as well as the two concerned currencies, without prejudice to the order in which he/she performs these operations, then the system calculates the conversion rate.

Categorizing Tasks. In order to clearly identify the responsibilities between human and system tasks, a categorization was proposed, distinguishing the tasks performed by humans without any interaction with the system (*human tasks*), those conducted by the system without human intervention (*system tasks*) and those involving both the user and the system (*interactive tasks*). In our example, the cognitive task that determines the amount of money to convert and both currencies is *human task*, while the two entering data tasks (amount and choice of currencies) are *interactive tasks*, and the calculation itself is a system task. Typically, a specific category of tasks (*abstract tasks*) is dedicated to the nodes of the task tree; it breaks down into tasks of different nature, here the main task “*Converting*”.

Some formalisms such as HAMSTERS offer much finer categories, differentiating interactive input or output tasks, cognitive human tasks, etc (Table 1).

Table 1. Examples of tasks in different notations

Task model	Human task	Interactive task	System task	Abstract task
CTT				
K-MAD				
HAMSTERS				

Temporal Dynamics. Historically, the concept of planning [3, 8] was associated to task/sub-task decomposition, giving task models the ability to express some kind of dynamics. The definition of the first tools that interpret and render this dynamics (CTTE, MAD*/Alacie [4]) quickly converged on the inclusion of a limited number of operators to determine the dynamic behavior of tasks between them. Four main operators relying on the LOTOS operators [11] have been defined, which allowed the specification of subtasks as *sequential*, *parallel* or *unordered*, or a *choice* between subtasks.

In the example, the conversion task of an amount of money between two currencies is described, according to the CTT formalism on Fig. 1, and K-MAD on Fig. 2. The behavior of these two models is exactly the same, the node tasks of the tree (*Converter*, *Choose Currency*, *Prepare*) being only used for structuring the model. Operators play a major role in the operational semantics of task models. Based on these operators, simulators offer an interactive simulation of task models. The user is able to dynamically explore the model, each elementary task is proposed according to the semantics of the operators. So when two tasks are linked in sequence, only the first is available to the user, and the second one becomes available only when the first one is "executed". Conversely, when several tasks are governed by a "no order" operator, they are all available at the same time: the user is supposed to choose which one to do first.

In CTT, operators are binary, and located between two sub-tasks of a same task. The "*Determine*" task that allows the user to provide the parameters of its conversion (amount, and starting and destination currencies conversion) is the first to be performed, because of the sequence operator (>>operator for "Activation" in CTT). Then the operator composition allows three interactive tasks ("*Enter...*") capture the different parameters of the conversion to be performed in any order (operator |=| for "OrderIndependance" in CTT). The task "*Calculate*", which calculates and displays the result, is a system task, and is connected through a sequence operator. In the K-MAD formalism, temporal operators are linked to the task decomposition, and apply to all subtasks of one super task. Written constraints are stronger, requiring the creation of intermediate tasks like "Prepare" where with CTT, the task "*Choose Currency*" is not mandatory. However, the bracketing is made implicit in K-MAD, while in CTT, operator precedence solves ambiguities. HAMSTER has meanwhile proposed the "expression tree" solution that avoids intermediate tasks for the only purpose of structuring operators.

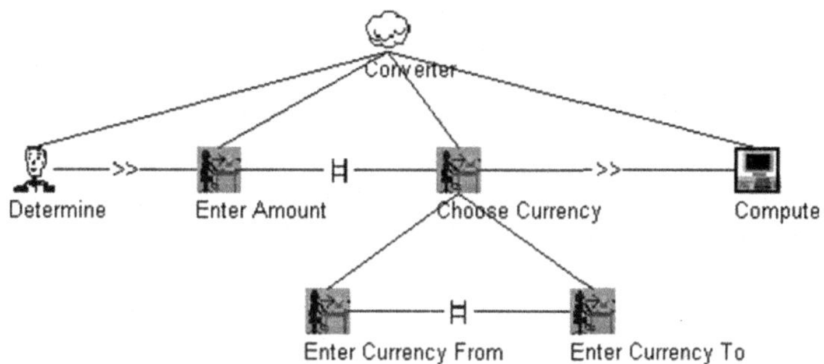

Fig. 1. A simple task with CTT

The dynamic behavior can be enriched as attributes with unary operators, which apply individually to the tasks. The first of them is the *optionality* operator; it establishes that, during the simulation, optional subtasks can be ignored by the human who performs the task. Thus, the optional tasks cannot belong to the system task category.

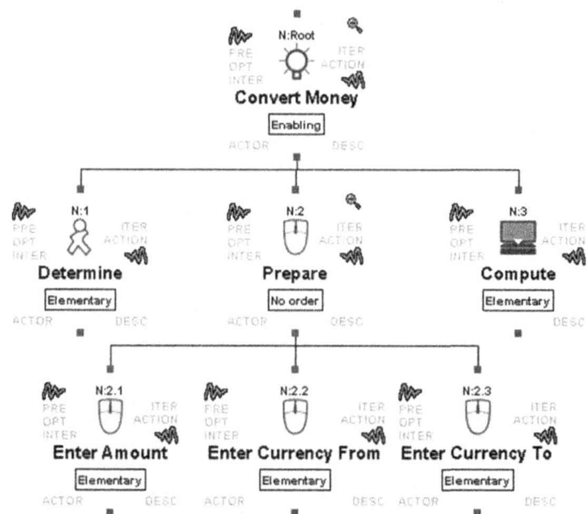

Fig. 2. A simple task with K-MAD

The Iteration Case. The different models all offer an iteration operator for describing a task that can/should happen repeatedly. Conforming to the strict hierarchical organization, this operator is a task attribute. If the concept of iteration is present in all models, how to express the condition of iterations (or iteration stop) differs greatly between models. While the first task model formalisms expressed iteration by the description of the task schedule leaving the whole of the human initiative (Johnson, MAD), the authors proposed two different ways to control iteration.

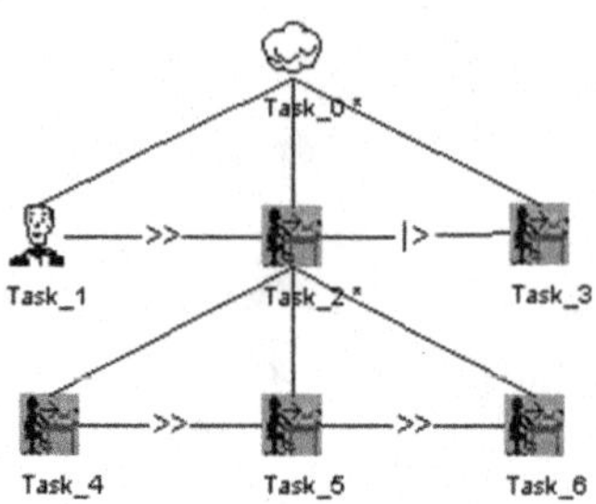

Fig. 3. Iteration with CTT

In CTT and HAMSTERS, the iteration stop is delegated to an external task, which role is to interrupt the current iteration. In Fig. 3, Task_2 is iterative (indicated by the asterisk next to the name of the task), and is divided into three sub-tasks that run in sequence. After Task_6, Task_4 becomes available again. The only way to stop the iteration consists in choosing Task_3, which is available at any time during the iteration thanks to the deactivation operator ([>), which aborts the task that precedes it (Task_2).

In K-MAD, where there is no disabling operator, the chosen option is an intrinsic condition that control the iteration, identical to a "while statement" in programming languages. This sets the task condition within the iterative task itself. For example, for a task that must take place a fixed number of times, it is possible to express the condition as [3]. However, the expression of more complex terms requires having objects and expressions.

Objects and Expressions. Since the early works on task models, the word "condition" was always used. However it was not formalized to a great extent in the tools that support the notations, as demonstrated in [2]. Recently, the simulators have become capable of taking into account the actual values of objects, thus conditioning the execution of tasks to the value of objects. K-MADe was the first widely accessible tools offering the ability to set pre-calculable conditions used by the simulator to allow or deny access to a task. CTTE offers the ability to set pre-conditions and post-conditions since version 2.5, released in 2011. However, K-MAD is the only notation proposing a "WHILE" construct. K-MADe and HAMSTERS propose a concept of edge effect (Assignment in HAMSTERS) to describe an operation performed on objects by the task. CTTE does not offer this feature, and the user must change the object values by hand to enable compliance with the conditions. However, CTTE is the only tool to manage the concept of post-condition, which corresponds to assertions on the value of objects at the end of tasks.

Objects can be independent or dependent from tasks. While K-MAD and HAMSTERS define them as independent from the tasks, CTT considers them as an integral part of the tasks, which forced its authors to add an operator to exchange objects between tasks.

If the way to express conditions changes from one formalism to another, treatment of pre-conditions by the simulator is universal: which the precondition is false, the task turns unavailable to the user, which can result in blocking the task model (K-MADe) or in its early termination (CTTE).

2.2 Task Model Limits

The primary objective of task models is to describe precisely a prescribed or observed activity. As we mentioned in the introduction, as part of the design of interactive applications, the clear separation of the roles or users from those played by the system is a key item. Furthermore, the precise semantics of notations is intended to guarantee a unique interpretation of the model. If this target is met by categorizing tasks, it is not the same as regards to the dynamic semantic models. The multiplicity of mechanisms can lead to inconsistencies in the model behavior, which prevents the building of precise and unambiguous descriptions.

In this section, we will describe, with the support of examples, the concrete problems one can meet when designing task models.

Not so Accurate Semantics. While authors of task models aim principally to avoid ambiguity, it is clear that firstly multiple mechanisms may lead to inconsistencies, and secondly gaps or unsaid things in the description of models can generate different interpretations of specific situations.

The first lack of precision concerns the notion of optional task. Is it a choice made by the system or only a choice given to the user? The second concerns the vagueness of the semantics of errors in task models: does it mean that the model is "stuck" running, or does it mean that the model is false? In general, the articles describing the task models do not focus on these issues, and only the tools can give an echo of the proposed dynamic behavior.

Case Study. To illustrate our study, consider the following example: model the task of keeping the score sheet of a volleyball match. The volleyball rules determine that a match consists of a maximum of five sets, the team that wins three of them wins the game. One way of describing the activity is to say that one must play three sets, then a fourth and a fifth if necessary. Both sets are optional, depending on system status (here, the current set score).

The use of CTT formalism[1] (Fig. 4) requires to manage the end of repetition as a creation of a task that will disable it. By the rules of the formalism, this task cannot be optional, hence the creation of the abstract task "Finish match." To achieve this task, sets 4 and 5 (if necessary) should be played, and then the score sheet needs to be

[1] In these three examples, the model is shown on only three levels of decomposition.

completed. These tasks are optional (as indicated by brackets around the name of the task), but not left to the user's choice: they must be based on the score result.

Figure 5 shows the same activity modeled with K-MAD. The ITER and OPT bold symbols respectively denote the existence of an iteration on the task 2 (N 2) "Mark normal set" and optional for tasks 3 and 3.2.

Figure 6 shows the same activity modeled with HAMSTERS. The iteration and optional symbols are noticed to the left and right of the assigned task.

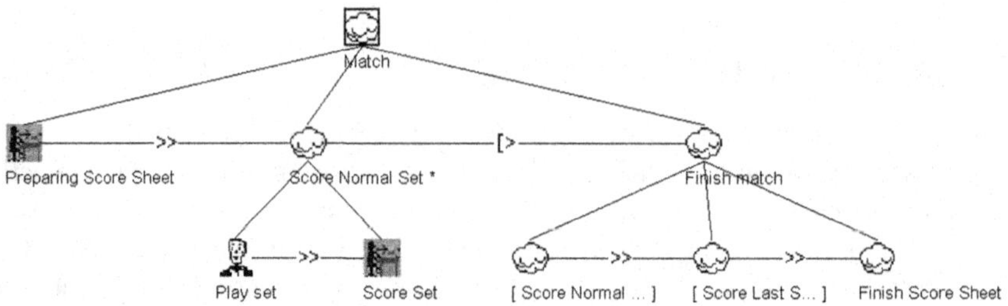

Fig. 4. "Keep the score sheet of a volleyball match" modeled with CTT

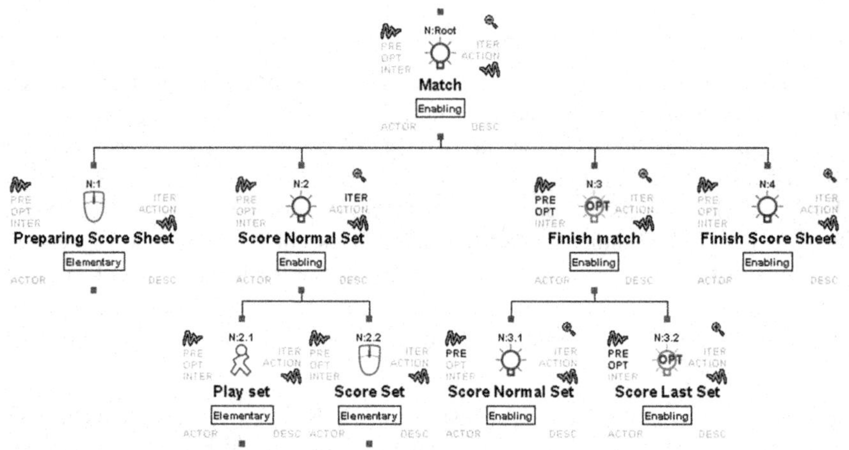

Fig. 5. "Keep the score sheet of a volleyball match" modeled with K-MAD

The difference in model decomposition is explained by a strict rule of CTT formalism: to get out of a repetitive task, the only way is to have a following mandatory task with a disabling operator. This prohibits the shape used in the K-MAD model, where the task following the repetition is optional (Fig. 5).

Limits of Optional Tasks. None of the three solutions is satisfactory from the point of view of volleyball rules. When interpreting the dynamic semantics of task models, we find that nothing prevents the user to "play" four or five sets with the same winner team.

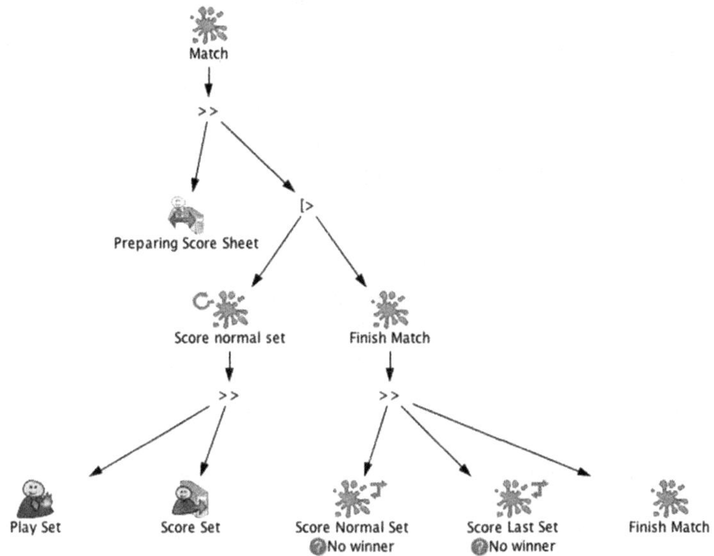

Fig. 6. "Keep the score sheet of a volleyball match" modeled with HAMSTERS

Using Pre-conditions. From the earliest works on task models, conditionality of tasks was highlighted. The concept of pre-condition, which allows conditioning the execution of a task to a condition expressed as a Boolean, has been proposed. According to his/her scenario choice, the task model user is able to guide the simulation of the model following his/her own perception of conditions. Thus, in our example, terms like "If no team has scored 3 sets" would correspond to a good pre-condition for the game tasks of the 4th and 5th sets. However, this condition is not based on any concrete evidence of the model, and cannot be formally exploited by simulators. In [2], the authors demonstrate the interest in the use of formal preconditions using computable expressions in the design of interactive systems based on task modeling. In fact, the three studied tools currently include computable expressions, based on more or less complex objects.

K-MADe manages digital objects, boolean or text that can be used to define pre-conditions attached to tasks or iteration terms (building "while" expressions). It also manages collections to handle objects in lists, stacks, tables, etc. CTTE manages objects of various types, which can be used for automatic generation of interfaces, but only offers the basic expression operators (equality, inequality, lower, upper).

In our case, the three tools can enrich the model description using calculable pre-conditions. It is possible to define such a condition in the form SetsA < 3 AND SetsB < 3 for both tasks matching the 4th and 5th sets, which will prohibit the realization of these tasks if the condition is not met.

One can notice that preconditions are completely invisible in the CTT model, while K-MAD and HAMSTERS give a feedback on their existence.

What Behavior? One might expect to have the same behavior for these models. It is not the case, as using the simulators can show. The way the simulators work is quite similar. At each step of the simulation, a framework offers the user a set of available/enabled tasks. Double-clicking on one of these tasks can "run" it and the simulator then recalculates all available tasks (Task Enabled Set) based on the operators of the model. In the case of CTTE simulator, actions for which preconditions are not checked do not appear among the available tasks. However, in the case of K-MADe, they are available, but not executable (i.e. a double-click on such a task does not result in change of state, a message informs that the pre-conditions is false).

Figure 7 shows the enabled tasks at the end of the repetition, in a situation where no team has won 3 sets (the game is not finished, you have to play the 4th set).

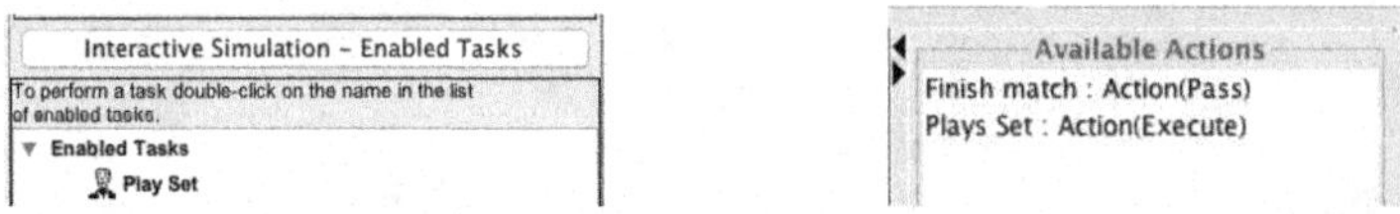

Fig. 7. Enabled tasks in CTTe (left) and K-MADe (right)

If the situation is properly managed in CTT thanks to taslk preconditions, K-MADe offers an illogical action that pass the action "Finish the game." This is due to the lack of consideration of the conditions in the node tasks.

Note also that the failure to carry out an optional task is translated differently in the simulators: in the case of K-MADe, you must explicitly "Pass" the action, while for CTTE, simply trigger the next task. Therefore, an optional task cannot be the last task of the model in CTT, because in this case one cannot complete the model without running the optional task.

In both cases, what can we observe? The only graphical representation of task models does not allows to predict the behavior of the model. Indeed, the only parameter that appears clearly on the graph is the optional nature of the task. Although, in some cases, the user must decide whether the optional task is done or not, in other cases, like here, not achieving the 4th and 5th sets it is not a user's choice, but is determined by the system status.

The combination of pre-conditions with the optional unary operator seems to solve the problem: in fact, adding a pre-condition on the system task "Calculate result", we can make it inaccessible until the conditions are not met. This solution is however not satisfactory for several reasons.

The Ambiguous Optional Attribute. What is the actual meaning of the optionality of tasks? Does it represent a decision to be made by the human operator who may or may not decide to do this task at this moment, or is it related to the system status, that is to say a situation in which the task should be performed if a condition is true, and omitted if not? Here, in the case of volleyball, the fourth set cannot be omitted if none of the teams has won more than 2 sets. The only way to prevent the user from validating the optional nature of the task is to put a precondition on the next task/s, to inactivate it/them. Besides the fact that this has no special meaning, it imposes a writing discipline that greatly complicates task model building and validation for modellers.

How do task models handle task optionality? In CTT, any task may be optional. During the simulation, if no pre-conditions are present, the task can be executed or ignored. In the absence of precondition definition, one can consider this choice as legal, because the task model user is supposed to master every aspect of the played scenario. However, if the preconditions are used, this behavior is no longer acceptable. Indeed, this would allow the user to override the pre-condition of a system task. In the case of K-MAD, a system task cannot be defined as optional, reducing the sense of optionality to a decision of the user of the model. But in this case, it is never possible to not execute…

The Failure Semantics. The third important point concerns the semantics of model failure. Using the only semantics of operators necessarily leads to a consistent state of the model, with one or more tasks to run (the model is still active) or not (the model is completed). The introduction of pre-conditions can lead to more complex situations. So what about a model where all possible tasks contain only tasks which pre-condition are false? CTTE ignore this case, considering that the list is empty, so that the model is completed. In contrast, K-MADe considers that the model is "blocked": it does not end in a normal situation.

3 Towards a More Accurate Semantics

We believe that the existence of "holes" in the task model semantics prevents task model authors to reach their main objective. An unambiguous semantics seems an essential prerequisite to any good modelling.

Some authors have noted a lack in the expressive possibilities of task models. This is the case of [10], which proposes to add some operators to CTT. Two of them are linked to our problem: the unary "Stop" operator and a modified choice operator. The "Stop" operator consists of an attribute that can manually interrupt the current task model during simulation. It allows taking into account one error that occurs during a task. The example given by the authors regard such a login task, where the user can decide to abort his task (user selectable, called deterministic), and where the system may fail the task if entering a wrong password (system selection, qualified non-deterministic).

Our proposal has two points: the definition of the concept of failure of the current activity, and the definition of a new attribute, in addition to the "Optional" attribute, to define the "Blocking" status of a task.

3.1 Current Task Failure

A task model describes a human activity. Ideally, this activity is always legal and valid. However, for the purpose of specifying interactive system (or parts of an interactive system), what does a deadlock mean, where no task is attainable because the conditions for their running are not met? The Sinnig's "Stop" operator [10] is intended to allow the incorporation of early termination of a task tree. It is an interruption provided explicitly by the task model developer. But what about the case where the model has a more attainable solution determined by the set of expressions that govern the pre-conditions tasks? In CTTE, the answer given is to consider that the model simulation is finished "normally". We believe that this solution is not suitable for using task models to validate interactive systems. We therefore propose the following rule: as one task remains present in the list of available tasks, the activity is completed. If a task cannot be activated, then the activity is in error. This notion, which does not currently exist in task models, allows us to consider the concept of validity or invalidity of scenarios.

3.2 Redefining Optionality

The examples discussed above demonstrate the lack of precision concerning the definition of the optional nature of the tasks in task models. Is this optionality only due to actions of the human actor in activity, should it be related to the system status, or the intrinsic nature of the task?

In our example, the 4th and 5th volleyball sets are not mandatory but depend on the system status. In a state, they are required, in another state, they are prohibited. The Sinnig's proposition, which consider the choice operator as either a user choice (deterministic as proposed) or a system choice depending on the system status (non deterministic) cannot therefore take into account all cases. Thus, it is not possible to define a task whose pre-condition determines the optional nature, but in the end, is also optional from the perspective of the user. Our proposal is to distinguish between two notions associated with the unsystematic character of a task.

- The optional nature of a task (attribute "Optional") is only attached to the choice of the human actor of the task model, which can freely choose to achieve the task or not. Therefore, a system task cannot be optional.
- We propose to define a new attribute, called "blocking." This attribute defines the behavior associated with the possible pre-condition expressed on tasks. So if "blocking" is true, the task cannot be omitted by the user. It shall be enforced if the pre-condition is true. However, if the pre-condition is false, the task will block the full model, which will then be in check. By default, a task is still "blocking" intrinsically, without precondition (which is always true to have a pre-condition) This task must be performed. Only the positioning of this task in a building with an 'alternative' operator unblocks the model.
  The advantage of this solution lies in the possibility of combining the two operators together. A blocking and optional task corresponds to the case where the user can override the completion of a task whatsoever.

4 Conclusion

In this article, we introduced and illustrated some inaccuracies of task models, which can be explained by the addition of new concepts in the originally defined formalism. We offer a solution to solve ambiguities generated by these inaccuracies.

Another field of study concerns the concept of interruption, and its link with the dynamic models as currently defined.

References

1. Baron, M., Lucquiaud, V., Autard, D., Scapin, D.: K-MADe : un environnement pour le noyau du modèle de description de l'activité IHM 2006, pp. 287–288. ACM (2006)
2. Caffiau, S., Scapin, D., Girard, P., Baron, M., Jambon, F.: Increasing the expressive power of task analysis: systematic comparison and empirical assessment of tool-supported task models. Interact. Comput. **22**(6), 569–593 (2010)
3. Diaper, D., Stanton, N.A.: The Handbook of Task Analysis for Human Computer Interaction. Lawrence Erlbaum Associates, Mahwah (2004)
4. Gamboa, R.F., Scapin, D.L., Hansmann, W., Hewitt, W.T., Purgathofer, W.: Editing MAD* task description for specifying user interfaces, at both semantic and presentation levels. In: Harrison, M.D., Torres, Jc (eds.) Design, Specification and Verification of Interactive Systems DSV-IS 1997, pp. 193–208. Springer, Heidelberg (1997)
5. Kieras, D.E.: GOMS models for task analysis. In: Diaper, D., Stanton, N. (eds.) The Handbook of Task Analysis, pp. 83–116 (2004)
6. Martinie, C.: Une approche à base de modèles synergiques pour la prise en compte simultanée de l'utilisabilité, la fiabilité et l'opérabilité des systèmes interactifs critiques, p. 236 (2011)
7. Paternò, F., Mancini, C., Meniconi, S.: Concurtasktrees: a diagrammatic notation for specifying task models. In: Howard, S., Hammond, J., Lindgaard, G. (eds.) Human-Computer Interaction Conference INTERACT 1997, pp. 362–369. Springer, Heidelberg (1997)
8. Scapin, D.L., Pierret-Golbreich, C.: Towards a method for task description: MAD. In: Berliguet, L., Berthelette, D. (eds.) Working with display units, pp. 371–380. Elsevier Science Publishers, North-Holland (1990)
9. Sebillote, S.: Task analysis and formalization according to MAD: Hierarchical task analysis, method of data gathering and examples of task description (1992)
10. Sinnig, D., Wurdel, M., Forbrig, P., Chalin, P., Khendek, F.: Task Models and Diagrams for User Interface Design. Springer, Heidelberg (2007)
11. Systems, I.S.O.I.P. Definition of the Temporal Ordering Specification Language LOTOS (1984)

Comparing Discrete Event and Agent Based Simulation in Modelling Human Behaviour at Airport Check-in Counter

Mazlina A. Majid[1(✉)], Mohammed Fakhreldin[2], and Kamal Z. Zuhairi[1]

[1] Faculty of Computer Systems and Software Engineering, Universiti Malaysia Pahang, 26300 Kuantan, Pahang, Malaysia
{mazlina,kamalz}@ump.edu.my

[2] Faculty of Computer Science and Information Systems, Jazan University, P.O. Box 114, Jizan, Saudi Arabia
mfakhreldin@jazanu.edu.sa

Abstract. Simulation is a well-established technique that uses what-if scenario analysis tool in Operational Research (OR). Discrete Event Simulation (DES) and System Dynamics Simulation (SDS) are the predominant simulation techniques in OR. However, in recent time, a new simulation technique, namely Agent-Based Simulation (ABS) is gaining more attention in the modelling of human behaviour. This research focused on modelling the human behaviour using DES and a combination of DES/ABS. The contribution made by this paper is the information unveiled as a result of comparing DES and a combination of DES/ABS for modelling both human reactive and human proactive behaviour in service systems; such as check-in services in an airport. The results of our experiments show that, the level of reactiveness considered in the combined DES/ABS model has a big impact on the simulation outputs. Therefore, for service systems of the type under investigation, we would suggest the use of hybridized DES/ABS as the preferred analysis tool.

Keywords: Simulation · Discrete event simulation · Agent based simulation · Human behaviour modelling · Reactive behaviour · Proactive behaviour

1 Introduction

Simulation has become a preferred tool in Operation Research for modelling complex systems [1]. Simulation is considered a decision support tool which has provided solutions to problems in industry since the early 1960s [2]. Studies in human behaviour modelling and simulation have received increased focus and attention from simulation research in the UK [3]. Human behaviour modelling and simulation refers to computer-based models that imitate either the behaviour of a single human or the collective actions of a team of humans [4]. Discrete Event Simulation (DES) and Agent Based Simulation (ABS) are simulation approaches often used for modelling human behaviour in Operational Research (OR). Examples can be found in [5, 6]. The capability of modelling human behaviour in both simulation approaches is due to their

M. Kurosu (Ed.): HCI 2016, Part I, LNCS 9731, pp. 510–522, 2016.
DOI: 10.1007/978-3-319-39510-4_47

ability to model heterogeneous entities with individual behaviour. Another simulation approach commonly used in OR is System Dynamic (SD). However, this approach focuses on modelling at an aggregate level and is therefore not well suited to model a heterogeneous population at an individual level. Because of this limitation, SD is not considered in the present study. Human behaviour can be categorised into different types, many of which can be found in the service sector. When talking about different kinds of human behaviour, we refer to reactive and proactive behaviour. Here, reactive behaviour is related to staff responses to the customer when something is being requested and is available. While proactive behaviour relates to a staff member's personal initiative to identify and solve an issue. When providing services, proactivity of staff plays an important role in an organisation's ability to generate income and revenue [7]. But the question here- *is it useful to consider proactive behaviour in models of service systems and which simulation techniques is the best choice for modelling such behaviour?* Thus, in this paper we investigate the impact of modelling different levels of proactive behaviour in DES and a combination of DES/ABS. This study compares both simulation techniques in term of simulation result using a real world case study: check-in services in the airport.

In some of our previous studies: the capabilities of DES and combined DES/ABS in representing the impact of reactive staff behaviour [8]; mixed reactive and proactive behaviour in a retail sector [9] and public sector [10]. In the present paper, we look at the capabilities of DES and a combination of DES/ABS in representing the impact of mixed reactive and proactive behaviour on another complex public sector system.

The paper is structured as follows: In Sect. 2 we explore the characteristics of DES and ABS and discuss the existing literature on modelling human behaviour in service sector. In Sect. 3 we describe our case study and the simulation models development and implementation. In Sect. 4 we present our experimental setup, the results of our experiments, and a discussion of these results. Finally, in Sect. 5 we draw some conclusions and summarise our current progress.

2 Literature Review

2.1 Human Behaviour Modelling in DES and ABS

This section reviews the existing research studies on modelling human behaviour using DES and ABS techniques. As explained by Pew and Mavor [4], Human Behaviour Representation (HBR), also known as human behaviour modelling, refers to computer-based models which imitate either the behaviour of a single person or the collective actions of a team of people. Nowadays, research into human behaviour modelling is well documented globally and discussed in a variety of application areas. Simulation appears to be the preferred choice as a modelling and simulating tool for investigating human behaviour [11]. This is because the diversity of human behaviours is more accurately depicted by the use of simulation \ [12].

In all the reviewed work, the best-known simulation techniques for modelling and simulating human behaviour are DES and ABS. Among existing studies on modelling human behaviour, the use of DES is presented by [5, 6, 13, 14], On the other hand, [15–19], recommend ABS for modelling human behaviour. [5] claims that, based on their experiments of modelling the emergency evacuation of a public building, it is possible to model human movement patterns in DES. However, the complex nature of DES structures where entities in the DES model are not independent and self-directed makes the DES model inappropriate for modelling large-scale systems. This characteristic of entities in DES is agreed by [13], who have used DES in planning the pedestrian movements of the visitor to the Istanbul Technical University Science Center. However, due to the dependent entities in the DES model, the pedestrian movement pattern in their simulation model is restricted to pre-determined routes. By contrast, [17, 18] have developed an agent-based fire evacuation model which models people-flow in free movement patterns. He states that the decision to use ABS is due to the fact that agent-based models can provide a realistic representation of the human body with the help of autonomous agents.

In addition to modelling human behaviour using DES, [12] have investigated methods of estimating the impact of imperfect situational awareness of military vehicle operators. They opined that, it is possible to use the DES model to understand human behaviour by matching the results from the DES model with human subjects. [15] comments that, modelling consumer behaviour when grocery shopping is easier using ABS because, this model has the ability to integrate communication among individuals or consumers. [16] asserts that, their research in applying ABS to simulate management practices in a department store appears to be the first research study of its kind. They argued that ABS is more suitable than DES due to the characteristics of the ABS model; specifically, it allows to model proactive and autonomous entities that can behave similar to humans in a real world system.

Instead of choosing only one simulation technique to model human behaviour, some researchers tend to combine DES and ABS in order to model a system which cannot be modelled by either method independently. Examples are [4] who studied the operation of courier services in logistics, who investigated manufacturing systems, who studied human travel systems. Others are [3] who looked at the operation of coffee shop services, [21] who is using SIMKIT to model both simulation models and [20], investigated the modelling of earth-moving operations. They all agree that DES and ABS modelling can complement each other in achieving their objectives. A combination of ABS and DES modelling is useful when human behaviour has to be modelled to represent the communication and autonomous decision-making.

The research into human behaviour using DES and ABS that has been carried out so far suggests that DES and ABS are able to model human behaviour but take different approaches (dependent entities vs. independent agents). The studies outlined above has shown that DES is suitable for capturing simple human behaviour, but is problematic when applied to more complex behaviours as the next event to occur in DES has to be determined. In contrast, ABS offers straightforward solutions to modelling complex human behaviour, i.e. free movement patterns or employee proactive behaviour, as agents can initiate an event themselves. However, for ABS, the resource requirements (computational power) are much higher and the modelling and implementation of the model is more complex.

2.2 The Simulation Choice

The comparison made in this study uses DES and a combination of DES/ABS. As the focus of this research was to investigate a service oriented system in the public sector, which involves queuing for the different services. The use of ABS is not the choice for the investigations carried out in this research, this is because in pure ABS models, the system itself is not explicitly modelled but emerges from the interaction of the many individual entities that make up the system. However, as ABS seems to be a good concept for representing human behaviour we use a combination of DES/ABS approach where we model the system in a process-oriented manner, while we models the actors inside the system (the people) as agents.

3 Case Study Description

The operation at the check-in counters in an airport has been chosen as third case study [9, 10] because it demonstrates a diversity of contact between counter staff and travellers, which is essential to this study of human behaviour. Information on this third case study is chosen from "Simulation with Arena" by [1].

Figure 1 illustrates the operation at the airport check-in service, the numbering and red arrow represents the sequence of operation. The operation at the airport check-in service of this case study starts from the point at which travellers enter the main entrance door of the airport and progress to the one from the five check-in counters of an airline company (represented by arrow number 1 in Fig. 1).

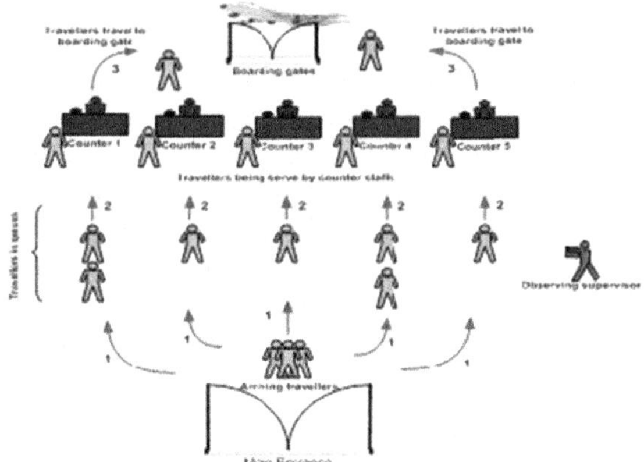

Fig. 1. The operation at the airport check-in service (Color figure online)

The operation at the five check-in counters is from 8.00 am to 12.00 am every day. If members of staff at the related check-in counters are busy, the travellers have to wait in the counter queue (represented by arrow number 2 in Fig. 1). If counter staff are available, then travellers will move to the check-in counter (represented by arrow number 3 in Fig. 1). Once their check-in is completed, the travellers are free to go to their boarding gates (represented by arrow number 3 in Fig. 1).

To model the human reactive and proactive behaviours, information on real human behaviours at the airport is gathered through secondary data sources such as books and academic papers.

The reactive behaviour that has been investigated relates to counter staff reactions to travellers in processing their check-in requests and their response to travellers waiting in queues during busy periods. The proactive behaviours that have been modelled are the behaviours of another member of staff (supervisor) who is responsible for observing and controlling the check-in services. The first proactive behaviour of a supervisor is a request to the counter staff to work faster in order to reduce the number of travellers waiting in queues. The decision to execute such proactive behaviour is based on their working experience. Identifying and removing any suspicious travellers from queues is the supervisor's second proactive behaviour to be modelled, their decision again based on observation and working experience. Suspicious travellers include those with overweight hand or cabin luggage, drunken travellers and unauthorised pregnant women. The proactive behaviour of travellers is related to their search for the shortest queue in order to be served more quickly. The decision by the travellers to execute such proactive behaviour is generated from knowledge that they gathered by observing other queues while checking-in.

After analysing the operation at the check-in counter, the level of detail to be modelled in the DES and the DES/ABS models, as well as conceptual modelling, is then taken to consideration.

4 Simulation Models

Both, the DES model and the combined DES/ABS model are based on the same conceptual model (Fig. 2) but the strategy of implementation in both cases is very different. DES modelling uses a process-oriented approach, i.e. the development begins by modelling the basic process flow of the check-in services operations as a queuing system. Then, the investigated human behaviours, reactive and proactive are added to the basic process flow (Fig. 2). Two different implementation approaches are used for developing the DES/ABS model: the process-oriented approach is used for the DES modelling (Fig. 2) and the individual-centric approach is used to model the agents. Figure 3 shows some state charts that represent the different types of agents in the model (travellers, counter staff and supervisor).

Two simulation models have been developed from the conceptual models and both are implemented in the multi-paradigm simulation software AnyLogic™ [22]. These simulation models consist of one arrival process (travellers), five single queues, and resources (five counters staff). Travellers, counter staff and supervisor are all passive objects in the DES model, while in a combination of DES/ABS model, they are all active objects. Passive objects are entities that are affected by the simulation‘s elements as they move through the system, while active objects are entities acting themselves by initiating actions [6].

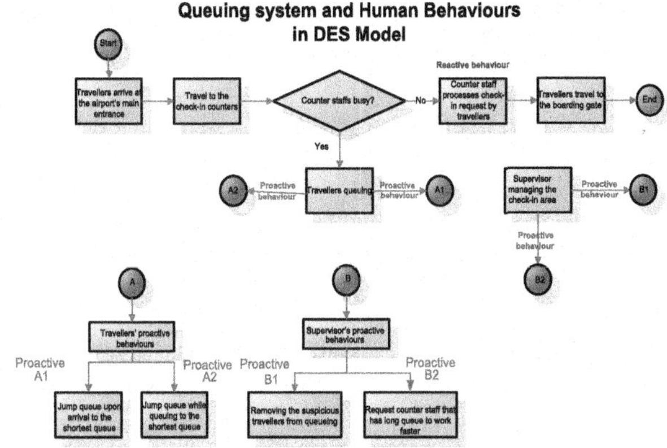

Fig. 2. The implementation of DES model

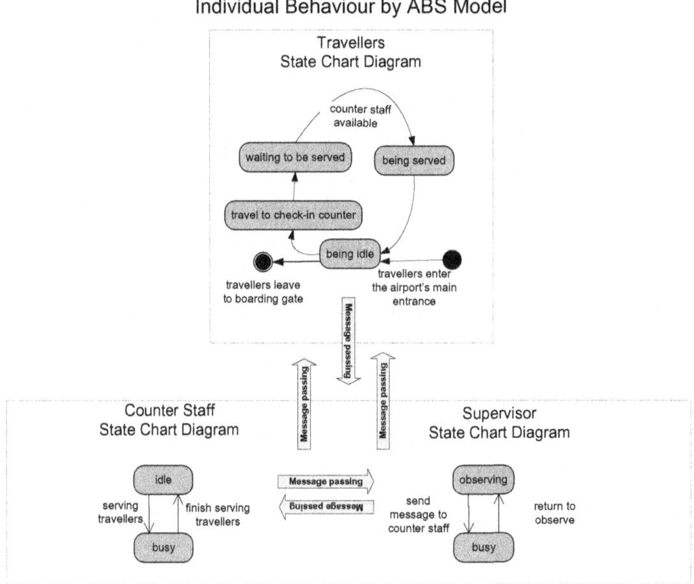

Fig. 3. The implementation of combined DES/ABS model

A discussion follows on how objects in DES model or agents in DES/ABS model are set up:

Travellers Object/Agent. The arrival rate of the simulation model is gathered from "Simulation with Arena" by [1]. In both DES and DES/ABS models, the arrival process is modelled using an exponential distribution with the arrival rate shown in Table 1. The arrival rate is equivalent to an exponentially distributed inter-arrival time with mean = 1/rate. The travel time as stated in Table 1 is the delay time for travellers moving from the airport entrance to the check-in counters.

Table 1. Travellers arrival rates

Arrival type	Time	Rate
Travellers arrival time	8.00–24.00 am	Approximately 30 people per hour
Travellers travel time	Upon arriving	Uniform (1,2)- minimum 1 min, maximum 2 min

Counter Staff Object/Agent. In both simulation models, five members of counter staff have been modelled performing the task of processing travellers' check-in requests. Task priority is allocated on a first-in-first-out basis according to the service time stated in Table 2.

Table 2. Counter staff service time

Service time parameters	Value
Counter staff service time	Weibull (7.78, 3.91)

Supervisor Agent (only in combined DES/ABS model). The supervisor agent is modelled in the combined DES/ABS model while in DES model the supervisor is imitated by a set of selection rules (programming function). This is because in the DES model the communication between the entities is not capable of being modelled. In both simulation models, the supervisor is not directly involved with the check-in process. He/she is there only to observe the situation at the check-in counter, so no service time is defined for the supervisor for both simulation models (DES and combined DES/ABS).

We conducted 100 replications for each set of parameters. Both simulation models use the same model input parameter values. Therefore, if we see any differences in the model outputs they will be due to the impact of the differences between the modelling techniques. The run length for this case study is 16 h, imitating the normal operation of the check-in counter at an airport. The verification and validation process are performed simultaneously with the development of the basic simulation models (DES and combined DES/ABS).

5 Experiment and Results

The purpose of the experiment is to compare the simulation results between DES and combined DES/ABS models when modelling human reactive and proactive behaviours. The experiment sought to find out what could be learnt from the simulation results when modelling complex proactive behaviours for the realistic representation of the real–life system using two different simulation techniques. The comparison of simulation results for DES and combined DES/ABS models is conducted statistically by performing a T-test. For our comparison we use the following hypotheses:

Ho 1:	Modelling human reactive behaviour in DES model produce statistically the same simulation results with combined DES/ABS model
Ho 2 :	Modelling human mixed reactive and proactive behaviour in DES model produce statistically the same simulation results with combined DES/ABS model

Four simulation models have been developed: 1. Reactive DES model 2. Reactive Combined DES/ABS model 3. Mixed Reactive and Proactive DES model and 4. Mixed Reactive and Proactive DES/ABS models. Two types of experiments have been conducted as shown in Table 3.

Table 3. Experiment description

Experiment	Description
Experiment 1	Reactive DES versus reactive combined DES/ABS
Experiment 2	Mixed reactive and proactive DES versus mixed reactive and proactive DES/ABS

In this experiment, the general idea of reactive (response to environment) and proactive behaviours as described in Sect. 4 were imitated and modelled. The first proactive behaviour that was modelled in this experiment is related to the behaviour of the supervisor, who is responsible for ensuring that the check-in process is under control. The supervisor's proactive behaviour is demonstrated by requesting counter staff to work faster in order to serve travellers who have been waiting a long time. The decision of requesting counter staff to work faster is based on the supervisor's awareness that some travellers would not move to another shorter queue. The second proactive behaviour is demonstrated by the behaviours of travellers who require faster service. Finding the shortest queue on arrival at the check-in services and moving from one queue to another shorter queue while queuing have exemplifies the proactive behaviours of travellers. Finally, the third proactive behaviour is exhibited in identifying suspicious travellers by the supervisor, based on their own experience and observation at the check-in counters.

To investigate the impact of modelling variation of proactive behaviours against reactive behaviours in DES and combined DES/ABS models, "customer waiting time" and "number of customers served" were used as our main performance measures. We have selected these measures as the literature recommends them as important measures to increase productivity in the service-oriented systems . In addition, we have used "counter staff utilisation" and "number of customers not served" as the additional performance measures. To execute the Experiment 2, the additional performance measures were used based on the investigated proactive behaviours (number of requests to work faster, number of travellers searching for shortest queue (upon arriving), number of travellers searching for shortest queue (while queuing) and number of travellers moved to the office). It is assumed that investigating these measures will provide sufficient evidence in understanding the impact of the simulation outputs for different behaviours in one simulation technique.

The sub-hypotheses were built for each performance measure in DES and combined DES/ABS according to the list of experiments to be compared. Finally, the results of the performance measures in the Experiment 1 and 2 were gathered and compared for both simulation models (Table 4).

Table 4. Results of experiment 1 and experiment 2

Performance measures		Experiment 1 DES	Experiment 1 Combined DES/ABS	Experiment 2 DES	Experiment 2 Combined DES/ABS
Travellers waiting times (minute)	Mean	18.64	18.46	6.44	3.12
	SD	23.91	24.84	10.18	8.17
Counter staff utilisation (%)	Mean	64	65	69	70
	SD	18.58	20.59	18.21	18.7
Number of travellers served (people)	Mean	473	473	462	459
	SD	22.35	22.81	24.19	25.1
Number of travellers not served (people)	Mean	4	4	0	0
	SD	2.25	4.71	0	0
Number of requests to work faster	Mean	–	–	1	0
	SD	–	–	1.25	0.19
Number of travellers searching for the shortest queue (upon arriving) (people)	Mean	–	–	477	478
	SD	–	–	25.18	50.89
Number of travellers searching for the shortest queue (while queuing) (people)	Mean	–	–	n/a	223
	SD	–	–	n/a	42.18
Number of travellers moved to the office (people)	Mean	–	–	15	17
	SD	–	–	10.15	11.83

The hypotheses for Experiment 1 are:

Ho1_1	:	The travellers waiting time resulting from the reactive DES model is not significantly different from the reactive combined DES/ABS model
Ho1_2	:	The number of travellers served resulting from the reactive DES model is not significantly different from the reactive combined DES/ABS model
Ho1_3	:	The counter staff utilisation resulting from the reactive DES model is not significantly different from the combined reactive DES/ABS model
Ho1_4	:	The number of travellers not served resulting from the reactive DES model is not significantly different from the reactive combined DES/ABS model

The hypotheses for T-test in Experiment 2 are the same with the four hypotheses in Experiment A1 but these hypotheses are tested with a name link to Experiment 2 as follows: Ho2_1, Ho2_2, Ho2_3, and Ho2_4, for the travellers waiting time, the counter staff utilisation, the number of travellers not served and the number of travellers served, respectively. To complete the Experiment 2, the following additional sub-hypotheses are needed.

Ho2_5	:	The number of requests to work faster resulting from the mixed reactive and proactive DES model is not significantly different from the mixed reactive and proactive combined DES/ABS model
Ho2_6	:	The number of travellers searching for the shortest queue (upon arrival) resulting from the mixed reactive and proactive DES model is not significantly different from the mixed reactive and proactive combined DES/ABS model
Ho2_7	:	The number of travellers searching for the shortest queue (while queuing) resulting from the mixed reactive and proactive DES model is not significantly different from the mixed reactive and proactive combined DES/ABS model
Ho2_8	:	The number of travellers moved to the office resulting from the mixed reactive and proactive DES model is not significantly different from the mixed reactive and proactive combined DES/ABS model

Results for the Experiment 1 and 2 are shown in Table 4 and the results of the T-test are shown in Tables 5 and 6. Referring to Table 4, Experiment 1 has revealed similarities in results between the DES and combined DES/ABS models. The test results in Table 5 show that the p-values for each performance measure are higher than the chosen level of significant value (0.05). Thus the Ho1_1, Ho1_2, Ho1_3, and Ho1_4, hypotheses are failed to be rejected. Results in this case study have revealed a similar impact on both simulation models when modelling similar reactive behaviour.

Table 5. Results of T-test in Experiment 1

Performance measures	DES vs. combined DES/ABS	
	P-value	Result
Travellers waiting time	P = 0.801	Fail to reject
Counter staff utilisation	P = 0.422	Fail to reject
Number of travellers served	P = 0.763	Fail to reject
Number of travellers not served	P = 0.851	Fail to reject

Hence, the simulation result for the reactive DES and combined DES/ABS models is statistically show no differences and the Ho1 hypothesis is failed to be rejected.

Similarities and dissimilarities of results between DES and combined DES/ABS were found in this combined-proactive experiment, as shown in Table 4. Significantly, the combined DES/ABS model has produced a shorter waiting time, a lower number of requests to work faster and a higher number of travellers searching for the shortest queue while queuing compared to the DES model. This impact is significant, probably due to the extra individual behaviour that is modelled in the combined DES/ABS

Table 6. Results of T-test in Experiment 2

Performance measures	DES vs. combined DES/ABS	
	P-value	Result
Travellers waiting times	P = 0.000	Reject
Counter staff utilisation	P = 0.486	Fail to reject
Number of travellers served	P = 0.612	Fail to reject
Number of travellers not served	P = 0.218	Fail to reject
Number of requests to work faster	P = 0.000	Reject
Number of travellers searching for shortest queue (upon arriving)	P = 0.766	Fail to reject
Number of travellers searching for shortest queue (while queuing)	Statistical test is not available	
Number of travellers moved to the office	P = 0.572	Fail to reject

model. Such behaviour (travellers searching for shortest queue while queuing) is frequent in the system under study and has affected the travellers' wish to be served more quickly; therefore no queue is longer than another. The statistical test (Table 6) has confirmed these three performance measures (customer waiting time, number of requests to work faster and number of travellers searching for the shortest queue while queuing) have shown lower p-values than the chosen level of significant value (0.05). Therefore, the Ho2_1, Ho2_5 and Ho2_7 hypotheses are rejected.

In addition, the statistical test has confirmed that there are no significant differences in both simulation models' results between counter staff utilisation, number of travellers served, number of travellers not served, number of travellers searching for shortest queue upon arrival and number of travellers moved to the office, as their p-values are higher than the level of significant value. The Ho2 _2, Ho2_3, Ho2_4, Ho2_6 and Ho2_8 hypotheses are therefore failed to be rejected. As an overall result, modelling human combined-proactive behaviour for both DES and combined DES/ABS models is statistically different in their simulation results performance. Therefore, the Ho2 hypothesis is rejected.

Modelling various proactive behaviours in the airport check-in services has proved that the behaviour of travellers who always seek faster service is the main reason that has influenced the performance of both simulation models. However, this is more noticeable in combined DES/ABS as modelling travellers' behaviours is more realistic than in the DES model. The performance of the combined DES/ABS model in modelling realistic human behaviours has a significant impact on the simulation study.

From the comparison investigation, new knowledge is obtained. The investigation has proven that DES is capable of producing similar results to those of combined DES/ABS when modelling the reactive human behaviour, but further complex proactive modelling produced different results. Modelling detail human behaviours in combined DES/ABS has demonstrated that modelling such behaviours produce significance impact on the simulation output performance. This study has shown that it is useful to model human proactive behaviour as detail as possible in the service industry in order to get a good understanding on the service-oriented systems performance. The best choice of simulation technique is combined DES/ABS.

6 Conclusions and Future Work

In this paper we have demonstrated the application of simulation to study the impact of human reactive and proactive behaviour service systems. The study in particular focusses on finding out more about the benefits of implementing only reactive or mixed reactive and proactive behaviours. More precisely, our investigations have been able to answer the question: Is it useful to model human proactive behaviour in service industry and which simulation techniques is the best choice for modelling such behaviour?

Previously, we have dealt with the reactive behaviour modelling [8] and mixed reactive proactive behaviour modelling [9] in a first case study based in the retail sector and a second case study based in the public service sector [10]. We found that modelling realistic proactive behaviours that habitually occur in the real system are worth modelling in the modelled situations as it has demonstrated a big impact to the overall system performance in DES and DES/ABS models.

Also in this paper, we have focused on modelling different level of proactive behaviour for check-in services in the airport. Modelling the service-oriented system as realistically (proactive behaviour) as possible is found important. This is because modelling such detail has a significant impact on the overall system performance, as it reduces the customer waiting time and the number of customers not served. We found a combination of DES/ABS model to be suitable for modelling the levels of proactive behaviour that was investigated in the proposed case study. In the future we would like to involve with more complex service-oriented systems, to test if we can generalise our findings regarding the comparison of modelling different level of proactive behaviours in DES and a combination of DES/ABS techniques.

Acknowledgement. This research is funded by Ministry of Higher Education and Universiti Malaysia Pahang under FRGS Research Grant.

References

1. Kelton, W.D., et al.: Simulation with ARENA. McGraw-Hill, New York (2007)
2. Shannon, R.E.: Systems Simulation – The Art and Science. Prentice-Hall, Englewood Cliff (1975)
3. Robinson, S.: Discrete-event simulation: from the pioneers to the present, what next? J. Oper. Res. Soc. **56**(6), 619–629 (2004)

4. Pew, R.W., Mavor, A.S. (Eds.): Modeling Human and Organizational Behavior: Application to Military Simulations. National Academy Press, National Research Council, Washington DC (1998)
5. Brailsford, S.C., et al.: Incorporating human behaviour in healthcare simulation models. In: Proceeding of the 38th Winter Simulation Conference, Monterey, California (2006)
6. Siebers, P.O., Aickelin, U., Celia, H., Clegg, C.: Towards the development of a simulator for investigating the impact of people management practices on retail performance. J. Simul. **5** (4), 247–265 (2010)
7. Rank, J., et al.: Proactive customer service performance: relationships with individual, task and leadership variable. Proc. J. Hum. Perform. **20**(4), 363–390 (2007)
8. Majid, M.A., et al.: Comparing simulation output accuracy of discrete event and agent based models: a quantitative approach. In: Summer Computer Simulation Conference (SCSC 2009), Istanbul, Turkey (2009)
9. Majid, M.A., et al.: Modelling reactive and proactive behaviour in simulation. In: 5th Simulation Workshop (SW10) Operational Research Society , Worcestershire, England (2010)
10. Majid, M.A., et al.: Modelling reactive and proactive behaviour in simulation: a case study in a university organisation. In: The International Conference on Modeling and Simulation 2012 (MAS 2012), 28–30 November 2012, Jeju, Korea (2012)
11. ProModel: Justifiying Simulation (2010)
12. Nehme, C., et al.: Using discrete-event simulation to model situational awareness of unmanned-vehicle operators. In: Virginia Modeling, Analysis and Simulation Center Capstone Conference, Norfolk, VA (2008)
13. Baysan, S., et al.: Modeling people flow: A real life case study in ITU science center. In: Proceedings of the Summer Computer Simulation Conference (2009)
14. Robinson, S.: Modelling without queues: adapting discrete-event simulation for service operations. J. Simul., 1–11 (2015)
15. Schenk, T.A., et al.: Agent-based simulation of consumer behavior in grocery shopping on a regional level. J. Bus. Res. **60**(8), 894–903 (2007)
16. Siebers, P.O., Aickelin, U., Celia, H., Clegg, C.: Using intelligent agents to understand management practices and retail productivity. In: Proceedings of the Winter Simulation Conference, pp. 2212–2220, 9–12 December, Washington DC, USA (2007)
17. Korhonen, T., et al.: FDS+Evac: an agent based fire evacuation model. In: Klingsch, W.W. F., Rogsch, C., Schadschneider, A., Schreckenberg, M. (eds.) Pedestrian and Evacuation Dynamics 2008, pp. 109–120. Springer, Heidelberg (2008)
18. Korhonen, T., et al.: FDS+Evac: modelling social interactions in fire evacuation. In: 7th International Conference on Performance-Based Codes and Fire Safety Design Methods (2008)
19. Sharma, V., et al.: A review of various agent based resolution modelling methods. Int. J. Comput. Sci. Inf. Technol. **5**(3), 4469–4472 (2014)
20. Zankoul, E, Khoury, H., Awwad, R.: Evaluation of agent-based and discrete-event simulation for modeling construction earthmoving operations. In: 32nd International Symposium on Automation and Robotics in Construction and Mining, At Oulu, Finland (2015)
21. Leng, T.B.: A study to model human behaviour in DES using SimKit. Thesis, Naval Postgraduate School, Monterey, California
22. Siebers, P.O., Wilkinson, I.: A first approach on modelling staff proactiveness in retail simulation models. J. Artif. Soc. Soc. Simul. **14**(2), 1–25 (2011)

An Automated Model Based Approach to Mobile UI Specification and Development

António Nestor Ribeiro(✉) and Costa Rogério Araújo

Departamento de Informática, Universidade Do Minho and HASLab / INESC TEC, Braga, Portugal
anr@di.uminho.pt, rogerio.ar.costa@gmail.com

Abstract. One of the problems of current software development lies on the existence of solutions to address properly the code portability for the increasing number of platforms. To build abstract models is one efficient and correct way to achieve this. The Model-Driven Software Engineering (MDSE) is a development methodology where models are the key for all project lifecycle, from requisites gathering, through modelling and to the development stage, as well as on testing. Pervasive computing demands the use of several technical specifications, such as wireless connections, advanced electronics, and the Internet, as well as it stresses the need to adjust the user interface layer to each one of the platforms. Using a model-driven approach it is possible to reuse software solutions between different targets, since models are not affected by the device diversity and its evolution.

This paper reports on a tool, which is highly parameterizable and driven to support Model-2-Model and Model-2-Code transformations. Also, instead of using a predefined technology, the tool was built to be scalable and extensible for many different targets and also by addressing the user interface layer generation.

Keywords: Model-Driven Software Engineering · Model transformation · Cross-platform generation · Pervasive software development

1 Introduction

The current trends about software development for mobile platforms, namely mobile apps development, are mainly focused on the portability for the rising number of devices to which user interface layers can be developed. This addresses the need to sustain this development by building abstract models as a mean to have an efficient and scalable way to achieve our purposes.

As its well known, model driving software engineering supplies a development methodology where models are the key for the entire project lifecycle, from requisites gathering, through modelling and development stage, as well as on testing. Using a model-driven approach it is possible to reuse software solutions between different targets, since models should not be affected by the device diversity and its evolution.

M. Kurosu (Ed.): HCI 2016, Part I, LNCS 9731, pp. 523–534, 2016.
DOI: 10.1007/978-3-319-39510-4_48

As said previously, actual technologies are developing up at great speed in a diversity of areas, such as hardware and software (middleware and user interface layer). Hardware has been evolving to standardized form factors, more powerful and cheaper, and software has become more complete, with increased functionalities at the user interface level.

However, this development led to the proliferation of platforms and technologies where constantly there is new base software with new features, which increasingly impose new restrictions to software portability. For example, each time a new Android smartphone is released, there is the risk of old released software become uncovered with problems such as fragmentation or "multiple screens". This is particularly true when dealing with the user interface layer source code.

The amount of complexity brought to the software side is only possible to be reasonably solved because of the notorious improvements around the development methodologies, which enables us to deliver software with lower production costs, longer lifecycle, and higher interoperability. Using models as basis of software development allows the overcome of the current platform proliferation and it also provides portability for new platforms that may appear in near future.

Model-Driven Architecture (MDA) [7], proposed in 2001 by the Object Management Group (OMG), encompass a set of standards for model-based software development. It is intended to support ever-changing business environments, minimising the software development time and project costs. MDA enables separating the system functionality from implementation details, keeping consistent glue between both elements.

Software development based on MDA starts with high-level models obtained in the specification phase. Gradually and automatically, the models should be transformed into more specific (low-level) models until source code is reached. The transition between models can be achieved by a set of well-defined rules (the models glue). Then, using a tool, it is possible to achieve automatic code generation from abstract (high-level) software models.

Tools supported by models make the software development more straightforward, because it enlaces the software portability, and the developer can choose the abstraction layer and programming language to be used. It is important to stress that data, behaviour and user interfaces can be modelled at adequate abstraction levels and then rely on transformation rules to generate the corresponding source code. Specific efforts on the development of each one of these layers usually implies that the models were not properly designed.

This paper uncovers the first results of a model-based tool, MDA SMARTAPP, which is driven to support highly parameterizable MDA transformation processes. The tool is to be used in the development of the application's business and user interface layers meant to be accessed by mobile apps (in a first approach Android specific) or hybrid web browser desktop applications.

The remaining document is structured as follows: in Sect. 2 it is exposed some related work; in Sect. 3 it is presented how Model-2-Model transformations are achieved; Sect. 4 is related to MDA SMARTAPP model editor; in Sect. 5 it is presented the tool architecture; Sect. 6 is related to the case study; and Sect. 7 presents the conclusions.

2 Related Work

To build a mature model-based tool, such as MDA SMART, it is important to overcome two major different points of view: what is expected from a model-based tool, and what could be done to support efficiently models transformation.

In a model-based tools space, there are some highly evolved tools, being the OutSystems Platform[1], or the IBM Rational Software Architect[2] two successful examples of such tools. Usually, these tools provide development environments with simple and high quality rendered interfaces, and a lot of features for drag-and-drop modeling. As a result, users becomes more concerned about the envisaged solution, instead of the implementation details. However, highly evolved tools have a restricted structure, and the user has sometimes some difficulty to custom and expand beyond their "sandbox". And the advantage of model portability is many times fully dependent on the tool ecosystem and not properly interoperable.

Several MDA implementations have already been proposed in the past [5,6]. In [2], for example, it is done a study on the applicability of MDA in the development of large-scale software. As a result, the study proved that MDA based approaches increases the quality and quantity of the deliverables and reduces the overall cost once it allows people to interact at a more abstract point of view. It is also important to note that using MDA models provides for some durability and resistance because they are not affected by the proliferation of available middlewares.

In [1] the development of a Fujaba [8] plugin to support Business Process Modeling (BPM) tasks is presented. The main goal is to port BPM models for UML activity diagrams and vice versa through Fujaba mechanisms "MoRTEn" (ModelRound-Trip Engineering) and "MoTE" (Model Transformation Engine). To support the transformations it was implemented a mechanism of Triple Graph Grammars (TGG) [12] in order to achieve bi-directionality and incremental model processing.

In [13] a prototype for the semi-automatic construction of Web Information Systems (WIS) was built. The objective is to achieve the tool architecture through other existent tools and some Model-Driven Development (MDD) components.

The most successful initiatives of MDA supported tools are the ones which use Domain-Specific Language (DSL) approaches to define model transformations. Here the tools are divided in several domains such as mobile devices, web services and applications, and standard desktop solutions.

Another work worth of mention is the one presented by Vaupel et al. [14]. It presents a modelling language and an infrastructure for the model driven development of Android apps. It also uses Ecore meta-models and it provides model transformation and source code generation using the Eclipse plugins. It defines a meta-model for the business layer, one for the user interface and another for

[1] http://www.outsystems.com/.
[2] http://www.ibm.com/developerworks/rational/products/rsa/.

specifying the application's behaviour. It uses simplified meta-models, in order to cope with complexity, for the transformation stages. One major difference from our approach is the fact that it only supports the transformation for Android applications not covering both the Web and hybrid clients.

3 Model to Model Transformation Engine

There are tools that manage web, mobile and desktop development at the same conceptual level. Even inside each one of these categories not all the existing tools support, or can be extended to the plethora of possible technological targets. In order to achieve this compatibility degree is the main objective of MDA SMARTAPP, a tool that allows the using of models and provides a way to support transformations for different target device families.

The kernel of MDA SMARTAPP is based on a model to model (Model-2-Model) transformation mechanism, the M2M Engine. The main purpose of M2M Engine is to iterate over all models of a MDA standard architecture until the models reach low-level abstraction layers. This is particularly useful when addressing the user interface controls and widgets, knowing that at model level the developer needs that technological particularities will not change the models, allowing to keep the discussion at a reasonably high and abstract level.

The DSL approach has been repeatedly used in model-based tools. There are well known cases where using a DSL become a success, such as is the case of ATLAS Transformation Language (ATL) from ATLAS Model Management Architecture (AMMA) platform.

ATL, proposed by the Group ATLAS INRIA & LINA, was aimed to implement Meta-Object Facility (MOF)/Query-View-Transformationg (QVT) [10,11] request standard from OMG. It's a hybrid language since it allows rules construction on both imperative an declarative paradigms. In a declarative way, simple mappings are implemented in a straightforward way. The imperative way to use the language is mostly used for higher complexity definitions.

The ATL virtual machine is properly equipped with a well-developed Object Constraint Language (OCL) [9] architecture. This feature provides flexibility in models manipulation (and respective meta-models) allowing it to cope with more

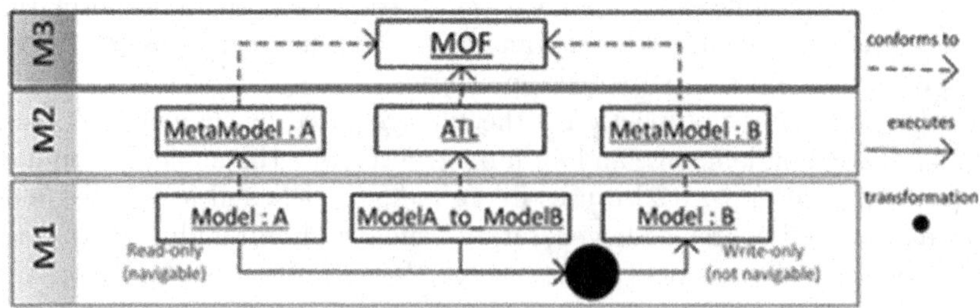

Fig. 1. EMF ATL - Operational context

complex models. Moreover, models can present problems in the transformation process, and these could be difficult to resolve if there is not a significant support from the OCL side.

As presented on Fig. 1, ATL operational context follows a MOF [10] compliant architecture. In this context, the input model (A) is translated to the output model (B) through a well defined set of ATL rules (ModelA_to_ModelB). The input model (A), the output model (B), and the set of ATL rules (ModelA_toModelB) conforms to the M2 (level) meta-models, MetaModel:A, MetaModel:B, and ATL, respectively. All three M2 meta-models are bridged by the (M3) MOF meta-meta-model.

MDA SMARTAPP takes advantage of this MOF compliant architecture to be extensible and scalable. For a new Model-2-Model configuration there is the need to provide the input and the output meta-model (written in the Ecore format), and the ATL set of rules. With only these three elements it is possible to achieve software portability for any device configuration.

4 M(odel) Editor

In order to give the end user a friendly environment to edit the models we developed a small scale graphical editor. The graphical editor component was built using the JGraph[3] library. This library presents good usability patterns, with a rich look and feel, it is well documented, and it has become used with success in a series of successful case studies [1]. However, it should be noted that our aim is not to replace other tools that can be used for model edition and manipulation, but to provide for prototyping purposes the means to easily create a model. We believe that most developers will use their preferred tool for model creation and through the existing formats for model interchange the models can exchanged with other applications.

In addition to the most well known functionalities, JGraph also provides a mechanism to implement the model validation. It is possible to reuse this mechanism to build "a priori" a model checker, and therefore by using this functionality, MDA SMARTAPP can validate the user actions and their conformity to the UML's meta-model. For example, it doesn't allow the user to specify an implementation of an UML class with respect to other class, as it should have been done to an interface definition.

In [2] is reported how hard and unmanageable is to restart a sequence of model transformations because of delayed detected errors. That is even more evident when dealing with very large and complex models, with a magnitude of several thousand objects (business and interface objects) as discussed in [3].

5 Tool Architecture

MDA SMARTAPP is intended to support the bottom layers from the MDA architecture: Platform Independent Model (PIM), Platform Specific

[3] http://www.jgraph.com/.

Model (PSM) and source code. Therefore, this tool provides one component dedicated for PIM models manipulation; one component for the PIM to PSM transformations; and one component for source code generation taking the PSM models as input. All three were designed to be abstract components, and can be extended by specific configurations.

The first component, the M(odel) Editor, is responsible for capturing the visual information (objects and locations) that describes the memory model representation. Similar to a CASE tool, this includes model manipulation according to the respective meta-model context. Also, it allows for a design environment with good usability patterns and without the need to the user to develop any source code.

The tool core component, the M2M Engine, is accomplished with an ATL configuration. This component is responsible for managing models definitions and to execute the instantiated Model-2-Model transformations.

The third component, the M2C Engine, covers the last step of a MDA architecture, and by using a template approach the PSM models are translated into source code.

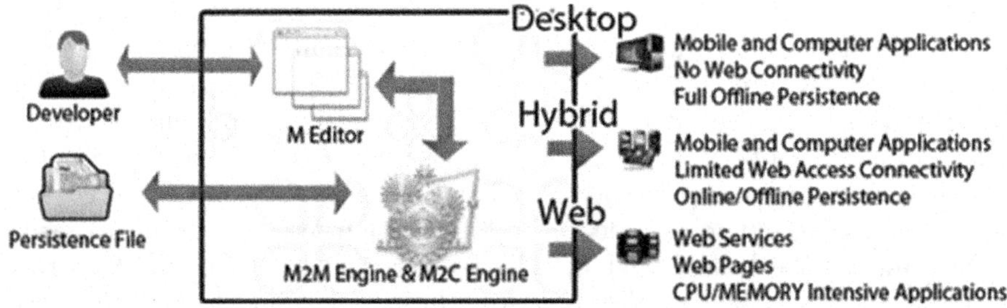

Fig. 2. MDA SMARTAPP - Tool logical architecture

MDA SMARTAPP supports UML2 for the PIM layer and Java and Android for the PSM and source code layer. Also, there are considered three main output targets (Fig. 2): Web applications, Hybrid clients with a server side and a client side components, and Desktop applications. Although the definitions of web and desktop applications are self-explanatory, it is important to define what we understand by hybrid applications. Hybrid applications are applications built specifically for native platforms (namely Android, iOS, or others) that exchange information with the server side using standard web protocols (eg. Web Services). At this stage we use Java as the platform for desktop applications and server side components and Android code will be generated to run in the mobile devices.

6 Case Study

As a proof of concept our case study is a simple Field Force Automation (FFA) application. The application objective is to retrieve lists of technical information shaped for different use cases. The biggest challenge in this domain lies on the definition of a usable Graphical User Interface (GUI) for the mobile devices, specially the smaller ones, that force the developer to think very carefully about the usability and the user experience. There's another significant challenge that arises from the fact that the source code portability is important especially when dealing with such constraints with the target hardware and base software.

This case study was solved with one unique abstract model, that later was derived for desktop (Java) and mobile (Android) applications.

First it was necessary to develop some primary MDA SMARTAPP features: this includes an UML2 domain editor (the M Editor component), UML to Java model transformations (the M2M Engine), and finally the source code generation for Java and Android targets (the M2C Engine).

For the UML2 domain editor it was developed a graphical view (V) of UML2 model using the JGraph library. This view is supported by a bespoke controller (C) and the UML2 meta-model[4] application program interface (M) available in the Eclipse platform.

To support the Model-2-Model transformation, it was considered a simplification of Java meta-model, in order to reduce the number of entities and relationships. Some ATL rules were specified, and strengthened with OCL definitions. In this particular case OCL allowed us, for example, to ensure that the UML2 packages are well unfolded to Java packages (Fig. 3), or the name of any Java element respects the reserved words, although other more complex restrictions could have been specified.

The source code generation of the user interfaces, from both desktop and mobile clients, was derived from the UsiXML [4] models of the interface layer.

```
helper context UML!Namespace def: getExtendedName() : String =
    if self.namespace.oclIsUndefined() then ''
    else if self.namespace.oclIsKindOf(UML!Model) then ''
    else self.namespace.getExtendedName() + '.'
    endif endif + self.name;
```

Fig. 3. UML2 to Java ATL rule - UML2 to Java package unfolding

Once we had a robust Java meta-model, two sets of Velocity templates were developed for Java and Android technologies. Since it is possible to build multiple template fragments and choose at runtime what best fits on the target device, it is possible to overcome the slight differences from similar targets with one unique PSM meta-model.

For our FFA application the simplified domain model is presented in Fig. 4 and it depicts the core business entities: the worker, the service and the client.

[4] http://www.eclipse.org/modeling/mdt/?project=uml2.

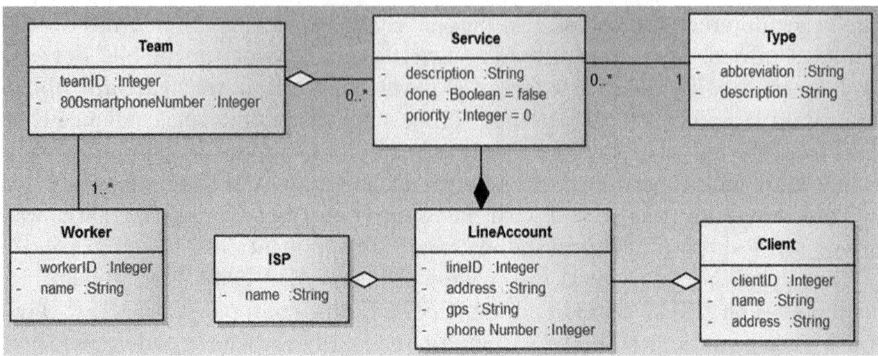

Fig. 4. Simplified domain model of a FFA application.

The domain model is transformed into a PIM model derived from the transformations needed to ensure the necessary compliance to the Java meta-model. Figure 5 shows MDA SMARTAPP platform independent model for the FFA application.

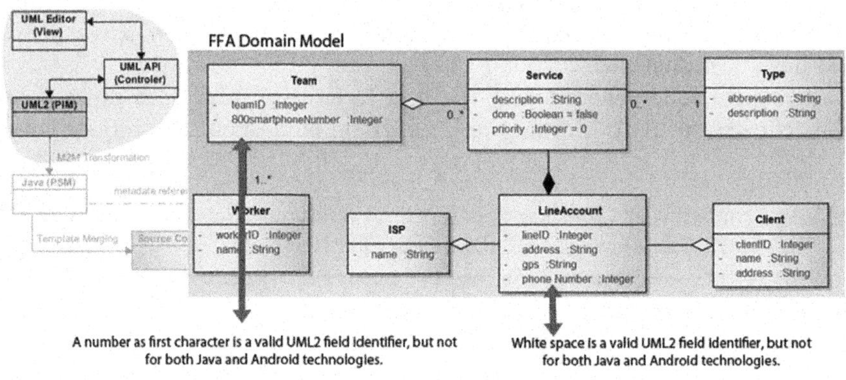

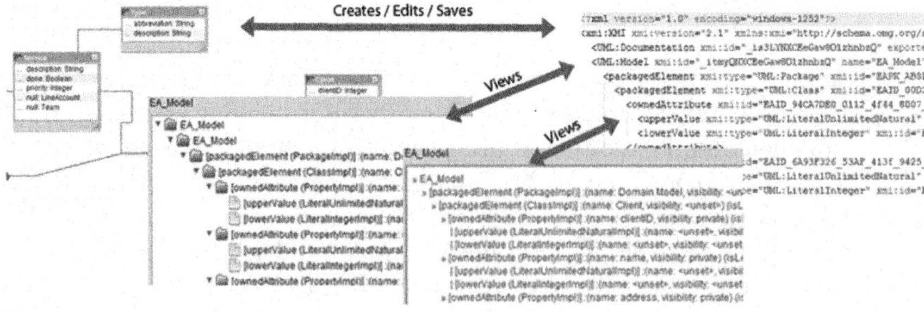

Fig. 5. PIM model construction.

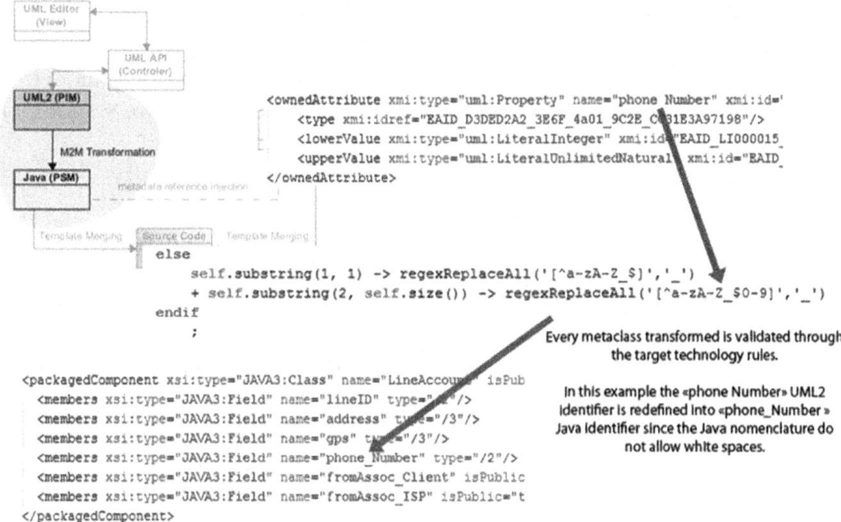
UML Editor (View)
UML API (Controler)
UML2 (PIM)
M2M Transformation
Java (PSM)
metadata reference injection
Template Merging
Source Code
Template Merging
<ownedAttribute xmi:type="uml:Property" name="phone Number" xmi:id='
<type xmi:idref="EAID_D3DED2A2_3E6F_4a01_9C2E_C31E3A97198"/>
<lowerValue xmi:type="uml:LiteralInteger" xmi:id="EAID_LI000015_
<upperValue xmi:type="uml:LiteralUnlimitedNatural" xmi:id="EAID_
</ownedAttribute>
else
self.substring(1, 1) -> regexReplaceAll('[^a-zA-Z_$]','_')
+ self.substring(2, self.size()) -> regexReplaceAll('[^a-zA-Z_$0-9]','_')
endif
;
Every metaclass transformed is validated through the target technology rules.
In this example the «phone Number» UML2 identifier is redefined into «phone_Number» Java identifier since the Java nomenclature do not allow white spaces.
<packagedComponent xsi:type="JAVA3:Class" name="LineAccount" isPub
<members xsi:type="JAVA3:Field" name="lineID" type="/2"/>
<members xsi:type="JAVA3:Field" name="address" type="/3"/>
<members xsi:type="JAVA3:Field" name="gps" type="/3"/>
<members xsi:type="JAVA3:Field" name="phone_Number" type="/2"/>
<members xsi:type="JAVA3:Field" name="fromAssoc_Client" isPublic
<members xsi:type="JAVA3:Field" name="fromAssoc_ISP" isPublic="t
</packagedComponent>

Fig. 6. PSM model construction.

The platform specific model, the PSM, will use the same target language (Java), so it is not necessary to change the existing UML model. Figure 6 shows the PSM model for the FFA application.

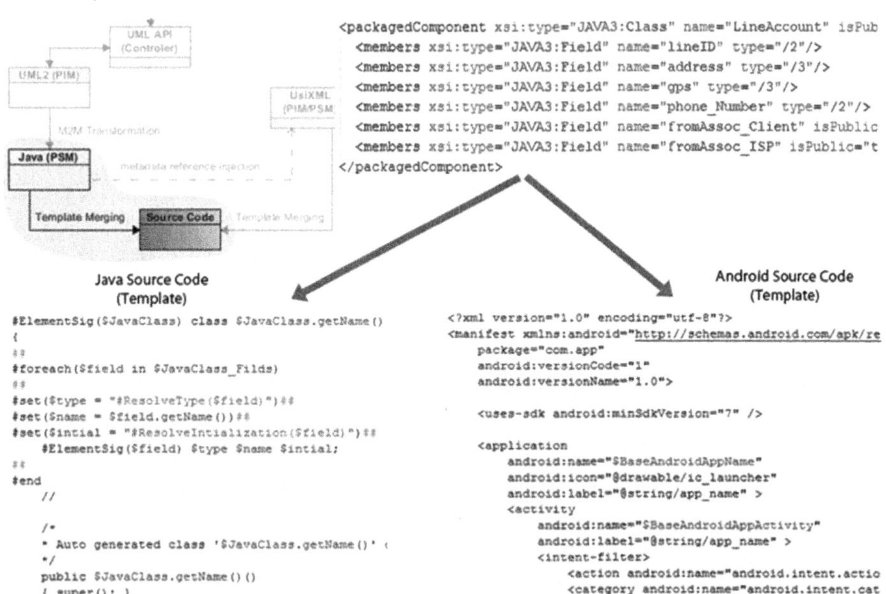
UML API (Controler)
UML2 (PIM)
UsiXML (PIM/PSM)
M2M Transformation
Java (PSM)
metadata reference injection
Template Merging
Source Code
Template Merging
<packagedComponent xsi:type="JAVA3:Class" name="LineAccount" isPub
<members xsi:type="JAVA3:Field" name="lineID" type="/2"/>
<members xsi:type="JAVA3:Field" name="address" type="/3"/>
<members xsi:type="JAVA3:Field" name="gps" type="/3"/>
<members xsi:type="JAVA3:Field" name="phone_Number" type="/2"/>
<members xsi:type="JAVA3:Field" name="fromAssoc_Client" isPublic
<members xsi:type="JAVA3:Field" name="fromAssoc_ISP" isPublic="t
</packagedComponent>
Java Source Code (Template)
#ElementSig($JavaClass) class $JavaClass.getName()
{
##
#foreach($field in $JavaClass_Filds)
##
#set($type = "#ResolveType($field)")##
#set($name = $field.getName())##
#set($intial = "#ResolveIntialization($field)")##
#ElementSig($field) $type $name $intial;
##
#end
//
/*
* Auto generated class '$JavaClass.getName()'
*/
public $JavaClass.getName() ()
{ super(); }
Android Source Code (Template)
<?xml version="1.0" encoding="utf-8"?>
<manifest xmlns:android="http://schemas.android.com/apk/re
package="com.app"
android:versionCode="1"
android:versionName="1.0">
<uses-sdk android:minSdkVersion="7" />
<application
android:name="$BaseAndroidAppName"
android:icon="@drawable/ic_launcher"
android:label="@string/app_name" >
<activity
android:name="$BaseAndroidAppActivity"
android:label="@string/app_name" >
<intent-filter>
<action android:name="android.intent.actio
<category android:name="android.intent.cat

Fig. 7. Source code generation for Java and Android.

Figure 7 illustrates the source code generation for both the Java and Android platforms.

Using the same template's strategy, and starting from a UsiXML model, the source code for the user interface layer is also generated. Figure 8 shows the usage of templates to generate this layer.

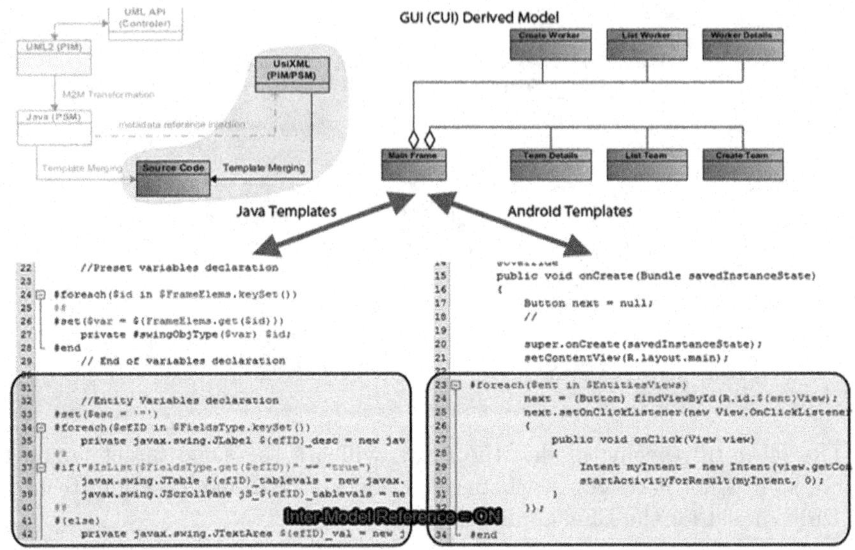

Fig. 8. User interface source code generation for Java and Android.

7 Conclusions

In this paper a model-based tool for hybrid systems development was presented. Through a DSL configuration the MDA SMARTAPP tool can translate abstract models in implementations artefacts for web, hybrid and desktop targets.

This paper described the first results of a model-based tool, MDA SMARTAPP, meant to support highly parameterizable MDA transformation processes. The tool is to be used in the development of business layer and user interface layers of applications that can be reached using mobile apps (in a first approach it is Android specific) or hybrid web browser desktop applications. Specifically, it supports PIM (Platform Independent Model) manipulation, PIM to PSM (Platform Specific Model) transformations, and automatic source code generation for both web and mobile clients. MDA SMARTAPP does the setup of a robust, extensible, and scalable model-based tool architecture where its skeleton is independent from any platform domain, having its main core based on model transformations.

The use of models, and the possibility of having them to parameterize the tool, ensures durability for any software and promote independency on changes of the base software of mobile devices. We presented a case study that covered this process as well as makes it possible to strive new application domains, since the tool can work with new target platforms, such as iOS or other custom fit solutions.

Also, this approach highlighted that with OCL it is possible to create robust and simple (not simpler) transformation processes, with business rules included, allowing us to shape better and target specific models, reducing the need to rearrange the generated lower-lever models.

The use of templates for source code generation allow us to easily reshape models in order to cover all the implementations variations from an original PSM specification. The work reported focused on a first set of components developed for MDA SMARTAPP and proves that highly parameterizable and complex user interface apps for mobile platforms can be specified using well known models and the transformations from models to source code can effectively deliver a ready to deploy product.

Acknowledgments. This work is financed by the ERDF - European Regional Development Fund through the Operational Programme for Competitiveness and Internationalisation - COMPETE 2020 Programme within project POCI-01-0145-FEDER-006961, and by National Funds through the FCT Fundação para a Ciência e a Tecnologia (Portuguese Foundation for Science and Technology) as part of project UID/EEA/50014/2013.

References

1. Altan, G.S.: On the Usability of Triple Graph Grammars for the Transformation of Business Process Models - An Evaluation based on FUJABA. Master's thesis, TU Wien, Austria (2008)
2. de Almeida, P.: MDA - Improving Software Development Productivity in Large-Scale Enterprise Applications. Master's thesis, University of Fribourg, Switzerland (2008)
3. Egyed, A.: Fixing inconsistencies in uml design models. In: Proceedings of the 29th international conference on Software Engineering, ICSE 2007, pp. 292–301. IEEE Computer Society, Washington, DC (2007)
4. Limbourg, Q., Vanderdonckt, J., Michotte, B., Bouillon, L., López-Jaquero, V.: USIXML: a language supporting multi-path development of user interfaces. In: Feige, U., Roth, J. (eds.) DSV-IS 2004 and EHCI 2004. LNCS, vol. 3425, pp. 200–220. Springer, Heidelberg (2005)
5. Ma, K., Yang, B.: A hybrid model transformation approach based on j2ee platform. In: 2010 Second International Workshop on Education Technology and Computer Science (ETCS), vol. 3, pp. 161–164, March 2010
6. Meads, A., Warren, I.: Odintools-model-driven development of intelligent mobile services. In: 2011 IEEE International Conference on Services Computing (SCC), pp. 448–455, July 2011

7. Miller, J., Mukerji, J.: Mda guide version 1.0.1. Technical report, Object Management Group (OMG) (2003)
8. Nickel, U., Niere, J., Zundorf, A.: The fujaba environment. In: Proceedings of the 2000 International Conference on Software Engineering, pp. 742–745 (2000)
9. Object Management Group. Object Constraint Language, v2.0. Technical report, May 2006. http://www.omg.org/cgi-bin/doc?formal/2006-05-01
10. OMG: Meta Object Facility (MOF) Core Specification Version 2.0 (2006)
11. Partners, Q.V.T.: Revised submission for MOF 2.0 Query / Views / Transformations RFP. Technical report, OMG (2003)
12. Schrr, A.: Specification of graph translators with triple graph grammars. In: Mayr, Ernst W., Schmidt, G., Tinhofer, G. (eds.) WG 1994. LNCS, vol. 903. Springer, Heidelberg (1995)
13. Vara, J.M.: M2DAT: a Technical Solution for Model-Driven Development of Web Information Systems. Ph.D. thesis, ETSII, University Rey Juan Carlos, Madrid, Spain, November 2009
14. Vaupel, S., Taentzer, G., Harries, J.P., Stroh, R., Gerlach, R., Guckert, M.: Model-driven development of mobile applications allowing role-driven variants. In: Dingel, J., Schulte, W., Ramos, I., Abrahão, S., Insfran, E. (eds.) MODELS 2014. LNCS, vol. 8767, pp. 1–17. Springer, Heidelberg (2014)

Modeling the Reliability of Man-Machine Systems with Sequential Interaction Gate

Bo Wang[1(✉)], Hong Yuan[2], Shujie Tian[2], Changhua Jiang[1], and Li Wang[1]

[1] National Key Laboratory of Human Factors Engineering, Astronaut Research and Training Center of China, Beijing 100094, China
{wowbob,jch08,wanglee}@139.com

[2] School of Mechanical Engineering, Xi'an Jiaotong University, Xi'an 710000, China
{yuanhong0624,sjtian}@139.com

Abstract. The reliability of man-machine system (MMS) depends upon the sequential interactions of the components. Conventional methods cannot take into account the dynamic evolution of the sequential interactions. Hence we propose a novel gate, sequential interaction gate, to model interactions in the MMS. The sequential interaction gate can graphically and mathematically address the sequential interactions in an adequate way to demonstrate interactive chains leading to the MMS's failure. An application case is given to show the validity of the proposed method.

Keywords: Man-machine system · Reliability · Sequential interaction

1 Introduction

The man-machine in this paper refers to a closed-loop control system comprising a machine and an actively participating human operator. For a man-machine system (MMS), unwanted occurrences should be reduced to the minimum. To achieve this goal the reliability of the MMS must be taken into account.

The reliability of the MMS has long served as a compelling target for reliability theory explanations. While many theoretical attempts have been found wanting, some classical theory concepts have been put forward. In the traditional view, the reliability of a MMS (RS) is the series of the machine's reliability (RM) and human's reliability (RH), and hence RS = RM • RH, where RM and RH are statistically independent.

Nevertheless, a typical characteristic of the MMS is interactive; hence it depends on the joint functioning of humans and machines [1, 2].

A simple MMS for instance is shown in Fig. 1.

The controller is operated by the human, and there is a controller monitor in the control system. When the human makes an error, the monitor will instantly detect and then let the controller refuse to perform or ring an alarm. If human error occurs, and the monitor sequentially fails, as a consequence, the MMS will fail.

The reliability of that system depends as much upon the sequential interactions as on the characteristics of the components. Conventional reliability analysis of the MMS, such as the Failure Mode and Effects Analysis (FMEA), Fault Tree Analysis (FTA),

M. Kurosu (Ed.): HCI 2016, Part I, LNCS 9731, pp. 535–541, 2016.
DOI: 10.1007/978-3-319-39510-4_49

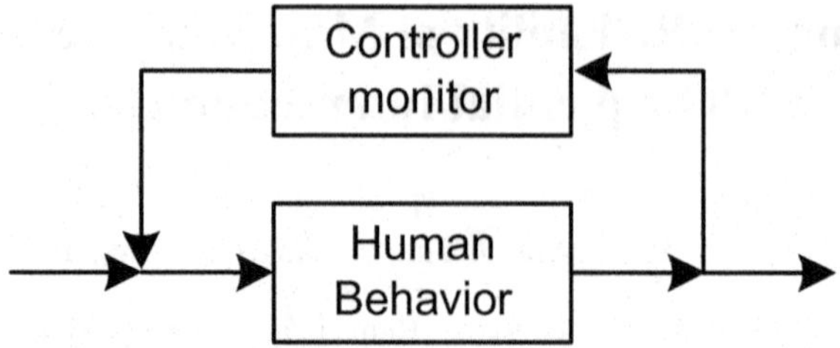

Fig. 1. A MMS example with controller monitor

Systematic Human Error Reduction and Prediction Approach (SHERPA) [3, 4], Cognitive Reliability and Error Analysis Method (CREAM) [5], Technique for Human Error Rate Prediction (THERP) [6], which separately consider the influence of humans and machines in the MMS, cannot take into account the dynamic evolution of the sequential interactions, methods are consequently needed which can address the sequential interactions in an adequate way to restrict the analysis to what actually happens.

However, few studies have met the requirements of adequately addressing the sequential interactions of the MMS.

Yagoda and Coovert [7] and Liu and Wang [8], with the aid of the Petri nets and Markov, provide methods to analyze the reliability of a MMS, which involve man-machine interactions. As is known to all, the exponential explosion is the main limitation for both the Petri nets and Markov. And, it's difficult to predict potential accident sequences in a safety-critical MMS so that vulnerable points can be disclosed and removed [9]. In addition, Petri nets and Markov model do not own a flexible, modular, intuitively structure, which cannot be constructed incrementally.

Conventional reliability analysis techniques cannot be applied directly and accurately to analyze the MMS. Therefore, we propose a sequential-interaction-gate-based model (SIGM), extended from our previous works [10, 11], for the reliability analysis of the MMS.

The proposed model is a formal approach to model the reliability of MMS as algebraic representation. It can provide reliability evaluation information to aid in the choice of different alternatives for man-machine interactions. During the operating state of a system, the model can also provide reliability information to improve system reliability.

2 Sequential-Interaction-Gate-Based Model

A main restrictive assumption in FTA is that basic events must be assumed to be statistically independent, and their interactions are depicted by means of Boolean OR/AND gates, so that only the combination of events is concerned, and not their dynamic interactions or sequences.

Those static gates cannot be applied directly and accurately for the MMS reliability; hence we provide a novel gate, sequential interaction gate (SIG), to model interactions in the MMS.

In this section, we recall the conventional static gates at first. Then, we define the SIG and put forward the SIG-based reliability qualitative analysis model.

2.1 Conventional Static Gates

The AND gate (with symbol .) and OR (with symbol +) gate with 2 events A and B are shown in Fig. 2. The AND gate occurs if all of the events occur, the OR gate occurs if at least one of the events occurs.

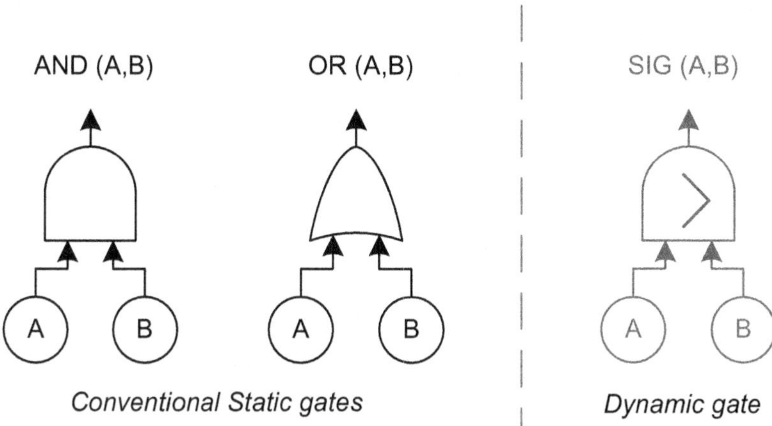

Fig. 2. Different gates in the SIGM

2.2 Sequential Interaction Gate (SIG)

The SIG (with symbol >) with 2 events A and B is also shown in Fig. 2. Events attached to a SIG must occur in the sequence that they appear from left to right in the graphical

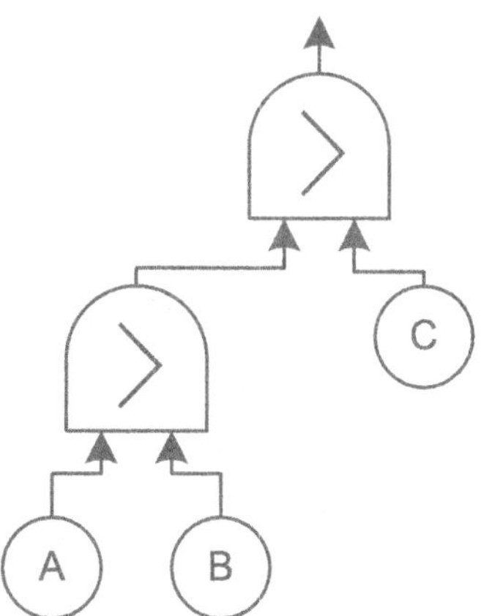

Fig. 3. Cascading SIGs

representation. As a consequence, in the case of a SIG with 2 events as showed in Fig. 2, A and B must occur and A must occur before B for the SIG to occur, which noted as A > B.

To represent the behavior that A occurs before B which occurs before C, the SIGs can be cascaded as showed in Fig. 3, which noted as (A > B) > C.

Fundamental theorems which allow developing and simplifying the algebraic representation of the cascading SIGs are defined.

- *RULE*1 $A.B \rightarrow A > B + B > A$
- *RULE*2 $(A + B) > C \rightarrow A > C + B > C$
- *RULE*3 $(A > B) > C \rightarrow A > B > C$
- *RULE*4 $A > (B > C) \rightarrow A > B > C + B > A > C$

The whole theorems and proofs can be found in our previous work [11].

3 Application

We propose modeling sequential interactions in a MMS which is depicted in Fig. 4.

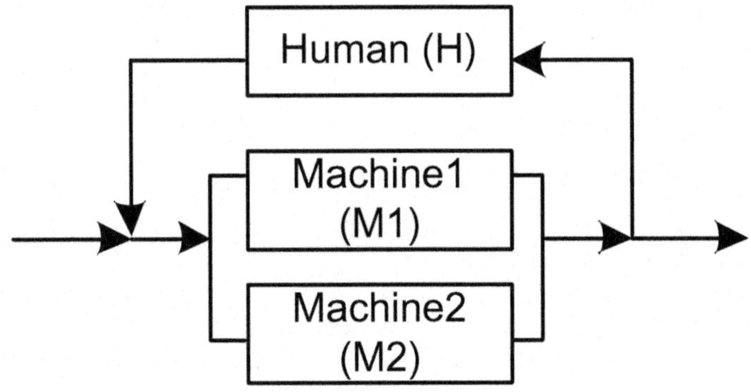

Fig. 4. An automatic, interactive MMS

There're two machines, M1 and M2, performing the control function. If M1 or M2 malfunctions, M2 or M1 can instantly detect it and will perform the correct instruction. The human monitors those two machines running conditions.

Therefore, if those two machines both fail, and the human sequentially makes error, as a consequence, the MMS will fail. Thus, the SIG-based model for the MMS is shown in Fig. 5.

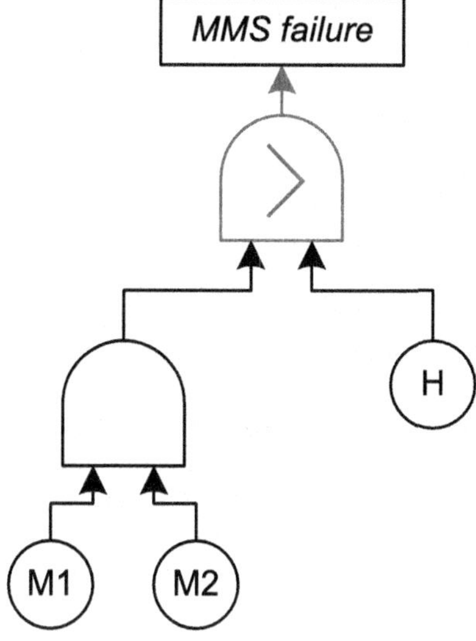

Fig. 5. The initial SIG-based model for the MMS

According to Rule 1, the equivalent model is shown in Fig. 6.

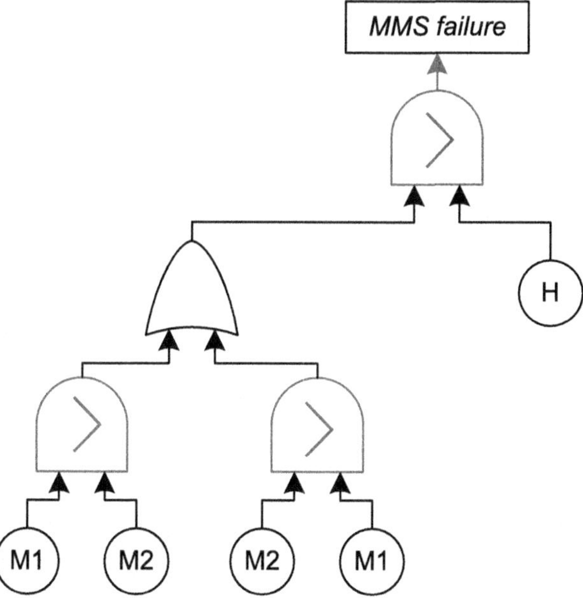

Fig. 6. The equivalent SIG-based model for the MMS

Significantly, the MMS with sequential interactions cannot be modeled exactly using usual techniques because the system failure criteria cannot be expressed in terms of combinations of basic events, all using the same time frame. The SIG-based models in Figs. 5 and 6 can distinctly and intuitively indicate interactions and sequences that may lead to the system's failure.

Further, we simplify the algebraic representation of the model as follows,

$$
\begin{aligned}
&\mathrm{SIG}(\mathrm{AND}(\mathrm{M1}, \mathrm{M2}), \mathrm{H}) \\
&\quad \to \mathrm{M1.M2} > \mathrm{H} \\
&\quad \to (\mathrm{M1} > \mathrm{M2} + \mathrm{M2} > \mathrm{M1}) > \mathrm{H} \qquad \mathit{RULE}1 \\
&\quad \to (\mathrm{M1} > \mathrm{M2}) > \mathrm{H} + (\mathrm{M2} > \mathrm{M1}) > \mathrm{H} \; \mathit{RULE}2 \\
&\quad \to \mathrm{M1} > \mathrm{M2} > \mathrm{H} + \mathrm{M2} > \mathrm{M1} > \mathrm{H}
\end{aligned}
$$

As shown in Fig. 7, M1 > M2 > H indicates that M1, M2 and H fail according to their positions in the expression, namely, M1 fails first, M2 fails next and H fails last, as a consequence, the MMS fails. This expression combines human and machine as a whole, and demonstrates interactive chains leading to the MMS's failure. In practice, cutting off the failure chain can, in some degree, reduce the failure of the MMS.

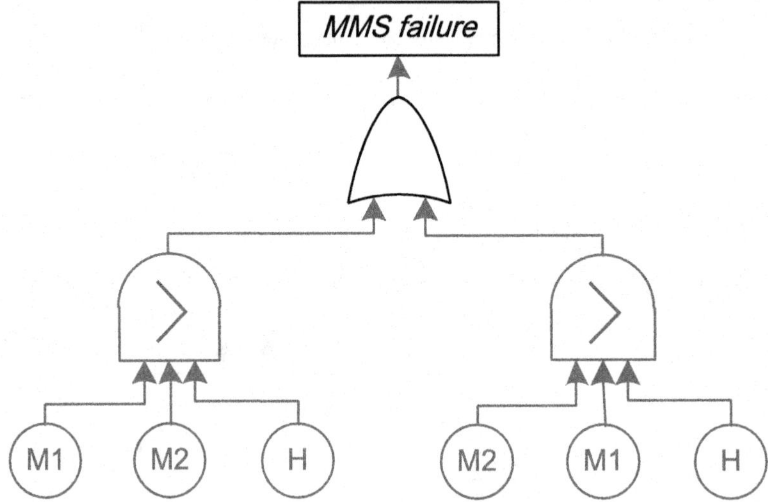

Fig. 7. The equivalent SIG-based simplification model for the MMS

4 Conclusion

This paper presents a novel method to analyze the MMS reliability using sequential interaction gate. The method is a new qualitative way that extends the existing the MMS reliability analysis models. Further quantitative analysis can be done to obtain the occurrence probability.

Acknowledgments. This work was supported by the foundation of National Key Laboratory of Human Factors Engineering, Grant NO. HF 2012-Z-B-05.

References

1. Hollnagel, E.: The reliability of man-machine interaction. Reliab. Eng. Syst. Saf. **38**(1–2), 81–89 (1992)
2. Hougaard, P.C., Hollnagel, E., Kjaer-Hansen, et al.: Fault identification in dynamic man-machine interaction. In: International Conference on Systems, Man and Cybernetics, pp. 387–391, 17–20 October 1993
3. Embrey, D.E.: SHERPA: a systematic human error reduction and prediction approach. In: Proceedings of the International Topical Meeting on Advances in Human Factors in Nuclear Power Systems (1986)
4. Harris, D., Stanton, N.A., Marshall, A., et al.: Using SHERPA to predict design-induced error on the flight deck. Aerosp. Sci. Technol. **9**(6), 525–532 (2005)
5. Hollnagel, E.: Cognitive Reliability and Error Analysis Method (CREAM), vol. 1. Elsevier, Amsterdam (1998)
6. Boring, R.L.: Fifty years of THERP and human reliability analysis. In: Proceedings of the Probabilistic Safety Assessment and Management and European Safety and Reliability Conference (PSAM 2011 and ESREL 2012) (2012)
7. Yagoda, R., Coovert, M.D.: Modeling human-robot interaction with petri-nets. In: 53rd Human Factors and Ergonomics Society Annual Meeting, San Antonio, TX, United States, 19–23 October 2009
8. Liu, C.M., Wang, A.H.: Reliability model of a man-machine system with human errors and its applications. J. Chin. Inst. Eng. **21**(2), 149–158 (1998)
9. Kontogiannis, T., Leopoulos, V., Marmaras, N.: Comparison of accident analysis techniques for safety-critical man-machine systems. Int. J. Ind. Ergon. **25**(4), 327–347 (2000)
10. Wang, B., Jiang, C.H., Wang, L., et al.: Universal probabilistic analysis for cut sequences in dynamic fault trees. In: Proceedings of 2014 10th International Conference on Reliability, Manta ability and Safety, pp. 741–745, Guangzhou, China, 6–8 August 2014
11. Wang, B., Li, Y., Xing, W.Y., Liu, D.: Algebraic modeling for dynamic gates in dynamic fault trees. In: International Conference on Mechanical and Aerospace Engineering, pp. 573–577, Paris, France, 7–8 July 2012

Development Methods and Techniques

AGILUS: A Method for Integrating Usability Evaluations on Agile Software Development

Renan Cavichi de Freitas[1(✉)], Luiz Antonio Rodrigues Jr.[1], and Adilson Marques da Cunha[2]

[1] Instituto Federal de Sao Paulo, Caraguatatuba, Brazil
{renancavichi,lrodrigues}@ifsp.edu.br
[2] Instituto Tecnologico Da Aeronautica, Sao Jose Dos Campos, Brazil
cunha@ita.br

Abstract. This paper presents a method for integrating usability evaluations on agile software development aiming to improve software quality and user satisfaction. The proposed method uses three different usability evaluations and user-centered design techniques, during the agile development process with the Scrum framework. The main results are presented in analyses and discussions about the use of the method on the development of two case studies: a Socio-pedagogical Monitoring System and an Event Management System.

Keywords: Integration of HCI and agile methods · Usability evaluation · Agile development · Scrum framework

1 Introduction

Agile methods have been used in Software Engineering as an alternative to tackle high rates of failure and project delays [1]. To improve software usability quality, new approaches have been studied to integrate User-Centered Design and Agile Development.

Previous studies [2–5] discuss approaches that aims to integrate usability evaluations on agile software development. In a first approach, Sy uses the parallel tracks of development technique to ensure that those responsible for implementation receive a prototype of interfaces with usability already evaluated.

In a second approach, Sy adopts the prototyping interfaces technique to refine interaction projects. Both approaches are also observed by Silva da Silva.

Crispin and Gregory use prototype evaluation methods to help teams to understand every system requirement, before starting source-code implementations and usability evaluation with users, to observe them in real use cases of the system.

Lars Nielsen uses heuristic evaluation to verify developed features implementation in each iteration.

This work presents the results obtained from a master degree research aiming to investigate, implement, and apply a method for usability evaluations on agile software development with Scrum framework [5], mainly to improve product quality and user satisfaction.

M. Kurosu (Ed.): HCI 2016, Part I, LNCS 9731, pp. 545–552, 2016.
DOI: 10.1007/978-3-319-39510-4_50

The proposed method, named AGILUS, was created based on the Agile Manifesto principles and values [7]. It uses usability evaluation methods and user-centered design techniques, both integrated to Scrum framework development process. In order to verify the AGILUS effectiveness, two case studies were performed, as well as some analyses and discussions.

Section 2 delimits the proposed method application scope on the agile development main stages. Section 3 describes the AGILUS mainly steps, pointing the objectives of each usability evaluation. Section 4 describes the use of the AGILUS method on agile development process. Section 5 describes two case studies where the method was used. Section 6 presents some analyses and discussions from method application results. Finally, conclusions are presented in Sect. 7.

2 AGILUS Method Application Scope

The AGILUS method scope starts after the Product Backlog definition and finishes when the Product Owner (PO) validates the software product increments, supported by the results of usability tests, involving representative system users.

Figure 1 highlights the AGILUS application method scope at the main agile development phases.

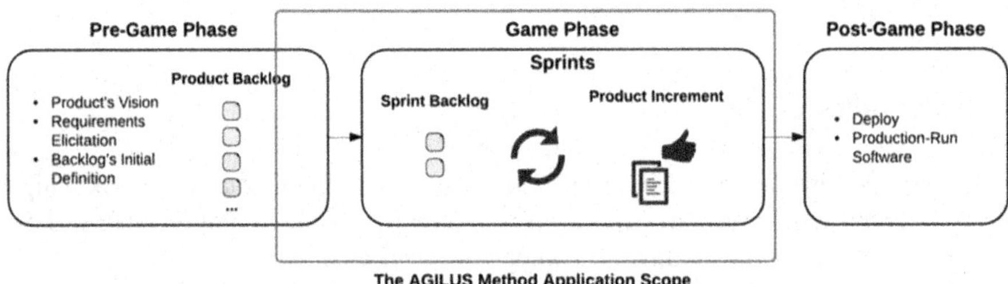

Fig. 1. The AGILUS method scope on agile development mainly phases

Thereby, usability evaluations that may be applied at the initial phases of the Pre-Game, such as Product's Vision, Requirements Elicitation, and Backlog's Initial Definition are out of the proposed method scope.

The Post-Game phase activities of the agile development process, which involves usability evaluations on production environment, are also out of scope.

3 Main AGILUS Method Steps

The proposed method, named AGILUS, is composed of three main steps, with three distinct and complementary usability evaluations adapted to the agile development, as shown in Fig. 2.

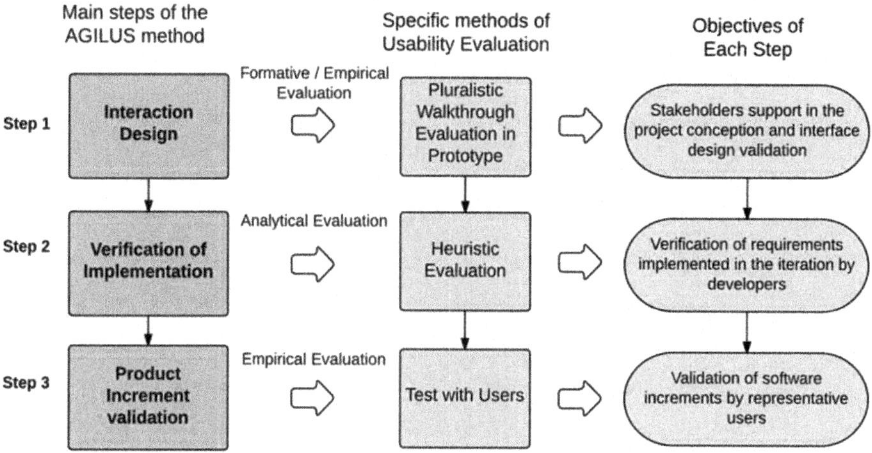

Fig. 2. The AGILUS method steps, usability evaluations and their objectives

The Pluralistic Walkthrough Evaluation in Prototype is responsible for the validation of Interaction Design in the initial step, where prototypes of interfaces are designed. We adopt this formative and empirical method to involve different stakeholders, including representative users in the evaluation. Thus, different project viewpoints contribute to the interaction design validation, that will be implemented in a parallel track of development.

The evaluation based on heuristics of usability, defined in the second step of the AGILUS method, is an analytical and exploratory testing to verify if implemented product increments meet usability principles.

As a final evaluation to support the validation of product increments, the Test with Users, defined in the third and final step of the proposed method, aims to measure the quality of usability as its efficiency, effectiveness, and user satisfaction.

4 AGILUS Method on Agile Development Process

This section aims to increase the understanding of the AGILUS method by identifying its steps on agile development with Scrum framework.

Figure 3 presents an overview of the agile development process where Scrum framework events were separated from the AGILUS method steps.

The first step of the AGILUS Method is the application of the Pluralistic Walkthrough Evaluation in Prototype. This evaluation must occur in at least one iteration before the implementation of a priority requirement, using the parallel tracks development technique of interaction design and implementation.

At the beginning of the project, the Pluralistic Walkthrough Evaluation should occur even in the Pre-Game Phase, after the initial prioritization of the Product Backlog.

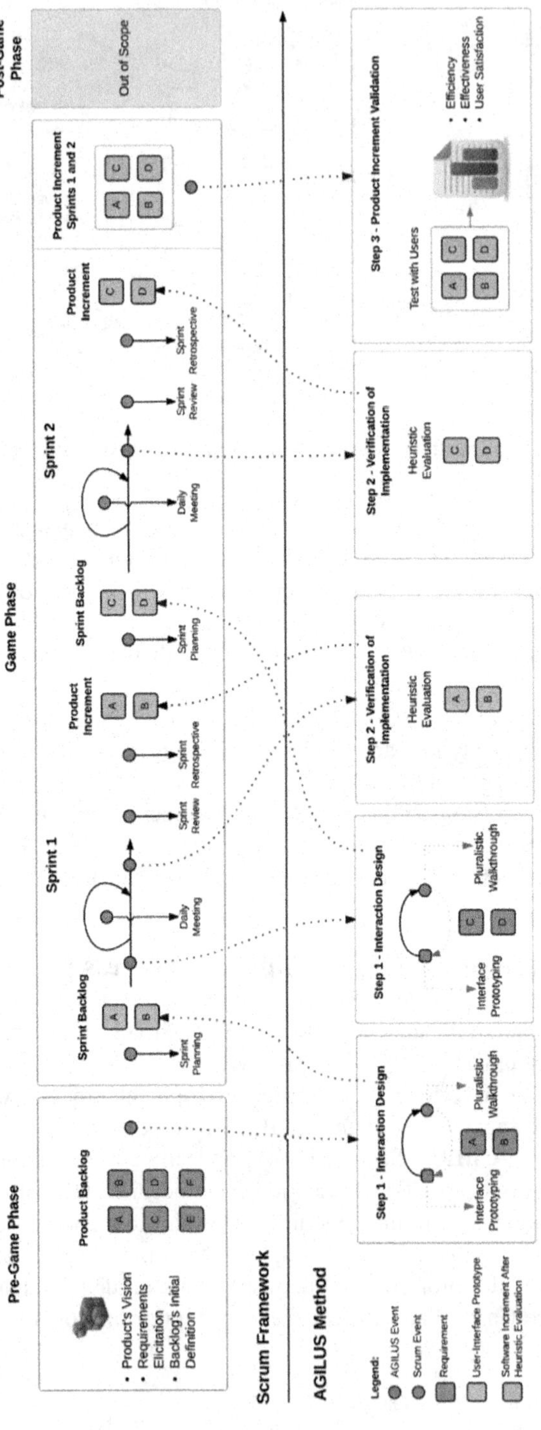

Fig. 3. The AGILUS method on agile development process with scrum

The User-Interface Prototyping and the Pluralistic Walkthrough Evaluation may occur in more than one cycle, refining the prototype until the Interaction Design is approved by the PO.

The approved prototype goes to the next Sprint Backlog, to be developed during the Sprint. As the developers begin coding the requirements, part of the team, responsible for the Interaction Design, starts in parallel, the prototyping of priority requirements interfaces, which are candidates to be implemented in the next Sprint, if any.

After code implementation, on the second step of the AGILUS method, the Implementation is verified by Heuristic Evaluation, before the end of the Sprint, as part of the definition of "Done".

Usability problems identified from Heuristic Evaluation should be resolved in the remaining time of the Sprint and before the Sprint Review. If the time for solutions implementation is insufficient, within the Sprint time, new usability requirements should be added to the Product Backlog, to be prioritized by the PO and, if possible, implemented in the next Sprint.

Likewise, sequentially, the following Sprints receive interfaces approved prototype, developed in the previous Sprint and, after its implementation, performs a Heuristic Evaluation.

After some Sprints or the development of a critical requirement for the project success, the PO must request a usability evaluation by Test with Users, as the third method step. In this evaluation to assess whether any usability problem was identified, one should measure the efficiency, effectiveness, and user satisfaction to evaluate the quality of the software usability.

As shown in Sect. 3, the Post-Game Phase is out of the AGILUS application scope.

5 Case Studies

To verify the usability quality of the developed software with the application of the AGILUS method, two case studies were conducted: A Socio-pedagogical Monitoring System (SMS); and an Event Management System (EMS), both developed for an educational institution.

These projects have been developed as follows: two weeks for the initial phase, two iterations of three weeks for development, and other two weeks for Tests with Users, involving six developers as volunteers from each team and twenty users also as volunteers being tested from each project.

To measure the usability of the developed systems, the following metrics were used: tasks runtime to measure efficiency; error and completion rate to measure effectiveness; and the System Usability Scale (SUS) [8] to measure user satisfaction.

Systems development were performed, as illustrated in Fig. 3. In each system, six tasks were set to perform the Test with Users in the final step of AGILUS method. For each task, it was measured its task runtime, error and completion rate, and, at the end of the test, the users were invited to answer the SUS questionnaire.

6 Analyses and Discussion of Results

In the Pluralistic Walkthrough Evaluation in Prototype step, significant results on improving projects usability were achieved:

- The diversity of viewpoints and opinions contributing to discussions;
- The product's vision maturation;
- The improvements on interaction design; and
- During discussions, the new user needs raising from those involved, being transformed into requirements. Therefore, the evaluation also has contributed to the new requirements elicitation.

The main detected difficulties on implementing the Pluralistic Walkthrough were:

- To find available schedule among the participants to undertake evaluations;
- The reduced number of tasks and the simplicity of user interfaces, in one evaluation have generated few improvements, becoming unproductive, considering the effort to bring stakeholders together;
- Discussions often have dispersed the task scope and demanded the moderator intervention to focus on its objectives; and
- Some users had to be encouraged by the moderator, during the test, in order to contribute with their opinions.

Considering the benefits and difficulties presented in this first step of the proposed method, it can be inferred that, whenever possible, the maximum of prioritized User Stories must be included in a Pluralistic Walkthrough Evaluation in Prototype without exceeding meeting time. Thus, a reduction in the number of meetings involving stakeholders has contributed to increase the AGILUS method efficiency.

The Heuristic Evaluation, the second AGILUS method step, was the evaluation that most allowed to identify usability problems with respect to: effort; number of involved persons; and evaluation time.

The main benefits noticed from this step highlighted:

- The deep exploration of software functionalities;
- The verification of several errors possibilities and system status feedbacks; and
- Standards consistency.

The main difficulties found were dependencies of expertise, skill, and experience from evaluators.

As the main empirical method for usability evaluation of the AGILUS method, the Test with Users, applied in the third step of each project at the end of the Game phase, aimed to measure the quality of usability and to identify problems by observing real system users performing software tasks.

Figure 4 shows the obtained results from the two case studies with average values of: 85 % and 84 % of efficiency, based on task runtime; 92 % and 85 % of effectiveness, based on the error rate; 98 % and 99 % of effectiveness, based on the completion rate; and 86 and 88 of SUS scores, for user satisfaction. These SUS scores results were considered "excellent", according to the grid interpretation from Sauro [9].

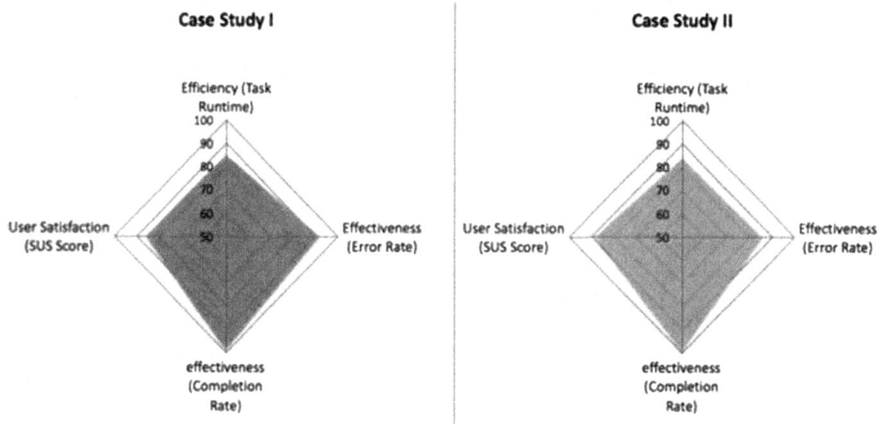

Fig. 4. The two case studies main results

7 Conclusion

Regarding usability quality and user satisfaction, from the two case studies, where the AGILUS method was applied, some significant results were obtained.

The main difficulties found from those two case studies were related to the application of the Pluralistic Walkthrough in Prototype method considering: the availability of those involved participants to arrange meetings; and the moderator need, to keep the participants focused on discussions of task goals, and to encourage them to give opinions during the test.

Depending on the achieved results with the application of the AGILUS method, the authors of this research believe that the proposed method can be successfully applied also in other knowledge domains involving the agile software development.

The authors also believe that, with few adaptations, the AGILUS method can be adopted by other agile development methods, besides the Scrum framework, providing software usability quality and user satisfaction.

Acknowledgments. The authors of this paper thank to the Federal Institute of Education, Science and Technology of Sao Paulo and to the Brazilian Aeronautics Institute of Technology, for accepting their challenges of innovation and for supporting the two case studies.

References

1. Standish Group International. The chaos manifesto (2013)
2. Sy, D.: Adapting usability investigations for agile user – centered design. J. Usability Stud. **2** (3), 112–132 (2007)
3. Silva da Silva, T., et al.: User-centered design and agile methods: a systematic review. In: Agile Conference, Salt Lake City, Proceedings, pp. 77–86. IEEE Computer Society, Washington, DC (2011)

4. Crispin, L., Gregory, J.: Agile testing: a practical guide for testers and agile teams. Addison-Wesley, Boston (2009)
5. Nielsen, L.L.: Usability requirements in agile development processes. Dissertation (Master in Science) – Technical University of Denmark, DTU Informatics and Mathematical Modeling, Lyngby (2011)
6. Schwaber, K., Sutherland, J.: Scrum Guide (2014)
7. Agile Manifesto. Manifesto for agile software development (2001)
8. Jeffries, R., et al.: User interface evaluation in the real world: a comparison of four techniques. In: SIGCHI Conference on Human Factors in Computing Systems, Proceedings, pp. 119–124. ACM, New York (1991)
9. Sauro, J.: A Practical Guide to the System Usability Scale: Background, Benchmarks & Best Practices. Create Space, Denver (2011)

Lean Communication-Centered Design: A Lightweight Design Process

Daniel V.C. Ferreira(✉) and Simone D.J. Barbosa

Departamento de Informática, PUC-Rio, Rio de Janeiro, Brazil
{dferreira,simone}@inf.puc-rio.br

Abstract. Lean Communication-Centered Design (LeanCCD) is a human-computer interaction (HCI) design process, which consists of conducting a workshop, detailing user goals, combining interaction models with paper sketches, and testing them with users, supported by guides and templates. This study adapted the Communication-Centered Design (CCD) and the eXtreme Communication-Centered Design (eXCeeD), other communication-centered design processes grounded in Semiotic Engineering (SemEng). SemEng defines user-system interaction as a computer-mediated communication process between designers and users. Approaches and processes based on SemEng are not used to directly yield the answer to a problem, but to increase the problem-solver's understanding of the problem itself and the implication that understanding brings about. Process evaluation in a case study, in the industry, proved itself difficult, both in carrying out LeanCCD activities and in the correct application of some techniques and concepts. However, unlike eXCeeD, we were able to observe a systematic use of support questions that contributed to the designers' reflection, aided by the proposed templates and guides.

Keywords: Agile design · Agile UX · Semiotic Engineering · Human-computer interaction · Communication-centered design · User Experience · Design methods for interactive software

1 Introduction

Human-Computer Interaction (HCI) is a field that studies the design and use of computer technology, especially the interaction between computers and people. Recently, several segments of the Brazilian industry have invested in HCI activities by hiring in-house experts and adjusting their business processes [1]. However, the low maturity in HCI, organizational culture, and the growing popularity of Agile Software Development (ASD) have reduced design time and decreased the odds of conducting research with end users [2].

To deal with these obstacles, many design practitioners have adopted solution-focused approaches aimed at synthesis. These approaches promote the definition and construction of solutions in short design cycles, increasing the understanding of the problem through the evaluation of candidate solutions. They are mostly adaptations to design approaches that leverage synthesis, analysis and evaluation [3, 4].

M. Kurosu (Ed.): HCI 2016, Part I, LNCS 9731, pp. 553–564, 2016.
DOI: 10.1007/978-3-319-39510-4_51

In 2007, Aureliano proposed eXCeeD – an adaptation of a Communication-centered Design approach that combined eXtreme Programming (XP) values with a streamlined HCI design process grounded in Semiotic Engineering (SemEng).

Communication-centered design approaches emerged as "an attempt to ensure that the domain concepts to be communicated to users are well represented and understood by every team member before proceeding to later design stages" [5].

In this approach, the search for understanding is supported by expressions used by the users when they interact with help systems (e.g.: "How do I do this?") [5]. Knowledge representation happens by building models that represent the interaction as a conversation between users and the system [6].

This study aimed to adapt eXCeeD, following its proponents' recommendations, and to contribute and increase the understanding of the communication-centered process. In order to achieve this goal, we observed the process adoption on a project in a corporate software development environment.

Among the suggested changes to eXCeeD, we can list: properly enabling the participants to carry out the activities, including an initial stage dedicated to user research and task analysis, besides investigating the explicit use of eXCeeD's questions to support semi-structured interviews with users and the study of the adoption of interaction models and regular notes.

Among many challenges of a study like this, we focus our discussion on the differences between a process like LeanCCD as proposed and how it is followed in practice. This discussion motivates us to reflect on how methodical (or not) such a process should be [7]. It also invites us to reflect on the designers' difficulties to follow prescribed procedures and to adopt specific techniques, particularly when they are not related to their previous experiences [8].

In the next section, we briefly present and compare the communication-centered approaches to interactive software design. In the third section, we present LeanCCD by detailing the adjustments made to eXCeeD. Next, we describe the case study that applied LeanCCD and a summary of the findings. Finally, we discuss some of these findings, concluding with some remarks and directions for future work.

2 Communication-Centered Design Processes

The CCD authors believe that in order to design the human-computer interaction, it is necessary to facilitate communication among designers to create a shared understanding of the domain and how the application should support users in that domain [9]. Communication-centered processes make use of questions used to build help systems [10] in order to capture this knowledge. On the other hand, design is achieved using MoLIC interaction models, among other representations.

A major contribution of SemEng to the HCI field was the proposal of a communicability evaluation method, representing breakdowns in the user-system communication (for instance, "I can do otherwise."). Silveira [10] used them to define expressions to access help systems (for instance, "Is there another way to do this?"). These expressions evolved in eXCeeD for questions that assist semi-structured interviews with users (for instance, “In what other ways would you {need/like} to do this?”).

With regard to the models, MoLIC has been used as a shared representation with two distinct goals: to represent the communication between the users and the designer (represented by the user interface, at interaction time) and to promote communication among members of the design team (at design time). The language proposes the creation of three representations: a model of user goals, an interaction model, and a conceptual sign schema.

Studies with MoLIC form the basis for the knowledge related to the adoption of CCD. eXCeeD, assuming that such an approach would generate extensive documentation and in order to adapt it to the development using eXtreme Programming [11], distributed activities, initially arranged in a waterfall model in the CCD, into design and development cycles.

Each cycle starts with prioritizing and detailing a user goal or a set of user’s goals. Then, the designers define the user interface and the system interaction through a combination of interaction models and user interface paper sketches. Finally, they evaluate the candidate solution with end users, using a technique called paper prototyping [12]. Figure 1 shows a summary of eXCeeD.

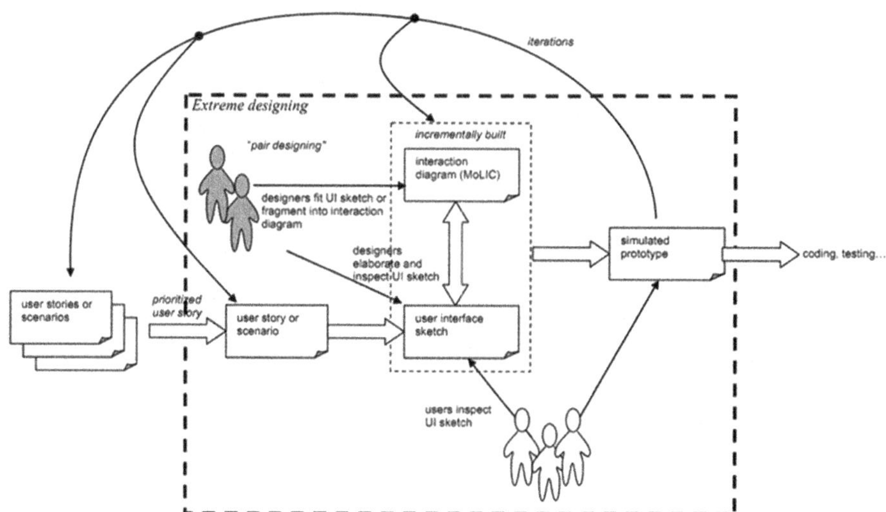

Fig. 1. Graphic summary from LeanCCD’s steps and activities

A case study evaluated the adoption of eXCeeD on a small project in an academic environment. The results pointed out a lack of understanding of the users’ needs during the description of the user goals, and the incorrect application of paper prototyping as defined by Snyder [12]. During interaction and interface modeling, disagreement among designers have resulted in the abandonment of both MoLIC diagrams and regular notes, weakening the conclusions regarding to the light documentation maintenance proposed by the process. Throughout the study, the designers did not use the questions explicitly, although subsequent tests have shown that designers addressed many of them intuitively.

3 Lean Communication-Centered Design

Based on the understanding reached by the evaluation of eXCeeD, we dedicate this section to describe how LeanCCD has responded to the study recommendations. In this proposal, the process can be summarized graphically in Fig. 2.

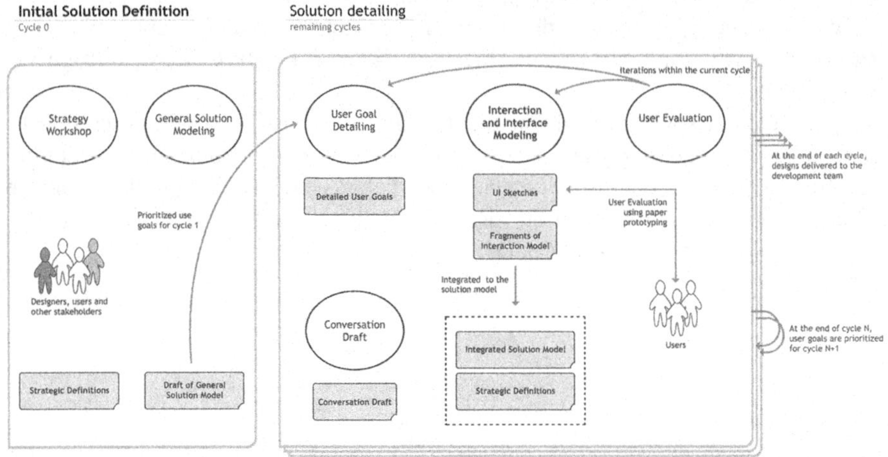

Fig. 2. Graphic summary from LeanCCD's steps and activities

- Enabling the participants to carry out the activities:

Due to the problems of carrying out some eXCeeD activities as proposed, we invested in defining ways of presenting the process by creating guides that supported the application of each activity. We also made a presentation to the participants before the case study that evaluated the LeanCCD. Then, both participants and the researcher practiced some LeanCCD activities on a dummy project.

- Include an initial step for the analysis of users and their tasks

Motivated by the lack of knowledge of the users' needs indicated by the study that evaluated eXCeeD, we included a brief preliminary analysis of users and their tasks in an initial cycle. The activities proposed by eXCeeD were accommodated in a step called "Solution Detailing," which is repeated in every cycle except the first, which happens in a step called "Defining an Initial Solution".

The initial cycle (also called cycle 0) proposes to carry out a workshop, – with the participation of users, sponsors, developers and other stakeholders – contextual inquiry and the creation of an initial broad solution model, which represents a preliminary draft of the users' goals and which answers the need for a comprehensive overall view of the solution, a deficiency pointed out by practitioners of agile methods [13]. The workshop is divided into three steps:

1. Product Vision Definition: activity inspired by the product vision statement, popular technique among practitioners of an agile method called Scrum [14]; it succinctly defines the product name, its class of product (e.g.: game, web application, website, portal, etc.), who should use it – with what goals and benefits and what the advantages over its competitor are. Unlike the vision statement, the target audience is divided between primary and secondary and a list of competitors and differentials can be articulated.
2. Target Audience Analysis: it is dedicated to expand the understanding of the primary and secondary target audience – defined in the previous activity. The activity makes use of empathy maps, a technique to promote co-creation, commitment, creativity, and innovation [15]. The goal is to define who these people that fit in that role are; what they do, say, hear, see, think, and feel. Through this reflection, it is possible to identify barriers and opportunities that can be addressed by the solution.
3. Definition of the Designer's Deputy's Profile: the goal is to make explicit the decisions on the communicative approach of a designer's deputy to each role or to a combination of a role and a user profile. The designer's deputy's profile consists of the important utterances, attitudes, posture, tone, dialogue length and the communication channels that the user users to communicate with the system.

After the strategy workshop, the General Solution Modeling is initiated. During the first iteration, LeanCCD proposes that a simplified version of MoLIC represent the overview of the solution from the perspective of a user role. LeanCCD proposes to create a user goals diagram and an interaction model in a single representation [16], unlike the initial strategy of creating MoLIC diagrams [17, 18].

Creating less detailed – or even incomplete – diagrams in the early design stages promotes the designer's reflection on alternative solutions. More elements are added as the interaction specification evolves [19].

At each solution detailing iteration, the designers refine the definitions made in the first stage. They also expand the general solution model, integrating the created interaction model fragments. Thus, the process defines a solution iteratively and incrementally. However, unlike eXCeeD, LeanCCD takes time to an Initial Solution Definition up-front, a common practice to design in agile software development [20].

- Investigate the explicit usage of questions that support conducting interviews with users

The designers have not adopted the questions explicitly in the study that has evaluated eXCeeD. LeanCCD maintained the questions, integrating them in a guide and using sticky notes in bulletin boards as an incentive strategy of their use.

The questions were mostly used during the detailing of user goals. LeanCCD also makes use of the questions proposed by Aureliano in order to detail a set of user goals. However, we propose a User Target Board that groups the questions into categories according to the related topic. Figure 3 shows the questions in the guide for each area where the notes should be posted.

- Investigate the adoption of models and regular notes

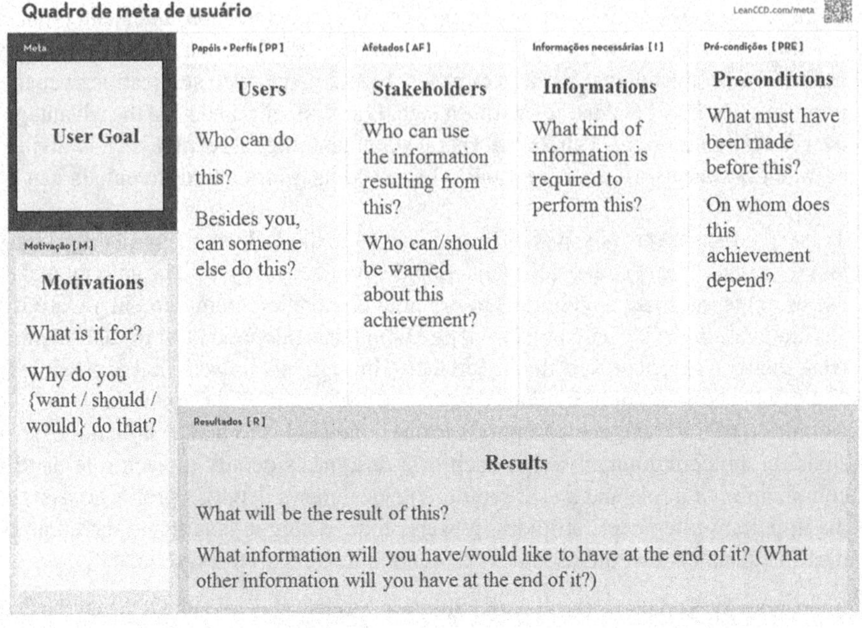

Fig. 3. User's goals detailed guide with questions contained in the respective guide.

The use of MoLIC models that were built in parallel with the user interface sketches is also part of LeanCCD. We kept this strategy as another opportunity to assess the adoption of MoLIC models in streamlined design approaches. We added to the regular notes the use of templates to record the information.

We also decided to propose the creation of conversation sketches, which are examples of conversations arranged in two lanes that represent, respectively, user utterances and system utterances, similar to essential use cases [21]. Instead of representing user intents and system responsibilities, conversation sketches are likely to represent a linearization of a path through a MoLIC interaction model.

The conversation sketches have two main objectives: to assist in the validation of the understanding with stakeholders that do not necessarily know the MoLIC language and to serve as rough sketches of interaction models, enabling the designer to explore alternatives through the simple manipulation of sticky notes.

4 Case Study

We evaluated LeanCCD happened in the software supply division of the Information Technology (IT) department of a multinational energy company. The division has a User Experience Center of Excellence founded with the goal of including HCI design techniques in the company's software development process. The UX Center of Excellence is composed by professionals with graduate degrees in Design, Computing and Psychology.

The study aimed to answer the questions: "How is interaction designed when adopting LeanCCD?" and "How can LeanCCD's evaluation collaborate to expand the understanding about communication-centered design processes?"

The study lasted three days. The first day was devoted to the presentation of the process and a survey of previous experiences of the designers. In the other two days, the researcher observed the designers working on a project that aimed to develop a dashboard that presents metrics of call center tickets of IT solutions. Two stages of evaluation were held, the first one at the end of the strategy workshop and the second one at the end of the project.

As the study aimed to evaluate a process with few participants, we decided to perform a mainly qualitative research, but with some quantitative indicators that offer an overview of the opinions of the participants. The choice of a mixed methods research allows the collection of data through different instruments in order to triangulate the results and to make a more comprehensive discussion about the process.

The evaluation covered the following topics: clarity, usefulness, ease and intention of adopting each process activity. Throughout the assessment, the designers completed a questionnaire by technique, in which they assigned values between 1 (negative extreme) and 7 (positive extreme) for each topic. The researcher also explored the opinions in depth through individual interviews. At last, the evaluation included an

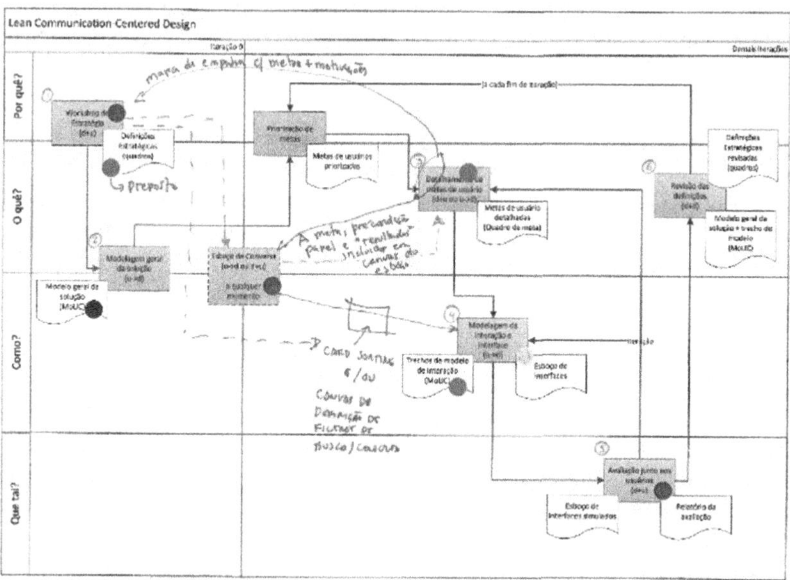

Fig. 4. Graphic summary of LeanCCD stages and activities

evaluation activity in which each participant could assign to the guides of each technique one out of eight stickers representing three strength points, three weak points, one extremely strong point and one extremely weak point of the technique. In the final evaluation, the same amount of stickers was available to attach to a process graphic summary, as presented in Fig. 4.

5 Findings

The main LeanCCD evaluation findings are: the positive assessment of the initial cycle, the difficulty of assessing the general model in a small project, the abandonment of MoLIC models and the subsequent adoption of conversation sketches, besides the explicit use of the questions by combining boards and guides during the detailing of the user goals.

The designers positively evaluated the workshop conclusion, although it was not possible to notice a more active collaboration of users in completing the boards, as intended. Moreover, the definition of the designer's deputy's profile was negatively assessed according to its utility, ease and intent to adopt it.

Given the limited scope of this study, it seems reasonable that the participants did not feel the lack of a representation of the entire solution. However, in order to prioritize and refine a user goal, designers consulted the product vision board. The hypothesis is that the product vision would sum up the solution in a more comprehensive way for small scopes.

The abandonment of MoLIC models – similar to what happened to the study that evaluated eXCeeD – and the designers' argument that the conversation draft is more aligned with a simplified approach raises a concern about the potential of the representation adopted in this study and the reasons and impacts behind the recurrent abandonment of the models.

The combination of boards and guides was an important step to investigate the explicit use of the questions in this study. However, we noticed that there is a small space for reflection within simplified approaches. In addition to that, the construction of the boards with A3 sheets was appointed as a limiting factor to the collaboration between designers and other participants. We suggest that, in future studies, they should be printed or drawn in larger dimensions, such as flipcharts and white boards.

6 Discussion

The findings presented in the previous section make us reflect on which factors influenced the behavior and opinions of the participants in this study. In this section, we will discuss the main factors highlighted, such as the over-theoretical approach adopted, the alignment of the proposal with simplified design processes, and the impacts of the strict sequencing of activities, which may have fostered the perception of an excessively methodical approach.

The perception of clarity on the activities of LeanCCD – expressed by the participating designers – was mainly harmed by the strategy of maintaining theoretical elements of the Semiotic Engineering and of MoLIC as proposed by their authors. Terms like "designer's deputy" and "perlocutionary effect" were not understood or properly interpreted.

This overuse of theory creates issues to be analyzed in future studies: What is the knowledge needed to apply the process, and how can it be transmitted to an HCI design team without prior knowledge of SemEng or MoLIC? How can this knowledge be simplified and be adapted to the language of designers, facilitating their understanding and application?

Since the theory was conceived as academic research, the presentation of Semiotic Engineering concepts – if necessary – should follow a more technical discourse and be more compatible with their interlocutors, designers in the software industry. Successful examples of the technical discussions involving developers can be observed in the research of communicability evaluation methods [22].

Regarding the adoption of models, the analysis of the participants' previous experiences pointed out prototyping as a common practice, but not combined with the construction of interaction models. As we could expect, designers have not adopted the interaction models. Once again, theory overuse may have influenced that decision. However, the participants of the study that have evaluated eXCeeD had an experience with the use of MoLIC and they also abandoned the use of the model. Would this repeated abandonment of MoLIC models on streamlined design processes indicate that the designers only see benefits in using this kind of models in projects with higher complexity?

Proponents of MoLIC pointed out that the main distinction is the representation of the entire system from the point of view of a user role. Although this is a gap of agile methods, the lack of such a representation has not been noticed in studies that have evaluated eXCeeD and LeanCCD.

It is possible to suppose that in streamlined contexts of design, the superficial view provided by the conversation sketches would be sufficient for designers. However, what would the designers lose by abandoning the modeling language or adopting less structured representations?

Further studies may investigate the effectiveness of the conversation sketches to represent the interaction and to analyze which elements from MoLIC would not be represented, and with what impact. The findings could point to the creation of a simplified version of MoLIC or to invest in expanding the use of conversation sketches in processes similar to eXCeeD.

During the final assessment using the process graphic summary, a designer scribbled and suggested changes to the order and combination of activities. This fact may highlight the need of flexibility to accommodate design preferences.

The sequencing of LeanCCD activity was more explicit during the evaluation process (Fig. 4) than in the graphic summary created subsequently (Fig. 2). That may have contributed to the perception of a methodical rigor in the way the process was introduced. Furthermore, the designers' opinions on the use of some techniques, such as the proposal of the designer's deputy profile, support the claim that some activities may have been executed only to fulfill a protocol.

7 Concluding Remarks

This article aims to contribute to an HCI design process that considers the communication between designers and users in the definition of a lightweight design process, the Lean Communication-Centered Design (LeanCCD). Among the main findings of this study were the positive assessment of the proposed initial cycle and the explicit use of the issues by combining boards and guides. However, we saw the non-adoption of MoLIC models – similar to what happened in the evaluation of eXCeeD – and we had difficulty in assessing the overall modeling of the solution due to the reduced scope of the projected system using the LeanCCD.

For future work, we recommend evaluating the general solution modeling in a study of broader scope – or in a less familiar area – and to conduct a few iterations to refine the model. A summary of the information obtained using the supporting questions is an interesting step, but it is necessary that some more comprehensive studies investigate their real use in agile contexts. Finally, they should invest in translating the boards and guides to other languages such as English and Spanish. This could expand the adoption of LeanCCD.

Among the factors that have most influenced the process execution are the theory overuse by the proponents of LeanCCD – indicating the investigation of a simplification of MoLIC and the concepts of SemEng. In addition to that, the rigid sequencing suggested by the graphic summary of the process may have encouraged the interpretation of an overly methodical approach, which goes against the principle of the studies that how designers usually behave [8]. By proposing a new graphic summary of the process activities, we attempted to avoid that impression (Fig. 2).

Giving up a methodical approach entirely implies to assume that we would always have experienced designers, working for companies able to deal with unpredictability, letting go of standardization, traceability and reproducibility, to list a few factors. We hypothesize that this is not a common scenario in which software development takes place in Brazil.

According to [7], "methods seem more like idealizations than prescriptions, and might better be presented as cases or exemplars rather than practical frameworks. This shift reveals the need to present a set of sound examples of how parts of various systems development method can be mixed and matched (perhaps with other, newly invented parts)".

Thus, CCD, eXCeeD, and LeanCCD can be considered examples of how you can adopt a communication-centered approach to the design of interactive systems. Studies such as the one reported in this paper would help to choose the approach to follow, to increase the understanding of the adoption of communication-centered processes.

Therefore, we suggest the interpretation of methodical and non-methodical approaches as extremes of a continuum, which can encourage us to find the balance that motivated the creation of LeanCCD. This balance point should be able to assist inexperienced designers to find design strategies, without losing the flexibility to accommodate individual preferences and to react to situations related to the environment in which these processes take place.

Acknowledgments. Simone D.J. Barbosa thanks CNPq (processes 453996/2014-0, 460627/2014-7, 309828/2015-5) for the financial support to her work. Daniel V. C. Ferreira thanks Petrobras S.A. for the support to his work.

References

1. Viera, A., Martins, S.: 2ª edição do Perfil do Profissional de UX no Brasil. World Usability Day 2013, São Paulo (2013)
2. do Pilar, D.R., Martins, F.: Rewards and Pains: User Research in Brazil User Experience Magazine. http://uxpamagazine.org/rewards-and-pains/
3. Beyer, H., Holtzblatt, K., Baker, L.: An agile customer-centered method: rapid contextual design. In: Zannier, C., Erdogmus, H., Lindstrom, L. (eds.) XP/Agile Universe 2004. LNCS, vol. 3134, pp. 50–59. Springer, Heidelberg (2004)
4. Obendorf, H., Schmolitzky, A., Finck, M.: XPnUE–defining and teaching a fusion of eXtreme programming and usability engineering. In: Proceedings of HCI Educators Workshop, Inventively: Teaching Theory, Design and Innovation in HCI (2006)
5. Silveira, M.S.: Metacomunicação designer-usuário na interação humano-computador (2002)
6. de Paula, M.G., da Silva, B.S., Barbosa, S.D.J.: Using an interaction model as a resource for communication in design. In: CHI 2005 Extended Abstracts on Human Factors in Computing Systems, pp. 1713–1716. ACM, New York (2005)
7. Truex, D., Baskerville, R., Travis, J.: Amethodical systems development: the deferred meaning of systems development methods. Acc. Manag. Inf. Technol. **10**, 53–79 (2000)
8. Cross, N.: Expertise in design: an overview. Des. Stud. **25**, 427–441 (2004)
9. Barbosa, S.D.J., Silveira, M.S., de Paula, M.G., Breitman, K.K.: Supporting a shared understanding of communication-oriented concerns in human-computer interaction: a lexicon-based approach. In: Feige, U., Roth, J. (eds.) EHCI-DSVIS 2004. LNCS, vol. 3425, pp. 271–288. Springer, Heidelberg (2005)
10. Silveira, M.S., Barbosa, S.D.J., de Souza, C.S.: Modelo e arquitetura de sistemas de help online. In: Proceedings of the III Workshop on Human Factors in Computational Systems, IHC, pp. 122–131 (2000)
11. Beck, K.: Extreme Programming Explained: Embrace Change. Addison-Wesley Professional, Boston (2000)
12. Snyder, C.: Paper Prototyping: The Fast and Easy Way to Design and Refine User Interfaces. Morgan Kaufmann, San Francisco (2003)
13. Sy, D., Miller, L.: Optimizing agile user-centred design. In: CHI 2008 Extended Abstracts on Human Factors in Computing Systems, pp. 3897–3900 (2008)
14. Schwaber, K.: Agile Project Management with Scrum. Microsoft Press, Redmond (2004)
15. Gray, D., Brown, S., Macanufo, J.: Gamestorming: A Playbook For Innovators, Rulebreakers, and Changemakers. O'Reilly Media Inc., Sebastapol (2010)
16. Barbosa, S.D.J., da Silva, B.S.: Design da interação humano-computador com MoLIC. Presented at the Companion Proceedings of the 13th Brazilian Symposium on Human Factors in Computing Systems (2014)
17. de Paula, M.G.: Projeto da interação humano-computador baseado em modelos fundamentados na engenharia semiótica: construção de um modelo de interação (2003)
18. Silva, B.S.: MoLIC segunda Edição: revisão de uma linguagem para modelagem da interação humano-computador (2005)

19. Barbosa, S.D.J., de Paula, M.G., de Lucena, C.J.P.: Adopting a communication-centered design approach to support interdisciplinary design teams. Presented at the 26th International Conference on Software Engineering - W1L Workshop "Bridging the Gaps II: Bridging the Gaps Between Software Engineering and Human-Computer Interaction", Edinburgh, UK (2004)
20. da Silva, T.S., Martin, A., Maurer, F., Silveira, M.: User-centered design and agile methods: a systematic review. Presented at the Agile Conference (AGILE), Salt Lake City (2011)
21. Constantine, L.L., Lockwood, L.A.D.: Software for Use: A Practical Guide to the Models and Methods of Usage-Centered Design. Addison-Wesley, New York (1999)
22. de Souza, C.S., Leitão, C.F., Prates, R.O., da Silva, E.J.: The semiotic inspection method. Presented at the Proceedings of VII Brazilian Symposium on Human Factors in Computing Systems (2006)

Multivariate Time Series ELM for Cloud Data Centre Workload Prediction

Salam Ismaeel(✉) and Ali Miri

Department of Computer Science, Ryerson University, Toronto, Canada
{salam.ismaeel,Ali.Miri}@ryerson.ca
http://www.ryerson.ca

Abstract. In existing Cloud Data Centres (CDCs), workload prediction plays an important role in energy conservation, as it allows for dynamic migration and consolidation of Virtual Machines (VMs) which are provisioned on these centres. In this paper, we propose a new multivariate time series Extreme Leaning Machine (ELM) algorithm, and use it in an efficient CDC workload prediction framework based on energy consumption. This prediction framework not only uses VM historical usage values, but also takes into account VM and user behaviour and current states of the data centre. We introduce a number of techniques to handle the problem of predicting window sizes to optimize Physical Machine (PM) utilization. The proposed ELM algorithm and prediction framework are implemented using Google Trace data, which represents a 29-day trace collected from a cluster that contains more than 12,500 PMs. The results indicate that our model performs better on a variety of time series patterns than other models in the literature.

Keywords: Cloud computing · Data centre management · Workload prediction · Extreme Leaning Machine (ELM)

1 Introduction

The last ten years have seen an exponential increase in the use of cloud computing to satisfy Information Technology (IT) requirements. Data centre power is among the largest commodity expenditure in IT services for most organizations. The global data centre electricity usage in 2012 was 300-400 TWh, or about 2 % of global electricity usage, and this usage is expected to triple by 2020 [1,18]. According to Environmental Protection Agency (EPA), each 1000kWh of power consumption also emits 0.72 tons of CO2 [16]. With 88 % of this usage going to powering and cooling of IT equipments, any reduction will have a significant impact on overall electricity consumption, and a better green technology.

Energy reduction in a data centre equipment is extremely challenging due to complexity of systems used in a CDC. Energy consumption is not only determined by hardware efficiency, but also by the resource management system deployed on the infrastructure and the efficiency of applications running on the system [8].

M. Kurosu (Ed.): HCI 2016, Part I, LNCS 9731, pp. 565–576, 2016.
DOI: 10.1007/978-3-319-39510-4_52

In a CDC, proactive dynamic consolidation of VM requests is one of the most effective way to increase resources utilization and reduce energy consumption. This is done through monitoring, use of historical data and prediction of future workload. Hence, VM request prediction plays a key role not only in efficient resource utilization strategies, but also in workload-scheduling and admission control for dynamic cloud computing environments. VM prediction module provides estimations to determine, whether or not to add more Physical Machine (PM) resources, rearrange the order of query execution, and admit or reject a new incoming query [7,8,15].

A formulation of VM request prediction problem can be addressed by the use of available historical data to forecast future requests. In other words, previous usage patterns are used to estimate future VM requests in a data centre.

In our previous work [7], we proposed a framework that combined k-means clustering and an Extreme Learning Machine (ELM) algorithm to forecast the VM requests. Although this framework showed promising results, it also did make an assumption that task requests made to a CDC are relatively stationary over time. But in some CDCs, the arriving rate of task requests can vary frequently, as applications are divided into one or more processes running in different VM with different life span. Additionally, run-time of the processes can change depending on the phases they are in [19]. Furthermore, workloads in CDCs are driven not only by tasks characteristics, but also by user behavioural patterns. User behaviours are significantly more diverse than task behaviours [12]. These rapid variations in VM requests and user behaviours make it difficult to use conventional machine learning algorithms with off-line learning, and including the standard ELM algorithm to obtain an accurate predication of VM requests. This suggest that a multivariate time series algorithm may provide a more suitable candidate for such applications. In this work, we introduce a new ELM prediction algorithm to be used for a multivariate time series CDC workload prediction. This algorithm will be combined with an efficient workload prediction framework for CDC based on energy consumption. In our framework, we have combined clustering algorithms for users and workload, and our proposed multivariate time series ELM to forecast VM requests. The main features of this approach are:

- We use clustering not only on VM requests, but also on user requests. This can result in proper filtering of unexpected VM requests caused by unpredictable users' actions.
- We overcome the problem of time varying VM requests, depending on the actual service demand.
- Our proposed multivariate time series ELM represents an online sequential framework which is able to eliminate the restrictions about observation window size and number of VM clusters (inputs) for the ELM predictor.

The rest of the paper is organized as follows: Sect. 2 summarizes the proposed general block diagram of the dynamic VM prediction framework. Section 3 will discuss VM and user clustering. Section 4 gives details on proposed multivariate time series ELM prediction algorithm. Experimental results and discussions can be found in Sect. 5. Conclusions is given in Sect. 6.

2 Proposed Prediction Framework

Our proposed real-time VM workload prediction system consists of the following main components (see Fig. 1):

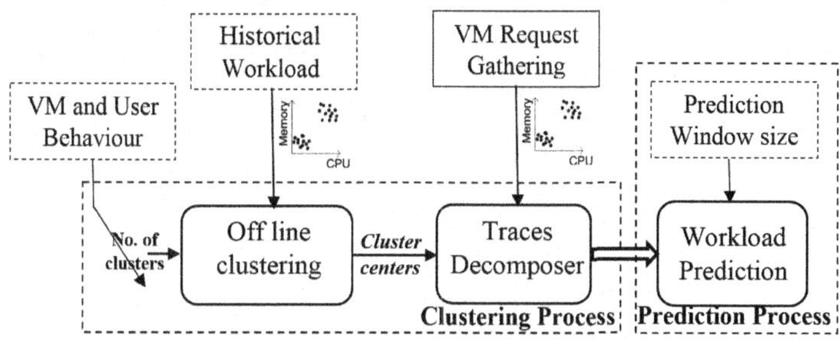

Fig. 1. Proposed prediction framework

Off-line clustering is used to create a set of clusters for different types of VMs and users form long term historical data. The centres of these clusters will be used to classify gathering data (new request and/or already exist VMs) during a specific time frame, or an *observation window.*

Trace decomposer is responsible for mapping each request received during a given observation window into one cluster according to long term cluster centres calculated off-line.

User and VM Behaviours have a strong influence on the overall cloud workload. Comprehensive workload models must consider both tasks and users and may even individual VM behaviour to reflect realistic conditions by excluding unwanted VMs or users form workload estimation process.

Historical Workload represents the historical data, which should updated periodically and used to predict the next period VM request for each observation window. It can also be used to calculate centres of clusters form time to time using long term observations.

VM Request Gathering includes types of monitoring which can help in detecting and tracing the variations or failure of resources and applications [6] during an observation window. For example in a large-scale CDC on an OpenStack platform, we can (a) use *OpenStack Ceilometer* to reliably collect measurements of the utilization of physical and virtual resources comprising deployed clouds [10], or (b) use *Data centre Infrastructure Manager (DCIM)* which provides detailed information about server configurations, hardware, network connections, and installed software [8].

Workload Prediction focuses on future VM request estimation, based on available monitoring and historical data. In other words, current and previous usage patterns are used to estimate future VM requests in the data centre. This will help the operator to place unneeded PMs in a low-power state to save energy.

Prediction Window size is the workload prediction time needed to decide whether PMs need to be switched to sleep mode [2]. It is totally depends on the configuration of CDC, specially the server hardware, and its values does effect workload prediction. From predication window and based on clustering and predication algorithm used, the monitoring frame is determined.

In the next section, and before we introduce our multivariate time series ELM prediction algorithm, we will give a brief description on data clustering components and algorithms used, together with some discussions on the Google Trace data [13] used to implement and compare our results to others.

3 Data Clustering

Data clustering consists of two components: a clustering algorithm and a trace decomposer, described in the previous section. They are responsible for mapping each request received during an observation window into one cluster for a predefined observation interval. The VM clustering is used to create set of clusters with different types of VMs or tasks during an observation window. In other words, VM clustering maps each VM request into one and only one cluster.

To compare our result with previous work in the literature [2,4,7], we have used the Google Trace data, and in particular the data provided in its Task event table. In the Task event table, each VM request represents a task. So our prediction algorithm is to estimate the future number of task requests and amount of resources associated with these requests.

The number of clusters should balance two conflicting objectives: (1) reducing errors and (2) maintaining low overhead. To compare and discuss the effect of the number of clusters, we used 10 h of Google data, where the total number of tasks was 1,029,342, each of which has an associated value of CPU and Memory.

We will plot the Sum of Squared Distances (SSD) error as a function of number of clusters. The SSD represents the error when each point in the data set is represented by its corresponding cluster centre, as shown in following equation [7]:

$$SSD = \sum_{i=1}^{\mathbf{k}} \sum_{r \in C_i} d(r, c_i)^2 \tag{1}$$

In this equation, C_i and c_i denote the ith cluster and it's centre, respectively, and $d(r, c_i)$ is the Euclidean distance between then new point r and the cluster centre c_i.

Figure 2 shows the comparison between k-means and fuzzy c-means (FCM) for different numbers of (a) VM clusters and (b) User clusters. We noticed that, although the FCM algorithm needs long off-line training time, it produces better results than the k-means based method for fewer number of clusters. This led

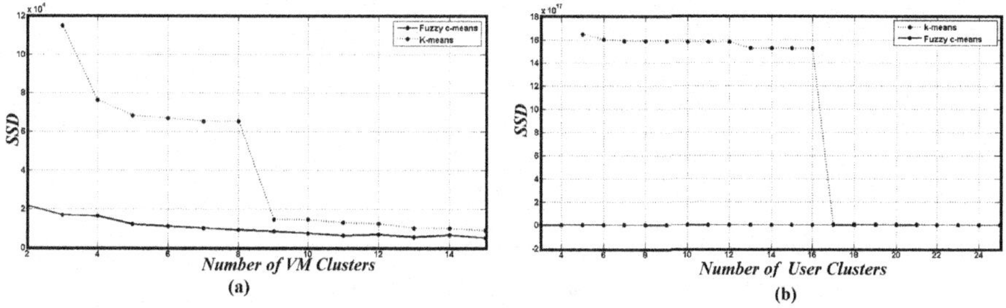

Fig. 2. SSD vs Number of cluster for (a) VMs (b) Users

us to choose FCM as clustering algorithm, which will provide fewer number of clusters with small error by balancing reducing errors and maintaining low overhead requirements through the use of minimize number of inputs in prediction algorithm [8].

Our observations shows greater variance of user cluster behaviours SSD error, when compared to its VM cluster behaviours. Also, results shows that in some cases user clusters have very small number of specific VM clusters. Hence, long term data during the off-line clustering can be used to identify and remove these types of user clusters from the predication computation. Such a filtering will then improve the accuracy of the predication, by removing the outliers from the dataset used.

4 Proposed Multivariate Time Series ELM

The mathematical model of the ELM is described as follow [9,11]:

Suppose there are N samples of data (x_i, t_i), where $x_i = [x_{i1}, ..., x_{in}] \in \mathbb{R}^n$ and $t_i = [t_{i1}, ..., t_{im}] \in \mathbb{R}^m$. The ELM algorithm is a Single-hidden Layer Feedforward Neural network (SLFN) with l hidden nodes and the activation function $g(x)$ and the output $Y(t)$:

$$Y(t) = \sum_{i=1}^{l} \beta_i g_i(x_j) = \sum_{i=1}^{l} \beta_i g_i(w_i.x_j + b_i), \quad j = 1, \dots, N \tag{2}$$

where $w_i = [w_{i1}, w_{i2}, \dots, w_{in}]^T$ is the weight vector of the connectors from the input node to the ith hidden node, and $\beta_i = [\beta_{i1}, \beta_{i2}, \dots, \beta_{im}]^T$ is the weight vector of the connectors between the ith hidden node and the output nodes. The variable b_i is the threshold of the ith hidden node. Approximating the samples with zero error, i.e.:

$$\sum_{i=1}^{l} \parallel y_j - t_j \parallel = 0 \tag{3}$$

one can find w_i, β_i, and b_i such that:

$$\sum_{i=1}^{l} \beta_i g_i(w_i.x_j + bi) = t_j, \quad j = 1, ..., N \tag{4}$$

Using the following substitutions: $\mathbf{H}(\mathbf{w}_1, ..., \mathbf{w}_l, b_1, \ldots, b_l, \mathbf{x}_1, \ldots, \mathbf{x}_Q) =$

$$\begin{bmatrix} g(\mathbf{w}_1\mathbf{x}_1 + b_1) & g(\mathbf{w}_2\mathbf{x}_1 + b_2) & \cdots & g(\mathbf{w}_l\mathbf{x}_1 + b_l) \\ g(\mathbf{w}_1\mathbf{x}_2 + b_1) & g(\mathbf{w}_2\mathbf{x}_2 + b_2) & \cdots & g(\mathbf{w}_l\mathbf{x}_2 + b_l) \\ \vdots & \vdots & \vdots & \vdots \\ g(\mathbf{w}_1\mathbf{x}_Q + b_1) & g(\mathbf{w}_2\mathbf{x}_Q + b_2) & \cdots & g(\mathbf{w}_l\mathbf{x}_Q + b_l) \end{bmatrix} \tag{5}$$

where $\beta = \left[\beta_1^T, \ldots, \beta_l^T\right]^T$ and $T = \left[t_1^T, \ldots, t_l^T\right]^T$, (5) can be written as:

$$H\beta = T. \tag{6}$$

The output weights β_i, $i = 1, 2, \cdots, m$ are determined through learning from the training instances by solving the following objective function:

$$\underbrace{min}_{\beta} \|\mathbf{H}\beta - \mathbf{T}\| \tag{7}$$

and its solution is:

$$\hat{\beta} = \left(\mu I + H^T H\right)^{-1} H^T \mathbf{T} \tag{8}$$

for $\boldsymbol{l} < N$, where I is the identity matrix; μ is a regularization parameter.

Equation 8 represent the optimal weight current sample, this weight can be updated for each previous time series samples to predict the one step ahead sample according to [17]:

$$\hat{\beta} = \hat{\beta} + \lambda \Delta \hat{\beta} \tag{9}$$

$$\Delta \hat{\beta} = \left(\mu I + H^T H\right)^{-1} H^T \mathbf{e} \tag{10}$$

where λ is a control parameter $(0, 1)$ and $\mathbf{e} = \left[e_1, e_2, \ldots, e_m\right]^T$ is the error vector.

The predicted output $\hat{Y}(k+1)$ will be calculated for the last estimated $\hat{\beta}$ for a new data set through:

$$\hat{Y}(k+1) = \mathbf{h}\hat{\beta} \tag{11}$$

where $\mathbf{h}$ is the $\mathbf{H}$ matrix for the new input.

Algorithm 1 describes the steps of the of Multivariate Time Series ELM predictor.

In this algorithm, ρ is an update parameter and P is the chunk data number. When $P > 1$, the improved ELM algorithm can update the output weights when every P samples are observed.

In terms of kth row of the hidden layer output matrix H denoted as h_k, we can write $H^T H$ in Eq. 8 as:

$$H^T H = \left[h_1^T \cdots h_N^T\right] \begin{bmatrix} h_1^T \\ \vdots \\ h_N^T \end{bmatrix} = \sum_{k=1}^{N} h_k^T h_k \tag{12}$$

Algorithm 1. Multivariate Time Series ELM Algorithm

Inputs:
  Normalize *X(k)* and *T(k)* to scales [0.1 0.9]
Initialization:
  Choose μ, $\boldsymbol{l}$; randomly generate w_{ij} and b_i; initial error E_{old}
while 1 **do** ▷ repeat for each estimation
  for $k = 1 : P$ **do** ▷ P is the number of observed samples
    Calculate $H(X(k), w, \beta)$ using Eq. 5
    Calculate $\mathbf{h}(z, w, \beta)$ where $z = X(k+1)$
    Calculate $\hat{Y}(k+1)$ using Eq. 11
    Calculate new error $e(k) = T(k) - Y(k)$
    $E_{new} = E_{old} + \frac{1}{2}\sum e^2(k)$
  end for
  Calculate $\Delta\hat{\beta}$ using Eq. 10
  Update weights using Eq. 9
  if $E_{new} < E_{old}$ **then**
    $\mu = \rho/\mu$;
  else
    $\mu = \rho\mu$
  end if
end while

So the sub-Hessian matrix is defined as [17]:

$$q_k = h_k^T h_k \tag{13}$$

and the accumulation of these sub-matrices of Eq. 13 is the quasi-Hessian matrix $\mathbf{Q}$ given by:

$$\mathbf{Q} = \sum_{k=1}^{Q} q_k \tag{14}$$

The main idea of these additional steps is to reduce the storage space by l elements required to calculate $\mathbf{Q}$ instead of storing the $Q \times l$ matrix. Additionally, it can be seen from Eq. 13 that the matrix $H^T H$ is symmetric, hence we only have to store its lower or upper triangular part. Therefore, only a scalar error e_k needs to be stored for each h_k [17].

5 Experimental Results

The main purpose of the prediction framework, Fig. 1, is to minimize CDC power and energy consumption through dynamic consolidation of VMs by reducing number of PM used. So, one of the most important parameters in workload predication is to select the length of the time period used. This time period should be long enough to switched off unnecessary PMs. This period is estimated based on the difference between the energy cost for keeping the PM idle and the PM OFF/ON power cost, as described in our previous work [7,8]. We can calculate the energy when the PM is in sleep mode E_{sleep} by:

$$E_{sleep} = E_0 + P_{sleep} \cdot (T_p - T_0) \tag{15}$$

where T_p is the length of the prediction window, P_{sleep} is the consumed power when in sleep mode, E_0 is the energy needed to switch the PM to sleep mode plus the energy needed to wake up it later, and T_0 is the transitional switching time. The estimated time required to keep the PM ON and idle (T_b) consumes an amount of energy that is equal to the energy consumed due to mode transition plus energy consumed, while the PM is in the sleep mode during that same period, i.e.

$$P_{idle} \cdot T_b = E_0 + P_{sleep} \cdot (T_b - T_0) \tag{16}$$

where T_b is the beak-even time. This means that energy can be saved by switching PM to sleep mode, if and only if the PM stay idle for a time period longer than T_b. That is, $T_p \geq T_b$ must hold in order for the power switching decision to be energy efficient.

According to the equation above, if we have the PM profiles, we can easily estimate the value of T_p. In our work, we utilized the approach taken by Dabbagh *et al.* [2,4], which used the energy measurement study of PMs conducted in [14] to estimate the break-even time, T_b.

Figures 3 and 4 represent the comparison of our result, based on the proposed ELM algorithm, and the related work in the literature [2,4,7,8]. In this comparison, we have used the data provided in the Task event table form Google data and a prediction windows of 5 min. We have also used the Root Mean Square Error (RMSE), defined by Eq. 17. We have used this error measure to compare different prediction models and scenarios with $\rho = 1$ and $P = 3$ in Algorithm 1.

$$RMSE = \sum_{i=1}^{4} \sqrt{\frac{1}{N} \sum_{k=1}^{N} \left(\hat{Y}_i(k) - Y_i(k) \right)^2} \tag{17}$$

where i is one of the 4 categories used, and N is total number of samples. In our implementation, we had to first select the number of hidden nodes $\boldsymbol{l}$ and the regulation parameter μ in the ELM predictor. Figure 3a shows the relation between the number of hidden neurons $\boldsymbol{l}$, while Fig. 3b represents the effect of regulation parameter μ for the proposed predictor. It is clear that RMSE is reduced, when increasing the number of hidden neurons $\boldsymbol{l}$, like any other conventional gradient descent algorithm, while the regulation parameter μ does not has a big effect on the value of RMSE. Therefore, we chose to use $\boldsymbol{l} = 100$ and $\mu = 1/5000$ for the proposed predictor.

In order to illustrate the effectiveness of our approach, we have compared the predictor accuracy with the followings: Simple ELM, Last minute predictors, Min predictors, Max predictors, Average predictor, Exponential Weighted Moving Average (EWMA) predictors, Linear Regression (LR) predictors, and Wiener filters [2,3,5,7]. These algorithms used to estimate number of request in each of 4

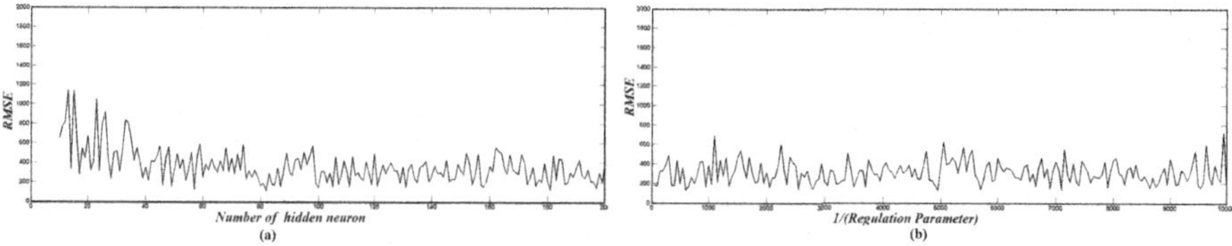

Fig. 3. RMSE vs (a) Number of hidden (b) regulation parameter

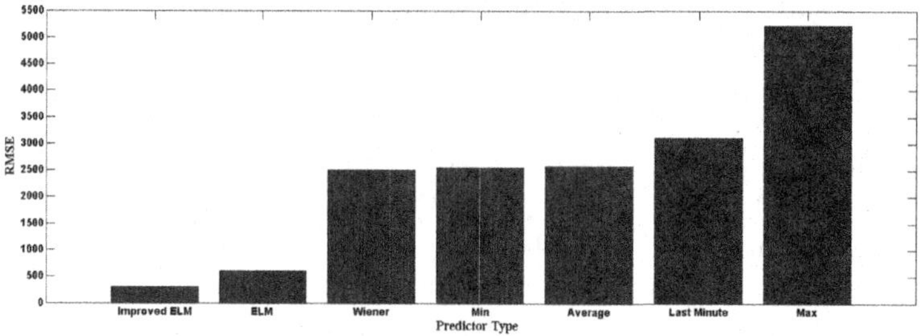

Fig. 4. RMSE comparisons of different predictive approaches

clusters of VMs. Figure 4 shows the RMSE of each of these prediction approaches, for 5 h test sample with 5 min prediction window. Our proposed predictor yields the lowest RMSE.

Figure 5 shows comparison of several scenarios in types and size of predictor inputs. Our investigation of the effect of inserting user behaviour (user clusters) and the VM request prediction was based on implementations of 6 user clusters and 4 VM clusters. The scenarios considered were: (1) ELM with 3 states of VM clusters; (2) ELM with 3 state VM and one state user clusters; (3) ELM with 3 state VM and user clusters; (4) ELM with one state VM and user clusters; and (5) improved ELM with one state VM clusters.

Our observations confirms that a long term filter can be used to remove VM requests that have less probability, based on the historical data. We also noticed

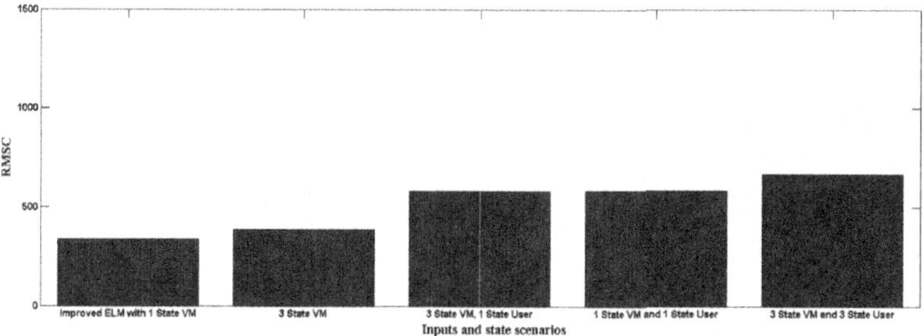

Fig. 5. RMSE comparisons of different ELM inputs and states scenarios

that adding only user clusters to a simple ELM prediction algorithm will not be effective. Such addition will increase the error, because the principle of ELM is to estimate the nonlinear function, and this estimation will have more error if we add more variables. On the other hand, our approach of using both user clusters and VM request together with the proposed ELM can provide as much as 20 % improvement in accuracy. Further improvement in accuracy may be obtained based on using a long term offline filter, given a set of data. Value selection for update parameter ρ and control parameter λ can also have an impact on the accuracy of results. In our experimentation, optimal values were found using a trial-and-error approach. Part of future work can focus on finding systematic way of finding off-line optimal values of ρ, λ and even type and number of hidden neuron l.

The on-line multivariate time series ELM is able to eliminate any restrictions on observation window size and number of VM clusters (inputs) for the predictor. In our online computation s, instead of using all the previous state for observation windows as inputs, we simply input the current state and used an iteration of previous states to cover all possible observation window states. This approach will also would reduce computational need of calculating of the inverse of Hessian matrix in Eq. 10.

6 Conclusion

In this paper, we have proposed a real-time CDC workload prediction framework that can be used for a better energy conservation strategy. A key component of this framework is a new multivariate time series ELM predication algorithm for VM request forecasting. The improve ELM can deal with the problem of time varying VM requests, and eliminates any restrictions on observation window sizes and the number of VM clusters for the ELM predictor. The framework is based on efficient use of historical VM request, user cluster algorithms, the current state of the data centre and an effective prediction window size. The long term historical workload time series data form cloud computing platforms can then be used to find the centre of VM size cluster and to filter the VM class-based on the probability of user behaviour class. These centres and filtered historical data with predefined window size, and the propose ELM-predictor will improve the accuracy of estimated number of requests in different VM categories. We evaluated the performance of the proposed framework using the Google trace data for different sampling rates and durations. The proposed ELM algorithm showed an improvement in accuracy of up to 20 %. Further improvement in accuracy may be obtained based on using a long term offline filter, given a set of data.

References

1. Belady, C.L.: Projecting annual new datacenter construction market size, global foundation services. Technical report, Global Foundation Services, March 2011
2. Dabbagh, M., Hamdaoui, B., Guizani, M., Rayes, A.: Energy-efficient resource allocation and provisioning framework for cloud data centers. IEEE Trans. Netw. Serv. Manage. **12**(3), 377–391 (2015)
3. Dabbagh, M., Hamdaoui, B., Guizani, M., Rayes, A.: Efficient datacenter resource utilization through cloud resource overcommitment. Memory **40**(50), 1–6 (2015)
4. Dabbagh, M., Hamdaoui, B., Guizani, M., Rayes, A.: Toward energy-efficient cloud computing: Prediction, consolidation, and overcommitment. IEEE Netw. **29**(2), 56–61 (2015)
5. Dabbagh, M., Hamdaoui, B., Guizani, M., Rayes, A.: Energy-efficient cloud resource management. In: Proceedings of the 2014 IEEE Conference on Computer Communications Workshops (INFOCOM WKSHPS), pp. 386–391. IEEE (2014)
6. Hameed, A., Khoshkbarforoushha, A., Ranjan, R., Jayaraman, P.P., Kolodziej, J., Balaji, P., Zeadally, S., Malluhi, Q.M., Tziritas, N., Vishnu, A., et al.: A survey and taxonomy on energy efficient resource allocation techniques for cloud computing systems. Computing, 1–24 (2014)
7. Ismaeel, S., Miri, A.: Using ELM techniques to predict data centre VM requests. In: Proceedings of the 2nd IEEE International Conference on Cyber Security and Cloud Computing (CSCloud 2015), pp. 80–86. IEEE, New York, November 2015
8. Ismaeel, S., Miri, A.: Energy-consumption clustering in cloud data centre. In: Proceedings of the 3rd IEEE MEC International Conference on Big Data and Smart City ICBDSC. IEEE, Muscut (2016, to appear)
9. Ismaeel, S., Miri, A., Chourishi, D.: Using the extreme learning machine (ELM) technique for heart disease diagnosis. In: Proceedings of The IEEE International Conference on Humanitarian Technology Conference (IHTC2015), pp. 1–3, May 2015
10. Ismaeel, S., Miri, A., Chourishi, D., Dibaj, S.R.: Open source cloud management platforms: a review. In: Proceedings of the 2nd IEEE International Conference on Cyber Security and Cloud Computing (CSCloud 2015), pp. 470–475. IEEE, New York, November 2015
11. Ismaeel, S., Miri, A., Sadeghian, A., Chourishi, D.: An extreme learning machine (ELM) predictor for electric arc furnaces' v-i characteristics. In: Proceedings of the 2nd IEEE International Conference on Cyber Security and Cloud Computing (CSCloud 2015), pp. 329–334. IEEE, New York, November 2015
12. Moreno, I., Garraghan, P., Townend, P., Xu, J.: Analysis, modeling and simulation of workload patterns in a large-scale utility cloud. IEEE Trans. Cloud Comput. **2**(2), 208–221 (2014)
13. Reiss, C., Wilkes, J., Hellerstein, J.L.: Google cluster-usage traces: format+ schema. Technical Report, Google Inc., Mountain View, CA, USA (2011)
14. Sarji, I., Ghali, C., Chehab, A., Kayssi, A.: Cloudese: energy efficiency model for cloud computing environments. In: Proceedings of The International Conference on Energy Aware Computing (ICEAC), pp. 1–6, November 2011
15. Song, A., Fan, W., Wang, W., Luo, J., Mo, Y.: Multi-objective virtual machine selection for migrating in virtualized data centers. In: Zu, Q., Hu, B., Elçi, A. (eds.) ICPCA 2012 and SWS 2012. LNCS, vol. 7719, pp. 426–438. Springer, Heidelberg (2013)

16. Uddin, M., Darabidarabkhani, Y., Shah, A., Memon, J.: Evaluating power efficient algorithms for efficiency and carbon emissions in cloud data centers: a review. Renew. Sustain. Energy Rev. **51**, 1553–1563 (2015)
17. Wang, X., Han, M.: Improved extreme learning machine for multivariate time series online sequential prediction. Eng. Appl. Artif. Intell. **40**, 28–36 (2015)
18. Yue, W., Chen, Q.: Dynamic placement of virtual machines with both deterministic and stochastic demands for green cloud computing. Math. Probl. Eng. **2014**, 1–11 (2014)
19. Zhang, Q., Boutaba, R.: Dynamic workload management in heterogeneous cloud computing environments. In: IEEE Network Operations and Management Symposium (NOMS), pp. 1–7, May 2014

Energy-Efficient Resource Allocation for Cloud Data Centres Using a Multi-way Data Analysis Technique

Raed Karim(✉), Salam Ismaeel, and Ali Miri

Department of Computer Science, Ryerson University,
350 Victoria Street, Toronto, ON M5B 2K3, Canada
{r2karim, salam.ismaeel, ali.miri}@ryerson.ca

Abstract. Cloud Data Centres (CDCs) are facilities used to host large numbers of servers, networking and storage systems, along with other required infrastructure such as cooling, Unsupervised Power Supplies (UPS) and security systems. With the high proliferation of cloud computing and big data, more and more data and cloud-based service solutions are hosted and provisioned through these CDCs. The increasing number of CDCs used to meet enterprises' needs has significant energy use implications, due to power use of these centres. In this paper, we propose a method to accurately predict workload in physical machines, so that energy consumption of CDCs can be reduced. We propose a multi-way prediction technique to estimate incoming workload at a CDC. We incorporate user behaviours to improve the prediction results. Our proposed prediction model produces more accurate prediction results, when compared with other well-known prediction models.

Keywords: Workload prediction · Cloud Data Centres · Tensor factorization · Energy Efficiency

1 Introduction

In CDCs, Physical Machines (PMs) use virtualization to host multiple Virtual Machines (VMs), where a wide range of applications (data-intensive and compute-intensive) are deployed and run [1]. Servers and storage systems in CDCs are used to host and run applications, and to process, store and provision data and contents to consumers in a client/server computing architecture. CDCs are equipped with different PMs brands (e.g. IBM, HP, Dell, etc.) with different compute resource specifications such as CPU cores with levels of performance, memory sizes, storage capacities and network bandwidths. It has been estimated that data centre energy consumption will reach 140 billion kilowatt-hours annually by 2020, costing US businesses $13 billion annually in electricity bills and emitting approximately 100 million metric tons of carbon pollution per year. This represents a significant increase from only 0.6 % of the global carbon emission in 2008 to 2.6 % in 2020 [2].

In CDCs, users often request compute resources to perform different IT-related tasks. However, not all of requested resources are used. According to Google [3], only a small segment of the provisioned VM instances are used during deployment. Lack of

M. Kurosu (Ed.): HCI 2016, Part I, LNCS 9731, pp. 577–585, 2016.
DOI: 10.1007/978-3-319-39510-4_53

knowledge of future resources needed by a CDC can lead to over-provisioning or under-provisioning problems [4].

To address the above problem, we propose a prediction model that estimates future incoming workload to a CDC. Our model predicates workload based on users' requirements, and in particular identifies required number and types of VMs, represented by vCPU and memory specifications. To test our model, we have utilized the available historical workload data collected from Google traces over a period of 29 days. The collected data represent Google compute cells. The tracelog contains over 25 millions tasks, submitted by 930 users who (previously) requested different types of VMs over different time slots. The number of recorded requests is 3295896. We will show how our model can improve workload prediction over this set of data using a Multi-Way Data Analysis (MWDA) approach that incorporates users' behaviour.

The rest of the paper is organized as follows. Section 2 provides an overview of the workload prediction process. Section 3 describes the proposed prediction model. Section 4 presents the experimental work. Section 5 discusses the related work. Section 6 concludes the paper and suggests some future work.

2 Related Work

Research on computing resource prediction and virtualization techniques in CDCs has gained lots of interest over the past few years, with a number of different techniques proposed in the literature to tackle the machine workload prediction problem. In [5], Qazi *et al.* used an autoregressive moving average technique (ARMA), whereas Dabbagh *et al.* [6] proposed the use of a weighted average of previous observations. Machine learning techniques, such as ELM [7] have also been used to predict future workload. These methods have a number of possible shortcomings because they do not consider of all the key inputs for obtaining accurate predications. In [5], both user behaviour and actual usage of CPU and memory were not considered. In [6], user behaviour was not considered during data processing and prediction computation. The main shortcoming of machine learning techniques is that adding user clusters (behaviours) as inputs to the prediction process increases the error in estimating the number of VM requests in each cluster. This is because adding more variables (users) to a nonlinear process can negatively affect estimation. This implies that traditional machine learning techniques cannot handle multi-dimensional problem domains.

The main consideration of our work is the optimal use of the available computing resources of PMs in CDCs. Our proposed model has the ability to capture multiple variables in a multi-dimensional environment. Since user behaviours have a large impact on improving prediction results, we incorporate users as one of the key model variables in order to improve prediction accuracy. Prediction accuracy, in turn, enables us to reduce the number of required PMs and hence to obtain better energy conservation.

3 Proposed Workload Prediction Process

As discussed in the previous section, our goal is to accurately estimate the right number and size of the required VMs based on future users' needs. This can in return result in reduction of power consumption in CDCs. To achieve this goal, we propose using the following three phases – data clustering (steps 1–3), data filtering (step 4) and workload prediction (step 5):

- **Data clustering**
  Step 1: We cluster VMs based on the calculated workload into different clusters. In our work and in line with other work [6, 7], we consider a case study of four VM clusters to demonstrate the effectiveness of our prediction model in which actual resources are utilized for the prediction process. We label clusters with ranges of workload percentages, as follows. The very big VMs cluster contains workload of 75 % and up, the big VMs cluster contains [50 %–74.9 %], the medium VMs cluster contains workload of [25 %–49.9 %] and the small VMs contains workload of [0.1 %–24.9 %]. We put users reported in the data set into different clusters based on the number of VM requests made in the past. Each cluster is characterized by request density. Based on the experimental work we have done [7], we observed that increasing the number of user clusters produces more accurate results. However, at a certain point no further improvement can be observed. We have performed the clustering process on different data sizes, and we have found that the number of clusters between 25 and 30 gives the best results.
  Step 2: According to the clustering outcome, we count the number of requests submitted by different users under each VM cluster. The calculated numbers represent historical workload data that we utilize during the prediction computation process.
  Step 3: We arrange the VMs' historical workload data in a tensor of three dimensions of users U_i, VM clusters V_j and time intervals t_n. Each entry of the tensor denotes the number of VMs of a particular VM cluster that a user has used within a specific time.
- **Data filtering**
  Step 4: We analyze recorded (historical) workload data by discovering their patterns and relationships. We consider user behaviours when used VMs in the past by calculating the linear correlations (dependencies) between users' clusters.
- **Workload prediction**
  Step 5: We employ a multi-way (tensor) technique to predict the incoming workload of VMs for a future time interval (i.e. the number of required VMs of each cluster based on users' requests). We sum up the predicted number of VMs of each cluster for all users to obtain the total number of VMs under each cluster for the future time interval.

3.1 Analyzing Workload Data for the Prediction Process

Our objective is to uncover hidden patterns (features) and dependencies among the available VMs, which are hosted on heterogeneous PMs, and dependencies among their users with respect to their workload information. In our previous work on web service domain [7], we have proven that learning hidden features can improve the prediction results.

In order to improve the prediction results, we analyze user behaviours which have used VMs in the past. Our analysis is done by calculating the correlation degrees among users using their workload values in series of time intervals. The correlation could be either positive or negative. We only consider users with positive correlation meaning that they had similar historical experiences in terms of workload they have applied on a same set of VMs. In this work and based on the available information, users' similarity is determined by two criteria: if users are geographically located close to each other and/or they have similar trends. User trends are determined by request characteristics (how often users request VMs, workload intensity, peak season time and off season time). We look into their historical invocations of the VMs, and then we calculate their correlations over the history with respect to request characteristics. We consider workload data of users with the highest degree of correlations. We denote the space of similar users as a user neighborhood. Users with negative correlations are those whose past experiences are dissimilar. Usually we are not interested in this type of users since they represent noise to the prediction computation process. We calculate the users' correlations using Pearson Correlation Coefficient (PCC) technique [8]. The neighborhood contains local information of workload data. In our proposed model, the local information is integrated in the global information (workload data of the whole tensor) during the prediction process.

4 Proposed Prediction Model (MWDA)

To address this problem, we propose a multiway low-rank Tensor Factorization (TF) model [9, 10]. In our model, we integrate three vectors (user-specific, VM-specific and time-specific) into a workload matrix. The TF factorizes the workload matrix and hence makes accurate prediction. Our goal is to map VMs and users information within sequential time intervals to a cooperative latent feature space of a low dimensionality, such that VM-time interactions can be captured as inner products in that space. The premise behind a low-dimensional TF technique is that there are only a few hidden features affecting the VM-time interactions, and a user's interactive experience is influenced by how each feature affects the user. TF can discover features underlying interactions between VMs as well as between users. It balances the overall information from all VMs (global information) and users, and information associated with users with similar behaviours (local information). We verify our proposed approach by conducting experiments. We use data of usage traces of a Google compute cell which is a set of PMs packed into racks in a data centre. We specifically extract the Task Event table that contains PMs ID, tasks sent to VMs, user ID and workload data represented by resource request for CPU and memory [3].

Let R denote the workload tensor. As we mentioned, R contains workload values based on different users requesting VMs of different time intervals. The future workload are predicted by minimizing the objective function as follows:

$$\frac{1}{2} \parallel R - \hat{R} \parallel_F^2 \tag{1}$$

where $\hat{R}$ denotes the predicted workload tensor; $\parallel . \parallel_F^2$ denotes the Frobenius form which is calculated as the square root of the sum of the absolute squares of $R - \hat{R}$.

Since R is very sparse, only VMs with recorded workload values are factorized. The tensor factorization term is minimized by applying the following function:

$$\min_{\text{U,V, A}} \zeta(R, U, V, A) = \frac{1}{2} \sum\nolimits_{e=1}^{i} \sum\nolimits_{f=1}^{j} \sum\nolimits_{g=1}^{n} I_{efg} (R_{ef} - \hat{R}_{ef})^2 \tag{2}$$

where I_{efg} is an indicator function that is equal to 1 if a VM is used, and a workload value is available; otherwise it is equal to 0.

$$\min_{\text{U,V, A}} \zeta(R, U, V, A) = \frac{1}{2} \sum\nolimits_{e=1}^{i} \sum\nolimits_{f=1}^{j} \sum\nolimits_{g=1}^{n} I_{efg} (R_{ef} - \hat{R}_{ef})^2 \tag{3}$$

Considering the original tensor factorization term, unknown workload values (the number of required VMs of each cluster) are predicted by learning the latent features of all known workload values through factorizing the user-specific, VM-specific and time-specific matrices. The main drawback for using only this term is that the prediction accuracy might be poor since workload values of all users are considered some of which could have caused noise into the prediction computation process [9]. To overcome this drawback, we propose to add an additional regularization term to the tensor factorization model. The new term considers the information of similar users in predicting future workload values. The premise is that neighbours have similar interactive experience when using VMs. This is due the fact that users within the same geographical locations and have similar workload patterns are more likely to have similar VM requests in the future. We incorporate the new regularization term into our tensor model as follows:

$$\begin{aligned} \min_{\text{U,V, A}} \zeta(R, U, V, A) = & \frac{1}{2} \sum_{e=1}^{i} \sum_{f=1}^{j} \sum_{g=1}^{n} I_{efg} \left(R_{efg} - \hat{R}_{efg}\right)^2 \\ & + \frac{\sigma}{2} \sum\nolimits_{e=1}^{i} \sum\nolimits_{f=1}^{j} \sum\nolimits_{g=1}^{n} \parallel \hat{R}_{efg(e)} - \sum\nolimits_{k \in K(e)} R_{efg(k)} P_{ek} \parallel_F^2, \end{aligned} \tag{4}$$

where $R_{efg(k)}$ denotes workload of similar users to V_e; $K(e)$ is a set of *top k* similar users and P_{ek} is the similarity weight of a similar users, and it is calculated as follows:

$$P_{ek} = \frac{sim(e,k)}{\sum_{k \in K(e)} sim(e,k)}, \tag{5}$$

Where $sim(e,k)$ is calculated using the PCC method.

A local minimum of the objective function in (9) can be found by performing the gradient descent algorithm in U_e, V_f and A_g as follows:

$$\begin{aligned}
\frac{\partial \zeta}{\partial U_e} &= \sum_{f=1}^{j} \sum_{g=1}^{n} I_{efg}(\hat{R}_{efg} - R_{efg})\left(V_f^T A_g\right) + \sigma(\hat{R}_{efg(i)} - \sum_{k \in K(e)} R_{efg(k)} P_{ek})\left(V_f^T A_g\right) \\
\frac{\partial \zeta}{\partial V_f} &= \sum_{e=1}^{i} \sum_{g=1}^{n} I_{efg}(\hat{R}_{efg} - R_{efg})(U_e^T A_g) + \sigma(\hat{R}_{efg(i)} - \sum_{k \in K(e)} R_{efg(k)} P_{ek})(U_e^T A_g) \\
\frac{\partial \zeta}{\partial A_g} &= \sum_{e=1}^{m} \sum_{f=1}^{n} I_{efg}(\hat{R}_{efg} - R_{efg})(U_e^T V_f) + \sigma(\hat{R}_{efg(i)} - \sum_{k \in K(e)} R_{efg(k)} P_{ek})(U_e^T V_f)
\end{aligned} \tag{6}$$

5 Experiments

In the experiments, we have used Google traces of CPU and memory data that are recorded for a period of 29 days. The data are recorded with timestamps in microsecond and it describes machines used and tasks requested by different users' requests. We specifically used the Task event table that contains time stamps, user information, CPU, memory and local disk resources requested by users. To demonstrate the effectiveness of our proposed prediction model, we have used a slice of the data trace of 24 h (1440 min) with a time interval of 5 min. We mapped the recorded CPU and memory workload data into multiple VM clusters so that each user request for a VM is mapped to a specific cluster. During the time frame, there were 3295896 requests as inputs to the clustering process. The number of VM clusters that we have selected is 4 which correspond to four VM categories (Small, Medium, Big and Very Big) according to our proposed prediction process described in Sect. 2. On the other hand, 426 users have been recorded within the specified time frame. We clustered the users based on their historical usages of requested VMs (i.e. the number of request users have made to VMs). We have used the fuzzy c-mean clustering algorithm. In our previous work [7], we demonstrated the efficiency of the fuzzy c-mean clustering algorithm compared to the traditional k-mean clustering algorithm. In this work, we used 25 clusters which produced the best results (the lowest error rate). The premise for clustering the users is to improve the efficiency of the correlation computation process described in Sect. 3.1.

5.1 Evaluation and Discussion

Our objective in conducting the experiments was to evaluate the prediction accuracy of our proposed model by comparing its results with the following well-known prediction algorithms available in the literature: (1) *Mean*: this method considers the average value of historical workload data. (2) *ARMA*: this method calculates the auto-regression moving average of the training data [11]. (3) *Weiner*: this method was proposed by [6]. It calculates the weighted average of the training data. (4) *Latest*: this method takes the training data as an input and returns the latest observation [7]. (5) *nUTF*: this method is a different version of our implemented algorithm that we used in our prediction model. It computes the tensor factorization without considering users' correlations (behaviours). (6) *MWDA*: this is our proposed prediction algorithm in this paper. We used a three dimensional multi-way technique to compute the prediction. We have calculated user clustering, and incorporated user correlations (behaviours) during the prediction process.

We have used the Mean Absolute Error (MAE) method to measure the prediction accuracy of each of the prediction algorithms including our proposed algorithm by computing the average absolute deviation of the predicted values from the actual data. The smaller MAE values indicate higher prediction accuracy. The MAE is defined as follows:

$$\mathrm{MAE} = \frac{\sum_{m,n,c} \left| \hat{\boldsymbol{R}}_{efg} - \boldsymbol{R}_{efg} \right|}{L}, \tag{7}$$

where, m, n, c denote the number of the user clusters, timestamps and VM components; R_{efg} denotes the actual workload value; $\hat{R}_{efg}$ denotes the predicted workload value; L is the number of the predicted values.

In this work, our objective is to estimate the future workload (the number of VMs of each type) based on historical workload values. Therefore, for the purpose of our experiments we removed the data of the future time interval (the next five minutes) from the tensor R. The remaining values are used for the learning purpose to predict the removed ones. We used the cross validation method during the MAE calculation process to obtain reliable error calculations. Table 1 shows the MAE values of the compared prediction methods. The observation was that our MWDA model outperformed all other models in terms of the accuracy of workload prediction results as it produces the lowest MAE values. The prediction accuracy is an important factor that determines how many VM needed for the next time frame and the types of these VMs. The better prediction results the better knowledge that is required to plan ahead of time for optimal placements of incoming VMs onto PMs in CDCs. Eventually, we can accurately estimate the number of PMs which can be turned off or used for other tasks. As a consequence, a considerable amount of energy can be conserved. Relying on users' knowledge or using poor prediction models can make the estimation of the number of unused PMs far from being accurate. Thus, it leads to a large percentage of energy waste or failing to meet users' QoS requirements. In our approach, we attempt to build a knowledge base that is dynamically updated and relies on the actual usages of computing resources. By training the historical workload data using a reliable prediction algorithm we can accurately estimate future workload. Accurately predicting workload can improve not only CDCs' providers' energy consumption but also users' QoS experience, which heavily rely on the adequacy of compute resources.

Table 1. Workload prediction comparisons (lower MAE values indicate better prediction accuracy).

	Mean	ARMA	Wiener	Latest	Minimum	nUTF	MWDA
MAE	13.92	7.41	7.38	9.70	9.81	6.28	3.42

6 Conclusions

In this paper, we proposed a model for predicting incoming workload in CDCs. Our prediction model solves the problems of machine overloading (a possible violation of users' QoS requirements) and underloading (unused computing resources lead to energy waste) by accurately predicting the number and the types of VMs based on user requirements. Using our model, we can accurately estimate the number and types of VMs required for the incoming workload. Hence, we can free up unused clusters that can be turned off or used for new VMs predicted by our model. Overall, the amount of energy consumed in CDCs is reduced for environmental and economy advantage. To the best of our knowledge, this is the first technique that incorporates user behaviours in a multi-way technique to improve the prediction of future incoming workload for energy saving purposes in CDCs. As an extension of this work, we plan to develop a placement mechanism that takes our prediction results as an input in order to optimally place the predicted VMs onto PMs in CDCs.

References

1. Dutta, S., Gera, S., Verma, A., Viswanathan, B.: SmartScale: automatic application scaling in enterprise clouds. In: Proceedings of IEEE Conference on Cloud Computing, pp. 221–228 (2012)
2. Delforge, P.: America's data centre consuming and wasting growing amounts of energy. http://www.nrdc.org/energy/data-centre-efficiency-assessment.asp
3. Reiss, C., Wilkes, J., Hellerstrin, J.L.: Google cluster-usage traces: format + schema. Google Inc. Technical report (2011)
4. Li, X., Qian, Z., Lu, S., Wu, J.: Energy efficient virtual machine placement algorithm with balanced and improved resource utilization in a data centre. Math. Comput. Model. **58**(5), 1222–1235 (2013)
5. Qazi, K., Li, Y., Sohn, A.: Workload prediction of virtual machines for harnessing data centre resources. In: Proceedings of IEEE International Conference on Cloud Computing, pp. 522–529 (2014)
6. Dabbagh, M., Hamdaoui, B., Guizani, M., Rayes, A.: Energy-efficient cloud resource management. In: Proceedings of IEEE Conference on Computer Communications Workshops (INFOCOM), pp. 386–391 (2014)
7. Ismaeel, S., Miri, A.: Energy-consumption clustering in cloud data centre. In: Proceedings of IEEE MEC International Conference on Big Data and Smart City (2016)
8. Karim, R., Ding, C., Miri, A.: End-to-end performance prediction for selecting cloud service solutions. In: Proceedings of IEE Symposium On Service-oriented System Engineering, pp. 69–77 (2015)

9. Karim, R., Ding, C., Miri, A.: End-to-end QoS prediction of vertically composed cloud services via tensor factorization. In: Proceedings of IEEE Cloud and Autonomic Computing, pp. 229–236 (2015)
10. Acar, E., Yener, B.: Unsupervised multiway data analysis: a literature survey. IEEE Trans. Knowl. Data Eng. **21**(1), 6–20 (2009)
11. Roy, N., Dubey, A., Gokhale, A.: Efficient autoscaling in the cloud using predictive models for workload forecasting. In: Proceedings of IEEE International Conference on Cloud Computing, pp. 500–507 (2011)

Agile and UCD Integration Based on Pre-development Usability Evaluations: An Experience Report

Jade Mendes Inácio de Carvalho[1], Tiago Silva da Silva[1(✉)], and Milene Selbach Silveira[2]

[1] ICT-UNIFESP, Universidade Federal de São Paulo, São Paulo, Brazil
jade.sj2@gmail.com, silvadasilva@unifesp.br
[2] PUCRS, Faculdade de Informática, Porto Alegre, Brazil
milene.silveira@pucrs.br

Abstract. Agile Methods and User-Centered Design have radically transformed the way people develop software, mostly by taking more focus on people than on processes. This study is focused on understanding the integration of Agile and User-Centered Design through usability evaluations before the development cycles. Based on a pilot study carried out in a Scrum web-based software development team, we observed great results regarding to rework decrease as well as the usability improvement of the developed system throughout its development cycle. In the context of this study, we concluded that, besides reducing rework and improving usability, pre-development usability evaluations resulted in a mindset change, affecting both the development team and stakeholders, helping them to understand the importance of this early integration of Agile and User-Centered Design.

Keywords: Agile · User-Centered Design · Evaluation · Pre-development

1 Introduction

Agile Methods have been transforming the way people work with software development mostly by taking more focus on people than processes. Similarly, the techniques that compose the User-Centered Design (UCD) methodology have been contributing to enable a simpler and more intuitive human-computer interaction, focusing on user experience and accessibility.

There are several studies around the integration of both methodologies, Agile and UCD, that aim to apply them together in a software development environment [11]. Basically because it is expected that once applied together they can bring great improvements to interactive computing systems. However, there is still a lot to be discussed about how to perform this integration.

One of them is applying usability evaluations on mockups before the development starts in order to anticipate possible defects and avoid rework. Based on

M. Kurosu (Ed.): HCI 2016, Part I, LNCS 9731, pp. 586–597, 2016.
DOI: 10.1007/978-3-319-39510-4_54

this statement, the main goal of this study is to understand if the integration of UCD and Agile through usability evaluations before development cycles is useful to eliminate rework.

The study was divided into two phases, the first dedicated to a systematic review based in the work of da Silva et al. [12] and the second dedicated to the implementation of a study using a set of methods identified in the review in order to collect results and lessons learned.

The review of da Silva et al. [12] concentrate papers about methods to integrate Agile Methodology and UCD from the most famous HCI conferences around the world. In order to select the studies that should be analyzed in the systematic review we filtered the papers according to the timing of usability evaluation execution. We considered only the papers related to methods that propose usability evaluations before the development cycles during the quantitative and qualitative analysis.

In the second phase, we ran a pilot study using a set of methods from the systematic review applied according to project's context. The lessons learned gathered during this experience transcended the expected benefits and brought not only rework reduction but also a new and collaborative mindset to the teams involved.

The remaining of this paper is organized into four sections as follows: the second section is regarding to the systematic review results, the third one is a description about the pilot study and the application of the methods, the fourth one is related to the results and lessons learned and the last section presents the conclusions of this study.

2 Systematic Review

As aforementioned, the first phase of this study was the implementation of a systematic review based on the study by da Silva et al. [12] in order to map usability evaluation methods applied in a pre-development stage in an agile environment.

Starting from a total of 46 papers about the integration of Agile and UCD, only 17 were identified by containing evaluation methods in the timing expected. The next two subsections present the quantitative and qualitative analyzes about the methods identified.

2.1 Quantitative Analysis

Regarding to the agile framework used in experiences reported in the papers, 4 of the 17 registered the use of XP, 3 registered Scrum, 2 used both and 4 did not mention which agile framework was used. The other 4 papers were not about a real experience but only a method proposal that did not mention any specific framework. This means that the most part of the analyzed methods that applies pre-development usability evaluations uses XP.

Regarding to the artifacts used in these evaluations, evolutive prototypes are the most used, in other words, prototypes that starts simple and evolves according to user tests results and requirements grooming. The second one is the low fidelity prototypes once the evaluations are being executed during a phase when nothing was developed yet. These results are presented in Fig. 1.

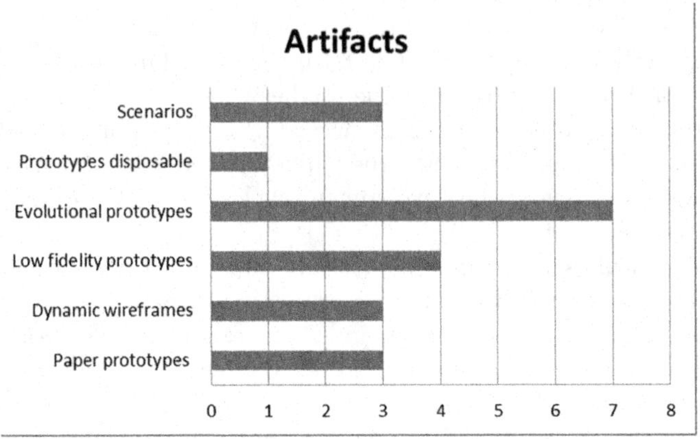

Fig. 1. Artifacts used per paper.

In relation to the distribution of papers based on the usability evaluation method applied, user tests are still the most used one, even before the development. The user tests are combined to the other methods (Figs. 2 and 3).

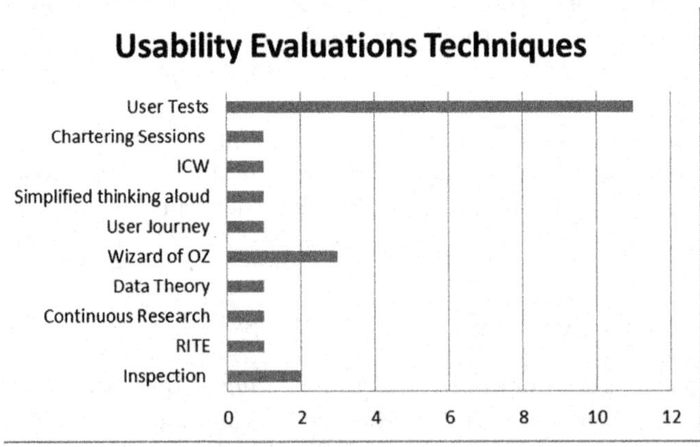

Fig. 2. Usability evaluation methods.

2.2 Qualitative Analysis

In this subsection we present the usability evaluation methods identified and the results presented by using each one of them.

User Tests. User Tests are mentioned as pre-development usability evaluation method in 11 – [1,2,4,6–8,10,13,14] – of the 17 papers.

The artifacts used are mainly different levels of prototypes used alone or combined with other artifacts such as scenarios and storyboards. About the prototype level, each study presents different advantages, for example, in low fidelity prototypes the users feel more comfortable to suggest changes, otherwise high fidelity prototypes allows a better feedback about what is working well or not.

The results presented by the papers that experienced user tests as main method, combined or not with other methods, were positive regarding to rework elimination which reflects directly in the reduce of project duration and cost [1,2,4,6,7,14]. Besides that, this method not only showed results in UCD but also in requirements grooming, setting users expectations about the project and allowing the development team to focus on implement a more valuable software.

Chartering Sessions. This method was quoted only in one – [14] – paper and combined with user tests based on low fidelity prototypes. The Chartering Sessions are sessions conducted after user tests focused on the discussion of feedback from user tests and on the analysis if the system meets users real needs.

Decrease of rework hours and improvement on requirements prioritization are the two most valuable results reached by using this method.

ICW - Informal Cognitive WalkThrough. This method is mentioned only in one paper – [5] – and it is used alone and not combined to user tests. The ICW main objective is to identify and correct usability issues easily and quickly. It is an inspection that is based on potential usability issues and the discussions around its solutions. The main results registered by using this are the decrease of user participation on the process besides the decrease of rework hours once the usability issues are fixed before the implementation.

Simplified Thinking Aloud. In the same way as the last method, this one is mentioned only in one paper – [7] – that describes it as a method of interviews, on which the users execute usability tests out loud exposing their objectives, feelings and worries during all evaluation execution in order to allow the observer to capture pain points, improvements and issues.

Once it promotes an easy language of iterative feedback, this method can or not count with the participation of a UCD specialist, what is a great benefit compared to the others that requires this role.

User Journey. This method is mentioned in a superficial way in only one paper – [2] – and it is composed by scenarios and its execution by different personas in order to obtain what are the paths taken when executing the software main tasks and to identify the issues that may be faced by users. The paper does not present any information about the results obtained when using it.

Wizard of Oz. Mentioned in three papers, this is the second most used method, one of these papers talks about its use and the others propose tools to use it [9].

The users are divided to play the roles of key users, system and help system, the last one offering instructions about how the system should answer based on each action and helping with key users' doubts.

Besides the reduction of rework hours, there is the identification of important features that should be absorbed in project scope and the assurance of users acceptance in Users/Usability Acceptance Tests (UAT).

Data Theory. It is assumed that the iterative planning affects user interface, also, this interactions guide usability tests that impacts on development cycle [4]. Taking this in mind, in order to prevent possible changes, the method proposes that UCD specialists must design prototypes and conduct usability tests in order to refine requirements two cycles ahead the first development cycle. The user requirements were better defined and comprehended guiding the prioritization what brings as results the decrease of rework hours.

RITE - Rapid Iterative Testing and Evaluation. The main problem that this method aim to solve is the identification of usability issues before the software implementation giving to the team a timebox to solve and improve it [3]. It is a user story maturity model based on usability tests that are watched by the development team that capture easily users needs and problems faced by them.

Usability Inspection. The usability inspection is usually applied within user tests. These inspections are not executed by users but by UCD specialists. The UCD specialists navigates in the prototypes searching by possibles usability problems based on this methodologies principles [6]. The main advantage of this model is the reduction of user tests cycle time once the specialists capture and solve usability problems during user tests.

3 Experience Report

This section presents the pilot study developed based on the application of pre-development evaluation methods identified during the first phase – systematic review.

3.1 The Research Site

The company where the study was carried out is a north American pharmaceutical multinational. More specifically in the sub-area responsible for web implementation that was transitioning from waterfall to Agile methods using Scrum as the main framework.

It is easy to understand that the team was not mature yet concerning agile implementation and they were institutionalizing a more people-centered mindset by taking the Agile Manifesto as basis.

About the User-Centered Design, the Latin America department does not have any focus on this neither specialists with background that covers this topic.

3.2 The Project

The software deliver area aimed to improve data collection to generate software engineering metrics. This collection has already been generated manually. A global team is in charge of this collection through excel files filled by all software development areas of the company.

The process of collecting these metrics presented a lot of problems to generate metrics in addition to the overtaxed process to consolidate all the gathered information, keeping the consistency and data standardization.

In order to optimize this process, the global team responsible by collect and generate these metrics requested an internal project to develop a web portal that allows project managers to input project information used to generate engineering metrics.

Besides that, the project scope was also composed by additional features as reporting calendar configuration, roles delegation for vacation or other out of office activities and alerts setting. The web portal should be accessed by people from around the world with different profiles and this implies in the importance and relevance of n UCD approach.

3.3 The People

The company implemented a new software development program composed by technicians hired through a process based on software development marathons. That way, the team was composed by young people with a low level of experience lead by a senior analyst.

The development team was composed by 5 people from the above cited program. On one hand, the team did not have maturity on software development, and some technical problems were faced. On the other hand, this lack of knowledge and experience provided a mindset change to this team and this fact facilitated the utilization of agile methods and UCD methods.

Regarding to the Scrum Master, he did not played this role before and did not know about UCD despite some trainings related to that. Also, the development team and Scrum Masters were allocated in the same room during the entire project.

The Product Owner also did not have any knowledge related to agile or UCD. He was a member of the global team accountable by software engineering metrics definition and consolidation. Also, this person was not even allocated in the same country as the rest of the team and participated remote in all meetings.

3.4 Methods Definition

During the Sprint 0, user stories and high fidelity prototypes were created besides the identification of the key users. Based on these artifacts and information available in this preparation phase, that occurs before the beginning of development cycle, the following methods identified during systematic review were chosen to be applied: user tests with high fidelity prototypes and usability inspections. Besides that, guidelines based on Nielsen's Heuristics were created to drive team's mindset implementation and UCD application.

About the other methods identified during the systematic review:

- Chartering Sessions could not be applied because the team did not count with any UCD specialist;
- ICW has as main motivator for its applicability decrease the hours of user participation, but it was not a problem in this context, contrariwise, the user engagement was really good once it was an internal project.
- The Wizard of Oz requires users together in some sessions, and it was discarded because once the users works in different projects, they had some difficult to participate in the same sessions.
- Once the project already had a set of high fidelity prototypes and user stories defined, Data Theory was also discarded.
- RITE was not used once it takes a lot of time from development team in usability evaluations and this fact goes against the conditions presented by leadership team – not use development teams time to usability methods in order to not impact project's implementation.

3.5 Methods Application

When presenting the proposal of applicability of UCD evaluation methods pre-development for the agile project stated here, the company allows the pilot execution using the two methods mentioned before, if the following conditions were respected:

- Development Team should not be allocated for too much time to work in the execution of UCD methods.
- Not all usability issues identified during the UCD evaluations would be corrected but only the prioritized ones.
- The usability evaluations should not generate rework to development team.

In order to start the application of evaluation methods, the first step to be performed was the definition of personas based on the stakeholders already identified by the product owner. Once the personas were defined, at least one person representing each persona was called to execute the user tests based on the high fidelity prototypes.

After the execution of user tests, the identified defects were organized in an artefact to be presented to the Product Owner in order to be prioritized. The artefact used was organized by dividing the defects by the total number of people who reported it, starting from those ones reported by the most part of the personas until those reported by only one.

Once the defects were prioritized, they were fixed according to the Product Owner definition. After the defects fixing, the prototypes were updated in order to reflect the changes applied and the first sprint development was based on them.

Once UCD was a method never used before by the development team, the absorption of its application importance took more time than expected. To aware the team and help them to apply this methods, a workshop was presented explaining UCD methodology, focusing mainly, in the Nielsen's Heuristics and how to use it in usability inspections. Examples using the interface of this project itself were used in the workshop as a way to facilitate team's engagement and learnability.

After the workshop, usability inspections were performed in the updated high fidelity prototypes and other versions were created to fix the issues identified. Also, as an alternative to help the team to develop the expected mindset, a guideline was developed contemplating Nielsen's heuristics and usability best practices (e.g. error messages standardization, buttons design, etc.).

After the guidelines implementation, every sprint from the second onwards followed the same rules. The team kept developing user stories until the product backlog be completed and the deploy was executed. During all the development cycle the team worked on the continuous improvement of the guidelines in order to cover all the rules that could help them to increase the use of usability methods and provide a portal that allows a better and easier experience to the user.

In order to gather conclusive information, after the deployment, the user tests were executed again and the results generated were analyzed and compared to the results obtained in the user tests executed in the prototypes in the preparation phase (Sprint 0).

4 Findings and Discussion

We observed great results with regards to the main goal of this experiment that is rework decreasing. Also, the integration of User-Centered Design and Agile Methodology worked very well even with this change in the way usability evaluations used to be applied.

Besides the expected results already mentioned, it was verified mindset changes from the stakeholders, Product Owner and the development teams regarding to the importance of usability matter.

Those results will be detailed in the next sections.

Rework Decrease. The results obtained regarding to the decrease of rework hours and the usability issues identified on each sprint were recorded and compared.

In the first sprint, one user test was already executed in the preparation phase but the workshop was not been executed yet. Therefore the team was still immature and the usability issues were bigger than in other phases. From the moment that the workshop ran and the team was presented to UCD concepts and methods, the usability issues number were decreasing, sprint by sprint, according to the team experience and the guidelines were being improved.

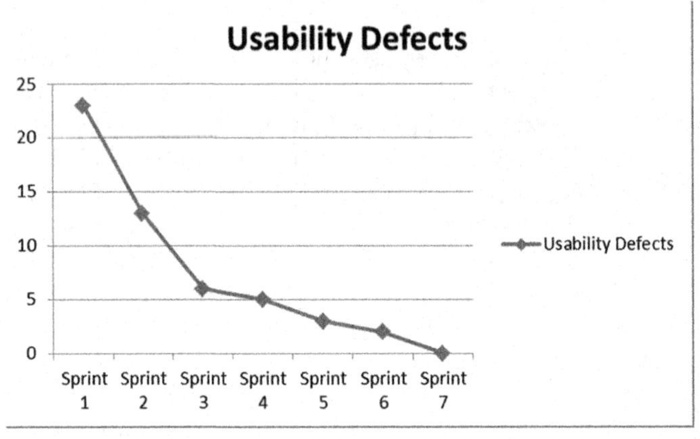

Fig. 3. Usability Defects per sprint

As expected, the usability issues were anticipated once the evaluations were been executed pre-development cycles and, this way, the most part of the user stories were fixed even before its implementation.

Usability Improvement. The results generated in the first user test – that occurred before the usability methods – were compared to results of the user tests that occurred after the pilot implementation and evaluation methods application.

It is important to mention the measure used to compare those two user tests. During the user tests, the key users representing personas executed 9 tasks. For each task it was registered if the key user had success on completing this or not. Also, for each task executed it was count the quantity of steps needed to finish the task. Comparing the results from both user tests, in the second round of tests, a hundred percent of the key users executed the tasks with less steps than in the first round.

Regarding the results, it can be observed in the Figs. 4 and 5 that the quantity of issues decreased substantially once the usability methods were applied and the improvements were made based on it.

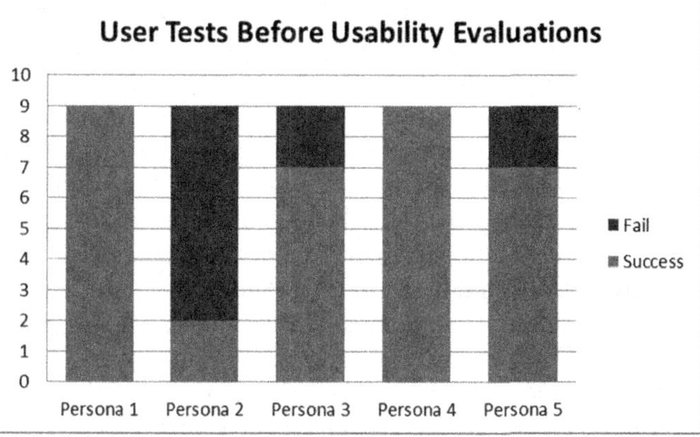

Fig. 4. User Tests before evaluations.

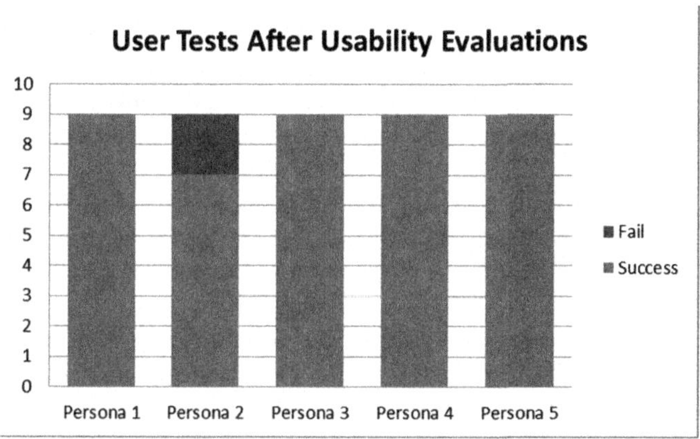

Fig. 5. User tests after evaluations.

Besides the counting of steps mentioned before, another used measure was to analyze if the user experience was improved or not. After the user tests, each key user provided feedback about the system usability. In the first user test, the team received a bad feedback from key users once they reported a lot of difficulties to complete the tasks and understand the system. In the second user tests, the feedback received were really positive and some of them mentioned how great was execute those test before development cycles.

5 Conclusion and Lessons Learned

We faced a lot of barriers to implement this method. Aware the team about the importance of usability quality and avoid rework by doing usability evaluations before the development begins was not a problem once the team was young and had already the mindset of continuous improvement pretty ingrained.

Still, one of the challenges faced was the defects report to development team. In the beginning there was a little discomfort with the quantity of usability defects reported. However, after the workshop presentation, the team learnt about usability evaluations, defects, and the importance of a good system usability. This was essential to change their behaviour with regards to the defects reported. After this workshop they created a critical opinion about system usability quality and the team itself started to report usability defects and fix them.

The main challenge faced to implement this model was the part of convincing the leadership board that it was an important matter and it has value including to spend time from development team. In order to go through this and receive the free pass to implement the proposed model, it was presented to them the results from user tests A, the comments added by key users in feedback sessions and mainly, all of this organized in the way to exposure how many defects were identified and tasks that were not completed.

Another interesting issue that should be mentioned is regarding to the project team profile: the team were not composed by any UX specialist and even this way, the team could execute usability evaluations and identify usability defects and, also, correct them before development what avoid rework, as mentioned before.

Another important issue is that, besides the team mindset change, the usability evaluations started to be appreciated also by the PO team and indirect stakeholders. We shared with them all work executed based on Usability heuristics and user tests and how the system was improved by that. This impacted the way they evaluate a system quality and even in UAT tests, they requested some changes regarding to the usability. In other words, their mindset changed and they also recognized the importance of this matter.

About the rework reduction, it is clear, based on the discussed results, that it was successful. Also, the goal to integrate Agile methods and UCD worked well even executing the usability evaluations before the development begins and the results exceeded the expectations affecting also the sphere of team and stakeholders mindset.

Acknowledgments. This research was supported by FAPESP, Brazil, proc. 2014/25779-3.

References

1. Beyer, H., Holtzblatt, K., Baker, L.: An agile customer-centered method: rapid contextual design. In: Zannier, C., Erdogmus, H., Lindstrom, L. (eds.) XP/Agile Universe 2004. LNCS, vol. 3134, pp. 50–59. Springer, Heidelberg (2004)
2. Chamberlain, S., Sharp, H., Maiden, N.A.M.D.: Towards a framework for integrating agile development and user-centred design. In: Abrahamsson, P., Marchesi, M., Succi, G. (eds.) XP 2006. LNCS, vol. 4044, pp. 143–153. Springer, Heidelberg (2006)

3. Fisher, K.G., Bankston, A.: From cradle to sprint: creating a full-lifecycle request pipeline at nationwide insurance. In: Proceedings of the 2009 Agile Conference, AGILE 2009, pp. 223–228. IEEE Computer Society, Washington, DC (2009)
4. Fox, D., Sillito, J., Maurer, F.: Agile methods and user-centered design: how these two methodologies are being successfully integrated in industry. In: Proceedings of the AGILE 2008, pp. 63–72. IEEE Computer Society, Washington, DC (2008). http://dx.doi.org/10.1109/Agile.2008.78
5. Grigoreanu, V., Mohanna, M.: Informal cognitive walkthroughs (icw): paring down and pairing up for an agile world. In: Proceedings of the SIGCHI Conference on Human Factors in Computing Systems, CHI 2013, pp. 3093–3096. ACM, New York (2013). http://dx.doi.acm.org/10.1145/2470654.2466421
6. Hussain, Z., Milchrahm, H., Shahzad, S., Slany, W., Tscheligi, M., Wolkerstorfer, P.: Integration of extreme programming and user-centered design: lessons learned. In: Abrahamsson, P., Marchesi, M., Maurer, F. (eds.) Agile Processes in Software Engineering and Extreme Programming. LNBIP, vol. 31, pp. 174–179. Springer, Heidelberg (2009)
7. Kane, D.: Finding a place for discount usability engineering in agile development: throwing down the gauntlet. In: Proceedings of the Agile Development Conference, ADC 2003, pp. 40–46, June 2003
8. Kollmann, J., Sharp, H., Blandford, A.: The importance of identity and vision to user experience designers on agile projects. In: Agile Conference, AGILE 2009, pp. 11–18, August 2009
9. Meszaros, G., Aston, J.: Adding usability testing to an agile project. In: Proceedings of the Conference on AGILE 2006, pp. 289–294. IEEE Computer Society, Washington, DC (2006). http://dx.doi.org/10.1109/AGILE.2006.5
10. Najafi, M., Toyoshiba, L.: Two case studies of user experience design and agile development. In: Proceedings of the AGILE 2008, pp. 531–536. IEEE Computer Society, Washington, DC (2008). http://dx.doi.org/10.1109/Agile.2008.67
11. Silva, T., Martin, A., Maurer, F., Silveira, M.: User-centered design and agile methods: a systematic review. In: Agile Conference, AGILE 2011, pp. 77–86 (2011)
12. Silva da Silva, T., Silveira, F.F., Silveira, M.S., Hellmann, T., Maurer, F.: A systematic mapping on agile UCD across the major agile and HCI conferences. In: Gervasi, O., Murgante, B., Misra, S., Gavrilova, M.L., Rocha, A.M.A.C., Torre, C., Taniar, D., Apduhan, B.O. (eds.) ICCSA 2015. LNCS, vol. 9159, pp. 86–100. Springer, Heidelberg (2015)
13. Ungar, J.: The design studio: interface design for agile teams. In: Proceedings of the AGILE 2008, pp. 519–524. IEEE Computer Society, Washington, DC (2008). http://dx.doi.org/10.1109/Agile.2008.51
14. Williams, H., Ferguson, A.: The ucd perspective: before and after agile. In: Proceedings of the AGILE 2007, pp. 285–290. IEEE Computer Society,Washington, DC (2007). http://dx.doi.org/10.1109/AGILE.2007.61

Can Situations Help with Reusability of Software?

Hua Ming[1(✉)] and Carl K. Chang[2]

[1] Oakland University, Rochester, MI 48309, USA
ming@oakland.edu
[2] Iowa State University, Ames, IA 50010, USA
chang@iastate.edu

Abstract. Software reusability is an important concept, as well as a powerful tool, to achieve modular solutions in the design and implementation of modern software systems. There is a wide array of research studies conducted in this area ranging from conceptual level to software construction level. Despite all these good pieces of work, software engineers still need to face the complications that strictly separate design time activities from those carried out at software construction time, to shift their mental gear between high level specification properties and low level implementation details. To bridge this gap, we propose a unified approach to facilitate software reuse. We seek to carry out this enterprise surrounding an abstraction, namely *Situation*. More specifically, we have created a computing environment and, under its runtime support, a functional programming language called $Situ^f$ in which domain experts can capture the features of a software system in terms of functional expressions. For each $Situ^f$ program, declarations and functional expressions provide essential definitions of *Situations*. Some language constructs of $Situ^f$, such as the import and include directives, are designed to make it easier to compose new software features by reusing existing ones.

1 Introduction and Related Work

Software reuse [9,10] is a powerful concept and realistic technique in the design and construction of modern software systems. Often in a mutually promotive relationship with modular programming [20], software reuse advocates a systematic embrace for the ideal of fully exploiting existing well tested code towards building new software under reduced development time, increased productivity and reliability.

The support for software reuse from modern programming languages, component-oriented and framework-based technologies, middleware, as well as from the state-of-the-art of modern software construction practices, has steadily improved over the years. All these advantages, among other factors such as psychology of programming and human factor improvement, are good preparations leading software reuse to a certain degree of success [19]. On the flip side however, problems such as idiosyncrasies and heterogeneities between different software

M. Kurosu (Ed.): HCI 2016, Part I, LNCS 9731, pp. 598–609, 2016.
DOI: 10.1007/978-3-319-39510-4_55

applications and application domains have been constraining the growing impact and effectiveness of software reuse.

1.1 The Power of Abstraction and the Abstraction of Situation

Through the development and maturation of software engineering, as well as of programming languages, we have fully witnessed the power of abstraction [11,13,14]. By introducing abstractions, e.g., data abstractions, iteration abstractions, procedural abstractions etc., and in particular, by relating modularity to abstraction [12], the composing, understanding, as well as the debugging and maintenance of a gigantic computer program can be carried out in separate manageable pieces. Consequently, the need for literally going through all the coding details has thus been mitigated.

We propose to utilize an abstraction called **situation**, which is distilled from our previous work on *Situ* framework [5,15–18]. The concept of situation can be traced back to its root in mathematical logic [2,3], and thereafter applied to AI [21] and theoretical computer science [4]. Situation as a concept also marched into the realm of human computer interaction, contributing to the success of situation awareness technologies [8].

Extending from the situation abstraction, we come up with an infrastructure and a functional, domain specific programming language called $Situ^f$ implemented to secure the situation abstraction into concrete and practical software engineering circumstances.

2 Functional Style Situation

From *Situ* framework [5], the behavioral context of a situation represented by A as in $(d, A, E)_t$, refers to the interaction of a software system through its interface, usually a GUI, with its human user. The concept of situation intimately portrays integrated use case scenarios, including the features of the software system.

Functional programming paradigm [1] is about computing with values, where the control flow of the entire program is deeply akin to the evaluation of a mathematical function, with little, or no side effect [1]. It is more of a **what** rather than **how** process. Due to its high expressive power and elegant computational effect, in recent years functional programming paradigm keeps gaining momentum, and has already been absorbed and built into some high impact computing technologies or well known infrastructures. Google's MapReduce [6] for the processing of big data is such an example.

In this work, we argue that functional situations present a powerful abstraction to model software features. The motivation behind this paper is this: **if we can program functional situations, where runtime environment**[1]

[1] Figure 4 is such an environment.

links situations with software features, then software reusability can be translated to situation reusability.

$$map\ (\ (submit\_review.download),\ [paper_1,\ paper_2,\ \dots\ paper_n]\ ) \tag{1}$$

(1) above is an example functional expression:

- It features a functional expression, where higher order function **map** is used;
- For **map**, the composite function *submit_review.download* is one of its inputs;
- The composite function *submit_review.download* intrinsically reflects a temporal order: *download* goes first, *submit_review* second;
- (1) specifies a paper review situation, corresponding to a software feature like in MyReview software[2], shown in Fig. 1.

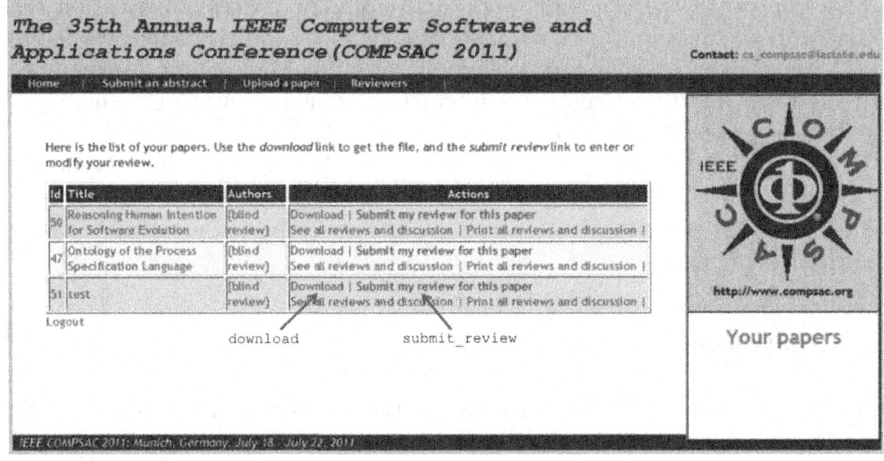

Fig. 1. Paper review situation vs. paper reivew software feature under MyReview software

The most important software features shown in Fig. 1 are marked by red arrows along with the names of the two functions in functional expression (1), i.e., "*dowload*" and "*submit_review*". Further, a moment's reflection reveals that the functional expression (1) captures the bareback essentials of the software features demonstrated in Fig. 1.

Indeed, functional expression (1) models the software features that allow the user, in this case a paper reviewer, to download papers and to submit reviews. It is a **situation** whose semantics is resulted by evaluating the functional expression (1).

It is a key observation from the preceding example that a situation may naturally take its form, or syntax, from extending a functional expression like (1).

[2] http://myreview.sourceforge.net.

In addition, a functional expression like (1) can semantically capture the essentials of the targeted software features. Situations thus proposed is a solid abstraction that carries both its syntax and semantics.

We further state that situation is an easy to use yet powerful abstraction for domain engineers. Using Fig. 1 again as an example: without the situation abstraction, Fig. 1 simply points to a bunch of software features for MyReview system; with the situation abstraction, Fig. 1 is simply one situation, namely paper review situation, for example. Its meaning is expressed via functional expression (1). The abstraction of situation is applied here in a natural and intuitive manner. On the following pages, we present a domain specific, functional programming language, named $Situ^f$ to further promote the abstraction of situations.

3 The Design of a Functional Domain Specific Language

To introduce $Situ^f$, we follow the reverse order: we will first present a program written in it, *i.e.,* Program 1 given in Fig. 2. Program 1 is a $Situ^f$ program for the paper review situation just discussed.

Program 1 A $Situ^f$ program for paper review situation

```
include GUI_Service_MyReview
import Context_Spec_MyReview

program paperReview
  data
    declare
      paper@129.186.93.0:/home/myreview/              \
            COMPSAC2011_Training/Review.php;
    declare
      Review@129.186.93.0:/home/myreview/             \
            COMPSAC2011_Training/Review.php;

  action
    declare
      download<None:paper>@129.186.93.0:/home/         \
          myreview/COMPSAC2011_Training/Review.php;
    declare
      submit_review<paper:Review>@129.186.93.0:/home/        \
          myreview/COMPSAC2011_Training/Review.php;

  situation
    map submit_review.download paper();
```

Fig. 2. A $Situ^f$ program for paper review situation

Program 1 defines context-oriented paperReview situation, following the original *Situ* framework, where all situations are based on behavioral and environmental contexts.

1. The notion of @ creates an IO channel in a $Situ^f$ program called *paperReview* to bind data and action to their real world counterparts: a paper can

be downloaded from Review.php, whose server-side url is specified; Review can be submitted and later on collected also through the same page. Each time a paper is downloaded or a review is submitted through Review.php, the contextual information will be captured by @ and sent back to program *paperReview.* @ is an I/O based language feature. Once declared, data and action can be used to construct a situation.

2. ( ) is another I/O based feature $Situ^f$ offers. It is a data constructor: at run-time paper() returns a list of papers resulted by a series of paper downloading actions performed on Review.php of the deployed MyReview system. Figure 3 helps illustrate this point.
3. Closely related with SituIO and its @ operator is the <program_url>[3] defined in the attribute grammar of $Situ^f$ at Table 1. This symbol specifies where $Situ^f$ runtime is able to find the external counterpart that supplies contextual information to declared data, actions and situations defined in Program 1 (Fig. 2.) Situation services provides the implementation.

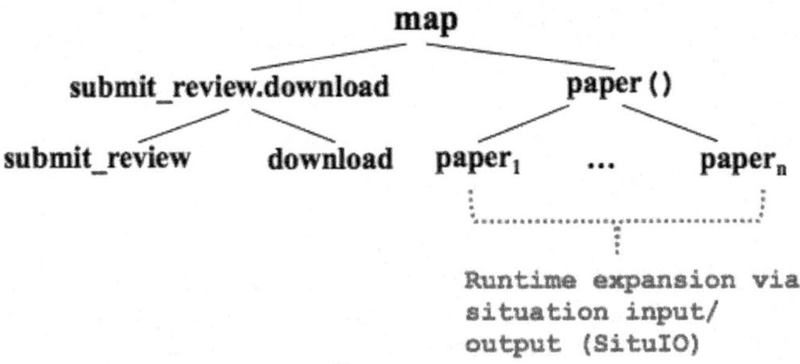

Fig. 3. Runtime expansion of "paper()"

3.1 Syntactical Features

The details of the attribute grammar for $Situ^f$ are given in Table 1. The data and action declarations in Program 1 (Fig. 2) set up the data, as well as the action to construct a situation. @ operator connects data structures like paper and Review to their real world data source. For Program 1 (Fig. 2) the source of data for paper and review is the server-side *Review.php*. This simply means that each time the user downloads a paper through Review.php, the context data related to that paper such as author list, email contact and abstract etc. ... will be collected over the Graphical User Interface and sent back to Program 1 runtime. More concretely, through paper(), context information of all assigned papers

[3] <prog_url> denotes a program url which takes the form of server_IP_address:serverside_absolute_directory. For programs on your local machine, simply use 255.255.255.255; .

are captured incrementally one after another and are given as input to review action. When the user finishes reviewing that paper and generates a *Review*[4], the *Review* will be captured in terms of its context ensemble: an aggregation of review comments, review score, suggestions to the Program Committee, etc. The communication is carried out while all intermediate results are recorded through XML intermediate representation.

Situ^f provides four built-in functional patterns as situation constructors to propagate contexts, or in attribute grammar's terms: *attributes*, to the entire parse tree. These four built-in patterns are **map, filter, reduce and apply**. The *map* pattern is used in Program 1 (Fig. 2) in statement "map submit_review.download paper()" to describe a situation where a reviewer needs to download and then review every paper assigned to her/him. The *map* pattern, commonly found in functional programming paradigm, applies its first input, i.e. the temporally combined action of downloading and then reviewing ("submit_review.download") to its second input, which is a list of papers. Readers familiar with functional programming know that *map* is a higher-order function that applies the first argument it accepts, which is a function or a composed function, to its second argument, usually a sequence of data such as the paper list aforementioned. *Situ*^{f} introduces *map* pattern so that its first argument can be re-used for all members in its second argument. Overall, applying *map* pattern over a list is to transform the list to another by working on each and every member of the list according to its first argument; in Specification (1), a list of reviewed papers that are attached with review comments and scores etc. are the end result for the main success scenario for Specification (1).

3.2 Situ^f-based Environment

The situation model that *Situ*^{f} is built upon is context-oriented, where context data are derived from actions exerted by a user over a software system. However a software system itself does not provide extra functionality to support context data collection tasks. The design of *Situ*^{f} keeps that in mind and proposes a special *include* directive to "include" situation services that provide context collection capabilities. Situation services are programs with implementation to collect context information for different *Situ*^{f} programs.

With concrete examples, this section elaborates on the technical details of context specification, situation services, their relationship with XML, their affiliation to a *Situ*^{f} program and finally the active roles they play towards a *Situ*^{f}-based environment.

According to the grammar of *Situ*^{f} language, the major constituents of a situation are *data* and *actions*. In a *Situ*^{f} program, the situation constructors, i.e., map, reduce, filter and apply, are used to assemble data and actions declared into a meaningful situation. This means that the context information in a *Situ*^{f} program is classified into two categories: data context and action context. Action context is built on top of data context, as the input and output of each action

[4] the data type declared in Program 1 (Fig. 2.) .

Table 1. Attribute grammar for $Situ^f$

(1) <program>	→ [**include** <service_list>][**import** <situation_spec_list>] **program** <identifier> **data** <dataDeclList> **action** <actionDeclList> **situation** <SituStmtList> $\{< SituStmtList >_{env} = < dataDeclList >_{env}$ $\cup < actionDeclList >_{env} \cup < service\_name >_{env}$ $\cup < situaion\_spec >_{env} \}$
(2)<identifier>	→ $[a \ldots \mid z \mid A \ldots \mid Z \mid \_]^{+}[0 \mid \ldots \mid 9 \mid a \ldots \mid z \mid A \ldots \mid Z \mid \_ \mid \backslash]^{*}$
(3)<dataName>	→ **None** $\{ < dataName >_{env} = \phi\}$
(4)<dataName>	→ <identifier> $\{ < dataName >_{env} = \{< identifier > .id\} \}$
(5)<dataDeclList>	→ **declare** <dataName>**@**<prog_url> $\{ \quad < dataDeclList >_{env} = < dataName > .env$ $\cup \{< prog\_url > .id\} \quad \}$
(6)<*dataDeclList*^{1}>	→ **declare**<dataName>**@**<prog_url>; <*dataDeclList*^{2}> $\{ \ < dataDeclList^1 >_{env} = < dataName > .env$ $\cup \{< prog\_url > .id\} \cup < dataDeclList^2 >_{env} \quad \}$
(7)<action>	→ **None** $\{< action >_{env} = \phi\}$
(8)<action>	→ <indentifier> $\{ < action >_{env} = \{< identifier > .id\} \}$
(9)<actionList>	→ <action> $\{ < actionList >_{env} = < action >_{env} \}$
(10)$< actionList >^1$	→ <action>.$< actionList >^2$ $\{ < actionList >^1_{env} = < action >_{env} \cup < actionList >^2_{env} \}$
(11)<input>	→ **None** $\{ < input >_{env} = \phi \}$
(12)<input>	→ <identifier> $\{ < input >_{env} = \{< identifier > .id\}\}$
(13)$< input >^1$	→ <identifier>,$< input >^2$ $\{ < input >^1_{env} = \{< identifier >_{id}\} \cup < input >^2_{env} \}$
(14)<output>	→ **None** $\{ < output >_{env} = \phi \}$
(15)<output>	→ <identifier> $\{ < output >_{env} = \{< identifier > .id\}\}$
(16)$< output >^1$	→ <idnetifier>,$< output >^2$ $\{ < output >^1_{env} = \{< identifier >_{id}\} \cup < output >^2_{env} \}$
(17)<actionDeclList>	→ **declare**<actionList>($< input >$:$< output >$) **@<prog_url>** $\{ \quad < actionDeclList >_{env} = < actionList > .env$ $\cup < input > .env \cup < output > .env$ $\cup \{< prog\_url > .id\} \quad \}$
(18)<actionDeclList>	→ **declare**<actionList>($< input >$:$< output >$) **@<prog_url>** ;<actionDeclList> $\{ < actionDeclList >_{env} = < actionList > .env$ $\cup < input >_{env} \cup < output >_{env}$ $\cup < prog\_url > .id \cup < actionDeclList >_{env} \}$
(19)<situStmtList>	→ <situStmt> $\{< situStmt >_{env} = < situStmtList >_{env}\}$
(20)<situStmtList^1>	→ <situStmt>;<situStmtList^2> $\{< situStmt >_{env} = < situStmtList >_{env}$ $< situStmtList^2 >_{env} = < situStmtList^1 >_{env}\}$
(21)<situStmt>	→ **map** <actionList> <dataName>() $\{map_{env} = < situStmt >_{env} \cup < actionList >_{env}$ $\cup < dataName > ()_{env}\}$
(22)<situStmt>	→ **filter** <actionList> <dataName>() $\{filter_{env} = < situStmt >_{env} \cup < actionList >_{env}$ $\cup < dataName > ()_{env}\}$
(23)<situStmt>	→ **reduce** <actionList> <dataName>() $\{reduce_{env} = < situStmt >_{env} \cup < actionList >_{env}$ $\cup < dataName > ()_{env}\}$
(24)<situStmt>	→ **apply** <actionList> <dataName> $\{apply_{env} = < situStmt >_{env} \cup < actionList >_{env}$ $\cup < dataName >_{env}\}$

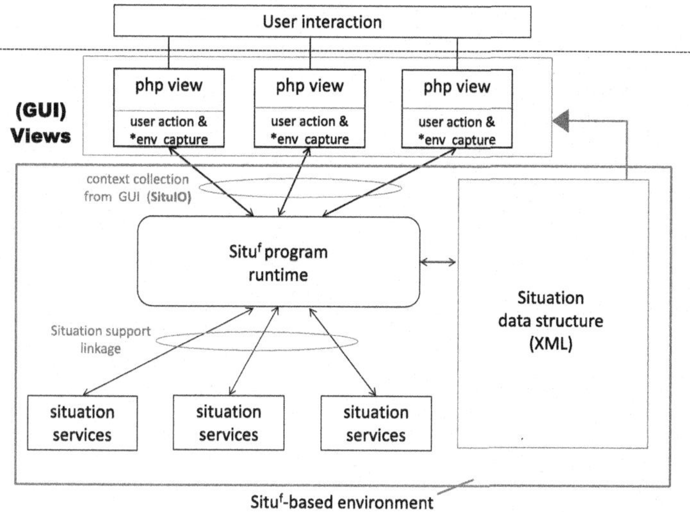

Fig. 4. *Situ*^{f}-based environment: the overview

come from data. We will concentrate on explaining data context, through which action context should seem easy.

In *Situ*^{f} environment, context information, either for data or for action, is represented and transmitted using XML format. We use XML Schema to configure "context" templates to synchronize the communication between a *Situ*^{f} program and the external context collection capabilities, i.e., situation services, under a *Situ*^{f}-based environment.

To provide concrete explanations and illustrations for key issues involved, let us revisit the paper review example given in Program 1 (Fig. 2.) The attribute grammar of *Situ*^{f} given in Table 1 requires that each declared *data*, represented by grammar symbol <dataName>, have an attribute called *env*, meaning *environment.* This is a composite attribute. Its runtime implication depends on the context specification the *Situ*^{f} program imports. In fact each paper declared in Program 1 (Fig. 2) contains the following attributes: *abstract*, *author_name*, *author_affiliation*, *email_contact*, *paperID*, *submitTime*, and *target_trackName.*

This detailed context information is generally beyond the concern or knowledge of a domain expert, but it is very important to answer the attribute grammar requests. *Situ*^{f}'s support of **separation of concerns** [7] bridges this gap. More concretely, *Situ*^{f} offers an *import* clause feature. As seen in Program 1 (Fig. 2), the "Context_Spec_MyReview" following the "import" directive is an instance of <situation_spec>, which is encoded as an XML Schema given in Fig. 5.

In fact, XML Schema enables *user-defined data types*, comprising *simple data types*, which cannot use elements or attributes, and *complex data types*, which can use elements and attributes [22]. Complex data types can also be defined from already existing data types. The XML Schema given in Fig. 5 essentially provides

```
<? XML version="1.0" encoding="UTF-16" ?>

<MyReview:schema xmlns:MyReview="http://www.w3.org/2001/XMLSchema"
version="1.0"s>
<MyReview:element name="paper" type="paperType">
     <MyReview:complexType name="paperType">
          <all>
               <element name="abstract" type="string" use="required"/>
               <element name="author_name" type='string" minOccurs="1"
                              maxOccurs="unbounded" />
               <element name="author_affiliation" type="string" minOccurs="1"
                              maxOccurs="unbounded" />
               <element name="email_contact" type="string" use="required"
                              maxOccurs="1" />
               <element name="paperID" type="integer" use="required" />
               <element name="submitTime" type="date" use="required" />
               <element name="targeted_trackName" type="string" use="required"
                              maxOccurs="1" />
               <element name="conference_name" type="string" use="required" />
          </all>
     </MyReview:complexType>
</MyReview:element>
</MyReview:schema>
```

Fig. 5. An XML schema-based context template for the paper data type

a template to help bind *paper*, a data variable declared in Program 2, and its closely related context. Note that Fig. 5 provides detailed attributes pertaining to the specific situations associated with the MyReview system. The associating power is further enhanced by the use of *namespace* MyReview in Fig. 5. That said, a paper under a different circumstance, such as the "EasyChair" software system, could involve completely different attributes, the use of which requires the importing of a different XML schema. Besides, the use of namespace in an XML Schema helps to disambiguate identical naming and to differentiate between separate situation domains, e.g., MyReview vs. EasyChair[5].

Upon the import of a context specification where relevant information for a paper is provided, the $Situ^f$ compiler automatically executes the following action (**Note**: the initial *env* attribute of paper only includes its id information. To see that, from production (4) given by the attribute grammar in Table 1: $< dataName >_{env} = < identifier > .id$, when paper is declared, it replaces <dataName>.):

$$paper_{env} = paper_{env} \cup \{ \text{abstract, author\_name, author\_affiliation, email\_contact, paperID, submitTime, targeted\_trackName} \}$$

In Fig. 5, "paper" is defined as a new type, where abstract, author_name, author_affiliation, email_contact, paperID, submitTime, targeted_trackName and conference_name are its built-in fields. Each field, corresponding to the respective context of a "paper", is of a precisely defined data type, such as string, integer, etc... The diverse data types available in XML Schema make XML Schema powerful enough to specify highly diverse data different $Situ^f$ programs may face.

5 For more background information on namespace mechanism of XML schema, please consult [22].

Figure 6 is a direct instantiation of the XML Schema based context template given in Fig. 5. Given that Fig. 6 strictly follows the format prescribed by Fig. 5, the latter is hence named Context Template.

```
<?xml version="1.0" encoding="UTF-16 ?>

<paper MyReview:schemaLocation="rs.cs.iastate.edu/myreview/context-
    Spec_MyReview">
    <abstract> This paper describes a novel testing approach for ...</abstract>
    <author_name>John Schneider</author_name>
    <author_affiliation> Oakland University </author_affiliation>
    <email_contact>jschneidre@oakland.edu</email_contact>
    <paperID>215</paperID>
    <submitTime>2015-08-31</submitTime>
    <targeted_trackName>Software Testing</targeted_trackName>
    <conference_name>ACM/IEEE ICSE</conference_name>
</paper>
```

Fig. 6. A sample runtime collected context value stored in XML

Figure 6 presents a concrete runtime example of a data value traveling through SituIO. This XML element is a value for the data variable "paper" declared in Program 1 (Fig. 2). It is generated under the governing of "Context_Spec_MyReview" file, which contains the XML Schema given in Fig. 5. The XML context information shown in Fig. 6 for "paper" also presents itself as a sample value for *env* attribute of <dataName>, a grammar symbol instantiated by "paper," from $Situ^f$'s attribute grammar in Table 1. Figure 6 shows a concrete instance of context values.

3.3 The Inclusion of Situation Services

Situation services extend the capability of a $Situ^f$ program that includes them. Situation services are either made by a third party provider and hosted on the cloud, or they can be hosted on the local machine. The default situation service for $Situ^f$ is called "common_service_GUI". The default service offers the capability that, once deployed at the targeted url site, it can capture and record a software user's action information, which is then sent back through SituIO to where the $Situ^f$ runtime is deployed. What is captured by the default service is *real time* behavioral and environmental contextual information, which is configured by the central $Situ^f$ program that generally contains program url addresses.

The design and runtime support environment for $Situ^f$ as introduced facilitate the domain experts, who have domain specific knowledge of existing software features, to compose new ones. Consider again the software features of MyReview shown in Fig. 1. The paper reviewers can use it to download the assigned papers for a conference and submit their reviews. The corresponding situation program in $Situ^f$ named "paperReview", is found in Program 1 (Fig. 2.)

Program 2 A $Situ^f$ program for review reminder

```
import paperReview

program reviewReminder

 action
   declare
     email<Review:String>@129.186.93.0:/home/        \
        myreview/COMPSAC2011_Training/Admin.php;
   declare
     check_count<Integer:Bool>@129.186.93.0:/home/        \
        myreview/COMPSAC2011_Training/Util.php;

   declare
     count_words<Review:Integer>@129.186.93.0:/home/   \
        myreview/COMPSAC2011_Training/Util.php;

 situation
    map email (filter check_count.count_words paperReview);
```

Fig. 7. A $Situ^f$ program for review reminder

Now that there is a need to add a new feature named *reviewReminder* to the MyReview system, which aims to send a reminder email, after certain date, to the reviewers who have not finished their review assignments. The overall requirement for the *reviewReminder* feature is to go through all paper reviews and to count the number of words in the review comments, by which empty reviews bear zero word count. Below a certain count value, the relative reviews will be considered incomplete. Correspondingly, a reminder message is emailed to the related reviewers.

A good question to ask is how to take full advantage of, or, **re-use**, the existing system features to compose *reviewReminder*. To this end, being able to **expressively and immediately** compose the essential linkage, between existing features and **reviewReminder**, gives the software designer a leg up towards a high quality software construction. Using $Situ^f$ language and with relative ease, the domain experts can propose a short solution, i.e., a $Situ^f$ program, shown in Fig. 7.

References

1. Backus, J.: Can programming be liberated from the von neumann style? a functional style and its algebra of programs. Commun. ACM **21**(8), 613–641 (1978)
2. Barwise, J.: The Situation in Logic. Center for the Study of Langauge and Information. Stanford University, Stanford (1989)
3. Barwise, J., Perry, J.: Situations and Attitudes. MIT Press, New York (1983)
4. Barwise, J., Seligman, J.: Information Flow: The Logic of Distributed Systems. Cambridge Tracts in Theoretical Computer Science. Cambridge University Press, Cambridge (1997)
5. Chang, C.K., Jiang, H., Ming, H., Oyama, K.: Situ: a situation-theoretic approach to context-aware service evolution. IEEE Trans. Serv. Comput. **2**(3), 261–275 (2009)

6. Dean, J., Ghemawat, S.: Mapreduce: simplified data processing on large clusters. In: OSDI, p. 1 (2004)
7. Dijkstra, E.W.: On the role of scientific thought. Selected Writings on Computing: A Personal Perspective. Texts and Monographs in Computer Science, pp. 60–66. Springer, New York (1982)
8. Endsley, M.R.: Toward a theory of situation awareness in dynamic systems. Hum. Factors **37**(1), 32–64 (1995)
9. Frakes, W.B., Kang, K.: Software reuse research: status and future. IEEE Trans. Softw. Eng. **7**, 529–536 (2005)
10. Krueger, C.W.: Software reuse. ACM Comput. Surv. (CSUR) **24**(2), 131–183 (1992)
11. Liskov, B., Guttag, J.: Abstraction and Specification in Program Development. MIT press, Cambridge (1986)
12. Liskov, B., Guttag, J.: Program Development in JAVA: Abstraction, Specification, and Object-oriented Design. Pearson Education, New York (2000)
13. Liskov, B., Snyder, A., Atkinson, R., Schaffert, C.: Abstraction mechanisms in clu. Commun. ACM **20**(8), 564–576 (1977)
14. Liskov, B.H., Zilles, S.: Specification techniques for data abstractions. IEEE Trans. Softw. Eng. **1**, 7–19 (1975)
15. Ming, H.: $Situ^f$: a domain specific language and a first step towards the realization of situ framework. PhD Dissertation. Iowa State University. ProQuest Dissertations & Theses Global. UMI 3539397 (2012)
16. Ming, H., Chang, C.K., Yang, J.: Dimensional situation analytics: from data towisdom. In: 2015 IEEE 39th Annual Computer Software and Applications Conference (COMPSAC), vol. 1, pp. 50–59. IEEE (2015)
17. Ming, H., Chang, C., Oyama, K., i Yang, H.: Reasoning about human intention change for individualized runtime software service evolution. In: 2010 IEEE 34th Annual Computer Software and Applications Conference (COMPSAC), pp. 289–296, July 2010
18. Ming, H., Oyama, K., Chang, C.: Human-intention driven self adaptive software evolvability in distributed service environments. In: 12th IEEE International Workshop on Future Trends of Distributed Computing Systems 2008, FTDCS 2008, pp. 51–57, October 2008
19. Morisio, M., Ezran, M., Tully, C.: Success and failure factors in software reuse. IEEE Trans. Softw. Eng. **28**(4), 340–357 (2002)
20. Parnas, D.L.: On the criteria to be used in decomposing systems into modules. Commun. ACM **15**(12), 1053–1058 (1972)
21. Reiter, R.: The frame problem in the situation calculus: a simple solution (sometimes) and a completeness result for goal regression. Artif. Intell. Math. Theor. Comput.: Papers in Honor of John McCarthy **27**, 359–380 (1991)
22. W3C: Extensible markup language (xml) (2003). http://www.w3.org/XML/

Cloud Security: A Virtualized VLAN (V2LAN) Implementation

Farid Shirazi(✉) and Alexander Krasnov

Ryerson University, Toronto, Canada
{f2shiraz,alexander.krasnov}@ryerson.ca

Abstract. Cloud computing is an emergent technology that brings together all aspects of IT infrastructure from software installation and upgrade to platform oriented services to network and to hardware and storage. However, there are various security concerns that prevent customers from taking benefits of the cloud. Many studies have offered a wide range of possible solutions to deal with cloud security issues. Some of these solutions are very expensive therefore not suitable for Cloud. For example, data encryption is considered as a vital tool and mechanism for securing business data. However, it is not feasible to deploy data encryption on every piece of data. Anthes argues that encryption is sometimes seen as the ultimate security measure, but in fact, encryption is a complex and costly process since encrypted data needs to be downloaded and decrypted for local use and then possibly uploading the results [1]. This study offers a robust, fast and cost effective security measures for protecting Cloud data residing on virtual machines (VMs) without the need for any additional monitoring package or introspection at VM level.

Keywords: Cloud computing · V2LAN · Virtualization · Identification · Authorization · Multi-tenancy

1 Introduction

Cloud technology is a radical IT innovation that brings together operational changes to every stage of computing from software installation, upgrade, maintenance and backups, to security [2]. This brings enormous possibilities of continuous innovation [3]. At the same time these changes are precarious [4], and need previsioning of complementary resources [5].

The Cloud technology completely redefines computing infrastructure, in which the infrastructure ownership is migrating to the subscription fees. There are many benefits of Cloud over the existing in-house IT infrastructure, including but not limited to: (1) On demand self-service, (2) Broad Network Access, (3) Resource Pooling, (4) Rapid elasticity, and (5) Measured services and (6) Platform Independency. Cloud computing offers also three main services: Software as a Service (SaaS), Platform as a Service (PaaS) and Infrastructure as a Service (IaaS). On the other hand there are many security and privacy issues discussed in literature associated with each of the above services.

M. Kurosu (Ed.): HCI 2016, Part I, LNCS 9731, pp. 610–621, 2016.
DOI: 10.1007/978-3-319-39510-4_56

Many customers desire to have the security, ethical and confidentiality principles provided by their LANs while connecting to a cloud. This is in particular important for mission critical applications such as financial data, R&D and clients private information among others. As such data management and data security is one of the core components concerning many organizations. As such understanding what is public cloud data and what is secure private data are among the most challenging and important tasks that face the adoption of cloud computing by businesses. In addition, cloud data is one of the main sources of today's "big data". Hemerly argues that the term big data not only describes size, it also describes the speed, volume and computational and analytical capacity required to manage data and derive insight [6]. It is important to secure as much as possible the processes and procedures about generating, computing, collecting, disseminating and securing data. Cloud security has always been the main concern for providers and for service consumers. Every provider implements its own best practices and security frameworks to serve customers' needs better and, at the same time, to comply with regulations and government requirements. According to a 2010 IBM Global IT Risk Study 77 % of respondents think that Cloud technology makes data privacy protection more difficult; the main concern of 50 % of respondents is data loss or breach, and only 23 % worry about corporate network security as the main concern [7]. In 2010, IBM started a new initiative to make the Cloud more secure. IBM understands that one security policy would not fit the variety of customer requirements, so IBM provides teams of security consultants that work with customers on their specific security needs.

The scope of Cloud security is massive by any measures. It is clear that all aspects of security including authorization, authentication, accountability, and endpoint-to-endpoint security are important, but broader considerations such as data protection, business continuity, and disaster recovery are very important to businesses as well. Customers' data storage and usage is an ongoing struggle for data privacy management, data misuse and violation.

2 Cloud Security Issues

Using Cloud computing brings significant benefits, including increased operations and economic efficiency, enhancing scalability and collaboration, and low start-up and maintenance costs. However, without proper security and privacy solutions the whole concept could be a big failure.

Identification and **authentication** define who can log into a system, while **authorization** provides permission for users to have access to specific resources based on individual or group memberships or assigned roles. Common authentication procedures provide at least one of the following factors: something you know, something you have, something you are, and where you are. **Accountability**'s role is to keep track of the users' and system log to help identify security violations and analyze security incident [8].

With the **SaaS** model, providers implement built-in security features. In the public Cloud end-users utilize features available for this application to protect data, while in the private Cloud organization is flexible to allow for the implementation of an acceptable level of security measures. In the **PaaP** model developers are responsible for securing their own applications, while providers hold the responsibility to secure the operating system and separate applications for tenants. In the **IaaS** model developers are in charge of the whole system and have to provide low-level system security and application level security.

Multi-tenancy is the Cloud concept of sharing resources among many end-users. This concept raises additional security concerns. Different Cloud providers resolve this problem in their own ways. For example, Salesforce.com separates users on a database level, securing data with carefully written databases queries, whereas Amazon implements virtualization on a hardware level to separate tenants [9].

A **Service level agreement** (SLA) defines the quality of service that a Cloud provider will deliver. While up time and bandwidth can be easily measured, security and privacy are not quantifiable. However, with proper monitoring and auditing, security incidents can be detected and brought to the SLA bargain process [9].

Compliance and regulations can potentially cause many jurisdictional problems in terms of which laws or regulations should apply depending on the data type or the user's residence. Also, depending on the business, companies have to comply with such regulations as the Health Insurance Portability and Accountability Act (HIPAA), Payment Card Industry Data Security Standards (PCI DSS), the Sarbanes Oxley Act on IT Security (SOX), Canada's Anti-Spam Legislation (Bill C-28) and others [10].

Security issues in Cloud are multiplied by issues at every individual service and application. Cloud computing virtual environments are independent domains with different privacy, security and trust relation approaches. Cloud service providers sometimes combine a few services to create new, better-quality application services. Such environmental domains use individually configured applications, services, and other settings. Hence, particular procedures have to be in place to guarantee that this dynamic structure is designed and maintained securely and security incidents and breaches are efficiently monitored and examined during the exploitation process. Even though each separate domain's policies are under control, security breaches can simply happen during integration [11].

3 Security Threats and Challenges

Cloud solutions integrate different parts of the computing infrastructure. As a whole, infrastructural security solutions are a product of all involved levels. Attacks can be accordingly divided by targeting levels as well: Data, Application, Host, and Network levels (Fig. 1) [9].

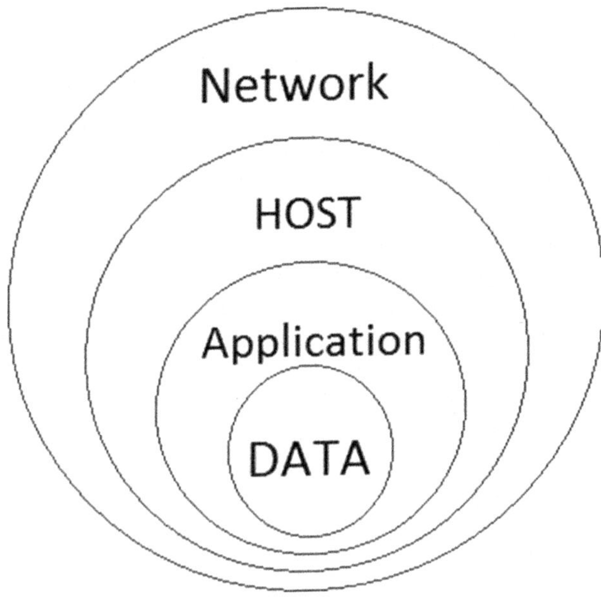

Fig. 1. Infrastructural levels of security

3.1 Network Level Attacks

At the Network level, security assumptions are different for Private and Public Clouds. In the Private Cloud, since the infrastructure lies within a company's premises, the firm has full control over this Cloud infrastructure. That means that all Cloud vulnerabilities and threats are the same as for corporate's services, and all firm's implemented threat mitigation measures can be applied to the Cloud infrastructure as well. For the public infrastructure security of access control, ensuring confidentiality, integrity, and availability (CIA) of data accessible through the Internet are the major risks on the Network level security [12].

Access control can be affected by reusable IP addresses. The IP v4 address pool is limited, and Cloud providers re-assign the same address to a new client when the address is released. At the same time there is some delay in updating DNS cash servers so a new customer may be exposed to some risk when accessing his/her Cloud resources through old DNS records to his/her new (re-assigned) IP address. Similar problems can occur with a reverse address resolution when the changed physical address is not updated at the ARP table. The Amazon Cloud provider offers elastic IP addresses where customers can fully control IP release. This helps avoid the aforementioned problem if the customer carefully manages their address space. However, this problem still cannot be resolved if customers use internal (non-routable) IP addresses within one Cloud provider [13]. An access control audit for network level logs in the Public Cloud is also cumbersome and may affect all types of Cloud services [13].

The **confidentiality and integrity** risks of customers' data that are exposed to the Internet are significant. When Amazon implemented Amazon Web Services (AWS)

Signature Version 1, a vulnerability report showed that the solution is insecure and many customers were unsatisfied with the provided level of security. Soon after that Amazon released AWS Signature Version 2, or suggested switching to HTTPS to mitigate integrity and confidentiality risk [14]. Secure Socket Layer/Transport Layer Security (SSL/TLS) is using to establish a protected, encrypted connection between a website and a client's web browser. Such connections are used to securely manage all features of provided Cloud services. The Internet researchers Juliano Rizzo and Thai Duong found a way to hack into the secured channel. They suggested using java script code built into a browser that acts as a Trojan horse, along with a network sniffer. This allows attackers to interfere with a secured tunnel, and to break SSL encryption. This attack was named BEASK (Browser Exploit against SSL/TLS) and has the potential to affect millions of websites [15].

The **availability** of data stored on the Cloud provider's premises is getting more important as more and more customer data is being saved on the Public Cloud. There are different types of attacks that can affect data availability. Some major attacks including but not limited to: DDoS attack on servers, DNS cash poising attack, IP spoofing attacks and ARP cache poisoning attacks [16, 17, 21].

3.2 Host Level Attacks

Security issues at the host level differ for Cloud models such as SaaS, PaaS, or IaaS and public or private deployment types. Threats at the host level are associated with its Virtual Machine (VM) vulnerabilities. For PaaS and SaaS services the Cloud provider does not share its platform with customers, therefore the provider is responsible for implementing the appropriate level of protection for VMs. A secure model of VM implementation which will be discussed in this paper is the main focus of this paper.

The following security threats are associated with IaaS services:

Hypervision Security Threats: When an attacker controls software that provides virtualization. The biggest threat is from "zero-day" vulnerabilities and can be anticipated by implementing the best security practices and frameworks that include, but are not limited to, host hardening, and patching and updating hosting software.

Perimeter Security: In some cases, virtual servers can reside outside of a firewall, which makes their securing more complex. Even when the servers are behind a Public Cloud provider's firewalls, they can be cracked by attackers inside the premises. A partial solution is to isolate virtual resources within their perimeters.

VM Security: Guest VMs are isolated from each other with hypervision software. Once a VM is allocated to customers, they are recommended to use a secured connection to manage their allocated resources. These are, for example, SSH and SSL/TLS. Other vulnerable services and protocols, such as FTP and NETBIOS, should be eliminated or substituted with their more secure analogs. Public Cloud providers should implement some operating procedures for properly deploying firewalls and enforce the use of strong passwords for user accounts [18].

3.3 Application Level Attacks

At this level customers have a lack of access control to audit logs, updates and patch management. In the public deployment model customers have to rely on providers' protection measures, while in the private model they can implement an appropriate amount of security at the host level. Security for hosting applications should be built into the software development life-cycle and provide quality assurance security testing at each stage of this cycle. The Open Web Application Security Project identifies ten security risks in web applications [19]. These security risks are: (1) Injection, (2) Cross-Site Scripting, (3) Broken Authentication and session management, (4) Insecure Direct Object References, (5) Cross-Site Request Forgery, (6) Security Misconfiguration, (7) Insecure Cryptographic storage, (8) Failure to Restrict URL Access, (9) Insufficient Transport Layer Protection, and (10) Invalidated Redirects and Forwards.

3.4 Data Level Attacks

Data level security is important for all Cloud models. Several aspects of data security have been discussed by [12]. These aspects including but not limited to: *Data-in-transit* is all data transferred across the network. *Data-at-rest* is data on file-servers and other storage areas. *Data lineage* is the process of tracking a data's origin and restricting that data's distribution to within defined premises for only audit and compliance purposes. *Data provenance* is the process of ensuring data integrity, which means precise and accurate data computation. *Data remanence* is the residual information present even after the data has been erased or moved to another location.

4 Virtualization Issues

Virtualization is a mechanism that connects physical hardware and virtual machines. It is also in charge of resource allocation and management for underlying services. The hypervisor or VM monitor compartmentalizes tenants on the physical computer and lets users run independent instances of VMs simultaneously and independently. This is fundamental for Cloud infrastructure, as providing a high level of security for virtualization is essential. The following types of VM vulnerabilities are most common [22].

4.1 VM Hopping

An attacker in such attacks resides on one of VMs and obtains access to a different instance of VM that is hosted on the same server, and the invader has to know target's IP address. There are different vectors of attacks and they are based on the type of host's hypervisor and other system vulnerabilities. After the attacker obtains access to the target's VM, he/she can modify the victim's configuration, and delete or tamper data. This type of attack targets IaaS and PaaS infrastructures, although it can indirectly strike SaaS since it uses the other types of infrastructure for its foundation. This type of attack is very common because it thrives on the basic Cloud principle of multi-tenancy [23].

4.2 VM Mobility

Almost all Cloud providers offer VM image replication features. Users can choose to use one of the pre-setup configurations from a repository. This feature facilitates quick configuration deployment but also distributes the same vulnerabilities that pertain to that particular setup. The attacker can know and use the configuration weaknesses. The results of this type of attack can lead to completely compromising a large number of new guest VMs. The attack mostly targets the IaaS model, as Cloud providers offer hardware resources and pre-installed VM images that users can customize. At the same time confidentiality, integrity and availability of the SaaS and PaaS models can be compromised, as they are exposed by the underlying IaaS vulnerabilities [24].

4.3 VM Diversity

Virtualization allows users to effortlessly deploy new virtual configurations in seconds. Users can choose different types of operating systems and pre-setup software configurations. That configuration diversity makes security management more challenging. The Service Level Agreement between a Cloud provider and a user can help to anticipate this issue. For the IaaS model, the Cloud provider obliges to supporting the hypervisor and servicing security, while the user has to strengthen his/her VM instances by applying patches, updates, and implementing best security practices. Similarly, for PaaS and SaaS models SLA can define and regulate a provider's and user's responsibilities for security management processes [25, 26].

4.4 VM Denial of Service

A Denial-of-service (DoS) attack happens after a guest's VMs occupies the CPU, network bandwidth, or hard drive throughput, and the hypervisor cannot allocate the resources to other guest machines. The base way to withstand this attack is to have a SLA that defines resource allocation to user's VMs. The SaaS Cloud model is less exposed to such attacks compare to the PaaS or IaaS models [25].

A Distributed Denial of Service (DDoS) attack happens when attackers take control over a number of computers with some vulnerability, and initiate a flood of traffic to the target machine.

4.5 The Insider Threat

All security counter-measures make sense only when attacks are external. However, data from VM can be compromised by anyone with administrative access, by whom all security precautions and efforts to monitor malicious activity can be circumvented. According to a VMworld magazine survey, 93 % of companies have mission-critical data at some virtual environment, and more than 70 % of respondents think that their colleagues could attack that data if they wanted to [27]. The only way to contend with the insider threat is to implement the same standards, audit practices, processes, and tools that a company uses in-house.

5 Virtualization and Multi-tenancy

Most articles so far already identified multi-tenancy and virtualization as main threats to cloud security. A paper called "A Distributed Access Control Architecture for Cloud Computing" discusses a possible solution to these problems using distributed architecture. The authors [28] discuss the system where both security management and software engineering techniques are used together. The authorization requirements are built using the following three components:

1) VRM (virtual resource manager) is located at each layer of the cloud and is responsible for providing and deploying virtual resources
2) DACM (distributed access control module) is also located at each layer and enforces access control policy
3) SLA (service level agreement) performs role mapping, prevents side-channel attacks by describing isolation constraints and presents a virtualized view of resources.

The only way to deliver secure multi-tenancy is to have some kind of isolation between tenant's data while at rest and in transition as well as physical location transparency where tenants can't determine where their data and resources are located to prevent side-channel attacks [30]. For example, Amazon Virtual Private Cloud allows the customer to specify set of virtual machines that can communicate only through an encrypted channel. There are some products on the market aimed at enhancing cloud security – IBM's Websphere Cast Iron and Cisco IronPort both provide among others secure messaging [30].

5.1 V2LAN

As indicated most of Cloud security discussed above are related to VMs (see Table 1). This study offers a Virtualized Virtual LAN (V2LAN) for protecting VMs locating on one or more physical servers. As we know each physical server is capable of providing many virtual machines providing computing resources to multiple organizations. Securing VMs against any data leak or unauthorized access is one of the main responsibilities of cloud providers. On the other hand customers should be aware of the importance of SLA in providing legal support in case unauthorized access to data and data leak occurs. We should not forget the fact that Cloud products and services are available to evry organization and to every individuals with the swipe of a credit card including hackers. This study offers a robust solution to secure VMs against any type of data leak.

A Virtual LAN defines a broadcast domain in which only those nodes that are grouped within a cluster are able exchange messages if desired. This feature provides a high level of abstraction and security at layer 2 level (as defined by OSI). For example, a common backbone connection shared across VLAN trunks or infrastructure can provide a very high level of security with great flexibilities. As such many Cloud features such as security, scalability and virtual machines are supported by VLAN. In fact a Cloud-aware switches have support for device virtualization at both layer 2 (datalink layer) and layer 3 (network layer). These types of switches are often referred to as a *layer 2.5* protocol. For example Cisco Nexus 7000 Series switches can be configured to

Table 1. Virtualization IT environments, security impacts.

Virtual machine vulnerability	Conventional environment	Cloud computing environment		
		SaaS	PaaS	IaaS
VM hopping	Confidentiality	No direct impact, though indirect affects are possible	Confidentiality	Confidentiality
	Integrity		Integrity	Integrity
	Availability		Availability	Availability
VM mobility	Confidentiality	—	Reduced occurrence of the vulnerability or alleviated impact	Confidentiality
	Integrity			Integrity
	Availability			Availability
	Security management			
VM diversity	Security management	—	×	×
VM denial of service	Availability	—	×	×

Source: Tsai *et al.*, 2012.

support Virtualized VLAN or V2LAN for short. They support the so called Virtual Device Contexts (VDCs). Each VDC runs as a separate logical entity comprising switching, security, and services that is designed for physical, virtual, and cloud environments. It uniquely integrates with servers, storage, and orchestration platforms for more efficient operations and greater scalability [31]. As shown in Fig. 2 each VDC is a complete unit capable of layer 3 routing via its virtual route forwarding (VRF) as well as layer 2 VLAN.

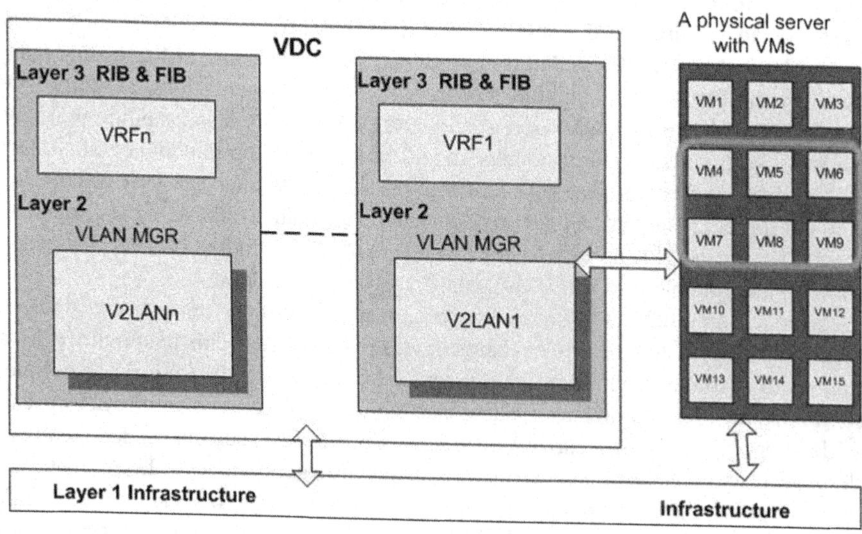

Fig. 2. Integrating V2LAN with VMs

5.2 V2LAN Implementation

The routing structure offered by VLANs in connection with VDC has a close and similar implementation with those of Multiprotocol Label Switching (MPLS) in which packet forwarding mechanism use Forwarding Information Base (FIB). FIB is based on a data structure called Routing Information Base (RIB). RIB is essentially a routing table. To make a decision about the best route, V2LAN FIB is relying on information provided by RIB for its outgoing traffic (traffic outside VM environment).

Figure 2 above shows a physical server containing some VMs (VM1 through VM15). Assume that only VM4 through VM9 are designed for Customer 1, and the rest of VMs belong to other clients. Our Cloud switch via its V2LAN1 component defines a unique broadcast domain that includes only these VMs; no other VMs can access or listen to message exchange within the domain of V2LAN1. V2LAN is acting as a buffer against data leakage within the context of virtual machines. This IaaS-based security feature is deployed in addition to SaaS-based VM security offered by the hypervisor. Anthes has noted that IBM Research deployed a method for securing VM known as "virtual machine introspection"; in which it puts security inside a protected VM running on the same physical machine [1]. Recent VM security employs a number of protective measures such as whitelisting and blacklisting of the guest kernel functions [1]. These activities are aimed to determine the operating system and the version of the VM. While V2LAN provides strong buffer against these types of activities, it eliminates the need of deploying or cloning such functions at VM levels.

V2LAN implementation is a secure and cost effective solution for increased business agility with VMs and their motilities [31]. It reduces capital and operational expenditures through more efficient use of hardware and storage devices and more efficient management, Create an architecture that supports futures growth, server performance, and storage and virtualization goals [31].

6 Conclusion

There are many advantages in using Cloud-based systems. However, there are also many technological problems that have not yet been solved. The Cloud is a technology that is widely used in the whole IT sector. Retaining factors such as data privacy and information security issues, computing power efficiency, and SLA related concerns are still holding back complete adoption of the technology.

Acceptance of the Cloud requires a shift in its perception and also the understanding of all its accompanying problems, especially security related ones. Although some security risks are already present at the traditional computing model, while using Cloud, the security risks might have a higher impact on businesses. Currently Cloud security has a lot of loose ends that deter potential Cloud customers from migration there. Until proper security mechanisms are in place, prospective customers are not going to leverage the advantages of Cloud technology.

As indicated above, VMs are one of the main sources of concern within the context of Cloud security. In this study we offered a cost effective solution to tackle this issue.

It offers a layer 2 and 3 solution to harden communication among interrelated VMs and prevent issues such as black listening or data leak.

Finally, it is important to note that this study is limited to VM issues and more specifically the issues related to data leak as such it does not claim that it has addressed all Cloud security issues as discussed in this paper.

References

1. Anthes, G.: Security in the cloud. Commun. ACM **53**(11), 16–18 (2010)
2. Truong, D.: How cloud computing enhances competitive advantages: a research model for small business. Bus. Rev. **15**(1), 59–65 (2010)
3. Carlo, J.L.: Internet computing as a disruptive information technology innovation: the role of strong order effects. Inf. Syst. J. **21**, 91–122 (2011)
4. Dewar, R., Dutton, E.J.: The adoption of radical and incremental innovations: an empirical analysis. Manag. Sci. **32**, 1422–1433 (1986)
5. Teece, D.P.: Dynamic capabilities and strategic management. Strateg. Manag. J. **18**, 509–533 (1997)
6. Hemerly, J.: Public policy considerations for data-driven innovation. IEEE Comput. Soc. **46**(6), 25–31 (2013)
7. Chisholm, T., Smigala, H.: IBM Advances Cloud Computing in Education; Unveils IBM Cloud Academy (2009). http://www-03.ibm.com/press/us/en/pressrelease/28749.wss
8. Katzan, H.: On the privacy of cloud computing. Int. J. Manag. Inf. Syst. **14**(2), 1–12 (2010)
9. Kulkarni, G., Gambhir, J., Patil, T., Dongare, A.: A security aspects in cloud computing. In: 2012 IEEE 3rd International Conference on Software Engineering and Service Science (ICSESS), pp. 547–550 (2012)
10. Takabi, H., Joshi, J.B., Ahn, G.J.: Security and privacy challenges in cloud computing environments. IEEE Secur. Priv. **8**(6), 24–31 (2010)
11. Jordan, J.: Climbing out of the box and into the cloud: building webscale for libraries. J. Libr. Adm. **51**(1), 3–17 (2011)
12. Mather, T., Kumaraswamy, S., Latif, S.: Cloud Security and Privacy: An Enterprise Edition on Risks and Compliance (Theory in Practice), O'Reilly Media, ISBN: 978-0596802769 (2009)
13. Rekhter: Address allocation for private internets (1996). Retrieved from Network Working Group. http://tools.ietf.org/html/rfc1918
14. Amazon AWS. AWS Signature Version 1 is Insecure (2008). http://www.daemonology.net/blog/2008-12-18-AWS-signature-version-1-is-insecure.html
15. The register. Hackers Break SSL Encryption Used by Millions of Sites (2011). http://www.theregister.co.uk/2011/09/19/beast_exploits_paypal_ssl
16. Atkins, D.: Threat Analysis of the Domain Name System (DNS) (2004). Retrieved from Network Working Group. http://tools.ietf.org/html/rfc3833
17. Evans, K.: IP Spoofing Attack and Defenses (2010). http://resources.infosecinstitute.com/ipspoofing-attack
18. Contextis. Assessing Cloud Node Security whitepapers@ (2011). Retrieved from Context Information Security: contextis.com
19. OWASP. The Ten Most Critical Web Application Security Risks (2010). Retrieved from Open Web Application Security Project. https://www.owasp.org/index.php/Category:OWASP_Top_Ten_Project

20. Sudha, S., Viswanathan, V.M.: Addressing security and privacy issues in cloud computing. J. Theor. Appl. Inf. Technol. **48**(2), 708–719 (2013)
21. Fewer, S.: ARP Poisoning an Investigation into Spoofing the Address Resolution Protocol (2009). http://www.harmonysecurity.com
22. Garfinkel,T., Rosenblum, M.: When virtual is harder than real: security challenges in virtual machine based computing environments. In: Proceedings of the 10th Workshop on Hot Topics in Operating Systems (2005). USENIX Association. https://www.usenix.org/legacy/events/hotos05/final_papers/garfinkel.html
23. Ristenpart, T. Tromer, E., Shacham, H., Savage, S.: Hey, you, get off of my cloud: exploring information leakage in third-party compute clouds. In: Proceedings of the 16th ACM Conference on Computer and Communications Security (CCS 09), pp. 199–212. ACM Press (2009)
24. Oberheide, C. J.: Empirical exploitation of live virtual machine migration. In: Proceedings of Black Hat DC 2008 Convention (2008). www.net-security.org/dl/articles/migration.pdf
25. Tsai, H., Siebenhaar, M., Miede, A., Huang, Y., Steinmetz, R.: Threat as a service?: virtualization's impact on cloud security. IEEE Comput. Soc. **14**(1), 32–37 (2012)
26. Yan, J., Early, S., Anderson, R.: The XenoService – A Distributed Defeat for Distributed Denial of Service. Proceedings of Information Survivability Workshop, Boston, Massachusetts, USA (2000)
27. Moss, H., Zierick, J.: Cloud providers will be better at security than you can ever be. Netw. World **28**(4), 27–28 (2011)
28. Almutairi, A., Sarfraz, M.I., Basalamah, S., Walid, G., Aref, W.G., Ghafoor, A.: A distributed access control architecture for cloud computing. IEEE Softw. **29**(2), 36–44 (2012)
29. Behl, A., Behl, K.: An analysis of cloud computing security issues. In: 2012 World Congress on Information and Communication Technologies (WICT), pp. 109–114 (2012)
30. Cachin, C., Schunter, M.: A cloud you can trust - IEEE Spectrum, December issue, pp. 28–33 (2011)
31. Cisco. Technical Overview of Virtual Device Contexts, Cisco Systems Inc. (2012)

Author Index

Printed in the United States
By Bookmasters